First Canadian Edition

Compensation

McGraw-Hill Ryerson

Series in Human Resource Management

George T. Milkovich
Cornell University

Jerry M. Newman
State University of New York—Buffalo

Nina Cole
Ryerson University

McGraw-Hill Ryerson

Toronto Montreal Boston Burr Ridge IL Dubuque IA Madison WI New York San Francisco
St Louis Bangkok Bogatá Caracas Kuala Lumpur Lisbon London Madrid Mexico City
Milan New Delhi Santiago Seoul Singapore Sydney Taipei

Compensation
First Canadian Edition

Statistics Canada information is used with the permission of the Minister of Industry, as Minister responsible for Statistics Canada. Information on the availability of the wide range of data from Statistics Canada can be obtained from Statistics Canada's Regional Offices, its World Wide Web site at <http://www.statcan.ca>, and its toll-free access number 1-800-263-1136.

ISBN: 0-07-0922020

1 2 3 4 5 6 7 8 9 10 QP 0 9 8 7 6 5

Printed and bound in Canada

Care has been taken to trace ownership of copyright material contained in this text; however, the publisher will welcome any information that enables them to rectify any reference or credit for subsequent editions.

Vice President, Editorial and Media Technology: Patrick Ferrier
Sponsoring Editor: Kim Brewster
Developmental Editor: Lori McLellan
Senior Marketing Manager: Kelly Smyth
Copy Editor: Jim Zimmerman
Senior Production Coordinator: Madeleine Harrington
Cover Design: Sharon Lucas
Cover Image Credit: Getty Images/Michael Banks
Interior Design: Greg Devitt
Page Layout: Lynda Powell
Printer: Quebecor Printing

Library and Archives Canada Cataloguing in Publication

Milkovich, George T.
    Compensation / George T. Milkovich, Jerry M. Newman, Nina Cole.—1st Canadian ed.

Includes bibliographical references and indexes.
ISBN 0-07-092202-0

    1. Compensation management--Textbooks. I. Newman, Jerry M. II. Cole, Nina D. (Nina Dawn) III. Title.

HF5549.5.C67M54 2004   658.3'2   C2004-905001-X

ABOUT THE AUTHORS

George T. Milkovich is the M. P. Catherwood Professor at the ILR School, Cornell University. He studies and writes about how people get paid and what difference it makes. People's compensation has been his interest for over 30 years. His research has resulted in numerous publications. Four have received national awards for their contributions. His books, *Compensation*, coauthored with Jerry Newman, now in its 8th edition, and *Cases in Compensation*, coauthored with Carolyn Milkovich, are the most widely adopted text and cases about pay in the world. His current research examines the globalization of compensation and reward systems.

Milkovich received the Keystone Award from the World at Work Association (formerly the American Compensation Association) for lifetime achievement. He also received the Distinguished Career Contributions Award from the Academy of Management HR Division, and is a Fellow in both the Academy of Management and the National Academy of Human Resources. He chaired the National Academy of Sciences Committee on Performance and Pay, and the Federal Joint Labor-Management Committee on Pay and Performance.

He has received three Outstanding Teacher Awards and is also on the faculties of Zhejiang University in China and Ljubljana University in Slovenia. He has served as a Visiting Professor at several leading international universities, including London Business School, Hong Kong University of Science and Technology, Charles University in Prague, Comenius University in Bratislava, and University of California in Los Angeles.

Jerry Newman (B.A., U of Michigan; M.A., Ph.D, U of Minnesota) is Distinguished Professor of Organization and Human Resources at the State University of New York at Buffalo. His research and teaching interests are in the areas of compensation, team effectiveness, and performance management. When not working he definitely does not sky dive.

Nina Cole is Associate Professor of Organizational Behaviour and Human Resources Management at Ryerson University in Toronto.

Prior to her academic career, she spent 12 years in the business world—eight years as a human resources consultant, and four years as a human resources manager. The last 15 years have been spent as an academic, teaching and conducting research on the application of organizational justice theories to human resource management. She is currently working on a research project, funded by the Social Sciences and Humanities Research Council, investigating the vicarious effect of employee discipline on co-workers.

Nina has published articles in both academic journals and industry publications, and has led seminars to assist managers in these challenging areas. She has spoken and written on these topics on numerous occasions, and also has co-authored textbooks on human resources management.

Nina has been active in the Administrative Sciences Association of Canada (ASAC) for many years. She chaired the 2005 annual conference, and will serve as president of ASAC in 2005-2006. She also is actively involved in Rotary International projects in the developing world.

BRIEF CONTENTS

CONTENTS

Contents

4 Job Analysis   64

5 Evaluating Work: Job Evaluation   88

Contents

Contents

8 Designing Pay Levels, Mix, and Pay Structures   176

9 Employee Benefits   214

Contents

PART III   242

Determining Individual Pay: Pay for Performance

10 Pay for Performance and the Role of Performance Appraisal   244

11 Pay-for-Performance Plans   280

Contents

PART IV   316

Managing the System

12 The Role of Government and Unions in Compensation   318

13 Budgets and Administration   341

Contents

PREFACE

Want to go for a walk? In space? If you are a Russian cosmonaut, you can earn a bonus of $1,000 for every space walk, up to three, per space trip. A contract listing specific tasks to be done on a space mission permits you to earn up to $30,000 above the $20,000 you earn while you are on the ground. Of course, this was only temporary. When those temporary, high-paying jobs were no longer available, you would go back to your usual occupation—hunting the whales. Conclusion: *Money matters*.

Many years ago, when Green Giant discovered too many insect parts in the pea pack from one of its plants, it designed a bonus plan that paid people for finding insect parts. Green Giant got what it paid for: insect parts. Innovative Green Giant employees brought insect parts from home to add to the peas right before they removed them and collected the bonus.

And speaking of bugs . . . a well-known software house designed a bonus plan that paid software engineers to find bugs in software code. Plan designers failed to realize that the people who found the bugs were the very same ones who wrote the buggy software code in the first place. Engineers joked about "writing me an SUV." The Russian cosmonauts claim that every spacewalk, report, experiment, and repair has a specific bonus attached. Tasks not done correctly incur penalties. Penalties and payments are totalled at the end of the trip. "We do not do anything extra unless we are paid for it. We don't want any black marks." Conclusion: *It matters what you pay for*.

Motorola trashed its old-fashioned pay system that employees said guaranteed a raise every six months if you were still breathing. They replaced it with a system that paid for learning new skills and working in teams. Sounded good. It wasn't. Employees resented those team members who went off for six weeks of training at full pay, while remaining team members picked up their work. Motorola was forced to trash its new-fashioned system, too. Conclusion: *It matters how you pay*.

We live in interesting times. Anywhere you look on the globe today, economic and social pressures are forcing managers to rethink how people get paid and what difference it makes. Traditional approaches to compensation are being questioned. But what is achieved by all this experimentation and change? We have lots of fads and fashions, but do they work? Where are the results?

In this book, we strive to separate beliefs from facts, wishful thinking from demonstrable results, and pay experts' opinions from research. Yet, when all is said and done, managing compensation is an art. As with any art, not everything that can be learned can be taught.

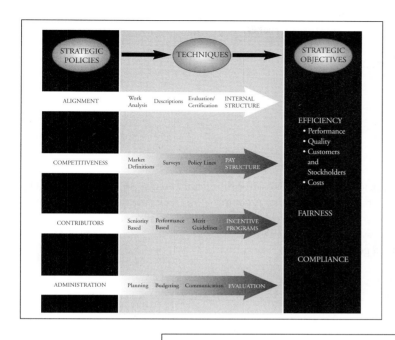

ABOUT THIS BOOK

The first Canadian edition of the classic Milkovich/ Newman compensation text has been written in response to a longstanding need on the part of Canadian students, and ever-increasing demand on the part of Canadian faculty, for a Canadian version of the Milkovich book. Very little has been changed, other than adapting the content and examples to a Canadian context. This approach is intended to preserve the unique perspective on compensation taken by Milkovich/Newman.

This book is based on the strategic choices in managing compensation. These choices, which confront managers in Canada and around the world, are introduced in the Total Compensation Model in Chapter 1. This model provides an integrating framework that is used throughout the book. Major compensation issues are discussed in the context of current theory, research, and practice. The practices illustrate new developments as well as established approaches to compensation decisions.

Each chapter contains a Web Exercise to point you to some of the vast compensation information on the Internet. Real-life Case Exercises ask you to apply the concepts and techniques discussed in each chapter. For example, the Case in Chapter 11 takes you through several exercises designed to explain how stock options work and how to value them. It also allows you to connect to real time stock prices for up-to-date stock option valuations.

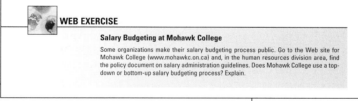

WEB EXERCISE

Salary Budgeting at Mohawk College

Some organizations make their salary budgeting process public. Go to the Web site for Mohawk College (www.mohawkc.on.ca) and, in the human resources division area, find the policy document on salary administration guidelines. Does Mohawk College use a top-down or bottom-up salary budgeting process? Explain.

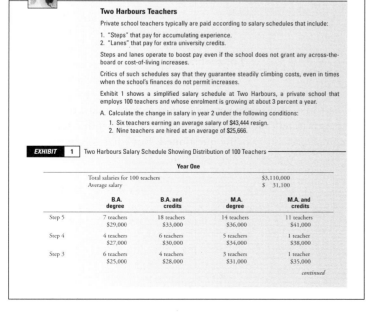

CASE

Two Harbours Teachers

Private school teachers typically are paid according to salary schedules that include:

1. "Steps" that pay for accumulating experience.
2. "Lanes" that pay for extra university credits.

Steps and lanes operate to boost pay even if the school does not grant any across-the-board or cost-of-living increases.

Critics of such schedules say that they guarantee steadily climbing costs, even in times when the school's finances do not permit increases.

Exhibit 1 shows a simplified salary schedule at Two Harbours, a private school that employs 100 teachers and whose enrolment is growing at about 3 percent a year.

A. Calculate the change in salary in year 2 under the following conditions:
   1. Six teachers earning an average salary of $43,444 resign.
   2. Nine teachers are hired at an average of $25,666.

EXHIBIT 1 Two Harbours Salary Schedule Showing Distribution of 100 Teachers

Year One

| | Total salaries for 100 teachers | | | $3,110,000 |
| | Average salary | | | $ 31,100 |

	B.A. degree	B.A. and credits	M.A. degree	M.A. and credits
Step 5	7 teachers $29,000	18 teachers $33,000	14 teachers $36,000	11 teachers $41,000
Step 4	4 teachers $27,000	6 teachers $30,000	5 teachers $34,000	1 teacher $38,000
Step 3	6 teachers $25,000	4 teachers $28,000	3 teachers $31,000	1 teacher $35,000

continued

.NET WORTH — What Attracts Employees to a Job?

The findings from a 2002 study of 765 Canadian companies by compensation consultants Towers Perrin illustrate the importance of both total compensation and relational returns. Although competitive base pay is the top attraction to a job, the second most important is opportunities for advancement. In third place is competitive health care benefits. The fourth and fifth most important factors that make a job attractive to Canadians are work/life balance and recognition for work, respectively. Other important factors include challenging work, learning and development opportunities, and a competitive retirement package.[1]

One Canadian company that promotes both total compensation and relational returns is IMS Health, a medical information and consulting company with offices in Montreal and Toronto. Their Web site highlights total compensation, including pay, benefits, incentives, recognition, social events, work/life balance arrangements, career growth, and more.[2]

Sources:
[1] *The Towers Perrin Talent Report: New Realities in Today's Workforce* (Canadian Report). Toronto, ON: Towers Perrin, 2002, p.11.
[2] www.imshealthcanada.com (June 23, 2003)

CHAPTER 7

DEFINING COMPETITIVENESS

LEARNING OUTCOMES

- *Describe* external competitiveness, and the two ways it is expressed in practice.
- *Discuss* the three major factors that shape external competitiveness.
- *Discuss* three labour demand theories and *explain* their predictions regarding pay.
- *Discuss* three supply side theories and *explain* their predictions regarding pay.
- *Explain* the three competitive pay policy alternatives.

WHAT'S NEW IN THE FIRST CANADIAN EDITION

The book has been reorganized into 13 chapters, to benefit Canadian instructors who generally teach 13-week courses. The first eight chapters are in the same order as those in the US text. Chapter 9 integrates the material on employee benefits from two chapters in the US text. Chapter 10 combines the theoretical material on pay-for-performance and the role of performance appraisal from two chapters in the US text. Chapter 11 combines the two US chapters on pay-for performance plans and compensation of special groups. Chapter 12 integrates the material on the role of governments and unions in compensation from two US chapters. The book concludes with Chapter 13 on budgets and administration, as did the US text. The material on international pay systems has been included as an appendix.

Each chapter includes a .NetWorth boxed feature, which highlights a comprehensive real-world example of the material in the chapter.

Learning Outcomes have been added at the beginning of each chapter, and the Chapter Summary relating to these learning outcomes is included at the end of the chapter.

CHAPTER SUMMARY

1. External competitiveness refers to the the relationship of one organization's pay to that of its competitors. External competitiveness is expressed in practice by (1) setting a pay level that is above, below, or equal to one's competitors, and (2) by considering the mix of pay forms relative to those of competitors.
2. The three major factors that shape external competitiveness are: (1) competition in the labour market for people with various skills; (2) competition in the product and service markets, which affects the financial condition of the organization; and (3) characteristics unique to each organization and its employees, such as its business strategy, technology, and the productivity and experience of its workforce.
3. Three labour demand theories are compensating differentials theory, efficiency wage theory, and signalling theory. Compensating differentials theory predicts that work with negative characteristics will require higher pay to attract workers. Efficiency wage theory predicts that above-market wages will improve efficiency by attracting workers who perform better and stay longer. Signalling theory predicts that pay policies will signal the kind of behaviour the employer wants.
4. Three supply-side theories are reservation wage theory, human capital theory, and job competition theory. Reservation wage theory predicts that job seekers will not take jobs when pay is below a certain level. Human capital theory predicts that the value of a person's skills and abilities will be related to the time and expense required to acquire them.

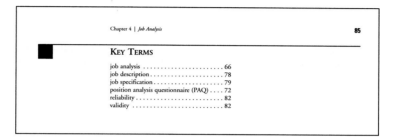

job specification

qualifications required to be hired for a job; may be included in the job description

fits into the organization: who is supervised by this jobholder, who supervises this jobholder, and the nature of any internal and external relationships. A job summary consists of a short paragraph that provides an overview of the job. The section on essential responsibilities elaborates on the summary. It includes the tasks. Related tasks may be grouped into task dimensions. This particular job description also includes very specific standards for judging whether an essential responsibility has been met, for example, "Provides a written assessment of patient within one hour of admission and at least once a shift." A final section lists the qualifications necessary to be hired for the job. These are the **job specifications** that can be used as a basis for hiring—the knowledge, skills, and abilities required to adequately perform the tasks. But keep in mind that the summary needs to be relevant to pay decisions and thus must focus on similarities and differences in content.

Definitions of Key Terms highlighted in each chapter are provided in the margins, and a list is provided at the end of the chapter.

KEY TERMS

REVIEW QUESTIONS

1. What are the two critical uses of job analysis for compensation decisions?
2. Describe the major decisions involved in job analysis.
3. Distinguish between task and behavioural data.
4. How should discrepancies between job analysis information provided by employees and supervisors be resolved?

 ## EXPERIENTIAL EXERCISES

1. Talk to several managers and find one or more who say that job analysis is a colossal waste of their time and the time of their employees. Find out what the reasons are for their opinion. Are they right?

2. **a)** Think of a specific job you presently hold or have held in the past (including a part-time job or volunteer work). Use the information in this chapter to develop a job analysis questionnaire that you believe would adequately capture all relevant information about that job. Then complete the questionnaire for your specific job.

   b) Pick a teammate (or the instructor will assign one) and exchange questionnaires with your teammate.

   c) Write a job description for your teammate's job. Does the questionnaire give you sufficient information? Is there additional information that would be helpful?

   d) Exchange descriptions. Critique the job description written by your teammate. Does it adequately capture all the important job aspects? Does it indicate which aspects are most important?

Review Questions and Experiential Exercises are suggested at the end of each chapter. A Web exercise has been included at the end of each chapter, in order to familiarize the student with the wealth of compensation-related material available on the Internet. Also included at the end of each chapter is a comprehensive case requiring application of the chapter material.

ACKNOWLEDGMENTS

Many people have contributed to our understanding of compensation and to the preparation of this textbook. In particular, we thank the following reviewers whose comments and suggestions greatly added to the value of this first Canadian edition:

Naresh Agarwal   *McMaster University*

Juris Svistunenko   *Georgian College*

John Hardisty   *Sheridan Institute of Technology and Advanced Learning*

Linda West   *University of Manitoba*

Suzanne Kavanagh   *George Brown College*

Holly Dwyer   *College of the North Atlantic*

David Morrison   *Durham College*

Gerald Hunt   *Ryerson University*

Brian Worth   *Georgian College*

Linda Yates Cameron   *Seneca College*

Linda Eligh   *University of Western Ontario*

Fred Mandl   *British Columbia Institute of Technology*

John L. Hall   *Concordia University*

Don Schepens   *Grant MacEwan College*

We also recognize the contributions of reviewers of the 7th edition of *Compensation* in the United States, upon which the first Canadian edition is based:

Tom Arnold   *Westmoreland Community College*

Lubica Bajzikova   *Comenius University, Bratislava*

Stuart Basefsky   *Cornell University*

Melissa Barringer   *University of Massachusetts*

Matt Bloom   *University of Notre Dame*

James T. Brakefield   *Western Illinois University*

Wayne Cascio   *University of Colorado*

Allen D. Engle Sr.   *Eastern Kentucky University*

Luis Gomez-Mejia   *Arizona State University*

Robert Heneman   *Ohio State University*

Peter Hom   *Arizona State University*

Greg Hundley   *Purdue*

W. Roy Johnson   *Iowa State University*

Jiri Kamenicek   *Charles University, Prague*

John G. Kilgour   *California State University, Hayward*

Frank Krzystofiak   *SUNY Buffalo*

David I. Levine   *Berkeley*

Janet Marler   *SUNY Albany*

Sarah Milkovich   *Brown University*

Ed Montemayer   *Michigan State University*

Atul Mitra   *Northern Iowa University*

Michael Moore   *Michigan State University*

J. Randall Nutter   *Geneva College*

Janez Prasnikar   *University of Ljubljana*

Yoko Sano   *Keio University*

Jennifer Stevens   *Cornell University*

Michael Sturman   *Cornell University*

Ningyu Tang   *Shanghai Jiao Tong University*

Zhong-Ming Wang   *Zhejiang University*

Yoshio Yanadori   *Cornell University*

Nada Zupan   *University of Ljubljana*

THE PAY MODEL

LEARNING OUTCOMES

- *Describe* how compensation is viewed differently by society, stakeholders, managers, and employees in Canada and around the world.
- *Discuss* major components of total returns for work.
- *Describe* the four strategic policies in the pay model and the techniques associated with them.
- *Discuss* the objectives of compensation in the pay model.

A friend of ours writes that she is in the touring company of the musical *Cats*. In the company are two performers called swings who sit backstage during each performance. Each swing must learn five different lead roles in the show. During the performance, the swing sits next to a rack with five different costumes and makeup for each of the five roles. Our friend, who has a lead in the show, once hurt her shoulder during a dance number. She signalled to someone offstage, and by the time she finished her number, the swing was dressed, in makeup, and out on stage for the next scene.

Our friend is paid $2,000 per week for playing one of the cats in the show. She is expected to do a certain number of performances and a certain number of rehearsals per week. She gets paid for the job she does. The swing gets paid $2,500 per week, whether she performs 20 shows that week or none. She is paid for knowing the five roles, whether she plays them or not.

Think of all the other employees, in addition to the performers, required to put on a performance of *Cats*. Electricians, trombonists, choreographers, dressers, janitors, nurses, vocal coaches, accountants, stagehands, payroll supervisors, ushers, lighting technicians, ticket sellers—the list goes on. Consider the array of wages paid to these employees. Why does the swing get paid more than other performers? Why does the performer get paid more (or less) than the trombonist? How are these decisions made, and who is involved in making them? Whether it's our own or someone else's, compensation questions engage our attention.

Does the compensation received by all the people connected with *Cats* matter? Most employers believe that how people are paid affects people's behaviour at work, which affects an organization's chances of success. Compensation systems can help an organization achieve and sustain competitive advantage.[1]

◼ COMPENSATION

What image does the word "compensation" bring to mind? It does not mean the same thing to everyone. Yet, how people view compensation affects how they behave at work. Thus, we must begin by recognizing different perspectives.

Society

Some people see pay as a measure of justice. For example, a comparison of earnings of women with those of men highlights what many consider inequities in pay decisions. The gender pay gap in Canada for full-time, full-year workers narrowed from 42 percent in 1967 to 30 percent in 2000. Despite this narrowing, and despite pay equity legislation, the gap persists, and always to the benefit of men. The latest studies show that, because women often withdraw temporarily from the labour force for family-related reasons, the resulting reduction in their experience has a serious impact on pay over the long term. For workers with less than two years' experience, the gap is only four percent, but it still exists.[2] However, a large portion of the wage gap still has yet to be explained.

Sometimes differences in compensation between countries are listed as a cause of loss of North American jobs to less developed economies. As **Exhibit 1.1(a)** reveals, labour costs in Mexico are about fourteen percent of those in Canada.[3] However, **Exhibit 1.1(b)** shows that when differences in productivity (the relative output for each dollar of pay) are factored in, the wage advantage of Mexico, Korea, and Taiwan disappears. Productivity is highest in France, the United States, and Germany.

EXHIBIT 1.1(a) Hourly Compensation Costs* ————————————————————

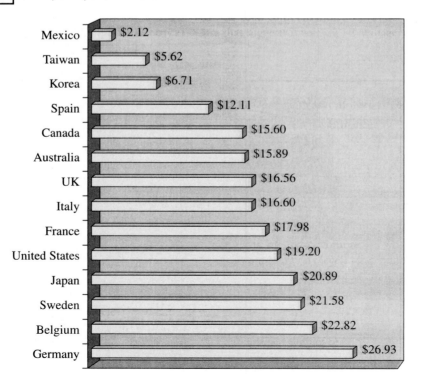

Country	Cost
Mexico	$2.12
Taiwan	$5.62
Korea	$6.71
Spain	$12.11
Canada	$15.60
Australia	$15.89
UK	$16.56
Italy	$16.60
France	$17.98
United States	$19.20
Japan	$20.89
Sweden	$21.58
Belgium	$22.82
Germany	$26.93

*U.S. Dollars

Voters may see compensation, pensions, and health care for public employees as the cause of increased taxes. Public policymakers and legislators may view changes in average pay as guides for adjusting eligibility for social services (provincial health care plans, welfare assistance, and the like).

Consumers sometimes see compensation as the cause of price increases. They may not believe that higher labour costs are to their benefit. On the other hand, other consumers have lobbied universities to insist on higher wages for labourers in Guatemala who sew shirts and caps bearing the university logo.[4]

Stockholders

To stockholders, executive pay is of special interest. In Canada, pay for executives is supposed to be tied to the financial performance of the company. Unfortunately, this does not always happen. For example, between 1990 and 2001, share prices increased about 300 percent, corporate profits increased 116 percent, but CEO pay increased by 535 percent. Consider the high pay–low performance of BCE Inc.'s CEO Jean Monty in 2001. In a year when returns to BCE shareholders declined by 14 percent, Monty's pay increased by 452 percent.[5]

Managers

Managers also have a stake in compensation: It directly influences their success in two ways. First, it is a major expense. Competitive pressures, both internationally and domestically, force managers to consider the affordability of their compensation decisions. Studies show that in many enterprises labour costs account for more than 50 percent of total costs.[6] Among some industries,

EXHIBIT 1.1(b) Output per Dollar* of Pay around the World

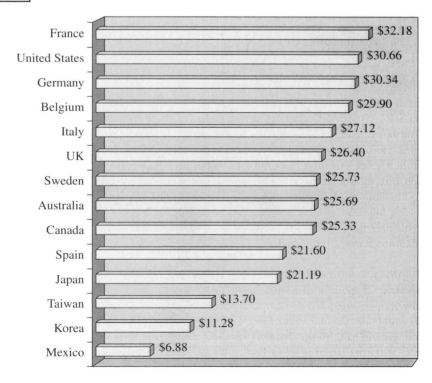

France $32.18
United States $30.66
Germany $30.34
Belgium $29.90
Italy $27.12
UK $26.40
Sweden $25.73
Australia $25.69
Canada $25.33
Spain $21.60
Japan $21.19
Taiwan $13.70
Korea $11.28
Mexico $6.88

*U.S. Dollars

such as financial or professional services or public employment such as education and government, this figure is even higher. However, even within an industry (e.g., automotive manufacturing, financial services), labour costs as a percent of total costs vary among individual firms.

In addition to treating pay as an expense, a manager also uses it to influence employee behaviours and improve organization performance. The way people are paid affects the quality of their work; their attitude toward customers; their willingness to be flexible or learn new skills or suggest innovations; and even their interest in unions or legal action against their employer. This potential to influence employees' behaviours, and subsequently the productivity and effectiveness of the organization, is another important reason to be clear about the meaning of compensation.[7]

Employees

The pay individuals receive in return for the work they perform is usually the major source of their financial security. Hence, pay plays a vital role in a person's economic and social well-being. Employees may see compensation as a *return in an exchange* between their employer and themselves, as an *entitlement* for being an employee of the company, or as a *reward* for a job well done. Compensation can be all of these things, though how many employees see their pay as a reward remains an open question.

Employees in large state-owned companies (e.g., in China) and in highly regulated countries (e.g., Sweden) sometimes believe their pay is an entitlement: their just due, regardless of their own performance or that of their employers. It is not uncommon for political leaders, trade unions, and employer federations in some countries such as Sweden and Germany to negotiate compensation policies that support their country's sociopolitical as well as economic priorities.[8]

Describing pay as a reward may sound farfetched to anyone who has reluctantly rolled out of bed to go to work. Even though writers and consultants use that term, do people really say, "They just gave me a reward increase," or "Here is my weekly reward check"? Sounds silly, doesn't it? Yet, if people see their pay as a return for their contributions and investments rather than a reward, and if writers and consultants persist in trying to convince them that pay is a reward, there is a disconnect that misleads both employees and managers. Employees invest in education and training; they contribute their time and energy at the workplace. Compensation is their return on those investments and contributions.[9]

Global

In English, compensation means to counterbalance, to offset, to make up for. However, if we look at the origin of the word in different languages, we get a sense of the richness of the meaning, which can combine entitlement, return, and reward.

In China, the traditional characters for compensation are based on the signs for logs and water; compensation provides the necessities in life. In today's China, however, the reforms of the last decade have led to use of a new word, *dai yu*, which refers to how you are treated or taken care of. When people talk about compensation, they ask each other "How about the 'dai yu' in your company?" rather than asking about the wages. So the benefits and training opportunities are very important.

Compensation in Japanese is *kyuyo*, which is made up of two separate characters (kyu and yo), both meaning "giving something." *Kyu* is an honourific used to indicate that the person doing the giving is someone of high rank, such as a feudal lord, an emperor, or a Samurai leader. Traditionally, compensation is thought of as something given by one's superior. Today, business consultants in Japan try to substitute the word *hou-syu*, which means reward, and has no associations with notions of superiors. The many allowances that are part of Japanese compensation systems translate as teate, which means "taking care of something." *Teate* is regarded as compensation that takes care of employees' financial needs. This concept is consistent

compensation

all forms of financial returns and tangible services and benefits employees receive as part of an employment relationship

with the family, housing, and commuting allowances that are still used in many Japanese companies.[10]

These contrasting perspectives of compensation—societal, stockholder, managerial, employee, and even global—add richness to the topic. But these perspectives can also cause confusion unless everyone is talking about the same thing. So let's define what we mean by compensation. **Compensation**, or pay (the words are used interchangeably in this book), refers to all forms of financial returns and tangible services and benefits employees receive as part of an employment relationship.

◾ FORMS OF PAY

relational returns

psychological returns employees believe they receive in the workplace

Exhibit 1.2 shows the variety of returns people may receive from work. They are categorized as *total compensation* and *relational returns*. The **relational returns** (development opportunities, status, opportunity to belong, challenging work, and so on) are the psychological returns people believe they receive in the workplace.[11] Total compensation includes pay received directly as cash (e.g., base, merit, incentives, cost-of-living adjustments) and indirectly as benefits (e.g., pensions, medical insurance, programs to help balance work and life demands, and so on). Programs to deliver compensation to people can be designed in a wide variety of ways, and a single employer typically uses more than one way. Both relational returns and total compensation can be designed to help the organization be successful. However, this book focuses on total compensation, which includes cash compensation and benefits.

Cash Compensation: Base

wage

pay calculated at an hourly rate

Base **wage** is the cash compensation that an employer pays for the work performed. Base wage tends to reflect the value of the work or skills and generally ignores differences attributable to individual employees. For example, the base wage for machine operators may be $12 an hour. However, some individual operators may receive more because of their experience and/or performance.

EXHIBIT 1.2 Total Returns for Work

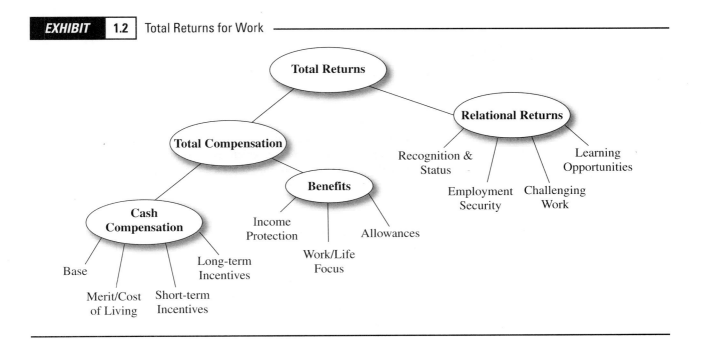

Some pay systems set base wage as a function of the skill or education an employee possesses; this is common for engineers and schoolteachers. A distinction is often made between a wage and a **salary**, with salary referring to pay that is calculated at an annual or monthly rate rather than hourly.

salary

pay calculated at an annual or monthly rate

Periodic adjustments to base wages may be made on the basis of changes in the overall cost of living, changes in what other employers are paying for the same work, or changes in experience or skill.

Cash Compensation: Merit Increases and Cost-of-Living Adjustments

merit increase

increment to base pay in recognition of past work behaviour

cost-of-living adjustment

percentage increment to base pay provided to all employees regardless of performance

Almost all Canadian firms use merit pay increases.[12] **Merit increases** are given as increments to the base pay in recognition of *past* work behavior. Some assessment of past performance is made, with or without a formal performance evaluation program, and the size of the increase is varied with performance. Thus, outstanding performers could receive an 8 to 10 percent merit increase 8 months after their last increase, whereas an average performer may receive, say, a 4 to 5 percent increase after 12 or 15 months. In contrast, a **cost-of-living adjustment** gives the same percentage increase across the board to everyone, regardless of performance, in order to maintain pay levels relative to increases in the cost of living.

Cash Compensation: Incentives

Incentives tie pay increases directly to performance. However, incentives differ from merit adjustments. First, incentives do not increase the base wage, and so must be re-earned each pay period. Second, the potential size of the incentive payment generally will be known beforehand. Whereas merit pay programs evaluate the past performance of an individual and then decide on the size of the increase, the performance objective for incentive payments is specified ahead of time. For example, an auto sales agent knows the commission on a BMW versus the commission on a Honda prior to making the sale. Thus, although both merit pay and incentives can influence performance, incentives do so by offering pay to influence future behaviour. Merit, on the other hand, recognizes and rewards past behaviours. The distinction is a matter of timing.

Incentives can be tied to the performance of an individual employee, a team of employees, a total business unit, or some combination of individual, team, and unit. The performance objective may be expense reduction, volume increases, customer satisfaction, revenue growth, return on investments, or increases in total shareholder value—the possibilities are endless.[13]

incentives/variable pay

one-time payments for meeting previously established performance objectives

Because **incentives** are one-time payments, they do not have a permanent effect on labour costs. When performance declines, incentive pay automatically declines, too. Consequently, incentives are frequently referred to as *variable pay*.

Long-Term Incentives

Incentives may be short or long term. Long-term incentives are intended to focus employee efforts on multi-year results. Although they could take the form of a cash bonus, more typically these returns are in the form of stock ownership or options to buy stock at specified, advantageous prices. Thus, they straddle the categories of cash compensation and benefits. Some argue that stock options are not compensation at all, that they are more accurately described as an "equity incentive" granted by owners to employees.[14] We will treat options as part of the financial returns employees receive from employers in exchange for their work and ideas.

The idea behind stock options is that giving employees a financial stake in how well the organization is doing will focus them on such long-term financial objectives as return on investment, market share, return on net assets, and the like. Magna grants shares of stock to selected key contributors who make outstanding contributions to the firm's success. Some companies have extended stock ownership beyond the ranks of managers and professionals. Sun Microsystems, Yahoo, Pepsi, Wal-Mart, and Starbucks offer stock options to all their employees. These companies believe that having a stake in the company supports a culture of ownership. They hope that employees will behave like owners.[15]

Benefits: Income Protection

Exhibit 1.2 shows that employee benefits, including income protection, work-life programs, and allowances, are also part of total compensation. Exhibit 1.2 shows that employee benefits, including income protection, work-life programs, and allowances, are also part of total compensation. Some income protection programs are legally required. For example, employers make contributions to the Canada/Quebec Pension Plan, Employment Insurance, and Workers' Compensation. Different countries have different lists of mandatory benefits.

Health insurance, dental insurance, pensions, and life insurance, are common benefits. They help protect employees from the financial risks inherent in daily life. Often, companies can provide these protections to employees more cheaply than employees can obtain them for themselves. Because the cost of providing benefits has been rising, they are an increasingly important form of pay.[16]

Benefits: Work-Life Programs

Programs that help employees better integrate their work and life responsibilities include time away from work (vacations, jury duty), access to services to meet specific needs (drug counselling, financial planning, referrals for child and elder care), and flexible work arrangements (telecommuting, nontraditional schedules, nonpaid time off). Responding to the tight labour market for highly skilled employees and the changing demographics of the work force (two-income families who demand employer flexibility so that family obligations can be met), many Canadian employers are giving a higher priority to these benefits forms. Husky Injection Molding in Bolton, Ontario offers a healthy workplace program with three main components—a wellness centre, a fitness centre, and a nutrition program.[17]

Benefits: Allowances

allowances

compensation to provide for items that are in short supply

Allowances often grow out of whatever is in short supply. In Korea and Japan, housing (dormitories and apartments) and transportation allowances are frequently part of the pay package. Some Japanese companies continue to offer a "rice allowance" based on number of dependents, a practice that grew out of post–World War II food shortages. Almost all companies starting operations in China discover that housing, transportation, and other allowances are expected. Companies that resist these allowances must come up with other ways to attract and retain talented employees. In many European countries, managers expect a car to be provided. The issue then becomes what make and model.

Total Earnings Opportunities: Present Value of a Stream of Earnings

Up to this point we have treated compensation as something paid or received at a moment in time. But compensation decisions have a temporal effect. Say you have a job offer of $30,000. If you stay with the firm five years and receive an annual increase of seven percent every five years, you will be earning $39,324 in five years. The expected cost commitment of the decision to hire you turns out to be $224,279 ($30,000 base compounded by seven percent for five years, plus benefits equal to 30 percent of base). So the decision to hire you implies a commitment of at least a quarter of a million dollars from your employer.

A present value perspective shifts the choice from comparing today's initial offers to consideration of future bonuses, merit increases, and promotions. Andersen Consulting, for example, says that their relatively low starting offers will be overcome by larger future pay increases. In effect, Andersen is selling the present value of the future stream of earnings. But few students apply that same analysis in calculating the future increases required to offset the lower initial offers. Hopefully, all students who get through Chapter One will now do so.

Relational Returns from Work

Why does Bill Gates still show up for work every morning? Why do all the Microsoft millionaires—relatively young employees made wealthy by the astounding performance of Microsoft stock—continue to write code? There is no doubt that nonfinancial returns from work create intrinsic motivation that has a substantial effect on employees' behaviour. Exhibit 1.2 includes recognition and status, employment security, challenging work, and opportunities to learn. Other relational forms might include personal satisfaction from successfully facing new challenges, teaming with great co-workers, and the like. Such factors are part of the total rewards, which is a broader umbrella than total compensation. So, although this book is about total compensation, let's not forget that compensation is only one of many factors affecting people's decisions about work. The .Net Worth box provides an example of a Canadian company using both total compensation and relational returns to attract new employees.

.NET WORTH   What Attracts Employees to a Job?

The findings from a 2002 study of 765 Canadian companies by compensation consultants Towers Perrin illustrate the importance of both total compensation and relational returns. Although competitive base pay is the top attraction to a job, the second most important is opportunities for advancement. In third place is competitive health care benefits. The fourth and fifth most important factors that make a job attractive to Canadians are work/life balance and recognition for work, respectively. Other important factors include challenging work, learning and development opportunities, and a competitive retirement package.[1]

One Canadian company that promotes both total compensation and relational returns is IMS Health, a medical information and consulting company with offices in Montreal and Toronto. Their Web site highlights total compensation, including pay, benefits, incentives, recognition, social events, work/life balance arrangements, career growth, and more.[2]

Sources:
[1] *The Towers Perrin Talent Report: New Realities in Today's Workforce* (Canadian Report). Toronto, ON: Towers Perrin, 2002, p.11.
[2] www.imshealthcanada.com (June 23, 2003)

■ A PAY MODEL

The pay model shown in **Exhibit 1.3** serves as both a framework for examining current pay systems and a guide to most of this book. It contains three basic building blocks: (1) the strategic compensation objectives, (2) the strategic policies that form the foundation of the compensation system, and (3) the techniques of compensation.

EXHIBIT | **1.3** | The Pay Model ————————————————————————

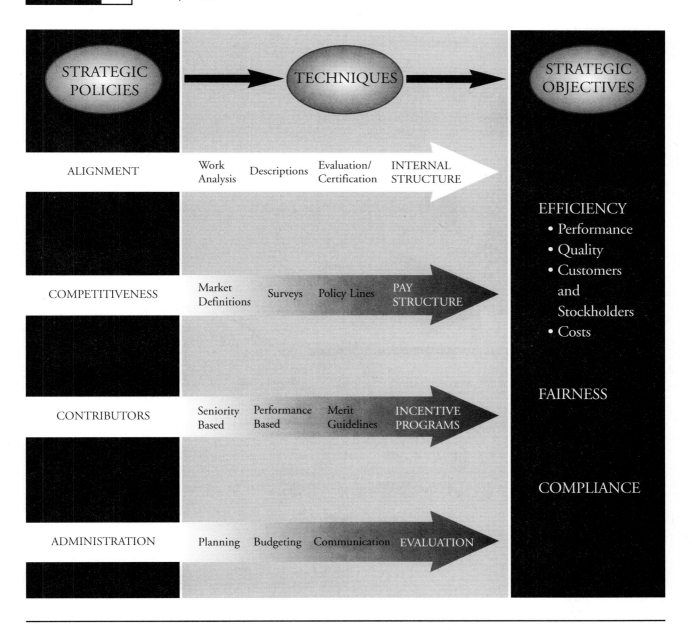

Strategic Compensation Objectives

strategic objectives

goals identified by an organization as necessary for the achievement of its strategy for success

Pay systems are designed and managed to achieve certain **strategic objectives**. The basic objectives, shown at the right side of the model, include efficiency, fairness, and compliance with laws and regulations. The efficiency objective can be stated more specifically: (1) improving performance, quality, delighting customers and stockholders, and (2) controlling labour costs. Compensation objectives at Medtronic and AES are contrasted in **Exhibit 1.4**. Medtronic is a medical technology company that pioneered cardiac pacemakers. Its compensation objectives emphasize performance, business success, and salaries that are competitive with other companies whose financial performance matches Medtronic's. AES generates and markets electricity around the world. Its goal is to "provide electricity worldwide in a socially responsible way." The notion of social responsibility pervades the company.

Fairness is a fundamental objective of pay systems. In Medtronic's objectives, fairness is reflected in "ensure fair treatment" and "be open and understandable." AES's mission statement acknowledges that, "Defining what is fair is often difficult, but we believe it is helpful to routinely question the relative fairness of alternative courses of action. It does not mean that everyone gets treated equally, but instead treated fairly or with justice given the appropriate situation."[18]

Thus, the fairness objective attempts to ensure fair treatment for all employees by recognizing both employee contributions (e.g., higher pay for greater performance, experience, or training) and employee needs (e.g., a fair wage as well as fair procedures). **Procedural fairness** is concerned with the processes used to make decisions about pay.[19] It suggests that the way a pay decision is made may be as important to employees as the results of the decision.

procedural fairness

fairness of the process used to make a decision

Compliance as a pay objective involves conforming to various federal, provincial, and territorial compensation laws and regulations. As these laws and regulations change, pay systems may need to be adjusted to ensure continued compliance.

There probably are as many statements of pay objectives as there are employers. In fact, highly diversified firms such as George Weston Ltd and Onex Corp, which compete in multiple lines of businesses, may have different pay objectives for different business units. Objectives at these companies emphasize the increased complexity of the business and importance of integrity

---

EXHIBIT   1.4   Comparison of Pay System Objectives at Medtronic and AES

Medtronic	AES
▪ Support objectives and increased complexity of business ▪ Minimize increases in fixed costs ▪ Emphasize performance through variable pay and stock ▪ Competitiveness aligned with financial performance: 50th percentile performance paid at 50th percentile of market, 75th percentile performance paid at 75th percentile of market	Our guiding principles are to act with integrity, treat people fairly, have fun, and be involved in projects that provide social benefits. This means we will ▪ Help AES attract self-motivated, dependable people who want to keep learning new things ▪ Hire people who really like the place and believe in the AES system ▪ Pay what others are paid both inside and and outside AES, but willing to take less to join AES ▪ Use teams of employees and managers to manage the compensation system ▪ Make all employees stockholders

(customers, quality), competitiveness (costs), ability to attract and retain quality people (performance), and having fun.

Objectives serve several purposes. First, they guide the design of the pay system. Consider the employer whose objective is to reward outstanding performance. That objective will determine the pay policy (e.g., pay for performance) as well as the elements of pay plans (e g., merit and/or incentives). Another employer's objectives may be to develop a flexible, continuously learning workforce through job design, training, and team-building techniques. A pay system that is aligned with this employer's objectives may have a policy of paying salaries that at least equal those of competitors and that go up with increased skills or knowledge. This pay system could be very different from our first example where the focus is on performance. Thus, different objectives guide the design of different pay systems.

Objectives also serve as the standards for judging the success of the pay system. If the objective is to attract and retain the best and the brightest, yet skilled employees are leaving to take higher paying jobs with other employers, the system may not be performing effectively. Although there may be many nonpay reasons for turnover, objectives provide standards for evaluating the effectiveness of a pay system.

Four Strategic Policies

Every employer must address the strategic policy decisions shown on the left side of the pay model: (1) internal alignment, (2) external competitiveness, (3) employee contributions, and (4) administration of the pay system. These policies form the foundation on which pay systems are built. These policies also serve as guidelines for managing pay in ways that accomplish the system's objectives.

Internal Alignment.   Internal alignment refers to comparisons between jobs or skill levels inside a single organization. Jobs and people's skills are compared in terms of their relative contributions to the organization's objectives. How, for example, does the work of the programmer compare with the work of the systems analyst, the software engineer, and the software architect? Does one contribute to providing solutions to customers and satisfying shareholders more than another? Does one require more knowledge or experience than another? Internal alignment refers to the pay rates both for employees doing equal work and for those doing dissimilar work. In fact, determining what is an appropriate difference in pay for people performing different work is one of the key challenges facing managers.

Internal alignment policies affect all three compensation objectives. Pay relationships within the organization affect employee decisions to stay with the organization, to become more flexible by investing in additional training, or to seek greater responsibility. By motivating employees to choose increased training and greater responsibility in dealing with customers, pay relationships indirectly affect the capabilities of the workforce and hence the efficiency of the entire organization. Fairness is affected in employees' comparisons of their pay to the pay of others in the organization. Basic fairness is provided by Canadian human rights laws, which make paying on the basis of race, gender, age, and other grounds, illegal.

External Competitiveness.   **External competitiveness** refers to compensation relationships external to the organization; i.e., comparison with competitors. How should an employer position its pay relative to what competitors are paying? *How much* do we wish to pay accountants in comparison to what other employers would pay them? *What mix* of pay forms—base, incentives, stock, benefits—will help achieve the compensation objectives? Employers have several policy options. Medtronic's policy is to pay competitively in its market based on its financial performance versus the financial performance of its competitors, while AES's policy is to expect people to be willing to take less to join the company.

Increasingly, organizations claim their pay systems are market driven, i.e., based almost exclusively on what competitors pay. However, "market driven" gets translated into practice in

external competitiveness

comparison of compensation with that of competitors

different ways. Some employers may set their pay levels higher than their competition, hoping to attract the best applicants. Of course, this assumes that someone is able to identify and hire the "best" from the pool of applicants.

What mix of pay forms a company uses is also part of its external competitive policy. Medtronic sets its base pay to match its competitors but ties incentives to performance. Plus it offers stock options to all its employees to promote a culture of ownership. The assumption is that owners will pay closer attention to the business. Further, Medtronic believes its benefits, particularly the emphasis on programs that balance work and life, make it a highly attractive place to work. Medtronic believes it is *how* it positions its pay, and *what forms* it uses, that gives it an advantage over its competitors. A Medtronic competitor, say MDS, may offer lower base pay but greater opportunity to work overtime or fatter bonuses. AES believes making all employees stockholders is consistent with its emphasis on social responsibility.

External competitiveness decisions—both how much, and what forms—have a twofold effect on objectives: (1) to ensure that the pay is sufficient to attract and retain employees—if employees do not perceive their pay as competitive in comparison to what other organizations are offering for similar work, they may be more likely to leave—and (2) to control labour costs so that the organization's prices of products or services can remain competitive. Thus, external competitiveness directly affects both efficiency and fairness. And it must do so in a way that complies with relevant legislation.

Employee Contributions.   The policy on employee contributions refers to the relative emphasis placed on performance. Should one programmer be paid differently from another if one has better performance and/or greater seniority? Or should all employees share in the organization's financial success (or failure) via incentives based on profit? Perhaps more productive teams of employees should be paid more than less productive teams.

The degree of emphasis to be placed on performance is an important policy decision, since it directly affects employees' attitudes and work behaviours. Employers with strong pay-for-performance policies are more likely to place greater emphasis on incentives and merit pay. Starbucks emphasizes stock options and sharing the success of corporate performance with the employees. General Electric emphasizes performance at the unit, division, and companywide level. Recognition of contributions also affects fairness, since employees need to understand the basis for judging performance in order to believe that their pay is fair.

Administration.   Policy regarding administration of the pay system is the last building block in our model. Although it is possible to design a system that is based on internal alignment, external competitiveness, and employee contributions, the system will not achieve its objectives unless it is managed properly.

The greatest system design in the world is useless without competent management. Managers choose what forms of pay to include and how to position pay against competitors. They must communicate with employees and judge whether the system is achieving its objectives. They must ask, Are we able to attract skilled workers? Can we keep them? Do our employees feel our system is fair? Do they understand how their pay is determined? How do the better-performing firms, with better financial returns and a larger share of the market, pay their employees? Are the systems used by these firms different from those used by less successful firms? How do our labour costs compare to our competitors? Answers to these questions are necessary in order to tune or redesign the system, to adjust to changes, and to highlight potential areas for further investigation. At AES, there is no compensation department, nor even a human resources management department. Instead, teams of employees make all the compensation decisions. The assumption is that this approach will ensure that everyone feels they are being treated fairly.

Pay Techniques

The remaining portion of the pay model in Exhibit 1.3 shows the pay techniques. The exhibit provides only an overview, since techniques are discussed throughout the rest of the book. Techniques tie the four basic policies to the pay objectives. Internal alignment typically is established through a sequence that starts with analysis of the work done and the people needed to do it. Information about the person and/or the job is collected, organized, and evaluated. Based on these evaluations, a structure of the work is designed.

This structure depicts relationships among jobs and skills or competencies inside an organization. It is based on the relative importance of the work in achieving the organization's objectives. The goal is to establish a structure that is aligned with and supports the organization's objectives. In turn, fairness of the pay system affects employee attitudes and behaviours as well as the organization's regulatory compliance.

External competitiveness is established by setting the organization's pay level in comparison with how much competitors pay for similar work and what pay forms they use. The total compensation is determined by defining the relevant labour markets in which the employer competes, conducting surveys to find out how and what other employers pay, and using that information in conjunction with the organization's policy decisions to generate a pay structure. The pay structure influences how well the organization is able to attract and retain a competent workforce and to control its labour costs.

The relative emphasis on employee contributions is established through performance and/or seniority-based increases, incentive plans, and stock options and other performance-based approaches. Increasingly, organizations in Canada and around the globe are using some form of incentive plan to share their success with employees. In addition to managing costs, these practices are intended to affect employee attitudes and behaviours, in particular the decisions to join the organization, to stay, and to perform effectively.

Uncounted variations in pay techniques exist; many are examined in this book. Surveys report differences in compensation policies and techniques among firms. Indeed, many consulting firms have Web pages in which they report their survey results. You can obtain updated information on various practices simply by surfing the Web.

■ BOOK PLAN

Compensation is such a broad and compelling topic that several books could be devoted to it. The focus of this book will be on the design and management of compensation systems. To aid in understanding how and why pay systems work, our pay model, which emphasizes the key strategic objectives, policies, and techniques, also provides the structure for much of the book.

Chapter 2 discusses how to formulate and implement a compensation strategy. We analyze what it means to be strategic about how people are paid and how compensation can help achieve and sustain an organization's competitive advantage.

The pay model plays a central role in formulating and implementing an organization's pay strategy. The pay model identifies four basic policy decisions that are the core of the pay strategy. After we discuss strategy, the next sections of the book will examine each in detail. The first, *internal alignment* (Chapters 3 through 6), examines pay relationships within a single organization. The next section (Chapters 7 and 8) examines *external competitiveness*—the pay relationships among competing organizations—and analyzes the influence of market-driven forces.

Once the compensation rates and structures are established, other issues emerge. How much should we pay each individual employee? How much and how often should a person's pay be increased, and on what basis—experience, seniority, or performance? Should pay increases be contingent on the organization's and/or the employee's performance? How should the organization share its success (or failure) with employees? Stock awards, profit sharing, bonuses, merit pay? These are examples of employee contributions, the third building block in the model (Chapters 9 and 10). After that, we cover employee services and benefits (Chapter 11). The role of governments and unions in compensation is examined in Chapter 12. We conclude with managing the compensation system (Chapter 13), which includes planning, budgeting, evaluating, and communicating. More detail on global compensation systems is provided in the Appendix.

Even though the book is divided into sections that reflect the pay model, that does not mean that pay policies and decisions are discrete. All policy decisions are interrelated. Together, they influence employee behaviours and organization performance, and can be a source of competitive advantage.

Our intention throughout the book is to examine alternative approaches. We believe that there rarely is a single correct approach; rather, alternative approaches exist or can be designed. The one most likely to be effective depends on the circumstances. We hope that this book will help you to become better informed about these options and how to design new ones. Whether as an employee, a manager, or an interested member of society, you should be able to assess effectiveness and fairness of pay systems.

■ CAVEAT EMPTOR—BE AN INFORMED CONSUMER

Our understanding of compensation management grows as research evidence accumulates. Nevertheless, evidence needs to be evaluated to determine its quality, relevance, and information value. Managers need to be informed consumers. Belief is a poor substitute for informed judgment.

Therefore, your challenge is to become an informed consumer of compensation information. How-to-do-it advice abounds, best-practices prescriptions are plentiful, and academic journals are packed with pay-related theory and research. We end the chapter with a brief consumer's guide that includes three questions.

1. Does the Research Measure Anything Useful?

How useful are the variables used in the study? How well are they measured? For example, many studies purport to measure organization performance. However, performance may be determined by accounting measures such as return on assets or cash flow, financial measures such as earnings per share or total shareholder return, operational measures such as scrap rates or defect indicators, or qualitative measures such as customer satisfaction. Performance may even be evaluated by the opinions of compensation managers, as in: How effective is your gain-sharing plan? (Answer choices are: highly effective, somewhat effective, somewhat ineffective, highly ineffective.) So the informed consumer must ask, Does this research measure anything important?

2. Does the Study Separate Correlation from Causation?

Correlation does not mean causation. For example, many studies investigate the relationship between the use of performance-based pay and performance. Just because the use of gain-sharing plans is related to improved performance does not mean that it caused the improvement. Other factors may be involved. Perhaps new technology, reengineering, improved marketing, or the general expansion of the local economy underlie the results.

Once we are confident that our variables are defined and measured accurately, we must be sure that they are actually related. Most often this is addressed through the use of statistical analyses. The correlation coefficient is a common measure of association that indicates how changes in one variable are related to changes in another. Many research studies use a statistical analysis known as regression analysis. One output from a regression analysis is the R^2. The R^2 is much like a correlation in that it tells us what percentage of the variation is accounted for by the variables we are using to predict or explain. For example, one study includes a regression analysis of the change in CEO pay due to change in company performance. The resulting R^2 of between 0.8 percent and 4.5 percent indicates that only a very small amount of change in CEO pay is related to changes in company performance.

Note that relation is not necessarily causation. For example, just because a manufacturing plant initiates a new incentive plan and the facility's performance improves, we cannot conclude that the incentive plan caused the improved performance. The two changes are associated or related, but causation is a tough link to make.

Too often, case studies, benchmarking studies of best practices, or consultant surveys are presented as studies that reveal cause and effect. They are not. Case studies are descriptive accounts whose value and limitations must be recognized. Just because the best-performing companies are using a practice does not mean the practice is causing the performance. For a long time, IBM pursued a full-employment policy. Clearly, that policy did not cause the value of IBM stock to increase or improve IBM's profitability. Arguably, it was IBM's profitability that enabled its full-employment policy. However, compensation research often attempts to answer questions of causality. Does the use of performance-based pay lead to greater customer satisfaction, improved quality, and better company performance? Causality is one of the most difficult questions to answer and continues to be an important and sometimes perplexing problem for researchers.

3. Are There Alternative Explanations?

Consider a hypothetical study that attempts to assess the impact of a performance-based pay initiative. The researchers measure performance by assessing quality, productivity, customer satisfaction, employee satisfaction, and the facility's performance. The final step is to see whether future performance improves over current performance. If it does, can we safely assume that it was the incentive pay that caused improved performance? Or is it equally likely that the improved performance has alternative explanations, such as the fluctuation in the value of currency, or perhaps a change in executive leadership in the facility? In this case, causal evidence seems weak.

If the researchers had measured the performance indicators several years prior to and after installing the plan, then the evidence of causality would be a bit stronger. Furthermore, if the researchers repeated this process in other facilities and found similar results, then the preponderance of evidence would be stronger. Clearly, the organization is doing something right, and incentive pay may be part of it.

The best way to establish causation is to account for these competing explanations, either statistically or through control groups. The point is that alternative explanations often exist. And if they do, they need to be accounted for in order to establish causality. It is very difficult to disentangle the effects of pay plans to clearly establish causality. However, it is possible to look at the overall pattern of evidence to make judgments about the effects of pay.

CONCLUSION

The model presented in this chapter provides a structure for understanding compensation systems. The three main components of the model include the objectives of the pay system, the policy decisions that provide the system's foundation, and the techniques that link policies and objectives. The following sections of the book examine each of the four policy decisions—internal alignment, external competitiveness, employee contributions, and administration—as well as techniques, new directions, and related research.

Two questions should constantly be in the minds of managers and readers of this text. First, Why do it this way? There is rarely one correct way to design a system or pay an individual.

Organizations, people, and circumstances are too varied. But a well-trained manager can select or design a suitable approach.

Second, So what? What does this technique do for us? How does it help achieve our organization goals? If good answers are not apparent, there is no point to the technique. Adapting the pay system to meet the needs of the employees and to help achieve the goals of the organization is what this book is all about.

The basic premise of this book is that compensation systems do have a profound impact. Yet, too often, traditional pay systems seem to be designed in response to some historic but long-forgotten problem. The practices continue, but the logic underlying them is not always clear or even relevant.

CHAPTER SUMMARY

1. Compensation is used by society as a measure of justice, a cause of increased taxes and price increases. Stockholders are concerned with executive pay relative to company performance. Managers see compensation as a major expense and a means to influence employee behaviour. Employees see compensation as a return in an exchange with their employer, an entitlement, or a reward. In other countries, compensation relates to being taken care of.
2. The two major components of total returns for work are total compensation and relational returns. Total compensation is composed of cash compensation (base pay and incentives) and benefits. Relational returns include psychological aspects of work such as recognition and status, challenging work, and learning opportunities.
3. The four strategic policies in the pay model are internal alignment, external competitiveness, employee contributions, and administration. The internal structure techniques associated with alignment are work analysis, descriptions, and evaluation/certification. The pay structure techniques associated with competitiveness are market definitions, surveys, and pay policy lines. The incentive program techniques associated with contributions are seniority-based, performance-based, and merit guidelines. The evaluation techniques associated with administration are planning, budgeting, and communication.
4. The strategic objectives of compensation are (1) efficiency in performance and quality, satisfying customers and stockholders, and controlling costs, (2) fairness, and (3) compliance with laws and regulations.

KEY TERMS

allowances 7
compensation. 5
cost-of-living adjustment 6
external competitiveness 11
incentives (variable pay) 6
merit increase. 6
procedural fairness 10
relational returns 5
salary. 6
strategic objectives 10
wage 5

REVIEW QUESTIONS

1. How do differing perspectives affect our views of compensation?
2. How does the pay model help organize one's thinking about compensation?
3. What can a pay system do for an organization? For an employee? Are these mutually exclusive?

EXPERIENTIAL EXERCISES

1. What is your definition of compensation? Which meaning of compensation seems most appropriate from an employee's view – return, reward, or entitlement? Compare your ideas with someone who has more experience, with someone from another country, with someone from another field of study.

2. List all the forms of pay you receive from work. Compare to someone else's list. Explain any differences.

3. Answer the three questions in Caveat Emptor for any study or business article that tells you how to pay people. Such articles can be found in the *WorldatWork Journal* or *Compensation and Benefits Review*.

WEB EXERCISE

Compensation on the Web

The WorldAtWork Web site www.worldatwork.org provides information on its compensation-related journals and special publications, as well as short courses aimed at practitioners. The Canadian Council of Human Resource Associations (CCHRA) www.cchra-ccarh.ca provides links to provincial HR associations that offer compensation-related information as well as more general HRM information. Some provinces have job boards for HR association members, including students. Both sites are good sources of information for people interested in careers in HRM. The Employee Benefits Research Institute (EBRI) includes links to other benefits sources on its Web site at www.ebri.org. Using the WorldAtWork and EBRI sites as a starting point, search for a list of five or more compensation magazines and journals.

CASE

Inside Internships

Many students work as unpaid interns as they begin their careers. Jaime Hurlbut completed a one-year internship at the Canadian Youth Business Foundation. The internship was provided through Career Edge, a private organization that arranges youth internships. Jaime found that when he graduated from university, most jobs he wanted required two to three years of experience. His internship gave him the means to succeed, and he was hired full-time as a Marketing and Communications Coordinator at the Canadian Youth Business Foundation. Jaime's satisfaction is obvious. He says: "I am finally doing what I have always dreamed of."

Questions

1. What do employers receive from summer interns? What returns do students get from the opportunities?

2. Should summer interns be paid? If so, how much? How would you recommend an employer decide the answers to both these questions?

3. What added information would you like to have before you make your recommendations? How would you use this information?

Source: "Inside Internships" www.careeredge.ca/testimonials.asp?sequence=3 (June 11, 2003).

STRATEGIC PERSPECTIVES

LEARNING OUTCOMES

- ■ *Explain* the four steps to develop a total compensation strategy.
- ■ *Explain* why managers should tailor their pay systems to support the organization's strategy.
- ■ *Describe* the two tests used to determine whether a pay strategy is a source of competitive advantage.
- ■ *Contrast* the "best fit" perspective on compensation with the "best practices" perspective.

You probably think you can skip this chapter. After all, what can be so challenging about forming and implementing a compensation strategy? Need a strategy? Just pay whatever the market rate is.

But a dose of reality quickly reveals that employers cannot behave so simply. As noted in the last chapter, companies compete very differently for very similar talent. Firepond, Microsoft, and Bristol-Myers Squibb (BMS) provide strategic perspectives. Firepond, a small startup, offers "software solutions" to large, traditional firms ("bricks and mortar") that are trying to grow e-businesses ("clicks"). As Exhibit 2.1 shows, Firepond, Microsoft, and BMS all emphasize employee performance and commitment, but each company does it differently. Firepond offers the potential of "hitting it big" by emphasizing stock options and deemphasizing cash (base and bonus) compared to its competitors.[1] This strategy is common among startup companies because it conserves cash for operating expenses (e.g., Friday beer and pizza, and paying the rent on the garage) and funding growth. In its earlier years, Microsoft explicitly asked its employees to "put some skin in the game,"[2] or accept less base pay to join a company whose stock options were increasing in worth exponentially.

But Microsoft changed. Facing fierce competition for software talent and litigation that depressed its stock value, Microsoft shifted its strategy to increase its base and bonus to the 65th percentile from the 45th percentile of competitors' pay, while still retaining its strong emphasis on options. So Microsoft not only changed *how much* (total compensation) it paid, but also *what mix of forms* it offers (relative importance of base, bonus, options, and benefits). Beyond this, Microsoft added a level to its internal structure, a new title of "Distinguished Engineers" for those whose jobs are critical to Microsoft success. It also started offering what

EXHIBIT **2.1** Strategic Perspectives toward Total Compensation ————————————

	Microsoft	Bristol-Myers Squibb	Firepond
Objectives	• Support the business objectives • Support recruiting, motivation, and retention of MS-calibre talent • Preserve MS core values	• Support business mission and goals • Develop global leaders at every level • Reinforce team-based culture • Reduce costs, increase productivity	• Demonstrate respect for individual talent and the limitless potential of a highly motivated team • Encourage high standards of excellence, original thinking, a passion for the process of discovery, and a willingness to take risks • Reward fresh ideas, hard work, and a commitment to excellence • Value diverse perspectives as a key to discovery
Internal Alignment	• Integral part of MS culture • Support MS performance-driven culture • Business/technology-based organization design structure	• Reflect responsibilities, required competencies, and business impact • Flexibility for development and growth	• Pay differences that foster a collegial atmosphere • Reinforce high expectations
Externally Competitive	• Lead in *total* compensation • Lag in base pay • Lead with bonuses, stock options	• Compare favourably to higher-performing competitors • Cash between the 50th and 75th percentile	• "Pay what others are paying"
Employee Contributions	• Bonuses and options based on individual performance	• Support high performance, leadership culture • Team-based increases • Options align employee and shareholder interest • Tailor to business and team results	• Bonus pool based on Firepond financial performance. Individual share of pool based on individual performance • Push stock ownership deep into company
Administration	• Open, transparent communications • Centralized administration • Software supported	• Performance and leadership feedback–everyone is a leader • Administrative ease	• Goal-focused, team-oriented, and self-managed

can only be called eye-popping performance-based stock options, at least five times what their competitors offered to outstanding people.

The approach at BMS, a global pharmaceutical, differs. BMS's mission is "to extend and enhance human life." Although it also uses options and bonuses tied to performance, the amounts are much smaller than at Firepond and Microsoft. BMS's strategy emphasizes greater balance among cash compensation (base and bonus), options, and a strong package of work/life balance programs. BMS uses its compensation to reinforce teamwork; it does not offer individual incentives except for a select few extraordinary contributors. BMS also focuses on developing skills and leadership at all levels in the organization. SAS Institute, the world's largest privately owned software company, provides yet a different mix. It emphasizes its work/life programs over cash compensation and gives only limited bonuses and no options. SAS headquarters provides free onsite child care centres, subsidized private schools for children of employees, two doctors on site for free medical care, plus recreation facilities. Working more than 35 hours per week is discouraged. In contrast, Microsoft built part of its mystique on stories of engineers sleeping under their desks and competing to be first in/last out of the company parking lot. These companies have very different strategic perspectives on total compensation.

A simple "let the market decide our compensation strategy" doesn't work internationally either. In many nations, markets do not operate as in North America or may not even exist. People either do not, or in some cases, cannot easily change employers. In China and some Eastern European countries, markets for labour are just emerging. Even in some countries with more developed economies, such as Germany and Sweden, the labour market is highly regulated. Consequently, there is less movement of people among companies than is common in Canada, the US, or even in Korea and Singapore.[3]

Understanding the differences in compensation strategies becomes important as well during acquisitions and mergers. Auto workers at the Volvo plant in Gothenburg, Sweden (recently acquired by Ford), can enjoy a gym, Olympic-sized swimming pool, tennis, track and tanning beds, along with a hot-water pool and physical therapy sessions after a hard day (30 hours per week) on the assembly line. Autoworkers at Ford's assembly plant in Oakville, Ontario, enjoy no such comparable facilities. Will Ford be able to continue such divergent compensation strategies at its Volvo and US operations? It is possible for different business units within the same company to adopt different compensation strategies. But if Volvo and Ford begin to share common parts and distribution channels and form global teams to design new cars, then these differences may become obstacles to achieving the needed cooperation and integration. The point is that a strategic perspective on compensation is more complex than it first appears. So we suggest that you continue to read this chapter.

■ STRATEGIC PERSPECTIVES

Because pay matters so much to most of us, it is sometimes too easy to become fixated on techniques: Sharing and examining so-called "best practices" becomes an end in itself. Questions such as "What does this technique do for (to) us?" or, "How does it help achieve our objectives?" are not asked. So, before proceeding to the particulars, think about how pay might support a business strategy. After completing this chapter, you should know how to develop a compensation strategy. More importantly, you should also know why you would bother doing so. Train yourself to ask the "So what?" question as you read this book. Once you do, you will be prepared to shine when your employer asks if your proposal makes sense.

■ SUPPORT BUSINESS STRATEGY

A currently popular theory found in almost every book and consultant's report tells managers to tailor their pay systems to support the organization's strategic directions. The rationale is based on contingency notions. That is, differences in a firm's strategy should be supported by corresponding differences in its human resource strategy, including compensation. *The underlying premise is that the greater the alignment, or fit, between the organization and the compensation system, the more effective the organization.*[4]

competitive advantage

■ a business practice or process that results in better performance than other competitors

what are we best at?

As Exhibit 2.2 depicts, compensation systems can be designed to support the organization's business strategy and to adapt to the sociopolitical, competitive, and regulatory pressures in the environment. The ultimate purpose—the "so what?"—is to gain and sustain **competitive advantage**.[5] It follows then that when business strategies change, pay systems need to change. A classic example is IBM's strategic and cultural transformation. IBM's emphasis on internal alignment (well-developed job evaluation plan, clear hierarchy for decision making, work/life balance benefits, policy of no layoffs) had served it well during the 1960s and throughout the 1980s

---

EXHIBIT   2.2   Strategic Choices

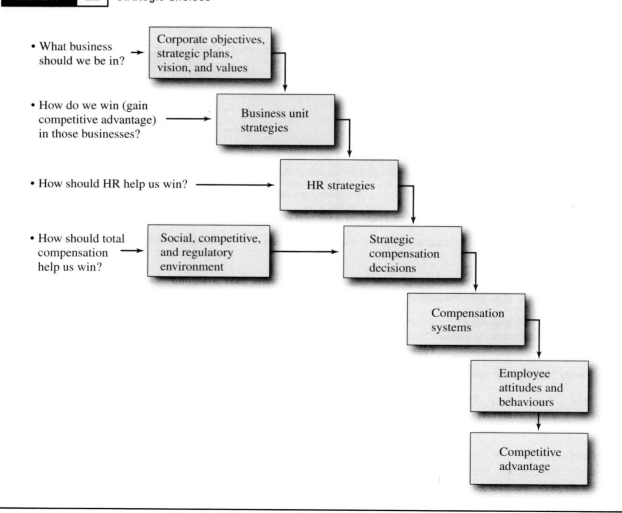

- What business should we be in? → Corporate objectives, strategic plans, vision, and values

- How do we win (gain competitive advantage) in those businesses? → Business unit strategies

- How should HR help us win? → HR strategies

- How should total compensation help us win? → Social, competitive, and regulatory environment → Strategic compensation decisions

Compensation systems

Employee attitudes and behaviours

Competitive advantage

when the company dominated the market for high-profit mainframe computers. But it did not provide flexibility to adapt to industry changes in the 1990s. A redesigned IBM now emphasizes cost control and a high performance culture (incentive pay), greater risk taking, and an increased focus on customers (product and service leadership). IBM's Web site now features information on "Innovations" and "e-Business." IBM changed its pay strategy and system to support its changed business strategy.[6]

strategic perspective

a focus on compensation decisions that help the organization gain and sustain competitive advantage

If the basic premise of a **strategic perspective** is to align the compensation system to the business strategy, then different business strategies will translate into different compensation approaches. Exhibit 2.3 gives an example of how compensation systems might be tailored to three different business strategies.[7] The *innovator* stresses new products and short response time to market trends. A supporting compensation approach places less emphasis on evaluating skills and jobs and more emphasis on incentives designed to encourage innovations. The *cost cutter's* efficiency-focused strategy stresses doing more with less by minimizing costs, encouraging productivity increases, and specifying in greater detail exactly how jobs should be performed. The *customer-focused* business strategy stresses delighting customers and bases employee pay on how well they do this. Different business strategies require different compensation approaches. One size does not fit all.[8]

EXHIBIT 2.3 Tailor the Compensation System to the Strategy

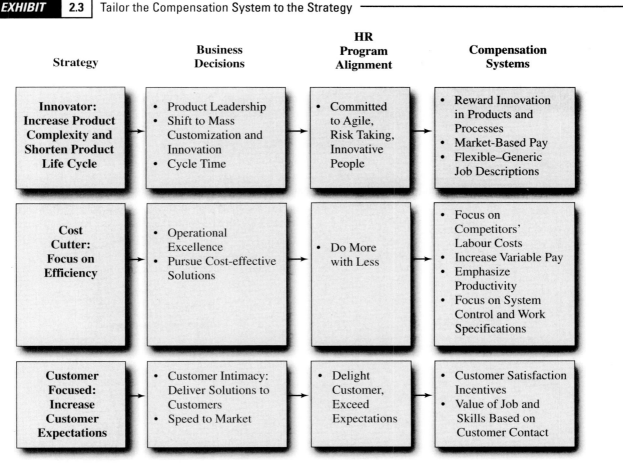

Strategy	Business Decisions	HR Program Alignment	Compensation Systems
Innovator: **Increase Product Complexity and Shorten Product Life Cycle**	• Product Leadership • Shift to Mass Customization and Innovation • Cycle Time	• Committed to Agile, Risk Taking, Innovative People	• Reward Innovation in Products and Processes • Market-Based Pay • Flexible–Generic Job Descriptions
Cost Cutter: **Focus on Efficiency**	• Operational Excellence • Pursue Cost-effective Solutions	• Do More with Less	• Focus on Competitors' Labour Costs • Increase Variable Pay • Emphasize Productivity • Focus on System Control and Work Specifications
Customer Focused: **Increase Customer Expectations**	• Customer Intimacy: Deliver Solutions to Customers • Speed to Market	• Delight Customer, Exceed Expectations	• Customer Satisfaction Incentives • Value of Job and Skills Based on Customer Contact

■ WHICH PAY DECISIONS ARE STRATEGIC?

strategy

■ the fundamental business decisions that an organization has made in order to achieve its strategic objectives, such as what business to be in and how to obtain competitive advantage

Strategy refers to the fundamental business decisions that an organization has made in order to achieve its strategic objectives. An organization defines its strategy through the tradeoffs it makes in choosing what (and what not) to do. Exhibit 2.2 relates these strategic choices to the quest for competitive advantage. At the corporate level, the fundamental strategic choice is, *What business should we be in?* At the business unit level, the choice shifts to, *How do we gain and sustain competitive advantage?* How do we win in those businesses? At the functional/systems level the strategic choice is, *How should total compensation help gain and sustain competitive advantage?*

The competitive advantage of Starbucks is apparent with the first sip of their specialty drink, mocha valencia. What started out as a Seattle seller of coffee beans has, through strategic decisions, grown to a familiar chain of coffeehouses stretching around the globe.[9] Along the way, Starbucks managers have designed a total compensation system to support this change in fundamental direction (from coffee bean importer to trendy coffeehouses) and growth (phenomenal, global). Their strategic perspective has led them to make compensation choices that help the organization gain and sustain competitive advantage.

Using our pay model, the strategic compensation decisions facing Starbucks managers can be considered in terms of the objectives and the four basic policies.

1. **Objectives:** How should compensation support the business strategy and be adaptive to the cultural and regulatory pressures in a global environment? (Starbucks objectives: Grow by making employees feel valued. Recognize that every dollar earned passes through employees' hands. Use pay, benefits, and opportunities for personal development to help gain employee loyalty and become difficult to imitate.)
2. **Alignment:** How differently should the different types and levels of skills and work be paid within the organization? (Starbucks: Deemphasize differences. Use egalitarian pay structures, cross-train employees to handle many jobs, and call employees "partners.")
3. **Competitiveness:** How should total compensation be positioned against our competitors? (Starbucks: Pay just slightly above other fast-food employers, a low-wage industry.) What forms of compensation should we use? (Starbucks: Provide health insurance and stock options, called bean stocks, for all employees including part-timers [even though most are relatively young and healthy, and few stay long enough to earn stock options], and give everyone a free pound of coffee every week.)
4. **Contributions:** Should pay increases be based on individual and/or team performance, on experience and/or continuous learning, on improved skills, on changes in cost of living, on personal needs (housing, transportation, health services), and/or on each business unit's performance? (Starbucks: Emphasize team performance and shareholder returns [options]. For new managers in Beijing and Prague, provide training opportunities in the United States.)
5. **Administration:** How open and transparent should the pay decisions be to all employees? Who should be involved in designing and managing the system? (Starbucks: As members of the Starbucks "family," our employees realize what is best for them. Partners can and do get involved.)

The decisions underlying these five issues, taken together, form a pattern that becomes an organization's compensation strategy.

Stated versus Unstated Strategies

All organizations that pay people have a compensation strategy. Some may have written, or stated, compensation strategies for all to see and understand. Others may not even realize they have a compensation strategy. Ask managers of these organizations what the compensation strategy is, and you might get a strange look. "We do whatever it takes" will be a pragmatic response. Their compensation strategy emerges from the pay decisions that they have made. Unstated compensation strategy is inferred from compensation practices.[10]

The point is that managers in all organizations make the five strategic decisions discussed earlier. Some do it in a rational, planned way, others do it more chaotically—as ad hoc responses to pressures from the economic, sociopolitical, and regulatory context in which the organization operates.

■ STEPS TO DEVELOP A TOTAL COMPENSATION STRATEGY

Developing a compensation strategy involves four simple steps. As Exhibits 2.2 and 2.4 reveal, the steps are familiar to any manager.

Although the steps are simple, executing them is complex. The process really becomes an art. Trial and error, experience, and insight play major roles. The process is dynamic, with the cycle being repeated as often as required.

Step 1: Assess Total Compensation Implications

Think about any organization's past, present, and most vitally, its future. What factors in its business environment have contributed to the company's success? Which of these factors are likely to

---

EXHIBIT 2.4 Key Steps to Formulate a Total Compensation Strategy

1. **Assess Total Compensation Implications**
   Competitive Dynamics
   Core Culture/Values
   Social and Political Context
   Employee/Union Needs
   Other HR Systems

2. **Fit Policy Decisions to Strategy**
   Objectives
   Alignment
   Competitiveness
   Contributions
   Administration

3. **Implement Strategy**
   Design System to Translate Strategy into Action
   Choose Techniques to Fit Strategy

4. **Reassess the Fit**
   Realign as Conditions Change
   Realign as Strategy Changes

become more (or less) important as the company looks ahead? Exhibit 2.4 classifies the factors as competitive dynamics, culture/values, social and political context, employee/union needs, and other HR systems.

Competitive Dynamics. This first step includes an understanding of the industry in which the organization operates and how it plans to compete. To cope with the turbulent competitive dynamics, focus on what factors in the business environment (i.e., changing customer needs, competitors' actions, changing labour market conditions, changing regulations, globalization) are important today. What will be important in the future? Start with the basics. What is your business strategy? How do you compete and win? How should the compensation system change to support and be part of that strategy? Learn to sense or read the underlying dynamics in your business (or build relationships with those who can). We have already discussed fitting different compensation strategies to different business strategies, using the business strategies of cost-cutter, customer centred, and innovator (Exhibit 2.3). But be cautious. Reality is more complex and chaotic. Organizations are not necessarily innovators, cost cutters, or customer centred. Instead, they are some of each, and more. So the rational, planned, and orderly image conveyed in Exhibit 2.3 does not adequately capture the turbulent and chaotic competitive dynamics underlying this process.[11]

Global pressures are an increasingly important component of competitive dynamics.[12] However, comparing pay between countries is complex. In Chapter 1, we noted differences in hourly labour costs and productivity (output per dollar of wages) between countries. But as we shall see later, countries also differ in the average length of the workweek, the average number of paid holidays, the kinds of social support programs, and even on how wages are set.[13] Different global competitors use different pay systems. Exhibit 2.5 describes Toshiba's total cash compensation for its managers. Thirty-seven percent of a Toshiba manager's pay is in the form of bonuses. Because they are paid out twice a year rather than in a biweekly paycheque, bonuses give Toshiba a cash flow advantage. In addition, because bonuses are not added into the employee's base pay, they do not become fixed costs. Japan levies payroll taxes on base wages only (in the exhibit, core salary), not on bonuses or allowances. Hence, the mix of forms at Toshiba (and most Japanese employers) emphasizes bonuses and allowances rather than core salary. A common

---

EXHIBIT 2.5 Toshiba's Managerial Compensation Plan Annual Amount (In Yen) ————————

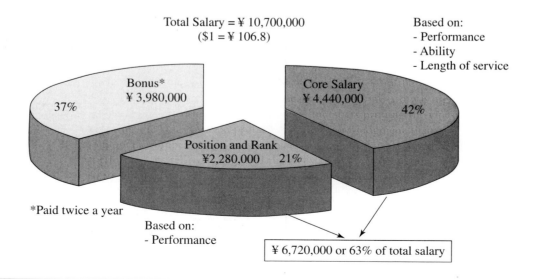

Total Salary = ¥ 10,700,000
($1 = ¥ 106.8)

Based on:
- Performance
- Ability
- Length of service

Bonus*
¥ 3,980,000

37%

Core Salary
¥ 4,440,000

42%

Position and Rank
¥2,280,000 21%

*Paid twice a year

Based on:
- Performance

¥ 6,720,000 or 63% of total salary

misperception is that Japanese pay systems are based solely on seniority. But, notice that Toshiba's managers' pay depends on educational level (ability), experience (i.e., seniority), and performance. Toshiba's use of performance-based pay is not unique in Japan. Toyota, Mitsubishi, and other traditional Japanese firms are also increasing their performance-based plans.[14] So managers do not simply face domestic competitors; they also must become knowledgeable in how their global competitors compete with pay.

Globalization's impact on compensation strategy was highlighted in Daimler-Benz's acquisition of Chrysler. At the time, the pay of the top 10 Daimler executives amounted to $10.7 million, compared to over $11 million paid to Chrysler's CEO alone. Such differences were not confined to the top executives. They rippled throughout the newly merged company. Exhibit 2.6 shows that at Chrysler as little as 25 percent of managers' pay was in the form of base salary. Performance-based bonuses and stock options made up the rest. At Daimler, up to 60 percent of managers' pay was in the form of base salary. Because of German tax codes at the time of the merger (since changed), stock options were used sparingly. So what difference does this make? If Daimler–Chrysler wants to win in the worldwide automobile market with a new global business strategy, it must consider the implications of how it compensates its company leadership worldwide rather than just nationwide.

Culture/Values. A pay system reflects the values that underlie an employer's treatment of its employees. In many organizations, core values guide employees' business behaviours and are reflected in the pay systems. The pay system mirrors the company's image and reputation. Exhibit 2.7 shows the values statements for Medtronic and AES. Medtronic's value number 5 recognizes employees' worth by fostering "personal satisfaction in work accomplished, security, advancement opportunity, and means to share in the company success." Its compensation strategy reflects this value by including work/life balance programs for security, incentives, and stock options to share in the company's success. AES gives stock to every single employee. They view this as part of their commitment to fairness and social responsibility.

But there are some skeptics out there. One study described mission statements as "an assemblage of trite phrases which impressed no one." On the other hand, Johnson and Johnson sees them as "the glue that holds our corporation together."[15]

Social and Political Context. In Exhibit 2.4, the sociopolitical context also affects compensation choices. Context refers to a wide range of factors, including legal and regulatory requirements, cultural differences, changing work force demographics, expectations, and the like. In the case of Starbucks, business is very people intensive. Consequently, Starbucks managers expect that an increasingly diverse workforce and increasingly diverse forms of pay (child care, chemical dependency counselling, educational reimbursements, employee assistance programs) may add value and be difficult for competitors (fast food outlets and other coffee shops) to imitate.[16]

EXHIBIT   2.6   Strategic Differences in Pay Forms at Daimler and Chrysler

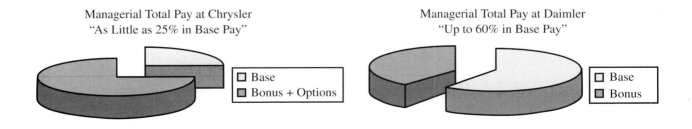

Managerial Total Pay at Chrysler
"As Little as 25% in Base Pay"

☐ Base
☐ Bonus + Options

Managerial Total Pay at Daimler
"Up to 60% in Base Pay"

☐ Base
☐ Bonus

EXHIBIT	2.7	Comparison of Medtronic and AES Mission and Values

Medtronic Values

Medtronic's mission imparts stability and provides a firm foundation for the company's growth. Written more than 30 years ago, our mission statement gives purpose to our work, describes the values we live by, and is the motivation behind every action we take.

1. To contribute to human welfare by application of biomedical engineering in the research, design, manufacture, and sale of instruments or appliances that alleviate pain, restore health, and extend life.
2. To direct our growth in the areas of biomedical engineering where we display maximum strength and ability; to gather people and facilities that tend to augment these areas; to continuously build on these areas through education and knowledge assimilation; to avoid participation in areas where we cannot make unique and worthy contributions.
3. To strive without reserve for the greatest possible reliability and quality in our products; to be the unsurpassed standard of comparison and to be recognized as a company of dedication, honesty, integrity, and service.
4. To make a fair profit on current operations to meet our obligations, sustain our growth, and reach our goals.
5. To recognize the personal worth of employees by providing an employment framework that allows personal satisfaction in work accomplished, security, advancement opportunity, and means to share in the company's success.
6. To maintain good citizenship as a company.

"Shared Principles" at AES

Integrity—We honour our commitments. Our goal is that the things AES people say and do in all parts of the Company should fit together with truth and consistency.
Fairness—It is our desire to treat fairly our people, customers, suppliers, stakeholders, governments, and the communities in which we operate. It does not mean that everyone gets treated equally but instead is treated fairly or with justice, given the appropriate situation.
Fun—We want all AES people and those people with whom we interact to have fun in their work. AES's goal is to create the most fun workplace since the industrial revolution.
Social Responsibility—involved in projects that provide social benefits, such as lower costs to customers, a high degree of safety and reliability, increased employment, and a cleaner environment.

As Starbucks begins to globalize by opening more shops in Beijing, Tokyo, Paris, and Prague, it will find that workforce diversity takes on a whole new meaning. Cultural norms about minorities' and women's work roles and pay may be at odds with Starbucks' core values and compensation strategy. Operating in different regions of the world requires more flexible approaches to pay.

Governments are major stakeholders in determining compensation. Hence, government relations to influence laws and regulations may also be part of compensation strategies. For example, as Starbucks enters the European Union, the EU's "social contract" becomes a matter of interest to the Starbucks leadership. And in China, Starbucks will discover that building relationships with government officials is essential. So, from a strategic perspective, managers of compensation may try to shape the sociopolitical environment as well as be shaped by it.

Employee Needs—Flexible.   The simple fact that employees differ is too easily overlooked in formulating a compensation strategy. Individual employees join the organization, make investment decisions, design new products, assemble components, and judge the quality of results.

Individual employees receive the pay. A major limitation of contemporary pay systems is the degree to which individual attitudes and preferences are ignored: Older, highly paid workers may wish to defer taxes by putting their pay into retirement funds, while younger employees may have high cash needs to buy a house, support a family, or finance an education. Dual career couples who are overinsured medically may prefer to use more of their combined pay for child care, automobile insurance, financial counselling, or other benefits such as flexible schedules. Employees who have young children or dependent parents may desire dependent care coverage.[17]

Perhaps it is time to consider letting employees specify their own pay forms. But putting people in the driver's seat is not going to happen overnight. Unlimited choice would be a challenge to administer. Employees offering greater choice to employees in different nations would face a bewildering maze of laws and regulations. Nevertheless, some pay systems are being designed to encourage some employee choices. Flexible benefit plans are examples, and increasing numbers of employers are adopting them.[18] A few organizations allow employees to trade cash received from incentives for stock options. These organizations believe that allowing employees their choice adds value and is difficult to imitate—it is a source of competitive advantage. Whether or not this belief is correct remains to be studied.

Unions.   Pay strategies also need to be adapted to the nature of the union–management relationship.[19] Strategies for dealing with unions vary widely. In early 2003, Noranda Inc.'s 345 unionized workers at their Belledune, New Brunswick, smelter agreed to a new three-year contract that froze wages and cut the workforce by 20 percent through early retirement incentives, rather than major layoffs.[20] On the other hand, in May 2003, Air Canada met with union resistance to its proposal for 10 percent wage cuts to keep the airline flying in the long term.[21]

Union influence on pay systems in Canada remains significant. Union preferences for different forms of pay (e.g., cost of living adjustments, improved health care) and their concern with job security affect pay strategy. Internationally, the role of unions in pay determination varies greatly.[22] In Europe, unions are major players in any strategic pay decisions. The point is that union interests are part of environmental pressures that help shape compensation strategies.

Role of Pay in Overall HR Strategy: Support, Catalyst of Change.   The pay system is just one of many systems that make up the HR strategy. Consequently, the pay strategy is also partially influenced by how it fits with other HR systems in the organization. A highly centralized and confidential pay system controlled by a few people in a corporate unit will not support a highly decentralized, flexible, open organization.

The importance of fit between pay programs and other HR management processes can be illustrated with examples of recruiting, hiring, and promoting. At Microsoft, the shift to greater base pay was a response to the tight labour market for software engineers. No matter the company's reputation, the pay linked with a job offer or a promotion must be sufficient to induce acceptance. Once people are in the door, pay programs must help keep them there. Some employers do not maintain significant pay differences between various skill levels or levels of responsibility. Lack of adequate differences in pay diminishes the incentive for employees to invest in the training required to become more skilled or to accept a promotion to supervisor. The situation is reversed for many engineering and research jobs, where the pay for managerial positions induces people to leave engineering and research positions. Again, Microsoft's addition of the Distinguished Engineer position is intended to help it hang onto technical talent. In the overall HR strategy, pay can take the role of a supporting player, or it can take the lead and become a catalyst for change. In either role, compensation is part of the total HR approach.

In sum, assessing the compensation implications of factors including the organization's business strategy, the global competitive dynamics, its culture and values, the sociopolitical context, employee needs, unions, and how pay fits with other HR systems is all necessary to better formulate a compensation strategy that "fits."

Step 2: A Total Compensation Strategy

The compensation strategy is made up of the five decisions outlined in the pay model: set objectives, and specify the four policies on alignment, competitiveness, contributions, and administration. This is Step 2 in developing a compensation strategy. It requires compensation decisions that fit the organization's business and environment. As we have already noted, compensation decisions support different business strategies. The objective is to make the right compensation decisions based on how the organization decides to compete. Exhibit 2.1 compares the compensation strategies crafted by Microsoft, Bristol-Myers Squibb, and Firepond to support their business strategies.

The rest of the book discusses these compensation decisions in detail. It is important to realize, however, that the decisions made on these five issues together form the compensation strategy.

Steps 3 and 4: Implement and Reassess

Step 3 is to implement the strategy through the design of the compensation system. The compensation system translates strategy into practice. Employees infer the underlying strategy based on how they are treated by the compensation system.

Step 4, reassess and realign, closes the loop. This step recognizes that the compensation strategy must change to fit changing conditions. Thus, periodic reassessment of the fit is needed.

.NET WORTH   Linking Total Rewards to the Johnson and Johnson Credo

Johnson & Johnson (J&J) is the largest and most diversified healthcare products company in the world. J&J's 112-year-old corporate credo dictates that its first responsibility is to customers, second to employees, third to communities, and finally to shareholders. This credo is literally carved in stone at the company's headquarters.

At J&J's technology-driven ETHICON subsidiary, which operates four business units, the first commitment is to ETHICON's overall objectives. Both their business strategy and their rewards are based on long-term performance. The rewards system focuses on retaining high potential employees, who are easily attracted to the company due to its status as one of the world's most respected and desirable corporations to work for.

ETHICON provides competitive base salary and benefits, but puts considerable focus on long-term security through retirement plans and stock options. Cash and stock awards are made to employees based on individual performance from a bonus pool based on achieving current financial targets and preparing the business for the future.

Other rewards, including on-site child care, family leave, flextime, and two-for-one matching of charitable donations, are aimed at retention of the high potential employees required for continued future achievement of the company's strategy. Relational rewards stem from a sense of caring for employees and for those less fortunate in the community, as well as attention to providing challenging work assignments.

Managing the links between the compensation strategy (those grand policy decisions) and the pay system (those procedures for paying people), as well as to people's perceptions and behaviours, is vital to implementing a pay strategy.

■ SOURCE OF COMPETITIVE ADVANTAGE: TWO TESTS

Designing and implementing a pay strategy that is a source of competitive advantage is easier said than done. Not all compensation decisions are strategic nor a source of competitive competitive advantage. Two tests determine whether a pay strategy is a source of competitive advantage: (1) Does it add value? and (2) Is it difficult to imitate?[23] These are high hurdles to overcome.

Adding Value

Pay decisions add value by helping to attract and retain critical talent, control costs, and motivate people to continue to learn and improve performance. Decisions about some pay techniques probably do not add value and thus are not strategic, nor do they seem to provide any advantage. Examples probably include how many levels in the performance evaluation rating scales, or whether to provide dental insurance (though a sauna and swimming pool may seem critical to those of us who work without them).

Difficult to Imitate

If the pay plan is relatively simple for any competitor to copy, then how can it possibly be a source of advantage? The answer, according to the strategic perspective, is that the real sustained advantage comes from (1) the way the organization's business strategy and compensation systems fit together, (2) the fit between compensation and other HR activities, and (3) how the systems are implemented.

WestJet Airlines of Calgary, Alberta, permits employees to receive up to 20 percent of their salaries in WestJet shares, and matches the amount dollar for dollar. They also provide profit-sharing cheques twice a year to all employees. This strategy adds value by linking the financial interests of the employees with those of WestJet's stockholders (both benefit if share value increases). It also helped secure WestJet's competitive advantage as a low-cost provider of frequent, no-frills flights. This strategy is difficult for competing airlines to imitate.

Are there advantages to an innovative compensation strategy? We do know that in products and services, first movers (innovators) have well-recognized advantages that can offset the risks involved—high margins, capturing market share and mindshare (brand recognition).[24] But we do not know whether such advantages accrue to innovators in total compensation. A recent Ford innovation was giving computers to its 360,000 employees around the world. Toyota and Honda responded by saying they did not see the value added by such a move, and General Motors and Daimler Chrysler claim to be "studying" it.[25] In the end, Ford Canada reneged on its promise to provide computers to its employees. What, if any, benefits accrued to Microsoft, one of the first to offer very large stock options to all employees, now that many competitors are doing the same thing? What about American Express, among the first to offer flexible benefit programs in Canada? Some companies sense opportunities in turbulent, competitive markets.[26] They take the risk and make their move. Some follow, and others do not. However, we simply don't know whether being an innovator in total compensation pays off. Does a compensation innovator attract more and better people? Induce people to stay and contribute? Are there cost advantages? Studies are needed to find the answers.

■ BASIC ISSUE: DOES "BEST FIT" PAY OFF?

best fit

■ aligning compensation decisions with the environment and the business strategy

The basic underlying premise of any strategic perspective is that if managers align pay decisions with the organization's strategy and values, are responsive to employees and union relations, and are globally competitive, then this **best fit** will mean that the organization is more likely to achieve competitive advantage.[27] The business strategy leads to the compensation plan, as illustrated in the following schematic:

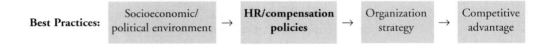

Best Fit: Socioeconomic/ political environment → Organization strategy → **HR/compensation policies** → Competitive advantage

The challenge is to design the "fit" with the environment, business strategy, and pay plan. The better the fit, the greater the competitive advantage.

Now let's rearrange this perspective so that HR/compensation policies precede organization strategies—this is the "best practices" premise.

Best Practices: Socioeconomic/ political environment → **HR/compensation policies** → Organization strategy → Competitive advantage

best practices

■ a set of pay practices that yields better performance with almost any business strategy

There are those who believe that (1) a set of best pay practices exists, and (2) these practices can be applied universally across situations.[28] They challenge the "best fit," "match-the-business-strategy" view. Rather than a better fit between business strategy and compensation plans yielding better performance, they say a set of **best practices** yields better performance with almost any business strategy.

The underlying premise in this perspective is that adopting the best pay practices will allow the employer to gain preferential access to superior employees. These superior human resources in turn will influence the strategy the organization adopts and be the source of its competitive advantage. This resource-based approach takes literally the oft-heard refrain from corporate public relations: Human resources are our most important asset. This may appear to be a chicken–egg discussion: Which comes first, the HR/compensation policies or the business strategy? Yet the answer is critical in the design of a pay plan.

If best practices do exist, what are they? It depends on whom you ask. Exhibit 2.8 summarizes two different views. One view is called the "new pay." Employee pay is based primarily on market rates; pay increases depend on performance (not cost of living or seniority increases), and the employment relationship is less secure. The logic is that the implicit contract is a partnership in which success (and risk) is shared.

A competing set of best practices, "high commitment," prescribes high base pay, sharing performance success only (not risk), guaranteeing employment security, promoting from within, and the like. These practices are believed to attract and retain a highly committed workforce, which will become the source of competitive advantage.

■ SO WHAT MATTERS MOST? BEST PRACTICES OR BEST FIT?

It would be nice to be able to say which compensation strategy best fits each situation, or which list of best practices truly represents the best. Unfortunately, little research has directly examined the competing views. However, there is some recent research that gets us beyond the theories and rhetoric.[29]

EXHIBIT **2.8** Best Practices Options

The New Pay*	High Commitment†
■ External market-sensitive-based pay, not internal alignment	■ High wages: You get what you pay for
■ Variable performance-based pay, not annual increases	■ Guarantee employment security
■ Risk-sharing partnership, not entitlement	■ Apply incentives; share gains, not risks
■ Flexible opportunities to contribute, not jobs	■ Employee ownership
■ Lateral promotions, not career path	■ Participation and empowerment
■ Employability, not job security	■ Teams, not individuals, are base units
■ Teams, not individual contributors	■ Smaller pay differences
	■ Promotion from within
	■ Selective recruiting
	■ Enterprisewide information sharing
	■ Training, cross-training, and skill development are crucial
	■ Symbolic egalitarianism adds value
	■ Long-term perspective matters
	■ Measurement matters

*Source: J. R. Schuster, The New Pay; E. Lawler, New Pay.
†Source: Pfeffer, *Competitive Advantage through People.*

One study examined eight years of data from 180 companies.[30] The authors reported that, although differences in relative pay levels (external competitiveness) existed among these companies, these differences were not related to their subsequent financial performance. However, differences in the percentage of bonuses and the percentage of people eligible for stock options (employee contributors) were related to future financial success of the organizations. It appears that it is not how much you pay, but how you pay, that matters; using performance bonuses and broadly based stock options are examples of best practices.

Another study not only found similar results, it also reported that the effect of the compensation strategy equalled the impact of all other aspects of the HR system (high involvement, teams, training programs, etc.) combined.[31] Again, performance-based bonuses and broadly based options appear to be a best practice.

Other studies also tend to confirm that compensation strategies affect organization performance.[32] One set of studies that focuses on specific industries, including auto, steel, and telecommunications, reports that high performance work systems (which include gainsharing and competitive pay levels plus training, teams, participation) all acting together are more effective than any single pay program.[33]

Further supporting the perspective that HR systems are interconnected, two researchers found relationships between compensation system design and employment security.[34] They report fewer layoffs and less downsizing in companies that have more performance-based (variable) pay strategies. The logic underlying their findings is that managers are less likely to lay off employees in bad times because labour costs are controlled through lower pay (fewer performance incentives) rather than lower head count.

So the research to date supports the use of bonuses and options tied to performance. What remains an open question is whether "best fit" matters. Do compensation systems that are aligned with the business, strategic, the environmental context, and other HR systems have greater effects? Much of the research suggests that "best practice" compensation strategies do have an impact; little seems to support a "best fit" model.

We believe that the preponderance of recent evidence supports the view that total compensation strategies influence employee behaviours and organization performance. We also believe that *the debate on best fit versus best practice is still unresolved*. Hence, taking a strategic perspective on pay remains a theory to be studied more fully.

Virtuous Circle.   Recent studies suggest that a total compensation package that emphasizes performance-based pay (bonuses and options) is related to firm performance only when the organization is performing well.[35] This phenomenon is like a virtuous circle: When there is success to share, success-sharing plans work best. As depicted in Exhibit 2.9, organizations that are successful (higher profits, greater market share, stronger total shareholder returns) are better able to offer incentives (bonuses and stock options) which reinforce employees' high performance and value of ownership. This in turn influences improved organization performance. Several studies also report that greater emphasis on performance-based practices in total compensation exposes employees to greater risk.[36] The logic is that when this risk is balanced by greater returns (in total compensation), this creates positive momentum for improved organization performance as well.

Vicious Circle.   However, as shown in the bottom half of Exhibit 2.9, when organization performance declines, total compensation packages that rely on stronger performance-based pay do not pay off; there are no bonuses, and the value of stock options declines.[37] Under these conditions an imbalance occurs between the risk employees face and their returns—with potentially negative effects on organization performance.

So, rather than one-time, simple relationships between total compensation systems and objectives, perhaps a circle better depicts the relationship. Positive performance yields positive returns, which in turn recycles to improve performance. Declining performance yields declining returns, which in turn reinforces declining performance. Unfortunately, we do not yet know what compensation strategy can be used to shift an organization caught in a vicious circle into a virtuous one. So caution and more evidence are required to interpret and apply many of these studies.

Surprisingly, we do not have much information about how people perceive various pay strategies. Do all managers "see" the total compensation strategy at Firepond or BMS the same way? There is some early evidence that suggests if you ask 10 managers about their company's HR

EXHIBIT 2.9   Virtuous and Vicious Circles

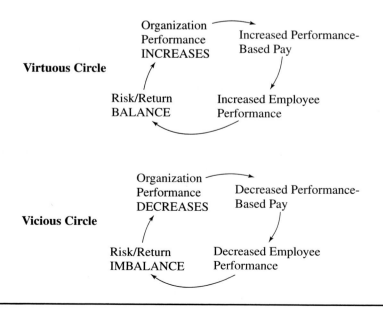

strategy, you might get 10 different answers. If the link between the strategy and people's perceptions is not clear, then maybe we are building on unstable ground.

■ SO WHAT'S THE DEAL?

implicit contract

an unwritten understanding between employers and employees about their reciprocal obligations and returns

Throughout this chapter, compensation and people, whether through strategic perspectives or finding the best practices, have been treated almost mechanically, like ingredients in a recipe. If only the right fit or the one right way or the right recipe can be found, people will respond and organizations will succeed. However, it cannot be overemphasized: It is the relationship with employees that is critical.

In the first pages of the book, we noted that compensation can be described as a return received in exchange for people's efforts and ideas given at their workplace. Exchange is a key part of the relationship. For most people, many of the terms and conditions of their employment exchanges are left unstated, forming an **implicit contract**, the deal.[38] Employees contribute toward achieving the goals of the employer in exchange for returns given by the employer and valued by the employee.

Compensation is an important part of this employment relationship. Unanticipated changes in compensation often breach this implicit understanding. Replacing annual pay increases with incentives, raising the deductibles on health care insurance, or tinkering with pension plans may have a negative influence on employee behaviour that is out of proportion to the financial impact of the change if employees feel the implicit contract has been breached.

Transactional and Relational Returns

Recall the total returns exhibit shown in the previous chapter (Exhibit 1.2). Returns take transactional and relational forms in the implicit employment deal.[39] These implicit deals signal the organization's compensation strategy. Transactional strategies emphasize total cash and benefits; relational strategies emphasize sociopsychological returns.

Exhibit 2.10 lays out a grid with transactional returns on one axis and relational returns on the other. It is possible to categorize compensation strategies in terms of their emphasis on transactional returns, relational returns, or both.

EXHIBIT 2.10 Framework for Analyzing Different "Deals"

	LOW ←————→ HIGH RELATIONAL	
TRANSACTIONAL LOW ←————→ HIGH	**HIGH PAY—LOW COMMITMENT** Hired Guns (Stockbrokers)	**HIGH PAY—HIGH COMMITMENT** Cult-like (Microsoft)
	LOW PAY—LOW COMMITMENT Workers as Commodity (Employers of Migrant Farm Workers)	**LOW PAY—HIGH COMMITMENT** Family (Starbucks)

In the grid, those organizations that pay low cash compensation and offer low relational returns are called "commodity." They view labour as a commodity, like any other input into the production process. In Canada, employers of migrant fruit pickers may offer this type of deal.

Organizations that offer both high compensation and high relational returns may be characterized as cultlike. Microsoft, Medtronic, and Toyota are examples. The strong commitment to the organization shows in the words and actions of employees: "Being at the center of technology, having an impact on the work, working with smart people, the sheer volume of opportunities, shipping winning products, beating competition."[40]

Some organizations offer a family relationship: high relational and less transactional returns. Starbucks may be an example; one writer calls them the "touchy-feely coffee company."[41] Finally, there are the "hired guns"—all transactional, "show-me-the-cash" relationships. Brokerage houses or auto dealerships may fit this category.

While labelling these companies is fun, and even convenient for describing different deals, it may be misleading. For example, the CEO of the Starbucks "family" states that he pays above his competitors and offers health insurance and "bean stock" to Starbuck partners/employees as part of the total relationship. In spite of this, Starbucks' turnover rate is about 60 percent, so most "partners" do not stay in the family very long. So, whether or not a deal is successful may depend on your criteria. Our point is that analyzing compensation strategies in terms of an implicit relationship highlights the fact that it is the relationship with employees that is strategic. Compensation is an important part, albeit not the only part, of the employment relationship.

CONCLUSION

A strategic perspective on compensation takes the position that how employees are compensated can be a source of sustainable competitive advantage. Two alternative approaches are highlighted: a "best fit"/contingent business strategy/environmental context approach, and a "best practices" approach. The "best fit" approach presumes that one size does not fit all. The art of managing compensation strategically involves fitting the compensation system to different business and environmental conditions. In contrast, the best practices approach assumes that there exists a universal, best way. The focus is not so much a question of what the best strategy is, but how best to implement the system. And agreement on what are the best practices does not exist, either.

Because the best fit approach is the most commonly used, we spent more time discussing it. The four-step process for forming and implementing a compensation strategy includes (1) assessing conditions, (2) deciding on the best strategic choices following the pay model (objectives, alignment, competitiveness, contributions, and administration), (3) implementing the strategy through the design of the pay system, and (4) reassessing the fit.

Recent studies have begun to research what aspect of the compensation relationship really does matter, but the answer is still fuzzy. Although more research is required before an answer emerges, we can say—yes, this IS our final answer—the notion of virtuous and vicious circles has some appeal.

Finally, an essential point is that the deal—the employment relationship—includes both transactional and relational forms of compensation. In this book we tend to focus more on the transactional returns—total compensation—but the relational returns matter, too. It is the total deal, the relationship with people, that makes an organization successful.

CHAPTER SUMMARY

1. The four steps to develop a total compensation strategy are: (1) assess total compensation implications, including competitive dynamics, culture/values, social and political context, employee needs for flexibility, unions, and the role of pay in overall HR strategy; (2) create a total compensation strategy from the five decisions in the pay model; (3) implement the compensation strategy; and (4) reassess and realign the strategy.

2. Managers should align the compensation strategy to the business strategy because the greater the alignment, or fit, between the organization and the compensation system, the more effective the organization will be.

3. The two tests used to determine whether a pay strategy is a source of competitive advantage are (1) Does it add value? and (2) Is it difficult to imitate?

4. The "best fit" perspective on compensation suggests that compensation should be aligned, or fit, with the specific business strategy adopted by the organization, given its environment, in order to maximize competitive advantage. The "best practices" perspective suggests that there is one set of best pay practices that can be applied universally across different situations and strategies, attracting superior employees who then create a winning strategy.

KEY TERMS

REVIEW QUESTIONS

1. Contrast the essential difference between the "best fit" (strategic business-based) and "best practice" perspectives on compensation.

2. Reread the culture/values statements in Exhibit 2.7. Discuss how, if at all, these values might be reflected in a compensation system. Are these values consistent with "let the market decide"?

3. Two tests for any source of competitive advantage are "adds value" and "difficult to imitate." Discuss whether these two tests are difficult to pass. Can compensation really be a source of competitive advantage?

EXPERIENTIAL EXERCISES

1. Select a company whose compensation system you are familiar with, or analyze the approach your college/university uses to pay teaching assistants and/or faculty. Infer the compensation strategy using the five issues (objectives, alignment, competitiveness, employee considerations, and administration). How does your organization compare to Microsoft? To Starbucks? What business strategy does it seem to "fit" (i.e., cost cutter, customer-centred, innovator, or something else)?

2. Set up a debate over the following proposition: "Best practices" is superior to the "best fit" approach when designing a compensation system.

3. So what is the deal between your instructor and the college/university? Is it more like hired gun, commodity, family, or cult? Discuss whether it would make any difference to teaching effectiveness if the deal were changed. What would you recommend and why?

WEB EXERCISE

Compensation Consultants on the Web

Compensation consultants are major players, and practically every organization uses at least one for data and advice. So learning more about services these consultants offer is useful. Go to the Web site of at least two of the following consulting firms, or find others.

Watson Wyatt	www.watsonwyatt.com (click on Canada)
Hay Group	www.haygroup.ca
Mercer	www.mercer.com (click on Mercer Human Resources Consulting)
Towers Perrin	www.towers.com (click on Canada)

1. Compare Web sites. From their Web sites, construct a chart comparing their stated core values and culture and their business strategy, and highlight the services offered.

2. Critically assess whether their strategies and services are unique and/or difficult to imitate. Which one would you select (based on the Web information) to help you formulate a company's total compensation strategy?

3. Based on the Web information, which one would you prefer to work for? Why?

4. Be prepared to share this information with others in class.
   Result: If everyone does a great job on this exercise, you will have useful information on consultants.

For more background, see L. Pinault, *Consulting Demons: Inside the Unscrupulous World of Global Corporate Consulting*. (New York: Harpers Business, 2000); and F. Cook, "A Personal Perspective of the Consulting Profession," *ACA News*, October 1999, pp 35–43.

CASE

Difficult to Copy?

Consider the Microsoft compensation strategy depicted in Exhibit 2.1. On the face of it, this strategy seems easy to copy (or at least to articulate). But determining which compensation strategy best fits an organization's business strategy and culture and the external pressures it faces may make the strategy more difficult to truly imitate. It is the relationship, the fit, with the way a pay system works with other aspects of the organization that makes it difficult to imitate and adds value. It is not the techniques themselves, but their interrelationships that make a strategic perspective successful.

Questions

1. Spend some time looking at the Web sites for Microsoft and Microsoft Canada. What can you infer about the business strategy and the organizational culture?

2. Find some information on the software industry in Canada. What are the external pressures Microsoft Canada is facing?

3. After you have a sense of what Microsoft Canada is like, decide whether you think its compensation strategy fits its business strategy, organizational culture, and external pressures.

4. How would you change compensation at Microsoft Canada?

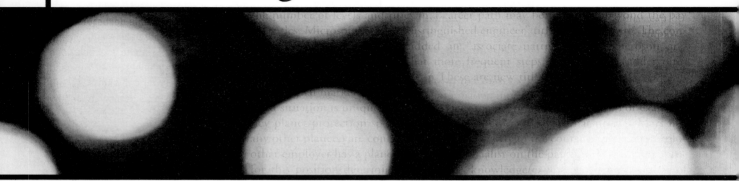

PART 1

Internal Alignment: Determining the Structure

Ford Motor Company employs a chief executive officer, drive train simulation engineers, software/mechanical/chemical and electrical engineers, plant managers, nurses, market analysts, pension fund managers, Web page designers, financial analysts, dashboard/ instruments installers, front/back seat assemblers, paint finishers, robotics technicians, dealer relations associates, accountants, guards, and even high voltage traction battery system engineers. How does Ford decide what to pay for all these different types of work? Is the financial analyst worth more (or less) than the accountant, or the seat installer more than the paint finisher? How much more (or less)? Should the potential consequences of errors, such as the use of allegedly faulty tires on the popular Ford Explorer, be considered in setting pay? If yes, then whose pay—the tire installer or the purchaser who ordered the tires from Firestone? The contract negotiator who entered into an agreement with Firestone? The quality control engineer who approved the tires? The CEO? Should the potential consequences of smart decisions, such as the design and marketing of the Explorer, which has made millions of dollars for Ford over the years, be considered in setting pay? Again, whose pay? How important are the characteristics of the employees—their competencies, knowledge, skills, or experience? How important are the characteristics of the work, the conditions under which it is done, or the value of what is produced? What about the employer's financial condition, or employee and union preferences?

Beyond understanding *how* pay is determined for different types of work, there are other critical questions in compensation management. Does *how much* we pay for different work make a difference? *Why* does Ford pay the financial analyst more than the accountant or the paint finisher more than the seat installer? Do these differences in pay support Ford's business strategy? Do they help Ford attract and retain employees? Do the procedures used support the work teams in Ford's Windstar plant in Oakville, Ontario? Or are the procedures bureaucratic burdens that hinder teamwork, customer satisfaction, and Ford's performance?

So many questions! Two of them lie at the core of compensation management. (1) How is pay determined for the wide variety of work performed in organizations? (2) How does pay affect employees' attitudes and work behaviours?

These questions are examined within the framework introduced in Chapter 1 and shown again in Exhibit I.1. This part of the book examines the strategic policy issue of internal alignment. The focus is within the organization. What internal alignment is, what affects it, and what is affected by it are considered in Chapter 3. Chapter 4 discusses how to assess the similarities and differences in work content. Chapters 5 and 6 scrutinize job-based, skill-based, and competency-based approaches for determining internal pay structures.

EXHIBIT   I.1   The Pay Model

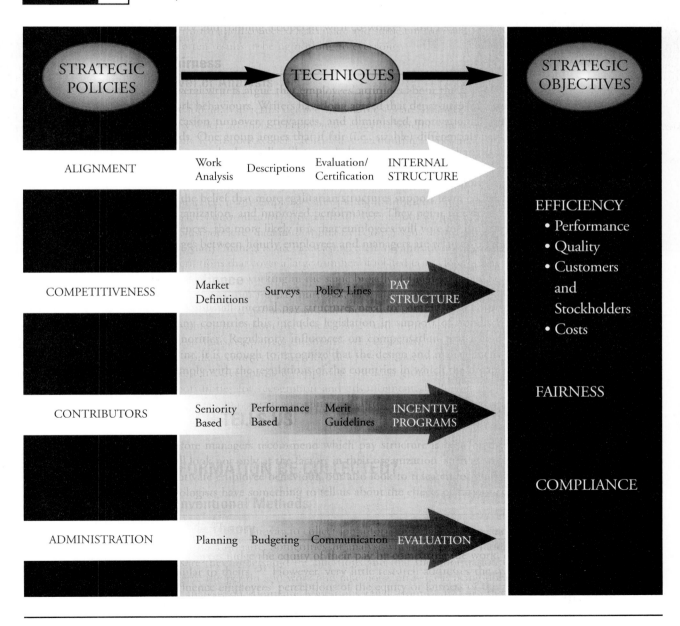

DEFINING INTERNAL ALIGNMENT

LEARNING OUTCOMES

- *Define* what is meant by internal alignment and pay structure.
- *Describe* the two types of factors that affect internal pay structures, and *discuss* at least two examples of each.
- *Explain* the two strategic choices involved in designing internal pay structures.
- *Describe* seven organizational outcomes of an internally aligned pay structure.
- *Explain* four theoretical approaches to determining which pay structure is best for an organization.

An ancient Christian parable describes a vineyard owner hiring labourers throughout the day and then paying them equally at the end of the day. The labourers hired at the beginning of the day question the fairness of those hired at the end of the day being paid the same amount for fewer hours of work.[1]

This parable raises age-old questions about internal alignment and pay structures within a single organization.[2] Clearly, the labourers in the vineyard felt that those who worked all day in the hot sun should be paid more, perhaps because they had contributed more to the householder's economic benefit. According to the labourers, "fair pay" should be based on two criteria: the value of contributions and the time worked. Perhaps the vineyard owner was using a third criterion: an individual's needs without regard to differences in the work performed.[3]

The parable doesn't tell us how the work in the vineyard was organized. Perhaps the labourers were organized into teams, with some members pruning the vines and others pulling weeds or tying the vines. Maybe pruning requires more judgment than tying. Pay structures in contemporary compensation plans are typically designed by assessing how the work is organized and performed, its relative value, and the skills and knowledge required to perform it. This is done through procedures acceptable to the parties involved. If the procedures used or the resulting pay structure is unacceptable to managers or employees, they'll probably murmur, too. Is pruning more valuable than tying? Today, murmuring may translate into turnover, unwillingness to try new technology, and maybe even a lack of concern about the quality of the grapes in the vineyard or the customer's satisfaction with them. This chapter examines the policy of internal alignment and its consequences.

■ COMPENSATION STRATEGY: INTERNAL ALIGNMENT

internal alignment (internal equity)

■ the pay relationships between the jobs/skills/ competencies within a single organization. The relationships form a structure that can *support the workflow*, is *fair to the employees*, and *directs their behaviour* toward organization objectives.

Setting objectives was our first pay policy issue in a strategic approach. **Internal alignment**, our second, addresses relationships *inside* the organization. How do the responsibilities and pay of a vine fastener, pruner, or weeder relate to each other? How do they relate to the responsibilities and pay of the cook, the wine steward, or the accountant employed in the same household? The relationships among different jobs inside an organization make up its internal structure. A policy on internal alignment addresses the logic underlying these relationships.

Exhibit 3.1 shows a structure for the engineering and scientific work at an engneering company. The structure includes six levels that range from entry to consultant. You can see the relationships among the titles in the descriptions of each level of work.

Deciding how much to pay the six levels creates a **pay structure**.

Supports Work Flow

pay structure

■ the array of pay rates for different work or skills within a single organization. The *number of levels*, *differentials* in pay between the levels, and the *criteria* used to determine those differences create the structure.

Work flow refers to the process by which goods and services are created and delivered to the customer. A company's work flow reflects how it is organized—its design. The challenge is to design a pay structure that supports the efficient flow of that work.[4] For example, drug companies traditionally base the size of their sales force on the number of physicians to be called on per day and the number of working days per year. The drug manufacturer Merck decided to take a nontraditional approach to organizing sales and marketing. Merck's analysis indicated that the ability of physicians to choose specific drugs was being constrained by government regulations and company health plan restrictions that control access to products for their members. With physicians no longer the sole decision makers, Merck created sales teams consisting of account executives, client representatives, and medical information scientists to serve a broader clientele of insurance companies and physicians. A cross-functional team responsible for a distinct geographic area (rather than a list of physician–clients) provides a relationship-building approach to selling products. Rather than hawking a specific drug and giving out free samples, the Merck teams got to know the clients and provided them with up-to-date information about trends and research. They became a source of knowledge useful to the physicians and the insurance companies. The teams keep clients apprised of regulations and cover drugs for a wider range of medical conditions. One team even translated brochures that explain a course of treatment into Chinese, Russian, and Spanish for a physician whose patients included non-English speaking immigrants. Such a response would have been beyond the resources of a single sales representative under Merck's old approach. (Of course, the recommended treatment did include Merck products.)

To support these new work teams, Merck designed a new compensation structure. The pay differences between account executives, customer representatives, and medical information scientists who served on the same teams were a major issue—just as they had been for the vineyard owner described in the parable, just as they are for the engineers.

Think globally as does Ford Motor Company. Ford acquired Volvo (Sweden), Jaguar and Land Rover (Britain), and most of Mazda (Japan). To leverage their new engineering and manufacturing knowledge, Ford is creating global teams. This changes the work flow and organization design at Ford. Ford also needs to design pay structures that enable people to make the new global organization work.

Supports Fairness

An internally aligned pay structure is more likely to be judged fair if it is based on the work and skills required to perform the work and if people have an opportunity to be involved in some way in determining the pay structure.[5]

EXHIBIT 3.1 Job Structure at an Engineering Company ————————————————————

Entry Level

Engineer
Limited use of basic principles and concepts. Develops solutions to limited problems. Closely supervised.

Senior Engineer
Full use of standard principles and concepts. Provides solutions to a variety of problems. Under general supervision.

Systems Engineer
Wide applications of principles and concepts, plus working knowledge of other related disciplines. Provides solutions to a wide variety of difficult problems. Solutions are imaginative, thorough, and practicable. Works under only very general direction.

Lead Engineer
Applies extensive expertise as a generalist or specialist. Develops solutions to complex problems that require the regular use of ingenuity and creativity. Work is performed without appreciable direction. Exercises considerable latitude in determining technical objectives of assignment.

Advisor Engineer
Applies advanced principles, theories, and concepts. Contributes to the development of new principles and concepts. Works on unusually complex problems and provides solutions that are highly innovative and ingenious. Works under consultative direction toward predetermined long-range goals. Assignments are often self-initiated.

Consultant Engineer
Exhibits an exceptional degree of ingenuity, creativity, and resourcefulness. Applies and/or develops highly advanced technologies, scientific principles, theories, and concepts. Develops information that extends the existing boundaries of knowledge in a given field. Often acts independently to uncover and resolve problems associated with the development and implementation of operational programs.

Recognized Authority

Two sources of fairness are important: the *procedures* for determining the pay structure, called *procedural justice*; and the *actual result* of those procedures, which is the pay structure itself, called **distributive justice**.

distributive justice

fairness of the result or outcome of a decision

Suppose you are given a ticket for speeding. *Procedural justice* refers to the process by which a decision is reached: the right to an attorney, the right to an impartial judge, and the right to receive a copy of the arresting officer's statement. *Distributive justice* refers to the fairness of the decision: guilty. Researchers report that employees' perceptions of procedural fairness significantly influence their acceptance of the results; employees and managers are more willing to accept low pay if they believe the way this result was obtained was fair. This research also strongly suggests that pay procedures are more likely to be perceived as fair (1) if they are consistently applied to all employees, (2) if employees participated in the process, (3) if appeals procedures are included, and (4) if the data used are accurate.

Applied to internal structures, procedural justice addresses how design and administrative decisions are made, and whether procedures are applied in a consistent manner. Distributive justice addresses whether the actual internal pay differences among employees are reasonable.

Directs Behaviour toward Organization Objectives

Internal pay structures influence employees' behaviour. Again, the challenge is to design the structures so they direct people's efforts toward organization objectives. At Merck, the new marketing teams needed to share unique knowledge with one another and with their clients. The same is

line-of-sight

■ link between an individual employee's work and the achievement of organizational objectives

true for Ford's global design teams. The criteria or rationale on which the structure is based ought to make clear the relationship between each job and the organization's objectives.[6] This is an example of **line-of-sight**. The more employees can "see" or understand links between their work and the organization's objectives, the more likely the structure will direct their behaviour toward those objectives. Internal alignment in pay structures helps create that line-of-sight.

WHAT SHAPES INTERNAL STRUCTURES?

The major factors that shape internal structures are shown in Exhibit 3.2. They include both external and organization factors, which are listed in the exhibit. The various factors might better be represented as a web, with all factors connected and interacting.

Exactly how these factors interact is not well understood. No single theory accounts for all factors. Some emphasize certain factors over others, others omit competing factors. As we discuss the factors that influence pay structures, we will also look at various theories.

EXHIBIT 3.2 What Shapes Internal Structures?

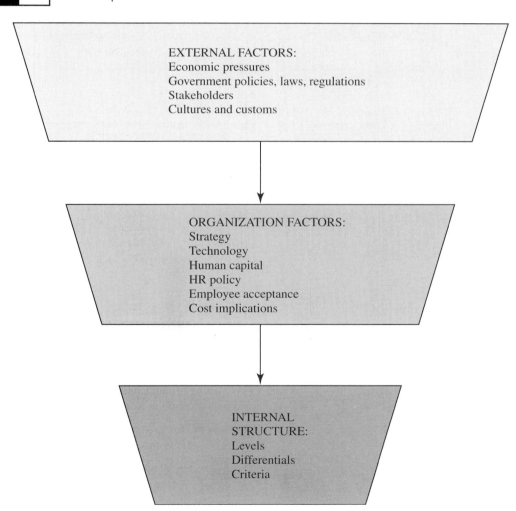

EXTERNAL FACTORS:
Economic pressures
Government policies, laws, regulations
Stakeholders
Cultures and customs

ORGANIZATION FACTORS:
Strategy
Technology
Human capital
HR policy
Employee acceptance
Cost implications

INTERNAL STRUCTURE:
Levels
Differentials
Criteria

External Factors: Economic Pressures

Adam Smith was an early advocate of letting economic market forces influence pay structures. Smith ascribed to human resources both an exchange value and a use value. *Exchange value* is whatever wage the employer and the employee agree on. *Use value* reflects the value of the goods or services labour produces. New technologies associated with the Industrial Revolution increased the use value of labour without a corresponding increase in exchange value.

Karl Marx accused capitalistic economic systems of basing pay structures on exchange value.[7] He said that employers unfairly pocketed the surplus value created by the difference between what owners were willing to pay workers and what owners earned from workers' efforts. He urged workers to overthrow capitalistic systems in order to reap the benefits of their labour and become owners themselves. In some sense, broad-based stock ownership by employees is following Marx's suggestion that employees become owners.

Smith and Marx concentrated on the supply of labour to explain pay structures. But in the face of rising wages in the last half of the 19th century, new theories began to examine the demand for labour. One of the best-known theories, the **marginal productivity theory**, says that employers do in fact pay use value.[8] Unless an employee can produce a value equal to the value received in wages, it will not be worthwhile for the employer to hire that worker. Pay differences among the job levels reflect differences in use value associated with different jobs. One job is paid more or less than another because of differences in relative productivity of the job and/or differences in how much a consumer values the output. Hence, differences in productivity provide a rationale for the internal pay structure.

However, the uncertainty in markets also affects internal structures. Rapid, often turbulent changes, in either competitors' products/services (as in the rise of the Internet for making purchases) or in customers' tastes (as in the popularity of sport utility vehicles) means organizations must be able to redesign workflow and employees must continuously learn new skills. Turbulent, unpredictable external conditions require pay structures that support agile organizations and flexible people.[9]

> **marginal productivity theory**
>
> ■ Unless an employee can produce something of value from his/her job equal to the value received in wages, it will not be worthwhile for an employer to hire that employee.

External Factors: Government Policies, Laws, and Regulations

In Canada, human rights legislation forbids pay systems that discriminate on the basis of gender, race, religion, sexual orientation, national origin, and many other grounds. Pay equity acts require "equal pay for work of equal value," based on skill, effort, responsibility, and working conditions. An internal structure may contain any number of levels, with differentials of any size, as long as the criteria for setting them are not gender, race, religion, or national origin.

Much pay-related legislation attempts to regulate economic forces to achieve social welfare objectives. The most obvious place to affect an internal structure is at the minimums (minimum wage legislation) and maximums (special reporting requirements for executive pay). But legislation also aims at the differentials.

In the Slovak Republic in Central Europe, an entire government agency is devoted to maintaining a 15-level pay structure that is required in all Slovak companies (but not foreign ones). The detailed procedures manuals and job descriptions fill a number of shelves. People dissatisfied with the pay rate for their jobs could appeal to this agency. Not surprisingly, few do. In nearby Slovenia, regulations require an 11-to-1 ratio between the top managers' pay and the average pay of the organization's workforce. However, a general manager concedes that it was impossible to recruit and retain sales and finance managers within these pay regulations. So how does he manage? He has established accounts for these managers in an Austrian bank, thereby circumventing the law.

In China, too, the government dictates that state-owned enterprises use a universal structure: Eight levels exist for industrial workers, 16 levels for technicians and engineers, and 26 for government administrators. Government agencies regulate and monitor compliance. However, reform plans have increased differentials and gotten rid of the "iron rice bowl"—the practice of paying all workers the same without regard to performance.

Most countries have various legal standards regulating pay structures. Whatever they are, organizations operating within those countries must abide by them.[10]

External Factors: Stakeholders

Unions, stockholders, and even political groups have a stake in establishing internal pay structures. Unions are the most obvious case. Most unions seek smaller pay differences among jobs and seniority-based promotions as a way to promote solidarity among members. At the minimum, unions seek to ensure that the interests of their members are well represented in decisions about structures. Stockholders also pay attention to executive pay. Research is beginning to document its effects on employees' behaviours and performance, and consequently, organization performance.

External Factors: Cultures and Customs

Culture is the mental programming for processing information that people share in common.[11] Such shared mindsets within a society may form a judgment of what size of pay differential is fair. In ancient Greece, Plato declared that societies are strongest when the richest earned a maximum of four times the lowest pay. Aristotle favoured a five-times limit.

Historians tell us that in 14th century Western Europe, the church endorsed a "just wage" doctrine, a structure of wages that supported the existing class structure in the society. The doctrine was an effort to end the economic and social chaos resulting from the death of one-third of the population from bubonic plague. The shortage of workers that resulted from the devastation led nobles and landholders to bid up the wages for surviving craftspeople. By allowing the church and royalty to determine wages, market forces such as scarcity of skills were explicitly denied as appropriate determinants of pay structures.

Even today cultural factors continue to shape pay structures around the world. Pay equity is a Canadian example in which advocates have been changing societal judgments about what wage is just. These judgments do change in response to pressures. For example, many traditional Japanese employers place heavy emphasis on seniority in their internal pay structures. But pressures from global competitors plus an aging workforce have made age-based pay structures very expensive. Consequently, many Japanese employers are changing their systems. This change is particularly irksome to us; as we have grown older, we seem to more fully appreciate the wisdom of paying for age.

Organization Factors: Strategy

You have already read in the last chapter how organization strategies influence internal pay structures. Different business strategies may require different pay structures to support them. The basic belief of a strategic perspective is that pay structures that are not aligned with the organization strategy may become obstacles to the organization's success.

Organization Factors: Human Capital

Human capital—the education, experience, knowledge, abilities, and skills that people possess—is regarded as a major influence on internal structures.[12] The stronger the link between those skills and experience and an organization's strategic objective, the more pay those skills will command. The engineering structure in Exhibit 3.1 results in paying consultant engineers more than lead engineers or senior engineers because the human capital of consultant engineers brings a greater return to the company. It is more crucial to the organization's success.

Organization Factors: Design of Work

Technology used in producing goods and services influences the *organizational design*, the *work* to be performed, and the *skills/knowledge* required to perform the work. Thus, the technology employed is another critical organization factor influencing the design of pay structures.[13]

A case in point is the difference in the number of levels in the engineering structure in Exhibit 3.1, with six levels for engineering alone—versus a plastics company, with five levels for all managerial/professional/technical employees (see Exhibit 3.4). The technology required to produce engineered products differs from that used to manufacture plastics. Manufacturing work is more labour intensive (more than 50 percent of operating expenses are labour costs) than is plastics (less than 20 percent); hence, different structures emerge.

Organization Factors: HR Policies

The organization's other *human resource policies* also influence pay structures. Most organizations tie money to promotions to induce employees to apply for higher-level positions.[14] However, in some organizations, offering a grander job title is considered a sufficient inducement, and little or no pay differential is offered.[15] If pay differentials are considered a key mechanism to encourage employees to accept greater responsibilities, then the pay structure must facilitate that policy.

Internal Labour Markets: Combining External and Internal Forces

Internal labour markets combine both external and organizational factors. As depicted in Exhibit 3.3, internal labour markets refer to the rules and procedures that (1) determine the pay for the different jobs within a single organization, and (2) allocate employees to those different jobs.[16] In many organizations, individuals tend to be recruited and hired only for specific entry-level jobs (an engineer would be hired right out of college; a senior engineer would have a few years' experience), and are later allocated (promoted or transferred) to other jobs. Because the employer competes in the external market for people to fill these entry jobs, their pay is linked to the external market. It must be high enough to attract a qualified pool of applicants. In contrast, pay for nonentry jobs (those staffed internally via transfer and promotions) is buffered from external forces and is more heavily influenced by internal factors such as the organization's strategy, technology, human capital required, and other HR systems. External factors are dominant influences on pay for entry jobs, but the differences for nonentry jobs tend to reflect the organization's internal factors.

Are Internal Labour Markets Dead?   There is a debate (at least among academics) over whether the concept of an internal labour market is still useful. Some say that the external market now dominates pay decisions.[17] There has been more rhetoric than research in this debate. But recent

EXHIBIT   **3.3**   Illustration of an Internal Labour Market

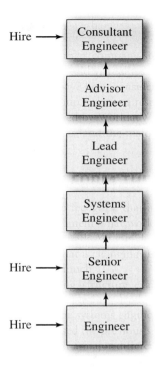

evidence indicates that, rather than dying, internal labour markets are adapting to more turbulent, uncertain external conditions by providing more agile, flexible structures. An internal alignment policy to guide the design of internal structures depends on the interplay of turbulent, uncertain external markets and adaptive, agile organizations.

Employee Acceptance: A Key Factor

A classic article on pay structures asserts that employees desire "fair" compensation.[18] Employees judge the fairness of their pay through comparisons with the compensation paid others for work related in some fashion to their own. Accordingly, an important factor influencing the internal pay structure is its *acceptability to the employees involved.*[19]

As we noted, pay structures change in response to changing external pressures such as skill shortages. Over time, the distorted pay differences become accepted as equitable and customary; efforts to change them are resisted. Thus, pay structures established for organizational and economic reasons at an earlier time may be maintained for cultural or other political reasons. It may take another economic jolt to overcome the cultural resistance. Then, new norms for employee acceptance are formed around the new structure. This "change and congeal" process does not yet support the continuous changes occurring in today's economy. New norms for employee acceptance probably will need to include recognition that people must get used to constant change, even in internal pay relationships.

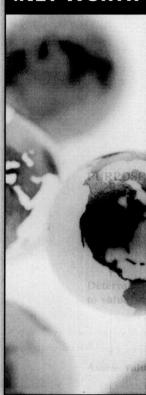

.NET WORTH

Internal Alignment in the Federal Government: An Impossible Task?

The federal government spent five years and millions of dollars working toward a new internal pay structure to apply to all government employees, and then trashed it in 2002 as "unworkable." The review began in 1997 in response to both external and organizational factors. The existing system, with more than 70 structures (called job classifications), was considered out of date relative to those of competing employers, and it was not meeting the requirements of pay equity legislation. The government's ability to compete in continuously changing labour markets is crucial, given that half of its workforce will be retiring in the next decade. However, the new system, with one structure, was too rigid to be effective.

The proposed one-structure system also was going to reduce the effectiveness of other HR systems, and faced ongoing difficulties with employee acceptance. The Public Service Alliance of Canada, the union representing government workers, was (and still is) ready to fight the government every step of the way if pay equity rights were diminished.

The Classification Division of the Treasury Board, where responsibility for compensation of the civil service rests, is now planning to implement a multi-year classification change program with several structures. The new approach will focus on individual occupations in the context of the government's strategic business objectives.

Source: A. Tomlinson, "Ottawa's Pay Equity Scheme Out the Window," *Canadian HR Reporter*, June 17, 2002, pp. 1, 11.

■ STRUCTURES VARY

An internal pay structure is defined by (1) the number of *levels* of work, (2) the pay *differentials* between the levels, and (3) the *criteria* used to determine those levels and differentials. These are the factors that a manager may vary to design a structure that supports the work flow, is fair, and directs employee behaviours toward objectives.

Levels

One feature of any pay structure is its hierarchical nature—the number of levels and reporting relationships. Because pay structures typically reflect the flow of work in the organization, some are more hierarchical with multiple levels; others are compressed with few levels.[20] As noted earlier, in comparison to the engineering company's six levels for a single job group (Exhibit 3.1), a plastics company uses five broad levels, described in Exhibit 3.4, to cover all professional and executive work.

Differentials

differentials

pay differences between job levels

The pay differences between levels are referred to as **differentials**. If we assume that an organization has a compensation budget of a set amount to distribute among its employees, there

EXHIBIT **3.4** Managerial/Professional Levels at a Plastics Company

Level	Description
Executive	Provides vision, leadership, and innovation to major business segments or functions
Director	Directs a significant functional area or smaller business segment
Leadership	Individual contributors leading projects or programs with broad scope and impact, or managers leading functional components with broad scope and impact
Technical/managerial	Individual contributors managing projects or programs with defined scope and responsibility, or first-tier management of a specialty area
Professional	Supervisors and individual contributors working on tasks, activities, and/or less complex, shorter duration projects

gini coefficient

statistic that varies between zero and one, increasing with pay differentials between job levels

are a number of ways to do so. It can divide the budget by the number of employees to give everyone the same amount. But few organizations in the world are that egalitarian. In most, pay varies among employees. Researchers use a statistic called the **gini coefficient** to describe the distribution of pay. A gini of zero means everyone is paid the identical wage. The higher the gini coefficient (maximum = 1), the greater the pay differentials between the levels.

Work that requires more *human capital*—knowledge, skills, abilities, is performed under less desirable working conditions, and/or whose results are more valued—is usually paid more than work with lesser requirements.[21] Exhibit 3.5 shows the differentials attached to the engineering company's structure.

Pay differentials of particular interest in managing compensation include those between adjacent levels in a career path, between team leaders and team members, between union and nonunion employees, and between executives and other employees.

Criteria: Job- or Person-Based

The criteria used to determine the number of levels and size of the pay differentials can be categorized as either *job-based* or *person-based*. A job-based structure looks at the work content—what tasks are done, what behaviours are expected, what results are expected. Person-based structures shift the focus to the employee: the *skills or knowledge* the employee possesses, whether or not they are used on the particular job the employee is doing, or the *competencies* an employee is assumed to possess.[22]

Although this theoretical division into person-based and job-based criteria is convenient, the two categories are not necessarily discrete. In the real world, it is hard to describe a job without reference to the jobholder's behaviour and skills. Conversely, it is hard to define a person's job-related knowledge or competencies without referring to work content. As we shall see in later chapters, both criteria require similar decisions. The engineering structure (Exhibit 3.1) uses the work performed as the criterion. The plastics structure (Exhibit 3.4) uses the competencies that are required at each level of work.

EXHIBIT | **3.5** | Engineering Pay Structure

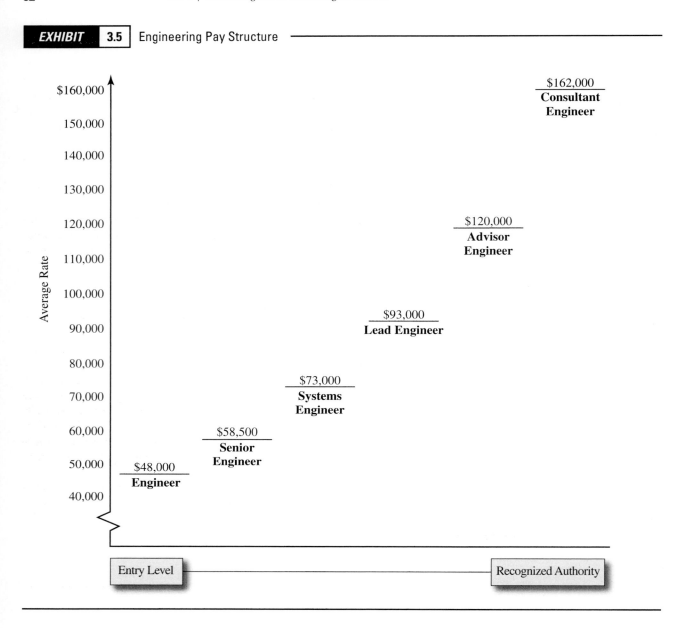

■ STRATEGIC CHOICES IN DESIGNING INTERNAL STRUCTURES

The basic premise underlying the strategic approach is that fit matters. Pay structures tailored to be aligned must support the way the work gets done, fit the organization's business strategy, and be fair to employees. Greater internal alignment—fit—is more likely to lead to success. Misaligned structures become obstacles. They may motivate employee behaviour that is inconsistent with the organization's strategy.

But what does it mean to fit or tailor the pay structure to be internally aligned? Two strategic choices are involved: (1) how tailored to organization design and work flow to make the structure, and (2) how to distribute pay throughout the levels in the structure.

Tailored versus Loosely Coupled

tailored structure

pay structure for well-defined jobs with relatively small differences in pay

A low-cost, customer-focused business strategy such as that followed by McDonald's or Wal-Mart may be supported by a closely **tailored structure**. Jobs are well defined, with detailed tasks or steps to follow. You can go into a McDonald's in Vancouver, Prague, or Shanghai and find they all are very similar. Their pay structures are, too. The customer representative and the food preparation jobs are very well defined in order to eliminate variability in how they are performed. The amount of ketchup that goes on the burger is premeasured, even the keys on the cash register are labelled with menu items rather than prices. And the differences in pay between jobs are relatively small.

loosely coupled structure

pay structure for jobs that are flexible, adaptable, and changing

In contrast to McDonald's, 3M's business strategy requires constant product innovation and short product design-to-market cycle times. Companies like 3M need to be very agile, constantly innovating and adapting. The competitive environment these organizations face is more turbulent and unpredictable. Their engineers may work on several teams developing several products at the same time. 3M's pay system needs to accommodate this flexibility. Hence, they need a more **loosely coupled structure** in order to facilitate constant change.

Egalitarian versus Hierarchical

Pay structures can range from egalitarian at one extreme to hierarchical at the other. Egalitarian structures have fewer levels and smaller differentials between adjacent levels and between the highest and lowest paid workers.

Exhibit 3.6 shows some variations in structures. Structure A has eight different levels, with relatively small differentials in comparison to structure B, which has only three levels. Structure A is hierarchical in comparison to the egalitarian structure of B; the multiple levels typically include detailed descriptions of work done at that level and delineate who is responsible for what. Hierarchical structures are consistent with a belief in the motivational effects of frequent promotions. Hierarchies value the differences in individual employee skills, responsibilities, and contributions to the organization.[23]

Structure B can also be characterized as "delayered" or compressed. Several levels of responsibility and supervision are removed so that all employees at all levels become responsible for a broader range of tasks but also have greater freedom to determine how best to accomplish what is expected of them. An egalitarian structure implies a belief that more equal treatment

EXHIBIT 3.6 Which Structure Has the Greatest Impact on Performance? On Fairness?

Structure A Layered	Structure B Delayered
Chief Engineer	Chief Engineer
Engineering Manager	
Consulting Engineer	
Senior Lead Engineer	
Lead Engineer	Consulting Engineer
Senior Engineer	
Engineer	
Engineer Trainee	Associate Engineer

will improve employee satisfaction, support cooperation, and therefore affect workers' performance.[24]

While it is hard to be against anything called egalitarian, if we instead use the word "averagism," as Chinese workers do when describing the pay system under socialism's state-owned enterprises, some of the possible drawbacks of this approach become clear.[25] Equal treatment can result in more knowledgeable employees with more responsible jobs (stars) going unrecognized and unrewarded, which may cause them to leave the organization. They may leave physically for another job (newly possible in China, with emerging labour markets). Or they may simply slack off or tune out and refuse to do anything that is not specifically required of them. Their change in behaviour will lower overall performance. So a case can be made for both egalitarian and hierarchical structures.

Exhibit 3.7 clarifies the differences between egalitarian and hierarchical structures. Keep in mind, though, that the choice is not either/or. Rather, the differences are a matter of degree. So levels can range from many to few, differentials can be large or small, and the criteria can be based on the job, the person, or some combination of the two.

At this point we will focus on the differentials between adjacent jobs in a career path within an organization. Other differentials such as those between gender and ethnic groups, CEOs and workers, union and nonunion employees, and high performers versus low performers are discussed throughout the book.

Career Path Differentials

Every April, like the tulips, stories about the large differentials in Canadian corporations appear in the business press. A famous example is Frank Stronach, the CEO of Magna International, who was paid $300,000 (U.S.) in base salary in 2002, plus $31.5 million in consulting fees. He also exercised $6 million in stock options.[26]

The Stronach pay package stands in sharp contrast to that earned by Magna employees earning union wages. Yet, more egalitarian structures are not problem free, either. For example, Ben and Jerry's Homemade, a purveyor of premium ice cream, tried to maintain a ratio of only 7 to 1 between its highest-paid and lowest-paid employee. The relatively narrow differential reflected the company's philosophy that the prosperity of its production workers and its management should be closely linked. The compressed structure also generated a great deal of favourable publicity. However, it eventually became a barrier to recruiting. Ben and Jerry's was

EXHIBIT 3.7 Strategic Choice: Hierarchical vs Egalitarian

	Hierarchical	Egalitarian
Levels	Many	Fewer
Differentials	Large	Small
Criteria	Person or Job	Person or Job
Supports:	Close Fit	Loose Fit
Work Organization	Individual Performers	Teams
Fairness	Performance	Equal Treatment
Behaviours	Opportunities for Promotion	Cooperation

forced to abandon this policy in order to hire an accounting manager and a new CEO. And only when the company was acquired by Unilever, a Dutch multinational, did the press publicize the fact that the value of stock increased the total compensation for founders Ben Cohen and Jerry Greenfield to much more than the 7 to 1 ratio. Like the Slovenian managers, they found a way to deal with economic reality. The Slovenian general manager established accounts outside the country; Ben and Jerry's changed their policy when necessary and focused attention on their cash compensation, rather than the value of their total compensation (including stock).

All this attention to CEO and employee differentials may interest some, but it shifts the focus away from pay differences within career paths—since it is unlikely that working as an auto machinist will prepare anyone for Stronach's CEO job. Look again at the engineering job structure in Exhibit 3.5. The question to be resolved is, What size should the pay differentials be between the adjacent engineering levels? Exhibit 3.8 shows that the differentials between engineering jobs range from $10,500 (Engineer to Senior Engineer) to $42,000 (Advisor to Consultant). Both the amount and the percentages increase at each level.

So what? To answer this we need to understand how differentials within the career path support work flow, motivate engineers to contribute to the company's success, and are considered fair by the engineers. The next several chapters discuss how these internal structures (the levels, differentials, and criteria) are designed and managed.

EXHIBIT 3.8 | Pay Differentials

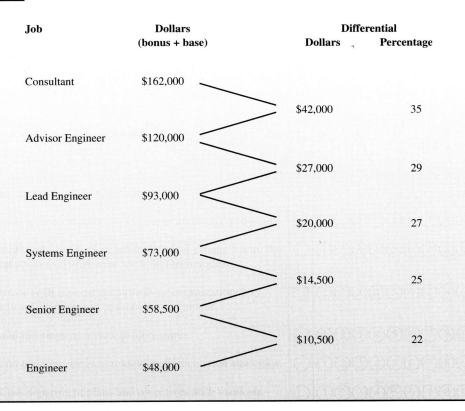

Job	Dollars (bonus + base)	Differential	
		Dollars	Percentage
Consultant	$162,000		
		$42,000	35
Advisor Engineer	$120,000		
		$27,000	29
Lead Engineer	$93,000		
		$20,000	27
Systems Engineer	$73,000		
		$14,500	25
Senior Engineer	$58,500		
		$10,500	22
Engineer	$48,000		

■ CONSEQUENCES OF ALIGNMENT

Let's turn again to that So What? question. Why worry about internal alignment at all? Why not simply pay employees whatever it takes to get them to take a job and to show up for work every day? Why not let external market forces and what competitors are paying determine internal wage differentials?

The answer can be found in several situations. The first is achieving and sustaining strategic competitive advantage. As discussed in Chapter 2, you want to be difficult to imitate. We noted that the number of levels and titles in a career path may be rewarding beyond the pay attached to the titles. Microsoft added a "distinguished engineer" title to its structure. The consulting firm McKinsey and Company added an "associate partner." Both Microsoft and McKinsey say that their rationale was that more frequent steps in the career ladder offer employees rewards and affect their behaviour. These are new titles and levels that are not yet reflected in the external market.

The second situation is unique jobs that reflect organization idiosyncracies. For example, a space agency planet protection specialist is responsible for ensuring that neither Mars nor Earth (nor any other planets) are contaminated inadvertently in the course of planetary exploration. No other employer has a planet protection specialist on the payroll. How is the appropriate pay for this position determined? The skills/knowledge/experience/responsibilities of the planet protection specialist were compared with requirements for other space agency jobs. Thus, the existing internal pay structure provides a basis for arriving at a rate for unique jobs.[27]

Another reason for paying attention to internal alignment is that some jobs are valued by a specific organization more or less than the rates for that job in the market. For example, top-notch compensation specialists may have greater value to a compensation consulting firm than to a heavy manufacturing company. The consulting firm may pay higher-than-market rates for the greater contribution of the particular job to organization goals.

Back to the practical question, Does any of this really matter? Recall the dimensions of internal pay structures. What difference do the number of levels, the size of pay differentials between levels, and the criteria (job versus person) make to the compensation system goals of efficiency, fairness, and compliance? Exhibit 3.9 suggests some of the organizational outcomes believed to be affected by internal pay structures.

EXHIBIT 3.9 Some Organizational Outcomes of Internally Aligned Structure ───────────

Efficiency: Competitive Advantage

Why manage the internal pay structure? Because it has the potential to lead to better organization performance. If the structure does not motivate employees to help achieve the organization's objectives, then it is a candidate for redesign.

Internal pay structures imply future rewards. The size of the pay differentials between the entry level and the highest level in the structure may induce employees to undertake the training and obtain the experience required for promotion. Consequently, a Senior Engineer job should pay more than an entry-level job. Without that pay difference, individuals are less likely to gain the additional knowledge and experience required. Similar logic can be applied to differentials between Lead Engineer, Advisor, and Consultant. Properly designed and managed pay differentials within organizations induce employees to remain with the organization, increase their experience and training, cooperate with co-workers, and seek greater responsibility.[28]

Fairness

Several writers argue that employees' attitudes about the fairness of the pay structure affect their work behaviours. Writers have long agreed that departures from an acceptable wage structure will occasion turnover, grievances, and diminished motivation.[29] But that is where the agreement ends. One group argues that if fair (i.e., sizable) differentials between jobs are not paid, individuals may harbour ill will toward the employer, resist change, change employment if possible, become depressed, and "lack that zest and enthusiasm which makes for high efficiency and personal satisfaction in work."[30] Others, including labour unions, argue for only small differentials, in the belief that more egalitarian structures support team cooperation, high commitment to the organization, and improved performance. They point to evidence that the greater the wage differences, the more likely it is that employees will vote for unions, and that smaller differences in wages between hourly employees and managers are related to greater product quality.

Compliance

Certainly, all internal pay structures need to comply with government laws and regulations. In many countries this includes legislation in support of nondiscriminatory pay for women and minorities. Regulatory influences on compensation management are examined later. At this point, it is enough to recognize that the design and management of internal pay structures must comply with the regulations of the countries in which the organization operates.

■ WHAT THE RESEARCH TELLS US

Before managers recommend which pay structure is best for their organizations, we hope they will look not only at the factors in their organization, such as work flow, what is fair, and how to motivate employee behaviour, but also look to research for guidance. Both economists and psychologists have something to tell us about the effects of various structures.

Equity Theory

Employees judge the equity of their pay by comparing the work, qualifications, and pay for jobs similar to theirs. [31] However, very little research addresses the question of what specific factors influence employees' perceptions of the equity or fairness of the *pay structure*, as opposed to the equity or fairness of the *pay*.[32] Consequently, equity theory could support both egalitarian and hierarchical structures.

Expectancy Theory

Employees make cognitive estimates of how much effort will be required to perform at a certain level and what that performance level will mean in terms of personal outcomes. Then, based on how appealing the outcomes are for the employee, a decision is made about how much effort to expend. Each employee may view a similar outcome differently. For example, a promotion may be very appealing to a junior manager who is highly motivated to take on more responsibility, but very unappealing to a more experienced senior manager who sees only the increase in headaches related to higher-level positions. Pay structure characteristics may have an impact on the effort of employees. For example, small differentials may be highly motivating for employees who place a high value on monetary rewards. Similarly, loosely coupled structures may appeal to employees who enjoy being innovative and creative in their work, whereas tailored structures may appeal to others who prefer the security of knowing exactly what they are being paid for. Thus this theory does not support the idea that there is one specific pay structure that is best for the organization.

Tournament Theory

Economists have focused more directly on the motivational effects of structures. Their starting point is a golf tournament where the prizes total, say, $100,000. How that $100,000 is distributed affects the performance of all players in the tournament. Consider three prizewinners, with the first-place winner getting over half the purse, versus ten prizewinners, with only slight differences in the size of the purse among the ten. According to tournament theory, *all* players play better in tournaments where the prize differentials are sizable.[33] Some research supports tournament theory. Raising the total prize money by $100,000 in the Professional Golf Association tournament lowered each player's score, on average, by 1.1 strokes over 72 holes.[34] And the closer the players got to the top prize, the more their scores were lowered.

Applying these results to organizations: The greater the differential from your present salary to your boss's salary, the harder you (and everyone else) will work. Suppose that the engineering structure contains 10 advisor engineers at the second-to-the-top level, each making $120,000, and each competing for two consultant positions, where the pay is $162,000. A tournament model says that if the consultants instead are paid $200,000, everyone will work even harder. Rather than resenting the big bucks paid to the consultants, engineers at all levels in the structure will be motivated by the greater differential to work harder to be a "winner"; i.e., get promoted to the next level.

But most work is not a round of golf, nor does it lead to the company presidency. Virtually all the research that supports hierarchical structures and tournament theory takes place in situations where individual performance matters most (auto racing, bowling, golf tournaments), or at best where the demand for cooperation among a small group of individuals is relatively low (professors, stockbrokers). In contrast, baseball provides a setting where both individual players' performance and the cooperative efforts of the entire team make a difference.[35] Using eight years of data on major league baseball, a recent study found that teams with egalitarian structures (practically identical player salaries) did better than those with hierarchical structures (very large differentials among players). In addition to affecting team performance (games won, gate receipts, franchise value, total income), internal structures had a sizable effect on players' individual performance (batting averages, errors, runs batted in, etc.). Thus, teams with more hierarchical structures performed worse than those with more egalitarian structures.

Another study looked at pay differentials among members of 460 organizations' executive teams.[36] It concluded that members of executive leadership teams were twice as likely to leave companies with larger pay differentials; hierarchy breeds turnover.

Institutional Model: Copy Others

Some organizations, just as some people, ignore the question of strategy altogether. Instead, they simply copy what others are doing. By extension, internal pay structures are sometimes adopted because they mimic so-called "best practices".[37]And it is still common for managers to bring back "the answers" discovered at the latest conference. Surveys that benchmark the practices of the best companies facilitate others' copying those practices. Recent examples of such behaviours include the rush to de-layer, to emphasize teams, to deemphasize individual contributions, and to shift to a competency-based pay system, often with little regard to whether any of these practices makes sense (fit) for the particular organization or its employees.[38]

◼ WHICH STRUCTURE FITS BEST?

In practice, the decision about which structure best fits a particular business strategy probably lies in our original definition of internal alignment: *An internally aligned structure supports the work flow, is fair to employees, and directs their behaviour toward organization objectives.* The lower part of Exhibit 3.7 summarizes the effects attributed to egalitarian and hierarchical structures.

How the Work Is Organized.　Work can be organized around teams, with all members on a team making roughly the same pay. Or it can be organized around individuals, with pay differences celebrated as a way to motivate performance. The pay structure should support the underlying organization structure. In organizations where work is highly interdependent and involves a larger group of people, the competition among workers for the higher pay fostered by hierarchical structures may work against organization performance.[39]

Fair to Employees.　George Meany, an early 20th century labour leader, is famous for his reaction to proposed pay innovations: "Tell me how much pay we will get, and I will tell you if I like it." Hierarchical structures evoke the same response. If I am at the top of the structure, I am probably persuaded that my high pay is an important signal to suppliers and customers that the company is doing well. If I am lower in the structure, I am probably less persuaded that the company ties its pay to employee contributions—at least, not my contributions.[40]

Directs Behaviour toward Organization Objectives.　We are learning more about the impact that pay ratios have on people's behaviours or an organization's success. The appropriate pay structure depends on the organization design and workflow. Those requiring greater collaboration, skill sharing, and interdependency generate greater performance with more egalitarian structures; those requiring strong individual contributions, more competition, and individual initiative generate greater performance with more hierarchical structures.

Research is beginning to offer some guidance in managing internal structures.

- More hierarchical structures are related to greater performance when the work flow depends more on individual contributors (e.g., consulting and law practices, surgical units, stock brokers, even university researchers).
- More egalitarian structures are related to greater performance when close collaboration and sharing of knowledge is required (e.g., fire fighting and rescue squads, manufacturing teams, hotel customer service staffs, global software design teams). The competition fostered in "winner-take-all" tournament hierarchies appears to have negative effects on performance when the work flow and organization design require teamwork.
- Structures that are not aligned with the work flow appear to be related to greater turnover.

So you decide: Is your workplace more like a round of golf or a baseball game? Note that, although these studies are very informative, there is still a lot we do not know. What about the appropriate number of levels, the size of the differentials, and the criteria to advance employees through a structure? We believe the answers lie in understanding the factors discussed in this chapter: the organization's strategic intent, organization design and work flow, human capital, and the external conditions, regulations, and customs it faces. We also believe that aligning the pay structures to fit the organization and the surrounding conditions is more likely to lead to competitive advantage for the organization and a sense of fair treatment for employees.

CONCLUSION

This chapter discusses the strategic policy of internal alignment and how it affects employees, managers, and employers. *Internal alignment* refers to the pay relationships among jobs/skills/competencies within a single organization. The potential consequences of internal pay structures are vital to organizations and individuals. Recent research and experience offer guidance concerning the design and management of these internal pay structures.

Pay structures—the array of pay rates for different jobs within an organization—are shaped by societal, economic, organizational, and other factors. Employees judge a structure to be equitable by comparing each job's pay with the qualifications required, the work performed, and the value of that work. Acceptance by employees of the pay differentials among jobs is a key test of an equitable pay structure.

Keep the goals of the entire compensation system in mind in thinking about internal pay structures. Widespread experience and increasing research support the belief that differences in internal pay structures, particularly employee career paths, influence people's attitudes and work behaviours, and therefore the success of organizations.

CHAPTER SUMMARY

1. *Internal alignment* refers to the pay relationships between jobs (or skills/competencies) within a single organization. The relationships form a structure that can support the workflow, is fair to employees, and directs their behaviour toward organization objectives. A *pay structure* is the array of pay rates for different work or skills. The number of levels, differentials in pay between the levels, and the criteria used to determine those differences create the structure.

2. Two types of factors that affect internal pay structures are (1) *external factors* such as economic pressures, government regulation, stakeholders, and culture; and (2) *organizational factors* such as strategy, technology, human capital, HR policies, employee acceptance, and cost implications.

3. The two strategic choices involved in designing internal pay structures are (1) how tailored to organization design and work flow to make the structure, and (2) how to distribute pay throughout the levels in the structure.

4. Seven organizational outcomes of an internally aligned pay structure are that they provide a basis to undertake training, increase experience, reduce turnover, facilitate career progression, facilitate performance, reduce pay-related grievances, and reduce pay-related work stoppages.

5. Four theoretical approaches to determining which pay structure is best for an organization are equity theory, expectancy theory, tournament theory, and the institutional model. *Equity theory* focuses on how employees compare their work, qualifications, and pay to those of others. *Expectancy theory* focuses on individual differences in perceptions, and suggests that no one structure will appeal to all employees. *Tournament theory* suggests that the greater the differences between salaries in the pay structure, the harder employees will work. The *institutional model* suggests that organizations copy the "best practices" of others.

KEY TERMS

REVIEW QUESTIONS

1. Why is internal alignment an important compensation policy?
2. Based on your own experience, which factors influenced the internal pay structure at your most recent employer? Provide examples that support your choice.
3. Explain the effect of internal alignment on work flow, fairness to employees, and effects on employee behaviour.
4. Would Palm Computing (maker of Palm Pilots) be better served by a tailored pay structure or a loosely coupled pay structure? Explain your answer.

EXPERIENTIAL EXERCISES

1. Look into any organization—your university/college, workplace, or the grocery store where you shop. Describe the flow of work. How is the job structure aligned with the organization's business, the workflow, and the organization objectives? How do you think it influences employee behaviours?

2. Prepare a list of at least five Canadian laws at various levels of government that impact pay rates.

3. Illustrate the internal labour market for faculty at your university/college, using Exhibit 3.3 as a guide.

WEB EXERCISE

Assessing Differentials in Major League Baseball

Go to the Web site http://www.canoe.ca/BaseballMoneyMatters/salaries_players.html, which lists salaries for all the players on all the major league baseball teams.

1. Pick some of your favourite teams and compare the highest and lowest paid player on the team.

2. Based on the differentials, which teams do the models and research discussed in this chapter predict will have the better record?

3. Click on the link for "Standings" and check it out. Suggestion: Don't bet your tuition on the relationship between player salary differentials on a team and the team's performance.

CASE

The Orchestra

Orchestras employ skilled and talented people, joined together as a team to create products and services. Job descriptions for orchestras look simple: Play the music. Violins play violin parts, trumpets play trumpet parts. Yet one study reported that orchestra players' job satisfaction ranks below that of prison guards. However, orchestra players were more satisfied than operating room nurses or hockey players.

The pay structure for a regional chamber orchestra is shown below. The pay covers six full orchestra concerts, one Carolling by Candlelight event, three Sunday Chamber Series Concerts, several Arts in Education elementary school concerts, two engagements for a flute quartet, and one "Ring in the Holidays" brass event, as well as regularly scheduled rehearsals.

Orchestra Compensation Schedule

Instrument	Fee
Violin, Concertmaster	$6,035
Principal Bass and Conductor	$4,390
Principal Viola	$4,360
Principal Flute	$3,755
Principal Trumpet	$3,665
Principal Cello	$3,620
Principal Clarinet	$3,590
Trumpet	$3,150
Principal Oboe	$3,130
Principal Violin II	$3,020
Principal Horn	$2,935

continued

CASE

Orchestra Compensation Schedule—continued

Instrument	Fee
Keyboard I	$2,910
Cello	$2,795
Principal Percussion	$2,640
Violin I	$2,510
Cello	$2,495
Principal Bassoon	$2,445
Violin I	$2,325
Violin I	$2,150
Violin I	$2,150
Violin I	$2,150
Violin II	$2,150
Violin II	$2,150
Viola	$2,150
Violin II	$1,710
Viola	$1,915
Oboe	$1,910
Trombone	$1,850
Viola	$1,760
Violin II/Viola	$1,545
Cello	$1,415
Clarinet	$1,340
Horn	$1,340
Flute	$1,260
Keyboard II	$1,205
Bassoon	$1,095
Violin II	$1,020

Questions

1. Describe the orchestra's pay structure in terms of levels, differentials, and job- or person-based.

2. Discuss what factors may explain the structure. Why does violinist I receive more than the oboist or trombonist? Why does the principal trumpet player earn more than the principal cellist and clarinetist, but less than the principal viola and flute players? What explains these differences? How does the relative supply versus demand for violinists compare to the supply versus demand for trombonists? Is it that violins play more notes?

3. How well do equity and tournament models apply?

 **Visit the Online Learning Centre at**
www.mcgrawhill.ca/college/milkovich

JOB ANALYSIS

LEARNING OUTCOMES

- *Explain* job analysis and why it has been called the cornerstone of human resources management.
- *Describe* the information that must be collected for job analysis and explain recent changes in how this information is collected.
- *Discuss* the differences between job descriptions and job specifications.
- *Explain* the pros and cons of job analysis, and different ways to judge job analysis.

Ten years ago, the cover story of *Fortune*, a leading business magazine, proclaimed "The End of the Job".[1] The story informed us that the use of "Jobs as a way of organizing work . . . is a social artifact that has outlived its usefulness." If organizations expected to be successful, they needed to "get rid of jobs" and "redesign to get the best out of the de-jobbed worker." If we no longer could expect to hold jobs, then could we at least hold a position? Unfortunately, no. Positions might be "too fixed." Roles? Nope. Too unitary, single-purposed. Skills and competencies then? Guess again; they would become obsolete.

Fortune told us that the postjob workers likely would be self-employed contract workers hired to work on projects or teams. Intel and Microsoft were suggested as examples of companies that design work around projects. People would work on 6 to 10 projects, maybe for different employers at one time. Well, maybe. But not yet. Look at the Web page for Microsoft or any other company. Almost all of them invite you to apply for (how quaint!) jobs. Microsoft and others are eager to hire employees who will work for no one but them. If you take one of these jobs, you may be working on 6 to 10 projects at once, but for different employers at one time? Not yet.[2]

Nevertheless, the concept of work is changing. Fluid organizations that require constant adaptations are no longer the exception. Sophisticated office equipment and computer software means clerical support employees don't need to worry about their spelling; however, they do need to know how to maintain the local area networks that link their machines and how to send e-mail attachments to Dublin and Caracas. Librarians who used to recommend and shelve books and provide guidance for research projects now show patrons how to run computerized searches to sort through an Internet world full of information. Auto assembly plants are replacing the retiring workers who were hired right out of high school with people trained to operate high-tech machinery and work well in teams. So, in addition to fluid organizations, fluid assignments are forcing employees to take responsibility for the objectives of what they are doing rather than for completing certain tasks. Authority is being pushed down to match the responsibilities.[3] Even the concept of the workplace has changed, as e-mail, cell phones, and frequent air travel have created "virtual" employees with no fixed location. Ford assemblers in India and car designers in Michigan can log on to their company-supplied computers to receive new training, exchange ideas and information, or hold virtual team meetings anytime, anyplace.

Yet, although there have been considerable changes in the way work is done, using a job as a way to organize and group tasks and responsibilities has not yet disappeared. A survey of over 200 organizations sponsored by WorldatWork found that more than 80 percent still use conventional job analysis programs, and the majority still use conventional job evaluation programs.[4]

■ SIMILARITIES AND DIFFERENCES FORM THE INTERNAL STRUCTURE

Organizations continue to recognize that if pay is to be based on the work performed, a systematic way is needed to document what work is performed and to assess the similarities and differences in different types of work. Yet it is clear that the nature of work is constantly changing. How do you assess something that is changing? If you answered, "very carefully," you have been watching Comedy Central too much.

Recall the engineering structure example in the previous chapter. When the company changed its marketing and product development strategy, it also redesigned its internal organization structure. Merging the systems engineer with the lead engineer and the entry engineer with the senior engineer collapsed the previous six levels of engineering work. Each distinct level in the structure corresponds with a major difference in the complexity of the work and the knowledge required to perform it.

The engineering company made these changes in order to remove obstacles to cross-functional cooperation and to permit its engineers to work more efficiently. Now, managers need to decide what kind of pay structure best supports this new organization structure. Should pay differences be based on the new levels in their engineering structure? If so, how much should these pay differences between levels be? Assessing similarities and differences in work and deciding whether these work differences justify pay differences is an important component of compensation.

■ STRUCTURES BASED ON JOBS OR PEOPLE

Managers are experimenting with a variety of responses to the challenge of constantly changing work. Some are describing work in more generic terms and grouping a wider variety of tasks together for pay purposes. The result is a de-layered structure, looser fitting, that allows employees to move among a wider range of tasks without having to adjust pay with each move. Others are switching from job-based to person-based approaches.[5] Rather than analyzing the tasks that make up a job, they analyze the skills or competencies a person must possess to perform the work. The objective is to create a work structure that supports more agile, changing organizations.

Exhibit 4.1 outlines the process for constructing a work-related internal structure. No matter the approach, the process begins by looking at people at work. Job-based structures look at the tasks the people are doing and the expected outcomes; skill- and competency-based structures look at the person. However, the underlying purpose of each phase of the process, called out in the left hand column of the exhibit, remains the same for both job- and person-based structures: (1) collect and summarize information that identifies similarities and differences, (2) determine what is to be valued, (3) quantify the relative value, and (4) translate relative value into an internal structure. (The blank boxes for the person-based structure will be filled in when we get to Chapter 6.) This chapter and the next focus on the job-based structure.[6]

EXHIBIT   **4.1**   Many Ways to Create Internal Structure ——————————————————

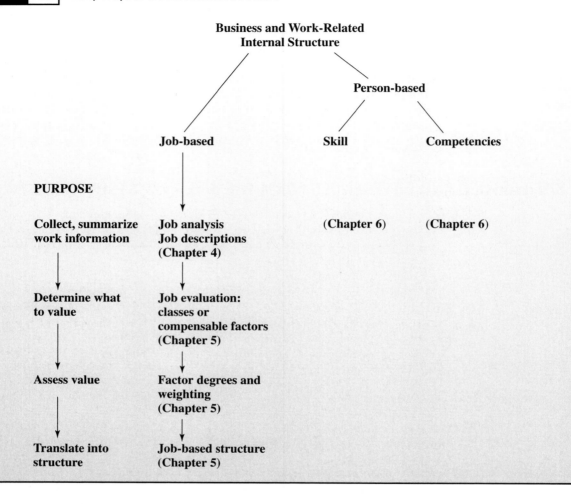

■ JOB-BASED APPROACH: MOST COMMON

job analysis

■ the systematic process
of collecting information
about the nature of
specific jobs

Exhibit 4.2 provides more detail about creating a job-based structure. Each step is defined and related to designing the structure. **Job analysis** provides the underlying information for preparing job descriptions and evaluating jobs. It is a prerequisite for job-based pay structures. The content of the job is identified via job analysis; this content serves as input for describing and valuing work.

Exhibit 4.2 also lists the major decisions in designing a job analysis: (1) Why are we collecting job information? (2) What information do we need? (3) How should we collect it? (4) Who should be involved? (5) How useful are the results?

Why Perform Job Analysis?

Historically, job analysis has been considered the cornerstone of human resources management. Potential uses for job analysis have been suggested for every major human resources function.[7] Often, the type of job analysis data needed varies by function. For example, job analysis identifies

EXHIBIT	4.2	Determining the Internal Job Structure

Internal relationships within the organization	→	**Job analysis** The systematic process of collecting information about the nature of specific jobs	→	**Job descriptions** Summary reports that identify, define, and describe the job as it is actually performed	→	**Job evaluation** Comparison of jobs within an organization	→	**Job structure** An ordering of jobs based on their content or relative value

Some Major Issues in Job Analysis
- Why collect information?
- What information is needed?
- How to collect information?
- Who should be involved?
- How useful are the results?

the skills and experience required to perform the work, which clarifies hiring and promotion standards. Training programs may be designed with job analysis data; jobs may be redesigned based on such data. In performance evaluation, both employees and supervisors look to the required behaviours and results expected in a job to help assess performance.

Although job analysis is not legally required, it provides managers a work-related rationale for pay differences. Employees who understand this rationale can better direct their behaviour toward organization objectives. Job analysis data also help managers defend their decisions when challenged.

In compensation, job analysis has two critical uses: (1) It establishes similarities and differences in the content of the jobs, and (2) it helps establish an internally fair and aligned job structure. If jobs have equal content, then in all likelihood, the pay established for them will be equal. If, on the other hand, the job content differs, then those differences, along with the market rates paid by competitors, are part of the rationale for paying jobs differently.

The key issue for compensation decision makers is still to ensure that the data collected serve the purpose of making decisions and are acceptable to the employees involved. As the arrows in Exhibit 4.2 indicate, collecting job information is only an interim step, not an end in itself.

JOB ANALYSIS PROCEDURES

Exhibit 4.3 summarizes some job analysis terms and their relationship to each other. Job analysis usually collects information about specific tasks or behaviours. A group of tasks performed by one person makes up a position. Identical positions make a job, and broadly similar jobs combine into a job family.[8]

Large organizations, often the biggest users of job analysis data, usually follow a step-by-step approach to conducting conventional job analysis.[9] Standard procedures, shown in Exhibit 4.4, include developing preliminary information, interviewing jobholders and supervisors, and then using the information to create and verify job descriptions. The picture that emerges from reading the steps in the exhibit is of a very stable workplace where the division from one job to the next is clear, with little overlap. In this workplace, jobs follow a steady progression in a hierarchy of increasing responsibility, and the relationship between jobs is clear. So is how to qualify for promotion into a higher-level job. Although some argue that such a traditional, stable structure

EXHIBIT | **4.3** | Job Analysis Terminology

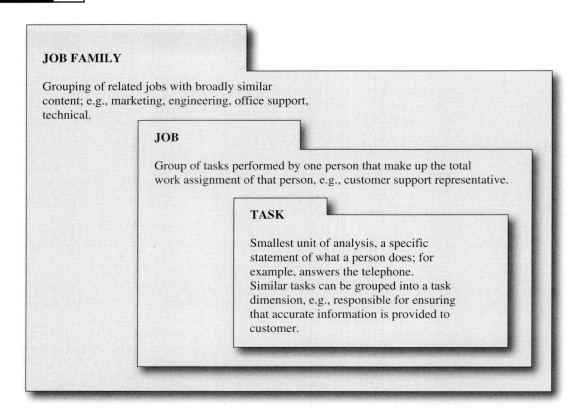

JOB FAMILY

Grouping of related jobs with broadly similar
content; e.g., marketing, engineering, office support,
technical.

JOB

Group of tasks performed by one person that make up the total
work assignment of that person, e.g., customer support representative.

TASK

Smallest unit of analysis, a specific
statement of what a person does; for
example, answers the telephone.
Similar tasks can be grouped into a task
dimension, e.g., responsible for ensuring
that accurate information is provided to
customer.

is a shrinking part of the workplace landscape, such structures nevertheless persist, in varying degrees, in many large organizations.[10] Thus, this depiction of conventional job analysis provides a useful description of the process.

WHAT INFORMATION SHOULD BE COLLECTED?

As the exhibit suggests, a typical analysis starts with a review of information already collected in order to develop a framework for further analysis. Job titles, major duties, task dimensions, and work-flow information may already exist. However, it may no longer be accurate. So the analyst must clarify existing information, too.

Generally, a good job analysis collects sufficient information to adequately identify, define, and describe a job. Exhibit 4.5 lists some of the information that is usually collected. The information is categorized as "related to the job" or "related to the employee."

Job Data: Identification

Job titles, departments, and the number of people who hold the job are examples of information that identifies a job. Although a job title may seem pretty straightforward, it may not be. For example, the federal government has hundreds of job titles, some of which are hard to interpret,

EXHIBIT 4.4 General Procedures for Conventional Job Analysis ——————————————

Step	Things to Remember or Do
1. Develop preliminary job information	a. Review existing documents in order to develop an initial "big-picture" familiarity with the job—its main mission, its major duties or functions, workflow patterns. b. Prepare a preliminary list of duties which will serve as a framework for conducting the interviews. c. Make a note of major items that are unclear or ambiguous or that need to be clarified during the data-gathering process.
2. Conduct initial tour of work site	a. The initial tour is designed to familiarize the job analyst with the work layout, the tools and equipment that are used, the general conditions of the workplace, and the mechanics associated with the end-to-end performance of major duties. b. The initial tour is particularly helpful for those jobs where a first-hand view of a complicated or unfamiliar piece of equipment may save the interviewee the thousand words required to describe the unfamiliar or technical. c. For continuity, it is recommended that the first level supervisor-interviewee be designated as the guide for the job-site observations
3. Conduct interviews	a. It is recommended that the first interview be conducted with the first-level supervisor who is considered to be in a better position than the jobholders to provide an overview of the job and how the major duties fit together. b. For scheduling purposes, it is recommended that no more than two interviews be conducted per day, each interview lasting no more than three hours.
Notes on selection of interviewees	a. The interviewees are considered subject matter experts by virtue of the fact that they perform the job (in the case of job incumbents) or are responsible for getting the job done (in the case of first-level supervisors). b. The job incumbent to be interviewed should represent the *typical* employee who is knowledgeable about the job (*not* the trainee who is just learning the ropes *nor* the outstanding member of the work unit). c. Whenever feasible, the interviewees should be selected with a view towards obtaining an appropriate diversity mix.
4. Conduct second tour of work site	a. The second tour of the work site is designed to clarify, confirm, and otherwise refine the information developed in the interviews. b. As in the initial tour, it is recommended that the same first-level supervisor-interviewee conduct the second walk through.
5. Consolidate job information	a. The consolidation phase of the job study involves piecing together into one coherent and comprehensive job description the data obtained from several sources—supervisor, jobholders, on-site tours, and written materials about the job. b. Past experience indicates that one minute of consolidation is required for every minute of interviewing. For planning purposes, at least five hours should be set aside for the consolidation phase. c. A subject matter expert should be accessible as a resource person to the job analyst during the consolidation phase. The supervisor-interviewee fills this role. d. Check your initial preliminary list of duties and questions—all must be answered or confirmed.
6. Verify job description	a. The verification phase involves bringing all the interviewees together for the purpose of determining if the consolidated job description is accurate and complete. b. The verification process is conducted in a group setting. Typed or legibly written copies of the job description (narrative description of the work setting *and* list of task statements) are distributed to the first-level supervisor and the job incumbent interviewees. c. Line by line, the job analyst goes through the entire job description and makes notes of any omissions, ambiguities, or needed clarifications. d. Collect all materials at the end of the verification meeting.

EXHIBIT **4.5** Typical Data Collected for Job Analysis

Data Related to Job

Job identification	Job content
Title	Tasks and activities
Department in which job is located	Effort (physical, mental, emotional)
Number of people who hold job	Constraints on actions
	Performance criteria
	Critical incidents
	Conflicting demands
	Working conditions
	Roles (e.g., negotiator, monitor, leader)
	Responsibility

Data Related to Employee

Employee characteristics	Internal relationships	External relationships
Professional/technical knowledge	Boss & other superiors	Suppliers
Manual skills	Peers	Customers
Verbal skills	Subordinates	Regulatory
Written skills		Professional/Industry
Quantitative skills		Community
Mechanical skills		Union/Employee Groups
Conceptual skills		
Managerial skills		
Leadership skills		
Interpersonal skills		

such as Specialist, Oral Literature; Detachment Quality Representative; Photogrammetrist; FRED Plan Administrator; and so on.[11] PepsiCo recently announced a new Chief Visionary Officer. Many organizations are scrambling to hire visionaries of one sort or another. A job title should be useful beyond providing fodder for the next *Dilbert* cartoon.

Job Data: Content

This is the heart of job analysis. Job content data involve the elemental tasks or units of work, with emphasis on the purpose of each task. An excerpt from a job analysis questionnaire that collects task data is shown in Exhibit 4.6. The inventory describes the job aspect of "Communication" in terms of actual tasks, for example, "read technical publications" and "consult with co-workers." The inventory takes eight items to cover "obtain technical information" and another seven for "exchange technical information." In fact, the task inventory from which the exhibit is excerpted contains 250 items and covers only systems and analyst jobs. New task-based questions need to be designed for each new set of jobs.

In addition to the emphasis on the task, the other distinguishing characteristic of the inventory in the exhibit is the emphasis on the objective of the task, for example, "read technical publications to keep current on industry" and "consult with co-workers to exchange ideas and techniques." Task data reveal the actual work performed and its purpose or outcome.

EXHIBIT | **4.6** | Communications: Task-Based Data

1. Mark the circle in the "Do This" column for tasks that you currently perform.

2. At the end of the task list, write in any unlisted tasks that you currently perform.

3. Rate each task that you perform for relative time spent by marking the appropriate circle in the "Time Spent" column.

Please use a No. 2 pencil and fill all circles completely.

Time spent in current position

Do This / Very small amount / Much below average / Below average / Slightly below average / About average / Slightly above average / Above average / Much above average / Very large amount

PERFORM COMMUNICATIONS ACTIVITIES

Obtain technical information

421. Read technical publications about competitive products. ○ ①②③④⑤⑥⑦⑧⑨

422. Read technical publications to keep current on industry. ○ ①②③④⑤⑥⑦⑧⑨

423. Attend required, recommended, or job-related courses and/or seminars. ○ ①②③④⑤⑥⑦⑧⑨

424. Study existing operating systems/programs to gain/maintain familiarity with them. ○ ①②③④⑤⑥⑦⑧⑨

425. Perform literature searches necessary to the development of products. ○ ①②③④⑤⑥⑦⑧⑨

426. Communicate with system software group to see how their recent changes impact current projects. ○ ①②③④⑤⑥⑦⑧⑨

427. Study and evaluate state-of-the-art techniques to remain competitive and/or lead the field. ○ ①②③④⑤⑥⑦⑧⑨

428. Attend industry standards meetings. ○ ①②③④⑤⑥⑦⑧⑨

Exchange technical information

429. Interface with coders to verify that the software design is being implemented as specified. ○ ①②③④⑤⑥⑦⑧⑨

430. Consult with co-workers to exchange ideas and techniques. ○ ①②③④⑤⑥⑦⑧⑨

431. Consult with members of other technical groups within the company to exchange new ideas and techniques. ○ ①②③④⑤⑥⑦⑧⑨

432. Interface with support consultants or organizations to clarify software design or courseware content. ○ ①②③④⑤⑥⑦⑧⑨

433. Attend meetings to review project status. ○ ①②③④⑤⑥⑦⑧⑨

434. Attend team meetings to review implementation strategies. ○ ①②③④⑤⑥⑦⑧⑨

435. Discuss department plans and objectives with manager. ○ ①②③④⑤⑥⑦⑧⑨

In Canada, it is very important to collect information relating to pay equity legislation. In particular, thorough information about the skill, effort, responsibility, and working conditions of each job is essential.

Employee Data

position analysis questionnaire (PAQ)

■ a structured job analysis questionnaire used for analyzing jobs on the basis of 194 job elements that describe generic work behaviours

Once we have specified the tasks and outcomes, we can look at the kinds of behaviours that will result in the outcomes. Exhibit 4.5 categorizes employee data as employee characteristics, internal relationships, and external relationships. Exhibit 4.7 shows how "Communications" can be described with verbs (e.g., negotiating, persuading). The verbs chosen are related to the employee characteristic being identified (e.g., bargaining skills, interpersonal skills). The rest of the statement helps identify whether the behaviour involves an internal or external relationship.

The excerpt in Exhibit 4.7 is from the **Position Analysis Questionnaire (PAQ)**, which groups work information into seven basic factors: information input, mental processes, work output,

---

EXHIBIT   4.7   Communications: Behaviour-Based Data (from the Position Analysis Questionnaire) ──────

Section 4 Relationships with Others
This section deals with different aspects of
interaction between people involved in
various kinds of work.

Importance to this Job (1)
N Does not apply
1 Very minor
2 Low
3 Average
4 High
5 Extreme

4.1 Communications
Rate the following in terms of how important the activity is to the completion of the job. Some jobs may involve several or all of the items in this section.

4.1.1 Oral (communicating by speaking)

 99 _____ Advising (dealing with individuals in order to counsel and/or guide them with regard to problems that may be resolved by legal, financial, scientific, technical, clinical, spiritual, and/or professional principles)

100 _____ Negotiating (dealing with others in order to reach an agreement or solution, for example, labour bargaining, diplomatic relations, etc.)

101 _____ Persuading (dealing with others in order to influence them toward some action or point of view, for example, selling, political campaigning, etc.)

102 _____ Instructing (the teaching of knowledge or skills, in either an informal or a formal manner, to others, for example, a public school teacher, a machinist teaching an apprentice, etc.)

103 _____ Interviewing (conducting interviews directed toward some specific objective, for example, interviewing job applicants, census taking, etc.)

104 _____ Routine information exchange: job related (the giving and/or receiving of *job-related* information of a routine nature, for example, ticket agent, taxicab dispatcher, receptionist, etc.)

105 _____ Nonroutine information exchange (the giving and/or receiving of *job-related* information of a nonroutine or unusual nature, for example, professional committee meetings, engineers discussing new product design, etc.)

106 _____ Public speaking (making speeches or formal presentations before relatively large audiences, for example, political addresses, radio/TV broadcasting, delivering a sermon, etc.)

4.1.2 Written (communicating by written/printed material)

107 _____ Writing (for example, writing or dictating letters, reports, etc., writing copy for ads, writing newspaper articles, etc.: does *not* include transcribing activities described in item 4.3, but only activities in which the incumbent creates the written material)

Source: E. J. McCormick, P. R., Jeanneret, and R. C. Mecham, *Position Analysis Questionnaire,* copyright © 1969 by Purdue Research Foundation, West Lafayette, IN 47907. Reprinted with permission.

relationships with other persons, job context, other job characteristics, and general dimensions. Similarities and differences among jobs are described in terms of these seven factors, rather than in terms of specific aspects unique to each job.[12] The communications behaviour in this exhibit is part of the "relationships with other persons" factor.

The entire PAQ consists of 194 items. Its developers claim that these items are sufficient to analyze any job. However, you can see by the exhibit that the reading level is quite high. A large proportion of employees need help to get through the whole thing. In addition, many employers believe that the information provided by the PAQ is too general for pay purposes.

However appealing it may be to rationalize job analysis as the foundation of all HR decisions, collecting all of this information for so many different purposes is very expensive. In addition, the resulting information may be too generalized for any single purpose, including compensation. If the information is to be used for multiple purposes, the analyst must be sure that the information collected is accurate and sufficient for each use. Trying to be all things to all people often results in being nothing to everyone.

Level of Analysis

The job analysis terms defined in Exhibit 4.3 are arranged in a hierarchy. The level in this hierarchy where an analysis begins may influence whether the work is similar or dissimilar. At the job family level, bookkeepers, tellers, and accounting clerks may be considered to be similar, yet at the job level, they are very different. An analogy might be looking at two grains of salt under a microscope versus looking at them as part of a serving of french fries. If job data suggest that jobs are similar, then the jobs must be paid equally; if jobs are different, they can be paid differently. In practice, many employers are finding it difficult to justify the time and expense of collecting task level information, particularly for flexible jobs with frequently changing tasks. They may collect just job-level data and emphasize comparisons in the external market for setting wages.

Many managers are increasing their organization's flexibility by adopting broad, generic descriptions that cover a large number of related tasks closer to the job family level in Exhibit 4.3. Two employees working in the same broadly defined jobs may be doing entirely different sets of related tasks. But for pay purposes, they are doing work of equal value. Employees working in very broadly defined jobs can easily be switched to other tasks that fall within the broad range of the same job, without the bureaucratic burden of making job transfer requests and wage adjustments. Thus, employees can more easily be matched to changes in the workflow.

Still, a countervailing view deserves consideration. More specific distinctions among jobs represent career paths to employees. Reducing the number of levels in a structure may reduce opportunities for recognition and advancement. Reducing titles or labelling all employees as "associates" may signal an egalitarian culture. But it also may sacrifice a sense of advancement and opportunity.[13]

■ HOW CAN THE INFORMATION BE COLLECTED?

Conventional Methods

The most common way to collect job information is to ask the people who are doing a job to fill out a questionnaire. Sometimes an analyst will interview the jobholders and their supervisors to be sure they understand the questions and that the information is correct. Or the analyst may observe the person and work and take notes on what is being done. Exhibit 4.8 shows part of a job analysis questionnaire. Questions range from "Give an example of a particularly difficult problem that you face in your work. Why does it occur? How often does it occur? What special skills and/or resources are needed to solve this difficult problem?" to "What is the nature of any

EXHIBIT 4.8 3M's Structured Interview Questionnaire

I. Job Overview

Job Summary	What is the main purpose of your job? (Why does it exist and what does the work contribute to 3M?)
	    Examples: To provide secretarial support in our department by performing office and administrative duties.
	        To purchase goods and services that meet specifications at the least cost.
	        To perform systems analysis involved in the development, installation, and maintenance of
	        computer applications.
	
	Hint: It may help to list the duties first before answering this question.

Duties and Respon-sibilities	What are your job's main duties and responsibilities? (These are the major work activities that usually take up a significant amount of your work time and occur regularly as you perform your work.) In the spaces below, list your job's five most important or most frequent duties. Then, in the boxes, estimate the percentage of the time you spend on each day.	**Percentage of Time Spent** (Total may be less than but not more than 100%)
	1.	

II. Skills/Knowledge Applied

Formal Training or Education	What is the level of formal training/education that is needed to start doing your job?
	    Example: High School, college diploma in Data Processing, Bachelor of Science in Chemistry.
	In some jobs, a combination of education and job-related experience can substitute for academic degrees.
	    Example: Bachelor's Degree in Accounting or completion of 2 years of general business plus 3–4 years' work
	        experience in an accounting field.

Experience	Months: Years: None
Skills/ Compet-encies	What important skills, competencies, or abilities are needed to do the work that you do? (Please give examples for each skill that you identify.) **A. Coordinating Skills** (such as scheduling activities, organizing/maintaining records) Are coordinating skills required? ☐ Yes ☐ No If yes, give examples of specific skills needed Example **B. Administrative Skills** (such as monitoring

III. Complexity of Duties

Structure and Variation of Work	How processes and tasks within your work are determined, and how you do them are important to understanding your work at 3M. Describe the work flow in your job. Think of the major focus of your job or think of the work activities on which you spend the most time. 1. From whom/where (title, not person) do you receive work? 2. What processes or tasks do you perform to complete it?
Problem Solving and Analysis	3. Give an example of a particularly difficult problem that you face in your work. Why does it occur? How often does it occur? What special skills and/or resources are needed to solve this difficult problem?

VI. General Comments

General Comments	What percentage of your job duties do you feel was captured in this questionnaire? ☐ 0–25% ☐ 26–50% ☐ 51–75% ☐ 76–100% What aspect of your job was not covered adequately by this questionnaire?

contact you have with individuals or companies in countries other than Canada?" These examples are drawn from the "Complexity of Duties" section of a job analysis questionnaire used by 3M. Other sections of the questionnaire are Skills/Knowledge Applied (19 to choose from), Impact This Job Has on 3M's Business, and Working Conditions. It concludes by asking respondents how well they feel the questionnaire has captured their particular job. The advantage of conventional questionnaires and interviews is that the involvement of employees increases their understanding of the process. However, the results are only as good as the people involved. If important aspects of a job are omitted, or if the job holders themselves either do not realize or are unable to express the importance of certain aspects, the resulting job descriptions will also be faulty. If you look at the number of jobs in an organization, you can see the difficulty in expecting a single analyst to understand all the different types of work and the importance of certain job aspects. Different people have different perceptions, which may result in differences in interpretation or emphasis. The whole process is open to bias and favouritism.[14]

As a result of this potential subjectivity, as well as the huge amount of time the process takes, conventional methods have given way to more quantitative (and systematic) data collection.

Quantitative Methods

Increasingly, an analyst will direct jobholders to a Web site where they complete a questionnaire on-line. Such an approach is characterized as quantitative job analysis, since the results can be analyzed arithmetically. A quantitative questionnaire typically asks jobholders to assess whether each item is or is not part of their job. If it is, they are asked to rate how important it is, and the amount of job time spent on it. The results can be machine scored like a multiple-choice test (except there are no wrong answers), and the results can be used to develop a profile of the job. Exhibit 4.9 shows part of an on-line job analysis questionnaire used by a United Kingdom consulting firm.[15] Questions are grouped around five compensable factors (discussed in Chapter 5): knowledge, accountability, reasoning, communications, and working conditions. Knowledge is further subcategorized as range of depth, qualifications, experience, occupational skills, management skills, and learning time. Assistance is given in the form of prompting questions and a list of jobs that have answered each question in a similar way. Results can be used to prepare a job profile based on the compensable factors. If more than one person is doing a particular job, results of several people in the job can be compared or averaged to develop the profile. Profiles can be compared across jobholders in the same or in different jobs. Exhibit 4.10 is a job profile prepared from the results of the questionnaire used in Exhibit 4.9. Exhibits 4.6 and 4.7 are excerpts from quantitative questionnaires.

Some consulting firms have developed quantitative inventories they can tailor to the needs of a specific organization or to a specific family of jobs, such as data/information processing jobs. Many organizations find it practical and cost effective to modify these existing inventories rather than develop their own analysis from ground zero. Turning over the analysis to a consulting shop does not necessarily mean that the organization and its employees are not involved in the process, both as sources of information, and as consumers who want to be sure the results are useful. The advantage of quantitative data collection is that more data can be collected faster. But keep in mind that the results are only as good as the items in the questionnaire. If important aspects of a job are omitted, or if the job holders themselves do not realize the importance of certain aspects, the resulting job descriptions will also be faulty.

Whether through a conventional analysis or a quantitative approach, completing a questionnaire requires considerable involvement by employees and supervisors. Involvement can increase their understanding of the process, which increases the likelihood that the results of the analysis will be acceptable.[16]

EXHIBIT 4.9   On-line Job Analysis Questionnaire

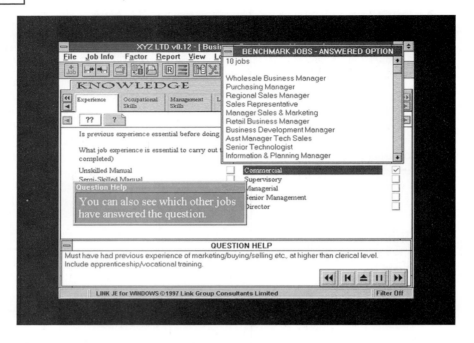

Source: Link Group Consultants, Limited. Used by permission. www.hrlink.co.uk

Who Collects the Information?

Collecting job analysis information through one-on-one interviews can be a thankless task. No matter how good a job you do, people will not always be happy with the resulting job descriptions. Although organizations frequently assign the task to a new employee, justifying the assignment on the grounds that it will help the new employee become familiar with the company's jobs, the analysis is better done by someone thoroughly familiar with the organization and its jobs.

Who Provides the Information?

The decision on the source of the data (job holders, supervisors, and/or analysts) hinges on how to ensure consistent, accurate, and acceptable data. Expertise about the work resides with the job holders and supervisors; hence, they are the principal sources. For key managerial/professional jobs, supervisors "two levels above" have also been suggested as valuable sources since they may have a more macro view of how jobs fit in the overall organization. In other instances, subordinates and employees in other jobs that interface with the job under study also are involved.

The number of incumbents per job from which to collect data probably varies with the stability of the job, as well as with the ease of collecting the information. An ill-defined or changing job will require either the involvement of more respondents or a more careful selection of respondents. Obviously, the more people involved, the more time-consuming and expensive the process, although computerization helps mitigate these objections.

EXHIBIT | **4.10** | On-line Job Profile

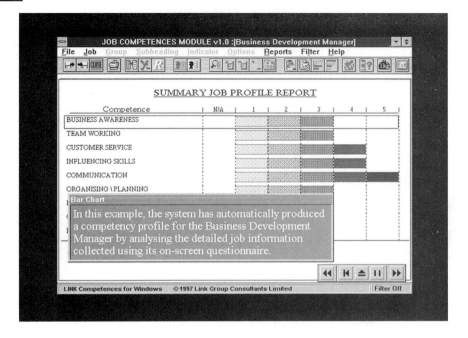

Source: Link Group Consultants, Limited. Used by permission. www.hrlink.co.uk

How to Resolve Discrepancies

What happens if the supervisor and the employees present different pictures of the job? Although supervisors, in theory, ought to know the jobs well, they may not, particularly if jobs are changing or ill-defined in the first place. People actually working in a job may change it. They may find ways to do things more efficiently, or they may not have realized that certain tasks were supposed to be part of their job. The crossfire from differing perspectives on the nature of a job indicates why conducting a job analysis can be a dangerous activity for a brand-new HR employee.

3M had an interesting problem when they collected job information from a group of engineers. The engineers listed a number of responsibilities that they viewed as part of their jobs; however, the manager realized that those responsibilities actually belonged to a higher level of work. The engineers had enlarged their jobs beyond what they were being paid to do. No one wanted to tell this highly productive group of employees to throttle back and slack off. So 3M looked for ways to recognize and reward these engineers rather than bureaucratize them.

What should the manager do if employees and their supervisors do not agree on what is part of the job? The answer is to collect more data. Enough data are required to ensure consistent, accurate, and acceptable results. In general, the more unusual the job, the more sources of data will be required. Discussing discrepancies with everyone, then asking both employees and supervisors to sign off on the proposed analysis helps ensure agreement, or at least understanding, of the results.

Top Management Support Is Critical.   In addition to involvement by analysts, job holders, and their supervisors, support of top management is absolutely essential. They must be alerted to the cost of a thorough job analysis, its time-consuming nature, and the fact that changes may result after it is completed. For example, jobs may be combined; pay rates may be adjusted. If top management is not willing to carry through, or at least seriously weigh, any changes suggested by the job analysis, the process is probably not worth the bother and expense.

◼ JOB DESCRIPTIONS SUMMARIZE THE DATA

job description

◼ written summary of a job, including responsibilities, qualifications, and relationships

So, now the job information has been collected, maybe even organized. But it still must be summarized in a way that will be useful for HR decisions, including job evaluation (Chapter 5). That summary of the job is the **job description**. The job description provides a word picture of the job. Exhibit 4.11 is part of a job description for a registered nurse. Trace the connection between different parts of the description and the job analysis data collected. The job is identified by title and its relationships to other jobs. The relationships demonstrate where the job

---

| **EXHIBIT** | **4.11** | Contemporary Job Description for Registered Nurse |

Job Title
Registered Nurse

Job Summary
Accountable for the complete spectrum of patient care from admission through transfer or discharge through the nursing process of assessment, planning, implementation, and evaluation. Each R.N. has primary authority to fulfill responsibility of the nursing process on the assigned shift and for projecting future needs of the patient/family. Directs and guides patient teaching and activities for ancillary personnel while maintaining standard of professional nursing.

Relationships
Reports to: Head Nurse or Charge Nurse.
Supervises: Responsible for the care delivered by L.P.N.'s, nursing assistants, orderlies, and transcribers.
Works with: Ancillary Care Departments.
External relationships: Physicians, patients, patients' families.

Qualifications
Education: Graduate of an accredited school of nursing.
Work experience: Critical care requires one year of recent medical/surgical experience (special care nursing preferred), medical/surgical experience (new graduates may be considered for noncharge positions).
Licence or registration requirements: Current R.N. licence or permit in the Province of Alberta.

Physical requirements: A. Ability to bend, reach, or assist to transfer up to 23 kilos.
                              B. Ability to stand and/or walk 80 percent of 8-hour shift.
                              C. Visual and hearing acuity to perform job-related functions.

Essential Responsibilities
1. Assess physical, emotional, and psycho-social dimensions of patients.
    Standard: Provides a written assessment of patient within one hour of admission and at least once a shift. Communicates this assessment to other patient care providers in accordance with hospital policies.

2. Formulates a written plan of care for patients from admission through discharge.
    Standard: Develops short-term and long-term goals within 24 hours of admission. Reviews and updates care plans each shift based on ongoing assessment.

3. Implements plan of care.
    Standard: Demonstrates skill in performing common nursing procedures in accordance with but not limited to the established written R.N. skills inventory specific to assigned area. Completes patient care activities in an organized and timely fashion, reassessing priorities appropriately.

Note: Additional responsibilities omitted from exhibit.

fits into the organization: who is supervised by this jobholder, who supervises this jobholder, and the nature of any internal and external relationships. A job summary consists of a short paragraph that provides an overview of the job. The section on essential responsibilities elaborates on the summary. It includes the tasks. Related tasks may be grouped into task dimensions. This particular job description also includes very specific standards for judging whether an essential responsibility has been met, for example, "Provides a written assessment of patient within one hour of admission and at least once a shift." A final section lists the qualifications necessary to be hired for the job. These are the **job specifications** that can be used as a basis for hiring—the knowledge, skills, and abilities required to adequately perform the tasks. But keep in mind that the summary needs to be relevant to pay decisions and thus must focus on similarities and differences in content.

job specification

qualifications required to be hired for a job; may be included in the job description

Describing Managerial/Professional Jobs

In addition to defining and describing jobs, descriptions of managerial/professional jobs often include more detailed information about the nature of the job, its scope, and accountability. One challenge is that an individual manager may influence the job content.[17] This is a classic example of how job-based and person-based approaches blend in practice, even though the distinctions are easy to make in a textbook. Professional/managerial job descriptions must capture the relationship between the job, the person performing it, and the organization objectives—how the job fits into the organization, the results expected, and what the person performing it brings to the job. Someone with strong information systems and computer expertise performing the compensation manager's job will probably shape it differently, based on this expertise, than someone with strong negotiation and/or counselling expertise. Exhibit 4.12 excerpts this scope and accountability information for a nurse manager. Rather than emphasizing the tasks to be done, this description focuses on the accountabilities (e.g., "responsible for the coordination,

EXHIBIT 4.12 Job Description for a Manager

Title: Nurse Manager

Department: ICU

Date Posted:

Status: Open

Position Description:
Under the direction of the Vice President of Patient Care Services and Directors of Patient Care Services, the Nurse Manager assumes 24-hour accountability and responsibility for the operations of defined patient specialty services. The Nurse Manager is administratively responsible for the coordination, direction, implementation, evaluation, and management of human resources and services. The Nurse Manager provides leadership in a manner consistent with the corporate mission, values, and philosophy and adheres to policies and procedures established by Saint Joseph's Hospital and the Division of Patient Care Services. The Nurse Manager participates in strategic planning and defining future direction for the assigned areas of responsibility and the organization.

Qualification:
Education: Graduate of accredited school of nursing. A bachelor's degree in Nursing or related field required. Master's degree preferred. Current licence in the Province of Nova Scotia as a Registered Nurse. Experience: A minimum of three year's clinical nursing is required. Minimum of two year's management experience or equivalent preferred.

direction, implementation, evaluation and management of personnel and services; provides leadership; participates in strategic planning and defining future direction").

Verify the Description

The final step in the job analysis process is to verify the accuracy of the resulting job descriptions (Step 6 in Exhibit 4.4). Verification often involves the interviewees as well as their supervisors to determine whether the proposed job description is accurate and complete. The description is discussed, line by line, with the analyst, taking note of any omissions, ambiguities, or needed clarifications (an often excruciating and thankless task). It would have been interesting to hear the discussion between our nurse from 100 years ago, whose job is described in Exhibit 4.13, and her

.NET WORTH

National Occupational Classification

In Canada, many companies turn to the federal government's National Occupational Classification (NOC) for reference when preparing job descriptions. The NOC is an excellent source of standardized job information, based on systematic field research by Human Resources Development Canada. It contains comprehensive descriptions and qualifications for about 30,000 occupations. NOC information is available on-line are www23.hrdc-drhc.gc.ca/2001/e/generic/welcome.shtml.

The NOC classifies occupations in Major Groups based on two key dimensions: skill level and skill type. The Major Groups, which are identified by two-digit numbers, are then broken down further into Minor Groups, with a third digit added, and Unit Groups, at which a fourth digit is added. For example, Major Group 64: Intermediate Sales and Service Occupations includes Minor Group 645: Occupations in Food and Beverage Service, which includes Unit Group 6452: Bartenders.

The Unit Group Description for Bartenders is:
Bartenders mix and serve alcoholic and non-alcoholic beverages. They are employed in restaurants, hotels, bars, taverns, private clubs, banquet halls, and other licensed establishments. Supervisors of bartenders are included in this unit group.

The main duties listed for Bartenders include:
- Take beverage orders from serving staff or directly from patrons
- Mix liquor, soft drinks, water, and other ingredients to prepare cocktails and other drinks
- Prepare mixed drinks, wine, draft or bottled beer, and non-alcoholic beverages for food and beverage servers or serve directly to patrons
- Collect payment for beverages and record sales
- Maintain inventory and control of bar stock and order supplies
- Clean bar area and wash glassware
- Ensure compliance with provincial/territorial liquor legislation and regulations
- May train and supervise other bartenders and bar staff
- May hire and dismiss staff

Source: Human Resources Development Canada, National Occupation Classification. Reproduced with the permission of the Minister of Public Works and Government Services Canada, 2004.

EXHIBIT | **4.13** | Job Description for Nurse 100 Years Ago

In addition to caring for your 50 patients, each nurse will follow these regulations:

1. Daily sweep and mop the floors of your ward, dust the patient's furniture and window sills.

2. Maintain an even temperature in your ward by bringing in a scuttle of coal for the day's business.

3. Light is important to observe the patient's condition. Therefore, each day, fill kerosene lamps, clean chimneys, and trim wicks. Wash the windows once a week.

4. The nurse's notes are important in aiding the physician's work. Make your pens carefully; you may whittle nibs to your individual taste.

5. Each nurse on the day duty will report every day at 7 a.m. and leave at 8 p.m. except on the Sabbath, on which day you will be off from 12:00 noon to 2:00 p.m.

6. Graduate nurses in good standing with the director of nurses will be given an evening off each week for courting purposes, or two evenings a week if you go regularly to church.

7. Each nurse should lay aside from each pay day a goodly sum of her earnings for her benefits during her declining years, so that she will not become a burden. For example, if you earn $30 a month you should set aside $15.

8. Any nurse who smokes, uses liquor in any form, gets her hair done at a beauty shop, or frequents dance halls will give the director good reason to suspect her worth, intentions, and integrity.

9. The nurse who performs her labours and serves her patients and doctors faithfully and without fault for a period of five years will be given an increase by the hospital administration of five cents a day, provided there are no hospital debts that are outstanding.

supervisor. The job description paints a vivid picture of expectations at that time, though we expect she probably did not have much opportunity for input 100 years ago.

JOB ANALYSIS: BEDROCK OR BUREAUCRACY?

HRNet, the world's largest Internet discussion group related to HR issues, provoked one of its largest responses ever to the query, "What good is job analysis?" Some felt that managers have no basis for making defensible, work-related decisions without it. Others called the process a bureaucratic boondoggle.

A large part of the disagreement centres on the issue of flexibility. Many organizations today are trying to become more competitive by reducing their costs. Using fewer employees to do a wider variety of tasks and jobs is part of that cost-reduction strategy. Streamlining job analysis and reducing the number of different jobs can reduce costs by making work assignments more fluid.

Generic descriptions that cover a larger number of related tasks (e.g., "associate") can provide flexibility in moving people among tasks without adjusting pay. Employees may be more easily matched to changes in the work flow; the importance of flexibility in behaviour is made clear to employees.

Traditional job analysis that makes fine distinctions between levels of jobs has been accused of reinforcing rigidity in the organization. Employees may refuse to do certain tasks that are not specifically called out in their job descriptions. It should be noted, however, that this problem arises mainly where employee relations are already poor. In unionized settings, union members may "work to rule" (i.e., not do anything that is not specifically listed in their job description) as a technique to put pressure on management. When work relationships are poor, both managers and employees can use a detailed job description as a "weapon."[18]

On the other hand, the hierarchies and distinctions between jobs also may represent career paths and opportunities. Changing jobs often means a promotion and/or recognition of performance, not to mention a fatter paycheque. Reducing the number of jobs reduces these opportunities for recognition and advancement. Some people value a title change from Engineer to Senior Engineer rather than the more generic Engineer Associate. In response to unhappy employees, some companies who have de-layered are "re-layering." Johnson & Johnson (J&J) in China sought to cut turnover from around 25 percent a year by re-layering. They went from 7 levels in their structure to 28, thereby responding to employees' desire for a greater sense of progress and promotion.

■ JUDGING JOB ANALYSIS

Beyond beliefs about its usefulness, or lack thereof, for satisfying both employees and employers, there are several ways to judge job analysis.

Reliability

reliability

consistency of results from repeated applications of a measure

If you measure something tomorrow and get the same results you got today, or if I measure and get the same result you did, the measurement is considered to be reliable. This doesn't mean it is right—only that repeated measures give the same result. **Reliability** is a measure of the consistency of results if the same measure is repeated many times.

Research findings on employee and supervisor agreement on the reliability of job analysis information are mixed. For instance, experience may change an employee's perceptions about a job, since the employee may have found new ways to do it or have added new tasks to the job. The supervisor may not realize the extent of change. In such cases, the job the employee is actually doing may not be the same job originally assigned by the supervisor. Obviously, the way to increase reliability in a job analysis is to reduce sources of variance. Quantitative job analysis helps reduce variance. But we need to be sure that we do not eliminate the richness or the nuances of a job while eliminating the variance.

Validity

validity

accuracy of a measure

Does the analysis create an accurate portrait of the work? There is almost no way of showing statistically the extent to which an analysis is accurate, particularly for complex jobs. Consequently, **validity** examines convergence of results among different sources of data and methods. If several job incumbents respond in similar ways to questionnaires, then it is considered more likely that the information they give is valid. However, a sign-off on the results does not guarantee validity. It may only mean everyone was sick to death of the process and wanted to get rid of the analyst so they could get back to work.

Acceptability

If job holders and managers are dissatisfied with the initial data collected or with the process, they are not likely to buy into the resulting job structure nor the pay rates that eventually are attached to that structure. An analyst collecting information through one-on-one interviews or observation is not always accepted because of the potential for subjectivity and favouritism. One writer says, "We all know the classic procedures. One (worker) watched and noted the actions of another . . . at work on (the) job. The actions of both are biased and the resulting information varied with the wind, especially the political wind."[19] However, more quantitative approaches also may run into difficulty, especially if they give in to the temptation to try to collect too much information for too many purposes. After four years in development, one application ran into such severe problems caused by its unwieldy size and incomprehensible questions that managers simply refused to use it.

Practicality

Practicality refers to the usefulness of the information collected. For pay purposes, job analysis provides work-related information to help determine how much to pay for a job—it helps determine whether the job is similar or different from other jobs. If job analysis does this in a reliable, valid, and acceptable way, then the technique is of practical use.[20]

As we have noted, some see job analysis information as useful for multiple purposes, such as hiring and training. But multiple purposes may require more information than is required to assess pay. The practical utility of all-encompassing quantitative job analysis plans, with their relatively complex procedures and analysis, remains in doubt. Some advocates get so taken with their statistics and computers that they ignore the role that human judgment must continue to play in job analysis. As Dunnette states, "I wish to emphasize the central role played in all these procedures by human judgment. I know of no methodology, statistical technique or objective measurements that can negate the importance of, nor supplement, rational judgment."[21]

A Judgment Call

In the face of all the difficulties, time, expense, and dissatisfaction, why on earth would you as a manager recommend that your employer bother with job analysis? Because work-related information is needed to determine pay, and differences in work determine pay differences. There is no satisfactory substitute that can ensure that the resulting pay structure will be work related or will provide reliable, accurate data to make and explain pay decisions.

If work information is required, then the real issue should be, How much detail is needed to make these pay decisions? The answer is: Enough to help set individual employees' pay, encourage continuous learning, increase the experience and skill of the workforce, and minimize the risk of pay-related grievances. The risk of omitting this detail is dissatisfied employees who drive away customers with their poor service, file lawsuits, or complain about management's inability to justify their decisions. The response to inadequate analysis ought not to be to dump the analysis; rather, the response should be more useful analysis.

CONCLUSION

Encouraging employee behaviours that help achieve an organization's objectives and foster a sense of fairness among employees are two hallmarks of a useful internal pay structure. One of the first strategic pay decisions is how much to align a pay structure internally as opposed to aligning it to external market forces. Do not be misled. The issue is *not* achieving internal alignment *versus* alignment with external market forces. Rather, the strategic decision focuses on sustaining the optimal balance of internally aligned and externally responsive pay structures that helps the organization achieve its mission. *Both are required.* This section of the book is about one of the first decisions you face in designing pay systems: how much to emphasize pay structures that are internally aligned with the work performed, the organization's structure, and its strategies. Whatever the choice, it needs to support (and be supported by) the organization's overall human resource strategy.

Next, managers must decide whether job and/or individual employee characteristics will be the basic unit of analysis supporting the pay structure. This is followed by deciding what data will be collected, what method(s) will be used to collect them, and who should be involved in the process.

A key test of an effective and fair pay structure is acceptance of results by managers and employees. The best way to ensure acceptance of job analysis results is to involve employees as well as supervisors in the process. At a minimum, all employees should be informed of the purposes and progress of the activity.

If almost everyone agrees about the importance of job analysis, does that mean everyone does it? Of course not. Unfortunately, job analysis can be tedious and time-consuming. Often the job is given to newly hired compensation analysts, ostensibly to help them learn the organization, but perhaps there's also a hint of "rite of passage" in such assignments.

Alternatives to job-based structures, such as skill-based or competency-based systems, are being experimented with in many firms. The premise is that basing structures on these other criteria will encourage employees to become more flexible, and fewer workers will be required for the same level of output. This may be the argument, but as experience increases with the alternatives, managers are discovering that they can be as time-consuming and bureaucratic as job analysis. Bear in mind, job content remains the conventional criterion for structures.

CHAPTER SUMMARY

1. Job analysis is the systematic process of collecting information about the nature of specific jobs. It has been called the cornerstone of human resources management because job analysis data are used in virtually every major HR function, including recruiting and selection, training, compensation, and so on.

2. The information that must be collected for job analysis includes job identification data, job content data, and data on qualifications necessary to do the job. Job content data are the heart of job analysis, and include the tasks involved, their purpose, reporting relationships, working conditions, and other specific job information. Conventional methods of collecting job analysis data such as questionnaires and interviews are being replaced by on-line questionnaires because they are more objective and less time-consuming.

3. Job descriptions provide a written summary of a job, including responsibilities, qualifications, and relationships. Job specifications are the qualifications required to be hired for a job, and may be included in the job description.

4. The benefit of traditional job analysis is that it provides the basis for defensible job-related decisions, and establishes a foundation for career paths. However, it is sometimes considered to be too rigid for today's more flexible organizations with fluid work assignments. Job analysis can be judged based on reliability (consistency) of the information obtained, validity (accuracy) of the information obtained, acceptability of the data and the process by employees and managers, and practicality (usefulness) of the information collected.

KEY TERMS

REVIEW QUESTIONS

1. What are the two critical uses of job analysis for compensation decisions?
2. Describe the major decisions involved in job analysis.
3. Distinguish between task and behavioural data.
4. How should discrepancies between job analysis information provided by employees and supervisors be resolved?

EXPERIENTIAL EXERCISES

1. Talk to several managers and find one or more who say that job analysis is a colossal waste of their time and the time of their employees. Find out what the reasons are for their opinion. Are they right?

2. **a)** Think of a specific job you presently hold or have held in the past (including a part-time job or volunteer work). Use the information in this chapter to develop a job analysis questionnaire that you believe would adequately capture all relevant information about that job. Then complete the questionnaire for your specific job.

    b) Pick a teammate (or the instructor will assign one) and exchange questionnaires with your teammate.

    c) Write a job description for your teammate's job. Does the questionnaire give you sufficient information? Is there additional information that would be helpful?

    d) Exchange descriptions. Critique the job description written by your teammate. Does it adequately capture all the important job aspects? Does it indicate which aspects are most important?

WEB EXERCISE

Job Analysis and On-line Job Postings

The number of on-line job boards has been expanding exponentially. Many companies post a sample of job openings on their Web sites. Compare the job postings from Workopolis.ca, Monster.ca, and several companies. How complete a job description is included with the posting? Are job titles specific or generic? Can you get any sense of a company's culture from its job postings?

CASE

Dual Ladders at 3M

"Dual ladders" provide two alternative career paths for technical employees. One ladder might start with an entry-level scientist and eventually go to the chief scientist for the company. An alternative ladder moves some scientists into managerial positions where promotions and pay increases come with increasing managerial responsibility. The purpose of the dual ladder is to offer technical employees opportunities for advancement without the requirement of managerial responsibility.

Two 3M scientists, John A. Martens and Gerald Niles, sued 3M, contending that the company held out its dual ladder compensation system to them as a promise that technical workers would be paid comparably to managerial employees. They claimed that the dual ladder system encouraged engineers and scientists to pursue technical careers by promising them that they did not need to switch to the managerial ladder, and that they would not forgo compensation and advancement by staying on the technical ladder.

Martens alleged that as he advanced at 3M, he was told that compensation and advancement were open-ended once he reached the top rung of the dual ladder system. Based on these representations, he stayed with the company. Once he reached the level of corporate scientist, however, he noticed that his peers and even subordinates on the management side of the ladder received greater compensation, responsibility, and recognition.

Niles contends that the dual ladder system appeared inequitable to him as well. He claims he was the lowest paid employee on a project management team, despite the fact the team was working solely on developing his inventions.

Questions

1. List the strengths and weaknesses of a dual ladder system. Be sure to focus on its work relatedness, market relatedness, and business-strategy relatedness. What argument would you make in favour of 3M's (and other companies') dual ladder?

2. How can organizations such as 3M reinforce the strategic importance of research and development?

CASE—*continued*

3. In light of the judgment inherent in defining career ladders, and the ambiguity of jobs in scientific management, what argument would you make against dual ladder systems?

4. What specific actions would you recommend to any company to minimize the vulnerabilities while retaining the notions of different labour markets and differences in types of work?

5. Should the top scientists and engineers at 3M be paid the same as top managers? How about top professors versus deans in your university? Or top high school teachers versus principals? On what basis do organizations make these decisions? Would you add additional criteria to these decisions?

Online Learning Centre   **Visit the Online Learning Centre at**
www.mcgrawhill.ca/college/milkovich

EVALUATING WORK: JOB EVALUATION

LEARNING OUTCOMES

- *Define* job evaluation and *explain* the different perspectives regarding this activity.
- *Describe* the ranking method of job evaluation and *explain* two specific methods of ranking.
- *Discuss* the classification method of job evaluation and how benchmark jobs are used in this method.
- *Explain* the six steps involved in the point method of job evaluation and *describe* the three common characteristics of point plans.
- *Discuss* who should be involved in job evaluation.

As soon as my daughter turned 14, she absolutely refused to go shopping with me. At first I thought it was because I like to hum along with the mall music. But she says it is because I embarrass her when I interrogate the assistant store manager about how he is paid—more precisely, how his pay compares to that of the stock clerks, the manager, and regional managers. My daughter claims I do this everywhere I go. "Compensationitis," she calls it. And I know it's contagious, because a colleague of mine grills his seatmates on airplanes. He's learned the pay rates for American Airlines captains who pilot Boeing 747 jets versus those who pilot the 101A Airbus.

Reporters often catch compensationitis, too, particularly when writing about other people's salaries. For example, gossip columnist Liz Hodgson reported that extras on movie director Steven Spielberg's film *Amistad* won a massive pay raise after complaining they should have been classified as singers.[1] The black actors, playing West African slaves being transported to the United States in the true story of a slave uprising in 1839, were originally paid just $79 a day, the union minimum. But they protested that they should have received $447, the singers' rate, because they had to learn and rehearse traditional tribal songs. Spielberg's DreamWorks SKG company worked out a deal with the Screen Actors Guild for extra pay totalling $250,000.

How does any organization go about valuing work? The next time you go to the supermarket, check out the different types of work there: store manager, produce manager, front-end manager, deli workers, butchers, stock clerks, checkout people, bakers—the list is long, and the work surprisingly diverse. If you managed a supermarket, how would you value work? Specifically, what techniques would you use, and would the techniques really matter? But be careful—compensationitis is contagious, and it can embarrass your friends.

This chapter and the next discuss techniques used to value work. Both chapters focus on "how to"—the specific steps involved. Job evaluation techniques are discussed in this chapter. Person-based techniques, both skill-based and competency-based, are in Chapter 6. The objective of all the techniques is an internally aligned pay structure. Ultimately, the pay structure helps the organization sustain its competitive advantage by influencing employee behaviours.

JOB-BASED STRUCTURES: JOB EVALUATION

job structure

hierarchy of all jobs based on value to the organization; provides the basis for the pay structure

Exhibit 5.1 is an elaboration of Exhibit 4.1 from the previous chapter. It orients us to the process of building a work structure and the techniques for building a job-based structure. Our job analysis and job descriptions (Chapter 4) collected and summarized work information. In this chapter, the focus is on how to determine what to value in the jobs, how to quantify that value, and how to translate that value into a **job structure**. **Job evaluation** is the process of determining and quantifying value. This potential to blend internal forces and external market forces is both a strength and a challenge to job evaluation.

Exhibit 5.2 shows how job evaluation fits into the process of determining the internal structure. You already know that the process begins with a job analysis, in which the information on jobs is collected, and that job descriptions summarize the information and serve as input for the evaluation. The exhibit calls out some of the major decisions in the job evaluation process.

DEFINING JOB EVALUATION: CONTENT, VALUE, AND EXTERNAL MARKET LINKS

Content and Value

job evaluation

the process of systematically determining the relative worth of jobs to create a job structure for the organization. The evaluation is based on a combination of job content, skills required, value to the organization, organizational culture, and the external market.

Perspectives differ on whether job evaluation is based on job content or job value. A structure based on job content refers to the skills required for the job, its duties, and its responsibilities. A structure based on job value refers to the *relative* contribution of the skills, duties, and responsibilities of a job to the organization's goals. But can this structure translate directly into pay rates, without regard to the external market, government regulations, or any individual negotiation process? Most people think not. Recall that internal alignment is just one of the building blocks of the pay model. Job characteristics matter, but they are not the only basis for pay. Job value may also include its value in the external market and/or its relationship to some other set of rates that have been agreed upon through collective bargaining or other negotiation process or to government legislation (minimum wage).

Not only may the content be described and valued differently by different observers (*Amistad* extras versus singers), but the value added by the same work may be more (or less) in one organization than in another. We observed in Chapter 3 that the value added by a compensation specialist to a firm whose earnings are generated through sales of manufactured goods or engineering expertise may differ from the value added by that specialist to a consulting firm whose revenues come through the sale of compensation expertise. So, although we talk about internal job value (contributions to organization objectives), external market value may differ. There is not a one-to-one correspondence with pay rates.

Linking Content with the External Market

Some see job evaluation as a process which links job content with external market rates. Aspects of job content (e.g., skills required and customer contacts) take on value based on their

EXHIBIT | **5.1** | Many Ways to Create Internal Structure

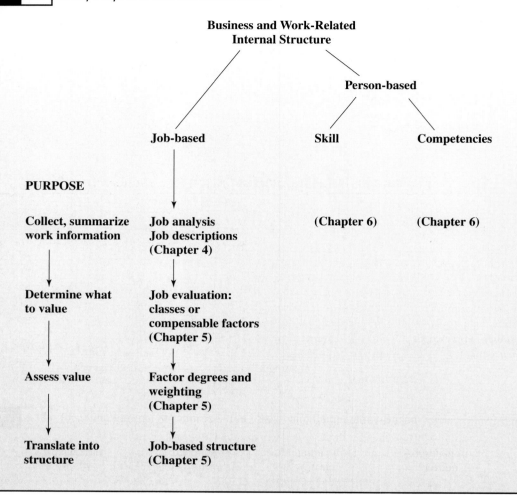

EXHIBIT | **5.2** | Determining an Internally Aligned Job Structure

Internal alignment: → Job analysis → Job descriptions → Job evaluation → Job structure
Work relationships
within the organization

Some Major Decisions in Job Evaluation
- Establish purpose of evaluation.
- Decide whether to use single or multiple plans.
- Choose among alternative approaches.
- Obtain involvement of relevant stakeholders.
- Evaluate plan's usefulness.

relationship to market wages. Because willingness to work more closely with customers or higher skill levels usually command higher wages in the labour market, nature of customer contacts and skill level become useful criteria for establishing differences among jobs. If some aspect of job content, such as working conditions, is not related to wages paid in the external labour market, then that aspect is excluded in the job evaluation. According to this perspective, the value of job content is based on what it can command in the external market; it has no intrinsic value.[2]

But not everyone agrees. A developer of the Hay job-evaluation plan (perhaps the plan most widely used by large corporations), states that the "measures are independent of the market and encourage rational determination of the basis for pricing job content."[3] Hay claims that job evaluation establishes the relative value of jobs based on their content, independent of a link to the market.

"Measure for Measure" versus "Much Ado about Nothing"

Researchers, too, have their own perspective on job evaluation. Some say that if job value can be quantified, then job evaluation takes on the trappings of measurement (objective, numerical, generalizable, documented, and reliable) and can be judged according to technical standards. Just as with employment tests, the reliability and validity of job evaluation plans can be compared; research will be able to tell us if 10 compensable factors is too many, or if 3 is too few.

Those involved in actually making pay decisions have a different view. They see job evaluation as a process which helps gain acceptance of pay differences between jobs—an administrative procedure through which the parties become involved and committed. The process invites give and take—an exchange of views. Employees, union representatives, and managers haggle over "the rules of the game" for determining the relative worth. As in sports and games, we are more willing to accept the results if we accept the rules and believe they are applied fairly.[4]

This interpretation is consistent with the history of job evaluation, which was begun as a way to bring labour peace and order to the wage-setting process.

Exhibit 5.3 summarizes the assumptions that underlie the perspectives on job evaluation. Some say the content of jobs has intrinsic value that the evaluation will uncover; others say the only fair measure of job value is found in the external market. Although some say contemporary job evaluation practices are just and fair, others say they are just fair. "Beneath the superficial orderliness of job evaluation techniques and findings, there is much that smacks of chaos."[5] We try to capture all these perspectives in this chapter.[6]

EXHIBIT 5.3 Perspectives on Job Evaluation

Job evaluation is:	Assumption
A measure of job content	Content has innate value outside of external market.
A measure of relative value	Relevant groups can reach consensus on relative value.
Link with external market	Job worth cannot be specified without external market information.
Measurement device	Honing instruments will provide objective measures.
Negotiation	Puts face of rationality onto a social/political process. Establishes rules of the game. Invites participation.

■ MAJOR DECISIONS

The major job evaluation decisions are depicted in Exhibit 5.2. They are: (1) establish the purpose(s), (2) decide on single versus multiple plans, (3) choose among alternative methods, (4) obtain involvement of relevant stakeholders, and (5) evaluate the usefulness of the results.

Establish the Purpose

Job evaluation is part of the process for establishing an internally aligned pay structure. Recall from Chapter 2 that an internally aligned pay structure supports the work flow, is fair to employees, and directs their behaviour toward organization objectives.

Support Work Flow.   The job evaluation process supports workflow by integrating each job's pay with its relative contributions to the organization and by setting pay for new, unique, or changing jobs.

Fair to Employees.   Job evaluation can reduce disputes and grievances over pay differences between jobs by establishing a workable, agreed-upon structure that reduces the role that chance, favouritism, and bias may play in setting pay.

Directs Behaviour toward Organization Objectives.   Job evaluation calls out to employees what it is about their work that the organization values, what supports the organization's strategy and its success. It can also help employees adapt to organization changes by improving their understanding of what is valued in their assignments and why that value may change.

   If the purpose of the evaluation is not called out, it becomes too easy to get lost in complex procedures, negotiations, and bureaucracy. The job evaluation process becomes the end in itself, instead of a way to achieve an objective. Establishing the objectives can help ensure that the evaluation actually is the rational and systematic process it was meant to be.

Single versus Multiple Plans

Rarely will an employer evaluate all jobs in the organization at one time. More typically, a related group of jobs, for example, production, engineering, or marketing, will be the focus. Many employers design different evaluation plans for different types of work. They do so because they believe that the work content is too diverse to be adequately evaluated by one plan. For example, production jobs may vary in terms of working conditions, manipulative skills, and knowledge of statistical quality control required. But engineering and marketing jobs do not vary on these factors, nor are those factors particularly important in engineering or marketing work. Rather, other factors such as technical knowledge and skills and contacts with customers may be relevant. Consequently, a single plan may not be acceptable to employees if a sizeable number of factors in the plan do not apply to their jobs.

   Rather than using either universal factors or entirely unique factors for each job family, some employers, notably Hewlett-Packard, use a core set of common factors and another set of factors unique to particular occupational or functional areas (finance, manufacturing, software and systems, sales). This approach is more likely to be acceptable to employees and managers and is easier to verify as work-related than is using generalized universal factors.

Choose among Methods

Ranking, classification, and point method are the most common job evaluation methods, though uncounted variations exist. Exhibit 5.4 compares the methods. *They all begin by assuming that an accurate job analysis has been translated into useful job descriptions.*

.NET WORTH | Universal Job Evaluation in the Federal Government

In 1997, the Canadian federal government decided to modernize its job classification and pay systems. The intent was to streamline the existing 77 occupational groups down to 29, and to design one job evaluation plan for all positions in the federal civil service. Five years later, the government announced that its goal of a universal classification system was unworkable, and that an alternative approach to classification reform would be taken instead.

According to the Treasury Board, "Applying a single standard and a single pay structure to the more than 150,000 positions in the federal public service would create too rigid and inflexible a management framework for the widely varied work of our employees. As a result, it could impede our ability to compete in the marketplace for the talent and skills needed to serve Canadians in the future. Furthermore, a universal approach:
- would not adequately recognize the diversity of work done by our employees
- could call into question the role of multiple unions; and
- might not guarantee compliance with the Canadian Human Rights Act."

The new approach will be a multi-year classification reform system that will tailor job evaluation by occupational group on a step-by-step basis. By 2006, the modernization plan will cover approximately 74 percent of the public service.

Source: Classification Reform: FAQ for HR Professionals, URL: http://www.tbs-sct.gc.ca/Classification/ FAQ/HRProf_e.asp, Treasury Board of Canada, Secretariat, 2004. Reproduced with the permission of the Minister of Public Works and Government Services, 2004.

EXHIBIT | 5.4 Comparison of Job Evaluation Methods

	Advantage	**Disadvantage**
Ranking	Fast, simple, easy to explain.	Cumbersome as number of jobs increases. Basis for comparisons is not called out.
Classification	Can group a wide range of work together in one system.	Descriptions may leave too much room for manipulation.
Point	Compensable factors call out basis for comparisons. Compensable factors communicate what is valued.	Can become bureaucratic and rule-bound.

RANKING

ranking

job evaluation method that ranks jobs from highest to lowest based on a global definition of value

alternation ranking method

ranking the highest- and lowest-valued jobs first, then the next highest- and lowest-valued jobs, repeating until all jobs have been ranked

paired comparison method

listing all jobs across columns and down rows of a matrix, comparing the two jobs in each cell and indicating which one is of greater value, then ranking jobs based on the total number of times each one is ranked as being of greater value

Ranking simply orders the job descriptions from highest to lowest based on a global definition of relative value or contribution to the organization's success. Ranking is the simplest, fastest, easiest method to understand and explain to employees, and the least expensive method, at least initially. However, it can create problems that require difficult and potentially expensive solutions because it doesn't tell employees what it is in their jobs that is important.

Two ways of ranking are common: alternation ranking and paired comparison. The **alternation ranking method** orders job descriptions alternately at each extreme. Agreement is reached among evaluators on which jobs are the most and least valuable, then the next most and least valued, and so on, until all jobs have been ordered. The **paired comparison method** uses a matrix to compare all possible pairs of jobs. The higher-ranked job is entered in the cell of the matrix. When all comparisons have been completed, the job most frequently judged "more valuable" becomes the highest-ranked job, and so on.

Alternation ranking and paired comparison methods may be more reliable (produce similar results more consistently) than simple ranking. Nevertheless, ranking has drawbacks. The criteria on which the jobs are ranked usually are so poorly defined—if they are specified at all—that the evaluations become subjective opinions that are impossible to justify in work-related terms. Furthermore, evaluator(s) using this method must be knowledgeable about every single job under study. The numbers alone turn what should be a simple task into a formidable one—50 jobs require 1,225 comparisons—and as organizations change, it is difficult to remain knowledgeable about all jobs. Some organizations try to overcome this difficulty by ranking jobs within single departments and merging the results. However, even though ranking appears simple, fast, and inexpensive, in the long run, the results are difficult to defend, and costly solutions may be required to overcome the problems created.

CLASSIFICATION

classification

job evaluation method based on job class descriptions into which jobs are categorized

benchmark job

a job whose contents are well known, relatively stable, and common across different employers

Picture a bookcase with many shelves. Each shelf is labelled with a paragraph describing the kinds of books on that shelf and, perhaps, one or two representative titles. This same approach describes the **classification system** of job evaluation. A series of classes covers the range of jobs. Class descriptions are the labels. A job description is compared to the class descriptions to decide which class is the best fit for that job. Each class is described in such a way that it captures sufficient work detail, yet is general enough to cause little difficulty in slotting a job description into its appropriate "shelf" or class.

The classes may be described further by including titles of benchmark jobs that fall into each class. A **benchmark job** has the following characteristics:

- Its contents are well known and relatively stable over time.
- The job is common across a number of different employers; i.e., it is not unique to a particular employer.

Writing class descriptions can be troublesome when jobs from several job families are covered by a single plan. Although greater specificity of the class definition improves the reliability of evaluation, it also limits the variety of jobs that can be easily classified. For example, class definitions written with sales jobs in mind may make it difficult to slot office or administrative jobs and vice versa. If you examine some of the class definitions of the Audit, Commerce, and Purchasing group of the federal government's 29-class evaluation system in Exhibit 5.5, you will see that the vagueness of the descriptions seems to leave a lot of room for judgment. The feds get around this issue by comparing compensable factors (proposed new factors are shown in

---

| **EXHIBIT** | **5.5** | Audit, Commerce, and Purchasing Group Description for the Federal Government |

The Audit, Commerce, and Purchasing Group comprises positions that are primarily involved in the application of a comprehensive knowledge of generally accepted accounting principles and auditing standards to the planning, delivery, and management of external audit programs; the planning, development, delivery, and management of economic development policies, programs, services, and other activities; and the planning, development, delivery, and management of policies, programs, systems, or other activities dealing with purchasing and supply in the Public Service.

Inclusions

Notwithstanding the generality of the foregoing, for greater certainty, the Audit, Commerce, and Purchasing Group includes positions that have, as their primary purpose, responsibility for one or more of the following activities:

1. audit the application of a comprehensive knowledge of generally accepted accounting principles and auditing standards to the auditing of the accounts and financial records of individuals, businesses, non-profit organizations, or provincial or municipal governments to determine their accuracy and reasonableness, to establish or verify costs, or to confirm the compliance of transactions with the provisions of statutes, regulations, agreements, or contracts;
2. commerce the planning, development, delivery, and management of economic development policies, programs, services, and other activities designed to promote the establishment, growth, and improvement of industry, commerce, and export trade; and the regulation of trade and commerce including:
   (a) the promotion of the more efficient use of resources in particular geographic areas through the conduct of studies and investigations and the implementation of programs and projects for this purpose;
   (b) the promotion of the development and use of modern industrial technologies;
   (c) the promotion of economic development directed towards groups, regions, industries, or the Canadian economy as a whole;
   (d) the promotion of the export of Canadian goods and services, including the tourist industry; the expansion of Canada's share of global trade by providing advice to Canadian companies, trade associations, or other agencies of government, by safeguarding and promoting Canadian trading relationships, or by bringing the export aspects to bear in Canada's aid and financing programs;
   (e) the study and assessment of developments in international trade and trading arrangements, and their implications for the Canadian economy;
   (f) the administration and enforcement of competition legislation and legislation relating to restraints of trade; and
   (g) the examination of records and reports of registered insurance, trust and loan companies, money lenders and small loan companies, fraternal benefit societies, and co-operative credit associations to ensure their solvency and compliance with legislation and regulations controlling their operations;
3. purchasing the planning, development, delivery, and management of purchasing and supply policies, programs, services, and other activities to meet the needs of Public Service departments and agencies, including one or more subsidiary activities, such as in the areas of asset management and disposal, contracting, procurement of goods or services, inventory management, cataloguing, warehousing, or traffic management;
4. the provision of advice in the above fields; and
5. the leadership of any of the above activities.

Exclusions

Positions excluded from the Audit, Commerce, and Purchasing Group are those whose primary purpose is included in the definition of any other group or those in which one or more of the following activities is of primary importance:

1. the evaluation of actuarial liabilities and the determination of premiums and contributions in respect of insurance, annuity, and pension plans;
2. the planning and conduct of internal financial audits;
3. the planning, development, delivery, or management of the internal comprehensive audit of the operations of Public Service departments and agencies;
4. the application of a comprehensive knowledge of agriculture to the promotion, development, and regulation of the agricultural industry and trade;

continued

EXHIBIT 5.5   Audit, Commerce, and Purchasing Group Description for the Federal Government—*continued*

5. the application of a comprehensive knowledge of economics, sociology, or statistics to the conduct of economic, socio-economic, and sociological research, studies, forecasts, and surveys;

6. the planning, development, delivery, and promotion of Canada's diplomatic, commercial, human rights, cultural, promotional, and international development policies and interests in other countries and in international organizations through the career rotational foreign service;

7. the design of trade exhibits or displays or activities dealing with the explanation, promotion, and publication of federal government programs, policies, and services;

8. the writing of specifications and technical descriptions that require the continuing application of technical knowledge; and

9. the receipt, storage, handling, and issue of items held in stores.

Source: URL: http://www.tbs-sct.gc.ca/Classification/OrgGroupStruct/OGD_e.asp, Treasury Board of Canada, Secretariat, 2002. Reproduced with the permission of the Minister of Public Works and Government Services, 2004.

Exhibit 5.6). Including titles of benchmark jobs for each class helps make the descriptions more concrete. So, in practice, the job descriptions are compared not only to the four compensable factors in Exhibit 5.6, the standard class descriptions, and benchmark jobs, but they also can be compared to one another to ensure that jobs within each class are more similar to each other than to jobs in adjacent classes. The final result is a series of classes with a number of jobs in each. The jobs within each class are considered to be equal (similar) work and will be paid equally. Jobs in different classes should be dissimilar and may have different pay rates.

EXHIBIT 5.6   Factor Evaluation System (with Subfactors) Proposed for the Federal Government

Responsibility

1. Information for the Use of Others
2. Well-Being of Individuals
3. Leadership of Human Resources
4. Money
5. Physical Assets and Products
6. Ensuring Compliance

Skill

7. Job Content Knowledge Application
8. Contextual Knowledge
9. Communication
10. Motor and Sensory Skills

Effort

11. Intellectual Effort
12. Sustained Attention
13. Psychological/Emotional Effort
14. Physical Effort

Working Conditions

15. Work Environment
16. Risks to Health

Source: www.tbs-sct.gc.ca/Classification/Tools/FactorElement_e.asp (August 4, 2003)

POINT METHOD

point method

job evaluation method that assigns a number of points to each job, based on compensable factors that are numerically scaled and weighted

Point methods have three common characteristics: (1) compensable factors, with (2) numerically scaled factor degrees, and (3) weights reflecting the relative importance of each factor.[7] Each job's relative value, and hence its location in the pay structure, is determined by the total points assigned to it.

Point plans are the most commonly used approach to establish pay structures in Canada. They represent a significant change from ranking and classification methods in that they make explicit the criteria for evaluating jobs—compensable factors.

Compensable factors are defined on the basis of the strategic direction of the business and how the work contributes to that strategy. The factors are scaled to reflect the degree to which they are present in each job, and weighted to reflect their overall importance to the organization. Points are then attached to each factor weight. The point total for each job determines its position in the job structure.

Exhibit 5.7 lists the steps involved in the design of a point plan.

- Conduct job analysis.
- Determine compensable factors.
- Scale the factors.
- Weight the factors according to importance.
- Communicate the plan and train users; prepare manual.
- Apply to nonbenchmark jobs.

The end product of this design process is an evaluation plan that helps develop and explain the pay structure.

EXHIBIT 5.7 | The Point Plan Process

Step One: Conduct Job Analysis
- A representative sample of benchmark jobs
- The content of these jobs is basis for compensable factors

Step Two: Determine Compensable Factors
- Based on the work performed (what is done)
- Based on strategy and values of the organization (what is valued)
- Acceptable to those affected by resulting pay structure (what is acceptable)

Step Three: Scale the Factors
- Use examples to anchor

Step Four: Weight the Factors
- Can reflect judgment of organization leaders, committee
- Can reflect a negotiated structure
- Can reflect a market-based structure

Step Five: Communicate the Plan
- Prepare manual
- Train users

Step Six: Apply to Nonbenchmark Jobs

Conduct Job Analysis

Just as with ranking and classification, point plans begin with job analysis. Typically, a representative sample of jobs, that is, benchmark jobs, is drawn for analysis. The content of these jobs serves as the basis for defining, scaling, and weighting the compensable factors.

Determine Compensable Factors

compensable factors

characteristics in the work that the organization values, that help it pursue its strategy and achieve its objectives

Compensable factors play a pivotal role in the point plan. These factors reflect how work adds value to the organization. They flow from the work itself and from the strategic direction of the business.

To select compensable factors, an organization asks itself, What is it about the work that adds value? One company chose *decision making* as a compensable factor. As shown in Exhibit 5.8, the definition of decision making is three-dimensional: (1) the risk and complexity (hence the availability of guidelines to assist in making the decisions), (2) the impact of the decisions, and (3) the time that must pass before the impact is evident.

In effect, this firm determined that its competitive advantage depends on decisions employees make in their work. And the relative value of the decisions depends on their risk, their complexity, and their impact on the company. Hence, this firm is signalling to all employees that jobs will be valued based on the nature of the decisions required by employees in those jobs. Jobs that require riskier decisions with greater impact have a higher relative worth than jobs that require fewer decisions of relatively little consequence.

To be useful, compensable factors should be

- Based on the work performed.
- Based on the strategy and values of the organization.
- Acceptable to the stakeholders affected by the resulting pay structure.

Based on the Work Itself.   Employees are the experts in the work actually done in any organization. Hence, it is important to seek their answers to what should be valued in the work itself. Some form of documentation (i.e., job descriptions, job analysis, employee and/or supervisory focus groups) must support the choice of factors. Work-related documentation helps gain acceptance by employees and managers, is easier to understand, and can withstand a variety of challenges to the pay structure. For example, managers may argue that the salaries of their employees are too low in comparison to those of other employees, or that the salary offered a job candidate is too low. Union leaders may wonder why one job is paid differently from another. Allegations of pay discrimination may be raised. Employees, line managers, union leaders, and compensation managers must understand and be able to explain why work is paid differently or the same. Differences in factors that obviously are based on the work itself provide that rationale, or even diminish the likelihood of the challenges arising.

Based on the Strategy and Values of the Organization.   The leadership of any organization is the best source of information on where the business should be going and how it is going to get there. Clearly, leadership's input into factor selection is crucial. So if the business strategy involves providing innovative, high-quality products and services designed in collaboration with customers and suppliers, then jobs with greater responsibilities for product innovation and customer contacts should be valued more highly. Or if the business strategy is more Wal-Mart-like, "providing goods and services to delight customers at the lowest cost and greatest convenience possible," then compensable factors might include impact on cost containment, customer relations, and so on.

Compensable factors need to reinforce the organization's culture and values as well as its business direction and the nature of the work. If that direction changes, then the compensable factors

EXHIBIT **5.8** Example of Compensable Factor Definition: Decision Making

Compensable Factor Definition: Evaluates the extent of required decision making and the beneficial or detrimental effect such decisions would have on the profitability of the organization.

Consideration is given to the:
- Risk and complexity of required decision making
- Impact such action would have on the company

What type of guidelines are available for making decisions?

_____ 1. Few decisions are required; work is performed according to standard procedures and/or detailed instructions.

_____ 2. Decisions are made within an established framework of clearly defined procedures. Incumbent is only required to recognize and follow the prescribed course of action.

_____ 3. Guidelines are available in the form of clearly defined procedures and standard practices. Incumbent must exercise some judgment in selecting the appropriate procedure.

_____ 4. Guidelines are available in the form of some standard practices, well-established precedent, and reference materials and company policy. Decisions require a moderate level of judgment and analysis of the appropriate course of action.

_____ 5. Some guidelines are available in the form of broad precedent, related practices, and general methods of the field. Decisions require a high level of judgment and/or modification of a standard course of action to address the issue at hand.

_____ 6. Few guidelines are available. The incumbent may consult with technical experts and review relevant professional publications. Decisions require innovation and creativity. The only limitation on course of action is company strategy and policy.

What is the impact of decisions made by the position?

_____ 1. Inappropriate decisions, recommendations or errors would normally cause minor delays and cost increments. Deficiencies will not affect the completion of programs or projects important to the organization.

_____ 2. Inappropriate decisions, recommendations or errors will normally cause moderate delays and additional allocation of funds and resources within the immediate work unit. Deficiencies will not affect the attainment of the organization's objectives.

_____ 3. Inappropriate decisions, recommendations, or errors would normally cause considerable delays and reallocation of funds and resources. Deficiencies will affect scheduling and project completion in other work units and, unless adjustments are made, could affect attainment of objectives of a major business segment of the company.

_____ 4. Inappropriate decisions, recommendations, or errors would normally affect critical programs or attainment of short-term goals for a major business segment of the company.

_____ 5. Inappropriate decisions, recommendations, or errors would affect attainment of objectives for the company and would normally affect long-term growth and public image.

The effectiveness of the majority of the position's decisions can be measured within:

_____ 1. One day.   _____ 4. Six months.
_____ 2. One week.   _____ 5. One year.
_____ 3. One month.   _____ 6. More than a year.

Source: Jill Kanin-Lovers, "The Role of Computers in Job Evaluations: A Case in Point," *Journal of Compensation and Benefits* (New York: Warren Gorham and Lamont, 1985).

also change. For example, strategic plans at many companies call for increased globalization. Both TRW (a global auto parts manufacturer) and 3M include a global factor similar to the one in Exhibit 5.9 in their managerial job-evaluation plan. Multinational responsibilities are defined in terms of the type of responsibility, the percentage of time devoted to international issues, and the number of countries covered. Do you suppose that any of these managers at 3M or TRW got raises when Czechoslovakia, Yugoslavia, and the Soviet Union rearranged themselves into a large number of smaller, independent countries?

Factors may also be eliminated if they no longer support the business strategy. The railway company Burlington Northern revised its job evaluation plan to omit the factor Number of Subordinates Supervised. It decided that a factor that values increases to staff runs counter to the organization's objective of reducing bureaucracy and increasing efficiency. Major shifts in the business strategy are not daily occurrences, but when they do occur, compensable factors should be reexamined to ensure they are consistent with the new directions.

Acceptable to the Stakeholders.   Acceptance of the compensable factors used to slot jobs into the pay structure may depend, at least in part, on tradition. For example, people who work in hospitals, nursing homes, and child care centres make the point that responsibility for people is used less often, and valued less, than responsibility for property.[8] This may be a carry-over from the days when nursing and child care service were provided by family members, usually women, without reimbursement. People now doing these jobs for pay say that properly valuing a factor for people responsibility would raise their wages. So, a frequently asked question is, Acceptable to whom? The answer ought to be to the stakeholders.

Adapting Factors from Existing Plans.   Although a wide variety of factors are used in standard existing plans, the factors tend to fall into four generic groups: skill, effort, responsibility, and

---

EXHIBIT 5.9 Compensable Factor Definition: Multinational Responsibilities

This factor concerns the multinational scope of the job. Multinational responsibilities are defined as line or functional managerial activities in one or several countries.

1. **The multinational responsibilities of the job can best be described as:**
   A. Approving major policy and strategic plans.
   B. Formulating, proposing, and monitoring implementation of policy and plans.
   C. Acting as a consultant in project design and implementation phases.
   D. Not applicable.

2. **Indicate the percentage of time spent on multinational issues:**
   A. 50%
   B. 25–49%
   C. 10–24%
   D. 10%

3. **The number of countries (other than your unit location) for which the position currently has operational or functional responsibility:**
   A. More than 10 countries
   B. 5 to 10 countries
   C. 1 to 4 countries
   D. Not applicable

working conditions. These four are required in pay equity legislation across Canada. The Hay Guide Chart–Profile Method of Position, used by 5,000 employers worldwide, is perhaps the most widely used. The classic three Hay factors—know-how, problem solving, and accountability—use guide charts to quantify the factors in more detail. In Exhibit 5.10, the Hay Factor Know-How is measured on three dimensions: scope (practical procedures vs. specialized techniques vs. scientific disciplines); depth (minimal vs. related vs. diverse vs. broad); and human relations skills (three levels). The cell that corresponds to the right level of all three dimensions for the job being evaluated is located in the guide chart. The cell gives the points for this factor. In the exhibit, the supervisor key punch position gets 152 points for Know-How.

How Many Factors?   A remaining issue to consider is how many factors should be included in the plan. Some factors may have overlapping definitions or may fail to account for anything unique in the criterion chosen. One writer calls this the "illusion of validity"—we want to believe that the factors are capturing divergent aspects of the job and that both are important.[9]

Another problem is called "small numbers."[10] If even one job in our benchmark sample has a certain characteristic, we tend to use that factor for the entire work domain. A common example is unpleasant working conditions. If even one job is performed in unpleasant working conditions, it is tempting to make it a compensable factor and apply it to all jobs. Once a factor is part of the system, others are likely to say their job has it, too. For example, office staff may feel that ringing telephones or leaky toner cartridges constitute unpleasant or hazardous conditions.

In one plan, a senior manager refused to accept a job evaluation plan unless the factor Working Conditions was included. The plan's designer, a recent college graduate, showed through statistical analysis that working conditions did not vary enough between 90 percent of the jobs to have a meaningful effect on the resulting pay structure. Nevertheless, the manager rejected this argument by pointing out that the plan designer had never worked in those jobs where working conditions mattered—in the plant's foundry. Working conditions were very meaningful to the people working in the foundry. In order to get the plan and pay decisions based on it accepted by the foundry workers, the plan was redesigned to include working conditions.

This situation is not unusual. In one study, a 21-factor plan produced the same job structure that could have been generated using only 7 of the factors. Furthermore, the jobs could be correctly slotted into classes using only three factors. Yet the company decided to keep the 21-factor plan because it was "accepted and doing the job." Research as far back as the 1940s demonstrates that the skills dimension explains 90 percent or more of the variance in job evaluation results; three factors generally account for 98 to 99 percent of variance.[11] But, as already noted, other factors often are included to ensure the plan's acceptance.

Scale the Factors

factor degree/level

description of several different degrees or levels of the factor in jobs. A different number of points is associated with each degree/level.

Once the factors are chosen, scales reflecting the different degrees within each factor are constructed. Each degree also may be anchored by the typical skills, tasks, and behaviours taken from the benchmark jobs that illustrate each **factor degree/level**. Exhibit 5.11 shows the federal government's scaling for the subfactor "Scope for Initiative and Judgment" of the factor "Problem Solving" for employees in the Social Services Support group.

A major problem in determining degrees is whether to make each degree equidistant from the adjacent degrees (interval scaling) in terms of the number of points for each level or degree. For example, with equidistant scaling, the maximum points for each of the four levels in Exhibit 5.11 might be 200, 300, 400, and 500. The actual scaling for this plan is not equal between the levels, because the difference in maximum points between levels ranges from 52 to 107. As another example, the intervals in the government plan for employees in the Technical Services group range from 75 to 175 points.[12]

EXHIBIT **5.10**   Hay Guide Chart–Profile Method of Job Evaluation

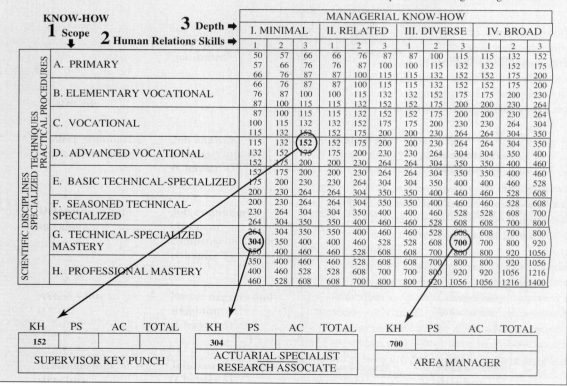

KNOW-HOW DEFINITIONS

DEFINITION: Know-How is the sum total to every kind of skill, however acquired, required for acceptable job performance. This sum total which comprises the overall savvy has 3 dimensions–the requirements for:

1 Scope: Practical procedures, specialized techniques, and scientific

2 Human Relations Skills: Know-How of integrating and harmonizing the diversified functions involved in managerial situations occurring in operating, supporting, and administrative fields. This Know-How may be exercised consultatively (about management) as well as executive, and involves in some combination the areas of organizing, planning, executing, controlling, and evaluating.

3 Depth: Active, practising, face-to-face skills in the area of human relationships (as defined at right).

MEASURING KNOW-HOW: Know-How has both scope (variety) and depth (thoroughness). Thus, a job may require some knowledge about a lot of things, or a lot of knowledge about a few things. The total Know-How is the combination of scope and depth. This concept makes practical the comparison and weighing of the total Know-How content of different jobs in terms of "how much knowledge about how many things."

2 HUMAN RELATIONS SKILLS

1. **BASIC:** Ordinary courtesy and effectiveness in dealing with others.

2. **IMPORTANT:** Understanding, influencing, and/or serving people are important, but not critical, considerations.

3. **CRITICAL:** Alternative or combined skills in understanding, selecting, developing, and motivating people are important in the highest degree.

KNOW-HOW
1 Scope   **2** Human Relations Skills ➡   **3** Depth ➡

	MANAGERIAL KNOW-HOW											
	I. MINIMAL			II. RELATED			III. DIVERSE			IV. BROAD		
	1	2	3	1	2	3	1	2	3	1	2	3
A. PRIMARY	50	57	66	66	76	87	87	100	115	115	132	152
	57	66	76	76	87	100	100	115	132	132	152	175
	66	76	87	87	100	115	115	132	152	152	175	200
B. ELEMENTARY VOCATIONAL	66	76	87	87	100	115	115	132	152	152	175	200
	76	87	100	100	115	132	132	152	175	175	200	230
	87	100	115	115	132	152	152	175	200	200	230	264
C. VOCATIONAL	87	100	115	115	132	152	152	175	200	200	230	264
	100	115	132	132	152	175	175	200	230	230	264	304
	115	132	152	152	175	200	200	230	264	264	304	350
D. ADVANCED VOCATIONAL	115	132	(152)	152	175	200	200	230	264	264	304	350
	132	152	175	175	200	230	230	264	304	304	350	400
	152	175	200	200	230	264	264	304	350	350	400	460
E. BASIC TECHNICAL-SPECIALIZED	152	175	200	200	230	264	264	304	350	350	400	460
	175	200	230	230	264	304	304	350	400	400	460	528
	200	230	264	264	304	350	350	400	460	460	528	608
F. SEASONED TECHNICAL-SPECIALIZED	200	230	264	264	304	350	350	400	460	460	528	608
	230	264	304	304	350	400	400	460	528	528	608	700
	264	304	350	350	400	460	460	528	608	608	700	800
G. TECHNICAL-SPECIALIZED MASTERY	264	304	350	350	400	460	460	528	608	608	700	800
	(304)	350	400	400	460	528	528	608	(700)	700	800	920
	350	400	460	460	528	608	608	700	800	800	920	1056
H. PROFESSIONAL MASTERY	350	400	460	460	528	608	608	700	800	800	920	1056
	400	460	528	528	608	700	700	800	920	920	1056	1216
	460	528	608	608	700	800	800	920	1056	1056	1216	1400

(Left axis labels: SCIENTIFIC DISCIPLINES / SPECIALIZED TECHNIQUES / PRACTICAL PROCEDURES)

KH	PS	AC	TOTAL
152			

SUPERVISOR KEY PUNCH

KH	PS	AC	TOTAL
304			

ACTUARIAL SPECIALIST
RESEARCH ASSOCIATE

KH	PS	AC	TOTAL
700			

AREA MANAGER

| **EXHIBIT** | **5.11** | Factor Scaling for Federal Government Social Science Support Employees |

Problem Solving – Scope for Initiative and Judgment

Level A (80-188 points) – Some judgment and initiative are required to select and apply established guidelines, including the adaptation of precedents.

Level B (133-295 points) – A moderate degree of judgment and initiative is required to identify the need to modify established guidelines to accommodate change in the subject area, and in applying principles to determine courses of action. Direction is sought if solutions are not within the intent of project objectives.

Level C (186-348 points) – A significant degree of judgment and initiative is required to determine the validity of guidelines for existing projects. Recommendations for changes are authoritative. The implications of courses of action on other projects are difficult to determine.

Level D (293-400 points) – A high degree of judgment and initiative is required to develop guidelines for various existing and new projects. Substantial contribution is made to the planning of major projects. Problems are solved within the intent of the objectives of the organization.

Source: Classification Reform: FAQ for HR Professionals, URL: www.tbs-sct.gc.ca/Classification/FAQ/HRProf_e.asp, Treasury Board of Canada, Secretariat, 2004. Reproduced with permission of the Minister of Public Works and Government Services, 2004.

The following criteria for scaling factors have been suggested: (1) limit the degrees to the number necessary to distinguish between jobs, (2) use understandable terminology, (3) anchor degree definitions with benchmark job titles, and (4) make it apparent how the degree applies to the job. Using too many degrees makes it difficult for evaluators to accurately choose the appropriate degree. This, in turn, reduces the acceptability of the system.

Weight the Factors According to Importance

factor weights

weighting assigned to each factor to reflect differences in importance attached to each factor by the employer

Once the degrees have been assigned, the **factor weights** must be determined. Different weights reflect differences in importance attached to each factor by the employer. Weights often are determined through an advisory committee that allocates 100 percent of the value among the factors.[13] In the illustration in Exhibit 5.12, a committee allocated 40 percent to skill, 30 percent to effort, 20 percent to responsibility, and 10 percent of the value to working conditions. Each factor has two subfactors, with five degrees each. For the bookstore manager, the subfactor Mental Skill gets half the 40 percent given to Skill; four degrees of Mental Skill times 20 equals 80 points, and three degrees of the subfactor Experience times 20 equals another 60 points. Effort is weighted 30 percent, so two degrees of physical effort times 15 gives 30 points, and four degrees of mental effort times 15 gives 60 points, and so on.

A supplement to committee judgment to determine weights is the use of a statistical analysis.[14] In this approach, the committee chooses the criterion pay structure, that is, a pay structure they wish to duplicate with the point plan. The criterion structure may be the current rates paid for benchmark jobs, market rates for benchmark jobs, rates for predominantly male jobs (in an attempt to eliminate gender bias), or union-negotiated rates.[15] Once a criterion structure is agreed on, statistical modelling techniques such as regression analysis are used to determine what weight for each factor will reproduce, as closely as possible, the chosen structure. The statistical approach is often labelled as *policy capturing* to contrast it to the *committee judgment* approach.

EXHIBIT | **5.12** | Job Evaluation Form

	Job _bookstore manager_			
	Check one: ☒ Administrative ☐ Technical			
Compensable Factors	**Degree** x	**Weight**	=	**Total**
Skill: (40%)	1 2 3 4 5			
Mental	[X in col 4]	20%		80
Experience	[X in col 2]	20%		60
Effort: (30%)				
Physical	[X in col 1]	15%		30
Mental	[X in col 2]	15%		60
Responsibility: (20%)				
Effect of Error	[X in col 3]	10%		40
Inventiveness/ Innovation	[X in col 2]	10%		30
Working Conditions: (10%)				
Environment	[X in col 1]	5%		5
Hazards	[X in col 1]	5%		5
				(310)

Criterion Pay Structure

The criterion structure used clearly makes a difference. Perhaps the clearest illustration can be found in the criterion structures used in municipalities. If only market rates were used, firefighters would be paid much less than police. Yet, many firefighters' unions have successfully negotiated a link between their pay and police rates. Hence, the negotiated pay structure deviates from a market structure. A second example occurs when unionized workers negotiate higher than market pay rates for lower-skill jobs. These two examples illustrate that the criterion pay structure on which job evaluation is based really matters.

Communicate the Plan

A job evaluation manual must be prepared for use by employees and managers charged with the responsibility of implementing job evaluation (usually a job evaluation committee). Users must be trained in how to use the manual.

Apply to Nonbenchmark Jobs

Recall that the compensable factors and weights were derived using a sample of benchmark jobs. The final step in the point plan process is to apply the plan to the remaining jobs. To do so, a manual usually is written that describes the method, defines the compensable factors, and provides enough information to permit users to distinguish varying degrees of each factor. The point of the manual is to allow users who were not involved in its development to apply the plan. Users require training and background information on the total pay system.

WHO SHOULD BE INVOLVED?

If the internal structure's purpose is to aid managers, and if ensuring high involvement and commitment from employees is important, those managers and employees with a stake in the results need to be involved in the process of designing it. A common approach is to use committees, task forces, or teams that include representatives from key operating functions, including nonmanagerial employees. In some cases, the group's role is only advisory; in others, it designs the evaluation approach, chooses compensable factors, and approves all major changes. Organizations with unions often find it advantageous to include union representation as a source of ideas and to help promote acceptance of the results. However, other union leaders believe that philosophical differences prevent their active participation. They take the position that collective bargaining yields more equitable results. So the extent of union participation varies. No single perspective exists on the value of active participation in the process, just as no single management perspective exists.

The Design Process Matters

Research suggests that attending to the fairness of the design process and the approach chosen (job evaluation, skill/competency-based plan, and market pricing) rather than focusing solely on the results (the internal pay structure) is likely to achieve employee and management commitment, trust, and acceptance of the results.[16] The absence of participation may make it easier for employees and managers to imagine ways the structure might have been rearranged to their personal liking. Two researchers noted, "if people do not participate in decisions, there is little to prevent them from assuming that things would have been better, 'if I'd have been in charge.'"[17]

Additional research is needed to ascertain whether the payoffs from increased participation offset potential costs (time involved to reach consensus, potential problems caused by disrupting current perceptions, etc.). For example, in multinational organizations the involvement of both corporate compensation and country managers raises the potential for conflict due to their differing perspectives. Country managers may wish to focus on the particular business needs in their country, whereas corporate managers may want a system that operates equally well (or poorly) across all countries. The country manager has operating objectives, does not want to lose key individuals, and views compensation as a mechanism to help accomplish these goals. Corporate, on the other hand, adopts a worldwide perspective and focuses on ensuring that decisions are consistent with the overall global strategy.

Appeals/Review Procedures

No matter the technique, no job evaluation plan anticipates all situations. It is inevitable that some jobs will be evaluated incorrectly, or at least that employees and managers may suspect that they were. Consequently, review procedures to handle such cases and to help ensure procedural fairness are required. Often the compensation manager handles reviews, but increasingly, peer or team reviews are being used. Sometimes these reviews take on the trappings of formal grievance procedures (e.g., documented complaints and responses and levels of approval). Problems may also be handled by managers and employee relations generalists through informal discussions with employees.[18]

When the evaluations are completed, approval by higher levels of management is usually required. An approval process helps ensure that any changes that result from evaluating work are consistent with the organization's operations and directions.

"I Know I Speak for All of Us When I Say I Speak for All of Us"

A recent study found that more powerful departments in a university (as indicated by number of faculty members and size of budget) were more successful in using the appeals process to get jobs paid more or reclassified (higher) than were weaker departments. The authors concluded that, in addition to assessing the worth of a job, the entire job evaluation process reflects the political and social context within the organization.[19] This result is consistent with other research that showed that a powerful member of a job evaluation committee could sway the results.[20] Using students as subjects, a "senior evaluator" alternately recommended valuing the shorthand typist over the cost clerk, and then the cost clerk over the shorthand typist with a different group of students. The students generally went along with either suggestion. Consequently, procedures should be judged for their susceptibility to political influences. "It is the decision-making process, rather than the instrument itself that seems to have the greatest influence on pay outcomes," writes one researcher.[21]

■ THE FINAL RESULT: STRUCTURE

The final result of the job analysis–job description–job evaluation process is a job structure; a hierarchy of work. This hierarchy translates the employer's internal alignment policy into practice. Exhibit 5.13 shows four hypothetical job structures within a single organization. These structures were obtained via different approaches to evaluating work. The jobs are arrayed within four basic functions: managerial, technical, manufacturing, and administrative. The managerial and administrative structures were obtained via a point job evaluation plan, and technical and manufacturing work via two different person-based plans (Chapter 6); the manufacturing plan was negotiated with the union. The exhibit illustrates the results of evaluating work: structures that support a policy of internal alignment.

EXHIBIT 5.13 Resulting Internal Structures—Job-, Skill-, and Competency-Based

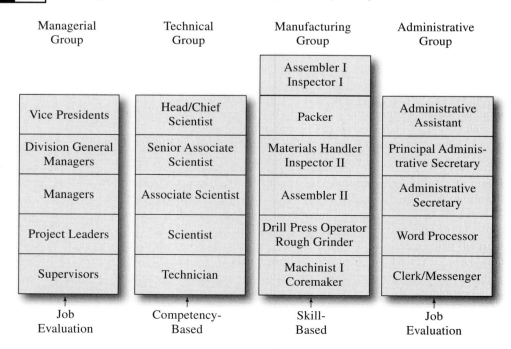

Managerial Group	Technical Group	Manufacturing Group	Administrative Group
		Assembler I / Inspector I	
Vice Presidents	Head/Chief Scientist	Packer	Administrative Assistant
Division General Managers	Senior Associate Scientist	Materials Handler Inspector II	Principal Administrative Secretary
Managers	Associate Scientist	Assembler II	Administrative Secretary
Project Leaders	Scientist	Drill Press Operator Rough Grinder	Word Processor
Supervisors	Technician	Machinist I Coremaker	Clerk/Messenger
Job Evaluation	Competency-Based	Skill-Based	Job Evaluation

Organizations commonly have multiple structures derived through multiple approaches that apply to different functional groups or units. Although some employees in one structure may wish to compare the procedures used in another structure to their own, the underlying premise in practice is that internal alignment is most influenced by fair and equitable treatment of employees doing similar work in the same skill group.

■ BALANCING CHAOS AND CONTROL

Looking back at the material we have covered in the past three chapters (determining internal alignment, job analysis, job evaluation), you may be thinking that we have spent a lot of time and a lot of our organization's money to develop some admirable techniques. But we have yet to pay a single employee a single dollar. Why bother with all this? Why not just pay whatever it takes, and get on with it?

Prior to the widespread use of job evaluation, employers in the 1930s and 1940s had irrational pay structures—the legacy of decentralized and uncoordinated wage-setting practices. Pay differences were a major source of unrest among workers. Employment and wage records were rarely kept; only the foreman knew with any accuracy how many workers were employed in his department and the rates they received. Foremen were thus "free to manage," but used wage information to vary the day rate for favoured workers or to assign them to jobs where piece rates were loose.

Job evaluation, with its specified procedures and documentable results, helped to change that. The technique provided work-related and business-related order and logic. However, over time, complex procedures and creeping bureaucracy can cause users to lose sight of the objectives. Instead, they focus on carefully prescribed and described activities. Specialists and researchers become so enamoured of their words and techniques that we slip into knowing more and more about less and less.

At the same time, the world of work is changing. The work of many if not most people now requires that they figure out what to do in a given situation instead of simply invoking a canned routine. They must identify problems and opportunities, make decisions, plan courses of action, marshal support, and, in general, design their own work methods, techniques, and tools. The challenge is to ensure that job-evaluation plans afford flexibility to adapt to changing conditions.

Generic factors and vague descriptions such as "associates" or "technicians" may be very attractive to managers coping with increased competitive pressures and the need to restructure work. This flexibility avoids bureaucracy and leaves managers "free to manage"—just like the foreman 100 years ago. But it also reduces control and guidelines, which in turn may make it harder to ensure that people are treated fairly. Some balance between chaos and control is required. History suggests that when flexibility without guidelines exists, chaotic and irrational pay rates too frequently result. Removing inefficient bureaucracy is important, but balanced guidelines are necessary to ensure that employees are treated fairly and that pay decisions help the organization achieve its objectives.

CONCLUSION

The differences in the rates paid for different jobs and skills affect the ability of managers to achieve their business objectives. Differences in pay matter. They matter to employees, because their willingness to take on more responsibility and training, to focus on adding value for customers and improving quality of products, and to be flexible enough to adapt to change all depend at least in part on how pay is structured for different levels of work. Differences in the rates paid for different jobs and skills also influence how fairly employees believe they are being treated. Unfair treatment ultimately is counterproductive.

So far we have examined the most common approach to designing pay differences for different work: job evaluation. In the next chapter, we will examine several alternative approaches. However, any approach needs to be evaluated according to how well it will help design an internal pay structure that is based on the work, will help achieve the business objectives, and will be acceptable to the key stakeholders.

Job evaluation has evolved into many different forms and methods. Consequently, wide variations exist in its use and how it is perceived. This chapter discussed some of the many perceptions of the role of job evaluation and reviewed the criticisms levelled at it. No matter how job evaluation is designed, its ultimate use is to help design and manage a work-related, business-focused, and agreed-upon pay structure.

CHAPTER SUMMARY

1. Job evaluation is the process of determining and quantifying the value of jobs. Different perspectives regarding job evaluation include:
   - job evaluation can determine the innate value of jobs
   - job evaluation can determine the relative value of jobs
   - it is not possible to value jobs without external market information
   - job evaluation is dependent on objective measurement instruments, and
   - job evaluation should be conducted participatively through a process of negotiation.

2. The ranking method of job evaluation rank orders the jobs from highest to lowest based on a global definition of value. Two methods of ranking are: (1) alternation ranking, where the most- and least-valued jobs are selected first, then the next most- and least-valued jobs, and so on; and (2) paired comparison, where each job is ranked against all other jobs.

3. The classification method of job evaluation uses class descriptions to categorize jobs. Descriptions of benchmark jobs (those that are well known, relatively stable, and common across different employers) are used as part of the class descriptions for clarification. The final result is a series of classes with a number of jobs in each.

4. The six steps involved in the point method of job evaluation are:
   - conduct job analysis
   - determine compensable factors
   - scale the factors
   - weight the factors according to importance
   - communicate the plan, and
   - apply the plan to nonbenchmark jobs.

   The three common characteristics of point plans are compensable factors, numerically scaled factor degrees/levels, and weights reflecting the importance of each factor.

5. Committees, task forces, or teams including nonmanagerial employees should be involved in job evaluation in an advisory or decision-making capacity. Union participation may also be desirable.

KEY TERMS

REVIEW QUESTIONS

1. How does job evaluation translate internal alignment policies (loosely coupled versus tight fitting) into practice? What does (a) flow of work, (b) fairness, and (c) directing people's behaviours toward organizational objectives have to do with job evaluation?
2. Why are there different approaches to job evaluation? Think of several employers in your area (hospital, Wal-Mart, manufacturing plant, bank, university/college, etc.) What approach would you expect each of them to use? Why?
3. What are the advantages and disadvantages of using more than one job evaluation plan in any single organization?
4. Why bother with job evaluation? Why not simply market price? How can job evaluation link internal alignment and external market pressures?

EXPERIENTIAL EXERCISES

1. Consider your university or college. Develop compensable factors for your institution to evaluate jobs. Would you use one job evaluation plan or multiple plans? Should the school's educational mission be reflected in your factors? Or are generic factors okay? Discuss. Ask your professor to help you identify the actual factors used (this likely will involve contacting the Human Resources Department compensation staff).

2. You are the manager of 10 people in a large organization. All become suspicious and upset when they receive a memo from the HR department saying their jobs are going to be evaluated. What would you say to try to reassure them?

WEB EXERCISE

The Foreign Service Classification Standard

The Canadian federal government has identified the Foreign Services Group as one of the three occupational groups most in need of classification reform. Go to the classification standard for the Foreign Service Group dated September 1972: (www.tbs-sct.gc.ca/Classification/Standards/FS/FS_e.asp).* If this page is not available, use the classification standards for the Economics and Social Science Services Group (EC) or the Program and Administrative Services (PA) Group (the other two groups in most need of reform). Write a brief report outlining problems with this classification standard, and make suggestions for improvement. Start by reviewing the seven "functional groupings" and degrees used for evaluating jobs. Are these "factors"? What is missing from this job evaluation plan? How can the matrix on page 2 be interpreted?

*at www.gc.ca; click English; click Departments and Agencies; click Treasury Board of Canada Secretariat; click English; click Classification Reform (under Highlights); click Work Tools; click Standards; click Classification Standards; click Foreign Service.

CASE

Job Evaluation for the Regional Municipality

Your regional municipality is enjoying economic growth. Tax revenues are up, but so is the workload for government employees. Recently there have been increasing complaints about pay. Some employees believe that their salary is out of line in comparison to the amount received by other employees. As a first step, the human resources director for the region has hired you to perform job analysis and write job descriptions. The results are shown below. Now a job structure is needed, based on a point system job evaluation technique.

1. Divide into teams of four to six students each. Each team should evaluate the eight jobs and prepare a job structure based on its evaluation. Assign titles to each job, and list your structure by title and job letter.

2. Each team should describe the process the group went through to arrive at that job structure. Job evaluation techniques and compensable factors used should be described, and the reasons for selecting them should be stated.

3. Each team should give each job a title and put its job structure on the board. Comparisons can then be made between job structures of the various teams. Does the job evaluation method used appear to affect the results? Do the compensable factors chosen affect the results? Does the process affect the results?

4. Evaluate the job descriptions. What parts were most useful? How could they be improved?

CASE

Job A

Kind of Work. Directs a large and complex fiscal management program in a large regional municipality department, agency, or institution. Provides technical and supervisory financial support to carry out policies and programs established by the department head. Serves as the chief liaison to activity managers to ensure coordination of their activities in planning with the accounting division. Maintains a close working relationship with the finance agency controller to ensure compliance with budgetary and financial planning requirements of the Department of Finance. Considerable latitude is granted employee in this class for developing, implementing, and administering financial methods and procedures. Typically reports to a high-level department manager with work reviewed through periodic conferences and reports.

Essential Responsibilities

- Directs all accounting functions of the department, agency, or institution so that adequate financial records and fiscal controls are maintained.
- Provides supervisory and high professional skills for the financial operations of the department consistent with the appropriate regional, provincial, and federal laws and regulations so that regional, provincial, and federal funds are utilized in the most efficient and effective manner.
- Provides coordination with other regional, provincial, and federal agencies relating to financial matters so that the department head and agency controller are informed as to matters pertaining to policies, procedures, and programs that may have an effect on the financial operation of the department.
- Develops authorized department budgets and financial plans, goals, and objectives for review and approval by the agency controller and the department head so that maximum use will be made of financial resources.
- Consults with and advises the department head, managers, supervisors, and the agency controller on financial policies and procedures, organizational changes, and interpretation of financial data and reports to ensure efficient and effective fiscal management.

Job B

Kind of Work. Keeps financial records where the accounts are relatively complex or assists higher-level accountants and accounting technicians when the accounts are complex and extensive.

Receives direction from higher level accounting personnel in the form of a review of work for accuracy and completeness. In some cases, may provide lead work direction to account clerks or clerical personnel engaged in the bookkeeping operation. Prepares relatively simple reports, makes preliminary analyses of financial conditions for use by other employees, and implements minor procedural and transactional changes in the fiscal operation. Emphasis is on bookkeeping procedures and the smooth transition of fiscal operations.

CASE

Essential Responsibilities

- Maintains the financial records of a moderate-sized department according to established procedures and makes adjustments to the records as directed.

- Prepares special analytical data for use by others in preparing budget requests or other reports.

- Approves and processes travel, account, invoice, and claim documents for payment.

- Codes and records all receipts and disbursement of funds.

- Reviews encumbrance or liquidation documents for accuracy and conformity with procedures and expedites financial transactions.

- Accesses or inputs information to the regionwide accounting system.

- Investigates errors or problems in the processing of fiscal transactions and recommends changes in procedures.

- Issues purchase orders.

- Provides lead work direction to other bookkeeping and clerical employees.

- Performs related work as required.

Job C

Kind of Work.   Serves as section chief or top assistant to an accounting director or other high-level fiscal management officer in a moderate- or large-sized regional municipality department. Directs the activities of an accounting or fiscal management section consisting of several subsections or assists the supervisor with the supervision of a very large and complex accounting operation. Works closely with the chief fiscal officer in formulating fiscal policies and independently establishes new accounts in payroll procedures to accomplish the department's program. Considerable independence of action is granted the employee, with work reviewed through reports and conferences.

Essential Responsibilities

- Prepares and administers the department budget, confers with operating officials on projected needs, and devises methods of adjusting budgets so that agency programs may be carried on efficiently and effectively.

- Provides technical accounting assistance and guidance to operational accounting units within a large- or medium-sized agency so that operating procedures and staff skills will be upgraded on a continuing basis with resultant improvement in quality and reduction in cost.

- Produces special accounting plans, reports, and analyses involving complex accounting methods and principles as a basis for decision making by the chief fiscal officer and the department head.

- Constructs and maintains the department's accounting structure and cost accounting capabilities so the department can conform to legislative intent, meet regional, provincial, and federal regulatory requirements, and provide the department with reporting capabilities.

CASE

- Assists in the coordination and ongoing analysis and control of fiscal matters relevant to satellite institutions under departmental supervision.

Job D

Kind of Work. Performs professional accounting work as the fiscal officer of a small department, institution, or major division, or as an assistant to a higher level accountant in a large fiscal operation. Work involves providing a wide range of accounting services to professional and managerial employees. Assists in the development and maintenance of broad fiscal programs. Regularly performs complex fiscal analysis, prepares fiscal reports for management, and recommends alternative solutions to accounting problems. May supervise account clerks, accounting technicians, or clerical employees engaged in the fiscal operation. Receives supervision from a higher level accountant, business manager, or other administrative employee.

Essential Responsibilities

- Helps administrative employees develop budgets to ensure that sufficient funds are available for operating needs.
- Monitors cash flow to ensure minimum adequate operating balance.
- Produces reports so that management has proper fiscal information.
- Submits reports to federal, regional, and provincial agencies to ensure that financial reporting requirements are met.
- Analyzes and interprets fiscal reports so that information is available in useful form.
- Instructs technicians and clerks in proper procedures to ensure smooth operation of accounting functions.
- Investigates fiscal accounting problems so that adequate solutions may be developed.
- Recommends and implements new procedures to ensure the efficient operation of the accounting section.
- Interprets regional and provincial laws and department policies to ensure the legality of fiscal transactions.

Job E

Kind of Work. Performs semiprofessional accounting work within an established accounting system. Responsible for maintaining accounting records on a major set of accounts, preauditing transactions in a major activity, or handling cash receipts in a major facility, and for classifying transactions, substantiating source documents, balancing accounts, and preparing reports as prescribed. Responsible for recognizing errors or problems in the fiscal transactions of an agency and recommending alternative solutions for consideration by other staff. Must regularly exercise initiative and independent judgment and may provide work direction to account clerks or clerical employees engaged in the fiscal operation. Receives supervision from other accounting personnel.

Essential Responsibilities

- Controls expenditures so they do not exceed budget totals and prepares allotment requests in the agency's budgetary accounts.

CASE

- Processes encumbrance changes of expenditures authorization and adjusts budget as necessary and desired.
- Reconciles department accounting records with the regionwide accounting system and records documents so that funds may be appropriated, allotted, encumbered, and transferred.
- Authorizes reimbursement for goods and services received by a major department.
- Develops and maintains a system of accounts receivable, including issuance of guidelines for participants and preparation of regional, provincial, and federal reports.
- Provides daily accounting on loans receivable or financial aids for a major college.
- Audits cost vendor statements for conformity within departmental guidelines.
- Supervises cash accounting unit and prepares reports on receipts and deposits.
- Performs related work as required.

Job F

Kind of Work.   Keeps financial records when the accounts are relatively simple, or assists others in assigned work of greater difficulty where accounting operations are more complex and extensive. The work involves a combination of clerical and bookkeeping responsibilities requiring specialized training or experience. Receives direction from higher-level accounting personnel in the form of detailed instructions and close review for accuracy and conformance with law, rules, or policy. Once oriented to the work, employee may exercise independent judgment in assigned duties.

Essential Responsibilities

- Maintains complete bookkeeping records independently when scope, volume, or complexity is limited or maintains a difficult part of an extensive bookkeeping operation.
- Codes and records all receipts and disbursement of funds.
- Prepares travel, account, invoice, and claim documents for payment.
- Reviews encumbrance or liquidation documents for accuracy and conformity with procedures and expedites financial transactions.
- Prepares financial information of reports and audits, invoices, and expenditure reports.
- Keeps general, control, or subsidiary books of accounts such as cash book appropriation and disbursement ledgers and encumbrance records.
- Accesses or inputs information to the provincial accounting system as directed.
- Performs related tasks as required.

Job G

Kind of Work.   Performs varied and difficult semiprofessional accounting work within an established accounting system. Maintains a complex set of accounts and works with higher management outside the accounting unit in planning and controlling expenditures. Works with higher level employees in providing technical fiscal advice and service

CASE

to functional activities. Receives supervision from higher level management or accounting personnel. May provide work direction to lower-level accounting, bookkeeping, or clerical personnel.

Essential Responsibilities

- Assists the chief accounting officer in the preparation of all budgets to ensure continuity in financial operations.
- Prepares and assembles the biennial budget and coordinates all accounting functions for a small department according to overall plan of department head and needs expressed by activity managers.
- Maintains cost coding and allocation system for a major department to serve as a basis for reimbursement.
- Provides accounting and budgetary controls for federal, provincial, regional, and private grants including reconciling bank statements and preparing reports on the status of the budget and accounts.
- Evaluates the spending progress of budget activities, ensures that budgetary limits are not exceeded, and recommends or effects changes in spending plans.
- Provides technical services to divisions of an agency in the supervision of deposits, accounts payable, procurement, and other business management areas.
- Performs related work as required.

Job H

Kind of Work.   Maintains a large and complex system of accounts. Serves as a section chief in the finance division of a very large department, maintains large regional, federal or regional–provincial accounts, and oversees a major regionwide accounting function in the Department of Finance. Responsible for coordinating and supervising the various phases of the accounting function. Responsibility extends to the development of procedure and policies for the work involved. Supervises a staff of accounting personnel.

Essential Responsibilities

- Provides regular budget review so that program managers have adequate funds to be effective.
- Conducts financial analysis for economical and equitable distribution or redistribution of agency resource.
- Prepares long- and short-range program recommendations for fiscal action so that agency policies are consistent.
- Plans and directs information technology related to fiscal services to ensure efficient operation.
- Develops and defines accounting office procedures to ensure the efficient delivery of fiscal services.
- Reviews and analyzes cost accounting data to ensure proper documentation of projected cost as required by policy and procedures.

CASE

- Prepares and supervises the preparation of federal budgets and grant requests, financial plans, and expenditure reports so that they accurately reflect needs and intent of the agency.

- Develops accounting and documentation procedures for the region's social services department so that regional, provincial, and federal auditing and reporting requirements are met.

- Establishes and maintains a financial reporting system for all federal and other non-regional funding sources so that all fiscal reporting requirements are adhered to on a timely and accurate basis.

- Assists grantee agencies in proper reporting procedures under federal grant programs so that requirements for reimbursement may be made on a timely basis.

- Determines the regionwide indirect costs so that all regional agencies are allocated their proportionate share of indirect costs.

- Supervises the review and processing of all encumbrance documents submitted to the Department of Finance so that necessary accounting information is recorded accurately and promptly in the accounting system.

PERSON-BASED STRUCTURES

LEARNING OUTCOMES

- *Explain* the difference between skill-based pay plans and competency-based pay plans, and *describe* the types of jobs each is commonly applied to.
- *Describe* the four basic steps in skill analysis.
- *Define* "competency," and *explain* what is meant by core competencies, competency sets, and competency indicators.
- *Explain* why employee acceptance is crucial for person-based pay plans, and how this acceptance can be obtained.
- *Describe* two potential sources of bias in internal pay structures.

History buffs tell us that some form of job evaluation was in use when the pharaohs built the pyramids. Chinese emperors managed the Great Wall construction with the assistance of job evaluation. The logic underlying today's job-based pay structures flows from scientific management, championed by Taylor in the 1910s. Work was broken into a series of steps and analyzed so that the "one best way," the most efficient way to perform every element of the job (right down to how to shovel coal), could be specified. Strategically, Taylor's approach fit with mass production technologies that were beginning to revolutionize the way work was done.

Taylorism pervades our lives. Not only are jobs analyzed and evaluated in terms of the "best way," but cookbooks and software manuals specify the methods for baking a cake or using a program as a series of simple, basic steps. Golf is analyzed as a series of basic tasks that can be combined successfully to lower one's handicap. Work, play, in all daily life, "Taylor's thinking so permeates the soil of modern life we no longer realize it is there."[1]

But in today's "new work culture," employees are told they must go beyond the tasks specified in their job descriptions. They must know more, think more on the job, and take personal responsibility for their results. Pay systems that support continuous learning and improvement, flexibility, participation, and partnership are essential for achieving competitive advantage today. Person-based structures hold out that promise.

The logic supporting person-based approaches is that structures based on differences in people's skills or competencies will be more flexible and thus encourage agility.

Person-based approaches are the topic of this chapter. At the end of this chapter, we shall discuss the usefulness of the various approaches—job- and person-based—for determining internal structures.

Exhibit 6.1 points out the similarities in the logic underlying job-based versus people-based approaches. No matter the basis for the structure, a way is needed to (1) collect and summarize information about the work, (2) determine what is of value to the organization, (3) quantify that value, and then (4) translate that value into internal structure. The previous two chapters discussed the process for job-based structures (job analysis and job evaluation). This chapter discusses the process for person-based structures. You will not be surprised to discover that similarities abound.

■ PERSON-BASED PAY STRUCTURES: SKILL PLANS

Skill-based pay plans are usually applied to so-called blue collar work and competencies to so-called white-collar work. The distinctions are not hard-and-fast. However, the majority of applications of skill-based pay have been in manufacturing and assembly work where the work

EXHIBIT   6.1   Many Ways to Create Internal Structure

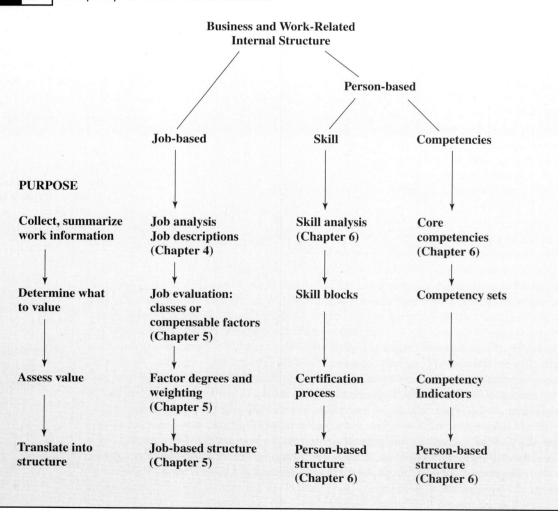

skill-based pay structures

link pay to the depth or breadth of the skills, abilities, and knowledge a person acquires that are relevant to the work

can be specified and defined. The advantage of a **skill-based pay structure** is that people can be deployed in a way that better matches the flow of work, thus avoiding bottlenecks as well as idle hands.[2] Structures based on skill pay individuals for all the skills for which they have been certified regardless of whether the work they are doing requires all or just a few of those particular skills. In contrast, a job-based plan pays employees for the job to which they are assigned, regardless of the skills they possess.

Types of Skill Plans

Skill plans can focus on depth (specialists in corporate law, finance, or welding and hydraulic maintenance) or breadth (generalists with knowledge in all phases of operations including marketing, manufacturing, finance, and human resources).

Specialist: In Depth.   The pay structures for your elementary or high school teachers were likely based on their knowledge as measured by education level. A typical teacher's contract specifies a series of steps, with each step corresponding to a level of education. A bachelor's degree in education is step one and is the minimum required for hiring. To advance a step to higher pay requires additional education. For example, the salary schedule included in the case at the end of this chapter requires 15 additional credits beyond the bachelor's degree to move to a higher step. Each year of seniority also is associated with a pay increase. The result can be that two teachers may receive different pay rates for doing essentially the same job—teaching English to high school students. The pay is based on the knowledge of the individual doing the job (measured by number of university credits and years of teaching experience) rather than job content or output (performance of students).[3] The presumption is that teachers with more knowledge are more effective and more flexible; i.e., able to teach all grades.

Generalist/Multiskill Based: Breadth.   As with teachers, employees in a multiskill system earn pay increases by acquiring new knowledge, but the knowledge is specific to a range of related jobs. Pay increases come with certification of new skills, rather than with job assignments. Employees then can be assigned to any of the jobs for which they are certified, based on the flow of work.[4] An example from Balzer's Tool Coating (a global tool manufacturer) makes the point. This company coats cutting tools by bombarding them with, among other things, titanium nitrate ions. This coating makes the sharp edge last much longer. Originally, eight different jobs were involved in the coating process. Everyone started at the same rate, no matter the job to which they were assigned. Employees received crosstraining in a variety of jobs, but without a specific training path or level. Different locations started new people in different jobs. In order to put some order into its system and make better use of its employees, Balzer moved to a skill-based plan for all its hourly workers, including administrative and sales employees. Its new structure includes four different levels, from Fundamental to Advanced. Exhibit 6.2 shows the new structure and the skill blocks in each level. New employees are hired into the Fundamental level. Fundamental skills include familiarity with company forms and procedures, basic product knowledge, safety, basic computer usage, and so on. Once they have been certified in all the skills at the Fundamental level, they receive a pay increase of $.50 an hour and move to the Basic skill level. Certification in each of the four skill blocks (blasting, cleaning, stripping, and degas) in this level is worth an additional $.50 an hour. Basic level employees can be assigned to any of the tasks for which they are certified; they will be paid whatever is their highest certification rate. The same approach is used to train and certify employees at the Intermediate and Advanced levels. A person certified at the very top of the structure, earning at least $10.50 an hour, could be assigned to any of the tasks in the structure. The advantage to Balzer is workforce flexibility and, hence, staffing assignments that can be better matched to the work flow. The advantage to employees is the more they learn, the more they earn.

EXHIBIT | **6.2** | Proposed Skill Ladder at Balzer Tool Coating

Skill-Based Salary Grades

Grade	Admin	Sales	Tool	Machine	Grade min	Grade max
		Skill Path				
Advanced					$10.50	$13.50
Advanced						
Advanced						
Advanced						
Advanced						
Advanced				Service		
Advanced	Office Admin	Inside Sales	Incoming Ins	Arc Tech		
					$9.50	$12.50
Intermed						
Intermed						
Intermed	Blueprint	Cust Serv	Outgoing Ins	Evap Tech		
Intermed	Expediting	Pricing- B	Shipping	Coating		
					$7.50	$11.50
Basic	Software	Van Driver	Receiving	Degas		
Basic	Pricing	Licensing	Racking	Stripping		
Basic	File/route	Packing	Packing	Cleaning		
Basic	Gen Office	Courier	Fixturing	Blasting		
Entry	Fundamental	Fundamental	Fundamental	Fundamental	$7.00	$7.50
# of skills	7	7	7	8	$0.50 per skill	

Source: Diana Southall, HR Foundations, Inc.

The system at Balzer differs from the system for teachers in that the responsibilities assigned to an employee in a multiskill system can change drastically over a short period of time, whereas teachers' basic job responsibilities do not vary on a day-to-day basis. Additionally, Balzer's system is designed to ensure that all the skills are clearly job related. Training improves skills that the company values. In contrast, a school district has no guarantee that courses taken actually improve teaching skills.

Purpose of the Skill-Based Structure

To evaluate the usefulness of skill-based structures, we shall use the objectives already specified for an internally aligned structure: support work flow, fair to employees, and directs their behaviour toward organization objectives. How well do skill-based structures do?

Support Work Flow. One of the main advantages of a skill-based plan is that it can more easily match people to a changing work flow.[5] For example, one national hotel chain moves many of its people to the hotel's front desk between 4 p.m. and 7 p.m., when the majority of guests check in. After 7 p.m., these same employees move to the food and beverage service area to match the demand for room service and dining room service. By ensuring that guests do not have to wait long to check in or to eat, the hotel provides a high level of service with fewer staff. (Yes, the same thought occurred to us on the tastiness of the resulting food, which reinforces the point that skill-based systems focus on inputs, not results.)

Fair to Employees.   Employees like the potential of higher pay that comes with learning. And by encouraging employees to take charge of their own development, skill-based plans may give them more control over their work lives.

However, favouritism and bias may play a role in determining who gets first crack at the training necessary to become certified at higher paying skill levels. Employees complain that they are forced to pick up the slack for those who are out for training. And the courts have not yet been asked to rule on the legality of two people doing the same task but for different (skill-based) pay.

Directs Behaviour toward Organization Objectives.   Person-based plans have the potential to clarify new standards and behavioural expectations. The fluid work assignments that skill-based plans permit encourage employees to take responsibility for the complete work process and its results, with less direction from supervisors.[6]

SKILL ANALYSIS

skill analysis

a systematic process to identify and collect information about skills required to perform work in an organization

Exhibit 6.3 depicts the process for determining a skill-based structure. It begins with a **skill analysis**, which is similar to the task statements in a job analysis. Related skills can be grouped into a skill block; skill blocks can be arranged by levels into a skill structure. To build the structure, a process is needed to describe, certify, and value the skills.

Exhibit 6.3 also identifies the major skill analysis decisions: (1) What information should be collected? (2) What methods should be used? (3) Who should be involved? (4) How useful are the results for pay purposes? These are exactly the same decisions managers face in job analysis.

What Information to Collect?

There is far less uniformity in the use of terms in person-based plans than in job-based plans. For example, food products manufacturer General Mills uses four skill categories corresponding to the steps in the production process: materials handling, mixing, filling, and packaging.[7] Each skill category has three blocks: (1) entry level, (2) accomplished, and (3) advanced. Exhibit 6.4 is a schematic of their plan. It shows that a new employee can start at entry level in materials handling and, after being certified on all skills included in skill block A1, can begin training for skills in either B1 or A2.

EXHIBIT 6.3 Determining the Internal Skill-Based Structure ─────────────

| Internal alignment work relationships within the organization | → | Skill analysis | → | Skill blocks | → | Skill certification | → | Skill-based structure |

Basic Decisions:
- What is the objective of the plan?
- What information should be collected?
- What methods should be used to determine and certify skills?
- Who should be involved?
- How useful are the results for pay purposes?

EXHIBIT **6.4** General Mills Skills-Based Structure

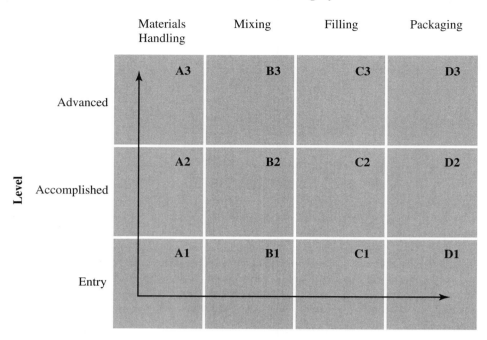

Skill Category

In contrast, FMC (a global chemical company with a manufacturing facility in Prince George, British Columbia) does not group skills into blocks. Instead, it assigns points and groups skills as foundation, core electives, and optional electives. FMC's plan for technicians is more fully developed in Exhibit 6.5.

- **Foundation Skills** include a quality seminar, videos on materials handling and hazardous materials, a three-day safety workshop, and a half-day orientation. All foundation skills are mandatory and must be certified to reach the Technician I rate ($11 per hour).
- **Core Electives** are necessary to the facility's operations (e.g., fabrication, welding, painting, finishing, assembly, inspection). Each skill is assigned a point value.
- **Optional Electives** are additional specialized competencies ranging from computer applications to team leadership and consensus building.

To reach technician II ($12 per hour), 40 core elective points (of 370) must be certified, in addition to the foundation competencies. To reach Technician III, an additional 100 points of core electives must be certified, plus three optional electives.

A fully qualified Technician IV (e.g., certified as mastering foundations, 365 points of core electives, and 5 optional electives) is able to perform all work in a cell at the facility. Technician IVs earn $14.50 per hour no matter the task they are doing. FMC's approach should look familiar to any college student: required courses, required credits chosen among specific categories, and optional electives. There is a minor difference, of course—FMC employees get paid for passing these courses, whereas college students pay to take courses!

The General Mills and FMC plans illustrate the kind of information that underpins the skill-based plans: very specific information on every aspect of the production process. This makes the plans particularly suited for continuous flow technologies where employees work in teams.

EXHIBIT 6.5 FMC Technician Skill-Based Structure

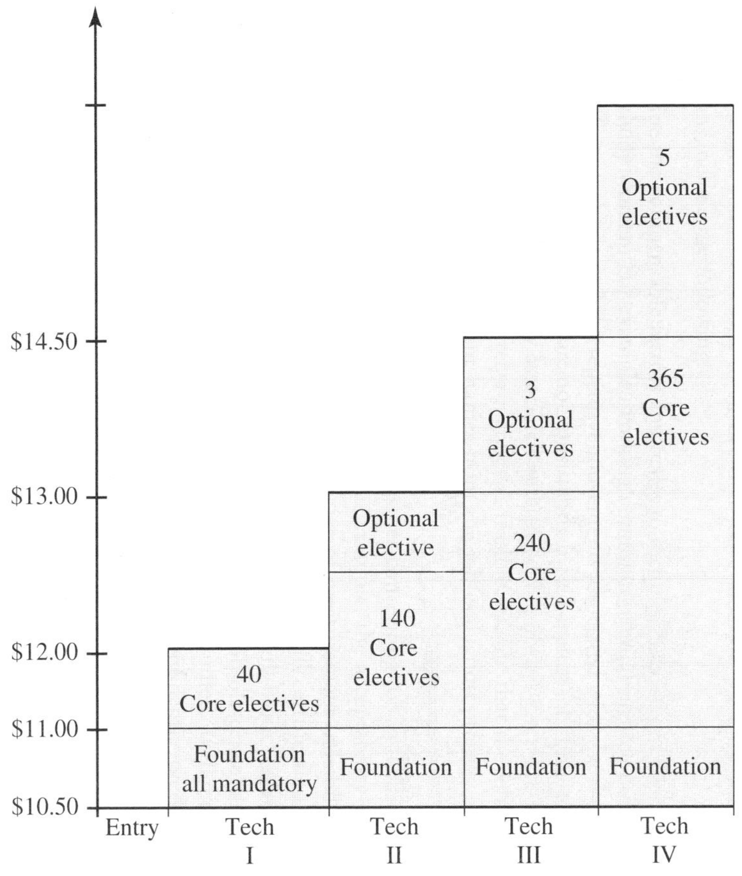

Foundations

Quality course
Shop floor control
Materials handling
Hazardous materials video
Safety workshop
Orientation workshop

Core Electives

Skills	Points		Skills	Points
Longeron Fabrication	10		Leak Check/Patch Weld	5
Panel Fabrication	15		Final Acceptance Test	10
Shell Fabrication	15		Welding Inspection	15
End Casting Welding	20		Flame Spraying	15
Finishing—Paint	20		Assembly Inspection	5
Finishing—Ablative/Autoclave	20		Safe % Arm Assembly	15
Finishing—Surface Prep	10		MK 13 Machining	25
MK 13 Assembly	15		MK 14 Machining	25
MK 14 Assembly	15		Tool Set Up	10
Finishing Inspection	5		NC1 Inspection	30
Machining Inspection	20		Degrease	10
Pad Welding	15		Guide Rail Assembly	5
			Receiving Inspection	5

Optional Electives

Maintenance
Logistics—JIT
Plant First Aid
Geometric Tolerancing
Computer-Spreadsheet
Computer-Database
Computer-Word Processing
Assessment Centre
Consensus Building

Career Development
Group Decision Making
Public Relations
Group Facilitator
Training
Group Problem Solving
Administration
Plant Security

Whom to Involve?

Employee involvement is almost always built into skill-based plans. Employees are the source of information on defining the skills, arranging them into a hierarchy, bundling them into skill blocks, and certifying whether a person actually possesses the skills. At Balzer and FMC, a committee comprised of managers from several sites developed the skill listing and certification process for each of the four skill ladders, with input from employees.

Establish Certification Methods

Practices for certifying that employees possess the skills and are able to apply them vary widely. Some organizations use peer review, on-the-job demonstrations, and tests for certification, similar to the traditional apprentice/journeyman/master path. Nortel uses a preassessment meeting between supervisor and employee to discuss skill accomplishments and training needs. Honeywell evaluates employees during the six months after they have learned the skills. Again, leaders and peers are used in the certification process. Still others require successful completion of formal courses. However, we do not need to point out to students that sitting in the classroom doesn't guarantee that anything is learned. School districts address this issue in a variety of ways. Some are more restrictive than others about which courses will increase teachers' pay. Some will certify for any courses; others only for courses in the teacher's subject area. However, no districts require evidence that the course makes any difference to results.

Newer skill-based applications appear to be moving away from an on-demand review and toward scheduling fixed review points in the year. Scheduling makes it easier to budget and control payroll increases. Other changes include ongoing recertifications, which replace the traditional one-time certification process and help ensure skills are kept fresh, and removal of certification (and accompanying pay) when a particular skill is deemed obsolete.[8] (This is the case with the national Certified Human Resources Professional designation in Canada). However, it can be difficult to change certification procedures once a system is in place. TRW faced this problem when using formal classes for their airbag facility. TRW felt that some employees were only putting in "seat time." Yet no one was willing to take the responsibility for refusing to certify, since an extra signoff beyond classroom attendance was not part of the original system design.

Many plans require that employees be recertified, since the skills may get rusty if they are not used frequently. Airplane pilots, for example, must go through an emergency-landing simulation every 12 months, since the airlines want to ensure that these skills are *not* actually demonstrated on the job with any frequency. Similarly, the introduction of new skill requirements and the obsolescence of previous skills require recertification. At its Ome facility in Tokyo, Toshiba requires all team members to recertify their skills every 24 months. Those who fail have the opportunity to retrain and attempt to recertify before their pay rate is reduced. However, the pressure to keep up to date and avoid obsolescence is intense.

Skill-based plans become increasingly expensive as the majority of employees become certified at the highest pay levels. As a result, the employer may have an average wage higher than competitors who are using conventional job evaluation. Unless the increased flexibility permits leaner staffing, the employer may also experience higher labour costs. Some employers are combatting this by requiring that employees stay at a rate for a certain length of time before they can take the training to move to a higher rate. Motorola abandoned its skill-based plan because, at the end of three years, everyone had topped out (by accumulating the necessary skill blocks). TRW, too, found that after a few years, people at two manufacturing plants on skill-based systems all had topped out. They were flexible and well trained. So now what? What happens in the next years out? Does everybody automatically receive a pay increase? In a firm with labour-intensive products, the increased labour costs under skill-based plans may also become a source of competitive disadvantage.

Research on Skill-Based Plans

Skill-based plans are generally well accepted by employees because it is easy to see the connection between the plan, the work, and the size of the paycheque. Consequently, the plans provide strong motivation for individuals to increase their skills. "Learn to earn" is a popular slogan used in these plans. A recent study connected the ease of communication and understanding of skill-based plans to employees' general perceptions of being treated fairly by the employer.[9] The design of the certification process is crucial in this perception of fairness. Two studies related use of a skills system to productivity. One found positive results, the other did not.[10] Another study found that younger, more educated employees with strong growth needs, organizational commitment, and a positive attitude toward workplace innovations were more successful in acquiring new skills.[11] On the other hand, for reasons not made clear, the study's authors recommend allocating training opportunities by seniority (i.e., to those who have a lower likelihood of benefiting from such training!).

So what kind of workplace seems best suited for a skill-based plan? Some of the early researchers on skill-based plans recently published the results of their survey on factors related to the longevity of skill-based plans. Sixty-one percent of the companies in their original sample were still using skill-based plans seven years later. One of the key factors that determined a plan's success was how well it was aligned with the organization's strategy. Plans were more viable in organizations following a defender strategy. Defender organizations focus on a relatively narrow, stable market niche, and grow by penetrating deeper into their current markets; they tend to establish a single core technology that they can operate continuously and efficiently, and they update technologies only to maintain efficiency and cost control. These characteristics favour the use of a skill-based plan. Although skill-based plans encourage employee flexibility, that flexibility must occur within the context of precisely defined skills. Precise definition is more possible when the production process is well understood and not vulnerable to rapid technological changes that force organizations to revamp the training and assessment, deal with obsolete skills, and reprice new skills. Organizations that prospect for new and different types of business or focus on innovation are likely to encounter these difficulties more often, making any skill plan difficult to sustain. In addition, skill-based plans are more likely to survive where employees participate in the day-to-day administration of the plan. This day-to-day participation was deemed more important than participation of the plan design. And, as with any HR program, commitment (from top management as well as supervisors) is essential.[12]

A final question is whether a multiskilled "jack-of-all-trades" might really be the master of none. Some research suggests that the greatest impact on results occurs after just a small amount of increased flexibility.[13] Greater increments in flexibility achieve fewer improvements. So, more skills may not necessarily improve productivity. Instead, there may be an optimal number of skills for any individual to possess. Beyond that number, productivity returns are smaller than the pay increases. Additionally, some employees may not be interested in giving up the job they are doing. Such "campers" create a bottleneck for rotating other employees into that position to acquire those skills. Organizations should decide in advance whether they are willing to design a plan to work around campers or force them into the system. Does the camper possess unique skills that cannot easily be learned by others? If so, perhaps that job should be carved out of the multiskill system. Either approach carries a price.[14]

The bottom line is that skill-based approaches may be only short-term initiatives for specific settings. They may refocus employees on learning new skills and adapting to a radically different work environment. They may also change how employees think about their work. However, as with any other pay technique, they do not appear suitable for all situations. The acceptability may vary, depending on how long the plan has been in place, and whether acceptability to the organization, to employees, or both, is important.

■ PERSON-BASED PAY STRUCTURES: COMPETENCIES

competencies

■ underlying, broadly applicable knowledge, skills, and behaviours that form the foundation for successful work performance

competency-based pay structure

■ links pay to work-related competencies

core competencies

■ competencies required for successful work performance in any job in the organization

competency sets

■ specific components of a competency

competency indicators

■ observable behaviours that indicate the level of competency within each competency set

There is confusion over what **competencies** are and what they are supposed to accomplish. As with job evaluation, perspectives proliferate. Are competencies a skill that can be learned and developed or a trait that is more difficult to learn and includes attitudes and motives? Do competencies focus on the minimum requirements that the organization needs to stay in business or on outstanding performance? Are they characteristics of the organization or of the employee? Unfortunately, the answer to all of these questions, is "yes."[15] A lack of consensus means that competencies can be a number of things; consequently, they stand in danger of becoming nothing.

Exhibit 6.6 shows the process of using competencies to address the need for internal alignment by creating a **competency-based pay structure**. All approaches to creating a structure begin by looking at the work performed in the organization. Although skill-and job-based systems hone in on information about specific tasks, **competencies** take the opposite approach. They look at the organization and try to abstract the underlying, broadly applicable knowledge, skills, and behaviours that form the foundation for successful work performance at any level or job in the organization. These are the **core competencies**. Core competencies are often linked to mission statements that express an organization's philosophy, values, business strategies, and plans.

Competency sets begin to translate each core competency into action. For the core competency of "business awareness," for example, competency sets might be related to organizational understanding, cost management, third-party relationships, and ability to identify business opportunities.

Competency indicators are the observable behaviours that indicate the level of competency within each set. These indicators may be used for staffing and evaluation as well as for pay purposes.

TRW's competency model for its human resource management department, shown in Exhibit 6.7, includes the four core competencies considered critical to the success of the business. All TRW HR employees are expected to demonstrate varying degrees of these competencies. However, not all individuals would be expected to reach the highest level in all competencies. Rather, the HR function would want to be sure it possessed all levels of mastery of all the core competencies within its HRM group, and individual employees would use the model as a guide to what TRW values and what capacities it wants people to develop.

The competency indicators anchor the degree of a competency required at each level of complexity of the work. Exhibit 6.8 shows five levels of competency indicators for the competency

EXHIBIT 6.6 Determining the Internal Competency-Based Pay Structure

Internal alignment work relationships within the organization → Core competencies → Competency sets → Competency indicators → Competency-based pay structure

Basic Decisions:
- What is objective of plan?
- What information to collect?
- Methods used to determine and certify competencies?
- Who is involved?
- How useful for pay purposes?

EXHIBIT | **6.7** | TRW Human Resources Competencies

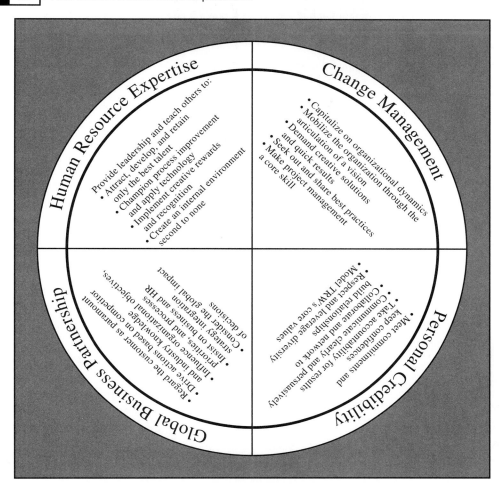

impact and influence. These behavioural anchors make the competency more concrete. The levels range from "uses direct persuasion" at level 1 to "uses experts or other third parties to influence" at level 5. Sometimes the behavioural anchors might include scales of the intensity of action, the degree of impact of the action, its complexity, and/or the amount of effort expended. Scaled competency indicators are similar to job analysis questionnaires and degrees of compensable factors, discussed in previous chapters.[16]

Defining Competencies

Because competencies are trying to get at what underlies work behaviours, there is a lot of fuzziness in defining them. Early conceptions of competencies focused on five areas:[17]

1. Skills (demonstration of expertise)
2. Knowledge (accumulated information)
3. Self-concepts (attitudes, values, self-image)
4. Traits (general disposition to behave in a certain way)
5. Motives (recurrent thoughts that drive behaviours).

| EXHIBIT | 6.8 | Sample Competency Indicator Description |

Impact and Influence: The intention to persuade, convince, or influence to have a specific impact. It includes the ability to anticipate and respond to the needs and concerns of others.

"Impact and Influence" is one of the competencies considered "most critical."

Level	Behaviours
0: Not shown	■ Lets things happen ■ Quotes policy and issues instruction
1: Direct persuasion	■ Uses direct persuasion in a discussion or presentation ■ Appeals to reason; uses data or concrete examples ■ Does not adapt presentation to the interest and level of the audience ■ Reiterates the same points when confronted with opposition
2: Multiple attempts to persuade	■ Tries different tactics when attempting to persuade without necessarily making an effort to adapt to the level or interest of an audience (e.g., making two or more different arguments or points in a discussion)
3: Builds trust and fosters win-win mentality (expected performance level)	■ Tailors presentations or discussions to appeal to the interest and level of other ■ Looks for the "win–win" opportunities ■ Demonstrates sensitivity and understanding of others in detecting underlying concerns, interests, or emotions, and uses that understanding to develop effective responses to objections
4: Multiple actions to influence	■ Takes more than one action to influence, with each action adapted to the specific audience (e.g., a group meeting to present the situation, followed by individual meetings) ■ May include taking a well-thought-out unusual action to have a specific impact
5: Influences through others	■ Uses experts or other third parties to influence ■ Develops and maintains a planned network of relationships with customers, internal peers, and industry colleagues ■ When required, assembles "behind the scenes" support for ideas regarding opportunities and/or solving problems

Reprinted from *Raising the Bar: Using Competencies to Enhance Employee Performance* with permission from the American Compensation Association (ACA), 14040 N. Northsight Blvd., Scottsdale, AZ USA 85260; telepnone (602) 483-8352. © ACA.

The first two areas—skills and knowledge—were considered the *essential characteristics that everyone needs to be effective in a job.* Examples might include effective listening or team problem solving. Such competencies are observable and measurable and can be acquired through training and development.

The other three competency categories—self-concepts, traits, and motives—are not directly measurable; rather, they must be inferred from actions. And it is these inferred characteristics that were judged to be the *differentiating competencies—critical factors that distinguish superior performance from average performance.*[18] In team settings, differentiating characteristics might include a strong identification with the team (self-concept), personal flexibility (trait), and the drive to produce results (motive). As experience with competencies has grown, organizations seem to be moving away from the vagueness of self-concepts, traits, and motives to place a greater emphasis on business-related descriptions of behaviours "that excellent performers exhibit much more consistently than average performers" and less on underlying inferences. Competencies are becoming "a collection of observable behaviours (not a single behaviour) that require no inference, assumption or interpretation."[19]

Purpose of the Competency-Based Structure

Do competencies help support an internally aligned structure? Using our by-now familiar yardstick, how well do competencies support the work flow, treat employees fairly, and direct their behaviour toward organization objectives?

Workflow.   As you can judge from reading the previous exhibits, competencies are chosen to ensure that all the critical needs of the organization are met. For example, TRW notes on its HR technical skills: "These skills are considered important for all HR professionals but the weighting of importance and the level of proficiency varies for different positions, organizations, and business conditions." So, rather than having the skills to smoothly perform today's work, the emphasis is on competence that will transcend work flow. This abstract quality is both competencies' strength and weakness.

Fair to Employees.   Advocates of competencies say they can empower employees to take charge of their own development. By focusing on optimum performance rather than average performance, competencies can help employees maintain their marketability.[20] On the other hand, critics of competencies worry that the field is going back to the 1950s and 1960s, when basing pay on personal characteristics was standard practice.[21] Basing pay on race or sex seems appalling today, yet was standard practice at one time. Basing pay on someone's judgment of another person's integrity raises a similar flag. Trying to justify pay differences based on inferred competencies creates risks that need to be managed.

Direct Behaviour toward Organization Objectives.   The main appeal of competencies is the direct link to the organization's strategy. Rather than platoons of employees on committees defining tasks, the process of identifying competencies starts with the company leadership deciding what will spell success for the company. So the process resembles identifying compensable factors as part of job evaluation.

The potential for refocusing and redirecting toward core issues is the biggest selling point for a competency approach.[22] Competencies can be the basis for a shared vision of the direction of the organization and the purpose of that direction. In effect, competencies provide guidelines for behaviour and keep people focused. They also can provide a common basis for communicating and working together. This latter possibility has become increasingly important as organizations go global, and as employees with widely differing viewpoints and experiences fill leadership positions in these global organizations.[23]

.NET WORTH

Leadership Competencies in the Federal Government

Competencies often are used, in addition to pay, as the basis for other human resource management initiatives. The Canadian federal government requires specific competencies for senior civil servants at the Assistant Deputy Minister (ADM) and Senior Executive levels:

> The Public Service Commission and deputy ministers recognize there are a certain number of competencies required to ensure an individual's success at senior management levels. These competencies form the basis of a standard of leadership behaviour that can be consistently applied across the executive community.
>
> Assistant deputy ministers are champions of the Canadian Public Service. In the midst of change and ambiguity, they elicit commitment and enthusiasm for the Public Service vision of the future. ADMs develop and carry out government policies that are in the best interests of the public. They plan strategies to help move toward the vision, committing to action and achieving their goals in the most efficient and effective manner. Working with others, ADMs are active in building a representative Public Service which is committed to learning and to becoming a workplace of choice. ADMs build partnerships with other organizations to better meet the objectives of all partners and in the interest of better serving the public.

The required competencies fall into five categories:

1. **Intellectual Competencies:** cognitive capacity, creativity
2. **Future Building Competency:** visioning
3. **Management Competencies:** action management, organizational awareness, teamwork, partnering
4. **Relationship Competencies:** interpersonal relations, communication
5. **Personal Competencies:** stamina/stress resistance, ethics and values, personality, behavioural flexibility, self-confidence

A subset of these competencies is used as a selection criterion for the Accelerated Executive Development Program (AEXDP) for high-potential employees, including developmental assignments, action learning groups, collective learning events, coaches, and mentors.

Source: Leadership Competencies in the Federal Government, developed by the Public Service Commission of Canada, http://www.psc-cfp.gc.ca/aexdp/leaders_e.htm. Reproduced with the permission of the Minister of Public Works and Government Services Canada, 2004.

■ COMPETENCY ANALYSIS

The bottom part of Exhibit 6.6 shows the basic decisions in creating a competency-based structure. These are:

- What is the objective of the plan?
- What information to collecct?
- Methods used to determine and certify competencies?
- Who is involved?
- How useful for pay purposes?

The first decision, and by far the most important, is to clarify the objective of the plan.

Objective

We have already pointed out that one of the pitfalls of competency systems is trying to do too many things with ill-suited systems. Competencies may have value for personal development and communicating organization direction. However, the vagueness and subjectivity (what exactly *are* this person's motives?) continue to make competencies a "risky foundation for a pay system."[24] The competency structure may exist on paper by virtue of the competency sets and scaled behavioural indicators, but bear little connection to the work employees do. On the other hand, perhaps paying for competencies is the only way to get people to pay attention to them. So the first issue is to conduct a **competency analysis** to clarify the purpose of the competency system.

What Information to Collect?

A number of schemes for classifying competencies have been proposed.[25] One of them uses three groups:

1. *Personal characteristics.* These have the aura of the Boy Scouts about them: trustworthy, loyal, courteous. In business settings, the relevant characteristics might be personal integrity, maturity of judgment, flexibility, and respect for others. Employees are expected to come in the door with these characteristics and then develop and demonstrate them in increasingly complex and ambiguous job situations.

2. *Visionary.* These are the highest level competencies. They might be expressed as possessing a global perspective, taking the initiative in moving the organization in new directions, and being able to articulate the implications for the organization of trends in the marketplace, in world events, and in the local community.

3. *Organization-specific.* Between these two groups are those competencies that are tied specifically to the particular organization and to the particular function where they are being applied. These generally include leadership, customer orientation, functional expertise (e.g., able to leap tall buildings and explain the difference between competencies and compensable factors), and developing others—whatever reflects the company values, culture, and strategic intent.

Exhibit 6.9 shows the leadership competencies that 3M developed internally for its global executives.[26] Behavioural anchors are used to rate an executive on each of these competencies. Exhibit 6.10 shows the behavioural anchors for the "Global Perspective" competency. Executives' ratings on these competencies are used to assess and develop executives worldwide. Because 3M relies heavily on promotion from within, competency ratings help develop executive talent for succession planning. Again, the link to development is clear; the link to pay is less clear.

Because they stem from each organization's mission statement or its strategy to achieve competitive advantage, you might conclude that the core competencies would be unique for each company. In fact, they are not. One analysis showed that most organizations appear to choose from the same list of 20 core competencies[27] (see Exhibit 6.11). So if the competencies do not differ, how can they be a source of competitive advantage? What does appear to differ among organizations is how they operationalize competencies. This parallels an issue we discussed in the strategy chapter: There may be only slight differences in the words, but the actions may differ. [28]

EXHIBIT **6.9** 3M Leadership Competencies

Fundamental

- **Ethics and Integrity**
  Exhibits uncompromising integrity and commitment to 3M's corporate values, human resource principles, and business conduct policies. Builds trust and instills self-confidence through mutually respectful, ongoing communication.
- **Intellectual Capacity**
  Assimilates and synthesizes information rapidly, recognizes the complexity in issues, challenges assumptions, and faces up to reality. Capable of handling multiple, complex, and paradoxical situations. Communicates clearly, concisely, and with appropriate simplicity.
- **Maturity and Judgment**
  Demonstrates resiliency and sound judgment in dealing with business and corporate challenges. Reorganizes when a decision must be made and acts in a considered and timely manner. Deals effectively with ambiguity and learns from success and failure.

Essential

- **Customer Orientation**
  Works constantly to provide superior value to the 3M customer, making each interaction a positive one.
- **Developing People**
  Selects and retains an excellent workforce within an environment that values diversity and respects individuality. Promotes continuous learning and the development of self and others to achieve maximum potential. Gives and seeks open and authentic feedback.
- **Inspiring Others**
  Positively affects the behaviour of others, motivating them to achieve personal satisfaction and high performance through a sense of purpose and spirit of cooperation. Leads by example.
- **Business Health and Results**
  Identifies and successfully generates product, market, and geographic growth opportunities, while consistently delivering positive short-term business results. Continually searches for ways to add value and position the organization for future success.

Visionary

- **Global Perspective**
  Operates from an awareness of 3M's global markets, capabilities, and resources. Exerts global leadership and works respectfully in multicultural environments to 3M's advantage.
- **Vision and Strategy**
  Creates and communicates a customer-focused vision, corporately aligned and engaging all employees in pursuit of a common goal.
- **Nurturing Innovation**
  Creates and sustains an environment that supports experimentation, rewards risk taking, reinforces curiosity, and challenges the status quo through freedom and openness without judgment. Influences the future to 3M's advantage.
- **Building Alliances**
  Builds and leverages mutually beneficial relationships and networks, both internal and external, which generate multiple opportunities for 3M.
- **Organizational Agility**
  Knows, respects, and leverages 3M culture and assets. Leads integrated change within a business unit to achieve sustainable competitive advantage. Utilizes teams intentionally and appropriately.

Source: Margaret E. Allredge and Kevin J. Nilan, "3M's Leadership Competency Model: An Internally Developed Solution, "*Human Resource Management* 39, Summer/Fall 2000, pp. 133–45. Reprinted by permission of John Wiley & Sons, Inc.

EXHIBIT | **6.10** | Competency Indicators for Global Perspectives Competency

Global Perspective: Behaviours

- Respects, values, and leverages other customs, cultures, and values. Uses a global management team to better understand and grow the total business: Able to leverage the benefits from working in multicultural environments.
- Optimizes and integrates resources on a global basis, including manufacturing, research, and businesses across countries, and functions to increase 3M's growth and profitability.
- Satisfies global customers and markets from anywhere in the world.
- Actively stays current on world economies, trade issues, international market trends and opportunities.

Source: Margaret E. Allredge and Kevin J. Nilan, "3M's Leadership Competency Model: An Internally Developed Solution," *Human Resource Management* 39, Summer/Fall 2000, pp. 133–45. Reprinted by permission of John Wiley & Sons, Inc.

EXHIBIT | **6.11** | The Top Twenty Competencies

Achievement orientation
Concern of quality
Initiative
Interpersonal understanding
Customer-service orientation
Influence and impact
Organization awareness
Networking
Directiveness
Teamwork and cooperation
Developing others
Team leadership
Technical expertise
Information seeking
Analytical thinking
Conceptual thinking
Self-control
Self-confidence
Business orientation
Flexibility

Source: Zingheim, Ledford, & Schuster, "Competencies and Competency Models," *Raising the Bar: Using Competencies to Enhance Employee Performance* (Scottsdale, AZ: American Compensation Association, 1996).

Whom to Involve?

Like compensable factors, competencies are derived from the executive leadership's beliefs about the organization and its strategic intent. However, anecdotal evidence indicates that not all employees understand that connection. Employees at one bank insisted that processing student tuition loans was a different competency from processing auto loans. The law department at Polaroid generated a list of over 1,000 competencies they felt were unique to the law department and that created value for the organization.

Exhibit 6.12 shows part of the competencies used by a major toy company. This is one of eight competencies for the marketing department. Other departments have separate competencies. Notice the mind-numbing level of detail. Although this approach may be useful for career development, it is doubtful that all this information is useful, much less necessary, for compensation purposes. The initial promise of simplicity and flexibility in person-based systems remains unfulfilled.

Establish Certification Methods

The heart of the person-based plan is that employees get paid for the relevant skills or competencies they possess, but not necessarily the ones they use. Skill-based plans assume that possessing these skills will make it easier to match work flow with staffing levels, so whether or not an individual is *using* a particular skill on a particular day is not an issue. Competency-based plans assume—what? That all competencies are used all the time? The assumptions are not clear. What is clear, however, is the requirement that if people are to be paid based on their competencies, then there must be some way to demonstrate or certify to all concerned that a person possesses that level of competency.

However, advocates of competencies are relatively silent on the topic of certification. Although consultants discuss competencies as compatible with 360-degree feedback and personal development, they are silent on objectively certifying whether a person possesses a competency, much less how to translate the competency into pay. Competency indicators can also become obsolete as strategies shift.[29] However, the same sense of urgency to avoid obsolescence that pervades skill-based systems does not affect competency systems since competencies are less specific to a particular job or project.

Research on Competencies

Although the notion of competencies may have value in identifying what distinguishes typical from truly outstanding performance, there is debate on whether competencies can be translated into a measurable, objective basis for pay. Much of the writing on competencies describes applications and the processes for arriving at the competencies; given the abstract nature of the topic, it is not surprising that little empirical research exists.

organizational agility

the capacity to be infinitely adaptable without having to change

One area that touches on the topic is the notion of **organizational agility**, which is "the capacity to be infinitely adaptable without having to change."[30] Advocates of agile organizations propose 20 competencies grouped into five categories. These competencies are needed not just at the top of the organization; employees at all levels and locations must be able to (1) take initiative to spot threats and opportunities in the marketplace, reconfiguring organization infrastructure to focus resources when and where they are needed to deal with serious threats and opportunities (rather than waiting for permission to act); (2) rapidly redeploy whenever needed; (3) spontaneously collaborate to pool resources for quick results; (4) innovate (move beyond old solutions unless they truly fit); and (5) learn rapidly and continuously.

EXHIBIT 6.12 Product Development Competency for Marketing Department at a Toy Company

Manages the product development process by:

- Analyzing and evaluating marketplace to identify niches/opportunities
- Evaluating product/concepts
- Developing marketing strategies
- Coordinating and evaluating research/testing
- Generating product recommendations and obtaining management support
- Driving product schedules/activities

Phase I: Baseline Expectation	Phase II: Competent/Proficient	Phase III: Advanced/Coach	Phase IV: Expert/Mentor
- Analyzes market/competitive data (e.g., TRST, NPD) and provides top-line trend analysis, with supervision - Evaluates products/concepts (see Toy Viability competency) - Contributes to product brainstorming sessions - Oversees market research activities and ensures timely completion - Obtains Account Management input to the product development effort - Develops and implements marketing strategy, with supervision: product, positioning, pricing/financial, promotion, packaging, merchandising, and advertising - Facilitates cost reductions to achieve price/profit goals; ensures execution of cost meeting next steps - Ensures adherence to produce schedules - Coordinates licensor approval of product concept/models	- Monitors and analyzes market/competitive data (e.g., TRST, NPD) with minimal supervision, and provides recommendations for product development opportunities - Makes substantial contributions in product brainstorming sessions - Analyzes market research results and makes appropriate product recommendations - Partners with Account Management group to obtain their buy-in to the product development effort - Develops and implements marketing strategy, with minimal supervision - Drives cost reductions to achieve price/profit goals - Drives product schedules and resolves product scheduling issues (late delivery, late debug) - Negotiates with licensors to obtain product approvals	- Independently monitors and analyzes market/competitive data (e.g., TRST, NPD), provides recommendations for product development opportunities, and coaches others to do so - Leads and facilitates formal product brainstorming sessions - Coaches others in analyzing market research results and making product recommendations - Develops innovative marketing plans (e.g., new channels of distribution, niche markets) - Independently develops and implements marketing strategy, and coaches others to do so - Identifies/evaluates cost reduction opportunities, and coaches others to do so - Identifies and implements product schedule improvement tactics - Coaches others to manage product schedules - Coaches others in managing licensor relationships - Shares product ideas/strategies with other teams/categories	- Reviews/approves recommendations for product development opportunities - Provides short- and long-term vision and goals for developing the corporate product portfolio across categories or brands - Reviews/approves marketing strategy, and proactively adjusts strategy in response to internal/external changes - Approves cost reduction recommendations - Anticipates critical issues that may impact product schedules and develops alternate plans - Ensures on-strategy delivery

According to advocates, competencies are enhanced by the extent to which people throughout the organization are business driven, focused, generative, adaptive, and values driven.[31] The key is to assure that all employees share a common vision, have a clear understanding of the business dynamics, and know how and why their contributions make a difference.

An area of research with potential application to competencies deals with intellectual capital and knowledge management.[32] Viewing the competencies of an organization's employees as a portfolio similar to a diversified investment portfolio highlights the fact that not all competencies are unique nor equally valuable strategically.[33] The focus then changes to managing existing competencies and developing new ones in ways that maximize the overall success of the organization. As organizations globalize, they may need globally balanced values and perspectives—a "mind matrix"—that allows a transnational strategy to function.[34] The right "mind matrix" depends on the right mix of competencies, and balances the range and depth of cultural, functional, and product competencies in the global organization.[35]

At the beginning of the section on competencies, we noted that multiple perspectives exist. The topic remains in a state of flux. One study of 286 competency models found that in higher-level technical, marketing, professional, and managerial positions, the distinguishing characteristics of success were motivation, interpersonal influence, and political skills.[36] In another study of systems programmers and analysts, where logic, mathematical, and programming skills previously had been thought to be the competencies for success, the competencies that distinguished superior performers were customer-service orientation, leveraging technical information, and influencing others.[37] So the notion of using competencies for developing higher level "knowledge workers" has some appeal. It fits with the staffing strategy of "hire smart people, give them the tools, then get out of the way." Unfortunately, "hiring smart" implies that these are hard-wired abilities rather than learned behaviours. As such, these may be ideal characteristics for selecting new hires, but it may not make sense to use them for pay beyond hiring offers.[38]

The basic question remains, Is it appropriate to pay you for what I believe you would *like to do or are capable of doing* versus what you are doing? As a Nobel physicist noted, "It is difficult to predict, especially the future." Human behaviour is celebrated for its variability and unpredictability. Isn't it "likely to be more effective, for *pay purposes*, to focus on what is easily measurable and directly related to organizational effectiveness" (i.e., knowledge and skills that are task/performance related)?[39]

ONE MORE TIME: STRUCTURE

Now that we have spent three chapters examining all the trees, let's look again at the forest. The purpose of job- and person-based procedures is really very simple—to design and manage an internal pay structure that helps achieve the organization's objectives.

As with job-based evaluation, the final result of the person-based plan is an internal structure of work in the organization. This structure should be aligned with the organization's internal alignment policy, which in turn supports its business operations. Furthermore, managers must ensure that the structure *remains* internally aligned by reassessing work/skills/competencies when necessary. Failure to do so risks structures that lack work- and performance-related logic and opens the door to bias and favouritism.

ADMINISTERING THE PLAN

Whatever plan is designed, a crucial issue is the fairness of its administration. Details of the plan should be described in a manual that includes all information necessary to apply the plan, such as definitions of compensable factors, degrees, or details of skill blocks, competencies, and certification methods. The manual will help ensure that the plan is administered as its designers intended.

We have mentioned the issue of employee acceptance throughout our discussion of job analysis and job evaluation. Employee acceptance of the process is crucial if the organization is to have any hope that employees will accept the resulting pay as fair. In order to build this acceptance, communication with all employees whose jobs are part of the process used to build the structure is required. This communication may be done through informational meetings, brochures, or other devices.[40]

RESULTS: HOW USEFUL?

The criteria for evaluating the usefulness of pay structures, whether job- or person-based, are much the same: how well they achieve their objectives, as well as their reliability and validity. Although there is vast research literature on job evaluation, most of it focuses on the procedures used rather than its usefulness or effects on employee behaviours. The research treats job-based evaluation as a measurement device and considers its reliability, validity, the costs involved in its design and implementation, and its compliance with laws and regulations. In contrast, research on person-based structures tends to focus on the effects and less on procedures or on the approach as a measurement device.

Reliability of Job Evaluation Techniques

A reliable evaluation would be one in which different evaluators produce the same results. Reliability can be increased by using evaluators who are familiar with the work. Many organizations use group consensus to increase reliability. Each evaluator makes a preliminary, independent evaluation. Then, meeting as a committee, evaluators discuss their results until consensus emerges. However, some studies report that results obtained through group consensus were not significantly different from those obtained by independent evaluators or by averaging individual evaluators' results. Nevertheless, the process may matter in terms of acceptability of results. Others report that a forceful or experienced leader on the committee can sway the results.[41]

Validity/Usefulness

Validity refers to the degree to which the evaluation achieves the desired results. Validity of job evaluation has been measured by "hit rates," or agreement of results with a predetermined benchmark structure. The agreed-upon structure may be the structure found in the external market, a structure negotiated with a union, a structure defined by a committee, market rates for jobs held predominantly by men (to try to eliminate any general discrimination reflected in the market), or a combination of these categories. Studies have reported hit rates ranging from 27 to 73 percent of jobs within one class in the benchmark structure.[42] The impact of such accuracy depends on the size of the salary discrepancy between classes. If being one class away translates into several hundred dollars in lost pay, then being "close" probably doesn't count. Except to statisticians.

Studies of the degree to which different job evaluation plans produce the same results start with the assumption that if different approaches produce the same results, then those results must be accurate. In other words, there is some innate structure at large in the universe; our job is to measure it. No, wait, that's physics, isn't it?

One study looked at three different job evaluation plans applied to the same set of jobs. The study found high consistency among raters using each method, but substantial differences in the plans' impact on pay decisions. For example, when different evaluators used a custom-designed point plan, their pay recommendations for the jobs agreed in only 51 percent of jobs.[43] Some studies have found pay discrepancies of up to $427 per month depending on the method used. So it is clear that the definition of reliability needs to be broadened to include impact on pay decisions.

In another study, three plans all gave the same result (they were reliable) but all three ranked a police officer higher than a detective (not valid).[44] But TV watchers know that in police departments, the detectives outrank the uniforms. What accounts for the reliability of invalid plans? Either the compensable factors did not pick up something deemed important in the detectives' jobs, or the detectives have more power to negotiate higher wages. So, although these three plans gave the same results, it is clear that they would have little employee acceptance. At least among detectives.

Acceptability

Several devices are used to assess and improve employee acceptability. An obvious one is to include a *formal appeals process*. Employees who believe their jobs are evaluated incorrectly should be able to request reanalysis and/or skills reevaluation. Most firms respond to such requests from managers, but few extend the process to all employees, unless those employees are represented by unions who have negotiated a grievance process.[45] *Employee attitude surveys* can assess perceptions of how useful evaluation is as a management tool. A third method is to *audit* how the plan is being used. Exhibit 6.13 lists examples of audit measures used by various employers. They range from the percentage of employees who understand the reasons for evaluation to the percentage of jobs with current descriptions, to the rate of requests for revaluation.

EXHIBIT 6.13 Illustrations of Audit Indexes

A. Overall indicators.

1. Ratio of number of current descriptions to numbers of employees.
2. Number of job descriptions evaluated last year and previous year.
3. Number of jobs evaluated per unit.
   (a) Newly created jobs.
   (b) Reevaluation of existing jobs.

B. Timeliness of job descriptions and evaluations.

1. Percentage of total jobs with current descriptions.
2. Percentage of evaluation requests returned within 7 working days, within 14 working days.
3. Percentage of reevaluation requests returned with changed (unchanged) evaluations.

C. Workability and acceptability of job evaluation.

1. Percentage of employees (managers) surveyed who know the purposes of job evaluation.
2. The number of employees who appeal their job's evaluation rating.
3. The number of employees who receive explanations of the results of their reevaluation requests.

BIAS IN INTERNAL STRUCTURES

The continuing differences in jobs held by men and women, and the accompanying pay differences, have focused attention on internal structures as a possible source of discrimination. Much of this attention has been directed at job evaluation as both a potential source of bias against women and a mechanism to reduce bias.[46] It has been widely speculated that job evaluation is susceptible to gender bias; that is, whether jobs held predominantly by women are undervalued relative to jobs held predominantly by men, simply because of the jobholder's gender. But evidence does not support the proposition that the gender of an individual *jobholder* influences the evaluation of the job.[47] Additionally, there is no evidence that the job *evaluator's* gender affects the results.

However, a study found that compensable factors related to job content (such as contact with others and judgment) did reflect bias, but that others pertaining to employee requirements (such as education and experience) did not.[48]

Wages Criteria Bias.   The second potential source of bias affects job evaluation indirectly, through the current wages paid for jobs. In this case, job evaluation results may be biased if the jobs held predominantly by women are underpaid. If this is the case, and if the job evaluation is based on the current wages paid, then the job evaluation results simply mirror any bias in the current pay rates. Considering that many job evaluation plans are purposely structured to mirror the existing pay structure, it should not be surprising that the current wages for jobs influence the results of job evaluation. One study of 400 compensation specialists revealed that market data had a substantially larger effect on pay decisions than did job evaluations or current pay data.[49]

This study is a unique look at several factors that may affect pay structures. If market rates and current pay already reflect gender bias, then these biased pay rates could work indirectly through the job evaluation process to deflate the evaluation of jobs held primarily by women.[50] Clearly, the criteria used in the design of evaluation plans need to be business and work related.

Several recommendations seek to ensure that job evaluation plans are bias free. The recommendations include the following:

1. Define the compensable factors and scales to include the content of jobs held predominantly by women. For example, working conditions should include the noise and stress of office machines and the repetitive movements associated with the use of computers.
2. Ensure that factor weights are not consistently biased against jobs held predominantly by women. Are factors usually associated with these jobs always given less weight?
3. Apply the plan in as bias-free a manner as feasible. Ensure that the job descriptions are bias-free, exclude incumbent names from the job evaluation process, and train diverse evaluators.

At the risk of pointing out the obvious, all issues concerning job evaluation also apply to both skill-based and competency-based plans. For example, the acceptability of the results of skill-based plans can be studied from the perspective of measurement (reliability and validity) and administration (costs, simplicity). The various points in skill certification at which errors and biases may enter into judgment (e.g., different views of skill-block definitions, potential favouritism toward team members, defining and assessing skill obsolescence) and whether skill block points and evaluators make a difference all need to be studied. In light of the detailed bureaucracy that has grown up around job evaluation, we confidently predict a growth of bureaucratic procedures around person-based plans, too. In addition to bureaucracy to manage costs, the whole approach to certification may be fraught with potential legal vulnerabilities if employees who fail to be certified challenge the process. Unfortunately, no studies of gender effects in skill-based or competency-based plans exist. Little attention has been paid to assessor training or validating the certification process. Just as employment tests used for hiring and promotion decisions must be demonstrably free of illegal bias, it seems logical that certification procedures used to determine pay structures should face the same requirement.

◼ THE PERFECT STRUCTURE

Exhibit 6.14 contrasts job-, skill-, and competency-based approaches. Pay increases are gained via promotions to more responsible jobs under job-based structures or by acquiring more valued skills/competencies under the person-based structures. Logically, employees will focus on how to get promoted (experience, performance) or on how to acquire the required skills or competencies (training, learning).

Managers whose employers use job-based plans focus on placing the right people in the right job. A switch to skill/competency-based plans reverses this procedure. Now, managers must assign the right work to the right people, that is, those with the right skills and competencies. A job-based approach controls costs by paying only as much as the work performed is worth, regardless of any greater skills the employee may possess. So as Exhibit 6.14 suggests, costs are controlled via job rates or work assignments and budgets.

In contrast, skill/competency-based plans pay employees for the highest level of skill/competency they have achieved, *regardless of the work they perform*. This maximizes flexibility. But it also encourages all employees to become certified at top rates. Unless an employer can either control the rate at which employees can certify skill/competency mastery or employ fewer people, the organization may experience higher labour costs than competitors using job-based approaches. The key is to offset the higher rates with greater productivity. One consulting firm claims that an average company switching to a skill-based system experiences a 15 to 20 percent increase in wage rates, a 20 to 25 percent increase in training and development costs, and initial *increases* in head count to allow people to cross-train and move around.[51] But a research study found that costs were no higher.[52]

In addition to potentially higher rates and higher training costs, skill/competency plans may have the additional disadvantage of becoming as complex and burdensome as job-based plans. Additionally, questions still remain about a skill/competency system's compliance with employment standards legislation. If a female worker has a lower skill-mastery level and lower pay than a male worker who is doing the same work, this would appear to violate the requirement in all Canadian jurisdictions for equal pay for equal work. Similarly, pay equity legislation could be violated if workers in a female-dominated job of equal value to a male-dominated job are not paid equally due to a skill/competency system.

So where does all this come out? What is the best approach to pay structures, and how will we know it when we see it? The answer is, it depends. The best approach may be to provide sufficient ambiguity to afford flexibility to adapt to changing conditions. Too generic an approach may not provide sufficient detail to make a clear link between pay, work, and results; too detailed an approach may become rigid.

On the one hand, bases for pay that are too strictly defined may miss changes in work that are inevitable in a changing economy; on the other hand, bases for pay that are too vaguely defined will have no credibility with employees, will fail to signal what is really important for success, and may lead to suspicions of favouritism and bias.

This chapter concludes our section on internal alignment. Before we move on to external considerations, let's once again address the issue, So what? Why bother with a pay structure? The answer should be, Because it supports improved organization performance. An internally aligned pay structure, whether strategically loosely coupled or tightly fitting, can be designed to (1) help determine pay for the wide variety of work in the organizations, and (2) ensure that pay influences peoples' attitudes and work behaviours and directs them toward organization objectives.

EXHIBIT 6.14 Contrasting Approaches

	Job-Based	Skill-Based	Competency-Based
What is valued **Quantify the value**	■ Compensable factors ■ Factor degree weights	■ Skill blocks ■ Skill levels	■ Competencies ■ Competency levels
Mechanisms to translate into pay	■ Assign points that reflect criterion pay structure	■ Certification and price skills in external market	■ Certification and price competencies in external market
Pay structure	■ Based on job performed/market	■ Based on skills certified/market	■ Based on competency developed/market
Pay increases	■ Promotion	■ Skill acquisition	■ Competency development
Managers' focus	■ Link employees to work ■ Promotion and placement ■ Cost control via pay for job and budget increase	■ Utilize skills efficiently ■ Provide training ■ Control costs via training, certification, and work assignments	■ Be sure competencies add value ■ Provide competency-developing opportunities ■ Control costs via certification and assignments
Employee focus	■ Seek promotions to earn more pay	■ Seek skills	■ Seek competencies
Procedures	■ Job analysis ■ Job evaluation	■ Skill analysis ■ Skill certification	■ Competency analysis ■ Competency certification
Advantages	■ Clear expectations ■ Sense of progress ■ Pay based on value of work performed	■ Continuous learning ■ Flexibility ■ Reduced work force	■ Continuous learning ■ Flexibility ■ Lateral movement
Limitations	■ Potential bureaucracy ■ Potential inflexibility	■ Potential bureaucracy ■ Requires costs controls	■ Potential bureaucracy ■ Requires cost controls

CONCLUSION

This section of the book started by examining pay structures within an organization. The importance placed on internal alignment in the pay structures is a basic strategic issue. The premise underlying internal alignment is that internal pay structures need to be aligned with the organization's business strategy and values, the design of the work flow, and a concern for the fair treatment of employees. The work relationships within a single organization are an important part of internal alignment. Structures that are acceptable to the stakeholders affect satisfaction with pay, the willingness to seek and accept promotions to more responsible jobs, the effort to keep learning and undertake additional training, and the propensity to remain with the employer; they also reduce the incidence of pay-related grievances.

The techniques for establishing internally aligned structures include job analysis, job evaluation, and person-based approaches for skill/competency-based plans. Although viewed by some as bureaucratic burdens, these techniques can aid in achieving the objectives of the pay system when they are properly designed and managed. Without them, our pay objectives of improving competitiveness and fairness are more difficult to achieve.

We have now finished the first part of the book. We have discussed strategic perspectives on compensation, the key strategic issues in compensation management, and the total pay model that provides a framework for the book. Managing compensation requires creating the pay system to support the organization strategies, its culture and values, and the needs of individual employees. We examined the internal alignment of the pay structure. We discussed the techniques used to establish alignment as well as its effects on compensation objectives. The next section of the book focuses on the next strategic issue in our pay model: external competitiveness.

CHAPTER SUMMARY

1. Skill-based pay plans and competency-based pay plans are conceptually identical, but skills are very specific and competencies are more general. Skill-based pay plans are usually applied to blue-collar jobs and competency-based plans to white-collar jobs.
2. The four basic steps in skills analysis are: (1) decide what information should be collected, (2) decide what methods should be used to collect the information, (3) decide who should be involved, and (4) ensure that the results are useful for pay purposes by establishing certification methods.
3. The term *competency* means the underlying, broadly applicable knowledge, skills, and behaviours that form the foundation for successful work performance at any level of job in the organization. Core *competencies* are competencies that are linked to the mission statement that expresses the organization's philosophy, values, business strategies, and plans. *Competency sets* translate the core competencies into specific actions. *Competency indicators* are the observable behaviours that indicate the level of competency in each competency set.
4. Employee acceptance is crucial for person-based plans because it is the key to employees' perceptions of fairness regarding the pay structure. Communication with employees during the building of the structure is the most important step to employee acceptance. Other important actions to enhance acceptability are a formal appeals process, employee attitude surveys, and audits of the pay plan.
5. Two potential sources of bias in internal pay structures are (1) bias in the job evaluation of traditionally female-dominated jobs, and (2) bias in current wages that may be perpetuated when job evaluation plans are structured to mirror existing pay rates.

KEY TERMS

REVIEW QUESTIONS

1. What are the similarities in the logic underlying job-based and person-based plans?
2. What is the difference between specialist skill plans and generalist skill plans?
3. Why is there not more variation in core competencies between organizations? What does differ?
4. If you were managing employee compensation, how would you recommend that your company evaluate the usefulness of its job evaluation or person-based plans?

EXPERIENTIAL EXERCISES

1. Conduct a skill analysis and design a skill certification plan for payroll administrators.

2. Find the mission statement for an organization with which you are familiar. Define core competencies, competency sets, and competency indicators for this organization.

3. David Tyson, author of the *Canadian Compensation Handbook*, states "There are a number of problems with skill-based pay. A major one is that, in my opinion, it does not comply with pay equity legislation anywhere in Canada." (pg. 27) Familiarize yourself with the basic components of pay equity legislation by visiting the Ontario Pay Equity Commission Web site (www.gov.on.ca/lab/pec). Survey the human resource management professors at your educational institution on the question, "Do you believe that skill/competency-based pay plans are consistent with pay equity legislation?" Then conduct a debate, starting with a summary of the reasons given on both sides of this issue.

WEB EXERCISE

Leadership Competencies

The Banff Centre for Leadership (www.banffcentre.ca/departments/leadership) provides detailed competency definitions for six different leadership situations: leading strategically, leading and managing for results, leadership challenge, team leadership and facilitation, managing in the middle, and building personal leadership capacity.

Compare and contrast the competencies in each of these. How much overlap is there? What competencies are unique to each of the six different situations? If these competencies can be applied at any company, how can they be strategic (difficult to imitate or unique)?

CASE

Targeting Teachers Pay

The pay schedule shown in Exhibit 6.15 is typical of many pay plans for teachers; it contains steps by which a teacher's salary increases with each year of experience as well as with additional university credits beyond a teaching certificate.

Say that Jane begins teaching in September of the current year. She has a bachelor's degree (Group III) and no experience. She will earn $41,457 during the current school year. Next year, she will move up one step in the new schedule and earn $44,338, a raise of $2881, or 6.9 percent.

Once she has received her Master's degree or qualified as a subject specialist, she will "move over" to the next column, (Group IV). Otherwise she will stay in the Group III column and advance one step each year until she reaches step 10 when she "tops out." Note that she will receive the step increase as well as any entire schedule increases that the school board gives each year. So any increase to the entire schedule translates into a larger increase for those teachers currently being paid according to the schedule.

1. Although the stepped salary schedule has many features of a knowledge-based pay system, not everyone agrees. Is this a knowledge-based pay system? How might you change it to make it more like the person-based plans discussed in this chapter? What features would you add/drop?

2. In the pay scale in the exhibit, notice that the column differentials increase with years of experience; for instance, the difference between Group III and Group IV at one year of experience is $2567, whereas the difference at year 10 is $4088. What message do these increasing differentials send to teachers? What pay theories address this issue? How would these differentials affect teacher behaviours? How would they affect school district costs?

3. Calculate the size of the pay differential for increased seniority versus increased ueducation. What behaviours do you believe these differentials will motivate; in other words, what pays more, growing older or taking courses?

4. Pay for performance for teachers is a hot topic in many school districts. How might the salary schedule be made compatible with a performance-based pay approach? Evaluate your ideas after you have completed Part III of this book, which discusses employee contributions.

CASE

EXHIBIT 6.15 Toronto Teachers' Pay Grid ($)

	Level of Education			
# Years Teaching	*Group I*	*Group II*	*Group III*	*Group IV*
Step 0	$36,706	$38,413	$41,457	$44,491
Step 1	38,646	40,451	44,338	46,905
Step 2	40,854	42,800	47,289	49,778
Step 3	43,141	45,155	50,234	52,659
Step 4	45,701	47,809	53,342	56,003
Step 5	48,255	50,481	56,443	59,343
Step 6	50,812	53,140	59,545	62,682
Step 7	53,375	55,794	62,650	66,031
Step 8	55,933	58,458	65,752	69,369
Step 9	58,490	61,117	68,858	72,713
Step 10	61,048	63,775	71,965	76,053

Source: www.osstf.on.ca/www/services/protective/bulletins/teachers/d12_toronto.html (August 8, 2003), and the Ontario Secondary School Teachers' Federation.

Visit the Online Learning Centre at
www.mcgrawhill.ca/college/milkovich

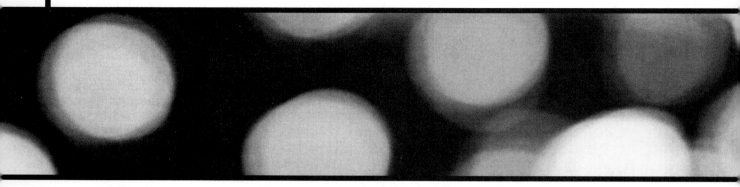

PART 2

External Competitiveness: Determining the Pay Level

Tiger Woods's golfing prowess is legendary. So are his earnings. In a single year, he won over $9 million dollars for playing (playing!) 76 rounds of golf. It took Mr. Woods 5152 strokes to win this money, or $1,783 per stroke. One of the fascinations of golf is that the more strokes you take, the less you earn. The #2 person in the PGA ranking, Phil Mickelson, managed to earn $4.8 million, but got only $856 per stroke. Other comparisons are equally fascinating. While a West Coast lifeguard earns only $800 per week, an actor who plays a lifeguard on television gets $100,000 per episode. David Letterman appears on television a few hours a week, and for this, CBS pays him $14 million a year. Compensation managers don't earn that much, no matter how well their decisions fit the organization's strategy.

Recent earnings for Mr. Woods and a host of others are shown in Exhibit II.1. To some people, these examples confirm what they always suspected: that pay is determined without apparent reason or justice. Nevertheless, there is logic. Mr. Letterman is able to command $14 million a year because (1) other networks are also interested in his services, and (2) CBS believes that his ability to attract young, hip (read: free-spending) viewers will create a stream of earnings for them that will be much greater than his pay.

The next two chapters discuss how employers set their pay level and decide forms of pay to use in comparison to their competitors. Exhibit II.2 shows that external competitiveness is the next strategic decision in the total pay model.

Two aspects of pay translate external competitiveness into practice: (1) How much to pay relative to competitors—whether to pay more than competitors, to match what they pay, or to pay less—and (2) what mix of base, bonus, stock options, benefits relative to the pay mix of competitors. In a sense, "What forms" to pay (base, bonus, benefits) are the pieces of the pie. "How much" is the size of the pie. External competitiveness includes both questions.

As we shall see in the next two chapters, a variety of answers exists. Chapter 7 discusses choosing the external competitiveness policy, the impact of that choice, and related theories and research. Chapter 8 has two parts. First, it discusses how to translate competitiveness policy into pay level and forms. Second, it discusses how to integrate information on pay level and forms with the internal structure from Part I.

EXHIBIT II.1 Who Makes How Much?

Tiger Woods	professional golfer (plus over $54 million in endorsements)	$9,000,000
Phil Mickelson	professional golfer	$4,800,000
Shaquille O'Neil	centre, LA Lakers (plus over $23 million in endorsements)	$22,000,000
Daniel and Henrik Sedin	Vancouver Canucks hockey players	(each) $1,227,500*
Jeff Bezos	CEO and founder, Amazon.com (plus stock options valued at $8 billion)	$81,840
Michael Don	CEO, France Telecom	$158,800
William Gates	chief engineer and founder, Microsoft (plus stock options valued at $70.9 billion)	$663,373
Frank Stronach	Chair, Magna International (plus over $51.8 million in stock options)	$314,080*
Belinda Stronach	CEO, Magna International (plus over $6.1 million in stock options)	$6,388,340*
Richard Dalzell	Internet technology chief, Amazon.com	$241,814
Adrienne Clarkson	governor general	$105,700*
Deborah Austin	Ontario provincial court judge	$177,583*
George W. Bush	president of the United States	$400,000
Major-General Bryan Dutton	last head of British military troops in Hong Kong; replaced by	$94,700
Major-General Zhou Borong	head of People's Liberation Army in Hong Kong	$1,730
Sandra Bullock	actress, in the movie hit Speed	$500,000
	actress, in the movie flop Speed 2	$12,500,000
"Judge Judy"	television star	$2,000,000
David Letterman	talk show host	$14,000,000
Regis Philbin	talk show host	$11,300,000
Kevin Spacey	actor, for his 16-week Broadway run of "The Iceman Cometh"	$14,755
Jack Spicer	stagehand for "The Iceman Cometh"	$46,475
Roger Martin	dean, Rotman School of Management, University of Toronto	$300,000*
William Getty	executive assistant, Ontario Elementary Teacher's Federation	$111,261*
Duncan Brown	CEO, Ontario Alcohol & Gaming Commission	$208,920*

* Canadian dollars

EXHIBIT **II.2** The Pay Model

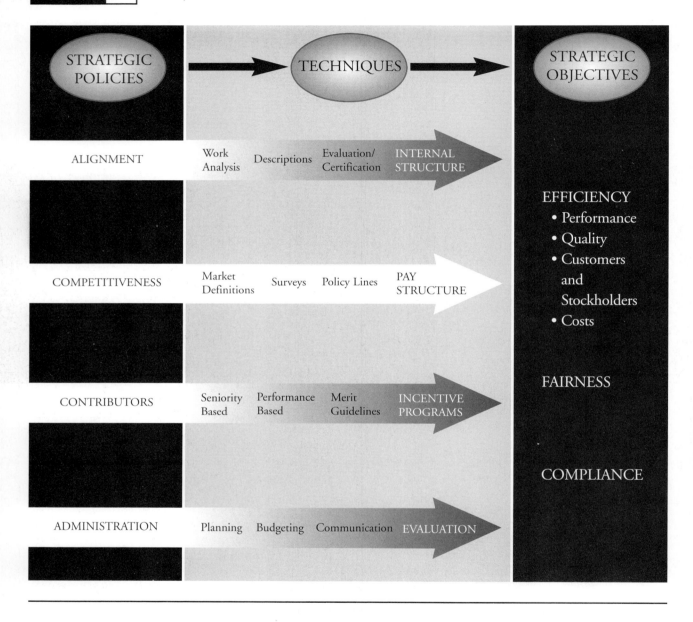

DEFINING COMPETITIVENESS

January is always a good month for travel agents in Montreal, Quebec. In addition to the permanent population eager to flee Montreal's leaden skies, graduating students from Montreal's various universities are travelling to job interviews with employers across the country—at company expense, full fare, no Saturday night stayovers required. When they return from these trips, students compare notes and find that even for people receiving the same degree in the same field from the same university, the offers vary from company to company. What explains the differences? Location has an effect: Firms in Toronto and New York City make higher offers. The work also has an effect: Jobs in employment pay a little less than jobs in compensation and employee relations. (Now aren't you glad you didn't drop this course?) And the industry to which the different firms belong has an effect: Pharmaceuticals, computer software, and petroleum firms tend to offer more than computer hardware, telecommunications, and natural resource firms.[1]

Students would like to attribute these differences to themselves: differences in grades, courses taken, interviewing skills, and so on. But as they accept offers and reject others, many companies whose offers were rejected by their first candidates now extend the identical offer to other students.

So it is hard to make the case that an individual's qualifications totally explain the offers. Why would companies extend identical offers to most candidates? And why would different companies extend different offers? This chapter discusses these choices and what difference they make for the organization.

The sheer number of economic theories related to compensation can make this chapter heavy going. Another difficulty is that the reality of pay decisions doesn't necessarily match the theories. The key to this chapter is to always ask, So what? How will this information help me? So grab the box of Timbits and let's find out.

■ COMPENSATION STRATEGY: EXTERNAL COMPETITIVENESS

pay level

■ the *average* of the array of rates paid by an employer: Σ base + bonuses + benefits + options/Σ employees

pay forms

■ the mix of the various types of payments that make up total compensation

In Part I, we looked at comparisons *inside* the organization. In external competitiveness, our second pay policy, we look at comparisons *outside* the organization—comparisons with other employers who hire the same kinds of employees. A major decision when designing a compensation strategy is whether to mirror what competitors are doing with pay. Or is there an advantage in being different? Competitiveness includes choosing the mix of pay forms (i.e., bonuses, stock options, flexible benefits) that is right for the business strategy.

External competitiveness refers to the pay relationships among organizations—the organization's pay relative to its competitors. It is expressed in practice by (1) setting a **pay level** that is above, below, or equal to competitors, and (2) by considering the mix of **pay forms** relative to those of competitors.

Both pay level and pay forms focus on two objectives: (1) to control costs and (2) to attract and retain employees.[2]

Control Costs

Pay level decisions have a significant impact on expenses. Other things being equal, the higher the pay level, the higher the labour costs:

$$\text{Labour Costs} \times \text{Pay Level} = \text{Number of Employees}$$

Furthermore, the higher the pay level relative to what competitors pay, the greater the relative costs to provide similar products or services. So you might think that all organizations would pay the same job the same rate. However, they do not. A survey of graduates of the MBA program at the Schulich School of Business at York University three months following their convocation in 2002 found that the average base salary for investment researchers was $74,750. The range of salaries for the same job ran from $40,000 to $172,000. Thus, some investment researchers were making four times what others were paid. The same work is paid differently. What could justify a pay level above whatever minimum amount is required to attract and retain investment researchers?

Attract and Retain Employees

One company may pay more because it believes its higher-paid investment researchers are more productive than those at other companies. They may be better trained; maybe they are more innovative in their research. Maybe they are less likely to quit, which saves recruiting and training costs. Different employers set different pay levels; that is, they deliberately choose to pay above or below what others are paying for the same work. That is why there is no single "going rate" in the labour market for a specific job.[3]

Not only do the rates paid for similar jobs vary between employers, a single company may set a different pay level for different job families.[4] The company in Exhibit 7.1 illustrates the point. The top chart shows that this particular company pays about 2 percent above the market for its entry-level engineer. (Market is set at zero in the exhibit.) However, they are 13 percent above the market for most of their marketing jobs and over 25 percent above the market for marketing managers. Office personnel and technicians are paid below the market. So this company uses very different pay levels for different job families.

These data are based on comparisons of *base* wage. When we look at *total compensation* in the bottom of the exhibit, a different pattern emerges. The company still has a different pay level for different job families. But when bonuses, stock options, and benefits are included, only marketing managers remain above the market. Every other job family is now substantially below the market. Engineering managers take the deepest plunge, from only 2 percent below the market to over 30 percent below.

EXHIBIT **7.1** One Company's Market Comparison: Base versus Total Compensation

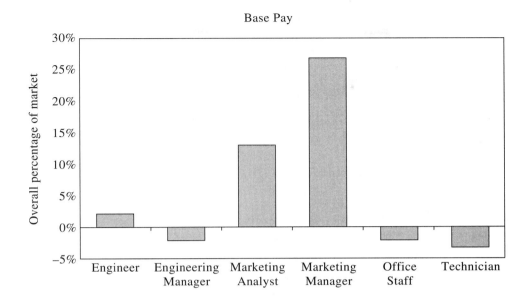

Base Pay

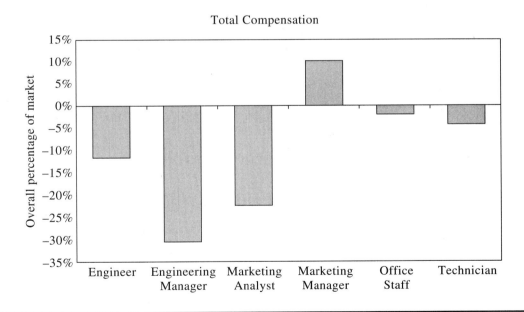

Total Compensation

The exhibit, based on actual company data, makes two points. First, companies often set different pay level policies for different job families. Second, how a company looks in comparison to the market depends on the companies they compare to and the pay forms included in the comparison. It is not clear whether this company deliberately chose to emphasize marketing managers and deemphasize engineering in its pay plan, or if it is paying the price for not hiring one of you readers to design their plan.[5] Either way, the point is that even though people love to talk about "market rates," there is no single "going rate" in the marketplace.

There is no single "going mix" of pay forms, either. Exhibit 7.2 compares the mix of pay forms for the same job (marketing manager) at two companies in the same geographic area. Both companies offer about the same total compensation. Yet the percentages allocated to base, bonuses, benefits, and options are very different.

EXHIBIT 7.2 | Two Companies, Same Total Compensation, Different Mixes ——————

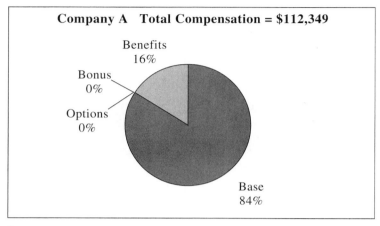

Company A   Total Compensation = $112,349

Benefits 16%
Bonus 0%
Options 0%
Base 84%

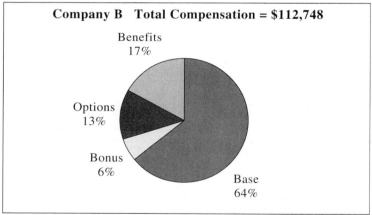

Company B   Total Compensation = $112,748

Benefits 17%
Options 13%
Bonus 6%
Base 64%

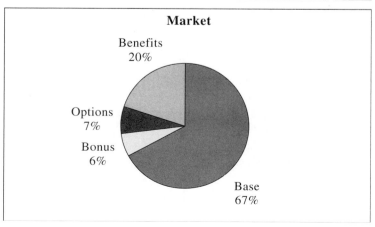

Market

Benefits 20%
Options 7%
Bonus 6%
Base 67%

WHAT SHAPES EXTERNAL COMPETITIVENESS?

Exhibit 7.3 shows the factors that affect a company's decision on pay level and mix. The factors include (1) competition in the *labour market* for people with various skills; (2) competition in the *product and service markets*, which affect the financial condition of the organization; and (3) characteristics unique to each organization and its employees, such as its business strategy, technology, and the productivity and experience of its workforce. These factors act in concert to influence pay-level and mix decisions.

LABOUR MARKET FACTORS

quoted price market

prices are specifically indicated

bourse market

prices are subject to barter or negotiation

Economists describe two basic types of markets: the **quoted price market** and the **bourse market**. Stores that label each item's price or ads that list a job opening's starting wage are examples of quoted price markets. You cannot name your own price when you order from Amazon, but Priceline says you can. However, Priceline does not guarantee that your price will be accepted, whereas an Amazon order arrives in a matter of days. In contrast to Amazon's quoted price, E-bay allows haggling over the terms and conditions until an agreement is reached. Graduating students usually find themselves in a quoted labour market, though minor haggling may occur.[6] In both the bourse and the quoted market, employers are the buyers and the potential employees are the sellers. If the inducements (total compensation) offered by the employer and the skills offered by the employee are mutually acceptable, a deal is struck. It may be formal contracts negotiated by unions, professional athletes, and executives, or it may be a brief letter, or maybe only the implied understanding of a handshake. All this activity makes up the labour market; the result is people and jobs match up at specified pay rates.

EXHIBIT 7.3 | What Shapes External Competitiveness?

LABOUR MARKET FACTORS
Nature of Demand
Nature of Supply

PRODUCT MARKET FACTORS
Degree of Competition
Level of Product Demand

ORGANIZATION FACTORS
Industry, Strategy, Size
Individual Manager

EXTERNAL COMPETITIVENESS

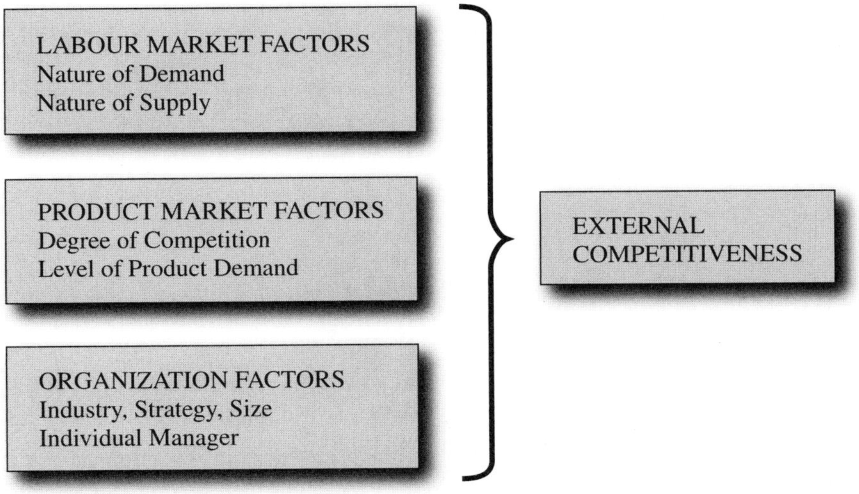

.NET WORTH   Marxian Economics and Compensation

Management consultant Niels Nielson contends that for more than a century, corporate North America has used Marxian theory in determining pay. In 1865, Marx wrote in *Das Capital* that the value of goods and services should be determined by the amount of labour that goes into them, not the marketplace. About 20 years after Marx's book, Frederick Taylor developed a system for setting the price of labour that was similar to Marx's theory. He evaluated (priced) jobs on the basis of abstract factors such as effort, skill, and working conditions. This concept was widely adopted by industry, and governments installed—and even legislated—a similar system. In 1935, Edward Hay developed the Hay point factor system based on the concept that the value of labour is determined by abstract and generic attributes of work, not supply and demand for the job.

There is noblility and purity to the ideals of compensation administration in its logic, structure, and stability, which are intended to override the turmoil of the marketplace. Even Lenin's ideal of a classless society has been adopted in our capitalist economy to minimize pay differences between employees in the same grade. However, job evaluation factors usually are vague, subjective, abstract, and often redundant, while the world is real, dynamic, and open. The attempt to produce both internal equity and external competitiveness involves compromises that violate both approaches.

Real equity is achieved by demonstrating to employees that their pay is competitive with what they would earn elsewhere. Market pricing is the nature and essence of capitalism. Admittedly, markets are imperfect, and other forces besides supply and demand are also at work in influencing prices. But, sooner or later, the market determines how much to pay. Even the largest and most powerful employers do check the market by using or conducting salary and wage surveys. The reality is that the market eventually governs. For example, a shortage of nurses caused the pay for this women's occupation to soar to such a point that men entered the profession.

Market pricing is efficient, fast, streamlined, and credible. A century of trying to make job content evaluation systems work has done little except to distort the economy. The time is long overdue to abandon these failed experiments in communist-style central planning in the capitalist labour market. Instead, compensation professionals should trust the method used to determine prices of all kinds of goods and services in a market economy: the marketplace law of supply and demand. It is better, faster, cheaper, and more effective. It is time to return to the laws of supply and demand in pricing jobs in the market.

How Labour Markets Work

Theories of labour markets usually begin with four basic assumptions:

1. Employers always seek to maximize profits.
2. People are homogeneous and therefore interchangeable; a business school graduate is a business school graduate is a business school graduate.

3. The pay rates reflect all costs associated with employment (e.g., base wage, bonuses, holidays, benefits, even training).
4. The markets faced by employers are competitive, so there is no advantage for a single employer to pay above or below the market rate.

Although these assumptions oversimplify reality, they provide a framework for understanding labour markets. As we shall see later, as reality forces us to change our assumptions, our theories change too.

Compensation managers often claim to be "market driven," that is, they pay competitively with the market or even are market leaders. Understanding how markets work requires analysis of the demand and supply of labour. The demand side focuses on the actions of the employer: how many employees they seek and what they are able and willing to pay. The supply side looks at potential employees: their qualifications and the pay they are willing to accept in exchange for their services.

Exhibit 7.4 shows a simple illustration of demand and supply for business school graduates. The vertical axis represents pay rates from $25,000 to $100,000 a year. The horizontal axis is the number of business school graduates in the market, ranging from 100 to 1,000. The line labelled "demand" is the sum of *all* employers' hiring preferences for business graduates at various pay levels. At $100,000, only 100 business graduates will be hired, because only a few firms will be able to afford them. At $25,000, companies can afford to hire 1,000 business graduates. However, as we look at the line labelled "supply," we see that there aren't 1,000 business graduates willing to be hired at $25,000. In fact, only 100 are willing to work for $25,000. As pay rates rise, more graduates become interested in working, so the labour supply line slopes upward. The point where the lines for labour demand and labour supply cross determines the market rate. In this illustration, the interaction among all employers and all business graduates determines the $50,000 market rate. Because any single employer can hire all the business graduates it wants at $50,000, and all business graduates are of equal quality (assumption #2), there is no reason for any wage other than $50,000 to be paid.

EXHIBIT 7.4 Supply and Demand for Business School Graduates in the Short Run

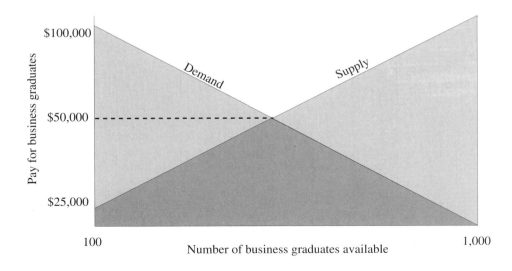

Labour Demand

So, if $50,000 is the market-determined rate for business graduates, how many business graduates will a specific employer hire? The answer requires an analysis of labour demand. In the short term, an employer cannot change any other factor of production (i.e., technology, capital, or natural resources). Thus, its level of production can change only if it changes the level of human resources. Under such conditions, a single employer's demand for labour coincides with the marginal product of labour.

Marginal Product

marginal product of labour

◾ the additional output associated with the employment of one additional human resources unit, with other production factors held constant

Assume that two business graduates form a consulting firm that provides services to 10 clients. The firm hires a third person who brings in five more clients. The **marginal product of labour** (the change in output associated with the additional unit of labour) of employing the third business graduate is five. But adding a fourth business graduate generates only four new clients. This diminishing marginal productivity results from the fact that each additional graduate has a progressively smaller share of the other factors of production with which to work. In the short term, other factors of production (e.g., office space, number of computers, telephone lines) are fixed. As more business graduates are brought into the firm without changing other production factors, the marginal productivity must eventually decline.

Marginal Revenue

marginal revenue of labour

◾ the additional revenue generated when the firm employs one additional unit of human resources, with other production factors held constant

Now let's look at **marginal revenue of labour**. Marginal revenue is the money generated by the sale of the marginal product; the additional output from the employment of one additional person. In the case of the consulting firm, it's the revenues generated by each additional business graduate. If the graduate's marginal revenue exceeds $50,000, profits are increased by the additional hiring. Conversely, if marginal revenue is less than $50,000, the employer would lose money on the last hire. Recall that our first labour market theory assumption is that employers seek to maximize profits. Therefore, the employer will continue to hire graduates until the marginal revenue generated by that last hire is equal to the costs associated with employing that graduate. Because other potential costs will not change in the short run, the level of demand that maximizes profits is that level at which the marginal revenue of the last hire is equal to the wage rate for that hire.

Exhibit 7.5 shows the connection between the labour market model and conditions facing a single employer. On the left is the same supply and demand model from Exhibit 7.4 showing that pay level ($50,000) is determined by the interaction of *all employers'* demand for business graduates. The right side of the exhibit shows supply and demand for an *individual employer*. At the market-determined rate ($50,000), the individual employer can hire as many business graduates as it wants. Therefore, supply is now an unlimited horizontal line. However, the demand line still slopes downward. The two lines intersect at 15. So for this employer, the marginal revenue of the 15th graduate is $50,000. The marginal revenue of the 16th graduate is less than $50,000 and so will not add enough revenue to cover costs. The point on the graph at which the incremental income from hiring the graduate—the *marginal revenue product*—equals the wage rate for that graduate is 15.[7]

A manager using the marginal revenue product model must do only two things: (1) determine the pay level set by market forces and (2) determine the marginal revenue generated by each new hire. This will tell the manager how many people to hire. Simple? Of course not.

The model provides a valuable analytical framework, but it oversimplifies the real world. In most organizations, it is almost impossible to quantify the goods or services produced by an individual employee, since most production is through joint efforts of employees with a variety of

EXHIBIT | **7.5** | Supply and Demand at the Market and Individual Employer Level ———————

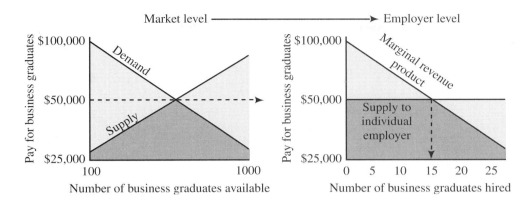

———

skills. Even in settings that use piece rates (i.e., 50 cents for each soccer ball sewn), it is hard to separate the contributions of labour from those of other resources (capital and raw materials).

So neither the marginal product nor the marginal revenue is directly measurable. However, managers do need some measure that reflects value. In the last two chapters, we discussed compensable factors, skill, and competencies. If compensable factors define what organizations value in work, then job evaluation reflects the job's contribution to the organization and may be viewed as a proxy for marginal revenue product. However, compensable factors are usually defined by organizations as input (skills required, problem solving required, responsibilities), rather than as the value of the output. This same logic applies to skills and competencies.

Labour Supply

We have already pointed out that in perfectly competitive markets, an individual employer faces a horizontal supply; that is, the market determines the price, and the individual employer can hire all the employees it wants, at that price. Now let us look more closely at the assumptions about the behaviour of potential employees. This model assumes that many people are seeking jobs, that they possess accurate information about all job openings, and that no barriers to mobility (discrimination, licensing provisions, or union membership requirements) between jobs exist.

As in the analysis of labour demand, these assumptions greatly simplify the real world. As the assumptions change, so does the supply. For example, the upward-sloping supply assumes that as pay increases, more people will be willing to take a job. But, if unemployment rates are low, offers of higher pay may not increase supply—everyone who wants to work is already working. If competitors quickly match a higher offer, the employer may face a higher pay level but no increase in supply, so that it ends up paying more for the employees it already has, but is still shorthanded.

An employer who dominates the local labour market, such as Algoma Steel in Sault Ste. Marie, Ontario, may also find that raising wages doesn't necessarily attract more applicants, simply because the supply has dried up. People who are conveniently located to Algoma Steel and interested in work are already there. Any additional applicants must be induced to enter the labour supply, perhaps from schools, retirement, or more distant areas. So a dominant employer has a relatively free hand in determining pay levels, since few local labour market competitors exist. However, once the local labour supply is exhausted, small increases in the pay levels may not attract more applicants. The supply still slopes upward, but it may take on the shape of a "step" function due to the large pay increases needed to attract additional people. Although many firms find lowering the job requirements and hiring less-skilled workers a better choice than raising wages, this choice incurs increased training costs (which were included in assumption #3).

MODIFICATIONS TO THE DEMAND SIDE

The story is told of the economics professor and the student who were strolling through campus. "Look," the student cried, "there's a $100 bill on the path!"

"No, that cannot be," the wiser head replied. "If there were a $100 bill, someone would have picked it up."

The point of the story is that economic theories frequently must be revised to account for reality. When we change our focus from all the employers in an economy to a *particular* employer, models must be modified to help us understand what actually occurs.

A particularly troublesome issue for economists is why an employer would pay more than what theory states is the market-determined rate. Exhibit 7.6 looks at three modifications to the model that address this phenomenon: compensating differentials, efficiency wage, and signalling.

Compensating Differentials Theory

compensating differentials theory

higher wages must be offered to compensate for negative features of jobs

More than 200 years ago, Adam Smith argued that individuals consider the "whole of the advantages and disadvantages of different employments" and make decisions based on the alternative with the greatest "net advantage."[8] **Compensating differentials theory** says that if a job has negative characteristics, that is, if the necessary training is very expensive (medical school), job security is tenuous (stockbrokers), working conditions are disagreeable (highway construction), or chances of success are low (professional sports), then employers must offer higher wages to compensate for these negative features.

Such compensating differentials explain the presence of various pay rates in the market. Although the notion is appealing, it is hard to document, due to the difficulties in measuring and controlling all the factors that go into a net advantage calculation.

EXHIBIT 7.6 Labour Demand Theories and Implications

Theory	Prediction	So What?
Compensating differentials	Work with negative characteristics requires higher pay to attract workers.	Job evaluation and compensable factors must capture these negative characteristics.
Efficiency wage	Above-market wages will improve efficiency by attracting workers who will perform better and be less willing to leave.	Staffing programs must have the capability of selecting the best employees; work must be structured to take advantage of employees' greater efforts.
Signalling	Pay policies signal the kinds of behaviour the employer seeks.	Pay practices must recognize desired behaviours with more pay, larger bonuses, and other forms of compensation.

Efficiency Wage Theory

efficiency wage theory

high wages may increase efficiency and lower labour costs by attracting higher-quality applicants who will work harder

Efficiency wage theory says that sometimes high wages may increase efficiency and actually lower labour costs if they:

1. Attract higher-quality applicants.
2. Lower turnover.
3. Increase worker effort.
4. Reduce "shirking "(what economists say when they mean "screwing around").
5. Reduce the need to supervise employees (academics say "monitoring").

So, basically, efficiency increases by hiring better employees or motivating present employees to work smarter or harder. The underlying assumption is that pay level determines effort—again, an appealing notion that is difficult to document.

There is some research on efficiency wage theory.[9] One study looked at shirking behaviour by examining employee discipline and wages in several auto plants. Higher wages were associated with lower shirking, measured as the number of disciplinary layoffs. Shirking was also lower when high unemployment made it more difficult for fired or disciplined employees to find another job. So, although the higher wages cut shirking, the authors were unable to say whether it was cut enough to offset the higher wage bill.[10]

Do higher wages actually attract more qualified applicants? Research says yes.[11] But they also attract more unqualified applicants. Few companies evaluate their recruiting programs well enough to show whether they do in fact choose only superior applicants from the larger pool. So an above-market wage does not guarantee a more productive workforce.

Does an above-market wage allow an organization to operate with fewer supervisors? Some research evidence says yes. For example, a study of hospitals found that those that paid high wages to staff nurses employed fewer nurse supervisors.[12] The researchers did not speculate on whether the higher wages attracted better nurses or caused average nurses to work harder, nor whether the hospital was able to reduce its overall nursing costs.

Notice that all the discussion so far has dealt with pay level. What forms to pay, the mix question, is virtually ignored in these theories. The simplifying assumption is that the pay level includes the value of different forms. Abstracted away is the distinct possibility that some people find more performance-based bonus pay or better health insurance more attractive. Signalling theory is more useful in understanding what pay mix influences.

Signalling Theory

signalling theory

pay levels and pay mix are designed to signal desired employee behaviours

Signalling theory says that employers deliberately design pay levels and mix as part of a strategy that signals to both prospective and current employees what kinds of behaviours are sought.[13] A policy of paying below the market for base pay yet offering generous bonuses or training opportunities sends a different signal, and presumably attracts different people, than a policy of matching market wage with no performance-based pay. An employer who combines lower base with high bonuses may be signalling that it wants employees who are risk takers. The proportion of people within the organization who are eligible for bonuses signals whether the same pay system is geared to all employees or to managers only and helps to communicate performance expectations. Check out Exhibit 7.3 again. It shows a breakdown of forms of pay for two competitors, as well as their relationship to the market. The pay mix at Company A emphasizes base (84 percent) more than at Company B (63.4 percent) or the market average (68 percent). Company A pays relatively smaller bonuses, no stock options, and somewhat lighter benefits. Company B's mix is closer to the market average. What is the message that A's pay mix is communicating? Which message appeals to you, A's or B's? The astute reader will note that at A, you can earn the $112,349 with very little apparent link to performance. Looks secure. Maybe just showing up is enough. Whereas for B, earning the $112,748 requires performance bonuses and options as well.

Riskier? Why would anyone work at B without extra returns for the riskier pay? Without a premium, it is surprising that B is able to attract and retain employees. Maybe B has interesting projects, flexible schedules, or more opportunity for promotion.

It may be that in the absence of complete and accurate information about the job, applicants make inferences about pay mix and nonmonetary elements (colleagues, job assignments) based on what they know about an employer's relative *pay level*. If this is so, then pay level signals a whole raft of information, both intended and unintended, accurate and inaccurate.

A study of college students approaching graduation found that both pay level and mix affected their job decisions.[14] Students wanted jobs that offered high pay, but they also showed a preference for individual-based (rather than team-based) pay, fixed (rather than variable) pay, job-based (rather than skill-based) pay, and flexible benefits. Job seekers were rated on various personal dimensions—materialism, confidence in their abilities, and risk aversion—which were related to pay preferences. Pay level was most important to materialists and less important to those who were risk averse. So applicants appear to select among job opportunities based on the perceived match between their personal dispositions and the nature of the organization, as signalled by the pay system. Both pay level and pay mix send a signal.

Signalling works on the supply side of the model, too, since suppliers of labour signal to potential employers. People who are better trained, have higher grades in relevant courses, and/or have related work experience signal to prospective employers that they are likely to be better performers. (Presumably they signal with the same degree of accuracy as employers.) So both characteristics of the applicants (degrees, grades, experience) and organization decisions about pay level (lead, match, lag) and mix (higher bonuses, benefit choices) act as signals that help communicate.

■ MODIFICATIONS TO THE SUPPLY SIDE

Three theories shown in Exhibit 7.7—reservation wage, human capital, and job competition—focus on understanding employee behaviour rather than employers—the supply side of the model.

Reservation Wage Theory

reservation wage theory

■ job seekers have a reservation wage level below which they will not accept a job

Economists are renowned for their great sense of humour. So it is not surprising that they describe pay as "noncompensatory,"[15] since **reservation wage theory** says that job seekers have a reservation wage level below which they will not accept a job offer, no matter how attractive the other job attributes. If pay level does not meet their minimum standard, no other job attributes can make up (i.e., compensate) for this inadequacy. Other theorists go a step further and say that some job seekers—satisfiers—take the first job offer they get where the pay meets their reservation wage. A reservation wage may be above or below the market wage. The theory seeks to explain differences in workers' responses to offers.

Human Capital Theory

human capital theory

■ higher earnings are made by people who improve their potential productivity by acquiring education, training, and experience

Human capital theory, perhaps the most influential economic theory for explaining pay level differences, is based on the premise that higher earnings flow to those who improve their potential productivity by investing in themselves (by acquiring additional education, training, and experience).[16] The theory assumes that people are in fact paid at the value of their marginal product. Improving productive abilities by investing in training or even in one's physical health will increase one's marginal product. The value of an individual's skills and abilities is a function of the time, expense, and resources expended to acquire them. Consequently, jobs that require long

| EXHIBIT 7.7 | Supply Side/ Theories and Implications |

Theory	Prediction	So What?
Reservation wage	Job seekers will not accept jobs whose pay is below a certain wage, no matter how attractive other job aspects.	Pay level will affect ability to recruit
Human capital	The value of an individual's skills and abilities is a function of the time and expense required to acquire them.	Higher pay is required to induce people to train for more difficult jobs.
Job competition	Workers compete through qualifications for jobs with established wages	As hiring difficulties increase, employers should expect to spend more to train new hires.

and expensive training (engineers, physicians) should receive higher pay levels than jobs that require less investment (clerical workers, elementary school teachers). As pay level increases, the number of people willing to overcome these barriers increases, which creates an upward-sloping supply.

So brain beats brawn. But there is a limit: Getting a PhD is not as sound an investment as getting a bachelor's and/or master's degree. Researchers also find that different types of education get different levels of pay. Degrees that require technical and software skills earn more than just any old university degree. But again, reality is complex. It is hard to believe that top managers' wages are increasing relative to others because bosses are more computer literate and are doing their own word processing and spreadsheets. It may be that recent technology changes have created exceptional demand not only for the power Web designers but also for managers with technical as well as "people skills." If so, then people with the ability to work with others, identify new opportunities, and innovate, coupled with new technological skills, should be paid even more than people with technological skills alone.

Job Competition Theory

job competition theory

workers compete through qualifications for jobs with established wages

A variation of the human capital model is the **job competition theory**, which says that workers do not compete for pay in labour markets. Rather, pay for jobs is "quoted" and a pool of applicants develops. Individuals in the pool are ranked by prospective employers according to the quality of their human capital (i.e., skills, abilities, and experience). As the employer dips further and further into the applicant pool, individuals require more training and are less productive, even though they receive the same pay as the higher-ranked applicant would have. Accordingly, the total cost (pay plus training) associated with each additional unit of labour in the pool increases as the market demand increases. This variation could explain the identical offers received by second- or third-choice students after first-choice candidates have rejected them.

A number of additional factors affect the supply of labour. Geographic barriers to mobility between jobs, union requirements, lack of information about job openings, the degree of risk involved, and the degree of unemployment also influence labour markets.

■ PRODUCT MARKET FACTORS AND ABILITY TO PAY

The supply and demand for labour are major determinants of an employer's pay level. However, any organization must generate, over time, enough revenue to cover expenses, including compensation. It follows that an employer's pay level is constrained by its ability to compete in the product/service market. So product market conditions determine to a large extent what the organization can afford to pay.

Product demand and the degree of competition are the two key product market factors. Both affect the ability of the organization to change what it charges for its products and services. If prices cannot be changed without decreasing sales, then the ability of the employer to set a higher pay level is constrained. For many years, North American automakers solved this affordability dilemma by routinely passing on increased pay in the form of higher car prices. Although competition among the "Big Three" automakers existed, they all passed on the pay increases. But global competitive pressures changed all this. Japanese automakers such as Toyota and Honda produced better-quality cars at lower cost. Faced with lower customer demand for their cars, North American automakers responded by restructuring. Some auto workers took pay cuts, accepted smaller wage increases, and agreed to job changes intended to improve productivity. The process is still continuing, with the result that both domestic and imported autos are of much better quality today than they were 10 years ago.

Product Demand.   Although labour market conditions (and legal requirements) put a floor on the pay level required to attract sufficient employees, the product market puts a lid on the maximum pay level that an employer can set. If the employer pays above the maximum, it must either pass on the higher pay level to consumers through price increases or hold prices fixed and allocate a greater share of total revenues to cover labour costs.

Degree of Competition.   Employers in highly competitive markets such as manufacturers of automobiles or generic drugs are less able to raise prices without loss of revenues. At the other extreme, single sellers of a Lamborghini or the drug Viagra are able to set whatever price they choose. However, too high a price often invites the eye of political candidates and government regulators.

Other factors besides product market conditions affect pay level. Some of these have already been discussed. The productivity of labour, the technology employed, the level of production relative to plant capacity available—all affect compensation decisions. These factors vary more across than within industries. The technologies employed and consumer preferences may vary between auto manufacturers, but the differences are relatively small when compared to the technologies and product demand of auto manufacturers versus the oil or financial industry.

A Dose of Reality: What Managers Say

Discussions with managers provide insight into how all of these economic factors translate into actual pay decisions. In one study, a number of scenarios were presented in which unemployment, profitability, and labour market conditions varied.[17] The managers were asked to make wage adjustment recommendations for several positions. Level of unemployment made almost no difference. One manager was incredulous at the suggestion: "You mean take advantage of the fact that there are a lot of people out of work?" (She must not have taken Economics 101.) The company's profitability was considered a factor for higher management in setting the overall pay budget but not something managers consider for individual pay adjustments. Although numerous indicators of ability to pay were mentioned, what the decision boiled down to was, "Whatever the chief financial officer says we can afford!" Managers were sympathetic to a company forced to pay less due to its own financial circumstances, but if a company had the resources, they thought it shortsighted to pay less, even though market conditions would have permitted lower pay. This mind-set probably helps explain wages' "downward stickiness," that pay goes up more easily than it falls. In direct contradiction to efficiency wage theory, managers believed that problems attracting and keeping people were the result of poor management rather than poor compensation. The managers did not recommend increasing wages to solve these problems. Instead, they offered the opinion that, "supervisors try to solve with money their difficulties with managing people."[18]

Another reality check comes from the low-wage, low-skill segment of the workforce, working at hotels, fast-food restaurants, food processors, or retail outlets. With unemployment low and turnover high, many employers have found it more useful to provide nonwage services to their employees rather than increase base pay. For example, McDonald's offers 50 percent food discounts for workers' families. Marriot offers a hotline to social workers who assist with child care and transportation crises. English language and citizenship courses are offered for recent immigrants. Seminars cover how to manage your chequebook and your life. This approach changes the mix from all base to base plus benefits and services.

Why do employers provide services rather than a wage increase? They claim that low-wage, low-skill employees value these services more than a wage increase. They would be unable to locate and purchase these services on their own, even if they had more money. Many of these services are tax-free, whereas wage increases are taxed. Additionally, because of competition for employees, a wage increase would likely be quickly matched by competitors. So everyone would be paying more but getting no advantage from it.[19]

The point is not that our theories are useless when applied to specific situations. Rather, the point is that reality is complex, and theories can help us better understand these complexities. But, in the day-to-day world, more than money matters.

ORGANIZATION FACTORS

Although product and labour market conditions create a range of possibilities within which managers create a policy on external competitiveness, organizational factors influence pay level and mix decisions, too.[20]

Industry

The industry in which an organization competes dictates the technologies used. Labour-intensive industries such as education and services tend to pay lower than technology-intensive industries such as petroleum or pharmaceuticals. On the other hand, professional services such as consulting firms pay well. The importance of qualifications and experience tailored to particular technologies is often overlooked in theoretical analysis of labour markets. But machinists and millwrights who build cars for General Motors in Oshawa, Ontario, have very different qualifications from those machinists and millwrights who build airplanes for Bombardier in Quebec.[21]

Employer Size

There is consistent evidence that large organizations tend to pay more than small ones. A study of manufacturing firms found that firms with 100 to 500 workers paid 6 percent higher wages than did smaller firms; firms of more than 500 workers paid 12 percent more than did the smallest firms.[22]This relationship between organization size, ability to pay, and pay level, is consistent with economic theory. It says that talented individuals have a higher marginal value in a larger organization because they can influence more people and decisions, which leads to more profits. Compare the advertising revenue that David Letterman can bring to CBS versus the potential revenue to station CHEX if his late-night show were seen only in Peterborough, Ontario. No matter how cool he is in Peterborough, CHEX could not generate enough revenue to be able to afford to pay Mr. Letterman $14 million; but CBS can. However, theories are less useful for explaining why practically everyone at bigger companies such as CBS, including janitors and compensation managers, is paid more. It seems unlikely that everyone has Letterman's impact on revenues.

People's Preferences

What pay forms (health insurance, eye care, bonuses, pensions) do employees really value? What forms should be changed (or started) to improve their value to employees? Better understanding of employee preferences is increasingly important in determining external competitiveness. Markets, after all, involve both employers' and employees' choices.[23] However, there are substantial difficulties in reliably measuring preferences. Who among us would be so crass as to (publicly) rank money over cordial co-workers or challenging assignments in response to the survey question, "What do you value most in your work?"

Organization Strategy

A variety of pay level and mix strategies exists. Some employers adopt a low-wage–no-mix strategy; they compete by producing goods and services with as little total compensation as possible. Nike and Reebok reportedly do this. Others select a low-base–high-services strategy. The Marriotts and McDonald's of the world do this. Still others use a high-base–high-services approach. Medtronic's "Fully present at work" approach is an example of high-base–high-services. Obviously, these are extremes on a continuum of possibilities.

■ RELEVANT MARKETS

Economists take "the market" for granted. As in, "the market determines wages." This strikes compensation managers as bizarrely abstract. They consider defining the relevant market a big part of figuring out how much to pay.

Although the notion of a single homogeneous labour market may be an interesting analytical device, each organization operates in many labour markets, each with unique demand and supply. Consequently, managers must define the markets that are relevant for pay purposes and establish the appropriate competitive positions in these markets. The three factors usually used to determine the relevant labour markets are the occupation (skill/knowledge required), geography (willingness to relocate and/or commute), and competitors (other employers in the same product/service and labour markets).

Occupations

The skills, knowledge, and qualifications required in an occupation are important because they tend to limit mobility among other occupations.[24] Qualifications include not only training and education, but also licensing and certification requirements. Accountants, for example, cannot become doctors without going to medical school. However, unless they bill themselves as *certified* public accountants, doctors would break no laws if they sold accounting services.

Geography

Qualifications interact with geography to further define the scope of the relevant labour markets. Top management is recruited globally; software engineers, due to their high demand, also are recruited globally. Most degreed professionals (accountants, HR specialists) typically are recruited nationally or regionally. Technicians, craftspeople, and operatives usually are recruited regionally; office workers are recruited locally. However, the geographic scope of a market is not fixed. It changes in response to workers' willingness to relocate or commute certain distances. This propensity to be mobile in turn may be affected by personal and economic circumstances as well as the employer's pay level. Local markets can even be shaped by the availability of convenient public transportation.

As Exhibit 7.8 shows, pay differentials vary between localities. A job that averages $67,200 nationally can range from $54,030 in Beausejour, Manitoba, to $74,790 in Baker Lake, Nunavut. However (there is always a however), some new findings suggest that larger firms ignore local market conditions.[25] Rather, they emphasize internal alignment across geographic locations to facilitate the use of virtual teams. Turns out that team members in different locations compare their pay. What a surprise!

Product Market Competitors

In addition to the occupation and geography, the industry in which the employer competes also affects the relevant labour markets by relating the qualifications required to particular technologies. Product market comparisons also focus on comparative labour costs.

Defining the Relevant Market

How do employers choose their relevant market? Surprisingly little research has been done on this issue. But, if the markets are incorrectly defined, the estimates of competitors' pay rates will be incorrect and the pay level and mix inappropriately established.

Two studies do shed some light on this issue.[26] They conclude that managers look at both their *competitors*—their products, location, and size—and the *jobs*—the skills and knowledge

---

EXHIBIT 7.8 | Pay Differences by Location

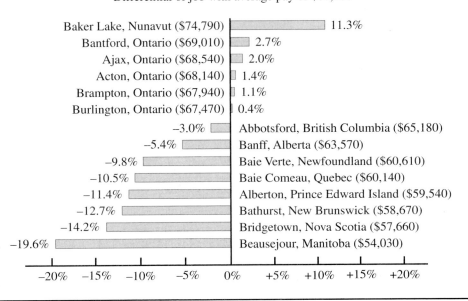

Differential of job with average pay of $67,200

required, and their importance to the organization's success (e.g., lawyers in law firms, software engineers at Microsoft). So, depending on its location and size, a company may be deemed a relevant comparison even if it is not a product market competitor. For example, an accounting firm in Sault Ste. Marie, Ontario, would be foolish to set pay rates for new accountants without knowing what Algoma Steel is paying its accountants.

The data from product market competitors (as opposed to labour market competitors) are likely to receive greater weight when:

1. Employee skills are specific to the product market (recall the differences in Bombardier millwrights versus GM millwrights).
2. Labour costs are a large share of total costs.
3. Product demand is responsive to price changes; that is, people won't pay $4.50 for a bottle of Leinenkugel; they'll have Molson's instead.
4. The supply of labour is not responsive to changes in pay (recall the earlier low-wage/low-skill example).

On the other hand, labour market comparisons gain importance if the organization is having difficulty attracting and retaining employees (e.g., keeping young lawyers from leaving law firms for startups).

Compensation theories offer some help in understanding the variations in pay levels we observe between employers. They are less helpful in understanding differences in the mix of pay forms. Relevant markets are shaped by pressures from the labour and product market and the organization. But so what? How, in fact, do managers set pay-level and pay-mix policy, and what difference does it make? In the remainder of this chapter, we will discuss these two issues.

■ COMPETITIVE PAY POLICY ALTERNATIVES

Recall that pay level is the average of the array of rates inside an organization. There are three conventional pay-level policies: to lead, to meet, or to follow competition. Newer policies emphasize flexibility: among policies for different employee groups, among pay forms for individual employees, and among elements of the employee relationship they wish to emphasize in their external competitiveness policy.

How do managers choose a policy?   A 1948 survey found that the most important factors in setting pay-level policies were rates paid by other employers in the area or industry, and union pressures.[27] The least important factors were the firm's financial position and company profits. When that survey was done, heavy manufacturing dominated the economy. By the early 1980s, however, the economy was transforming to an emphasis on knowledge workers. A 1983 Conference Board survey reported a shift in the relative importance of pay-setting factors.[28] Industry patterns had dropped to fourth place, whereas a firm's specific financial situation was most important.

We expect that many of our readers consider 1983 as ancient as 1948. We hope that one of them will do a new survey. Although the factors considered in setting pay level may be stable, their relative importance varies over time. It would be interesting to rank the factors in the current globalizing economy.

What difference does the pay level policy make?   The basic premise is that the competitiveness of pay will affect the organization's ability to achieve its compensation objectives, which in turn will affect the organization's performance. The probable effects of alternative policies are shown in Exhibit 7.9 and discussed in more detail below. The problem with much pay level research is that it focuses on base pay and ignores bonuses, incentives, options, employment security, benefits, or other forms of pay. Yet the exhibits and discussion in this chapter should have

EXHIBIT **7.9** Probable Relationships between External Pay Policies and Objectives

Policy	Compensation Objectives				
	Ability to Attract	Contain Ability to Retain	Reduce Labour Costs	Pay Dissatisfaction	Increase Productivity
Pay above market (lead)	+	+	?	+	?
Pay with market (match)	=	=	=	=	?
Pay below market (lag)	–	?	+	–	?
Hybrid policy	?	?	+	?	+
Employer of choice	+	+	+	–	?

convinced you that base pay represents only a portion of compensation. Comparisons on base alone can mislead. In fact, managers seem to believe they get more bang for the buck by allocating dollars away from base pay and into variable forms that more effectively shape employee behaviour.[29]

Pay with Competition (Match)

Given the choice to match, lead, or lag, the most common policy is to match rates paid by competitors.[30] Managers historically justify this policy by saying that failure to match competitors' rates would cause dissatisfaction among present employees and limit the organization's ability to recruit. Many nonunionized companies tend to match or even lead competition to head off unions.[31] A pay-with-competition policy tries to ensure that an organization's wage costs are approximately equal to those of its product competitors and that its ability to attract applicants will be approximately equal to its labour market competitors. Although this policy avoids placing an employer at a disadvantage in pricing products, it may not provide an employer with a competitive advantage in its labour markets. Classical economic models predict that employers will meet competitive wages.

Lead Policy

A lead policy maximizes the ability to attract and retain quality employees and minimizes employee dissatisfaction with pay. It also may offset less attractive features of the work, à la Adam Smith's "net advantage." Combat pay premiums paid to military personnel offset some of the risk of being killed. The higher pay offered by brokerage firms offsets the risk of being fired when the market tanks.

As noted earlier, sometimes an entire industry can pass high pay rates on to consumers if pay is a relatively low proportion of total operating expenses or if the industry is highly regulated. But what about specific firms within a high-pay industry? Do any advantages actually accrue to them? If all firms *in the industry* have similar technologies and operating expenses, then the lead policy must provide some competitive advantage that offsets the higher costs.

A number of researchers have linked high wages to ease of attraction, reduced vacancy rates and training time, and better-quality employees.[32] Research also suggests that high pay levels reduce turnover and absenteeism. Several studies found that the use of variable pay (bonuses and long-term incentives) is related to an organization's improved financial performance, but that pay level is not.[33]

A lead policy can have negative effects, too. It may force the employer to increase the wages of current employees, too, to avoid internal misalignment and murmuring against the employer. Additionally, a lead policy may mask negative job attributes that contribute to high turnover later on (e.g., lack of challenging assignments or hostile colleagues). Remember the managers' view that high turnover was likely to be a managerial problem rather than a compensation problem.[34]

Lag Policy

A policy to pay below market rates may hinder a firm's ability to attract potential employees. However, if pay level is lagged in return for the promise of higher future returns (e.g., stock ownership in a high-tech startup firm), such a promise may increase employee commitment and foster teamwork, which may increase productivity. Additionally, it is possible to lag competition on pay level but to lead on other returns from work (e.g., hot assignments, desirable location, outstanding colleagues, cool tools).

Flexible Policies

In practice, many employers go beyond a single choice among the three policy options. They may vary the policy for different occupational families, as did the company in Exhibit 7.2. Or they may vary the policy for different forms of pay, as did the companies back in Exhibit 7.3. One insurance company describes its policy: "It is our goal to position ourselves competitively above market value in total compensation, slight-to-somewhat-below in base salary, and well-above average in incentive compensation."[35] Praxair offers employees the opportunity to earn a bonus of up to 40 days' pay if the division's operating profits exceed certain targets. However, Praxair repositioned its base pay to 5 percent below its previous "match" policy. So, in effect, Praxair lags the market, but pays a bonus in good years that yields a slight lead position. Praxair's hybrid policy is intended to focus employee attention on the firm's financial performance and motivate productivity improvements. It also signals to potential job seekers that Praxair wants people willing to perform and able to tolerate some risk. In the meantime, the 5 percent lag helps control labour costs.

Limited attention has been devoted to pay mix policies. Some obvious alternatives include *performance driven*, *market match*, *work life balance*, and *security*. Exhibit 7.10 illustrates these four alternatives. Incentives and stock options make up a greater percentage of total compensation in *performance driven* than in the other three. The *market match* simply mimics the pay mix competitors are paying. How managers actually make these mix decisions is a ripe issue for more research.

How managers position their organization's pay against competitors is changing. Some alternatives that are emerging focus on total returns from work (beyond financial returns) and offering people choices among these returns. Rather than flexible, perhaps a better term would be "fuzzy" policies.

Employer of Choice.   An employer of choice policy goes beyond pay level and forms to focus on all returns from employment. Just as companies compete for customers by offering a choice of product features, quality, and services at the right price, some employers also compete for employees by offering choices in the mix of base salary, incentives, benefits, and work environment. For example, IBM leads its competitors with its extensive training opportunities, opportunities for global assignments, and the like. But it matches or even follows with its base pay, matches performance bonuses, and may even lag on benefits. Microsoft matches base and performance bonus, leads on benefits, and is off the chart with its wealth-creating stock options (depending on the direction of its stock price). Both companies offer supremely challenging work opportunities. Both incorporate pay level and mix as part of their total compensation strategy.

EXHIBIT | 7.10 | Pay Mix Policy Alternatives

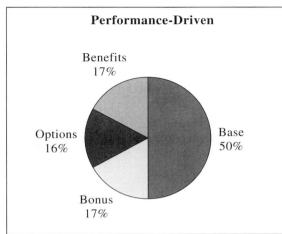

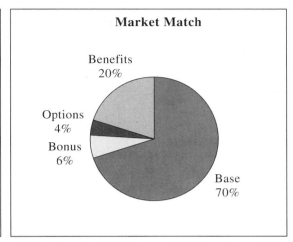

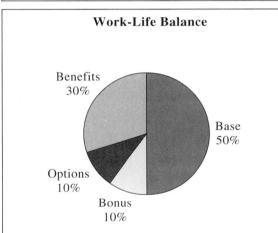

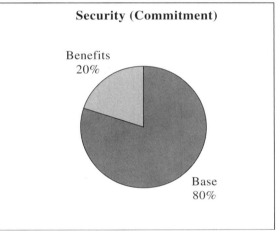

Shared Choice.   This approach begins with the traditional alternatives of lead, meet, or lag. But it then adds a second part, which is to offer *employees choices* (within limits) in the pay mix. This shared choice alternative is similar to the employer of choice in that it recognizes the importance of both pay level and mix. The difference is who gets to choose. An employer of choice aligns the pay level and mix with its business strategy and market competitors. With shared choice, employees have more say in the forms of pay they receive.

This "employees as customer" perspective is not all that revolutionary. Many employers offer choices on health insurance (individual versus dependant coverage), retirement investments (growth or value), and so on.[36] (See information on flexible benefits in Chapter 9.) However, NCR is studying how to extend an "employees as customer" approach. NCR believes its employees value the freedom to make these choices for themselves. Choosing will also make clear the costs of each pay form. One risk to NCR is that employees will make "wrong" choices that will jeopardize their financial well-being without realizing it (e.g., inadequate health insurance). Similarly, in an effort to slow the stream of employee defections, Coke shifted its traditional compensation system. Under the new plan, employees are offered the choice of taking more cash and fewer stock options.[37]

Which Policy Achieves Competitive Advantage?

Research on the effect of pay-level policies is difficult because companies' stated policies often do not correspond to reality. For example, HR managers at 124 companies were asked to define their firm's target pay level. All 124 of them reported that their companies paid above the median![38]

Beyond opinions, there is little evidence of the consequences of different policy alternatives. We do know that pay level affects costs; we do not know whether any effects it might have on productivity or attracting and retaining employees are sufficient to offset costs. Nor is it known how much of a pay level variation makes a difference to employees; will 5 percent, 10 percent, or 15 percent be a noticeable difference? Although lagging competitive pay could produce a noticeable reduction in short-term labour costs, it is not known whether this savings is accompanied by a reduction in the quality and performance of the workforce. It may be that an employer's pay level will not gain any competitive *advantage*; however, the wrong pay level may put the organization at a serious *disadvantage*. Similarly, we simply do not know the effects of the different pay mix alternatives or the financial results of shifting the responsibility to choose the mix to employees. The possibility of achieving competitive advantage lies more in the message that pay level and mix signal to people. That is our belief, anyway.

So where does this leave the manager? In the absence of convincing evidence, the least-risk approach may be to set both pay level and pay mix to match competition. They may adopt a lead policy for skills that are critical to the organization's success, a match policy for less critical skills, and a lag policy for jobs that are easily filled in the local labour market. An obvious concern with flexible policies is to achieve some degree of business alignment and fair treatment for employees among the choices.

Pitfalls of Pies

Thinking about the mix of pay forms as pieces in a pie chart has limitations. These are particularly clear when the value of options are volatile. The pie charts in Exhibit 7.11 show a well-known software company's mix before and after a major stock market decline (stock prices plummeted

EXHIBIT 7.11 Volatility of Stock Value Changes Total Pay Mix

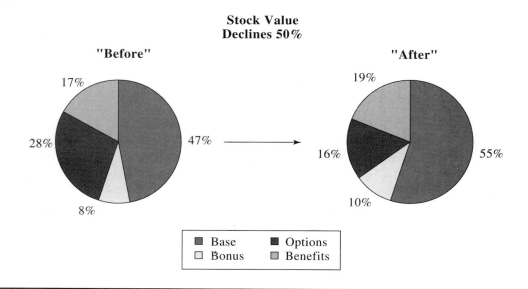

50% within a month). Note the effects on the composition of the pay forms. Base pay went from 47 percent to 55 percent of total compensation, whereas the value of stock options fell from 28 percent to 16 percent. (The reverse has happened in this company, too.) But wait, it can get worse. One technology company was forced to disclose that three-quarters of all its stock options were "under water," that is, exercisable at prices higher than their market price. Due to stock market volatility, the options had become worthless to employees. So what is the message to employees? To competitors? Has the compensation strategy changed? Not the company's intended strategy, but in reality, the mix has changed. So the possible volatility in the value of different pay forms needs to be anticipated.

Some prefer to report the mix of pay forms using a "dashboard," as depicted in Exhibit 7.12. The dashboard changes the focus from emphasizing the relative importance of each form within a single company to comparing each form by itself to the market (many companies). In the example, the value of stock options is 78 percent of competitors' median, base pay is at 95 percent of competitors' median, and overall total compensation is 102 percent of (or 2 percent above) the market median. Pies, dashboards—different focus, both recognizing the importance of the mix of pay forms.

CONSEQUENCES OF PAY LEVEL AND MIX DECISIONS

Earlier we noted that external competitiveness has two major consequences: It affects (1) operating expenses and (2) employee attitudes and work behaviours. Exhibit 7.13 summarizes these consequences, which have been discussed throughout this chapter. The competitiveness policy directly affects the compensation objectives of efficiency, fairness, and compliance.

Efficiency

Compensation represents an expense, so any decisions that affect its level and mix are important. A variety of theories make assumptions about the effects of relative pay levels on an

---

EXHIBIT 7.12 Dashboard: Total Pay Mix Breakdown vs. Competitors

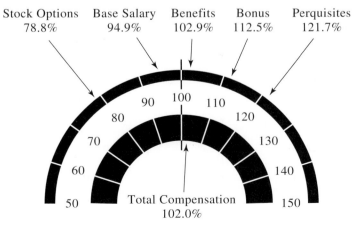

100 = chosen market position, e.g., Market Median

EXHIBIT | **7.13** | Some Consequences of Pay Levels

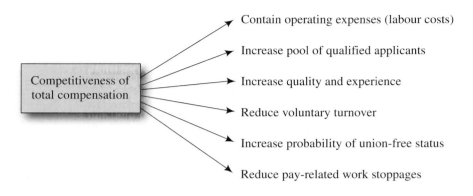

organization's effectiveness. Some recommend lead policies to diminish shirking and permit hiring better-qualified applicants. Others—marginal productivity—recommend matching. A utility model even supports a lag policy.[39] Virtually no research suggests under what circumstances managers should choose which pay mix alternative.

Pay level and mix indirectly affect revenues through the quality of the workforce induced to join and the productivity and experience levels of those who stay. Reduction in turnover of high performers, increased experience levels, increased probability of remaining union-free, and reduction of pay-related grievances and work stoppages are examples of the work behaviours presumed to be affected by pay level decisions. The freedom for employees to choose which forms their pay may take could be related to efficiency. However, if they make the wrong choices—well, it could be still related, only in this case to lower results.

Fairness

Satisfaction with pay is directly related to the pay level: More is better.[40] But employees' sense of fairness is also related to how others are paid. A friend at another business school claims that if all but one of the faculty in the school got $1,000,000 and one person received $1,000,001, the others would all be murmuring for an explanation.

Compliance

It's not enough to say that an employer must pay at or above the legal minimum wage. Provisions of prevailing wage laws and equal rights legislation must also be met. In fact, we will return to the subject of market wages again when we discuss pay discrimination. In addition to pay level, various pay forms also are regulated. Pensions and health care are considered part of every citizen's economic security and are regulated to some degree in most countries. This is discussed again when we look at international practices and benefits.

No matter the competitive pay policy, it needs to be translated into practice. The starting point is measuring the market through use of a salary survey. For this, we turn to the next chapter.

CONCLUSION

One reviewer of this book told us that "there are three important contributions of this chapter. (1) That there is no 'going rate' and so managers make conscious pay level and mix decisions influenced by several factors; (2) that there are both product market and labour market competitors that impact the pay level and mix decisions; and (3) that alternative pay level and mix decisions have different consequences." That is a great summary of the key points.

The pay model used throughout this book emphasizes strategic policy issues: objectives, alignment, competitiveness, contributions, and administration. Policies need to be designed to achieve specific pay objectives. This section is concerned with external competitiveness, or pay comparisons between organizations. Does Research in Motion pay its accountants the same wage that B.C. Hydro pays its accountants? Probably not. Different companies pay different rates; the average of the overall array of rates in an organization constitutes the pay level. Different companies also use different forms of pay. To achieve the objectives stipulated for the pay system, both the pay level and mix must be properly positioned relative to competitors. Each integrated job structure or career path within the organization may have its own competitive position in the market. The next chapter considers the decisions involved and the variety of techniques available to implement decisions.

Before we proceed, let us reemphasize that the major reason we are interested in the external competitiveness policy—pay level and mix of forms—is that they have profound consequences on the organization's objectives. Theories and practical experience support this belief. But as we have noted also, more research is needed to guide us in making decisions. We have clearly established that differences between organizations' competitive policies and their pay levels and forms exist. We have examined the factors that determine these differences. What remains to be better understood is the potential effects of various policies.

CHAPTER SUMMARY

1. External competitiveness refers to the the relationship of one organization's pay to that of its competitors. External competitiveness is expressed in practice by (1) setting a pay level that is above, below, or equal to one's competitors, and (2) by considering the mix of pay forms relative to those of competitors.
2. The three major factors that shape external competitiveness are: (1) competition in the labour market for people with various skills; (2) competition in the product and service markets, which affects the financial condition of the organization; and (3) characteristics unique to each organization and its employees, such as its business strategy, technology, and the productivity and experience of its workforce.
3. Three labour demand theories are compensating differentials theory, efficiency wage theory, and signalling theory. Compensating differentials theory predicts that work with negative characteristics will require higher pay to attract workers. Efficiency wage theory predicts that above-market wages will improve efficiency by attracting workers who perform better and stay longer. Signalling theory predicts that pay policies will signal the kind of behaviour the employer wants.
4. Three supply-side theories are reservation wage theory, human capital theory, and job competition theory. Reservation wage theory predicts that job seekers will not take jobs when pay is below a certain level. Human capital theory predicts that the value of a person's skills and abilities will be related to the time and expense required to acquire them.

Job competition theory predicts that workers will compete through qualifications for jobs with established wages.

5.   Three competitive pay alternatives are to match the market/competition, lag the market, and lead the market.

KEY TERMS

REVIEW QUESTIONS

1.   Distinguish policies on external competitiveness from policies on internal alignment. Why is external competitiveness so important?
2.   What factors shape an organization's external competitiveness?
3.   What does marginal revenue product have to do with pay?

EXPERIENTIAL EXERCISES

1.   Using efficiency wage theory, find an organization (major league sports teams may make the relevant information publicly available) that offers above-market wages, and investigate whether the theory accurately predicts behaviour such as workers with better performance and lower turnover.

2.   What is a relevant market for university professors? For Wal-Mart associates? For politicians? Gather information on market pay for politicians in your municipality.

3.   Find a company that follows a lag policy. Why do they believe it pays to pay below market? Can you find any companies that follow performance-driven and/or work-life balance policies?

WEB EXERCISE

External Competitiveness Comparisons

Select three organizations that you believe might be labour market competitors; e.g., Microsoft, IBM, Oracle, or federal government (http://jobs.gc.ca), Quebec government (www.tresor.gouv.qc.ca/ressources/emplois.htm), Ontario government (www.gojobs.gov.on.ca). Compare their job postings. How many of these organizations list salaries for the job openings? Do they quote a single salary or a range? Do they allow room for salary negotiation? What information is provided about the mix of different pay forms?

CASE

External Competitiveness Decisions at Two Firms

A. Sled Dog Software

Software engineers are critical resources. They directly affect the success of many start-up companies. Suppose you faced a clean slate: A group of investors is about to invest in a new startup, a specialty software company based in Vancouver, B.C.

These investors hired you to help them determine software engineers' pay. Go back to Exhibit 7.2. What would you advise?

1. What policy regarding external competitiveness would you advise? List the options and the pros and cons of each policy option. Offer the rationale for your recommendation.

2. What forms of pay would you recommend? Again, offer your rationale.

3. Consider the theories and research presented in this chapter. Which ones did you use to support your recommendation?

4. List three pieces of additional information you would like to have to refine your recommendation. Explain how this information would help you.

B. Managing a Low-Wage, Low-Skill Workforce

Take another look at the section about practices of the low-wage, low-skill employers such as Marriott and McDonald's. Then look again at the alternative mix of pay forms policies.

1. Which pay mix policy would you recommend McDonald's adopt?

2. What results do you anticipate? Don't forget efficiency, including costs, fairness, and compliance.

3. How, if at all, do the theories discussed help you understand what the anticipated results will be?

Visit the Online Learning Centre at
www.mcgrawhill.ca/college/milkovich

DESIGNING PAY LEVELS, MIX AND PAY STUCTURES

LEARNING OUTCOMES

- *Describe* the seven decisions involved in setting externally competitive pay and designing the corresponding pay structure.
- *Explain* the steps involved in survey design.
- *Describe* what is meant by "updating" survey data.
- *Explain* the difference between a market pay line and a pay policy line.
- *Discuss* how pay grades are created, the relationship of pay ranges to pay grades, and the concept of broadbanding.
- *Explain* how to adjust a pay structure to balance internal and external pressures.

"Average pay of benchmark jobs set to average pay of similar jobs in comparable companies."—3M

"A move to market-based pay to allow a closer alignment with market rates. We set pay by job family rather than having the same pay policy for all jobs."—IBM

"Pay among the leaders. Base pay will be fully comparable (50th percentile of competitors). Total compensation, including benefits and performance incentives, will bring our compensation to the 75th percentile of competitors."—Colgate

"Our competitive strategy is based on commitment, performance, and winning. Base salaries are similar to what our competitors pay, our bonuses equal our competitors, but our long-term incentives (stock options) are paid to everyone and far exceed our competitors."—Microsoft[1]

All these statements refer to different organizations' external competitiveness policies—comparison of the compensation offered by an employer relative to its competitors. In the last chapter, we discussed the factors that influenced these policies. The levels and types of compensation that competitors offer—base salary, bonuses and stock options, benefits—are critical. Market factors that influence policy include the supply of qualified workers and the demand for these workers from other firms. Organizational factors such as the employer's financial condition, technology, size, strategy, productivity, and the influence of unions and employee demographics may also affect a firm's competitive pay policies. In this chapter, we examine how managers use these factors to design pay levels, mix of forms, and structures.

MAJOR DECISIONS

The major decisions involved in setting externally competitive pay and designing the corresponding pay structures are shown in Exhibit 8.1. They include: (1) specify the employer's external pay policy, (2) define the purpose of the survey, (3) choose relevant market competitors, (4) design the survey, (5) interpret survey results and construct the market line, (6) construct a pay policy line that reflects external pay policy, and (7) balance competitiveness with internal alignment through the use of ranges, flat rates, and/or bands. This is a lengthy list. Think of Exhibit 8.1 as a road map through this chapter. The guideposts are the major decisions you face in designing a pay structure. Don't forget to end with, So what? "So what" means understanding how pay structures support business success and ensure fair treatment for employees.

SET COMPETITIVE PAY POLICY

The first decision, specifying the external competitive pay policy, was covered in the previous chapter. To translate any external pay policy into practice requires information on the external **market**. **Surveys** provide the data for translating that policy into pay levels, pay mix, and structures.

THE PURPOSE OF A SURVEY

survey

the systematic process of collecting and making judgments about the compensation paid by other employers

Most firms conduct or participate in several different pay surveys every year. Large employers may participate in up to 100 surveys in a single year, although they base their own compensation decisions on data from only a few surveys.

An employer conducts or participates in a survey for a number of reasons: (1) to adjust the pay level in response to changing competitor pay rates, (2) to set the mix of pay forms relative to those paid by competitors, (3) to establish or price its pay structure, (4) to analyze pay-related problems, or (5) to estimate the labour costs of product market competitors.

EXHIBIT 8.1 Determining Externally Competitive Pay Levels and Structures

External competitiveness: Pay relationships among organizations → **Set policy** → **Define market** → **Conduct survey** → **Draw policy lines** → **Merge internal & external pressures** → **Competitive pay levels, mix, and structures**

Some Major Decisions in Pay Level Determination
- Determine pay level policy
- Define purpose of survey
- Define relevant market
- Design and conduct survey
- Interpret and apply results
- Design grades and ranges or bands

Adjust Pay Level—How Much to Pay?

Most organizations make adjustments to employees' pay on a regular basis. Such adjustments may be based on the overall upward movement of pay rates caused by the competition for people in the market. Or, adjustments may be based on performance, ability to pay, cost of living, or seniority. Monitoring the changes in rates paid by competitors is necessary to maintain or adjust how much a firm pays—its pay level in relation to these competitors.

Adjust Pay Mix—What Forms?

Adjustments to the different forms of pay competitors use (base, bonus, stock, benefits) and the relative importance they place on each form occur less frequently than adjustments to overall pay level. The mix of forms and their relative importance makes up the "pay package." It is not clear (absent good research) why changes to this package occur less frequently than changes in the pay level. Perhaps the message (signal) to employees is in the mix—and changing the message about what is valued confuses people. More likely, insufficient attention has been devoted to mix decisions. Instead, the mix organizations use was based on external pressures such as government regulations, union demands, and mimicking what others did. Managers today recognize that total compensation involves many types of pay, and some pay forms may affect employee behaviour more than others. So collecting accurate information on total compensation, the mix of pay competitors use, and costs of various forms is increasingly important.

Adjust Pay Structure?

Many employers use market surveys to validate their own job evaluation results. For example, job evaluation may place purchasing assistant jobs at the same level in the job structure as some secretarial jobs. But if the market shows vastly different pay rates for the two types of work, most employers will recheck their evaluation process to see whether the jobs have been properly evaluated. Some may even establish a separate structure for different types of work. Recall IBM's policy to set pay by job families. Thus, the job structure that results from internal job evaluation may not match the pay structures found in the external market. Reconciling these two pay structures is a major issue. Informed judgment and accurate information are vital for making these judgments.

As organizations move to more generic jobs that focus on the person more than the job, the need for accurate market data increases. Former relationships between job evaluation points and dollars no longer hold.

Special Situations

Information from specialized surveys may shed light on specific pay-related problems. Many special studies appraise the starting salary offers or current pay practices for targeted groups, such as patent attorneys, retail sales managers, or software engineers.[2] Managers must decide whether they are going to match (or exceed) their competitors or use other returns to lure or hold particular employees.[3]

Estimate Competitors' Labour Costs

Some firms, particularly those in highly competitive businesses such as retailing, auto, or specialty steel production, use salary survey data to benchmark against competitors' product pricing and manufacturing practices. Industrywide labour cost estimates are reported by Statistics Canada.

■ DEFINE RELEVANT MARKET COMPETITORS

We are up to the third of our major decisions shown in Exhibit 8.1. Relevant markets were also discussed in Chapter 7, where we pointed out that employers compete in many labour markets. A survey of the labour market differs from the usual notion of a statistically accurate sample of a population. Salary surveys focus on a narrower population, and the relevant population depends on the purpose of the survey. To make decisions about pay levels, mix, and structures, the relevant labour market includes those employers who are competitors for employees, with emphasis on product/service market-specific skills (machinists for airplanes versus locomotives, financial analysts from consumer products rather than the federal government).[4] As we observed in Chapter 7, the relevant market includes:

1. employers who compete for the same occupations or skills required
2. employers who compete for employees within the same geographic area
3. employers who compete with the same products and services

Exhibit 8.2 shows how qualifications interact with geography to define the scope of relevant labour markets. As the importance and complexity of qualifications increase, the geographic limits also increase. Competition tends to be national for managerial and professional skills, but local or regional for clerical and production skills.

However, these generalizations do not always hold true. In areas with high concentrations of scientists, engineers, and managers (e.g., Toronto, Ottawa, or Calgary), the primary market comparison may be regional, with national data used only secondarily.

EXHIBIT 8.2 Relevant Labour Markets by Geographic and Employee Groups

Geographic Scope	Production	Office and Clerical	Technicians	Scientists and Engineers	Managerial Professional	Executive
Local: Within relatively small areas such as cities or metropolitan areas	Most likely	Most likely	Most likely			
Regional: Within a particular area of the province or several provinces (e.g., the wheat-producing region of western Canada)	Only if in short supply or critical	Only if in short supply or critical	Most likely	Likely	Most Likely	
National: Across the country				Most likely	Most likely	Most likely
International: Across several countries				Only for critical skills or those in very short supply	Only for critical skills or those in very short supply	Sometimes

Some writers argue that if the skills are tied to a particular industry, as underwriters, actuaries, and claims representatives are to insurance, it makes sense to define the market on an industry basis, and some research agrees.[5] If accounting, sales, or clerical skills are not limited to one particular industry, then industry considerations are less important. From the perspective of cost control and ability to pay, including competitors in the product/service market is crucial.[6] The pay rates of product/service competitors will affect both costs of operations and financial condition (e.g., ability to pay). However, this becomes a problem when the major competitors are based in countries with far lower pay rates, such as China or Mexico. In fact, the increasingly international character of business has spawned interest in global survey data, particularly for managerial and professional talent.[7]

This creates additional complexities because legal regulations and tax policies, as well as customs, vary between countries. For example, because of tax laws, executives in Korea and Spain receive company credit cards that can be used for personal expenses (groceries, clothing). In the United States, these purchases would count as taxable income, but they do not in Korea and Spain. Although the quality of data available for international comparisons is improving, using the data to adjust pay still requires a lot of judgment. Labour markets are just emerging in some regions (China, Eastern Europe). Historically, in these countries, state agencies set nationwide wage rates, so there was no need for surveys. Japanese companies historically shared information among themselves but did not share such information with outsiders, so no surveys were available. Companies with worldwide locations use local surveys for jobs filled locally and international surveys for top managers.

But even if an employer possesses good international survey data, utilizing that data still requires careful judgment. For example, Sun Microsystems pays its Russian engineers in Moscow between $260 and $320 a month. Although these salaries are absurdly low by Western standards, they are 25 to 30 times the salaries paid to other engineers outside the Sun-funded unit at the same institute. Sun probably can afford to pay more, even in light of all the other expenses and bureaucratic headaches associated with such an undertaking.[8] But does it make sense to inflate salaries for some to a North American level, when colleagues at other institutes or support staff at the same institute do not receive comparable salaries? Software engineers working for IBM in India told us that although they are paid very well by Indian standards, they feel underpaid compared to IBM engineers in the United States with whom they work on virtual project teams.[9]

Fuzzy Markets

New e-businesses are often created by a "fusion" of industries. Walk through a bay of cubicles (plastered with *Dilbert* cartoons) at Yahoo and you are likely to find former kindergarten teachers, software engineers, and former sales representatives all collaborating on a single team. Yahoo combines technology, media, and commerce into one company. What is the relevant labour market (skill/geography)? Which firms should be included in Yahoo's surveys? Or, look at Wine.com, which sells wine on the Web. This company includes people from traditional wine shops, Web developers, and marketers. These new fusion organizations possess unique and diverse knowledge and experience, making "relevant" markets appear more like fuzzy markets.[10]

Even outside e-business, as person-based structures, contract and temporary employees, outsourcing, and other nontraditional approaches become traditional, customized surveys, or at least flexibility to analyze data from competitors using skill/competencies or contract workers will be required. Presently, managers with unique structures face the double bind of finding it hard to get comparable market data, when at the same time they are placing more emphasis on external market data.

■ DESIGN THE SURVEY

Consulting firms offer a wide choice of ongoing surveys covering almost every job family and industry group imaginable. Their surveys are getting better and better.[11] Although we would like to attribute the improvement to the fact that our textbook has improved the sophistication of compensation education in North America, it is more likely that the improvement is the result of technological advances. Increasingly, consultants offer clients the option of electronically accessing the consultants' survey database. The client then does the special analysis it desires. General Electric conducts most of its market analysis in this manner. Hay PayNet permits organizations to tie into Hay's vast survey data 24/7.[12]

So if surveys from consultants are getting easier to use, why bother with all this detail? Because expertise is still necessary to judge the quality of information, no matter where it comes from. Plus, some of our readers may wish to join these consulting firms.

Designing a survey requires answering the following questions: (1) Who should be involved in the survey design? (2) How many employers should be included? (3) Which jobs should be included? and (4) What information should be collected?

Who Should Be Involved?

In most organizations, the responsibility for managing the survey lies with the compensation manager. But, since compensation expenses have a powerful effect on profitability, including managers and employees on task forces makes sense.

Hiring a third-party consultant instead of managing the survey internally buys expertise but may trade off some control over the decisions that determine the quality and usefulness of the data.

How Many Employers?

There are no firm rules about how many employers to include in a survey.[13] Large firms with a lead policy may exchange data with only a few (6 to 10) top-paying competitors. A small organization in an area dominated by two or three employers may decide to survey only smaller competitors. National surveys conducted by consulting firms often include more than 100 employers. Clients of these consultants often stipulate special analyses that report pay rates by selected industry groups, geographic region, and/or pay levels (e.g., top 10 percent).

Publicly Available Data.   In Canada, Statistics Canada is the major source of publicly available compensation data. It publishes extensive information on pay for various occupations and industries.

Word-of-Mouse.   Once upon a time (about five years ago) individual employees had a hard time accessing salary data. Confidentiality (secrecy) was the policy of the land. Salary data with which to compare one's own salary was gathered via word of mouth. Today, a click of the mouse makes a wealth of data available to everyone. Employees are comparing their compensation to data from Statistics Canada or salary.monster.ca.[14] This ease of access means that managers must be able to explain (defend?) the salaries paid to employees compared to those a mouse click away. Unfortunately, the quality of much salary data on the Web is highly suspect. Few of the sites offer any information about how the data were collected, what pay forms were included, and so on. Exhibit 8.3 shows the level of detail provided by salary.monster.ca.

Where Are the Standards?   Opinions about the value of consultant surveys are rampant; research is not. Do Hay, Mercer, Towers Perrin, or Watson Wyatt surveys yield significantly different results? Many firms select one survey as their primary source and use others to cross-check or "validate" the results.

EXHIBIT	8.3	Salary Data on the Web

Salary Wizard

A manager, Compensation and Benefits, working in Vancouver earns a median total cash compensation of $81,813. The top half of earners are paid an average of $93,517 and the lower half of earners are paid an average of $74,806. (*These data as of August 2003*)

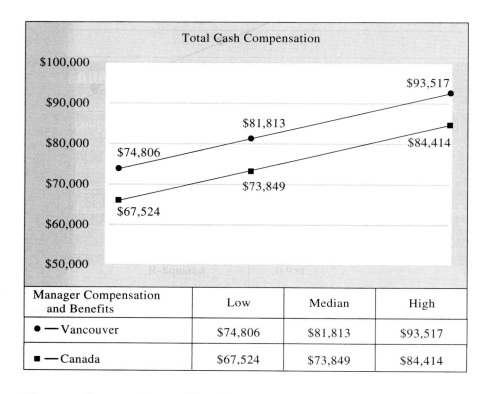

Manager Compensation and Benefits	Low	Median	High
●—Vancouver	$74,806	$81,813	$93,517
■—Canada	$67,524	$73,849	$84,414

Manager, Compensation and Benefits

Designs, plans, and implements corporate benefits and compensation programs, policies, and procedures. Requires a bachelor's degree in a related area and at least seven years' experience in the field. Generally manages a group of compensation and/or benefits analysts. Relies on experience and judgment to plan and accomplish goals. Typically reports to an executive.

For staffing decisions, employment test designers report the test's performance against a set of standards (reliability, validity, etc.). Accountants have generally accepted practices. Even lawyers have standards of practice. For pay decisions, professional standards do not exist. Issues of sample design and statistical inference are seldom considered. Some employers routinely combine the results of several surveys and weight each survey in this composite according to some person's judgment of the quality of the data reported.[15] No systematic study of differences in market definition, participating firms, types of data collected, quality of data, analysis performed, and/or results is available.

Which Jobs to Include?

A general guideline is to keep things as simple as possible. Select as few employers and jobs as necessary to accomplish the purpose. The more complex the survey, the less likely other employers are inclined to participate. There are several approaches to selecting jobs for inclusion.

Benchmark Jobs Approach. In Chapter 5 we noted that benchmark jobs have stable job content and are common across different employers. If the purpose of the survey is to price the entire structure, then benchmark jobs can be selected to include the entire job structure—all key functions and all levels. The employer in Exhibit 8.4, for example, organizes work into four structures. Benchmark jobs are chosen from as many levels in each of these structures as can be matched with the descriptions of the benchmark jobs that are included in the survey.

The degree of match between the survey's benchmark jobs and each company's jobs is assessed by various means. The Hay Group, for example, has installed the same job evaluation plan in many companies that participate in their surveys. Consequently, jobs in different organizations can be compared on their job evaluation points and the distribution of points among the compensable factors. Other surveys simply ask participants to judge the degree of match, using a scale similar to the following:

Please check ( ) degree to which your job matches the benchmark job described in the survey.

My company's job is:

Of much less value	( )
Of slightly less value	( )
Of equal value	( )
Of slightly more value	( )
Of much more value	( )

However, a consultant friend insists that when the compensation manager changes, the job matches often change, too.

EXHIBIT 8.4 Benchmarks

Managerial Group	Technical Group	Manufacturing Group	Administrative Group
		Assembler I Inspector I	
Vice Presidents	Head/Chief Scientist	Packer	Administrative Assistant
Division General Managers	Senior Associate Scientist	Material Handler Inspector II	Principal Administrative Secretary
Managers	Associate Scientist	Assembler II	Administrative Secretary
Project Leaders	Scientist	Drill Press Operator Rough Grinder	Word Processor
Supervisors	Technician	Machinist I Coremaker	Clerk/Messenger

More heavily shaded jobs have been selected as benchmarks.

Global Approach.   Rarely are all the jobs identical among organizations. For many organizations, the way they design the work and the underlying technology is part of their competitive advantage. Exxon Mobil's project teams, for example, include unique combinations of disciplines, including chemical and software engineers, geophysicists, and government relations people. The fusion of these disciplines is unique and difficult to survey. The global approach may be better suited in these situations. A global approach uses the rates paid to every individual employee in an entire skill group or discipline (e.g., all chemical engineers or all software engineers). Exhibit 8.5 shows external market data for chemical engineers with bachelor's degrees and demonstrates that, in general, pay increases with years of experience. Exhibit 8.6 translates those data into percentiles. A survey user can determine the rates paid to engineers (Exhibit 8.5) as well as the rate's relationship to years since degree (YSD) (Exhibit 8.6). Because of this relationship to YSD, the curved lines in Exhibit 8.6 are often referred to as **maturity curves**. A global approach simply substitutes a particular skill (represented by a BS in engineering in the example) and experience or maturity (YSD) for detailed descriptions of work performed.

Low-High Approach.   If an organization is using skill/competency-based structures or generic job descriptions, it may not be able to match jobs with competitors who use a traditional job-based approach. Job-based market data must be converted to fit the skill or competency structure. The simplest approach is to identify the lowest and highest paid benchmark jobs for the relevant skills in the relevant market and to use the wages for these jobs as anchors for the skill-based structures. Work at various levels within the structure then can be slotted between the anchors. For example, Exhibit 8.7 graphs a structure that begins with market rates for entry-level unskilled labour and goes up to market rates for team leaders at the high end. A straight line connects the rates. Wage rates for the rest of the structure can then be slotted along this line. For example, if the entry market rate for operator A is $12 per hour and the rate for a team leader is $42 per hour, then the rate for operator B can be somewhere between $12 and $42 per hour.

The usefulness of this approach depends on how well the extreme benchmark jobs match the organization's work, and whether they really do tap the entire range of skills. Hanging a pay system on two pieces of market data raises the stakes on the accuracy of those data.

Market Basket Approach.   This approach to pricing a skill or competency system uses more data than the low–high approach, but it requires more judgment. Again, skills and competencies are converted to a wide-ranging job, and then multiple market matches are found for that "super-job." Each related survey job is weighted by the percentage by which it overlaps the superjob. Exhibit 8.8 shows the math. Notice that the precision of the mathematical calculation is offset by the "adjustment" for "unique value" based on the judgment of the survey user. The absence of professional standards beyond "rule of thumb" becomes more troubling as the opportunity to manipulate results via "judgment" increases.

Benchmark Conversion Approach.   If an employer is finding it hard to match survey jobs, it can apply its plan for creating internal alignment to the descriptions of survey jobs. For example, if an organization uses job evaluation, then its job evaluation system can be applied to the survey jobs. The magnitude of difference between job evaluation points for internal jobs and survey jobs provides a "guideline" for adjusting the market data. Again, a "judgment."

So, the real issue is to ensure that the survey data will be useful. Depending on the purpose of the survey, either the benchmark, the global, the low–high, market basket, or benchmark conversion approach can help.

---

maturity curves

curves on a graph depicting the relationship between salaries and years of work experience since attaining a degree

EXHIBIT 8.5   Frequency Distribution—All Engineers, All Companies

Years Since BS

Monthly Salary $

Monthly Salary $	0	1	2	3	4	5	6	7	8	9	10	11	12	13	14	15	16	17	18	19	20	21	22	23	24	25	26	27	28	29	30	31	32	33	34	35	36	37	TOTAL
8950-OVER																													2		6		3		1	1	1	10	40
8825-8949																					2			1	2	2					1	1	3		1	1	1	1	9
7700-8824																				2	1				2		1	1	1	2	2			3	1			2	12
8575-8699									1							1		1		1	2		1					1		1			1		1	1		2	14
8450-8574								1							1		1		1	2	1	2	1	1		2	1	1	4	2	1	2	1	3	2	2	2	9	31
8325-8449								4		2				2	1	2	2	3	3	1		3	6	1	3	3	2		4	1		4	3		2	1	4	5	24
8200-8324					4	4	1	10	1	1		4	2		2		1	2	3	1	4	4	2	5	2	4	2	3	3	2	2	3	1	5	2	3	4	5	42
8075-8199				2			5	8	5	2		8	2	3	2			3	3		3	3	2	5	2	7	2	3	4	3	3	2	4	5	2	3	2	6	43
7950-8074			4	3	4	4	6	18	16	2	2	8	5	5	6	10	6	5	6		4	4	10	4	3	2	4	4	5	2	2	4			5	4	2	8	44
7825-7949				5	5	8	13	21	13	1	3	8	8	4	7	11	13	10	6	3	3	2	5	5	3	7	6	8	6	3	3	4	4	5	3	3	2	6	63
7700-7824			2	3	8	8	13	13	20	2	3	8	9	9	8	11	8	5	5	3	6	4	5	4	3	2	6	7	8	4	4	5	2	3	5	3	6	14	70
7575-7699				6	12	4	14	22	7		14	10	6	5	9	11	8	9	6	5	4	6	13	7	10	9	10	8	6	6	7	4	6	3	3	4	3	11	97
7450-7574		2			4	4	8	19	18	3	2	8	10	10	7	7	19	11	12	2	6	3	5	6	9	5	7	6	8	4	5	4	2	4	5	4	3	10	102
7325-7449					11	11	10	13	10	4	8	8	11	17	17	21	14	9	14	12	6	10	5	5	8	4	2	3	8	4	4	4	1	6	3	3	4	15	116
7200-7324					8	12	7		11	5	14	12	13	9	13	21	8	13	15	7	8	4	13	15	11	9	7	5	7	9	6	8	7	4	3	5	7	16	151
7075-7199		8	6	6	1	1	1	10	14	7	14	15	16	15	16	16	14	12	10	11	7	10	8	4	8	5	8	7	9	4	7	7	10	3	3	4	3	21	173
6950-7074		8	6			5	5	10	18	12	8	15	13	10	6	10	8	9	4	11	8	4	7	13	8	8	8	5	7	4	6	7	2	3	3	4	1	17	178
6825-6949		6	3				6	8	16	10	12	15	13	5	7	11	6	5	9	12	10	9	8	6	9	6	8	5	5	6	3	4	2	3	4	2	2	18	180
6700-6824				2	4	4	6	18	13	10	16	12	15	10	8	10	13	10	6	7	7	4	7	7	11	6	8	8	5	8	10	4	11	3	4	2	2	27	210
6575-6699				3	4	5	13	8	9	9	9	8	8	4	9	11	6	5	6	6	11	8	8	8	9	6	10	8	6	8	3	6	6	3	5	5	2	10	192
6450-6574		2		6	8	8	14	21	19	10	9	13	8	9	11	11	8	5	6	5	7	11	7	7	16	9	10	7	4	12	7	4	2	3	3	3	4	19	232
6325-6449		1	3	4	4	4	14	22	7	8	2	8	10	10	7	7	19	11	12	9	7	8	3	3	9	5	7	6	6	8	5	4	2	4	5	7	6	20	216
6200-6324					11	10	8		4	4	8	5	10	17	19	21	14	12	14	12	9	11	13	13	11	9	7	8	8	12	4	10	3	4	2	7	3	24	290
6075-6199			6	1		7	2	4	2	5	14	12	11	9	17	21	8	9	15	7	10	8	15	15	5	9	8	6	8	9	7	7	10	6	4	9	7	18	281
5950-6074				2	7	3	10	10	11	7	8	12	13	15	13	21	8	13	10	11	9	8	7	4	5	5	2	7	6	4	7	7	2	3	4	1	3	9	262
5825-5949				4	1	4	1	10	14	8	8	15	13	15	16	16	14	10	11	11	8	8	13	13	8	4	4	5	5	4	4	6	2	2	3	2	12	12	255
5700-5824				1			5	8	9	10	9	12	16	10	14	14	13	9	4	6	10	4	6	6	8	4	3	5	2	4	6	6	3	4	3	3	8	8	234
5575-5699			2		4	4	6	8	16	10	12	15	8	10	16	5	4	5	5	6	7	3	5	3	4	4	4	4	4	2	3	6	2	3	4	3	2	7	205
5450-5574			3	2	5	5	13	18	13	9	16	12	8	2	9	14	6	9	6	5	3	6	3	6	4	7	3	5	3	4	4	6	3	3		2	8	3	193
5325-5449			6	3	8	8	13	21	19	10	9	10	8	11	8	5	6	5	5	6	6	3	6	3	5	2	2	4	6	3		4	4	4		1		7	176
5200-5324				6		4	14	19	7	9	14	9	9	5	9	14	4	4	4	4	7	4	5	6	2	3	2	2	2	3	1			3	4	3		3	155
5075-5199		1		6	8	11	8	13	18	8	8	5	8	5	8	5	2	2	2	4	4	6	3	3	3	2	2	1	2	2	3		4		1	2		5	174
4950-5074						4	8	7	10	7	14	8	6	5	6	2	2	2	2	5	4	1	4	5	3	2	2	1	2	1	1	3			1				172
4825-4949		2	2	6	9	8	14	13	8	8	4	3	5	5	2	3	5	2	2	2	4		3		2		2	2	2				3						158
4700-4824	4	8	17	19	20	15	8	4	10	8	8	2	4	5		3	3		2		5	1	4	5	3	2		1		2	1								172
4575-4699	29	11	19	22	25	12	12	2	8	7	3	3	3		1	2	1	2			3				2		2		2	1	3	3			1	2		1	116
4450-4574	16	42	17	17	14	7	8	4	2			3				1			1			1						1								1			48
4325-4449	16	37	22	10	4	10	5	2	3									2		1																			29
4200-4324	13	11	8	6	1		1	2																															
UNDER 4200	10	6	3	4	4		2	2																															
TOTAL	62	120	142	117	105	87	116	167	165	131	139	166	145	154	193	221	187	170	174	164	179	148	183	170	168	137	128	119	131	124	111	109	103	89	74	91	82	354	5425
MEDIAN	2458	2455	2553	2703	2728	2804	2976	3195	3295	3429	3455	3658	3688	3908	4005	4089	4186	4188	4304	4422	4429	4432	4512	4503	4524	4595	4630	4551	4762	4669	4656	4585	4682	4762	4950	4637	5012	4748	4035
MEAN	2433	2477	2564	2711	2752	2854	3008	3199	3332	3434	3501	3665	3698	3924	4041	4189	4209	4239	4421	4466	4476	4438	4637	4502	4583	4638	4665	4629	4741	4669	4821	4657	4738	4851	4828	4772	4899	4860	4090
STD. DEV.	110	170	243	275	289	344	388	428	479	491	513	583	527	673	678	699	729	798	791	856	932	861	951	807	839	859	819	826	897	979	1097	929	965	1010	1011	943	887	963	1051

| **EXHIBIT** | **8.6** | Percentile Curves: Years since First Degree versus Monthly Salary—All Engineers, All Companies |

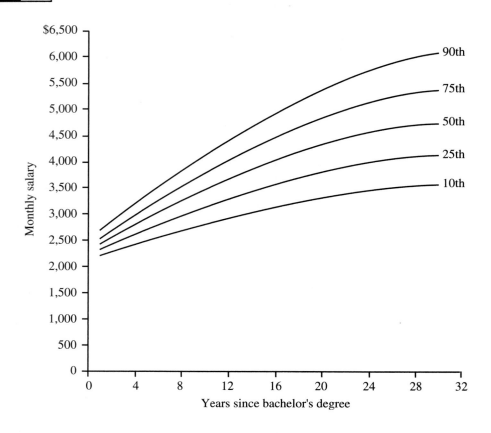

| **EXHIBIT** | **8.7** | Pricing a Skill-Based Structure |

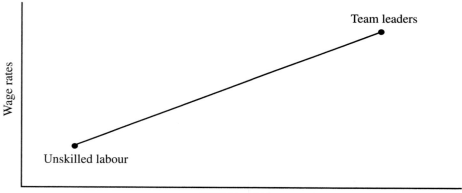

EXHIBIT | **8.8** | Pricing a Competency-Based Structure

Related survey jobs	Degree to which this survey job reflects our "job" of MARKETER		Market Rate for survey job		Contribution to our MARKETER
Entry-Level Engineer	.20	×	$46,500	=	$9,300
Marketing Manager	.35	×	$88,000	=	$30,800
Financial Analyst	.45	×	$60,000	=	$27,000
	1.00				$67,100
Adjustment for "unique value" (10%)					$6,710
Suggested Wage for Competency-Based "Job" of Marketer					$73,810

What Information to Collect?

Three basic types of data typically are requested: (1) information about the nature of the organization, (2) information about the total compensation system, and (3) specific pay data on each incumbent in the jobs under study. Exhibit 8.9 lists the basic data elements and the logic for including them. No survey includes all the data that will be discussed. Rather, the data collected depend on the purpose of the survey and the jobs and skills included.

Organization Data. This information assesses the similarities and differences between survey users. Surveys for executive and upper-level positions include more detailed financial and reporting relationships data, since compensation for these jobs is more directly related to the organization's financial performance. More often than not, the financial data are simply used to group firms by size expressed in terms of sales or revenues rather than considering the performance of competitors.

Total Compensation Data. All the basic forms of pay need to be covered in a survey to assess the similarities and differences in the total pay packages and to accurately assess competitors' practices.[16] The list shown in Exhibit 8.9 reveals the range of forms that could be included in each company's definition of total compensation. As a practical matter, it can be hard to include *all* the pay forms. Too much detail on benefits, such as medical coverage deductibles and flexible schedules, can make a survey too cumbersome to be useful. Alternatives range from a brief description of a benchmark benefit package to including only the most expensive and variable benefits or asking for an estimate of total benefit expenses as a percentage of total labour costs. Three alternatives—base pay, total cash (base, profit sharing, bonuses), and total compensation (total cash plus benefits and perquisites)—are the most commonly used.

Exhibit 8.10 draws the distinction between three different compensation forms and highlights the usefulness and limitations of these alternatives as a survey measure. Keep in mind that we are interested in gathering data on how much pay and what forms of pay competitors use to pay their people. Exhibit 8.11 shows some results of survey analysis using these three different measures on a sample of seven jobs from an internal job structure. The "going market rate" varies, depending on what forms are included.

EXHIBIT 8.9	Data Elements to Consider for Surveys and Their Rationale

Basic Elements	Examples	Rationale
Nature of Organization		
Identification	Company, name, address, contact person	Further contacts
Financial performance	Assets, sales, profits (after taxes), cash flow	Indicates nature of the product/service markets, the ability to pay, size, and financial viability
Size	Profit centres, product lines	Importance of specific job groups to business success
	Total number of employees	Impact on labour market
Structure	Organizational charts	Indicates how business is organized and how important managerial jobs are
Nature of Total Compensation System		
Cash forms used	Base pay, pay increase schedules, long- and short-term incentives, bonuses, cost of living adjustments, overtime and shift differentials	Indicate the mix of compensation offered; used to establish a comparable base
Noncash forms used	Composition of benefits and services, particularly the degree of coverage and contributions to medical and health insurance and pensions	
Incumbent and Job		
Date	Date survey data in effect	Need to update rates to current date
Job	Match generic job description	Indicates degree of similarity with survey's key jobs
	Number of employees supervised and reporting levels	Describes scope of responsibilities
Individual	Years since degree, education, date of hire	Indicates training and tenure of incumbents
Pay	Actual rates paid to each individual, total earnings, last increase, bonuses, incentives	

A. *Base pay.* This is the amount of *cash* the competitors decided *each job and incumbent* is worth. A company might use this information for its initial observations of how "good" the data appear to fit a range of jobs. In Exhibit 8.11, Line A is a market line based on base pay. Focusing only on base pay reveals how competitors may value similar jobs or skills but does not include the opportunity to earn performance-based bonuses.

B. *Total cash* is base plus bonus. This reflects the *cash* value of the job and incumbent *plus bonuses* (Line B in the exhibit).

C. *Total compensation* includes total cash plus stock options and benefits. Total compensation reflects the total overall value of the employee (performance, experience, skills, etc.) plus the value of the work itself.

EXHIBIT	8.10	Advantages and Disadvantages of Measures of Compensation

Base Pay	Tells how competitors are valuing the work in similar jobs	Fails to include performance incentives and other forms, so will not give true picture if competitors offer low base but high incentives
Total Cash (base + bonus)	Tells how competitors are valuing work; also tells the cash pay for performance opportunity in the job	All employees may not receive incentives, so it may overstate the competitors' pay; plus, it does not include long-term incentives
Total Compensation (base + bonus + stock options + benefits)	Tells the total value competitors place on this work	All employees may not receive all the forms. Be careful; don't set base equal to competitors' total compensation. Risks high fixed costs.

EXHIBIT	8.11	Salary Graphs Using Different Measures of Compensation

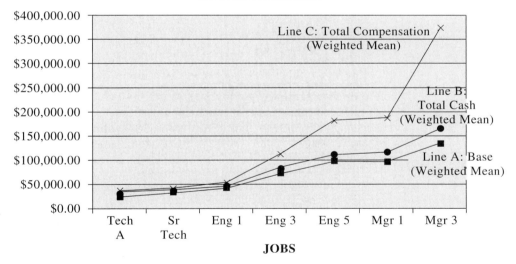

ACTUAL SALARIES

	A: Base, Wtd Mean	B: Cash, Wtd Mean	C: Total Comp, Wtd Mean
Tech A	$22,989.17	$24,554.61	$30,831.04
Sr Tech	$37,748.74	$42,510.23	$51,482.48
Eng 1	$46,085.21	$48,289.66	$56,917.08
Eng 3	$73,134.74	$81,285.93	$112,805.98
Eng 5	$102,415.07	$112,587.43	$179,449.81
Mgr 1	$95,260.05	$115,304.66	$188,509.84
Mgr 3	$134,173.33	$171,030.50	$378,276.71

It is no surprise that for all seven jobs, total compensation is higher than base pay alone or base plus bonus. However, the variability and magnitude of the difference may be a surprise: from $7,842 ($30,8 – 12$22,989, or 34 percent) for the job of Technician A, to $244,103.38 (182 percent) for the Manager 3. Base pay is, on average, only 35 percent ($134,173/$378,277) of total compensation for the Manager 3s in this survey. So what kinds of compensation to include is an important decision in designing a survey design. Misinterpreting competitors' pay practices can lead to costly mispricing of pay levels and structures.

Rather than mailed questionnaires, survey data today frequently are exchanged on-line. Technology has made processing data and spitting out reports easy. The greatest challenge of total compensation surveys may be to understand how to disaggregate and evaluate all the information. A well-designed total compensation database will allow each participating firm to determine the models, financial assumptions, and demographic profiles that best reflect its view of the world. In the best total compensation projects, each firm sees the survey as a customizable database project by which they can specify the characteristics of the employers and jobs to include.

■ INTERPRET SURVEY RESULTS AND CONSTRUCT A MARKET LINE

After the survey data are all collected, the next step is to analyze the results and use statistics to construct a market line. Twenty years ago, researcher David Belcher interviewed compensation professionals to discover how survey data are actually analyzed. He reported:

> Every organization uses its own methods of distilling information from the survey; uses different surveys for different purposes; and uses different methods for company surveys. I could find no commonality in these methods of analysis by industry, by firm size, or by union presence. For example, some did nothing except read the entire survey, some emphasized industry data, others geographic competitors (commuting distances), some made comparisons with less than five competitors, some emphasized only large firms, others throw out the data from large firms.[17]

His conclusion still holds today. Diversity rules in analyzing survey data. We hope diversity reflects flexibility in dealing with a variety of circumstances. We worry that diversity reflects expediency and a lack of business- and work-related logic.

Verify Data

So the survey report has arrived in the mail (or, more likely, been posted to a secure Web-site). Now what? A common first step is to check the *accuracy* of the job matches, then check for *anomalies* (i.e., an employer whose data are substantially out of line with those from others), age of data, level of abstractness (i.e., standard occupations versus job descriptions), and the nature of the organizations (e.g., "old" economy versus "new" economy). Exhibit 8.12 is an excerpt from the survey used to prepare Exhibit 8.11. The survey was conducted at the behest of FastCat, a small startup.[18] Although there were a number of jobs included in the survey, we use information for just one job—Engineer 1—to illustrate. As you can see, surveys do not make light reading. However, they contain a wealth of information. To extract that information, let us enter the portal . . . on being the FastCat analyst.

survey levelling

multiplying survey data by a factor to adjust for differences between the company job and the survey job

Accuracy of Match.   Part A of the survey contains the job description for which survey participants were asked to report data. Does the description match a job at FastCat? If the job is similar but not identical, some companies use **survey levelling**, that is, they multiply the survey data by some factor that corresponds to the analyst's judgment of the differences between the company and survey job. Levelling is another example of the use of judgment in the survey analysis process. It clearly leaves the objectivity of the decisions open to challenge.

EXHIBIT **8.12** Survey Data

A. Job Description: Engineer 1

Participates in development, testing, and documentation of software programs. Performs design and analysis tasks as a project team member. Typical minimum requirements are a bachelor's degree in a scientific or technical field or the equivalent and up to two years of experience.

B. Individual Salary Data (partial data; for illustration only)

Job	Base	Bonus	Total Cash	Stock Option	Benefits	Total Comp
Engineer 1					*JE Points:*	50
					Number of Incumbents:	585
Company 1						
Engineer 1	$79,000	$500	$79,500	$0	$8,251	$87,751
Engineer 1	$65,500	$2,500	$68,000	$0	$8,251	$76,251
Engineer 1	$65,000	$0	$65,000	$0	$8,251	$73,251
Engineer 1	$58,000	$4,000	$62,000	$0	$8,251	$70,251
Engineer 1	$57,930	$3,000	$60,930	$0	$8,251	$69,181
Engineer 1	$57,200	$2,000	$59,200	$0	$8,251	$67,451
Engineer 1	$56,000	$1,100	$57,100	$0	$8,251	$65,351
Engineer 1	$54,000	$0	$54,000	$0	$8,251	$62,251
Engineer 1	$52,500	$0	$52,500	$0	$8,251	$60,751
Engineer 1	$51,500	$1,500	$53,000	$0	$8,251	$61,251
Engineer 1	$49,000	$3,300	$52,300	$0	$8,251	$60,551
Engineer 1	$48,500	$0	$48,500	$0	$8,251	$56,751
Engineer 1	$36,500	$0	$36,500	$0	$8,251	$44,751
Company 2						
Engineer 1	$57,598	$0	$57,598	$28,889	$8,518	$95,004
Engineer 1	$57,000	$0	$57,000	$31,815	$8,518	$97,332
Engineer 1	$55,000	$0	$55,000	$20,110	$8,518	$83,628

C. Company Data (partial data; for illustration only)

	# Incumbents		Base	Short Term	Total Cash	LTI	Benefits	Total Comp
Company 1								
	13	Avg.	56,202.31	1,376.92	57,579.23	0.00	8,250.89	65,830.12
		Min.	36,500.00	0.00	36,500.00	0.00	8,250.89	44,750.89
		Max.	79,000.00	4,000.00	79,500.00	0.00	8,250.89	87,750.89
Company 2								
	13	Avg.	52,764.80	1,473.56	54,238.36	21,068.91	8,517.56	83,824.83
		Min.	47,376.20	0.00	50,038.33	4,878.98	8,517.56	65,416.54
		Max.	57,598.21	3,716.89	58,494.01	31,814.83	8,517.56	97,332.39
Company 4								
	2		56,004.00	0.00	56,004.00	0.00	9,692.56	65,696.56
			55,016.00	0.00	55,016.00	0.00	9,692.56	64,708.56
		Avg.	55,510.00	0.00	55,510.00	0.00	9,692.56	65,202.56
Company 8								
	14	Avg.	54,246.00	4,247.21	58,493.21	0.00	7,204.50	65,697.71
		Min.	45,000.00	860.00	48,448.00	0.00	7,204.50	55,363.50
		Max.	62,000.00	8,394.00	68,200.00	0.00	7,204.50	75,404.50

EXHIBIT 8.12 | Survey Data (*continued*)

	# Incumbents		Base	Short Term	Total Cash	LTI	Benefits	Total Comp
Company 12								
	35	Avg.	50,459.34	1,123.26	51,582.60	1,760.05	7,693.11	61,035.76
		Min.	42,000.00	0.00	43,092.00	0.00	7,693.11	52,606.26
		Max.	64,265.00	1,670.89	65,935.89	9,076.52	7,693.11	73,629.00
Company 13								
	5	Avg.	48,700.80	400.00	49,100.80	2,050.00	8,001.00	59,152.20
		Min.	45,456.00	0.00	45,456.00	0.00	8,001.00	53,458.00
		Max.	54,912.00	2,000.00	54,912.00	8,506.00	8,001.00	66,507.00
Company 14								
	10	Avg.	44,462.40	863.43	45,325.83	0.00	7,337.00	52,662.83
		Min.	37,440.00	372.95	37,812.95	0.00	7,337.00	45,149.95
		Max.	47,832.00	1,197.12	49,029.12	0.00	7,337.00	56,366.12
Company 15								
	71	Avg.	49,685.92	8,253.61	57,939.52	1,762.97	8,404.00	68,106.48
		Min.	44,900.00	0.00	49,022.00	0.00	8,404.00	57,426.00
		Max.	57,300.00	14,132.00	68,357.00	63,639.00	8,404.00	125,471.00
Company 51								
	4	Avg.	46,193.88	1,399.75	47,593.63	41,954.39	7,640.89	97,188.90
		Min.	42,375.06	0.00	44,988.75	20,518.14	7,640.89	75,159.23
		Max.	48,400.04	2,985.31	51,385.35	74,453.00	7,640.89	133,479.24
Company 57								
	226	Avg.	44,091.57	1,262.43	45,354.00	0.00	6,812.00	52,166.00
		Min.	38,064.00	0.00	39,372.00	0.00	6,812.00	46,184.00
		Max.	60,476.00	2,179.00	62,655.00	0.00	6,812.00	69,467.00
Company 58								
	107	Avg.	44,107.18	1,367.04	45,474.21	0.00	6,770.00	52,244.21
		Min.	36,156.00	0.00	37,569.00	0.00	6,770.00	44,339.00
		Max.	57,600.00	2,147.00	58,913.00	0.00	6,770.00	65,683.00
Company 59								
	71	Avg.	44,913.63	1,152.85	46,066.48	0.00	6,812.00	52,878.48
		Min.	39,156.00	407.00	40,473.00	0.00	6,812.00	47,285.00
		Max.	57,000.00	1,639.00	57,407.00	0.00	6,812.00	64,219.00

D. Summary Data for Engineer 1

Base Salary		Total Cash		Total Compensation		Bonuses	Stock Options
Wtd Mean:	$46,085.21	*Wtd Mean:*	$48,289.66	*Wtd Mean:*	$56,917.08	*Avg* $2,370.59	*Avg* $16,920.18
Mean:	$49,092.71	*Mean:*	$50,940.53	*Mean:*	$65,524.22	*As a % of Base*	*As a % of Base*
50th:	$45,000.00	*50th:*	$46,422.00	*50th:*	$53,271.00	5.18%	33.96%
25th:	$42,600.00	*25th:*	$43,769.00	*25th:*	$50,593.11	*% who Receive*	*% who Receive*
75th:	$48,500.00	*75th:*	$51,854.04	*75th:*	$60,750.89	92.99%	8.38%

Anomalies.   Part B of the survey gives actual salaries received by actual Engineer 1s. Perusal of actual salary data gives the analyst an initial sense of the nature and quality of the data and helps identify any areas for additional consideration. For example, Part B of Exhibit 8.12 shows that no Engineer 1s at Company 1 receive stock options, and five receive no bonuses. The bonuses that are paid range from $500 to $4,000. Because there are 585 Engineer 1s in this survey, we have not included all their salary information. Nevertheless, individual level data provide a wealth of information about specific practices. Unfortunately, many surveys provide only summary information such as company averages. Understanding minimums, maximums, and what percentage actually receive bonuses and/or options is essential.

Part C of Exhibit 8.12 provides company data. Again, the first step is to look for anomalies.

Does any one company dominate? For example, company 57 employs 226 Engineer 1s, whereas four of the companies report only one Engineer 1. A separate analysis of the largest company's data will isolate that employer's pay practices and clarify the nature of its influence.

Do all employers show similar patterns? The base pay for a single job at Company 1 ranges from $36,500 to $79,000. This raises the possibility that this company might use broad bands (discussed later in this chapter). Although seven of the companies have a bonus-to-base pay ratio of around 2 to 3 percent, Company 15 pays an average bonus of $8,254. Company 51 gives one of its engineers options valued at $74,453 on top of base pay. Because they are such outliers (anomalies) compared to other companies, the FastCat analyst might consider dropping these companies. What difference will it make if Company 15 or 51 is dropped? What difference will it make if they are included?

Part D at the bottom of Exhibit 8.12 contains summary data: five different measures of base pay, cash, and total compensation, as well as the percentage of engineers who receive bonuses (92.99%) and options (8.38%). The data suggest that most of FastCat's competitors use bonuses but are less likely to use options for this particular job. Summary data help reduce all the survey information into a smaller number of measures for further statistical analysis.

Becoming familiar with the actual survey data is a necessary first step in judging their accuracy and usefulness. Before we proceed with our process of interpreting the results, a review of some simple statistics is required.

Statistical Analysis

All the statistics necessary to analyze survey data, including regression, are covered in any basic statistics class or textbook. Understanding regression analysis equips you to make sound compensation judgments. We shall focus on how these statistics help FastCat get from the raw survey data shown in Exhibit 8.12 to a market line that reflects the competitors' pay in the market: frequency distributions, and measures of central tendency and variation.

Frequency distributions.   Exhibit 8.13 shows two frequency distributions created from the data in the Exhibit 8.12 survey. The top one shows the distribution of the *base wages* for the 585 Engineer 1s. The X axis shows base wages in increments of $1,000, ranging from $36,000 to $80,000. The second frequency distribution shows the *total compensation* for 719 Engineer 5s from the same survey. *Total compensation* for Engineer 5s is shown in increments of $10,000 and ranges from under $90,000 to over $900,000. This wide range of dollars is the reason that many surveys switch to logs of dollars for higher level positions. Frequency distributions help visualize the information in the survey and may highlight nonconformities. For example, the one base wage above $79,000 may be considered an **outlier**—an extreme that falls outside the majority of the data points. Is this a unique person? Or an error in reporting the data? Whether or not to include outliers is a judgment call.

The exhibit shows that frequency distributions can vary in their shape. Unusual shapes may reflect problems with job matches, widely dispersed pay rates, or employers with widely divergent

outlier

a data point that falls outside the majority of the data points

EXHIBIT	8.13	Frequency Distributions

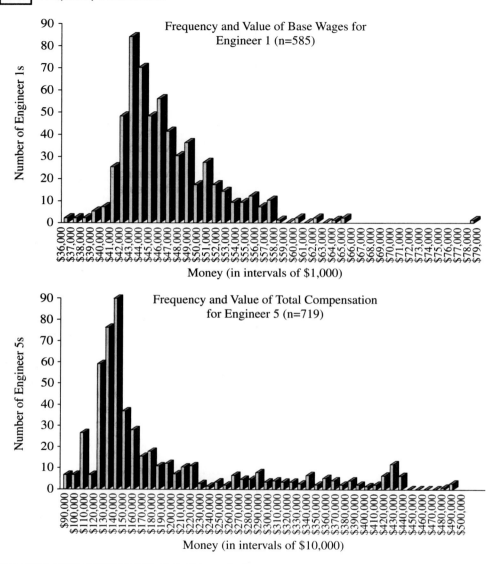

pay policies. If the data look reasonable at this point, one wag suggests it's probably the result of two large, offsetting errors.

Central Tendency.   A measure of central tendency reduces a large amount of data to a single number. The frequency distributions show the *mode*—the most common measure (in Exhibit 8.13, the most common base wage is the interval of $43,000 to $43,999). Other measures of central tendency include the mean, weighted mean, and median. The *weighted mean* is calculated by adding the base wages for all 585 engineers in the survey and then dividing by 585 ($46,085). This measure gives equal weight to *each individual employee's* wage. On the other hand, if only company averages are reported in the survey, then a *mean* may be calculated by adding one measure of base wage per company and dividing by the number of companies. In the survey in Exhibit 8.12, the mean base wage is $49,912 (calculated by adding the average base wage for each of the 16 companies and then dividing by 16 companies). Although use of the mean is common, it may not accurately reflect actual labour market conditions, since the base wage of the largest employer is given the same weight as that of the smallest employer. The *median* is another measure of central tendency: It is the middle of all reported rates. In our sample of 585 engineers, the median base wage would be whatever rate is halfway down a list of all 585 rates arranged from highest to lowest ($45,000). (Since half of 585 is 292.5, the 292nd and 293rd rate are averaged.) Medians dampen the effect of outliers. Some analysts calculate several measures of central tendency before deciding which one best represents the "going rate." In general, the weighted mean gives a fairly accurate picture of actual labour market conditions, since it captures the size of the supply and demand. The bottom of Exhibit 8.12 includes the weighted mean, mean, and 50th percentile, which is the same as the median.

Variation.   The distribution of rates around a measure of central tendency is called variation. The two frequency distributions in Exhibit 8.13 show very different patterns of variation. The *standard deviation* is probably the most common statistical measure of variation, although its use in salary surveys is rare. Standard deviation refers to how far from the mean (or weighted mean) each of the items in a frequency distribution is located. One standard deviation of the base wages for Engineer 1 is $4,863, which means that 68 percent of the salaries lie between $41,222 ($46,085 − $4,863) and $50,948 ($46,085 + $4,863). Information about variation tells us about how similar (dissimilar) competitors pay in the market.

Quartiles and percentiles are more common measures of dispersion in salary survey analysis. Recall from the chapter introduction that someone's policy was "to be in the 75th percentile nationally." A 75th percentile means that 75 percent of all pay rates are at or below that point, and 25 percent are above. The survey in Exhibit 8.12 gives 50th, 25th, and 75th percentiles (also called "quartiles"). To calculate percentiles, the measures are ordered from lowest to highest, then converted to percentages. We shall use quartiles later in the chapter in setting pay ranges.

These are among the most common statistics used in survey reports. Now that everyone is up to speed on statistics, let us go back to applying the survey results to FastCat. Next step is to update the survey data.

Update the Survey Data

Because they reflect decisions of employers, employees, unions, and government agencies, wages paid by competitors are constantly changing. And competitors adjust their wages at different times. Universities typically adjust to match the academic year. Unionized employers adjust on dates negotiated in labour agreements. Many employers adjust each employee's pay on the anniversary of the employee's date of hire. Even though these changes do not occur smoothly and uniformly throughout the year, as a practical matter it is common practice to assume that they do. Therefore, a survey that requires three months to collect, code, and analyze is probably outdated before it becomes available. Consequently, the pay data usually are updated to forecast the competitive rates for the future date when the pay decisions will be implemented.

The amount to update (often called *aging or trending*) is based on several factors, including historical trends in market economic forecasts, prospects for the economy in which the employer operates, and the manager's judgment, among others.

Exhibit 8.14 illustrates updating. In the example, the base pay rates collected in the survey were in effect at January 1 of the *current year*. Because this company's stated policy is to "match at the 50th percentile," the median base pay for the Engineer 1 job ($45,000) is the 50th percentile of the base wage in the market. The compensation manager will use these data for pay decisions that will go into effect on January 1 of the **plan year**. Assume that base pay has been increasing by approximately 5 percent annually. If we assume that the future will be like the past, then the market data are multiplied by 105 percent, to account for the rise in pay that is expected to occur by the end of the *current year*. The $45,000 this past January 1 is updated to $47,250 by the end of the *current year*.

To estimate what the market rates will be by the *end* of the *plan* year, a judgment is made about the rate of increase expected during the plan year, and survey results are updated again on the basis of this judgment.

Construct a Market Pay Line

Turn back and look again at Exhibit 8.11. It shows the results of the FastCat analyst's decisions on which benchmark jobs to include (seven jobs on the X [the horizontal] axis), which companies to include, and which statistics to use to measure pay. Three different compensation metrics are included: base wage, total cash, and total compensation. For each of these metrics, a line has been drawn connecting the rates for the seven jobs. Why were the seven jobs arranged in this order on the graph? In other words, why isn't the Technician A in the middle or on the

---

EXHIBIT **8.14**   Choices for Updating Survey Data to Reflect Pay Policy

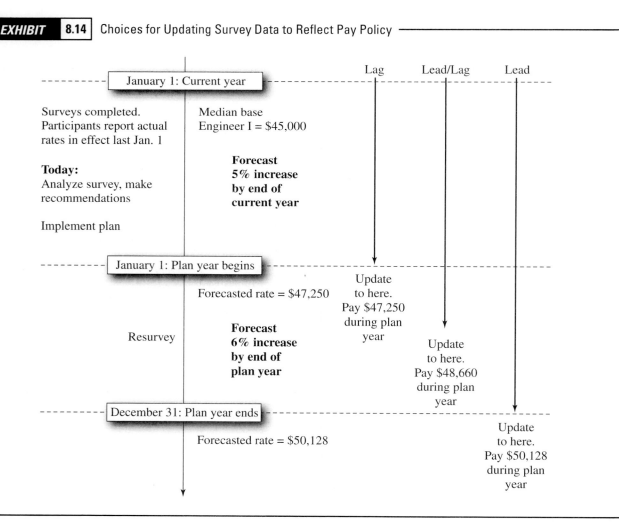

market pay line

links a company's benchmark jobs on the horizontal axis (internal structure) with market rates paid by competitors (market survey) on the vertical axis

right? Because the ordering on the graph reflects the internal structure at FastCat. Jobs are ordered on the horizontal (X) axis according to their position in the internal structure. In our example, job evaluation points are the basis for this ordering. Consequently, a **market pay line** links a company's benchmark jobs on the horizontal axis (internal structure) with market rates paid by competitors (market survey), which are on the vertical axis.

A market line may be drawn freehand by connecting the data points, as was done in Exhibit 8.11. Or, statistical techniques such as regression analysis may be used. Exhibit 8.15 shows the regression lines that used the same data as in Exhibit 8.11. Regression generates a straight line that best fits the data by minimizing the variance around the line. Regression provides a statistical *summary of the distribution of going rates paid by competitors in the market—in this case, the market line.* The appendix contains more information about regression analysis.

To understand what the regression lines mean, compare the data tables in Exhibit 8.11 and 8.15. Exhibit 8.11 tells the *market rates for seven survey jobs.* Exhibit 8.15 shows the *job evaluation points for the FastCats jobs that match* each of these seven survey jobs, and the *regression's "prediction"* of the salary of each job. The actual base wage for the survey job Tech A is $22,989 (Exhibit 8.11). The "predicted" base for the matching FastCat job is $23,058 (Exhibit 8.15). Why use the regression results rather than the actual survey data? Regression "smooths" large amounts of data while minimizing variations in it. In Exhibit 8.16, the diamonds are the actual results of the survey, and the solid line is the regression result.

EXHIBIT | **8.15** | From Regression Results to a Market Line

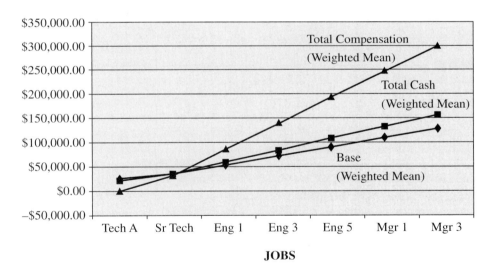

Job	JEPts	Predicted Base, Wtd Mean	Predicted Cash, Wtd Mean	Predicted Total Comp
Tech A	10	$23,057.96	$20,543.71	−$1,330.36
Sr Tech	25	$34,361.06	$35,116.51	$31,172.24
Eng 1	50	$53,199.56	$59,404.51	$85,343.24
Eng 3	75	$72,038.06	$83,692.51	$139,514.24
Eng 5	100	$90,876.56	$107,980.51	$193,685.24
Mgr 1	125	$109,715.06	$132,268.51	$247,856.24
Mgr 3	150	$128,553.56	$156,556.51	$302,027.24

EXHIBIT 8.16 Understanding Regression

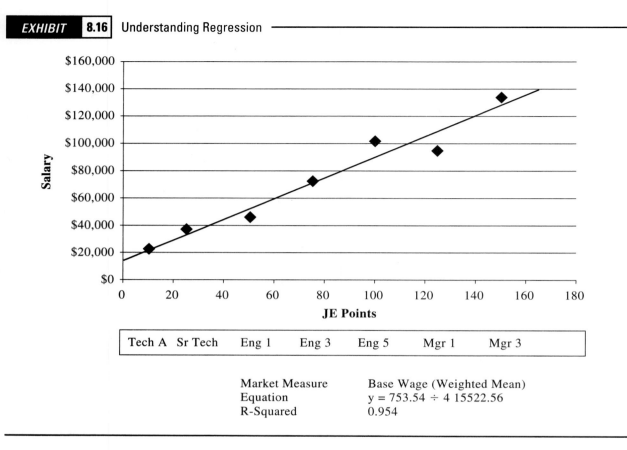

Tech A	Sr Tech	Eng 1	Eng 3	Eng 5	Mgr 1	Mgr 3

Market Measure	Base Wage (Weighted Mean)
Equation	y = 753.54 ÷ 4 15522.56
R-Squared	0.954

Before we leave survey data analysis, it is important to emphasize that not all survey results look like those in this chapter, and not all companies use the statistical and analytical techniques discussed in this chapter. There is no one "right way" to analyze survey data. It has been our intent to provide some insight into the kinds of calculations that are useful and the assumptions that underlie salary surveys.

Combine Internal Structure and External Market Rates

At this point, two parts of the total pay model have merged. Their relationship to each other can be seen in Exhibit 8.17.

- The *internally aligned structure* developed in Part One is shown on the horizontal axis. For this illustration, our structure consists of jobs A through P, with P being the Engineering Manager 3, the most complex job in this structure. Jobs B, F, G, H, J, M, and P are the seven benchmark jobs that have been matched in the survey. Job F is our Engineer 1.
- The salaries paid by relevant competitors for those benchmark jobs, as measured by the survey—*the external competitive data*—are shown on the vertical (Y) axis.

These two components—internal alignment and external competitiveness—come together in the pay structure. The pay structure has two aspects: the *pay policy line*, and *pay ranges*.

| EXHIBIT | 8.17 | Develop Pay Grades

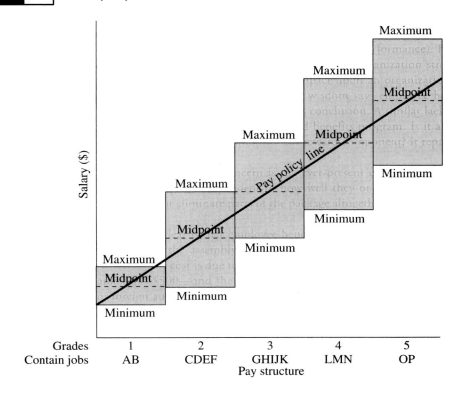

■ SET COMPETITIVE POSITION: THE PAY POLICY LINE

pay policy line

pay line representing an adjustment to the market pay line to reflect the company's external competitive position in the market (i.e., lead, match, lag)

The next major decision is to set the external competitive position by constructing a **pay policy line**. This line reflects external competitive position in the market. The previous chapter discussed why employers might choose different external competitive pay policies. Here, the organization must put its chosen competitive pay policy into effect. You are already familiar with some of the choices that went into creating that policy (e.g., lead, match, lag).

Choice of Measure.   There are a number of ways to translate a pay level policy into practice. The *choice of the measure* to use in the regression analysis is one. Exhibit 8.16 used the weighted mean of base pay. If Colgate practises what it claims at the beginning of the chapter, then Colgate might use a weighted mean for base pay and the 75th percentile for total compensation.

Updating.   A pay level policy may also affect how an employer *updates* the survey data. Look again at Exhibit 8.14. The arrows on the right side of the exhibit show how updating reflects policy. If the company chooses a "match" policy, but then updates survey data to the end of the current year/start of the plan year and keeps this rate in effect throughout the plan year, the company actually will be lagging the market. It will match its desired market pay level only at the beginning of the plan year. The market rates continue to rise throughout the year; the company's rates do not.

Aging the market data to a point halfway through the plan year (middle arrow in Exhibit 8.14) is called *lead/lag*. The original survey rates are updated to the end of the current year plus half the projected amount for the plan year ($48,660). An employer that wants to lead the market may age data to the *end* of the plan year ($50,128), then pay at this rate throughout the plan year.

Flat Percentage.   A third approach to translate pay level policy into practice is simply to *specify a percentage* above or below the regression line (market line) that an employer intends to match, and then draw a new line at this higher (or lower) level. This would carry out the policy statement, "We lead the market by 10 percent." Other possibilities exist. An employer might lead by including only a few top-paying competitors in the analysis and then matching them. Or lead for some job families and lag for others. The point is that just as there are alternatives among competitive pay policies (lead, match, lag, etc.), so there are alternative ways to translate policy into practice. If the practice does not match the policy (i.e., we say one thing but do another), then employees receive the wrong message.

■ SET COMPETITIVE POSITION: GRADES AND RANGES

The next step is to design pay grades and ranges. These analyses usually are done with base pay data, since base pay reflects the basic value of the work (or relevant skill sets).

Why Bother with Grades and Ranges?

Grades and ranges offer managers the flexibility to deal with pressures from external markets and within the organization. External market pressures include many already discussed such as those created by supply and demand. Beyond this, ranges permit managers to recognize other differences. These include:

1. Differences in quality (skills, abilities, experience) between individuals applying for work (e.g., Microsoft may have stricter hiring requirements for engineers than FastCat, even though job descriptions appear identical).
2. Differences in the productivity or value of these quality variations (e.g., the value of the results from a software engineer at Microsoft probably differs from the results of a software engineer at Best Buy).
3. Differences in the mix of pay forms competitors use (e.g., Oracle uses more stock options than IBM, so IBM managers may need to offer more base when competing with Oracle).

In addition to offering flexibility to deal with these external differences in rates, an organization may desire differences in rates paid to employees on the same job. *A pay range exists whenever two or more rates are paid to employees in the same job*. Hence, ranges provide managers the opportunity to:

1. Recognize individual performance differences with pay.
2. Meet employees' expectations that their pay will increase over time, even while holding the same job.
3. Encourage employee commitment to remain with the organization.

From an internal alignment perspective, the range reflects the differences in performance or experience the employer wishes to pay for a given level of work. From an external competitiveness perspective, the range also acts as a control device. A range maximum sets the lid on what the employer is willing to pay for that work; the range minimum sets the floor.

Not all employers use ranges. Skill-based plans establish single *flat rates* for each skill level regardless of performance or seniority. And many collective bargaining contracts establish single flat rates for each job (e.g., all Senior Machinists II receive $14.50 per hour regardless of performance or seniority). This flat rate is often set to correspond to some midpoint on a survey of that job. And increasingly, *broad bands* (think really fat ranges) are being adopted. Broad bands offer employers even greater flexibility to treat employees differently and to deal with external pressures. Banding is discussed below.

Develop Grades

pay grade

■ grouping of jobs considered substantially equal for pay purposes

The first step in building flexibility into the pay structure is to group different jobs that are considered substantially equal for pay purposes into a **pay grade**. Grades enhance an organization's ability to move people between jobs within a grade with no change in pay. In Exhibit 8.17 the jobs are grouped into five grades on the horizontal axis.

The question of which jobs are substantially equal and therefore slotted into one grade requires the analyst to reconsider the original job evaluation results. Each grade will have its own pay range, and *all the jobs within a single grade will have the same pay range*. Jobs in different grades (e.g., jobs C, D, E, and F in Grade 2) should be dissimilar to those in other grades (Grade 1 jobs A and B) and will have a different pay range.

Although grades permit flexibility, they are challenging to design. The objective is that all jobs that are similar for pay purposes be placed within the same grade. If jobs with relatively close job evaluation point totals fall on either side of grade boundaries, the magnitude of difference in salary treatment may be out of proportion to the magnitude of difference in the value of the job content. Resolving such dilemmas requires an understanding of the specific jobs, career paths, and workflow in the organization. Designing the grade structure that fits each organization involves the use of trial and error until one structure is found to fit the best without too many problems. Considerable judgment is involved.

Establish Range Midpoints, Minimums, and Maximums

pay range

■ an upper and lower limit on pay for all jobs in a pay grade

Grades group job evaluation data on the horizontal axis; ranges group salary data on the vertical axis. **Pay ranges** set an upper and lower limit between which all wages for all jobs in that particular grade are expected to fall. A range has three salient features: a midpoint, a minimum, and a maximum. The midpoints for each range usually correspond to the point where the pay policy line crosses each grade. The competitive pay level for each grade, established earlier, becomes the midpoint of the pay range for that grade. The midpoint for Grade 2 in Exhibit 8.17, which contains the Engineer job, is $54,896 (i.e., the point where the pay policy line crosses the centre of the grade).

What Size Should the Range Be?   The size of the range is based on some judgment about how the ranges support career paths, promotions, and other organization systems.[19] Top-level management positions commonly have ranges of 60 to 120 percent; entry to midlevel professional and managerial positions, between 35 and 60 percent; office and production work, 10 to 25 percent. The underlying logic is that larger ranges in the managerial jobs reflect the greater opportunity for individual discretion and performance variations in the work. Grade 2 has a range that extends 20 percent above and 20 percent below the midpoint. An alternative formula for calculating minimum = midpoint / [100%+(1/2 range)]; for calculating maximum = minimum + (range × minimum). This approach gives a different result from adding 20 percent above and below the midpoint. The important point is to be consistent in whatever approach you choose and to be sure other users of the survey are apprised of how range minimums and maximums are calculated.[20]

Another, perhaps better, basis on which to determine the desired range is what makes good sense to the particular employer. Surveys usually provide data on both the actual maximum and minimum rates paid, as well as the ranges established by policy. Some compensation managers use the actual rates paid, particularly the 75th and 25th percentiles in the survey data, as their maximums and minimums. Others examine alternatives to ensure that the proposed spread includes at least 75 percent of the rates in the survey data. Still others establish the minimum and maximum separately. The amount between the minimum and the midpoint can be a function of the amount of time it takes a new employee to become fully competent. Jobs quickly learned may have minimums much closer to the midpoints. The maximum becomes the amount above the midpoint that the company is willing to pay for sustained performance on the job. In the end, the size of the range is based on judgment that weighs all these factors.

Promotion Increases Matter.   An issue related to ranges is the size of pay differentials between managers and the employees they manage. A managerial job typically would be at least one pay range removed from the jobs it supervises. Although a 15 percent pay differential has been offered as a rule of thumb, large range overlap, combined with possible overtime or incentive pay available in some jobs but not in managerial jobs, could make it difficult to maintain such a differential. On the other hand, some argue that differentials are counterproductive if they force good technical talent (e.g., engineers) to become managers solely because managers command higher incomes. The issue is one of overlap.

Overlap

If A and B are two adjacent pay grades, with B the higher of the two, the degree of overlap is defined as 100 × [(Maximum Rate Grade A − Minimum Rate Grade B)/ (Maximum Rate Grade A − Minimum Rate Grade A)]. What difference does overlap make? Exhibit 8.18 shows two extremes in the degree of overlap between adjacent grades. The high degree of overlap and low midpoint differentials in Figure A indicate small differences in the value of jobs in the adjoining grades. Being promoted from one grade to another may include a title change but not much change in pay. On the other hand, the smaller ranges in Figure B create less overlap, which permits the manager to reinforce a promotion into a new grade with a larger pay increase. What is the optimal overlap? The differential between grades must be large enough to induce employees to seek and/or accept promotion or to undertake the necessary training required to move into a higher grade. However, there is virtually no research to indicate how much differential is necessary to influence employees to do so.

EXHIBIT | **8.18** | Range Overlap ————————————————————————————————————

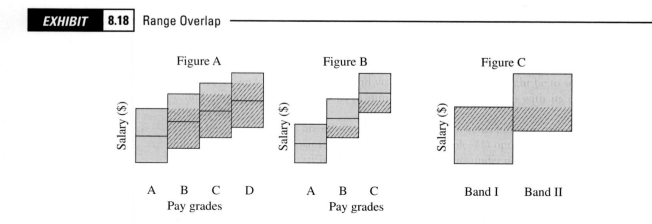

SET COMPETITIVE POSITION: BROADBANDING

broadbanding

a large band of jobs containing several pay grades

Figure C in Exhibit 8.18 collapses salary grades into only a few broad bands, each with a sizeable range. This technique, known as **broadbanding**, consolidates as many as four or five traditional grades into a single band with one minimum and one maximum. Because the band encompasses so many jobs of differing values, a range midpoint usually is not used.[21]

Contrasts between ranges and broad bands are highlighted in Exhibit 8.19. Supporters of broad bands list several advantages over traditional approaches. First, broad bands provide flexibility to define job responsibilities more broadly. They support redesigned, downsized, or boundaryless organizations that have eliminated layers of managerial jobs. They foster cross-functional growth and development in these new organizations. Employees can move laterally across functions within a band in order to gain depth of experience. Companies with global operations use bands to aid in moving managers among worldwide assignments. The emphasis on lateral movement with no pay adjustments tied to such movement helps manage the reality of fewer promotion opportunities in flattened organization structures. The flexibility of banding eases mergers and acquisitions since there are not many levels to argue over.[22]

Broad bands are often combined with more traditional salary administration practices by using midpoints or other control points within bands to keep the system more intact structurally.[23] Perhaps the most important difference between grades-and-ranges and broad banding is where the controls are located. The "grade-and-range" approach has guidelines and controls designed right into the pay system. Range minimums, maximums, and midpoints guide managers' decisions to ensure consistency across managers. Under bands, managers have only a total salary budget limiting them. But as experience with bands has advanced, some guidelines increasingly are designed into them.

Bands may add flexibility to the compensation system. Less time will be spent judging fine distinctions between jobs and building barriers. On the other hand, some say that the time avoided judging jobs now will be spent judging individuals, a prospect managers already try to avoid. How will an organization avoid the appearance of salary treatment based on personality and politics rather than objective criteria?[24] Ideally, with a strong performance-based system.

Broadbanding takes two steps.

1. **Set the number of bands.** Surveys report companies are using three to eight bands for pay purposes. Merck uses six bands for its entire structure, with titles ranging from contributor to executive. A unit of General Electric replaced 24 levels with five bands.

EXHIBIT 8.19 Contrasts between Ranges and Bands

Ranges support	Bands support
Some flexibility within controls	Emphasis on flexibility within guidelines
Relatively stable organization design	Global organizations
Recognition via titles or career progression	Crossfunctional experience and lateral progression
Midpoint controls, comparatives	Reference market rates, shadow ranges
Controls designed into system	Controls in budget, few in system
Give managers "freedom with guidelines"	Give managers "freedom to manage" pay
To 150 percent range-spread	100–400 percent spreads

Usually bands are established at the major "breaks," or differences in work or skill/competency requirements. Titles used to label each band reflect these major breaks, such as associates (entry level individual contributor), professional (experienced, knowledgeable team member), leader (project or group supervisor), director, or "coach," or even "visionary"(we don't make this up).

The four bands in Exhibit 8.20 (associates, professionals, lead professionals, senior professionals) include multiple job families within each band. Each band might include jobs from finance, purchasing, software development and engineering, marketing, and so on. The challenge is how much to pay people who are in the same band but in different functions performing different work.

Do associates and professionals at companies such as General Electric in purchasing (with degrees in business) receive the same pay as engineers (with degrees in computer science)? Not likely. Usually external market differences exist, so the different functions or groups within bands must be priced differently.

2. **Price the bands: reference rates.** As the bottom of Exhibit 8.20 depicts, different market rates may be identified within each band for each job family. In the professionals band in the exhibit, the three job families (purchasing, finance, and engineering) have

---

EXHIBIT 8.20 | Four Bands

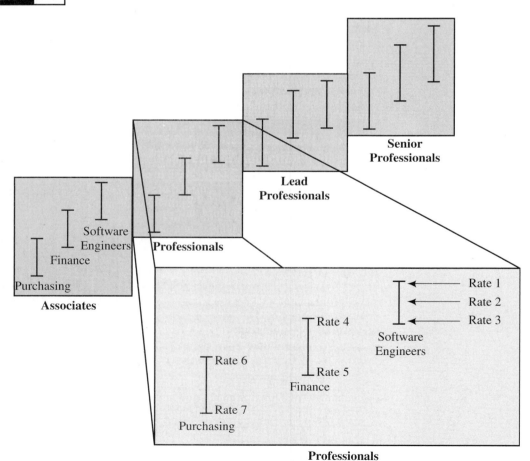

.NET WORTH — Broadbanding

A May 2002 AON Consulting e-survey of 52 organizations using broadbanding found that 78 percent were satisfied or somewhat satisfied with their broadbanding job structure. The top three reasons for implementing a broadbanding system were (1) more flexible pay and career movement processes, (2) a flatter organization structure, and (3) replacing an outdated compensation structure.

When it came to structuring pay within the broad bands, 50 percent used market reference points/ranges for job groups; 44 percent used market reference points/ranges for individual jobs; and 28 percent simply provided market data to managers to make local pay decisions. Thus, in the tradeoff between internal equity and market competitiveness, the market was the winner. Despite the common beliefs that pay structures consist of grades and that benchmark jobs are the ones that should be analyzed relative to the market, 44 percent of respondents used market reference points/ranges for individual jobs, suggesting that organizations might be giving up on clustering jobs for pay purposes.

Source: A.S. Rosen & D. Turetsky, "Broadbanding: The Construction of a Career Management Framework," *WorldatWork Journal*, Fourth Quarter 2002, pp. 45-55.

reference rates
pay rates from market data used in pricing broad bands

different **reference rates.** The reference rates are drawn from market data and managers' intimate knowledge of going rates (especially in volatile e-business companies); they reflect rates paid by competitors.

You might say, "This is beginning to look a lot like 'ranges' within each band." You would be correct. The difference is that ranges traditionally serve as controls, whereas reference rates act as guides. Today's guides grow into tomorrow's bureaucracy.

Flexibility—Control. Broadbanding encourages employees to move cross-functionally (e.g., purchasing to finance, between development and systems design) to increase the cross-fertilization of ideas. Hence, a career move is more likely to be within a band and less likely between bands.

According to supporters, the principal payoff of broadbanding is flexibility. Flexibility is one side of the coin; chaos and favouritism is the other. Banding presumes that managers will manage employee pay to accomplish the organization's objectives (and not their own) and treat employees fairly. Historically, this is not the first time greater flexibility has been shifted to managers and employees. Indeed, the rationale underlying the use of ranges and grades was to reduce inconsistencies and favouritism that were destructive to employee relations in previous generations.[25] The challenge today is to take advantage of flexibility without increasing labour costs or leaving the organization vulnerable to charges of favouritism or inconsistent and illegal practices.

BALANCING INTERNAL AND EXTERNAL PRESSURES: ADJUSTING THE PAY STRUCTURE

Establishing the pay ranges/bands for work reflects a balance between competitive pressures and pressures for internal alignment and fairness. Up until now, we have tended to make a distinction between the job structure and the pay structure.

A *job structure* orders jobs on the basis of internal organizational factors (reflected in job evaluation or skill certification). The *pay structure*, on the other hand, is anchored by the organization's external competitive position, reflected in its base pay policy lines.

Reconciling Differences

The problem with using two bases (internal and external) to create a structure is that they are likely to result in two different structures. The order in which jobs are ranked on internal and external factors probably will not agree completely. Differences between market structures and rates and job evaluation rankings warrant a review of the basic decisions in evaluating and pricing that particular job. This may entail a review of the job analysis, the job description, and the evaluation of the job, or the market data for the job in question. Often this reanalysis solves the problem. Sometimes, however, discrepancies persist; sometimes survey data are discarded; sometimes benchmark job matches are changed.

One study of how differences are actually reconciled found that managers weigh external market data more heavily than internal job evaluation data. In light of all the judgments that go into internal evaluation, market data often are considered to be more objective.[26] Yet this chapter and recent research shows that market data are also based on judgments.

Sometimes differences arise because a shortage of a particular skill has driven up the market rate. But reclassifying a market-sensitive job (one in which a supply-and-demand imbalance exists) into a higher salary grade, where it will remain long after the imbalance has been corrected, creates additional problems. Creating a special range that is clearly designated as *market responsive* may be a better approach. However, decisions made on the basis of expediency run the risk of undermining the integrity of the pay decisions.

■ MARKET PRICING

market pricing

■ establishing pay structure by relying almost exclusively on external market pay rates

Many organizations in the Canada are adopting pay strategies that emphasize external competitiveness and deemphasize internal alignment. Called **market pricing**, this approach sets pay structures by relying almost exclusively on rates paid by competitors in the external market. Organizations that fill a large proportion of their job vacancies with hires from the outside may also become market pricers. Market pricers match a large percentage of their jobs with market data and collect as much market data as possible.[27] They *rank to market* to determine the pay for jobs unique to their firms. The competitive rates for positions for which external market data are available are first calculated, then the remaining (nonbenchmark) jobs are blended into the pay hierarchy created, based on external rates. Pfizer, for example, begins with job analysis and job descriptions. These are immediately followed by labour market analysis and market pricing for as many jobs as possible. After that, the remaining jobs are blended in and the internal job relationships are reviewed to be sure they are "*reasonable in light of organization work flow and other uniqueness.*" The final step is pricing those jobs not priced directly in the market. This is done by comparing the value of these jobs to Pfizer to Pfizer jobs already priced in the market.

Market pricing goes beyond the use of benchmark jobs and then slotting nonbenchmarks. The objective of market pricing is to base most if not all of the internal pay structure on external rates paid by competitors, breaking down the boundaries between the internal organization and external market forces. Some companies even match all forms of pay for each job to their competitors in the market. For example, if the average rate paid by competitors for a controller job is $150,000, then the company pays $150,000. If 60 percent of the $150,000 is base pay, 20 percent is annual bonus, 5 percent is stock options, and 15 percent is benefits, the company matches not only the amount but also this mix of pay forms. Another $150,000 job, say director of marketing, may have a different pattern among market competitors, which is also matched.

Pure market pricing carried to this extreme deemphasizes internal alignment completely. Gone is any attempt to align internal pay structures with the business strategy and the work performed. Rather, the internal pay structure is aligned with competitors' decisions that are reflected in the market. In a very real sense, the decisions of its competitors determine an organization's pay structure.

This approach raises several issues. Among them: Just how valid are the market data?[28] Do they really lend themselves to such decisions? Why should competitors' pay decisions be the sole or even primary determinant of another company's pay structure? If they are, then *how much or what forms* a company pays no longer constitute a competitive advantage. They are not unique, nor are they difficult to imitate.

Any unique or difficult-to-imitate aspects of the organization's pay structure, which may have been based on its unique technology or its unique flow of work, are deemphasized by market pricers. Fairness is presumed to be reflected by market rates; employee behaviour is presumed to be reinforced by totally market-priced structures, which are the very same as those of competitors.

In sum, the process of balancing internal and external pressures is a matter of judgment, made with an eye to the strategic perspectives and objectives established for the pay system.[29] Deemphasizing pay alignment within an organization may lead to feelings of unfair treatment among employees and inconsistency with the fundamental culture of the organization. This in turn may reduce employees' willingness to share new ideas about how to improve the work or the product. Unaligned and inequitable pay relationships may also lead employees to seek other jobs, file grievances, form unions, go out on strike, or refuse to take on increased job responsibilities. Neglecting external competitive pay practices, however, will affect both the ability to attract applicants and the ability to hire applicants who match the organization's needs. External pay relationships also impact labour costs and hence the ability to compete in the product/service market.

■ REVIEW

The end of Part Two of the textbook is a logical spot for a midterm exam. Exhibit 8.21 has been designed to help you review.

EXHIBIT 8.21 Mid-Term Exam ───

Open-book mid-term exam: Answer true or false to the following questions:

You know you are spending too much time working on compensation when you

- Use the terms "pay mix" and "external competitiveness" when you e-mail home for money.
- Think that paying for lunch requires a strategic approach.
- Ask your date to specify his/her competencies.
- Think that copying your classmate's answers on this exam is benchmarking.
- Can explain the difference between traditional pay grades and ranges and new broad bands with shadow ranges.
- Believe your answer to the above.
- Would cross the street to listen to economists and psychologists discuss the "likely effects of alternative external competitiveness policies."
- Consider your Phase II assignment a wonderful opportunity to increase your human capital.
- Think adding points to your project grade creates a "balanced scorecard."
- Are willing to pay your instructor to teach any other course.
- Are surprised to learn that some people think a COLA is a soft drink.
- Turn your head to listen rather than roll your eyes when someone talks about being "incentivized" with pay.
- Believe that instead of your mom, "the market" knows best.

How did you do? Good. Now let's move on to the next chapters.

CONCLUSION

This chapter has detailed the basic decisions and techniques involved in setting pay levels and mix and designing pay structures. Most organizations survey other employers' pay practices to determine the rates competitors pay. An employer using survey results considers how it wishes to position its total compensation in the market: to lead, to match, or to follow competition. This policy decision may be different for different business units and even for different job groups within a single organization. The policy on competitive position is translated into practice by setting pay policy lines; they serve as reference points around which pay grades and ranges or bands are designed.

The use of grades and ranges recognizes both external and internal pressures on pay decisions. No single "going rate" for a job exists in the market; instead, an array of rates exists. This array results from conditions of demand and supply, variations in the quality of employees, and differences in employer policies and practices. It also reflects the fact that employers differ in the value they attach to the jobs and people. And, very importantly, it reflects differences in the mix of pay forms different companies emphasize.

Internally, the use of ranges is consistent with variations in the discretion present in jobs. Some employees will perform better than others; some employees are more experienced than others. Pay ranges permit employers to value and recognize these differences with pay.

Managers increasingly are interested in broadbanding, which offers even greater flexibility than grades and ranges to deal with the continuously changing work assignments required in many successful organizations. Broadbanding offers freedom to adapt to changes without requiring approvals, but risks self-serving and potentially inequitable decisions on the part of the manager. Recently, the trend has been toward approaches with greater flexibility to adapt to changing conditions. Such flexibility also makes mergers and acquisitions easier and global alignment possible.

Let us step back for a moment to review what has been discussed and preview what is coming. We have examined two strategic components of the total pay model. A concern for internal alignment meant that analysis and perhaps descriptions and evaluation were important for achieving a competitive advantage and fair treatment. A concern for external competitiveness required competitive positioning, survey design and analysis, setting the pay policy line (how much and what forms), and designing grades and ranges or broad bands. The next part of the book is concerned with employee contributions—paying the people who perform the work. This is perhaps the most important part of the book. All that has gone before is mere prelude, setting up the pay levels, mix, and structures by which people are to be paid. Now it is time to pay the people.

CHAPTER SUMMARY

1.   The seven decisions involved in setting externally competitive pay and designing the corresponding pay structure are: (1) specify the employer's external pay policy, (2) define the purpose of the survey, (3) choose relevant market competitors, (4) design the survey, (5) interpret survey results and construct the market line, (6) construct a pay policy line that reflects external pay policy, and (7) balance competitiveness with internal alignments through the use of ranges, flat rates, and/or bands.

2. The steps involved in survey design are deciding: a) whether to do the survey in-house or to involve consultants, b) how many employers to survey, c) on standards for assessing survey results, d) which jobs to include in the survey, and e) what information to collect.

3. Survey data reported will change after they are collected when pay is increased at various organizations at various points throughout the year. Therefore, data are updated to forecast competitive rates for the date when the pay decisions will be implemented.

4. A market pay line links a company's benchmark jobs on the horizontal axis (internal structure) with market rates paid by competitors (market survey) on the vertical axis. A pay policy line represents external competitive position in the market (i.e., lead, match, lag).

5. Pay grades are created by grouping jobs considered substantially equal for pay purposes. Pay ranges provide an upper and lower limit for pay for all jobs in a pay grade. Broadbanding is the practice of establishing large bands of jobs containing several pay grades.

6. Differences between market structures and rates and job evaluation rankings warrant a review of the basic decisions in evaluating and pricing jobs. Pay structures often are adjusted to balance these internal and external pressures by reviewing job analysis, the job description, and the job evaluation or market data for the job in question. Market data often are weighted more heavily than internal job evaluation data when making adjustments to pay structures.

KEY TERMS

REVIEW QUESTIONS

1. What are the three main categories of employers in the relevant market for pay surveys?
2. Describe five approaches to selecting jobs for inclusion in a survey.
3. What do surveys have to do with pay discrimination?
4. Contrast pay ranges and grades with bands. Why would you use either? Does their use assist or hinder the achievement of internal alignment? External competitiveness?

EXPERIENTIAL EXERCISES

1. Determine the relevant market for a survey of university professors. Explain the factors you considered in order to arrive at this determination. Why is the definition of the relevant market so important?

2. Draft a recommendation regarding a competitive pay policy for Wal-Mart. Explain why this particular recommendation has been made. Does it depend on circumstances faced by the employer? Which ones? What policy would you recommend to your provincial government?

3. Design a survey for setting pay for welders, and another for financial managers. Do the issues differ? Will the techniques used and the data collected differ? Why or why not?

WEB EXERCISE

Statistics Canada Pay Survey

For a demonstration of Canadian government earnings data, go to the Statistics Canada Web site www.statcan.ca and search for "earnings" (free information only). Find report 97F 0024 X1E 2001 013 called "Earnings of Canadians: Highlight Tables, 2001 Census." Click on "Earnings Groups, Full-Year, Full-Time Workers by Level of Education" for all of Canada (provinces and territories). Draw up two charts comparing the average salary Canadawide and in your province/territory for men and women in each education category. What do these earnings data say about the value of higher education? Does the site give information about how many people were included and how they were selected? What other background information would you like to have regarding the data collection?

CASE

Word-of-Mouse: Compensation Comparisons

Click on the Web site http://salary.monster.ca. This site provides pay data on hundreds of jobs in many different industries in cities all over Canada. Identify several jobs of interest to you, such as Compensation and Benefits Manager, Occupational Health and Safety Manager, Training and Development Manager, Marketing Manager, or Investment Analyst. Select specific cities or use the Canadian national average. Obtain the median, the low and high base, and total cash compensation rates for each job. Then consider the following questions:

1. Which jobs are paid more or less? Is this what you would have expected? Why or why not? What factors could explain the differences in salaries?

2. Do the jobs have different bonuses as a percentage of their base salaries? What could explain these differences?

3. Do the data include the value of stock options? What are the implications of this?

4. How could you use this information in negotiating your salary in your job upon graduation? What data would you provide to support your "asking price"? What factors will influence whether or not you might get what you ask for?

5. What is the relevant labour market for these jobs? How big are the differences between salaries in different locations?

6. For each job, compare the median salary to the low and high averages. How much variation exists? What factors might explain this variation in pay rates for the same job?

7. Look for a description of how these salary data are developed. Do you think there is enough information? Why or why not? Discuss some of the factors that might impair the accuracy of these data. What are the implications of using inaccurate salary data for individuals or companies?

8. With this information available free, why would you bother with consultants' surveys?

■ APPENDIX 8–A
STATISTICS TO CALCULATE A MARKET LINE USING REGRESSION ANALYSIS

Using the mathematical formula for a straight line,

$$y = a + bx$$

where

y = dollars
x = job evaluation points
a = the y value (in dollars) at which $x = 0$ (i.e., the straight line crosses the y-axis)
b = the slope of the line

If $b = 0$, the line is parallel to the x-axis and all jobs are paid the same, regardless of job evaluation points. Using the dollars from the market survey data and the job evaluation points from
the internal job structure, solving this equation enables the analyst to construct a line based on
the relationship between the internal job structure and market rates. An upward sloping line
means that more job evaluation points are associated with higher dollars. The market line can be
written as

Pay for job A = a + (b × Job evaluation points for job A)

Pay for job B = a + (b × Job evaluation points for job B), etc.

The issue is to estimate the values of a and b in an efficient manner, so that errors of prediction
are minimized. This is what "least squares" regression analysis does.

For many jobs, particularly high-level managerial and executive jobs, job evaluation is not
used. Instead, salaries are related to some measure of company size (sales, volume, operating revenues) as a measure of responsibility through the use of logarithms. In such situations, x and y
are converted to logarithms (in base 10), and the equation for a straight line becomes

$$\log y = a + b(\log x)$$

where

x = sales or revenues (in millions of dollars)
y = current compensation (in thousands of dollars)

Example

Given sales and compensation levels for a sample of jobs, assume that

$a = 1.7390$
$b = 0.3000$

Using the equation $\log y = 1.7390 + 0.3000 (\log x)$, one can calculate the current market rate
for the chief executive in a company with sales of $500 million.

1.   First, set $x = 500$, that is 500,000,000 with six zeros dropped.
2.   Log $x = 2.6990$.
3.   Multiply log x by 0.3000, which is the coefficient of the variable log x in the given equa-
     tion. This results in a value of 0.8997.
4.   Add to 0.8097 the constant in the equation, 1.7390. The result, 2.5487, is the value
     of log y.

5. The chief executive's total current compensation is the antilog of log *y*, which is 354. Read in thousands of dollars, it is $354,000.

Equation: log *y* = 1.7390 1 0.3000 (log *x*)

x = $500,000,000 = 500

log *x* = 2.6990

log *y* = 1.7390 1 0.3000 (2.6990)

log *y* = 1.7390 1 0.8097

log *y* = 2.5487

antilog *y* = 354

y = $354,000

EMPLOYEE BENEFITS

LEARNING OUTCOMES

■ *Explain* why employee benefits are such a significant component of total compensation.

■ *Discuss* key issues in benefits planning, design, and administration.

■ *Describe* three important functions in benefits administration.

■ *Summarize* the legally required benefits in Canada.

■ *Explain* the difference between defined benefit and defined contribution pension plans.

■ *Describe* the two general strategies for controlling medical benefit costs.

Consider the kinds of things that are common in companies that made the *Maclean's* magazine list of "Canada's Top 100 Employers."[1] These companies recognize the importance of taking care of employees' needs as a key factor in attracting and retaining the best employees. A first-class benefits plan includes some mix of the following benefits: education reimbursement and employee training; on-site child care services, financial counselling, and concierge services; retirement benefits; and noncostly benefits such as casual dress policies.[2] Some examples from specific companies include:

■ SaskTel, headquartered in Regina, has a pool table, big-screen TV, and an exercise room in their training facility.
■ l'Union Canadienne, an insurance company headquartered in Quebec City, provides an employee lounge with couches, music, a TV, a pool table, and the services of a massage therapist.
■ Joseph Brant Memorial Hospital in Burlington, Ontario, offers a bonus up to $500 for new hire referrals and tops up maternity benefits to 93 percent of an employee's salary for 27 weeks.

■ INTRODUCTION TO EMPLOYEE BENEFITS

Clearly these firms would argue that these extra services are important benefits of employment, perhaps making attraction, retention, and motivation of employees just that much easier. But the truth is, we don't know if even ordinary benefits have positive payoffs. Until we can clearly identify the advantages of employee benefits, we need to find ways to control their costs, or at least slow their growth. There has been a rapid rise in employee benefit costs, moving from about 15 percent of payroll costs in 1953 to the 40 percent range today.[3]

However, think about what we know that is fact—not faith—in the benefits area. Which of the issues covered in the pay model, for example, can we answer with respect to benefits? Does effective **employee benefits** administration facilitate organization performance? The answer is unclear. We do know that benefit costs can be cut, and this affects the bottom line (admittedly an important measure of organization performance). But what about other design and administrative efforts? Do they complement organization strategy and performance? We don't know. Or do employee benefits impact upon an organization's ability to attract, retain, and motivate employees? Conventional wisdom says employee benefits can affect retention, but there is little research to support this conclusion. A similar lack of research surrounds each of the other potential payoffs to a sound benefits program. Is it any wonder, then, that firms are increasingly paying attention to this reward component? It represents a labour cost with no apparent returns.

Compounding this concern is the ever-present entitlement problem. Employees perceive benefits as a right, independent of how well they or the company perform. Efforts to reduce benefit levels or eliminate parts of the package altogether meet with employee resistance and dissatisfaction.

What is clear is that employee benefits are costly. As an example, visualize a $20,000 car rolling down the assembly line at General Motors. A cost accountant would tell you that $1,300 of this cost is due to pension cost alone. Compare this to the cost of all the steel for the same car—$500—and the impact is evident. Now compare this to much lower pension costs for foreign automakers in their North American factories (with their younger, healthier workers and hardly any retirees), and the global implications of benefit costs are all too frightening.[4]

Over one 20-year period (1955–1975), employee benefit costs rose at a much greater rate than employee wages or the consumer price index.[5] A similar comparison for the period 1963–1987 showed that the rate of growth had slowed somewhat. Organizations must control the growth and cost of benefits, particularly with the aging, and increasingly costly, baby boomer generation.

■ WHY THE GROWTH IN EMPLOYEE BENEFITS?

Government Impetus

The government has played an important role in the growth of employee benefits. Three employee benefits are mandated by either the provincial or federal government: workers' compensation (provincial), employment insurance (federal), and Canada/Quebec Pension Plan (federal and Quebec). In addition, most other employee benefits are affected by such laws as the Income Tax Act, human rights acts, pension benefits acts, etc. For example, Canadian human rights laws require that family and survivor benefits be offered to an employee's unmarried partner, whether of the same or opposite sex, wherever they are provided to a legal spouse.

Unions

Unions have fought for the introduction of new benefits and the improvement of existing benefits. Largely through the efforts of unions, most notably the auto and steelworkers, several benefits common today were given their initial impetus: pattern pension plans, supplementary unemployment compensation, and extended vacation plans.[6]

Employer Impetus

Many of the benefits in existence today were provided at employer initiative. Much of this initiative can be traced to pragmatic concerns about employee satisfaction and productivity. Rest

employee benefits

part of the total compensation package, other than pay for time worked, provided to employees in whole or in part by employer payments, such as life insurance, pension plan, worker's compensation, vacation, etc.

breaks often were implemented in the belief that fatigue increased accidents and lowered productivity. Savings and profit-sharing plans (e.g., Procter & Gamble's profit-sharing plan was initiated in 1885) were implemented to improve performance and provide increased security for worker retirement years. Indeed, many employer-initiated benefits were designed to create a climate in which employees perceived that management was genuinely concerned for their welfare. Notice, though, that these supposed benefits were taken on faith. But their costs were quite real. And, absent hard data about payoffs, employee benefits slowly became a costly entitlement of the North American workforce.

Cost Effectiveness of Benefits

Another important and sound impetus for the growth of employee benefits is their cost effectiveness in two situations. The first cost advantage is that most employee benefits are not taxable. Provision of a benefit rather than an equivalent increase in wages avoids payment of personal income tax. A second cost effectiveness component of benefits arises because many group-based benefits (e.g., life, health, and legal insurance) can be obtained at a lower rate than could be obtained by employees acting on their own. Group insurance also has relatively easy qualification standards, giving security to a set of employees who might not otherwise qualify.

■ THE VALUE OF EMPLOYEE BENEFITS

Exhibit 9.1 shows the relative importance employees attached to different types of benefits across three different studies.[7] In general, the three studies reported in Exhibit 9.1 show fairly consistent results. For example, medical payments regularly are listed as one of the most important benefits employees receive. These rankings have added significance when we note over the past two decades that health care costs are the most rapidly growing and the most difficult to control of all the benefit options offered by employers.[8]

These costs would not seem nearly so outrageous if we had evidence that employees place high value on the benefits they receive. Unfortunately, there is evidence that employees frequently are unaware of, or undervalue, the benefits provided by their organization.

The lack of knowledge about the value of employee benefits inferred from these studies can be traced to both attitudinal and design problems. Looming largest is the attitude problem.

EXHIBIT 9.1   Ranking of Different Employee Benefits ────────────────

	Study		
	1	*2*	*3*
Medical	1	1	3
Pension	2	3	8
Paid Vacation and Holidays	3	2	X
Sickness	4	X	5
Dental	5	X	6
Profit-Sharing	6	X	2
Long Term Disability	7	X	7
Life Insurance	8	X	4

X = not rated in this study

Benefits are taken for granted. Employees view them as a right, with little comprehension of, or concern for, employer costs.[9]

One possible salvation from this money pit comes from recent reports that employees are not necessarily looking for more benefits, but rather greater choice in the benefits they receive.[10] In fact, up to 70 percent of employees in one study indicated they would be willing to pay more out of pocket for benefits if they were granted greater choice in designing their own benefits package. Better benefits planning, design, and administration may offer an opportunity to improve benefits effectiveness. Indeed, preliminary evidence indicates employers are making serious efforts to educate employees about benefits, with an outcome of increased employee awareness.[11]

■ KEY ISSUES IN BENEFITS PLANNING, DESIGN, AND ADMINISTRATION

Benefits Planning and Design Issues

First and foremost, the benefits planning process must address the vital question: "What is the relative role of benefits in a total compensation package?"[12] For example, if a major compensation objective is to attract good employees, we need to ask, "What is the best way to achieve this?" The answer is not always, nor even frequently, "Let's add another benefit."

Consider a company that needs to fill some clerical and administrative jobs. One temptation might be to set up a daycare centre to attract more mothers with preschool children. Certainly this is a popular response today, judging from all the press daycare centres are receiving. A more prudent compensation policy would ask the question: "Is daycare the most effective way to achieve my compensation objective?" Can the necessary workers be attracted to the company using some other compensation tool that better meets company needs? For example, we know that daycare is relatively popular in the insurance industry. If we went to compensation experts in that industry they might say (and we would be impressed if they did): "Seventy-five percent of our workforce is female, and one-third have pre-school children. Surveys of this group indicate daycare is an extremely important factor in the decision to accept a job." If we heard this kind of logic it would certainly illustrate the kind of care firms should use before adopting expensive benefit options.

As a second example, how do we deal with undesirable turnover? We might be tempted to design a benefits package that improves progressively with seniority, thus providing a reward for continuing service. This would only be the preferred option, though, if other compensation tools, such as increasing wages or introducing incentive compensation, were less effective.

In addition to integrating benefits with other compensation components, the planning process also should include strategies to ensure external competitiveness and adequacy of benefits. Competitiveness requires an understanding of what other firms in your product and labour markets offer as benefits. Firms conduct benefits surveys much as they conduct salary surveys. Either our firm must have a package comparable to survey participants, or there should be a sound justification of why deviation makes sense for the firm.

In contrast, ensuring that benefits are adequate is a somewhat more difficult task. Most organizations evaluating adequacy consider the financial liability of employees with and without a particular benefit (e.g., employee medical expenses with and without medical expenses benefits). There is no magic formula for defining benefits adequacy.[13] In part, the answer may lie in the relationship between benefits adequacy and the third plan objective, cost of effectiveness. More organizations need to consider whether employee benefits are cost justified. All sorts of ethical questions arise when we start asking this question. How far should we go with eldercare? Can we justify a $50,000 expense for a new drug treatment that will likely buy only a few months more of life? Companies face these impossible questions when designing a benefits system.

Benefits Administration Issues

Three major administration issues arise in setting up a benefits package: (1) Who should be protected or benefited? (2) How much choice should employees have among an array of benefits? (3) How should benefits be financed?[14]

The first issue—who should be covered—ought to be an easy question. Employees, of course. But every organization has a variety of employees with different employment statuses. Should these individuals be treated equally with respect to benefits coverage? Companies often differentiate treatment based on employment status. The dollar value of benefits is much lower, even when we factor in the difference in hours worked, for part-timers than for full-time employees.

As a second example, should retired automobile executives be permitted to continue purchasing cars at a discount price, a benefit that could be reserved solely for current employees? In fact, a whole series of questions need to be answered:

1. What probationary periods (for eligibility of benefits) should be used for various types of benefits? Does the employer want to cover employees and their dependents immediately upon employment or to provide such coverage for employees who have established more or less permanent employment with the employer? Is there a rationale for different probationary periods with different benefits?
2. Which dependents of active employees should be covered?
3. Should retirees (as well as their spouses and perhaps other dependents) be covered, and for which benefits?
4. Should survivors of deceased active employees (and/or retirees) be covered? And if so, for which benefits? Are benefits for surviving spouses appropriate?
5. What coverage, if any, should be extended to employees who are suffering from disabilities?
6. What coverage, if any, should be extended to employees during layoff, leaves of absence, strikes, and so forth?
7. Should coverage be limited to full-time employees?[15]

The answers to these questions depend on the policy decisions regarding adequacy, competition, and cost effectiveness discussed in the last section.

The second administrative issue concerns choice (flexibility) in plan coverage. In the standard benefits package, employees typically have not been offered a choice among employee benefits. Rather, a package is designed with the average employee in mind, and any deviations in needs simply go unsatisfied. The other extreme (discussed in greater detail later) is represented by **flexible benefit plans**. Under this concept employees are permitted great flexibility in choosing the benefits options of greatest value to them. Picture an individual allotted x dollars choosing benefits according to their attractiveness and cost. The flexibility in this type of plan is apparent. Exhibit 9.2 illustrates a typical choice among packages offered to employees under a flexible benefits system. Imagine an employee whose spouse works and already has family coverage for health, dental, and vision. The temptation might be to select package A. A second employee with retirement in mind might select option B with its contributions to a pension plan.

Even companies that are not considering a flexible benefits program are offering greater flexibility and choice. Such plans might provide, for example, (1) optional levels of group term life insurance; (2) the availability of death or disability benefits under pension or profit-sharing plans; or (3) choices of covering dependents under group medical expense coverage.

Exhibit 9.3 summarizes some of the major advantages and disadvantages of flexible benefits. Judging from increased adoption of flexible benefits over the past decade, it seems that employers consider that the advantages noted in Exhibit 9.3 far outweigh the disadvantages. Current estimates put the rate of flexible benefit adoption at somewhere between 13–33 percent of medium-to-large employers.[16]

flexible benefit plans

benefit plans in which the employee is provided with a specified amount of money and then chooses which benefits to spend the money on, according to their attractiveness and cost

EXHIBIT	**9.2**	Example of Possible Options in a Flexible Benefits Package

	Package			
	A	*B*	*C*	*D*
Health Care	No	Basic	Enhanced	Premium
Dental Care	No	Basic	Enhanced	Premium
Vision Care	No	No	No	Yes
Life Insurance	1 × AE*	2 × AE	2 × AE	3 × AE
Dependent Care	Yes	No	No	No
Pension	No	Basic	Enhanced	Premium

*AE = Average Earnings

The level at which an organization finally chooses to operate on this choice/ flexibility dimension really depends on its evaluation of the relative advantages and disadvantages of flexible plans, as noted in Exhibit 9.3.[17] Many companies cite the cost savings from flexible benefits as a primary motivation. Companies also offer flexible plans in response to cost pressures related to the increasing diversity of the workforce. Flexible benefits plans, it is argued, increase employee awareness of the true costs of benefits, and therefore, increase employee recognition of benefits value.[18]

The final administrative issue involves the question of financing benefits plans. Alternatives include:

1. Noncontributory (employer pays total costs)
2. Contributory (costs shared between employer and employee)
3. Employee financed (employee pays total costs for some benefits, e.g., long-term disability)

In general, organizations prefer to make benefits options contributory, reasoning that anything free, no matter how valuable, is less valuable to an employee. Furthermore, employees have no personal interest in controlling the cost of a free good.

EXHIBIT	**9.3**	Advantages and Disadvantages of Flexible Benefit Programs

Advantages
1. Employees choose packages that best satisfy their unique needs.
2. Flexible benefits help firms meet the changing needs of a changing workforce.
3. Increased involvement of employees and families improves understanding of benefits.
4. Flexible plans make introduction of new benefits less costly. The new option is added merely as one among a wide variety of elements from which to choose.
5. Cost containment: Organization sets dollar maximum. Employee chooses within that constraint.

Disadvantages
1. Employees make bad choices and find themselves not covered for predictable emergencies.
2. Administrative burdens and expenses increase.
3. Adverse selection. Employees pick only benefits they will use. The subsequent high benefit utilization increases costs.

■ COMPONENTS OF A BENEFITS PLAN

Exhibit 9.4 outlines a model of the factors influencing benefits choice, from both the employer and employee perspective. We will now briefly examine each of these factors.

Employer Preferences

As Exhibit 9.4 indicates, a number of factors affect employer preference in determining desirable components of a benefits package.

Relationship to Total Compensation Costs. A good compensation manager considers employee benefit costs as part of a total package of compensation costs. Frequently employees think that just because an employee benefit is attractive, the company should provide it. A good compensation manager thinks somewhat differently: "Is there a better use for this money? Could we put the money into some other compensation component and achieve better results?" Benefit costs are only one part of a total compensation package. Decisions about outlays have to be considered from this perspective.

Costs Relative to Benefits. A major reason for the proliferating cost of benefits programs is the narrow focus of benefits administrators. Too frequently the costs/advantages of a particular benefit inclusion are viewed in isolation, without reference to total package costs or forecasts of rising costs in future years. To control spiralling benefit costs, administrators should adopt a broader, cost-centred approach. As a first step, this approach would require policy decisions on the level of benefit expenditures which are acceptable both in the short and long run. Historically, benefits managers negotiated or provided benefits on a package basis rather than

---

EXHIBIT 9.4   Factors Influencing Choice of Benefits Package ─────────────

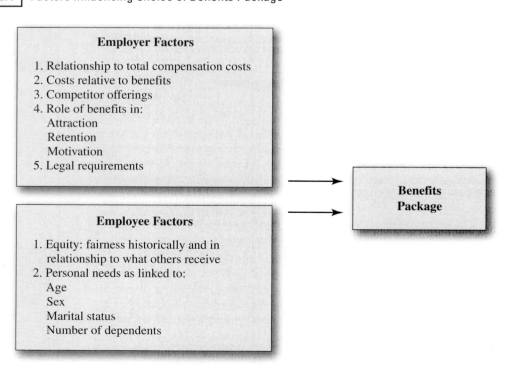

a cost basis. The current cost of a benefit would be identified and, if the cost seemed reasonable, the benefit would be provided for or negotiated with employees. This failed to recognize that rising costs of this benefit were expected to be borne by the employer. The classic example of this phenomenon is health care coverage. An employer considering a community-based medical plan such as Blue Cross during the early 1960s no doubt agreed to pay all or most of the costs of one of the Blue Cross options. As costs of this plan skyrocketed during the 60s and 70s, the employer was expected to continue coverage at the historical level. In effect, the employer became locked into a level of coverage, rather than negotiating a level of cost. In subsequent years, then, the spiralling costs were essentially out of the control of the benefits manager.

A cost-centred approach would require benefits administrators, in cooperation with insurance carriers and armed with published forecasts of anticipated costs for particular benefits, to determine the cost commitments for the existing benefits package. Budget dollars not already earmarked might then be allocated to new benefits that best satisfy organizational goals. Factors affecting this decision include an evaluation of benefits offered by other firms and the competitiveness of the existing package. Also important is compliance with various legal requirements as they change over time (Chapter 12). Finally, the actual benefit of a new option must be explored in relation to employee preferences. Those benefits that top the list of employee preferences should be evaluated in relation to current and future costs. Because future cost estimates may be difficult to project, it is imperative that benefits administrators reduce uncertainty.

If a benefit forecast suggests future cost containment may be difficult, the benefit should be offered to employees only on a cost-sharing basis. Management determines what percentage of cost it can afford to bear within budget projections, and the option is offered to employees on a cost-sharing basis, with projected increases in both employer and employee costs communicated openly. In the negotiation process, then, employees or union representatives can evaluate their preference for the option against the forecasted cost burden. In effect, this approach defines the contribution an employer is willing to make, in advance. And it avoids the constraints of a defined benefit strategy that burdens the employer with continued provision of that defined benefit level despite rapidly spiralling costs.

Competitor Offerings. Benefits must be externally equitable, too. This raises the question, What is the absolute level of benefits payments relative to important product and labour market competitors? A policy decision must be made about the position (market lead, market lag, or competitive) the organization wants to maintain in its absolute level of benefits relative to the competition. One of the best strategies to determine external equity is to conduct a benefits survey. Alternatively, many consulting organizations, professional associations, and interest groups collect benefits data that can be purchased.

Role of Benefits in Attraction, Retention, and Motivation. Given the rapid growth in benefits and the staggering cost implications, it seems only logical that employers would expect to derive a fair return on this investment. In fact, there is at best only anecdotal evidence that employee benefits are cost justified. This evidence falls into three categories.[19] First, employee benefits are widely claimed to help in the retention of workers. Benefit schedules are specifically designed to favour longer-term employees. For example, retirement benefits increase with years of service, and most plans do not provide for full employee eligibility until a specified number of years of service has been reached. Equally, amount of vacation time increases with years of service; and finally, employees' savings plans, profit-sharing plans, and stock purchase plans frequently provide for increased participation or benefits as company seniority increases. By tying these benefits to seniority, it is assumed that workers will be more reluctant to change jobs.

There is also some research to support this common assumption that benefits increase retention. Two studies found that higher benefits reduced mobility.[20] More detailed follow-up studies, though, found only two specific benefits curtailed employee turnover: pensions and medical coverage.[21] Virtually no other employee benefit had a significant impact on turnover.

We've been assuming here that turnover is bad and stability is good. In fact, there are times when turnover may be good—something we may not want to discourage. Some employees may stay in a job they wanted to leave simply because the pension plan is so generous. This job lock probably is not a desirable outcome for employers.

Employee benefits also might be valued if we could prove that they increase employee satisfaction. Unfortunately, though, today only 50 percent of workers consider their benefits adequate. This is down from 83 percent in the early 80s.[22] The lowest satisfaction marks go to disability, life, and health insurance.[23] Why have satisfaction ratings fallen? One view holds that benefits satisfaction falls as cost-cutting companies attempt to reduce coverage and to shift more of the costs to employees.[24] A second view is more pessimistic, arguing that benefits plans fail to meet either employer or employee needs. In this view, simply pumping more money into benefits is inappropriate. Rather, employers must make fundamental changes in the way they approach the benefits planning process. Companies must realize that declining satisfaction with benefits is a result of long-term changes in the workforce. Ever-increasing numbers of women in the labour force, coupled with increasing numbers of dual-career families and higher educational attainments, suggest changing values of employees.[25] Changing values, in turn, necessitate a reevaluation of benefits packages.

Finally, employee benefits also are valued because they may have an impact on the bottom line. Although supporting evidence is slim, there are some glimmers of potential. For example, employee stock ownership plans (Chapter 11), according to some reports, improve company productivity.[26] Presumably, owning stock motivates employees to be more productive. After all, part of the reward returns to them in the form of dividends and increased stock value. Similar productivity improvements are reported for employee assistance programs (e.g., alcohol and drug treatment programs for employees), with reports of up to 25 percent jumps in productivity after their implementation.[27]

Legal Requirements. Employers obviously want a benefits package that complies with all aspects of the law. For example, **vesting** of pension benefits, which occurs when employees become entitled to the employer-paid portion of pension benefits upon termination of employment, is required by law after no more than two years of employment. There is an increasingly complex web of legislation in the benefits area. Greater details on legally mandated benefits including Workers' Compensation, Canada/Quebec Pension Plan, and employment insurance are provided later in this chapter.

vesting

waiting period for entitlement to the employer-paid portion of pension benefits

Absolute and Relative Compensation Costs. Any evaluation of employee benefits must be placed in the context of total compensation costs. Cost competitiveness means the total package must be competitive—not just specific segments. Consequently, decisions about whether to adopt certain options must be considered in light of the impact on total costs and in relationship to expenditures of competitors as determined in benefits surveys.

Employee Preferences

Employee preferences for various benefit options are determined by individual needs. Those benefits perceived to best satisfy individual needs are most highly desired. In part these needs arise from feelings of perceived equity or inequity.

Equity. To illustrate the impact of equity, consider the example of government employees working in the same neighbourhood as auto workers. Imagine the dissatisfaction with government holidays that arises when government employees leave for work every morning, knowing that the auto workers are home in bed for the whole week between Christmas and New Year's Day. The perceived unfairness of this difference need not be rational. But it is, nevertheless, a factor that must be considered in determining employee needs. Occasionally this comparison process leads to a "bandwagon" effect, whereby new benefits offered by a competitor are adopted without careful consideration, simply because the employer wants to avoid hard feelings. This phenomenon is particularly apparent for employers with strong commitments to maintaining a totally or partially nonunion workforce. Benefits obtained by a unionized competitor or a unionized segment of the firm's workforce are frequently passed along to nonunion employees. Although the effectiveness of this strategy in thwarting unionization efforts has not been demonstrated, many nonunion firms prefer to provide the benefit as a safety measure.

Personal Needs of Employees. A major assumption in empirical efforts to determine employee preferences is that preferences are somehow systematically related to what are termed demographic differences. The demographic approach assumes that demographic groups (e.g., young versus old, married versus unmarried) can be identified for which benefits preferences are fairly consistent across members of the group. Furthermore, this approach assumes that meaningful differences exist between groups in terms of benefit preferences.

There is evidence that these assumptions are only partially correct. In an extensive review of employee preference literature, Glueck traced patterns of group preferences for particular benefits.[28] As one might expect, older workers showed stronger preferences than younger workers for pension plans.[29] Also, families with dependents had stronger preferences for health/medical coverage than did families with no dependents.[30] The big surprise in all these studies, though, is that many of the other demographic group breakdowns failed to result in differential benefit preferences. Traditionally, it has been assumed that benefit preferences ought to differ between males and females, blue collar and white collar, and married and single workers. Few of these expectations have been borne out by these studies. Rather, the studies have tended to be more valuable in showing preference trends that are characteristic of all employees. Among the benefits available, health/medical and stock plans are highly preferred benefits, whereas such options as early retirement, profit sharing, shorter hours, and counselling services rank among the least-preferred options. Beyond these conclusions, most preference studies have shown wide variation in individuals with respect to benefits desired.

The weakness of this demographic approach has led some organizations to undertake a second and more expensive empirical method of determining employee preferences: surveying individuals about needs. One way of accomplishing this requires development of a questionnaire on which employees evaluate various benefits. For example, Exhibit 9.5 illustrates a questionnaire format.

Although other strategies for scaling are available (e.g., paired comparison), the most important factor to remember is that a consistent method must be used in assessing preferences on a questionnaire. Switching between a ranking method and a Likert-type scale could, by itself, affect the results.[31]

A third empirical method of identifying individual employee preferences is commonly known as a flexible benefit plan. As previously noted, employees are allotted a fixed amount of money and permitted to spend that amount in the purchase of benefit options. From a theoretical perspective, this approach to benefits packaging is ideal. Employees directly identify the benefits of greatest value to them, and, by constraining the dollars employees have to spend, benefits managers are able to control benefits costs. NCR has adopted a variant on flexible benefits that is part of their new "customer-oriented" benefits promotion. Employees who wish to can exchange some of their base salary for greater coverage on desired benefits, as illustrated in Exhibit 9.6.

| EXHIBIT | 9.5 | Questionnaire Formats for Benefits Surveys |

Employee Benefit Questionnaire

1. In the space provided in front of the benefits listed below indicate how important each benefit is to you and your family. Indicate this by placing a "1" for the most important, and "2" for the next most important, etc. Therefore, if life insurance is the most important benefit to you and your family, place a "1" in front of it.

Importance		*Improvement*
_____	Dental insurance	_____
_____	Disability (pay while sick)	_____
_____	Educational assistance	_____
_____	Holidays	_____
_____	Life insurance	_____
_____	Medical insurance	_____
_____	Retirement plan	_____
_____	Savings plan	_____
_____	Vacations	_____
_____	_____	_____
_____	_____	_____

   Now, go back, and in the space provided after each benefit, indicate the priority for improvement. For example, if the savings plan is the benefit you would most like to see improved, give it a "1," the next a priority "2," etc. Use the blank lines to add any benefits not listed.

2. Would you be willing to contribute a portion of your earnings for new or improved benefits beyond the level already provided by the Company?
    ❑ Yes   ❑ No
    If yes, please indicate below in which area(s):
    ❑ Dental insurance   ❑ Medical insurance
    ❑ Disability benefits   ❑ Retirement plan
    ❑ Life insurance   ❑ Savings plan

Source: Pfizer Corporation

ADMINISTERING THE BENEFITS PROGRAM

The job description for an employee-benefits manager found in Exhibit 9.7 indicates that administrative time is spent on three functions requiring further discussion: (1) communicating the benefits program, (2) claims processing, and (3) cost containment.[32]

Employee Benefits Communication

Much of the effort to achieve benefit goals focuses on identifying methods of communication. Benefits communication, particularly regarding retirement plans, is increasingly important because a large number of employees are approaching retirement. Accurate information must be provided to these employees in a timely manner. Pension legislation across Canada specifies the information that must be disclosed to plan members and their spouses/domestic partners. Court challenges concerning erroneous information on benefit statements are more and more frequent, as employees' awareness of their right to information increases.[33]

| **EXHIBIT** | **9.6** | Administering the Benefits Program |

Costs. Please modify this "base" benefit package into another which you would most prefer, bearing in mind that selecting different levels will impact your cash pay (see box to right).

Base Benefit Package	**$11,460**
Current Benefit Package Chosen	**$11,760**
Change in cash pay	−$300

FEATURE   ALTERNATIVE LEVELS

Medical Plan	Opt Out −$4,800	Traditional-Basic (family) Current **Base**	Traditional-Basic (single) −$800	Traditional-Enhanced (single) +$1,000	Traditional-Enhanced (family) +$1,300
Long-term Disability Plan	Opt Out −$840	50% of Your Salary Current **Base**	60% of Your Salary +$240	70% of Your Salary +$480	
Life Insurance	None **Base**	1 Times Your Salary +$240	2 Times Your Salary Current +$480	3 Times Your Salary +$720	4 Times Your Salary +$960
Pension Plan	None −$1,800	3% Match 2-Year Vesting +$1,200	6% Match 2-Year Vesting Current **Base**	6% Match 1-Year Vesting $900	10% Match Immediate Vesting $2,400
Paid Parental/ Family Leave	None Current −$180	3-Day Leave **Base**	12-Week Leave ½ Salary +$540	12-Week Leave Full Salary +$1,800	

Adapted from "Employee a Customer" by Lynn Gaughan and Jorg Kasparek, NCR Corp., and John Hagens and Jeff Young, *Workspan*, September 2000, p. 31–37.

The most frequent method for communicating employee benefits today probably is still the employee benefits handbook.[34] A typical handbook contains a description of all benefits, including levels of coverage and eligibility requirements. To be most effective, this benefits manual should be accompanied by group meetings and videotapes.[35] Although some organizations may supplement this initial benefits discussion with periodic refreshers once per year, a more typical approach involves one-on-one discussions between the benefits administrator and an employee seeking information on a particular benefit. The benefits handbook is often supplemented with personalized benefits statements generated by computer. These tailor-made reports provide a breakdown of package components and list selected cost information about the options.[36] Annual benefits statements increasingly are being provided using real-time e-statements. These statements provide a current view of an employee's total compensation package and clearly communicate the value of the employer's benefit programs and the firm's commitment to the well-being of its workforce.[37]

EXHIBIT 9.7 Job Description for Employee-Benefits Executive

Position

The primary responsibility of this position is the administration of established company benefits programs. Develops and recommends new and improved policies and plans with regard to employee benefits. Assures compliance with legislative requirements and regulations.

Specific Functions

1. Plans and directs implementation and administration of employee benefits programs designed to insure employees against loss of income due to illness, injury, layoff, or retirement.
2. Directs preparation and distribution of written and verbal information to inform employees of benefits programs, such as insurance and pension plans, paid time off, bonus pay, and special employer-sponsored activities.
3. Analyzes existing benefits policy of organization, and prevailing practices among similar organizations, to establish competitive benefits programs.
4. Evaluates services, coverage, and options available through insurance and investment companies, to determine programs best meeting needs of organization.
5. Plans modification of existing benefits programs, utilizing knowledge of laws concerning employee insurance coverage and agreements with labour unions to ensure compliance with legal requirements.
6. Recommends benefits plan changes to management.
7. Notifies employees and labour union representatives of changes in benefits programs.
8. Directs performance of critical functions, such as updating records and processing insurance claims.
9. May interview, select, hire, and train employees.

In addition, the employee-benefits executive may be responsible for various employee services, such as recreation programs, advisory services, credit unions, and savings bond purchase programs.

Source: *Dictionary of Occupational Titles*, Vol. 1, 4th ed. (U.S. Dept. of Labor 1991), p. 109.

Despite this and other innovative plans to communicate employee benefit packages, failure to understand benefits components and their value is still one of the root causes of employee dissatisfaction with a benefits package.[38] We believe an effective communications package must have three elements. First, an organization must spell out its benefit objectives and ensure that any communications achieve these objectives.

The second element of an effective communications package is to match the message with the appropriate medium. Technological advances have made tremendous improvements to employee benefits communication. In today's corporations, benefits administrators are aiming to maintain communication with employees in a timely, consistent, and accurate manner, and many are selecting an intranet as their chosen avenue of communication.[39] Advantages of an intranet include: employee access to benefits information 24 hours a day, seven days a week without added cost; employee ability to post changes directly to their accounts without completing lengthy paperwork; and increased ease of updating information.[40]

Employers such as Hewlett-Packard (Canada) Ltd. increasingly are posting their employee benefits handbook components on their intranets.[41] This change is beneficial to employers because of the decreased cost and increased ease of making revisions in the employee benefits handbook components. Experts say e-benefits are a huge trend waiting to reinvent human resource practices.[42] However, employee benefits handbook disclaimers are one component that probably should remain in paper form.[43] The disclaimer is significant because it clearly states that the employee benefit handbook is not an employment contract, and that the employer reserves the right to change, modify, or discontinue its policies, rules, and benefits at any time, usually with or without notice.

Benefits administration over the Internet is also growing at a rapid pace. A wide range of applications is available, from simple on-line benefits information to annual benefits enrolment processing to personal data changes to complete employee self-service.[44]

Another example of recent advances in benefits communication is the use of a call centre operation.[45] Call centres can decrease costs while improving service levels and maintaining close employee interaction. At Kellogg's, for example, for a cost equal to approximately one-fifth of its paper-based predecessor (which required specialists to be located at every location in the United States and Canada), the call centre allows users to access benefit plan information, to download and print documents, and to retrieve basic information regarding Kellogg's 45 benefit vendors. Employees and retirees dial in to the call centre, where an automated phone tree connects them to the specific information that they are looking for. For convenience, the call centre has a quick option that exits the phone tree, allowing the caller to speak directly with a call centre specialist. The call centre operates highly efficiently, providing the caller with the information sought within just a few minutes. Annual cost savings of this system equal $500,000. Kellogg's anticipates that future technological initiatives will include setting up kiosks, Web-enabled personal computers that allow employees to access information they presently access over the telephone and to contact specialists over the Internet in live chat rooms.

And finally, element three: The content of the communications package must be complete, clear, and free of the complex jargon which so readily invades benefits discussions. The amount of time/space devoted to each issue should vary closely with both the perceived importance of the benefit to employees and with the expected difficulty in communicating option alternatives.[46]

Claims Processing

As noted by one expert, claims processing arises when an employee asserts that a specific event (such as disability or hospitalization) has occurred, and requests that the employer fulfill a promise of payment.[47] A claims processor first must determine whether the act has, in fact, occurred. If the answer is yes, the second step involves determining whether the employee is eligible for the benefit. If payment is approved at this stage, the claims processor calculates the payment level. It is particularly important at this stage to ensure coordination of benefits. If multiple insurance companies are liable for payment (e.g., working spouses covered by different insurers), a good claims processor can save from 10 to 15 percent of claims cost by ensuring that the liability is paid jointly.[48]

Although these steps are time consuming, most of the work is quite routine in nature. The major job challenges come from approximately 10 percent of all claims in which payment is denied. A benefits administrator must then become an adroit counsellor, explaining the situation to the employee in a manner that conveys the equitable and consistent procedures used.

Cost Containment

Increasingly, employers are auditing their benefits options for cost containment opportunities. The most prevalent practices include:

1. Probationary periods—excluding new employees from benefits coverage until some term of employment (e.g., three months) is completed.

benefit maximums

limitations on benefit payable

2. **Benefit maximums**—it is not uncommon to limit disability income payments to some maximum percentage of income, and to limit medical/dental coverage for specific procedures to a certain fixed amount.

coinsurance

percentage of insurance premiums paid for by the employer

deductible

specified dollar amount of claims paid by the employee each year before insurance benefits begin

coordination of benefits

reduction of benefits by any amount paid under a spouse's plan

3. **Coinsurance**—the employer pays a fixed percentage of insurance premiums; employees pay the remainder

4. **Deductibles**—a specified dollar amount of claims to be paid each year by the employee before the insurance plan begins paying (e.g., $25 deductible means that the employee pays the first $25 in claims submitted each year).

5. **Coordination of Benefits**—when two spouses both have employee benefits coverage, benefits are reduced by any benefits payable under the spouse's plan (i.e., both spouses cannot receive benefits to cover the same expenses).

6. Administrative cost containment—includes such things as seeking competitive bids for program delivery.

So prevalent is the cost issue today that the terminology of cost containment is becoming a part of every employee's vocabulary. Exhibit 9.8 provides definitions of some common cost-containment terms.

Probably the biggest cost-containment strategy in recent years is the movement to outsourcing. By hiring vendors to administer their benefits programs, many companies have achieved greater centralization, consistency, and control of costs and benefits.[49] Companies such as Digital Equipment Corporation outsource so they can focus on their core businesses, "leaving benefits to the benefits experts."[50]

Given continuing escalation in the cost of employee benefits, organizations would do well to evaluate the effectiveness of their benefits adoption, retention, and termination procedures. Specifically, how does an organization go about selecting appropriate employee benefits? Are the decisions based on sound evaluation of employee preferences, balanced against organizational goals of legal compliance and competitiveness? Do the benefits chosen serve to attract, retain, and/or motivate employees? Or are organizations paying for indirect compensation without any tangible benefit? The benefits determination process identifies major issues in selecting and evaluating particular benefit choices. Next, we will catalogue the various benefits available and discuss some of the decisions confronting a benefits administrator.

EXHIBIT 9.8 A Basic Primer of Cost-Containment Terminology

Deductibles—an employee claim for insurance coverage is preceded by the requirement that the first $x dollars claimed be paid by the claimant.

Coinsurance—the proportion of insurance premiums paid by the employer.

Benefit Cutbacks—wage concessions some employers are negotiating with employees to eliminate or reduce employer contributions to selected options.

Defined Contribution Pension Plans—employers establish the limits of their responsibility for employee benefits in terms of a dollar contribution maximum.

Defined Benefit Pension Plans—employers establish the limits of their responsibility for employee benefits in terms of a specific benefit and the options included. As the cost of these options rises in future years, the employer is obligated to provide the benefit as negotiated, despite its increased cost.

Coordination of Benefits—in families where both spouses work, benefits are reduced by any amount payable under the spouse's plan.

Benefit Maximums—establishing a maximum payout for specific health-related claims.

BENEFITS OPTIONS

Sometimes the number of benefits options and choices can be overwhelming. A widely accepted categorization of employee benefits is shown in Exhibit 9.9.

LEGALLY REQUIRED BENEFITS

Virtually every employee benefit is somehow affected by law (many of the limitations are imposed by tax laws). In this section the primary focus will be on benefits that are required by law: Workers' Compensation, Canada/Quebec Pension Plan, and Employment Insurance.

| EXHIBIT 9.9 | Categorization of Employee Benefits |

Type of Benefit

1. **Legally required payments**
    a. Canada/Quebec Pension Plan
    b. Employment Insurance
    c. Workers' Compensation
    d. Government-sponsored medical plans

2. **Retirement and savings plan payments**
    a. Defined benefit pension plan contributions
    b. Defined contribution plan payments
    c. Profit-sharing
    d. Employee stock ownership plans (ESOP)
    e. Administrative and other costs

3. **Life insurance and death benefits**

4. **Medical insurance**
    a. Employer-sponsored medical plans
    b. Dental insurance
    c. Vision care

5. **Income Security**
    a. Short-term disability
    b. Sick leave
    c. Long-term disability

6. **Payments for time not worked**
    a. Paid rest periods, coffee breaks, lunch periods, wash-up time, travel time, clothes-change time, get-ready time, etc.
    b. Payments for vacations
    c. Payments for holidays

7. **Miscellaneous benefits**
    a. Parental leave
    b. Child care services
    c. Eldercare services
    d. Employee assistance plans
    e. Other

Workers' Compensation

Workers' Compensation is a form of no-fault insurance (employees are eligible even if their actions caused the accident) that covers injuries and diseases that arise out of, and while in the course of, employment. Workers' Compensation is legislated by each province and territory, but the variations in benefits and costs are relatively minor. The focus of Workers' Compensation has been shifting from the provision of compensation to injured workers to prevention of accidents through promoting occupational health and safety and facilitating recovery and return to work for injured workers.

All jurisdictions provide benefits for:

- loss of earnings due to temporary disability (total or partial)
- loss of earnings due to permanent disability (total or partial)
- health care expenses (including those normally paid under provincial health care plans)
- survivor benefits for fatal injuries.

The amount of compensation varies by jurisdiction from 75 percent to 90 percent of net earnings, with two jurisdictions providing 75 percent of gross earnings. Workers' Compensation benefits are non-taxable. The complete cost of administering and paying out compensation for work-related injuries and illnesses is borne by employers under a collective liability fund. Employers are placed in different rate groups, or classes, according to the nature of their business, and all members of the class pay the same assessment rates, based on a percentage of payroll, into the fund. Some jurisdictions offer "experience rating" plans that partially link assessment rates to a company's level of claims.

In 2001, just over one million Workers' Compensation claims were reported in Canada. Just over 373,000 were lost-time claims, and 919 were fatalities. The average cost of benefits per claim was $11,500, and the average administration cost per lost-time claim was $3,500. Workers' Compensation costs are an ongoing concern for employers, who bear the entire cost, but have limited control over administration. The continuing increase in medical costs, together with an aging workforce experiencing longer claims duration, means that no relief can be expected for some time. Some progress has been made in controlling costs in Ontario, where the $11.5 billion unfunded liability for future benefit payments faced in the mid-1990s was decreased to $6.6 billion by 2002.[51]

Canada/Quebec Pension Plan (C/QPP)

The **Canada/Quebec Pension Plan** came into effect on January 1, 1966. This government-sponsored plan is designed to replace employment income in case of retirement, death, or disability. All employees and self-employed persons must contribute to the plan, and employers match their employees' contributions. Both contributions and benefits are calculated on earnings between the Year's Basic Exemption (YBE), now fixed at $3,500, and the Year's Maximum Pensionable Earnings (YMPE), set at $40,500 in 2004, approximately the average Canadian wage. Contribution rates were increased considerably between 1997 and 2003 in order to ensure adequate financing and sustainability of the plan over the long run, and to ensure a manageable financial burden for future generations.

The retirement pension benefit beginning at age 65 is 25 percent of average pensionable earnings over the retiree's working life, adjusted for inflation up to the average inflation rate during the last five years prior to retirement. Plan members can choose to begin receiving benefits at any time between the ages of 60 and 70. Benefits are reduced upon retirement prior to age 65 and increased upon retirement after age 65. Disability benefits are payable to contributors who sustain a severe, prolonged mental or physical disability, and are payable until age 65 when the retirement pension begins. If a plan member dies, a lump sum death benefit is payable to the survivor, and a survivor pension benefit is payable to the surviving spouse/partner. An additional death benefit in the form of a pension is also payable to any dependent children until they reach the age of 18. All benefits are indexed to the Consumer Price Index and are taxable.[52]

Employment Insurance

Employment Insurance

a mandatory government-sponsored plan for all employed Canadians that provides workers with temporary income replacement as a result of employment interruptions due to circumstances beyond their control, funded by employer and employee contributions

Employment insurance provides workers with temporary income replacement as a result of employment interruptions due to work shortages, sickness, non-occupational accidents, maternity leave, parental leave, and adoption leave. It does not apply to workers who are self-employed. Benefits are not payable when an employee is terminated for just cause or quits without good reason.

Originally known as Unemployment Insurance when first introduced in 1940, the focus of the legislation was changed in 1996 to reduce the penalties for accepting lesser hours or wages when steady work is not available, and to create a more level playing field for the growing number of Canadians operating outside of traditional full-time employment.

Minimum eligibility criteria for employment insurance benefits vary from 420 to 700 hours of work during the qualification period of the 52 weeks immediately before the start of the claim (or the period since the start of a previous claim during the qualifying period). The number of hours required for eligibility decreases as the regional unemployment rate increases.

The maximum insurable earnings is $39,000, and will remain at that level until the average industrial wage catches up, at which time the maximum insurable earnings will become the average industrial wage. The maximum insurable earnings level provides the basis for the calculation of contributions and benefits. The EI program is funded entirely by contributions from employees and employers. The employee contribution is made on earnings up to the maximum insurable earnings, and varies over time, depending on the funded status of the program. In 2003, the employee contribution was $2.20 per $100 of weekly insurable earnings. Employers contribute 1.4 times their employees' contributions. Employers who provide a wage loss replacement plan for illness that pays at least as much as the EI benefit qualify for a rate reduction.

The basic benefit is 55 percent of the individual's average insured earnings, and is included in taxable income. A waiting period of two weeks applies before the first benefit payment is made. EI benefits are payable for a maximum of 45 weeks (up to 65 weeks for combined sickness, maternity, and parental leave). In 2003, the maximum weekly benefit was just over $400. Low-income claimants with children receive a Family Supplement, but their total benefit cannot exceed the maximum weekly benefit.

Some firms also offer a Supplementary Unemployment Benefit (SUB) plan, a self-insured program to supplement benefits received under the EI plan. Maternity and parental SUB plans can supplement up to 100 percent of earnings, and all other SUB plans can supplement up to 95 percent of earnings. EI benefits are not reduced by any SUB benefits received. Work-sharing programs are a related arrangement by which employees work a reduced workweek and receive EI benefits for the remainder of the week. The EI Commission must approve SUB plans and work-sharing programs.[53]

Government-Sponsored Medical Plans

All provinces and territories sponsor health care plans that provide basic medical and hospital services with no direct fee to patients. British Columbia, Alberta, and now Ontario finance their health-care plans by requiring monthly premiums to be paid by each resident; Quebec, Manitoba, and Newfoundland levy an employer payroll tax to partially fund the cost of their health care plans; the rest use general tax revenues to pay for their plans.

The services paid for by these plans include medically required procedures provided by physicians, nurses, and other health care professionals, standard ward hospital accommodation, drugs and medication administered in the hospital, laboratory and diagnostic procedures, and hospital facilities such as operating rooms. Some of the services not covered by provincial/territorial plans are prescription drugs, dental care, eyeglasses, private-duty nursing, cosmetic surgery, and semi-private or private hospital accommodation.

■ RETIREMENT AND SAVINGS PLAN PAYMENTS

pension plan

plan that provides income to an employee at retirement as compensation for work performed now

There is a strong relationship between employee age and preference for a **pension plan**. Although this need for retirement security may become more pronounced as workers age, it is evident among younger workers as well.

Pension programs provide income to an employee at retirement as compensation for work performed now. The security motive and certain tax advantages have also fostered this growth in pension programs. The vast majority of employers choose to provide this benefit as part of their overall package. Perhaps because of their prevalence, pension plans are also one of the targets for cost control.

Retirement issues are ranked as top priorities by employee benefits specialists—both as employees themselves, and as employee benefit managers. The importance of employer-provided retirement plans is demonstrated by one recent study, which showed that employees with employer-provided retirement plans are more likely to have sufficient savings for a comfortable retirement than are others who do not have these plans.[54]

Two types of pension plans will be discussed to varying degrees here: (1) defined-benefit and (2) defined-contribution plans. A third type of plan is a hybrid of the first two.

Defined-Benefit Plans

defined-benefit plan

pension plan in which an employer agrees to provide a specific level of retirement pension, the exact cost of which is unknown

In a **defined-benefit plan**, an employer agrees to provide a specific level of retirement pension, which is expressed either as a fixed dollar or percentage-of-earnings amount that may vary (increase) with years of seniority in the company. The firm finances this obligation by following an actuarially determined benefits formula and making current payments that will yield the future pension benefit for a retiring employee.[55]

Defined-benefit plans generally follow one of three different formulas. The most common approach is to calculate average earnings over the last (or best) 3–5 years of service for a prospective retiree and to offer a pension of about one-half this amount, adjusted for years of seniority. The second formula for a defined-benefits plan uses average career earnings rather than earnings from the last few years: Other things being equal, this would reduce the level of benefit for pensioners. The final formula commits an employer to a fixed (flat) dollar amount that is not dependent on earnings data. This figure generally rises with seniority level.

The level of pension a company chooses to offer depends on the answer to several questions. First, What level of retirement compensation would a company like to set as a target, expressed in relation to preretirement earnings? Second, Should Canada/Quebec Pension Plan payments be factored in when considering the level of income an employee should have during retirement? Third, Should other post-retirement income sources (e.g., savings plans that are partially funded by employer contributions) be integrated with the pension payment? Fourth, a company must decide how to factor seniority into the payout formula. The larger the role played by seniority, the more important pensions will be in retaining employees. Most companies believe that the maximum pension payout for a particular level of earnings should be achieved only by employees who have spent an entire career with the company. As Exhibit 9.10 vividly illustrates, job hoppers are hurt financially by this type of strategy. In our example—a very plausible scenario—job hopping cuts final pension amounts in half.

EXHIBIT	9.10	The High Cost of Job Hopping

		Years in Company	Percentage of Salary for Pension	×	Salary at Company (final)	Annual Pension
Sam's Career History	Job 1	10	10%	×	$ 35,817	= $ 3,582
	Job 2	10	10%	×	$ 64,143	= $ 6,414
	Job 3	10	10%	×	$114,870	= $11,487
	Job 4	10	10%	×	$205,714	= $20,571
					Sam's Total Pension	= $42,054
Ann's Career History	Job 1	40		×	$205,714	= $82,286
					Ann's Total Pension	= $82,286

Assumptions: 1. Starting salary of $20,000 with 6 percent annual inflation rate. 2. Both employees receive annual increases equal to inflation rate. 3. Pensions based on one percentage point (of salary) for each year of service multiplied by final salary at time of exit from company.
Source: Federal Reserve Bank of Boston.

Defined-Contribution Plans

defined-contribution plan

pension plan in which an employer agrees to provide specific contributions but the final benefit is unknown

Defined-contribution plans require specific contributions by an employer. In some cases, contributions may be required from employees or offered on an optional basis. The final benefit received by employees is unknown, depending on the investment success of those charged with administering the pension fund.

The advantages and disadvantages of these two generic categories of pensions (defined-benefit and defined-contribution) are outlined in Exhibit 9.11. Possibly the most important of the factors noted in Exhibit 9.11 is the differential risk borne by employers on the cost dimension. Defined contribution plans have known costs from year one. The employer agrees to a specific level of payment that only changes through negotiation or through some voluntary action. This allows for quite realistic cost projections. In contrast, defined-benefit plans commit the employer to a specific level of benefit. Variations from actuarial projections can add or reduce costs over the years and make the budgeting process much more uncertain. Perhaps for this reason, defined-contribution plans have been more popular for new adoptions over the past 15 years.[56]

EXHIBIT	9.11	Relative Advantages of Different Pension Alternatives

	Defined-Benefit Plan	Defined-Contribution Plan
1.	Provides an explicit benefit which is easily communicated	Unknown benefit level is difficult to communicate
2.	Company absorbs risk associated with changes in inflation and interest rates which affect cost	Employees assume these risks
3.	More favourable to long-service employees	More favourable to short-term employees
4.	Employer costs unknown	Employer costs known up front

Pension Legislation

Each province across Canada, as well as the federal government, has legislation regarding pension benefits. In addition, the Income Tax Act has detailed requirements regarding pension plans that must be met in order for employer and employee contributions to be tax deductible up to the limits provided in the Act. Pension plans must be registered both with the Canada Customs and Revenue Agency (CCHRA) and with the applicable provincial pension commission. Plans covering employees in more than one jurisdiction must comply with the funding standards of the jurisdiction of registration, but must also apply the rules of each jurisdiction for employees working in that jurisdiction. Some of the areas covered by these laws include eligible service, maximum contributions, early and late retirement benefits, pre-retirement and post-retirement death benefits, vesting on termination of employment, portability of pension benefits between plans, regulations regarding investment of pension fund assets, etc.[57]

◼ LIFE INSURANCE

One of the most common employee benefits offered by organizations is some form of life insurance. Typical coverage is a group insurance policy with a face value of one to two times the employee's annual salary. Most plan premiums are paid completely by the employer. Some plans include retiree coverage, and many include accidental death and dismemberment clauses. To discourage turnover, almost all companies make this benefit forfeitable at the time of departure from the company.

Life insurance is one of the benefits heavily affected by movement to a flexible benefits program. Flexibility is introduced by providing a core of basic life coverage (e.g., $25,000). The option then exists to choose greater coverage (usually in increments of $10,000–$25,000) as part of the optional package.

◼ MEDICAL INSURANCE

Employer-sponsored medical insurance provides coverage for expenses not payable under provincial/territorial plans. A 2000 Angus Reid poll showed that Canadian employees consider drug plans to be their most important employee benefit.[58] Dramatic increases in health care costs, particularly prescription drugs (which represent 75 percent of employer medical benefit costs in Canada), are the biggest issue facing benefits managers in Canada today.[59] The main reasons for these increases are increased use of expensive new drugs, rising drug utilization by an aging population, and reductions in coverage under provincial/territorial health care plans.[60]

Health Care: Cost Control Strategies   There are two general strategies available to benefit managers for controlling the rapidly escalating costs of health care.[61] First, organizations can motivate employees to change their demand for health care, through changes in either the design or the administration of health insurance policies.[62] Included in this category of control strategies are: (1) deductibles (the first x dollars of health care cost are paid by the employee); (2) coinsurance rates (the percentage of premium payments paid by the company); (3) maximum benefits (defining a maximum payout schedule for specific health problems); (4) coordination of benefits (ensuring no double payment when coverage exists under the employee's plan and a spouse's plan).

The second cost strategy involves promotion of preventive health programs. Incentives for quitting smoking are popular inclusions here. But there is also increased interest in healthier food in cafeterias and vending machines, on-site physical fitness facilities, and early screening to identify possible health problems before they become serious. One review of physical fitness programs found that fitness led to better mental health and improved resistance to stress; there also was some evidence of increased productivity and commitment, and decreased absenteeism and turnover.[63]

Dental Insurance

A rarity 25 years ago, dental insurance is now quite prevalent. Dental care plans typically cover the full cost of basic preventive maintenance such as checkups and fillings; 50 to 80 percent of major restorative work such as bridges and crowns; and sometimes orthodontics, usually at 50 percent coverage. Benefits payable are usually linked to the dental fee guide in each province for the current year or a previous year (when fees were lower so that employer costs can be controlled—employees pay any additional charge up to the current fee level).

Vision Care

Vision care dates back only to the 1976 contract between the Auto Workers and the Big 3 automakers. Since then, this benefit has spread throughout the private and public sectors. Most plans are noncontributory and cover part or all of the costs of eye examinations, lenses, frames, and contact lenses.

■ INCOME SECURITY

short-term disability plans/salary continuation plans

■ employer-sponsored plans that provide a continuation of all or part of an employee's earnings when the employee is absent from work due to an illness or injury that is not work-related

sick leave plans

■ employer-sponsored plans that grant a specified number of paid sick days per month or per year

long-term disability plans

■ employer-sponsored plans that provide income protection due to long-term illness or injury that is not work-related

Short-term disability plans (also known as **salary continuation plans**) provide a continuation of all or part of an employee's earnings when the employee is absent from work due to an illness or injury that is not work-related. Usually a medical certificate is required if the absence extends beyond two or three days. These plans typically provide full pay for some period of time (often two or three weeks) and then gradually reduce the percentage of earnings paid as the period of absence lengthens. The benefits cease when the employee returns to work or when the employee qualifies for long-term disability (often after 26 weeks of absence).

Sick leave plans operate quite differently from short-term disability plans. Most sick leave policies grant full pay for a specified number of paid sick days per month or per year (usually about one per month). A common problem with sick leave is that, although many employees use their sick days only when they are legitimately sick, others simply use their sick leaves as extra vacation days, whether they are sick or not. Worse still, seriously ill or injured employees get no pay once their sick days are used up until long-term disability benefits, if any, begin.

Employers have tried several tactics to eliminate or reduce the use of sick leave days by employees who are not sick. Some buy back unused sick leave at the end of the year by paying their employees a daily equivalent pay for each sick leave day not used, a practice which can encourage legitimately sick employees to come to work despite their illness.[64] Others have experimented with holding monthly lotteries in which only employees with perfect monthly attendance are eligible to win a cash prize. Still others aggressively investigate all absences, for example, by calling the absent employees at their homes when they are off on sick leave.

Long-term disability plans provide income protection due to long-term illness or injury that is not work-related. The payments typically begin after 26 weeks of disability and continue to age 65 (when pension plan benefits begin) or for life. Benefits usually range from 50 percent to 75 percent of the employee's base pay, and are not taxable if the employee pays the full cost of the plan (any employer contributions result in taxable benefits for the disabled employee).

The number of long-term disability claims in Canada is rising sharply. Psychiatric disabilities are the fastest growing of all occupational disabilities, with depression being the most common. A Harvard University study projects that by 2020, depression will be the biggest source of lost workdays in developed countries.[65] Due to the rising numbers of disability claims, disability management programs with a goal of returning disabled employees safely back to work are becoming a priority in many organizations.

■ PAYMENT FOR TIME NOT WORKED

Included within this category are several self-explanatory benefits:

1. Paid rest periods, lunch periods, wash-up time, travel time, clothes-change time, and get-ready time benefits
2. Paid vacations and payments in lieu of vacation
3. Payments for holidays not worked
4. Other (payments for armed forces duty; jury duty allowances; payments for time lost due to death in family or other personal reasons)

Judging from employee preferences discussed in the last chapter and from analysis of negotiated union contracts, pay for time not worked continues to be a high-demand benefit. Twenty years ago it was relatively rare, for example, to grant time for anything but vacations, holidays, and sick leave. Now, many organizations have a policy of ensuring payments for civic responsibilities and obligations. Any outside pay for such civic duties usually is nominal, so companies often supplement this pay, frequently to the level of 100 percent of wages lost.

■ MISCELLANEOUS BENEFITS

Parental Leave

There is also increasing coverage for parental leave. Paternity and adoption leaves are much more common than they were 25 years ago.

Child Care Services

Companies increasingly are offering child care services to their employees as a paid benefit. Working is often not optional for women with pre-school children—most contribute significantly

.NET WORTH   Business Year for Addiction and Mental Health

The period from May 14, 2003 to May 14, 2004 was declared the first Business Year for Addiction and Mental Health. The Global Business and Economic Roundtable on Addiction and Mental Health used the year to promote and generate support for its Charter on Mental Health. The goal was to get CEOs to sign the charter and commit to workplace practices that minimize the disabling and even deadly effects of depression, anxiety, and addiction.

The Charter includes goals specifically tied to employee assistance plans (EAPs) including:

- the redesign of present-day EAPs and group health plans to target and reduce the effects of depression at work
- dramatic improvement in the rate of employee utilization of EAPs to 25 to 35 percent, up from the current rates of 7 to 10 percent
- increased training for managers/executives at all levels to play a fundamental role in the early identification of a troubled employee
- employee education and screening modules to increase early access through the workplace to appropriate care for depression

Source: "Business Year for Addiction and Mental Health," *Canadian HR Reporter*, June 2, 2003, p.7.

to their household earnings. Many employers are offering some form of child care benefits to their employees, including resource and referral services, sick or emergency child care programs, and on-site daycare centres.

One fast-growing employee benefit is emergency child care. Companies can lose significant working-hours as a result of last-minute child care problems, and, therefore, more and more companies are offering this low-cost benefit. Emergency child care services generally are offered either at on-site child care centres or at centres that are near the workplace, or through company-paid babysitters.

Eldercare

Given longer life expectancy than ever before and the aging of the baby-boom generation, one benefit that will become increasingly important is eldercare assistance. The programs that are available so far provide only referral services.

Employee Assistance Plans (EAPs)

employee assistance plan (EAP)

employer-sponsored program that provides employees with confidential counselling and/or treatment programs for personal problems including addiction, stress, and mental health issues

An **employee assistance plan** is a formal employer program that provides employees with confidential counselling and/or treatment programs for problems such as mental health issues, marital/family problems, work/career stress, legal problems, and substance abuse. These programs are particularly important for helping employees who suffer workplace trauma ranging from harassment to physical assault.[66] The number of EAPs in Canada is growing because they are a proactive way to reduce absenteeism and disability costs. The percentage of employees using EAPs is difficult to determine due to confidentiality, but is estimated to be in the order of 10 percent.

■ BENEFITS FOR CONTINGENT WORKERS

Contingent work relationships include working through a temporary help agency, working for a contract company, working on call, and working as an independent contractor. Contracting offers a viable way to meet rapidly changing environmental conditions, both by reducing costs and by permitting easier expansion and contraction of production/services.

Contingent workers cost less primarily because the benefits offered, if any, are lower than for regular employees. As Exhibit 9.12 shows, the fewer hours employees work in a week, the more severe is the benefits' penalty.

EXHIBIT 9.12 Benefits Received: Full-Time versus Contingent Employees

	Small Companies		Medium Companies		Large Companies	
	Full Time	Contingent	Full Time	Contingent	Full Time	Contingent
Vacation	98%	40%	100%	100%	100%	80%
Health Insurance	96	21	100	56	100	67
Holidays	97	48	100	77	100	67
Life Insurance	85	21	100	47	100	67
Pension	89	43	98	91	100	71
Sick leave	70	26	83	53	96	58

CONCLUSION

Since the 1940s, employee benefits have been the most volatile area in the compensation field. From 1940 to 1980 these dramatic changes came in the form of more and better forms of employee benefits. The result should not have been unexpected. Employee benefits are now a major—and many believe prohibitively expensive—component of doing business. In the new millennium, cost-saving efforts to improve the competitive position of North American industry are widespread. A part of these cost savings will come from tighter administrative controls on existing benefit packages. But another part may come from a reduction in existing benefits packages. If this does evolve as a trend, benefits administrators will need to develop a mechanism for identifying employee preferences (in this case "least preferences") and use these as a guideline to meet agreed-upon savings targets.

CHAPTER SUMMARY

1. Employee benefits have been increasing in cost for the last 50 years, and now constitute a significant amount of compensation expense in all Canadian organizations, on the order of 40 percent of payroll.
2. Key issues in benefits planning, design, and administration are: (i) the relative role of benefits in a compensation package, (ii) external competitiveness, (iii) benefits adequacy and cost justification, (iv) who should be included in these plans, (v) level of choice for employees, and (vi) employee-employer cost sharing.
3. Three important functions in benefits administration are communication, claims processing, and cost containment.
4. There are three legally required benefits in Canada, in addition to government-sponsored health care plans: Workers' Compensation, Canada/Quebec Pension Plan, and Employment Insurance. Workers' Compensation provides compensation for injuries and diseases that arise out of, and while in the course of, employment. The Canada/Quebec Pension Plan is a pension plan for all employed Canadians. Employment Insurance provides workers with temporary income replacement as a result of employment interruptions due to circumstances beyond their control.
5. In a defined-benefit plan, the employer agrees to provide a specific level of retirement pension, the exact cost of which is unknown. In a defined-contribution pension plan, the employer agrees to provide specific contributions, but the final benefit is unknown.
6. The two general strategies for controlling medical benefit costs are: (i) motivating employees to change their demand for health care through changes in the design or administration of the plan, and (ii) the promotion of preventive health programs.

KEY TERMS

REVIEW QUESTIONS

1. How does the concept of external equity differ when discussing pay versus benefits?
2. Describe how a flexible benefits plan might increase worker satisfaction with benefits at the same time that costs are being reduced.
3. Explain how an employee assistance plan could reduce costs for several other benefits.

EXPERIENTIAL EXERCISES

1. Your CEO is living proof that a little bit of knowledge is a dangerous thing. He just read in the *Globe and Mail* that employee benefits cost, on average, 38 percent of payroll. To save money, he suggests that the company fire its two benefits administrators, do away with all benefits, and give employees a 38 percent pay raise. What arguments could you provide to persuade the CEO that this is not a good idea?

2. Your company has a serious turnover problem among employees with fewer than five years' seniority. The CEO wants to use employee benefits to lessen this problem. What might you do, specifically in the areas of pension vesting, vacation and holiday allocation, and life insurance coverage, in an effort to reduce turnover?

3. Assume you are politically foolhardy and decide to challenge your CEO's decision in the previous question to use benefits as a major tool for reducing turnover. Before she fires you, what arguments might you use to try to persuade her? (Hint: Are there other compensation tools that might be more effective in reducing turnover? Might the changes in benefits have unintended consequences for more-senior employees?)

WEB EXERCISE

Certified Employee Benefits Specialist Program (CEBS)

The Certified Employee Benefits Specialist Program is sponsored by the International Foundation of Employee Benefits Plans in Wisconsin (www.ifebp.org). In Canada, CEBS is co-sponsored by Dalhousie University (www.dal.ca/~henson/pd/prof-des.html). Review these two sites and then go to the Canadian CEBS site www.ifebp.org/cebs/cebscanada. What are the course requirements? Where are CEBS courses offered in Canada? What is the difference between the CEBS designation and the three other designations— Group Benefits Associate, Retirement Plans Associate, and Compensation Management Specialist? Would you recommend CEBS to your classmates who are interested in a career in employee benefits?

CASE

Romance Novels, Inc.

Romance Novels, Inc., has a distribution centre in Baie d'Urfé, Quebec, a suburb of Montreal. Books are shipped there from the publisher and orders are processed from this distribution centre. In recent years RNI has been plagued by two problems that are becoming more serious. First, Amazon. com continues to prove a powerful competitor, particularly because they can process and ship a book order in a maximum of two days. RNI still has difficulty hitting this turnaround time, but has managed to meet a three-day timeline for all books. Second, RNI finds itself—as do many organizations in a tight labour market— increasingly dependent on contingent (temporary) workers. Approximately 25 percent of RNI's work force are "temps," and they are disproportionately placed in the pick-and-pack division, the division that competes with Amazon.com for Internet sales. Recent attitude surveys show these workers feel no loyalty to the organization, and their performance and turnover rates demonstrate this (Exhibit 1). John Meindl, plant manager, has called you in to help solve these two, perhaps interrelated, problems. Given the following information, make suggestions about what to do. Note: John is unwilling, absent persuasive arguments, to hire temps full time. He feels it is important to retain flexibility to terminate quickly should there be an economic downturn.

EXHIBIT 1 Productivity, Quality, and Turnover Data, by Employment Status

	Pieces shipped/hr	Customer complaints/1000 orders	Annual turnover
Full-time Workers	327	6.32	14%
Contingent Workers	287	6.68	43%

EXHIBIT 2 Base Wage, Variable Compensation, and Benefits Expenditures, by Employment Status for Order Fillers (all temps are hired as order fillers)

	Base Wg (avg)	Variable Comp	Benefits (% payroll)	Seniority (yrs)
Full-Time Workers	8.85	max 4%	33%	6.5
Contingent Workers	8.05	max 4%	17%	1.8

CASE

| **EXHIBIT** | **3** | Performance Appraisal Form Used for All Full-time and Temporary Employees |

Scale

Dimension	Well Below Average 1	Below Average 2	Average 3	Above Average 4	Well Above Average 5
Quality of Work					
Job Knowledge					
Initiative					
Dependability					
Overall Performance					

Interviews with supervisory staff and John Meindl disclose the following information:

Contingent workers feel like second-class citizens.

Kelly Services, the temp agency used by RNI, charges 10% per hour for every contingent (temporary) worker.

Contributions for legally required benefits (17% of payroll) are made by Kelly Services. So, in effect, RNI bears the cost burden for legally mandated benefits.

John Meindl is thinking about extending some combination of the following benefits to contingent workers. Decide which benefits should be extended, and whether they should be given to all contingent workers, or based on some factor such as seniority or performance. John Meindl is not averse to trying merit-(performance-)based benefits. Indeed, the high-tech firm he came from was a pioneer in that area in the early 90s.

Benefit	Cost per hour	Cost for level of current coverage of full-time employees	Temp. worker rating of benefit
5 vacation days (max)	.03/day of vacation	.18	high
Life Ins ($10,000)	.01/$1000 insurance	.07	low
Pension contribution (max 5%match)	.01/1% match	.11	medium
Sick days (5 max)	.03/day sick	.21	high

Which of these benefits should be extended? You may give any combination of 0–5 days of vacation and/or sick days, any amount of insurance in $1000 increments between 0–$10,000, and any amount of match on pension from 0%–5%. Keeping in mind equity issues with full-time workers, rating of benefits, and the goal of being competitive with Amazon.com, how do you want to allocate these benefits, and in what proportions? Justify your answer. If you could change John's mind about how to proceed, what recommendations would you make to him, and why?

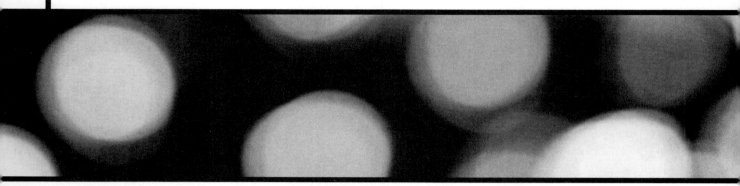

PART 3

Determining Individual Pay: Pay for Performance

Thus far we have concentrated on two components of the pay model (Exhibit III.1). Internal consistency and the practices to ensure it—job analysis and job evaluation—provide guidance in relating jobs to one another in terms of the content of the work and the relative contribution to the organization's objectives. External competitiveness, or comparisons with the external labour market, raises issues of proper survey definitions, setting policy lines, and arriving at competitive pay levels and equitable pay structures. This part of the book deals with a third critical dimension of the pay system design and administration—paying individual employees performing the job.

How much should one employee be paid relative to another when they both hold the same job in the same organization? If this question is not answered satisfactorily, all prior efforts to evaluate and price jobs will have been in vain. For example, the compensation manager determines that all systems analysts should be paid between $49,000 and $60,000. But where in that range is each individual paid? Should a good performer be paid more than a poor performer? If the answer is yes, how should performance be measured and what should be the differential reward? Similarly, should the systems analyst with more years' experience (i.e., higher seniority) be paid more than a co-worker with less time on the job? Again, if the answer is yes, what is the tradeoff between seniority and performance in assigning pay raises? As Exhibit III.1 suggests, all these questions involve the concept of employee contribution. In the next two chapters we will be discussing different facets of employee contribution.

Chapter 10 considers how pay affects performance. Is there evidence that companies should invest in pay-for-performance plans? In other words, does paying for performance result in higher performance? The answer may seem obvious, but there are many ways to complicate this elegant notion. We acknowledge that performance can't always be measured objectively. What do we do to ensure that subjective appraisal procedures are as free from error as possible? Much progress has been made here, and we provide a tour of the different strategies to measure performance.

Chapter 11 looks at actual pay-for-performance plans. The compensation arena is full of programs that promise to link pay and performance. We identify these plans and discuss their relative advantages and disadvantages. Pay for special groups that require the design of compensation programs that sometimes differ from more traditional designs are also discussed.

EXHIBIT **III.1** The Pay Model

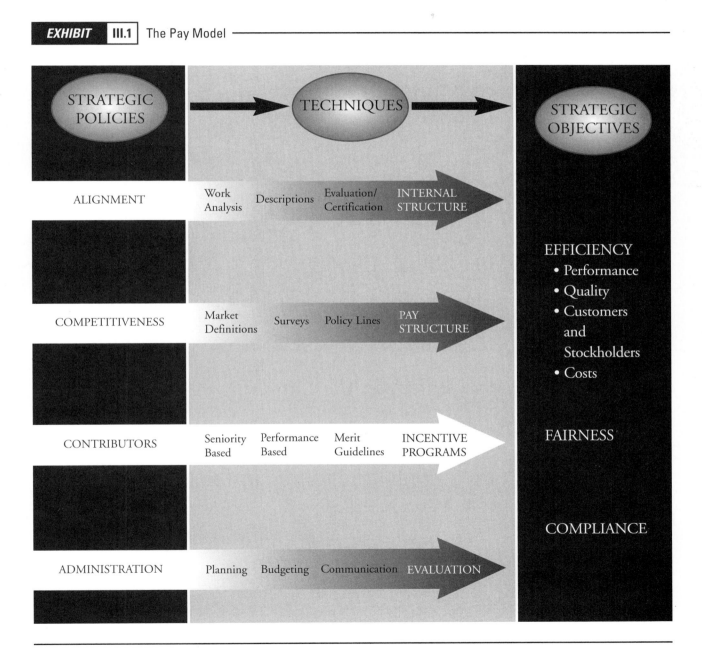

PAY FOR PERFORMANCE AND THE ROLE OF PERFORMANCE APPRAISAL

LEARNING OUTCOMES

- *Explain* the three factors on which employee performance depends.
- Briefly *describe* the difference between motivation theories that focus on content and those that focus on the nature of the exchange, and those that focus on desired behaviour.
- *Discuss* the ways in which compensation motivates behaviour.
- *Describe* at least five common errors in the appraisal process.
- *Explain* three strategies to better understand and measure job performance.
- *Discuss* the key elements of an effective performance appraisal process.
- *Explain* the three factors that determine the effectiveness of a pay-for-performance plan.

pay-for-performance plan

a pay plan that links individual pay to some measure of performance on the job

The primary focus of the last section was to determine the worth of jobs, independent of who performed those jobs. Job analysis, job evaluation, and job pricing all have a common theme. They are techniques to identify the value a firm places on its jobs. Now we introduce people into the equation. Now we declare that different people performing the same job may have different value to the organization. Jim is a better programmer than Sam. Sally knows more programming languages than John. Companies often link individual pay to performance through a **pay-for-performance plan**—in this case, paying Sally more than John, and Jim more than Sam.

Entering people into the compensation equation greatly complicates the compensation process. There is growing evidence that the way we design HR practices, like performance management, strongly affects the way employees perceive the company. The simple (or not so simple as we will discuss) process of implementing a performance appraisal system that employees find acceptable goes a long way towards increasing trust in top management.[1] So, as we discuss pay for performance, remember there are other important outcomes that also depend on building good performance measurement tools.

In Chapter 1 we talked about compensation objectives complementing overall human resources objectives, and both of these helping an organization to achieve its overall strategic objectives. But this raises the question, "How does an organization achieve its overall strategic objectives?" In this section of the book we argue that organizational success ultimately depends on human behaviour. Our compensation decisions and practices should be designed to increase the likelihood that employees will behave in ways that help the organization achieve its strategic objectives. This chapter is organized around employee behaviours. First, we identify the four kinds of behaviours organizations are interested in. Then we note what theories say about our ability to motivate these behaviours. And finally, we talk about our success, and sometimes lack thereof, in designing compensation systems to elicit these behaviours.

WHAT BEHAVIOURS DO EMPLOYERS CARE ABOUT? LINKING ORGANIZATION STRATEGY TO COMPENSATION AND PERFORMANCE MANAGEMENT

The simple answer is that employers want employees to perform in ways that lead to better organizational performance. Our focus in this chapter, then, is on employee performance. There is growing evidence that employee performance depends on three general factors:[2]

$$\text{Employee performance} = f(S,K,M) \text{ where}$$

S　=　Skill and ability to perform task
K　=　Knowledge of facts, rules, principles, and procedures
M　=　Motivation to perform

Wanting to succeed isn't enough. Having the ability without the desire also isn't enough. For an organization to succeed, it needs employees who perform well. And, as we noted in Chapter 2, this involves not only good compensation strategy and practice, but also other well-developed HR practices.[3] We need to hire people with skill and ability (S). We need to make sure the good employees (high S) stay with the company. If we can succeed at these first two things, we can then concentrate on building further knowledge and skills (K & S). And finally, we need to find ways to motivate (M) employees to perform well on their jobs—to take their knowledge and abilities and apply them in ways that contribute to organizational performance.

Apparent through all of this is the need to accurately measure performance. *We can't reward performance if we can't measure it!* As a simple example, think about where piece-rate systems are used to pay people. Why do many sales jobs use commissions (a form of piece rate) as the primary compensation vehicle? Conventional wisdom has always been that performance in a sales job is relatively easy to measure—dollar sales. There is little ambiguity in the measure of performance, and this makes it easy to create a strong link between units of performance and amount of compensation. One of the biggest recent advances in compensation strategy has been to document and extend this conventional wisdom. Initial evidence suggests that the way we design compensation systems is intimately linked to the stability of our performance measures. Exhibit 10.1 builds on the results of two studies to speculate about the following relationship.[4]

Think about what each of the cells suggests in terms of compensation practices under different performance conditions. First, what might cause wide swings in corporate performance—often this occurs when something in the external environment fluctuates widely too (e.g., exchange rate with a major foreign customer, raw material costs). It probably wouldn't be fair, and employees would certainly object, if a large part of pay were incentive based in this kind of environment. Things the employees don't control (in the external environment) would be dictating a big part of pay. Lack of employee control translates into perceptions of unfair treatment. Cells B and D both suggest that a low incentive component is appropriate in organizations with highly variable annual performance. Conversely, as cells A and C indicate, larger incentive components are appropriate in companies with stable annual performance.

Employee performance also can vary. Some jobs are fairly stable, with expectations fairly consistent across time. In other jobs, though, there might be a great deal of fluctuation in the

EXHIBIT **10.1** Performance Measurement Relates to Compensation

Variability/ease of measurement in individual performance	Variability in Organizational Performance	
	Low Variability: few swings in overall corporate performance	*High Variability: regular and large swings in overall corporate performance*
Unstable, unclear, and changing objectives	Cell A—provide wide range of rewards beyond just money. Include significant incentive component.	Cell B—provide wide range of rewards beyond just money. Emphasize base pay with low incentive portion.
Stable and easily measured	Cell C—emphasize monetary rewards with large incentive component.	Cell D—emphasize monetary rewards. Large base pay with low incentive portion.

kinds of things expected of employees, requiring employees who are willing to be flexible and adjust to changing demands. Evidence suggests that companies are best able to get employees to adjust, be flexible, and show commitment when a broader array of rewards, rather than just money, is part of the compensation package.[5]

When we distill all of this, what can we conclude? We think the response depends on how we answer the following four questions:

How do we get good employment prospects to *join* our company?

How do we *retain* these good employees once they join?

How do we get employees to *develop skills* for current and future jobs?

How do we get employees to *perform well* on their current job?

First, how do we get good people to join our company? How did Ford get Wayne Gretzky to serve as corporate spokesperson? Part of the answer is rumoured to be a contract worth millions of dollars. The long-run success of any company depends on getting good people to accept employment. And the compensation challenge is to figure out what components of our compensation package are likely to influence this decision to join.

The obvious complement to the decision to join is the decision to stay. How do we retain employees? It doesn't do much good to attract exceptional employees to our company only to lose them a short time later. Once our compensation practices get a good employee in the door, we need to figure out ways to ensure it's not a revolving door.

We also need to recognize, though, that what we need employees to do today may change literally overnight. A fast-changing world requires employees who can adjust more quickly. How do we get employees, traditionally resistant to change, to willingly develop skills today that may not be vital on the current job but which are forecast to be critical as the company's strategic plan adjusts to change? Another compensation challenge!

Finally, we want employees to do well on their current jobs. This means both performing, and performing well, tasks that support our strategic objectives. What motivates employees to succeed? The compensation challenge is to design rewards that enhance job performance.

■ WHAT DOES IT TAKE TO GET EMPLOYEES TO BEHAVE IN DESIRED WAYS? WHAT MOTIVATION THEORY AND RESEARCH SAYS

motivation

a process involving the determination of what is important to a person, and offering it in exchange for desired behaviour

Another way of asking the same question is, "What motivates employees?" In the simplest sense, **motivation** involves three elements: (1) what's important to a person, and (2) offering it in exchange for some (3) desired behaviour. On the first question, there are data that suggest that employees prefer pay systems that recognize: individual performance, changes in the cost of living, seniority, and the market rate, to name the most important factors.[6] To narrow down specific employee preferences, though, there has been some exciting new work on what's important to employees. The new idea is called flexible total compensation—a takeoff on flexible benefits, as described in Chapter 9. Flexible compensation develops the idea that only the individual employee knows what package of rewards would best suit his or her personal needs. The key ingredient in this yet-to-be-tried program—careful cost analysis to make sure the dollar cost of the package an employee selects meets employer budgetary limits.[7]

In Exhibit 10.2 we briefly summarize some of the important motivation theories. Pay particular attention to the last column where we talk about the implications for employee behaviour.

Some of the theories in Exhibit 10.2 focus on content—identifying what is important to people. Maslow and Herzberg, for example, both fall in this category. People have certain needs, such as physiological, security, and self-esteem, that influence behaviour. Presumably, if we offer rewards that satisfy one or more needs, employees will behave in desired ways. These theories often drive compensation decisions about the breadth and depth of compensation offerings. Flexible pay, whereby employees choose from a menu of pay and benefit choices, clearly is driven by the issue of needs. Who best knows what satisfies needs? The employee!

A second set of theories, best exemplified by expectancy theory, equity theory, and agency theory, focus less on need states and more on the second element—the nature of the exchange. Many of our compensation practices recognize the importance of a fair exchange. We evaluate jobs using a common set of compensable factors in part to let employees know that an explicit set of rules governs the evaluation process. We collect salary survey data because we want the exchange to be fair compared to external standards. We design incentive systems to align employee behaviour with the needs of the organization. All these pay decisions, and more, owe much to understanding how the employment exchange affects employee motivation.

expectancy theory

motivation theory stating that people cognitively evaluate potential behaviours in relation to rewards offered in exchange

Expectancy theory argues that people behave as if they cognitively evaluate what behaviours are possible (e.g., the probability that they can complete the task) in relation to the value of rewards offered in exchange. According to this theory, we choose behaviours that yield the most satisfactory exchange. **Equity theory** focuses also on what goes on inside an employee's head. Equity theory argues that people are highly concerned about equity, or fairness of the exchange process. Employees look at the exchange as a ratio between what is expected and what is received. Some theorists say we judge transactions as fair when others around us don't have a more (or less) favourable balance between the give and get of an exchange.[8] Even greater focus on the exchange process occurs in the last of this second set of theories, **agency theory**.[9] Here employees are depicted as agents who enter an exchange with principals—the owners or their designated managers. It is assumed that both sides to the exchange seek the most favourable exchange possible, and will act opportunistically if given a chance (e.g., try to "get by" with doing as little as possible to satisfy the contract). Compensation is a major element in this theory, because it is used to keep employees in line: Employers identify important behaviours and important outcomes and pay specifically for achieving desired levels of each. Such incentive systems penalize employees who try to shirk their duties by giving them proportionately lower rewards.

equity theory

motivation theory stating that people are concerned about fairness of the reward outcomes exchanged for employee inputs

agency theory

motivation theory stating that employees and management/owners both will act opportunistically to obtain the most favourable exchange possible

Finally, at least one of the theories summarized in 10.2 focuses on the third element of motivation: desired behaviour. A review of this literature indicates that the vast majority of studies on goal setting find a positive impact of goal setting on performance. Workers assigned "hard" goals consistently do better than workers told to "do your best."[10]

| **EXHIBIT** | **10.2** | What Motivation Theories Say |

Theory	Essential Features	Predictions about Performance-Based Pay	So What?
Maslow's Need Hierarchy	People are motivated by inner needs. Needs form a hierarchy from most basic (food and shelter) to higher-order (e.g., self-esteem, love, self-actualization). Needs are never fully met; they operate cyclically. Higher-order needs become motivating after lower-order needs have been met. When needs are not met, they become frustrating.	1. Base pay must be set high enough to provide individuals with the economic means to meet their basic living needs. 2. An at-risk program will not be motivating since it restricts employees' ability to meet lower-order needs. 3. Success-sharing plans may be motivating to the extent they help employees pursue higher-order needs.	A. Performance-based pay may be de-motivating if it impinges upon employees' capacity to meet daily living needs. B. Incentive pay is motivating to the extent it is attached to achievement, recognition, or approval.
Herzberg's 2-Factor Theory	Employees are motivated by two types of motivators: hygiene factors and satisfiers. Hygiene or maintenance factors, in their absence, prevent behaviours, but in their presence cannot motivate performance. These are related to basic living needs, security, and fair treatment. Satisfiers, such as recognition, promotion, and achievement motivate performance.	1. Base pay must be set high enough enough to provide individuals with the economic means to meet hygiene needs, but it cannot motivate performance. 2. Performance is obtained through rewards; payments in excess of that required to meet basic needs. 3. Performance-based pay is motivating to the extent it is connected with meeting employees' needs for recognition, pleasure attainment, achievement, and the like. 4. Other factors such as interpersonal atmosphere, responsibility, type of work, and working conditions influence the efficacy of performance-based pay.	A. Pay level is important—must meet minimum requirements before performance-based pay can operate as motivator. B. Security plans will induce minimum, but not extra, performance. Success-sharing plans will be motivating. At-risk plans will be demotivating. C. Other conditions in the working relationship influence the effectiveness of performance-based pay.
Expectancy	Motivation is the product of three perceptions: expectancy, instrumentality, and valence. Expectancy is employees' assessment of their ability to perform required job tasks. Instrumentality is employees' beliefs that requisite job performance will be rewarded by the organization. Valence is the value employees attach to the organization rewards offered for satisfactory job performance.	1. Job tasks and responsibilities should be clearly defined. 2. The pay-performance link is critical. 3. Performance-based pay returns must be large enough to be seen as rewards. 4. People choose the behaviour that leads to the greatest reward.	A. Larger incentive payments are better than smaller ones. B. Line-of-sight is critical—employees must believe they can influence performance targets. C. Employee assessments of their own ability are important—organizations should be aware of training and resource needs required to perform at target levels.

continued

EXHIBIT	**10.2**	What Motivation Theories Say (*continued*)

Theory	Essential Features	Predictions about Performance-Based Pay	So What?
Equity	Employees are motivated when perceived outputs (i.e., pay) are equal to perceived inputs (e.g., effort, work behaviours). A disequilibrium in the output-to-input balance causes discomfort. If employees perceive that others are paid more for the same effort, they will react negatively (e.g., shirk) to correct the output-to-input balance.	1. The pay-performance link is critical; increases in performance must be matched by commensurate increases in pay. 2. Performance inputs and expected outputs must be clearly defined and identified. 3. Employees evaluate the adequacy of their pay via comparisons with other employees.	A. Performance measures must be clearly defined and employee must be able to affect them through work behaviours. B. If payouts do not match expectations, employees will react negatively. C. Fairness and consistency of performance-based pay across employees in an organization is important. D. Since employees evaluate their pay-effort balance in comparison to other employees, relative pay matters.
Reinforcement	Rewards reinforce (i.e., motivate and sustain) performance. Rewards must follow directly after behaviours to be reinforcing. Behaviours which are not rewarded will be discontinued.	1. Performance-based payments must follow closely behind performance. 2. Rewards must be tightly coupled to desired performance objectives. 3. Withholding payouts can be a way to discourage unwanted behaviours.	A. Timing of payouts is very important.
Goal Setting	Challenging performance goals influence greater intensity and duration in employee performance. Goals serve as feedback standards to which employees can compare their performance. Individuals are motivated to the extent that goal achievement is combined with receiving valued rewards.	1. Performance-based pay must be contingent upon achievement of important performance goals. 2. Performance goals should be challenging and specific. 3. The amount of the incentive reward should match the goal difficulty.	A. Line-of-sight is important; employees must believe they can influence performance targets. B. Performance targets should be communicated in terms of specific, difficult goals. C. Feedback about performance is important. D. Performance-based payouts should be contingent upon goal achievement.
Agency	Pay directs and motivates employee performance. Employees prefer static wages (e.g., a salary) to performance-based pay. If performance can be accurately monitored, payments should be based upon satisfactory completion of work duties. If performance cannot be monitored, pay should be aligned with achieving organizational objectives.	1. Performance-based pay must be tightly linked to organizational objectives. 2. Employees dislike risky pay and will demand a wage premium (e.g., higher total pay) in exchange for accepting performance-based pay. 3. Performance-based pay can be used to direct and induce employee performance.	A. Performance-based pay is the optimal compensation choice for more complex jobs where monitoring employees' work is difficult. B. Performance targets should be tied to organizational goals. C. Use of performance-based pay will require higher total pay opportunity.

■ WHAT DOES IT TAKE TO GET EMPLOYEES TO BEHAVE IN DESIRED WAYS? WHAT COMPENSATION PEOPLE SAY

In the past, compensation people didn't ask this question very often. Employees learned what behaviours were important as part of the socialization process or as part of the performance management process.[11] If it was part of the culture to work long hours, you quickly learned this. If your performance appraisal at the end of the year stressed certain types of behaviours, or if your boss said certain things were important to her, then the signals were pretty clear: Do these things! Compensation might have rewarded people for meeting these expectations, but usually the compensation package wasn't designed to be one of the signals about expected performance. Now compensation people talk about pay in terms of a neon arrow flashing: "Do these things." Progressive companies ask the question, "What do we want our compensation package to do?" "How, for example, do we get our product engineers to take more risks?" Compensation then is designed to support this risk-taking behaviour. In the next section we begin to talk about the different types of reward components, acknowledging that pay isn't the only reward that influences behaviour.

■ TOTAL REWARD SYSTEM

Compensation is but one of many rewards that influence employee behaviour. Depending on the survey you consult, workers highly value such other job rewards as empowerment, recognition, and opportunities for advancement.[12] Please note that at least 13 general categories of rewards are provided by organizations (Exhibit 10.3) as part of their **total reward system**.

total reward system

■ all rewards (in at least 13 general categories) provided by organizations

Now consider an example that shows how compensation decisions have to be integrated with total reward system decisions. If we don't think about the presence or absence of other rewards than money in an organization, we may find the compensation process producing unintended consequences. In a team-based work environment where the culture of the organization strongly supports empowerment of workers, empowerment is a form of reward. In Exhibit 10.3 we identify the dimensions of empowerment (see #9) as *authority* to make decisions, some *control* over factors that influence outcomes, and the *autonomy* to carry out decisions without overregulation by upper management. Some people find empowerment a very positive inducement, making coming to work each day a pleasure. Others may view empowerment as just added responsibility—legitimizing demands for more pay. In the first case adding extra compensation may not be necessary. Some have even argued it can lessen motivation.[13] In the second case, extra compensation may be a

---

EXHIBIT   10.3   Components of a Total Reward System

1. Compensation	Wages, Commissions, and Bonuses
2. Benefits	Vacations, Health Insurance
3. Social Interaction	Friendly Workplace
4. Security	Stable, Consistent Position and Rewards
5. Status/Recognition	Respect, Prominence Due to Work
6. Work Variety	Opportunity to Experience Different Things
7. Workload	Right Amount of Work (Not too much, not too little)
8. Work Importance	Is Work Valued by Society
9. Authority/Control/Autonomy	Ability to Influence Others; Control Own Destiny
10. Advancement	Chance to Get Ahead
11. Feedback	Receive Information Helping to Improve Performance
12. Work Conditions	Hazard Free
13. Development Opportunity	Formal and Informal Training to Learn New Knowledge/Skills/Abilities

necessity. Is it any wonder that companies are having trouble finding one right answer to the team compensation question?

Exhibit 10.4 outlines the different types of wage components, ordered from least risky to most risky for employees. We define risky in terms of stability of income, or the ability to accurately

EXHIBIT 10.4 Wage Components

Wage component	Definition	Level of Risk to Employee
Base Pay	The guaranteed portion of an employee's wage package.	As long as employment continues, this is the secure portion of wages.
Across the Board	Wage increase granted to all employees, regardless of performance. Size related to some subjective assessment by employer about ability to pay. Typically an add-on to base pay in subsequent years.	Some risk to employee since at discretion of employer. But not tied to performance differences, so risk lower in that respect.
Cost-of-Living Increase	Same as across-the-board increase, except magnitude based on change in cost of living (e.g., as measured by CPI).	Same as across-the-board increases.
Merit Pay	Wage increase granted to employee as function of some assessment of employee peformance. Adds on to base pay in subsequent years.	Two types of risk faced by employees. Size of total merit pool at discretion of employer (risk element), and individual portion of pool depends on performance, which also is not totally predictable.
Lump-Sum Bonus	As with merit pay, granted for individual performance. Does not add into base pay, but is distributed as a one-time bonus.	Three types of risks faced here. Both types mentioned under merit pay, plus not added into base —requires annually "re-earning" the added pay
Individual Incentive	Sometimes this variable pay is an add-on to a fixed base pay. The incentive component ties increments in compensation directly to extra individual production (e.g., commission systems, piece rate). Although measures of performance typically are subjective, with merit and lump-sum components, this form of variable pay differs because measures of performance are objective (e.g., sales volume).	Most risky compensation component if sole element of pay, but often combined with a base pay. No or low fixed base pay means each year employee is dependent upon number of units of performance to determine pay.
Success-Sharing Plans	A generic category of pay add-on (variable pay) which is tied to some measure of group performance, not individual performance. Not added into base pay. Distinguished from risk-sharing plans below because employees share in any success—performance above standard—but are not penalized for performance below standard.	All success-sharing plans have risks noted in above pay components plus the risk associated with group performance measures. Now individual worker is also dependent upon the performance of others included in the group.
■ Gain-Sharing	Differs from profit sharing in that goal to exceed is not financial performance of organization, but some cost index (e.g., labour cost is most common, might also include scrap costs, utility costs).	Less risk to individual than profit sharing because performance measure is more controllable.

continued

EXHIBIT 10.4	Wage Components (*continued*)

Wage component	Definition	Level of Risk to Employee
■ Profit Sharing	Add-on linked to group performance (team, division, total company) relative to exceeding some financial goal.	Profit measures are influenced by factors beyond employee control (e.g., economic climate, accounting write-offs). Less control means more risk.
Risk-Sharing Plans	Generic category of pay add-on (variable pay) that differs from success sharing in that employee shares not only in the successes, but is also penalized during poor performance years. Penalty is in form of lower total compensation in poor corporate performance years. Reward, though, is typically higher than for success-sharing programs in high performance years.	Greater risk than success-sharing plans. Typically, employees absorb a "temporary" cut in base pay. If performance targets are met, this cut is neutralized by one component of variable pay. Risk to employee is increased, though, because even base pay is no longer totally predictable.

predict income level from year to year. Over the last several decades, companies have been moving more towards compensation programs higher on the risk continuum. New forms of pay are less entitlement-oriented and more linked to the uncertainties of individual, group, and corporate performance.[14] Employees increasingly are expected to bear a share of the risks that businesses have borne solely in the past. It's not entirely clear what impact this shifting of risk will have in the long run, but some authors are already voicing concerns that efforts to build employee loyalty and commitment may be an early casualty of these new pay systems.[15] Some research suggests that employees may need a risk premium (higher pay) to stay and perform in a company with pay-at-risk.[16] To explore what impact these new forms of pay have, we now summarize what we know about the ability of different compensation components to motivate the four general behaviours we noted earlier.

■ DOES COMPENSATION MOTIVATE BEHAVIOUR? GENERAL COMMENTS

Although there are exceptions, generally, linking pay to behaviours of employees results in better individual and organizational performance.[17] One particularly good study looked at the HR practices of over 3,000 companies.[18] One set of questions asked: (1) whether the company had a formal appraisal process, (2) was the appraisal tied to the size of pay increases, and (3) did performance influence who would be promoted. Organizations significantly above the mean (by one standard deviation) on these and other "High Performance Work Practices" had annual sales that averaged $27,000 more per employee. So, rewarding employees for performance pays off.

In a more comprehensive review, Heneman reports that 40 of 42 studies looking at merit pay claim performance increases when pay is tied to performance.[19] Gerhart and Milkovich took the performance-based pay question one step further. They found, across 200 companies, there was a 1.5 percent increase in return on assets for every 10 percent increase in the size of a bonus.[20] Furthermore, they found that the variable portion of pay had a stronger impact on individual and corporate performance than did the level of base pay.

■ DOES COMPENSATION MOTIVATE BEHAVIOUR? SPECIFIC COMMENTS

This section looks at the role of compensation in motivating the four types of behaviour outlined earlier: the decision to join, to stay, to develop skills, and to perform well.

Do People Join a Firm because of Pay?

That level of pay and pay system characteristics influence a job candidate's decision to join a firm shouldn't be too surprising.[21] Pay is one of the more visible rewards in the whole recruitment process. Job offers spell out level of compensation and may even include discussions about kind of pay such as bonuses and profit participation. Other rewards are subjective, and tend to require actual time on the job before we can decide whether they are positive or negative features of the job. Not so for pay. Being perceived as more objective, it's more easily communicated in the employment offer.

Recent research suggests job candidates look for organizations with reward systems that fit their personalities.[22] Below we outline some of the ways that "fit" is important.

Person Characteristics	Preferred Reward Characteristics
Materialistic	Relatively more concerned about pay level[23]
Low Self-Esteem	Low self-esteem individuals want large, decentralized organization with little pay for performance[24]
Risk Takers	Want more pay based on performance[25]
Individualists ("I control my destiny")	Want pay plans based on individual performance, not group performance[26]

None of these relationships is particularly surprising. People are attracted to organizations that fit their personalities. Evidence suggests talented employees are attracted to companies that have strong links between pay and performance.[27]

It's not a big jump, then, to suggest organizations should design their reward systems to attract people with desired personalities and values. For example, if we need risk takers, maybe we should design reward systems that have elements of risk built into them.

Do People Stay in a Firm (or Leave) because of Pay?

There is clear evidence that poor performers are more likely to leave an organization than good performers.[28] How does pay affect this relationship? Much of the equity theory research in the 1970s documented that workers who feel unfairly treated in pay react by leaving the firm for greener pastures.[29] This is particularly true under incentive conditions. Turnover is much higher for poor performers when pay is based on individual performance. Conversely, group incentive plans may lead to more turnover of better performers—clearly an undesirable outcome. When AT&T shifted from individual to team-based incentives a number of years ago, star performers either reduced their output or quit. Out of 208 above-average performers, only one continued to report performance increases under the group incentive plan. The rest felt cheated because the incentives for higher individual performance were now spread across all group members.[30]

Clearly, pay can be a factor in decisions to stay or leave.[31] Too little pay triggers feelings of unfair treatment. Result? Turnover. Supporting this, pay that employees find reasonable can help reduce turnover.[32] Even the way we pay has an impact on turnover. Evidence suggests that some employees are uncomfortable with pay systems that put any substantial future earnings at risk, or pay systems that link less to personal effort and more to group effort. We need to make sure, as one critic has noted, that we don't let our design of new reward systems rupture our relationships with employees.[33] Recent efforts to use different types of compensation as a tool for retaining workers has focused on what is called scarce talent. For example, information technology employees have been scarce for much of the past decade, at least. One way to retain these workers is to develop a variable pay component for each project.

For example, reports of variable pay linked to individual length of stay on a project, to peer ratings and to project results, suggest that this pay-for-performance combination might appeal to scarce talent.[34]

Do Employees More Readily Agree to Develop Job Skills because of Pay?

We don't know the answer to this question. Skill-based pay (Chapter 6) is intended, at least partially, to pay employees for learning new skills—skills that hopefully will help employees perform better on current jobs and adjust more rapidly to demands on future jobs. Whether this promise is fulfilled is unclear. Evidence is starting to accumulate that pay for skill may not increase productivity, but that it does focus people on believing in the importance of quality and in turning out significantly higher quality products.[35]

Do Employees Perform Better on Their Jobs because of Pay?

Recent critics, led by Alfie Kohn, argue that incentives are both morally and practically wrong.[36] The moral argument suggests that incentives are flawed because they involve one person controlling another. The counter-argument to this notes that employment is a reciprocal arrangement. Workers can choose whether they want to work under compensation systems with strong pay-to-performance linkages (as in the case of incentive systems). Perhaps Kohn's greatest contribution is here, in recognizing that we don't know if the presence of incentive systems affects people's interest in being recruited or, if already employed, their willingness to stay under such incentive conditions.

Kohn also suggests that incentive systems can actually harm productivity, a decidedly negative practical outcome. His rationale is that rewarding a person for performing a task reduces interest in that task—extrinsic rewards (money) reduce intrinsic rewards (enjoyment of the task for its own sake).[37] Critics of this interpretation point out at least two important flaws in Kohn's conclusions.[38] First, the pragmatics of business demand that some jobs be performed—indeed, many jobs—that aren't the most intrinsically interesting. If it requires incentives to get real world jobs completed and thus to create value for an organization and its consumers, this may simply be one of the costs of doing business. Second, Kohn's studies frequently looked at people in isolation. In the real world people interact with each other, know who is performing and who isn't, and react to this when rewards are allocated.

An obvious but often overlooked question is: Do employees think any link at all should be made between pay and performance? Substantial evidence exists that management and workers alike believe pay should be tied to performance. Dyer and colleagues found that workers believed the most important factor for salary increases should be job performance. Following close behind is a factor that presumably would be picked up in job evaluation (nature of job) and a motivational variable (amount of effort expended).[39]

Other research supports these findings.[40] Once we move away from the managerial ranks, though, other groups express a different view of the pay–performance link. The role that performance levels should assume in determining pay increases is less clear-cut for blue-collar workers.[41] As an illustration, consider the frequent opposition to compensation plans that are based on performance (i.e., incentive piece-rate systems). Unionized workers prefer seniority rather than performance as a basis for pay increases.[42] Part of this preference may stem from a distrust of subjective performance measurement systems. Unions ask, "Can management be counted on to be fair?" In contrast, seniority is an objective index for calculating increases. Some evidence also suggests that women might prefer allocation methods not based on performance.[43]

It's probably a good thing that, in general, workers believe pay should be tied to performance, because it appears to help the bottom line (profits). Numerous studies indicate that tying pay to individual performance has a positive impact on employee performance.[44] One recent study of over 3,000 companies provided convincing evidence that linking pay to performance has a positive impact on the bottom line. Over a five-year period such practices can increase per-employee sales by as much as $100,000.[45]

When we turn to the impact of pay on group performance, the evidence is somewhat clearer: Pay matters! A number of recent studies provide strong evidence that pay for performance has a direct and, at times substantial, impact on firm performance. Those that pay for performance have stronger corporate earnings![46]

Most well-controlled studies in which companies base part of pay on some measure of corporate or division performance report increases in performance of about 4–6 percent per year.[47] Typical of these studies is a utility company that placed one division on an experimental group incentive plan and left the other division with no pay changes (the control group).[48] The goal in the experimental division was to lower unit cost of electricity. After implementing this variable pay plan (or group incentive plan), performance improved significantly over the control division on 11 of 12 objective performance measures. As an example, unit production costs fell 6 percent.

Compensation experts estimate that every dollar spent on any performance-based pay plan yields $2.34 more in organizational earnings.[49] Put differently, there is further documented evidence that every 10 percent increase in bonus paid yields a 1.5 percent increase in R.O.A. (return on assets) to the firm.[50]

Before we rush out and develop a variable pay component for the compensation package, though, we should recognize that such plans can, and do, fail. Sometimes the failure arises, ironically, because the incentive works too well, leading employees to exhibit rewarded behaviours to the exclusion of other desired behaviours. But often the problem relates to the definition and measurement of performance.

◾ THE ROLE OF PERFORMANCE APPRAISALS IN COMPENSATION DECISIONS

performance appraisal

process of evaluating or appraising an employee's performance on the job

We can't reward performance if we can't measure it. Clearly, a key element of pay-for-performance plans is some measure of performance obtained through a **performance appraisal** process. Sometimes this measure is objective and quantifiable. Certainly, when we are measuring performance for a group incentive plan, objective financial measures may be readily available. As we move down to the level of the individual and the team, these "hard" measures are not as readily available.

Performance reviews are used for a wide variety of outcomes in organizations—only one of which is to guide the allocation of merit increases. Unfortunately, as we will discover, the link between performance ratings and these outcomes is not always as strong as we would like. In fact, it's common to make a distinction between performance judgments and performance ratings.[51] Performance ratings—the things we enter into an employee's permanent record—are influenced by a host of things besides the employee behaviours observed by raters. Such things as organization values (e.g., value technical skill or interpersonal skills more highly), competition among departments, differences in status among departments, economic conditions (labour shortages make for less willingness to terminate employees for poor performance)—all influence the way raters rate employees.

At times, measurement of performance can be quantifiable. Indeed, some good estimates suggest that between 13 percent of the time (hourly workers) and 70 percent of the time (managerial employees), employee performance is tied to these quantifiable measures.[52] Just because something is quantifiable, though, doesn't mean it is an objective measure of performance. As any accounting student knows, financial measures are arrived at through a process that involves some subjective decision making. Such potential for subjectivity has led some experts to warn that so-called objective data can be deficient and may not tell the whole story.[53] Despite these concerns, most HR professionals probably would prefer to work with objective data. Sometimes, though, objective performance standards are not feasible. Either job output is not readily quantifiable or the components that are quantifiable do not reflect important job dimensions.

The end result, all too often, is a performance appraisal process that is plagued by errors. Edwards Deming, the grandfather of the quality movement here and in Japan, launched an attack of appraisals because, he contended, the work situation (not the individual) is the major determinant of performance.[54] Variation in performance arises many times because employees don't have the necessary information, technology, or control to adequately perform their jobs.[55] Furthermore, Deming argued, individual work standards and performance ratings rob employees of pride and self-esteem.

Some experts argue that we should apply total quality management principles to improving the process.[56] A first step, of course, is recognition that part of performance is influenced more by the work environment and system than by employee behaviours. For example, sometimes when students say the computer ate my disk . . . it really happened.

A second step in this direction concerns identifying strategies to understand and measure job performance better. This may help us reduce the number and types of rating errors illustrated in Exhibit 10.5.

EXHIBIT | 10.5 | Common Errors in the Appraisal Process ───────────────────

Halo error	An appraiser giving favourable ratings to all job duties based on impressive performance in just one job function. For example, a rater who hates tardiness rates a prompt subordinate high across all performance dimensions *exclusively because of this one characteristic.*
Negative halo error	The opposite of a halo error. Downgrading an employee across all performance dimensions *exclusively because of poor performance on one dimension.*
First impression error	Developing a negative or positive opinion of an employee early in the review period and allowing that to influence negatively or positively all later perceptions of performance.
Recency error	The opposite of first impression error. Allowing performance, either good or bad, at the end of the review period to play too large a role in determining an employee's rating for the entire period.
Leniency error	Consistently rating someone higher than is deserved.
Strictness error	The opposite of leniency error. Rating someone consistently lower than is deserved.
Central tendency error	Avoiding extremes in ratings across employees.
Similar-to-me error	Giving better ratings to individuals who are like the rater in behaviour and/or personality.
Spillover error	Continuing to downgrade an employee for performance errors in prior rating periods.

COMMON ERRORS IN APPRAISING PERFORMANCE

Suppose you supervised 1,000 employees. How many would you expect to rate at the highest level? How many would be average or below? If you're tempted to argue that the distribution should look something like a normal curve, you might get an A in statistics, but fail Reality 101. One survey of 1,816 organizations reported the following distribution of performance ratings (Exhibit 10.6) for its managers.

The truth is, as raters we tend to make mistakes. Our ratings differ from what would occur if we could somehow, in a moment of clarity, divine the truth. We make errors in ratings. Recognizing and understanding the errors are the first steps in communicating and building a more effective appraisal process.

Not surprisingly, the potential for error causes employees to lose faith in the performance appraisal process. There are several factors that lead raters to give inaccurate appraisals: (1) guilt, (2) embarrassment about giving praise, (3) taking things for granted, (4) not noticing, (5) halo effect, (6) dislike of confrontation, or (7) spending too little time on preparation of the appraisal.[57] To counter such problems, companies and researchers alike have expended considerable time and money to identify ways to improve performance ratings.

STRATEGIES TO BETTER UNDERSTAND AND MEASURE JOB PERFORMANCE

Efforts to improve the performance rating process take several forms.[58] First, researchers and compensation people alike devote considerable energy to defining job performance—what exactly should be measured when we evaluate employees? We generally identify factors such as task knowledge, knowledge of correct procedures, skill, and motivation.[59] More specific factors include such performance dimensions as planning and organizing, training, coaching, developing subordinates, and technical proficiency.[60]

A second direction for performance research notes that the definition of performance and its components is expanding. Jobs are becoming more dynamic, and the need for employees to adapt and grow increasingly is stressed. This focus on individual characteristics, or personal competencies, is consistent with the whole trend toward measuring job competency.[61]

A third direction for improving the quality of performance ratings centres on identifying the best evaluation format. More recently, attention has focused less on the rating format and more on the raters themselves. One branch of this work identifies possible categories of raters (supervisor, peers, subordinates, customers, self) and examines whether a given category leads to more or less accurate ratings. The second branch of this research about raters attempts to identify how raters process information about job performance and translate it into performance ratings. Finally, data also suggest that raters can be trained to increase the accuracy of their ratings. The following sections discuss each of these different approaches to better understand and measure performance.

EXHIBIT 10.6 Ratings of Managers

Rating Received	Percentage of Managers Receiving Rating
Above average employee	46.4
Average employee	49.0
Below average	4.6

Strategy One: Improve Evaluation Formats

evaluation format

the method used to evaluate an employee's performance, either ranking against other employees or rating on one or more performance criteria

alternation ranking

ranking the best employee, then the worst employee, then the next best and worst, and so on

paired comparison performance ranking

ranking each employee against all other employees, one pair at a time

Types of Formats.   **Evaluation formats** can be divided into two general categories: ranking and rating.[62] Ranking formats require the rater to compare employees to one another to determine the relative ordering of the group on some performance measure (usually some measure of overall performance). Exhibit 10.7 illustrates three different methods of ranking employees.

The straight ranking procedure is just that: Employees are ranked relative to one another. **Alternation ranking** recognizes that raters are better at ranking people at extreme ends of the distribution. Raters are asked to indicate the best employee and then the worst employee. Working at the two extremes permits a rater to get more practice prior to making the harder distinctions in the vast middle ground of employees. Finally, the **paired comparison performance ranking** method simplifies the ranking process by forcing raters to make ranking judgments about discrete pairs of people. Each individual is compared separately with all others in the work group. The person who "wins" the most paired comparisons is ranked top in the group, and so on. Unfortunately, as the size of the work group goes above 10 to 15 employees, the number of paired comparisons becomes unmanageable.

The second category of appraisal formats, ratings, is generally more popular than ranking systems. The various rating formats have two elements in common. First, in contrast to

EXHIBIT 10.7 | Three Ranking Formats

Straight Ranking Method

Rank	Employee's Name
Best	1. _____
Next Best	2. _____
Next Best	3. _____
etc.	

Alternation Ranking

Rank	Employee's Name
Best performer	1. _____
Next best	2. _____
Next best	3. _____
etc.	4. _____
Next worst	3. _____
Next worst	2. _____
Worst performer	1. _____

(alternate identifying best then worst, next best then next worst, etc.)

Paired Comparison Performance Ranking Method

	John	Pete	Sam	Tom	# times ranked higher
Bill	x	x	x	x	4
John		x	x	x	3
Pete			x	x	2
Sam				x	1

x indicates person in row ranked higher than person in column. Highest ranking goes to person with most "ranking wins."

ranking formats, rating formats require raters to evaluate employees on some absolute standard rather than relative to other employees. Second, each performance standard is measured on a scale on which appraisers can check the point that best represents the employee's performance. In this way, performance variation is described along a continuum from good to bad. The types of descriptors used in anchoring this continuum provide the major difference in rating scales.

These descriptors may be adjectives, behaviours, or outcomes. When adjectives are used as anchors, the format is called a standard rating scale. Exhibit 10.8 shows a typical rating scale with adjectives as anchors ("well above average" to "well below average").

Behaviourally anchored rating scales (BARS) seem to be the most common behavioural format. BARS help to rate an employee's performance more completely. Manager A and manager B could both have met their individual objectives, but we don't know what means they used to attain them, nor do we know how difficult these objectives were in comparison to each other. Without this knowledge, ratings can't be used to compare the achievements of these two managers.[63] By anchoring scales with concrete behaviours, firms adopting a BARS format hope to make evaluations less subjective. When raters try to decide on a rating, they have a common definition (in the form of a behavioural example) for each of the performance levels.

This evaluation format directly addresses a major criticism of standard rating scales: Different raters carry with them into the rating situation different definitions of the scale levels (e.g., different raters have different ideas about what "average work" is). Exhibit 10.9 illustrates a behaviourally anchored rating scale. In both the standard rating scale and BARS, overall performance is calculated as some weighted average (weighted by the importance the organization attaches to each dimension) of the ratings on all dimensions. The appendix to this chapter (shown on the text Web site) gives an example of rating scales and the total appraisal form for Pfizer Pharmeceutical. As a brief illustration, though, consider Exhibit 10.10.

The employee evaluated in Exhibit 10.10 is rated slightly above average. An alternative method for obtaining the overall rating would be to allow the rater discretion not only in rating performance on the individual dimensions, but in assigning an overall evaluation. Then, the weights (shown in the far right column of Exhibit 10.10) would not be used, and an overall evaluation would be based on a subjective and internal assessment by the rater.

In addition to adjectives and behaviours, outcomes also are used as a standard. The most common form is **management by objectives (MBO)**. As a first step, organization objectives are identified from the strategic plan of the company. Each successively lower level in the organizational hierarchy is charged with identifying work objectives that will support attainment of organizational goals. Exhibit 10.11 illustrates a common MBO objective. Notice that the emphasis is on outcomes achieved by employees. At the beginning of a performance review

behaviourally anchored rating scale (BARS)

performance rating scale using behavioural descriptions as anchors for different levels of performance on the scale

management by objectives (MBO)

performance rating method based on meeting objectives set at the beginning of the performance review period

---

EXHIBIT 10.8 Rating Scales Using Absolute Standards ——————————————

Standard Rating Scale with Adjective Anchors

Communications skills:	Written and oral ability to clearly and convincingly express thoughts, ideas, or facts in individual or group situations.				
Circle the number that best describes the level of employee performance	1 well above average	2 above average	3 average	4 below average	5 well below average

EXHIBIT	10.9	Standard Rating Scale with Behavioural Scale Anchors

Teamwork:		Ability to contribute to group performance, to draw out the best from others, to foster activities building group morale, even under high pressure situations.
Exceeds Standards	1	Seeks out or is regularly requested for group assignments. Groups this person works with inevitably have high performance and high morale. Employee makes strong personal contribution and is able to identify strengths of many different types of group members and foster their participation. Wards off personality conflicts by positive attitude and ability to mediate unhealthy conflicts, sometimes even before they arise. Will make special effort to insure credit for group performance is shared by all.
	2	Seen as a positive contributor in group assignments. Works well with all types of people and personalities, occasionally elevating group performance of others. Good ability to resolve unhealthy group conflicts that flare up. Will make special effort to insure strong performers receive credit due them.
Meets Standards	3	Seen as a positive personal contributor in group assignments. Works well with most types of people and personalities. Is never a source of unhealthy group conflict and will encourage the same behaviour in others.
	4	When group mission requires skill this person is strong in, employee seen as strong contributor. On other occasions will not hinder performance of others. Works well with most types of people and personalities and will not be the initiator of unhealthy group conflict. Will not participate in such conflict unless provoked on multiple occasions.
	5	Depending on the match of personal skill and group mission, this person will be seen as a positive contributor. Will not be a hindrance to performance of others and avoids unhealthy conflict unless provoked.
Does Not Meet Standards	6	Unlikely to be chosen for assignments requiring teamwork except on occasions when personal expertise is vital to group mission. Not responsive to group goals, but can be enticed to help when personal appeals are made. May not get along with other members and either withdraw or generate unhealthy conflict. Seeks personal recognition for team performance and/or may downplay efforts of others.
	7	Has reputation for noncontribution and for creating conflicts in groups. Cares little about group goals and is very hard to motivate towards and goal completion unless personal rewards are guaranteed. May undermine group performance to further personal aims. Known to seek personal recognition and/or downplay efforts of others.
Rating:		Documentation of Rating (optional except for 6 and 7):

period, the employee and supervisor discuss performance objectives (column 1).[64] Months later, at the end of the review period, the two meet again to record results formally (of course, multiple informal discussions should have occurred before this time). Results are then compared to objectives, and a performance rating is then determined based on how well objectives were met.

Exhibit 10.12 shows some of the common components of an MBO format and the percentage of experts who judge this component vital to a successful evaluation effort.

| EXHIBIT | 10.10 | An Example of Employee Appraisal |

Employee: Kelsey T. Mahoney
Job Title: Supervisor, Shipping and Receiving

Performance Dimension	Dimension Rating					Dimension Weight	Rating × Weight
	Well Below Average 1	Below Average 2	Average 3	Above Average 4	Well Above Average 5		
Leadership Ability				X		0.2	0.8
Job Knowledge					X	0.1	0.5
Work Output				X		0.3	1.2
Attendance		X				0.2	0.6
Initiative		X				0.2	0.6

Sum of Rating 3 weight = 3.7
Overall Rating = 3.7

| EXHIBIT | 10.11 | Example of MBO Objective for Communications Skill |

1. Performance objective	2. Results
By July 1 of this year Bill will complete a report summarizing employee reactions to the new performance appraisal system. An oral presentation will be prepared and delivered to all non-exempt employees in groups of 15–20. All oral presentations will be completed by August 31, and reactions of employees to this presentation will average at least 3.0 on a 5-point scale.	Written report completed by July 1. All but one oral presentation completed by August 31. Last report not completed until September 15 because of unavoidable conflicts in vacation schedules. Average rating of employees (reaction to oral presentation) was 3.4, exceeding minimum expectations.

Evaluating Performance Evaluation Formats. Evaluation formats are generally evaluated against five criteria: (1) employee development potential (amount of feedback about performance that the format offers), (2) administrative ease, (3) HR research potential, (4) cost, and (5) validity. Admittedly, different organizations will attach different weights to these criteria. These criteria are explained below.[65]

Employee Development Criterion. Does the method communicate the goals and objectives of the organization? Is feedback to employees a natural outgrowth of the evaluation format so that employee developmental needs are identified and can be attended to readily?

Administrative Criterion. How easily can evaluation results be used for administrative decisions concerning wage increases, promotions, demotions, terminations, and transfers? Comparisons between individuals for personnel action require some common denominator for

EXHIBIT 10.12 Components of a Successful MBO Program

	Total Number of Responses*	Percentage of Authorities in Agreement
1. Goals and objectives should be specific.	37	97%
2. Goals and objectives should be defined in terms of measurable results.	37	97
3. Individual goals should be linked to overall organization goals.	37	97
4. Objectives should be reviewed "periodically."	31	82
5. The time period for goal accomplishment should be specified.	27	71
6. Wherever possible, the indicator of the results should be quantifiable; otherwise, it should be at least verifiable.	26	68
7. Objectives should be flexible; changed as conditions warrant.	26	68
8. Objectives should include a plan of action for accomplishing the results.	21	55
9. Objectives should be assigned priorities of weights.	19	50

*In this table the total number of responses actually represents the total number of authorities responding; thus, percentages also represent the percentage of authorities in agreement with the statements made.

Source: Mark L. McConkie, "A Clarification of the Goal Setting and Appraisal Process in MBO," *Academy of Management Review* 4, no. 1 (1979), pp. 29–40. © 1979, Academy of Management Review.

comparison. Typically this is a numerical rating of performance. Evaluation forms that do not produce numerical ratings cause administrative headaches.

HR Research Criterion.   Does the instrument lend itself well to validating employment tests? Can applicants predicted to perform well be monitored through performance evaluation? Similarly, can the success of various employees and organizational development programs be traced to impacts on employee performance? As with the administrative criterion, though, evaluations typically need to be quantitative to permit the statistical tests common in HR research.

Cost Criterion.   Does the evaluation form require a long time to develop initially? Is it time-consuming for supervisors to use in rating their employees? Is it expensive to use? All these factors increase the format cost.

Validity Criterion.   The most research by far on formats in recent years has focused on reducing error and improving accuracy. Success in this pursuit would mean that decisions based on performance ratings (e.g., promotions, merit increases) could be made with increased confidence. In general, the search for the perfect format to eliminate rating errors and improve accuracy has been unsuccessful. For example, the high acclaim accompanying the introduction of BARS has not been supported by research.[66]

Exhibit 10.13 provides a report card on the five most common rating formats relative to the criteria just discussed. Which of these appraisal formats is the best? Unfortunately, the answer is a murky "it depends." Keeley suggests that the choice of an appraisal format is dependent on the type of tasks being performed.[67] He argues that tasks can be ordered along a continuum from those that are very routine to those for which the appropriate behaviour for goal accomplishment is very uncertain. At one extreme of the continuum are behaviour-based evaluation procedures that define specific performance expectations against which employee performance is evaluated. Keeley argues that behaviourally anchored rating scales fall into this category.

At the other extreme of the continuum are tasks that are highly uncertain in nature. A relatively low consensus exists about the characteristics of successful performance, and it may be

EXHIBIT 10.13 An Evaluation of Performance Evaluation Formats

	Employee Development Criterion	Administration Criterion	HR Research Criterion	Economic Criterion	Validity Criterion
Ranking	Poor—ranks typically based on overall performance, with little thought given to feedback on specific performance dimensions.	Poor—comparisons of ranks across work units to determine merit raises are meaningless. Other administrative actions similarly hindered.	Average—validation studies can be completed with rankings of performance.	Good—inexpensive source of performance data. Easy to develop and use in small organizations and in small units.	Average—good reliability but poor on rating errors, especially halo.
Standard Rating Scales	Average—general problem areas identified. Some information on extent of developmental need is available, but no feedback on necessary behaviours/outcomes.	Average—ratings valuable for merit increase decisions and others. Not easily defended if contested.	Average—validation studies can be completed, but level of measurement contamination unknown.	Good—inexpensive to develop and easy to use.	Average—content validity is suspect. Rating errors and reliability are average.
Behaviourally Anchored Rating Scales	Good—extent of problem and behavioural needs are identified.	Good—BARS good for making administrative decisions. Useful for legal defence because job relevant.	Good—validation studies can be completed and measurement problems on BARS less than many other criterion measures.	Average—expensive to develop but easy to use.	Good—high content validity. Some evidence of inter-rater reliability and reduced rating errors.
Management by Objectives	Excellent—extent of problem and outcome deficiencies are identified.	Poor—MBO not suited to merit income decisions. Level of completion and difficulty of objectives hard to compare between employees.	Poor—nonstandard objectives across employees and no overall measures of performance make validity studies difficult.	Poor—expensive to develop and time-consuming to use.	Excellent—high content validity. Low rating errors.

difficult to specify expected goals. For this type of task, Keeley argues that judgment-based evaluation procedures—as exemplified by standard rating scales—may be most appropriate.

Strategy Two: Select the Right Raters

A second way that firms have tried to improve the accuracy of performance ratings is to focus on who might conduct the ratings and which of these sources is more likely to be accurate. To lessen the impact of one reviewer, and to increase participation in the process, a method known as **360-degree feedback** has grown more popular in recent years. Generally, this system is used in conjunction with supervisory reviews.[68] This method assesses employee performance from five points of view: supervisor, peer, self, customer, and subordinate. Let's take a closer look at the role and benefit of each of these raters.

Supervisors as Raters. Some estimates indicate that more than 80 percent of the input for performance ratings comes from supervisors.[69] Supervisors are knowledgeable about the job and the dimensions to be rated. Also, supervisors frequently have considerable prior experience in rating employees, thus giving them some pretty firm ideas about what level of performance is required for any given level of performance rating.[70] Supervisor ratings also tend to be more reliable than those from other sources.[71] On the negative side, though, supervisors are particularly prone to halo and leniency errors.[72]

Peers as Raters. One of the major strengths of using peers as raters is that they work more closely with the ratee and probably have an undistorted perspective of typical performance. Balanced against this positive are at least two powerful negatives. First, peers may have little or no experience in conducting appraisals, leading to rather mixed evidence about the reliability of this rating source. Second, in a situation in which teamwork is promoted, placing the burden of rating peers on co-workers either may create group tensions (in the case of low evaluations) or yield ratings second only to self-ratings in level of leniency.[73]

Self as Rater. Some organizations have experimented with self-ratings. Obviously self-ratings are done by someone who has the most complete knowledge about the ratee's performance. Unfortunately, though, self-ratings are generally more lenient and possibly more unreliable than ratings from other sources.[74] One compromise in the use of self-ratings is to use them for developmental rather than administrative purposes.

Customer as Rater. This is the era of the customer. The drive for quality means that more companies are recognizing the importance of customers. One logical outcome of this increased interest is ratings from customers. For example, Burger King surveys its customers, sets up toll-free numbers to get feedback, and hires mystery customers to order food and report back on the service and treatment they receive.

Subordinate as Rater. The notion of subordinates as raters is appealing since most employees want to be successful with the people who report to them. Research shows that subordinates prefer, not surprisingly, to give their feedback to managers anonymously. If their identity is known, subordinates give artificially inflated ratings of their supervisors.[75]

Strategy Three: Understand Why Raters Make Mistakes

A third way to improve job performance ratings is to understand how raters think. When we observe and evaluate performance, what else influences ratings besides an employee's performance?[76] We know, for example, that feelings, attitudes, and moods influence raters. Hope

360-degree feedback

performance appraisal method including feedback from up to five sources: supervisor, peers, self, customers, and subordinates for a rater who is generally cheerful rather than grumpy; it could influence how you are evaluated.[77]

Researchers continue to explore how raters process information about the performance of the people they rate. In general, we think the following kinds of processes occur. First, the rater observes behaviour of a ratee. Second, the rater encodes this behaviour as part of a total picture of the ratee. Third, the rater stores this information in memory, which is subject to both short- and long-term decay. Fourth, when it comes time to evaluate a ratee, the rater reviews the performance dimensions and retrieves stored observations/impressions to determine their relevance to the performance dimensions. Finally, the information is reconsidered and integrated with other available information as the rater decides on the final ratings.[78] This process can produce information errors quite unintentionally, and they can occur at any stage.

Errors in the Rating Process.   Ideally raters should notice only performance-related factors when they observe employee behaviour. Unless a behaviour affects performance it should not influence performance ratings. Fortunately, studies show that performance actually does play an important role, perhaps the major role, in determining how a supervisor rates a subordinate.[79] On the negative side, though, performance-irrelevant factors appear to influence ratings, and they can cause errors in the evaluation process.[80]

Errors in Observation (Attention).   Generally, researchers have varied three types of input information to see what raters pay attention to when they are collecting information for performance appraisals. First, it appears that raters are influenced by general appearance characteristics of the ratees.[81] In general, it seems that if supervisors see ratees as similar to themselves, there is a positive influence on performance ratings, independent of actual performance.[82]

Researchers also look at change in performance over time to see if this influences performance ratings. Both the pattern of performance (performance gets better vs. worse over time) and the variability of performance (consistent vs. erratic) influence performance ratings, even when the overall level of performance is controlled.[83]

Errors in Storage and Recall.   Research suggests that raters store information in the form of traits.[84] More importantly, people also tend to recall information in the form of trait categories, such as laziness. Specific instructions to recall information about the ratee, as for a performance review, elicit the trait—lazy. The entire rating process, then, may be heavily influenced by the trait categories the rater adopts, regardless of their accuracy. Errors in storage and recall also appear to arise from memory decay. Some research suggests that memory decay can be avoided if raters keep a diary and record information about employee performance as it occurs.[85]

Errors in the Actual Evaluation.   The context of the actual evaluation process also can influence evaluations.[86] For example, performance appraisals sometimes serve a political end. Supervisors have been known to deflate performance to send a signal to an employee—You're not wanted here.[87] Supervisors also tend to weigh negative attributes more heavily than positive attributes; you are likely to receive a much lower score if you perform poorly than you are to receive a proportionally higher score if you perform well.[88]

If the purpose of evaluation is to divide up a fixed pot of merit increases, ratings also tend to be less accurate. Supervisors who know that ratings will be used to determine merit increases are less likely to differentiate among subordinates than when the ratings will be used for other purposes.[89] Being required to provide feedback to subordinates about their ratings also yields less accuracy than a secrecy policy.[90] However, when raters must justify their scoring of subordinates in writing, the rating is more accurate.[91]

.NET WORTH

Current Performance Management Practices

A recent research study of 55 medium and large companies investigated what factors contribute to performance management system effectiveness. The results showed that a large number of practices are involved, including goal setting, communication, competency models, reward system practices, behaviour of managers, and training. All of these have a potentially positive impact on the effectiveness of performance appraisals. Perhaps the most surprising omission from the list of positive practices is 360-degree appraisal. Despite its growing popularity and the attention it has received in the literature, it is neither correlated with the effectiveness of the appraisal process nor is it used frequently by the companies in the sample.

The practices most highly correlated with effectiveness and most widely used are:

1. performance goals that are driven by business strategy
2. jointly set performance goals for individuals
3. close tie between appraisal results and salary increases
4. leadership by senior management
5. development planning

The practices that are high in impact on effectiveness but low in usage are:

1. competency models based on business strategy
2. appraisal of how well managers do appraisals
3. measures of the effectiveness of the system
4. training for individuals being appraised
5. e-HR systems

It is important to remember that creating an effective performance management system is not simply a matter of picking a number of best practices and putting them into place. There are critical interface and system design issues that need to be taken into account. The individual performance management practices need to be driven by the business strategy and to fit with each other and with the overall human resource management system of the organization. The data confirmed this by showing a significant relationship between the degree to which the performance management system is integrated with other HR systems and the effectiveness of the performance management system. Thus a performance management system is not a stand-alone item.

Although there is no magic formula for the design of a performance management system, the practices identified in the study as having a positive impact on performance management effectiveness should be considered by every organization.

Source: E. E. Lawler III & M. McDermott, "Current Performance Management Practices," *WorldatWork Journal*, Second Quarter 2003, pp. 49-80.

TRAINING RATERS TO RATE MORE ACCURATELY

Most research indicates that rater training is an effective method for reducing appraisal errors.[92] Rater-training programs can be divided into three distinct categories:[93] (1) Rater-error training, in which the goal is to reduce psychometric errors (e.g., leniency, severity, central tendency, halo) by familiarizing raters with their existence; (2) performance dimension training, which exposes supervisors to the performance dimensions to be used in rating; and (3) performance-standard training, which provides raters with a standard of comparison or frame of reference for making appraisals.

The greatest success has come from efforts to reduce halo errors and improve accuracy. Leniency errors are the most difficult form of error to eliminate because giving inflated ratings avoids complaints and, possibly, reduced employee morale.

PUTTING IT ALL TOGETHER: THE PERFORMANCE EVALUATION PROCESS

A good performance evaluation doesn't begin on the day of the performance interview. We outline here some of the key elements in the total process, from day one, that make for a good outcome in the appraisal process.[94] First, we need a sound basis for establishing the performance appraisal dimensions and scales associated with each dimension. Performance dimensions should be relevant to the strategic plan of the company. Unclear job expectations are one of the most significant barriers to good performance. If an employee doesn't know what you expect of him, how can he possibly please you?[95]

Second, we need to involve employees in every stage of developing performance dimensions and building scales to measure how well they perform on these dimensions. Third, we need to make sure raters are trained in use of the appraisal system and that all employees understand how the system operates and what it will be used for. Fourth, we need to make sure raters are motivated to rate accurately. One way to achieve this is to ensure that managers are rated on how well they utilize and develop human resources.

Fifth, raters should maintain a diary of employee performance, both as documentation and to jog the memory.[96] This will help ensure that supervisors are knowledgeable about subordinate performance.[97] Sixth, raters should attempt a performance diagnosis to determine in advance whether performance problems arise because of motivation, skill deficiency, or external environmental constraints;[98] this process in turn tells the supervisor whether the problem requires motivation building, training, or efforts to remove external constraints. Lastly, the actual appraisal process should follow the guidelines outlined in Exhibit 10.14.[99] At a minimum this performance measurement system should provide:

1. A clear sense of direction.
2. An opportunity for employees to participate in setting the goals and standards for performance.
3. Prompt, honest, and meaningful feedback.
4. Immediate and sincere reinforcement.
5. Coaching and suggestions for improving future performance.
6. Fair and respectful treatment.
7. An opportunity for employees to understand and influence decisions which affect them.

Only when we are satisfied with our performance evaluation system can we then move on to designing a pay-for-performance plan.

EXHIBIT | **10.14** | Tips on Appraising Employee Performance

Preparation for the Performance Interview

1. Keep a weekly log of individual's performance. Why?
   A. It makes the task of writing up the evaluation simpler. The rater does not have to strain to remember six months or a year ago.
   B. It reduces the chances of some rating errors (e.g., recency, halo).
   C. It gives support/backup to the rating.
2. Preparation for the interview should *not* begin a week or two before it takes place. There should be continual feedback to the employee on his/her performance so that (*a*) problems can be corrected before they get out of hand, (*b*) improvements can be made sooner, and (*c*) encouragement and support are ongoing.
3. Allow sufficient time to write up the evaluation. A well-thought-out evaluation will be more objective and equitable. Sufficient time includes (*a*) the actual time necessary to think out and write up the evaluation, (*b*) time away from the evaluation, and (*c*) time to review and possibly revise.
4. Have employees fill out an appraisal form prior to the interview. This prepares employees for what will take place in the interview and allows them to come prepared with future goal suggestions, areas they wish to pursue, and suggestions concerning their jobs or the company.
5. Set up an agreed-upon, convenient time to hold the interview (at least one week in advance). Be sure to pick a nonthreatening day.
6. Be prepared!
   A. Know what you are going to say. Prepare an outline (which includes the evaluation and future goal suggestions).
   B. Decide on developmental opportunities *before* the interview. Be sure you know of possible resources and contacts.
   C. Review performance interview steps.
7. Arrange the room in such a way as to encourage discussion.
   A. Do not have barriers between yourself and the employee (such as a large desk).
   B. Arrange with secretary that there be no phone calls or interruptions.

Performance Appraisal Interview (Steps)

1. Set the subordinate at ease. Begin by stating the purpose of the discussion. Let the individual know that it will be a two-way process. Neither the superior nor subordinate should dominate the discussion.
2. Give a general, overall impression of the evaluation.
3. Discuss each dimension separately. Ask the employee to give his/her impression on own performance first. Then explain your position. If there is a problem on some, try *together* to determine the cause. When exploring causes, urge the subordinate to identify three or four causes. Then, jointly determine the most important ones. Identifying causes is important because it points out action plans which might be taken.
4. Together, develop action plans to correct problem areas. These plans will flow naturally from the consideration of the causes. Be specific about the who, what, and when. Be sure to provide for some kind of follow-up or report back.
5. Close the interview on an optimistic note.

Communication Technique Suggestions

1. Do not control the interview—make it two-way. Do this by asking open-ended questions rather than submitting your own solutions. For example, rather than saying, "Jim, I'd like you to do these reports over again," it would be better to say, "Jim, what sort of things might we do here?" Avoid questions that lead to one-word answers.
2. Stress behaviours and results rather than personal traits. Say, "I've noticed that your weekly report has been one to two days late in the last six weeks," rather than, "You tend to be a tardy, lazy person."
3. Show interest and concern. Instead of saying, "Too bad, but we all go through that," say, "I think I know what you're feeling. I remember a similar experience."

continued

EXHIBIT **10.14** Tips on Appraising Employee Performance (*continued*) ——————————————

4. Allow the subordinate to finish a sentence or thought. This includes being receptive to the subordinate's own ideas and suggestions. For example, rather than saying, "You may have something there, but let's go back to the real problem," say, "I'm not certain I understand how that relates to this problem. Why don't you fill me in on it a bit more?"

These last four suggestions emphasize problem analysis rather than appraisal. Of course, appraisal of past performance is a part of the problem analysis, but these suggestions should lead to a more participative and less defensive subordinate role. These suggestions will also help improve creativity in problem solving. The subordinate will have a clearer understanding of why and how he/she needs to change work behaviour. There should be a growth of climate of cooperation, which increases motivation to achieve performance goals.

DESIGNING A PAY-FOR-PERFORMANCE PLAN

As the pay model suggests, the effectiveness of reward systems is dependent on three things: efficiency, equity, and legislative compliance.

Efficiency

Efficiency involves three general areas of concern.

Strategy: Does the pay-for-performance plan support corporate objectives? For example, is the plan cost effective, or are we making payouts that bear no relation to improved performance on the bottom line? Similarly, does the plan help us improve quality of service? Some pay-for-performance plans are so focused on quantity of performance as a measure that we forget about quality.

The plan also should link well with HR strategy and objectives. If other elements of our total HR plan are geared to select, reinforce, and nurture risk-taking behaviour, we don't want a compensation component that rewards the status quo.

Finally, we address the most difficult question of all—How much of an increase makes a difference? What does it take to motivate an employee? Is 4 percent, the recent average of pay increases, really enough to motivate higher performance? Although there are few hard data on this question, most experts agree that employees don't begin to notice incentive payouts unless they are at least 10 percent, with 15–20 percent more likely to evoke the desired response.[100]

Structure: Is the structure of the organization sufficiently decentralized to allow different operating units to create flexible variations on a general pay-for-performance plan? Different operating units may have different competencies and different competitive advantages. We don't want a rigid pay-for-performance system that detracts from these advantages, all in the name of consistency across divisions. For example, recent efforts by IBM to adapt performance reviews to the different needs of different units and managers in them has resulted in a very flexible system. In this new system, managers get a budget, some training on how to conduct reviews, and a philosophical mandate: Differentiate pay for stars relative to average performers, or risk losing stars. Managers are given a number of performance dimensions. Which dimensions are used for which employees is totally a personal decision. Indeed, managers who don't like reviews at all can input merit increases directly, anchored only by a brief explanation for the reason.[101]

Standards: Operationally, the key to designing a pay-for-performance plan rests in standards. Specifically, we need to be concerned about:

Objectives: Are they specific, yet flexible? Can employees see that their behaviour influences ability to achieve objectives (called the "line-of-sight" issue in industry)?

Measures: Do employees know what measures (individual appraisals, peer reviews of team performance, corporate financial measures, etc.) will be used to assess whether performance is sufficiently good to merit a payout?

Eligibility: How far down the organization will the plan run? Companies such as Pepsico believe all employees should be included. Others think only top management can see how their decisions affect the bottom line.

Funding: Will you fund the program out of extra revenue generated above and beyond some preset standard? If so, what happens in a bad year? Many employees become disillusioned when they feel they have worked harder, but economic conditions or poor management decisions conspire to cut or eliminate bonuses.

Equity or Fairness

distributive justice

perceived fairness of pay or other work outcomes received

Our second design objective is to ensure that the plan is fair to employees. Two types of fairness are concerns for employees. The first type is fairness in the amount that is distributed to employees. Not surprisingly, this type of fairness is labelled **distributive justice**.[102] Perceptions of fairness here depend on the amount of compensation actually received relative to input (e.g., productivity) compared to some relevant standard. Notice that several of the components of this equity equation are frustratingly removed from the control of the typical supervisor or manager working with employees. A manager has little influence over the size of an employee's paycheque. This is influenced more by external market conditions, pay policy decisions of the organization, and the occupational choice made by the employee.

procedural justice

perceived fairness of the procedures used to determine pay or other work outcomes

Managers do have somewhat more control, though, over the second type of equity. Employees also are concerned about the fairness of *procedures* used to determine the amount of rewards they receive. Employees expect **procedural justice**. Evidence suggests that organizations that use fair procedures and supervisors who are viewed as fair in the means they use to allocate rewards are perceived as more trustworthy and command higher levels of commitment.[103] Some research even suggests that employee satisfaction with pay may depend more on the procedures used to determine pay than on the actual level distributed.[104] A key element in fairness is communication. Employees want to know in advance what is expected of them. They want the opportunity to provide input into these standards or expectations, too. And, if performance is judged lacking relative to these standards, they want a mechanism for appeals. In a union environment, this is the grievance procedure. Something similar needs to be set up in a nonunion environment.[105]

Legislative Compliance

Finally, our pay-for-performance plan should comply with existing laws. We want a reward system that maintains and enhances the reputation of our firm. Think about the companies that visit a college campus. Some of them students naturally gravitate to—the interview schedule fills very quickly indeed. Why? Because of reputation. We tend to undervalue the reward value of a good reputation. To guard this reputation we need to make sure we comply with compensation laws.

■ TYING PAY TO SUBJECTIVELY APPRAISED PERFORMANCE

Think, for a moment, about what it really means to give employees merit performance increases. Bill Peterson makes $40,000 per year. He gets a merit increase of 3 percent, the approximate average increase over the past few years. Bill's take-home increase (adjusted for taxes) is a measly $16 per week more than he used to make. Before we console Bill, though, consider Jane Krefting, who is a better performer than Bill, and receives a 6 percent merit increase. Should she be thrilled by this pay-for-performance differential and motivated to continue as a high achiever? Probably not. After taxes, her paycheque (assuming a base salary similar to Bill's) is only $15 dollars per week more than Bill's cheque.

The central issue involving merit pay is: How do we get employees to view raises as a reward for performance? Very simply, organizations frequently grant increases that are not designed or communicated to be related to performance. Perhaps the central reason for this is the way merit pay is managed. Many companies view raises not as motivational tools to shape behaviour, but as budgetary line items to control costs.[106] Frequently this results in pay increase guidelines with little motivational impact. Pay increase guidelines that fit with low motivation will be discussed briefly before outlining a standard that attempts to link pay to performance.[107]

One type of pay increase guideline with low motivation potential provides equal increases to all employees regardless of performance, e.g., across-the-board increases and cost-of-living increases. These are typically found in unionized firms.

Another form of guideline comes somewhat closer to tying pay to performance. Seniority increases tie pay increases to a preset progression pattern based on seniority. To the extent that performance improves with time on the job, this method has the rudiments of paying for performance.

By far the most prevalent form of pay guideline is one intended to link pay and performance.[108] Of course, the first problem we run into is, What is our measure of performance? If the measure is objective, our ability to link pay to performance is a bit easier. But here we talk about subjective measures. One set of subjective measures, as we discussed in Chapter 6, involves the competencies that people possess or acquire. Increasingly, companies assert that corporate performance depends on having employees who possess key competencies. Xerox identifies 17 core competencies. As a company with strong strategic objectives linked to customer satisfaction and quality, it's not surprising to find that Xerox values such competencies as quality orientation, customer care, dependability, and teamwork. Recent trends in compensation centre on finding ways to build competencies in employees. Merit increases may be linked to employee ability and willingness to demonstrate key competencies. For example, demonstrating more of the following behaviours might be tied to higher merit increases.

Competency: Customer Care

1. Follows through on commitments to customers in a timely manner
2. Defines and communicates customer requirements
3. Resolves customer issues in a timely manner
4. Demonstrates empathy for customer feelings
5. Presents a positive image to the customer
6. Displays a professional image at all times
7. Communicates a positive image of the company and individuals to customers

In practice, tying pay to performance requires three things. First, we need some definition of performance. Second, we need some continuum that describes different levels from low to high on the performance measure. And third, we need to decide how much of a merit increase will be given for different levels of performance. Decisions about these three questions lead to some form of merit pay guide. In its simplest form a guideline specifies pay increases permissible for different levels of performance (see Exhibit 10.15).

A more complex guideline ties pay not only to performance but also to position in the pay range. Exhibit 10.16 illustrates such a system for a food market firm. The percentages in the cells of Exhibit 10.16 are changed yearly to reflect changing economic conditions. Despite these changes, though, two characteristics remain constant. First, as would be expected in a pay-for-performance system, lower performance is tied to lower pay increases. In fact, in many organizations the poorest performers receive no merit increases. The second relationship is that pay increases at a decreasing rate as employees move through a pay range. For the same level of performance, employees low in the range receive higher percentage increases than employees who have progressed farther through the range. In part this is designed to forestall the time when employees reach the salary maximum and have salaries frozen. In part, though, it is also a cost-control mechanism tied to budgeting procedures, as discussed in Chapter 13.

Performance- and Position-Based Guidelines

Given a salary increase matrix, merit increases are relatively easy to determine. As Exhibit 10.16 indicates, an employee at the top of his pay grade who receives a "competent" rating would receive a 4 percent increase in base salary. A new trainee starting out below the minimum of a pay grade would receive a 10 percent increase for a "superior" performance rating.

Designing Merit Guidelines

Designing merit guidelines involves answering four questions. First, what should the poorest performer be paid as an increase? Notice that this figure is seldom negative. Wage increases are, unfortunately, considered an entitlement. Wage cuts tied to poor performance are very rare. Most organizations, though, are willing to give no increases to very poor performers.

The second question involves average performers. How much should they be paid as an increase? Most organizations try to ensure that average performers are kept whole (wages will still have the same purchasing power) relative to the cost of living. This dictates that the midpoint of the merit guidelines equal the percentage change in the local or national consumer price index (CPI). Following this guideline, the 6 percent increase for an average performer in the second

EXHIBIT 10.15 Performance-Based Guideline

	1	2	3	4	5
Performance Level	Very Outstanding	Satisfactory	Marginally Satisfactory	Unsatisfactory	Unsatisfactory
Merit Increase	6–8%	5–7%	4–6%	2–4%	0 %

EXHIBIT 10.16 Performance Rating Salary Increase Matrix

Position in Range	Performance Rating — Unsatisfactory	Needs Improvement	Competent	Commendable	Superior
Fourth quartile	0%	0%	4%	5%	6%
Third quartile	0	0	5	6	7
Second quartile	0	0	6	7	8
First quartile	0	2	7	8	9
Below minimum of range	0	3	8	9	10

quartile of Exhibit 10.16 would reflect the change in CPI for that area. In a year with lower inflation, all the percentages in the matrix probably would be lower.

Third, how much should the top performers be paid? In part, budgetary considerations (Chapter 13) answer this question. But there is also growing evidence that employees do not agree on the size of increases that they consider meaningful (Chapter 8). Continuation of this research may help determine the approximate size of increases needed to make a difference in employee performance.

Finally, matrices can differ in the size of the differential between different levels of performance. Exhibit 10.16 basically rewards successive levels of performance with one percent increases (at least in the portion of the matrix in which any increase is granted). A larger jump between levels would signal a stronger commitment to recognizing performance with higher pay increases. Most companies balance this, though, against cost considerations. Larger differentials cost more. When money is tight this option is less attractive. Exhibit 10.17 shows how a merit grid is constructed when cost constraints (merit budget) are known.

PROMOTIONAL INCREASES AS A PAY-FOR-PERFORMANCE TOOL

Let's not forget that firms have methods of rewarding good performance other than raises. One of the most effective is a promotion accompanied by a salary increase, generally reported as being in the 8 to 12 percent range. This method of linking pay to performance has at least two characteristics that distinguish it from traditional annual merit pay increases. First, the size of the increment is approximately double a normal merit increase. A clearer message is sent to employees, both in the form of money and promotion, that good performance is valued and tangibly rewarded. Second, promotion increases represent, in a sense, a reward to employees for commitment and exemplary performance over a sustained period of time. Promotions generally are not annual events. They complement annual merit rewards by showing employees that there are benefits to both single-year productivity and to the continuation of such desirable behaviour.

EXHIBIT 10.17 Merit Grids

Merit grids combine 3 variables: level of performance, distribution of employees within their job's pay range, and merit increase percentages.

Example:

1. Assume a performance rating scale of A through D: 30 percent of employees get A, 35 percent get B, 20 percent get C, and 15 percent get D. Change to decimals.

A	B	C	D
.30	.35	.20	.15

2. Assume a range distribution as follows: 10 percent of all employees are in the top (fourth) quartile of the pay range for their job, 35 percent are in the third quartile, 30 percent in second quartile, and 25 percent in lowest quartile. Change to decimals.

1	.10
2	.35
3	.30
4	.25

3. Multiply the performance distribution by the range distribution to obtain the percentage of employees in each cell. Cell entries = Performance × Range.

   Performance Rating Scale

Pay Range Quartile	A	B	C	D
1	.30 × .10 = .03	.35 × .20 = .035	.30 × .10 = .02	.15 × .10 = .015
2	.30 × .35 = .105	.35 × .35 = .1225	.20 × .35 = .07	.15 × .35 = .0525
3	.30 × .30 = .09	.35 × .30 = .105	.20 × .30 = .06	.15 × .30 = .045
4	.30 × .25 = .075	.35 × .25 = .1225	.20 × .25 = .05	.15 × .25 = .0375

   Cell entries tell us that 3 percent of employees are in top quartile of pay range AND received an A performance rating, 10.5 percent of employees are in second quartile of pay range AND received an A performance rating, etc.

4. Distribute increase percentage among cells, varying the percentages according to performance and range distribution, for example, 6 percent to those employees in cell A1, 5 percent to those employees in B1.

5. Multiply increase percentages by the employee distribution for each cell. Sum of all cells should equal the total merit increase percentage.

   Example: 6% × cell A1 = .06 × .03 = .0018

                            5% × cell B1 = .05 × .035 = .00175

                                       etc. _____

           Targeted merit increase percentage = Sum

6. Adjust increase percentage among cells if needed in order to stay within budgeted increase.

CONCLUSION

We know that employee performance depends upon some blend of skill, knowledge, and motivation. Absent any of these three ingredients, performance is likely to be suboptimal. Rewards must help organizations attract and retain employees, make high performance an attractive option for employees, encourage employees to build new skills, and foster commitment to the organization. We are just starting to realize all the different things that can serve as rewards to motivate employees.

The process of appraising employee performance can be both time consuming and stressful. Development of sound appraisal systems requires an understanding of organizational objectives balanced against the relative merits of each type of appraisal system. For example, despite its inherent weaknesses, an appraisal system based on ranking of employee performance may be appropriate in small organizations which, for a variety of reasons, choose not to tie pay to performance; a sophisticated MBO appraisal system may not be appropriate for such a company.

Training supervisors effectively to appraise performance requires an understanding of organizational objectives. We know relatively little about the ways raters process information and evaluate employee performance. However, a thorough understanding of organizational objectives combined with a knowledge of common errors in evaluation can make a significant difference in the quality of appraisals.

CHAPTER SUMMARY

1. The three factors on which employee performance depends are: (1) skill and ability to perform the task, (2) knowledge of facts, rules, principles, and procedures, and (3) motivation to perform.
2. Content theories focus on human needs that influence behaviour. Motivation theories that focus on the nature of the exchange look at the cognitive processes used to assess a situation and choose behavior that yields the most satisfactory exchange. Goal setting theory focuses on desired behaviour.
3. Compensation motivates behaviour because it affects decisions about whether to join a firm, to stay or leave, to agree to develop job skills, and to perform better.
4. Common errors in the performance appraisal process include the halo error (overall high rating due to one characteristic), the negative halo error (overall low rating due to one characteristic), first-impression error (rating based only on first impression), recency error (rating based only on most recent impression), leniency error, strictness error, central tendency error (rating all employees as average), similar-to-me error (high ratings for individuals similar to the rater), and spillover error (low ratings related to poor performance in a prior rating period).
5. Three strategies to better understand and measure job performance are: (1) improving the appraisal format, (2) selecting the right raters, and (3) understanding why raters make mistakes.
6. The key elements of an effective performance appraisal process are a sound basis for establishing performance dimensions, involving employees in developing performance dimensions and building measurement scales, ensuring that raters are trained and motivated to rate accurately, ensuring that raters maintain a diary of employee performance, having raters attempt a performance diagnosis to identify solutions for performance problems, and

following established guidelines for the actual appraisal process between the supervisor and the employee.

7. Three factors that determine the effectiveness of a pay-for-performance plan are: (1) efficiency in supporting corporate objectives, (2) equity and fairness, and (3) legal compliance.

KEY TERMS

REVIEW QUESTIONS

1. If you wanted workers to perceive their compensation package as secure, which components would you include and which would you avoid?

2. How does procedural justice differ from distributive justice? Defend the position that supervisors have considerable control over procedural justice in their departments, but little control over distributive justice. How might you use the principle of procedural justice to avoid having an employee quit because she believes her boss gave her an unfair evaluation?

3. Shaw Corporation manufactures specialty equipment for the auto industry (e.g., seat frames). One job involves operation of machines that form heat-treated metal into various seat shapes. The job is fairly low-level and routine. Without any further information, which of the five types of appraisal formats do you think would be most appropriate for this job? Justify your answer.

4. Employees in your department have formed semi-autonomous work teams (they determine their own production schedule and individual work assignments). Individual performance is assessed using four performance dimensions: quantity of work, quality of work, interpersonal skills, and teamwork. Should the supervisor have a role in the rating process? What role, if any, should other members of the work team have in the assessment process?

EXPERIENTIAL EXERCISES

1. Roycroft Industries makes CD cases that are particularly well received on the international market. Because of currency fluctuations, the profits Roycroft generates vary widely from year to year. Jim McVeigh, who works for Roycroft, is in charge of a large product development group where the emphasis is on flexible performance, creativity, and "doing whatever it takes to get the job done." What kind of reward system would you recommend for this group of employees? In particular, should there be a large incentive component? Should rewards focus mostly on money, or should Roycroft work hard to incorporate the other 12 rewards noted in this chapter?

2. Assume you have one employee fall into each of the cells in Exhibit 10.16 (25 employees in the company). How much would base salary increase in dollars if the current average salary in the company is $15,000? (Assume that ratings are randomly distributed by salary level; you can use $15,000 as your base salary for calculation in each of the cells.)

WEB EXERCISE

360-Degree Performance Appraisal On-line

Several Web-based products have been developed in order to reduce the administrative burden associated with 360-degree performance appraisal. Go to the MindSolve site at www.mindsolve.com and click on "download demos." Then click on "MVP Multi-source feedback" and view the presentation. Go back and click on "Three easy steps to 360 assessments." Next, go to the Halogen Software site at www.halogensoftware.com and under "Products," select Halogen e-360 and take the on-line tour. Compare and contrast these two 360-degree appraisal products. What are the strengths and weaknesses of each? Which would you select for employee development purposes? Why? Would you select one of these products for performance appraisal purposes? If so, which one? Explain.

CASE

Policy Implications of Merit Pay Guides

Canadian Snow Vehicles (CSV) is a manufacturer of snowmobiles. During the past four years, profits have plummeted 43 percent. This decline is attributed to rising costs of production and is widely believed to have triggered the resignation of CSV's long-time president, C. Milton Carol. The newly hired CEO is Winston McBeade, a former vice president of finance and of human resources management at Longtemp Enterprises, a producer of novelty watches. As his first policy statement in office, Mr. McBeade declared a war on high production costs. As his first official act, Mr. McBeade proposed implementing a new merit pay guide (see Exhibits 1 and 2 for former and revised pay guides). What can you deduce about Mr. McBeade's "philosophy" of cost control from both the prior and newly revised merit guides? What implications does this new philosophy have for improving the link between pay and performance and, hence, productivity?

EXHIBIT   1   Merit Pay Guide for Last Year

Performance

	Well Below Average	Below Average	Average	Above Average	Well Above Average
Above Grade Maximum (red circle)	0 / 0	2 / 0	3 / 10	4 / 5	6 / 15
Q4	0 / 0	3 / 0	4 / 5	5 / 10	7 / 15
Q3	0 / 0	4 / 0	5 / 10	6 / 25	8 / 10
Q2	2 /	5 / 2	6 / 9	7 / 9	9 / 10
Q1	2 / 0	6 / 3	7 / 6	8 / 5	10 / 9

Position in Salary Range (rows Q4, Q3, Q2, Q1). In each cell the upper-left number is the merit increase and the lower-right number is the number of employees.

Notes: 1. Cost of living rose 3 percent last year.
2. The number at the lower right corner of each cell represents the number of employees falling into that cell during the previous year.

CASE

EXHIBIT **2** Revised Pay Guide

Performance

Position in Salary Range		Well Below Average	Below Average	Average	Above Average	Well Above Average
	Above grade maximum (red circle)	0	0	0	0	0
	Q4	0	0	2	3	4
	Q3	0	0	3	4	5
	Q2	0	0	4	5	6
	Q1	0	0	5	6	7

Note: Cost of living is expected to rise 3 percent this year.

PAY-FOR-PERFORMANCE PLANS

LEARNING OUTCOMES

- *Describe* three short-term individual pay-for-performance plans.
- *Describe* four categories of performance measures and *identify* two examples of each.
- *Discuss* the five causes of problems with team compensation systems.
- *Explain* seven key issues in designing a gain-sharing plan.
- *Explain* the difference between employee stock ownership plans, stock options, and broad-based option plans.
- *Describe* three possible explanations for extremely high levels of CEO compensation.
- *Identify* the five basic elements of executive compensation packages.
- *Define* dual career ladders and maturity curves and *explain* how these are used in compensating scientists and engineers in high-tech industries.

What's in a name? The answer is . . . confusion, at least if we are talking about pay-for-performance/variable pay plans. Listen long enough and you will hear about incentive plans, variable pay plans, compensation at risk, earnings at risk, success sharing, and others. Sometimes these names are used interchangeably. They shouldn't be. The major thing all these names have in common is a shift in thinking about compensation. We used to think of pay as primarily an entitlement—if you went to work and did well enough to avoid being fired, you were entitled to the same size paycheque as everyone else.

■ WHAT IS A PAY-FOR-PERFORMANCE PLAN?

Pay-for-performance plans signal a movement away from entitlement—sometimes a very slow movement—towards pay that varies with some measure of individual or organizational performance. Of the pay components we discussed in Chapter 10, only base pay and across-the-board increases don't fit the pay-for-performance category. Curiously, though, many of the surveys on pay for performance tend to omit the grandfather of all these plans, merit pay. Merit pay is still a pay-for-performance plan used for more than three-quarters of all exempt, clerical, and administrative employees.[1] Although more innovative pay-for-performance plans may get more and better press, there is still no widespread evidence of their adoption.

A wide variety of variable pay plans is in use today. What used to be primarily a compensation tool for top management is gradually becoming more prevalent for lower-level employees too. Exhibit 11.1 indicates that variable pay is commanding a larger share of total compensation for all employee groups.

The greater interest in variable pay probably can be traced to two trends. First, the increasing competition from foreign producers forces North American producers to cut costs and/or increase productivity. Well-designed variable pay plans have a proven track record of motivating better performance and helping cut costs. Second, today's fast-paced business environment means that workers must be willing to adjust what they do and how they do it. There are new technologies, new work processes, new work relationships. All these require workers to adapt in ways and with a speed that is unparalleled. Failure to move quickly means market share goes to competitors. If this happens, workers face possible layoffs and terminations. To avoid this scenario, compensation experts are focusing on ways to design reward systems so that workers will be able and willing to move quickly into new jobs and new ways of performing old jobs. The ability and incentive to do this come partially from reward systems that more closely link worker interests with the objectives of the company.

DOES VARIABLE PAY IMPROVE PERFORMANCE RESULTS? THE GENERAL EVIDENCE

As the evidence pointed out in Chapter 10, pay-for-performance plans—those that introduce variability into the level of pay you receive—seem to have a positive impact on performance if designed well. Notice, we qualified our statement that variable pay plans can be effective—*if they are designed well*. In the next sections we talk about issues in design and the impacts they can have.

EXHIBIT 11.1 Base vs. Variable Pay

| | Percentage of Total Compensation | | | |
| | Today | | Expected in 3 Years | |
Employee Group	Base	Variable	Base	Variable
Hourly	98%	2	96%	4
Salaried	92	8	87	13
Executive	76	24	71	29

■ SPECIFIC PAY-FOR-PERFORMANCE PLANS: SHORT TERM

Merit Pay

merit pay

increase in base pay related to performance

A **merit pay** system links increases in base pay (called merit increases) to how highly employees are rated on a subjective performance evaluation. Chapter 10 covers performance evaluation, but as a simple illustration consider the following typical merit pay setup.

	Well Above Average	Above Average	Average	Below Average	Well Below Average
Performance Rating	1	2	3	4	5
Merit Pay Increase	6%	5%	4%	3%	0%

At the end of a performance year, the employee is evaluated, usually by the direct supervisor. The performance rating, 1 to 5 in the above example, determines the size of the increase added into base pay. This last point is important. In effect, what you do this year in terms of performance is rewarded *every year* you remain with your employer. By building into base pay, the dollar amount, just like the Energizer bunny, keeps on going! With compounding, this can amount to tens of thousands of dollars over an employee's work career.[2]

Increasingly, merit pay is under attack. Not only is it expensive, but many argue it doesn't achieve the desired goal: improving employee and corporate performance.[3] In a thorough review of merit pay literature, though, Heneman concludes that merit pay does have a small, but significant, impact on performance.[4]

If we want merit pay to live up to its potential, it needs to be managed better.[5] This requires a complete overhaul of the way we allocate raises: improving the accuracy of performance ratings, allocating enough merit money to truly reward performance, and making sure the size of the merit increase differentiates across performance levels. To illustrate this latter point, consider the employee who works hard all year, earns a 6 percent increase as our guidelines above indicate, and compares himself with the average performer who coasts to a 4 percent increase. First we take out taxes on that extra 2 percent. Then we spread it out over 52 paycheques. It's only a slight exaggeration to suggest that the extra money won't pay for a good cup of coffee. Unless we make the reward difference larger for every increment in performance, many employees are going to say "Why bother?"

Lump-Sum Bonuses

Lump-sum bonuses are an increasingly used substitute for merit pay. Based on employee or company performance, employees receive an end-of-year bonus that does not build into base pay. Because employees must earn this increase every year, it is viewed less as an entitlement than is merit pay. As Exhibit 11.2 indicates, lump-sum bonuses also can be considerably less expensive than merit pay over the long run.

Notice how quickly base pay rises under a merit pay plan. After just five years, base pay is almost $14,000 higher than under a lump-sum bonus plan. It should be no surprise that cost-conscious firms report switching to lump-sum pay. Forty-five percent of all companies reported using lump-sum bonuses in 1999, up from 30 percent in 1996.[6] It also should be no surprise that employees aren't particularly fond of lump-sum bonuses. After all, the intent of lump-sum bonuses is to cause shock waves in an entitlement culture. By giving lump-sum bonuses for several years, a company is essentially freezing base pay. Gradually this results in a repositioning relative to competitors. The message becomes loud and clear: "Don't expect to receive increases in base pay year after year—new rewards must be earned each year."

EXHIBIT 11.2 Relative Cost Comparisons

	Merit Pay	**Lump-Sum Bonus**
Base Pay	$50,000	$50,000
Year 1 payout 5%	(2,500)	5% (2,500)
New Base Pay	52,500	50,000
Extra Cost Total	2,500	2,500
Year 2 Payout 5%	($2,625 = .05 × 52,500)	5% (2,500 = .05 × 50,000)
New Base Pay	55,125 (52,500 + 2,625)	50,000
Extra Cost Total	5,125	5,000
After 5 years. . . .		
Year 5 Payout	3,039	2,500
New Base Pay	63,814	50,000

Individual Spot Awards

Technically, spot awards should fall under pay-for-performance plans. About 30 percent of all companies use spot awards.[7] Usually these payouts are awarded for exceptional performance, often on special projects or for performance that so exceeds expectations as to be deserving of an add-on bonus. The mechanics are simple. After the fact, someone in the organization alerts top management to the exceptional performance. If the company is large, there may be a formal mechanism for this recognition, and perhaps some guidelines on the size of the spot award (so named because it is supposed to be awarded on the spot). Smaller companies may be more casual about recognition and more subjective about deciding the size of the award. One creative user of spot awards is Mary Kay Cosmetics. Top saleswomen get pink Cadillacs, mink coats, and diamond rings.[8]

Individual Incentive Plans: Types

These plans differ from the above because they offer a promise of pay for some objective, preestablished level of performance. A standard is established against which worker performance is compared in order to determine the magnitude of the incentive pay. For individual incentive systems, this standard is compared to individual worker performance. From this basic foundation, a number of seemingly complex and divergent plans have evolved. Before discussing the more prevalent of these plans, however, it is important to note that each varies along two dimensions and can be classified into one of four cells, illustrated in Exhibit 11.3.

The first dimension on which incentive systems vary is in the *method of rate determination*. Plans either set up a rate based on units of production per time period or in time period per unit of production. On the surface, this distinction may appear trivial but, in fact, the deviations arise because tasks have different cycles of operation.[9] Short-cycle tasks, those that are completed in a relatively short period of time, typically have as a standard a designated number of units to be produced in a given time period. For long-cycle tasks, this would not be appropriate. It is entirely possible that only one task or some portion of it may be completed in a day. Consequently, for longer cycle tasks, the standard is typically set in terms of time required to complete one unit of production. Individual incentives are based on whether or not workers complete the task in the designated time period.

EXHIBIT 11.3 Individual Incentive Plans ───────────────────────────

Relationship between production level and pay	Method of Rate Determination	
	Units of production per time period	Time period per unit of production
Pay constant function of production level	(1) Straight piecework plan.	(2) Standardhour plan.
Pay varies as function of production level	(3) Taylor differential piece rate system. Merrick multiple piece rate system.	(4) Halsey 50-50 method.

The second dimension on which individual incentive systems vary is the specified relationship between production level and wages. The first alternative is to tie wages to output on a one-to-one basis, so that wages are some constant function of production. In contrast, some plans vary wages as a function of production level. For example, one common alternative is to provide higher dollar rates for production above the standard than for production below the standard.

Each of the plans discussed in this section has as a foundation a standard level of performance determined by some form of time study or job analysis completed by an industrial engineer or trained human resources administrator. (Exhibit 11.4 provides an illustration of a time study.) The variations in these plans occur either in the way the standard is set or in the way wages are tied to output. As in Exhibit 11.3, there are four general categories of plans.

1. *Cell 1*. The most frequently implemented incentive system is a *straight piecework* system (Exhibit 11.5). Rate determination is based on units of production per time period, and wages vary directly as a function of production level. The major advantages of this type of system are that it is easily understood by workers and, perhaps consequently, more readily accepted than some of the other incentive systems.

2. *Cell 2*. Another relatively common plan called a *standard hour plan* sets standards based on time per unit and ties incentives directly to level of output. A common example can be found in any neighbourhood gasoline station or automobile repair shop. Let us assume that you need a new transmission. The estimate you receive for labour costs is based on the mechanic's hourly rate of pay, multiplied by a time estimate for job completion derived from a book listing average time estimates for a wide variety of jobs. If the mechanic receives $60 per hour and a transmission is listed as requiring four hours to remove and replace, the labour cost would be $240. All this is determined in advance of any actual work. Of course, if the mechanic is highly experienced and fast, the job may be completed in considerably less time than indicated in the book. However, the job is still charged as if it took the quoted time to complete. Standard hour plans are more practical than a straight piecework plan for long-cycle operations and jobs that are nonrepetitive and require numerous skills for completion.[10]

3. *Cell 3*. The two plans included in cell 3 provide for variable incentives as a function of units of production per time period. Both the *Taylor plan* and the *Merrick plan* provide different piece rates, depending on the level of production relative to the standard. The Taylor plan establishes two piecework rates. One rate goes into effect when a worker

EXHIBIT 11.4 | Example of a Time Study

Task: Drilling operation.
Elements: 1. Move part from box to jig.
           2. Position part in jig.
           3. Drill hole in part.
           4. Remove jig and drop part in chute.

Notes and Remarks	Observation Number	Elements			
		(1)	*(2)*	*(3)*	*(4)*
	1	.17	.22	.26	.29
	2	.17	.22	.27	.34
	3	.16	.21	.28	.39
	4	.18	.21	.29	.29
	5	.19	.20	.30	.36
	6	.25	.21	.31	.31
	7	.17	.23	.29	.33
Observed time		.17 (mode)	.21 (mode)	.29 (median)	.33 (mean)
Effort rating	(130%)	1.30	1.30	1.30	1.30
Corrected time		.2210	.2730	.3370	.4290
Total corrected time					1.2600

Allowances:
Fatigue	5%	
Personal needs	5%	
Contingencies	10%	
Total	20% (of total corrected time of 1.2600)	.2520
Total allotted time for task		1.5120

Source: From Stephen J. Carroll and Craig E. Schneider, *Performance Appraisal and Review Systems* (Glenview, IL: Scott, Foresman, 1982). Copyright © 1982 by Scott, Foresman and Company. Reprinted by permission.

EXHIBIT 11.5 | Illustration of a Straight Piece Rate Plan

Piece rate standard (e.g., determined from time study): 10 units/hour
Guaranteed minimum wage (if standard is not met): $5/hour
Incentive rate (for each unit over 10 units): $.50/unit

Examples of Worker Output	Wage
10 units or less	$5.00/hour (as guaranteed)
20 units	20 × $.50 = $10/hour
30 units	30 × $.50 = $15/hour

exceeds the published standard for a given time period. This rate is set higher than the regular wage incentive level. A second rate is established for production below standard, and this rate is lower than the regular wage.

The Merrick system operates in the same way, except that three piecework rates are set: (1) high—for production exceeding 100 percent of standard; (2) medium—for production between 83 and 100 percent of standard; and (3) low—for production less than 83 percent of standard. Exhibit 11.6 compares these two plans.

4. *Cell 4.* Plans included in cell 4 provide for variable incentives linked to a standard expressed as time period per unit of production, such as the *Halsey 50-50 method*. This plan features a shared split between worker and employer of any savings in direct cost. An allowed time for a task is determined via time study. The savings resulting from completion of a task in less than the standard time are allocated 50–50 (the most frequent division) between the worker and the company.

Individual Incentive Plans: Advantages and Disadvantages

A common problem with incentive plans is that employees and managers end up in conflict because the incentive system often focuses only on one small part of what it takes for the company to be successful.[11] Employees, being rational, do more of what the incentive system pays for. Exhibit 11.7 outlines some of the other problems, as well as advantages, of individual incentive plans.

Individual Incentive Plans: Examples

Even though incentive systems are less popular than they used to be, there are still notable successes. Of course, most sales positions have some part of pay based on commissions, a form of individual incentives. Perhaps the longest running success with individual incentives, going back to before World War I, belongs to a company called Lincoln Electric in Cleveland, Ohio. We describe the compensation package for factory jobs at Lincoln Electric in Exhibit 11.8. Notice how the different pieces fit together. This isn't a case of an incentive plan operating in a vacuum. All the pieces of the compensation and reward package fit together. Lincoln Electric's success is so striking that it's the subject of many case analyses.[12]

EXHIBIT 11.6 Illustrations of the Taylor and Merrick Plans ————————————————

Piece rate standard: 10 units per hour
Standard wage: $5.00/hour
Piecework rate:

Output	Taylor Rate per Unit	Taylor Wage	Merrick Rate per Unit	Merrick Wage
7 units/hour	$.50/unit	$3.50	$.50/unit	$3.50
8 units/hour	$.50/unit	$4.00	$.50/unit	$4.00
9 units/hour	$.50/unit	$4.50	$.60/unit	$5.40
10 units/hour	$.50/unit	$5.00	$.60/unit	$6.00
11 units/hour	$.70/unit	$7.70	$.70/unit	$7.70
12 + units	Calculations at same rate as for 11 units.			

EXHIBIT | **11.7** | Advantages and Disadvantages of Individualized Incentive Plans ——————

Advantages

1. Substantial contribution to raise productivity, to lower production costs, and to increase earnings of workers.
2. Less direct supervision is required to maintain reasonable levels of output than under payment by time.
3. In most cases, systems of payment by results, if accompanied by improved organizational and work measurement, enable labour costs to be estimated more accurately than under payment by time. This helps costing and budgetary control.

Disadvantages

1. Greater conflict may emerge between employees seeking to maximize output and managers concerned about deteriorating quality levels.
2. Attempts to introduce new technology may be resisted by employees concerned about the impact on production standards.
3. Reduced willingness of employees to suggest new production methods for fear of subsequent increases in production standards.
4. Increased complaints that equipment is poorly maintained, hindering employee efforts to earn larger incentives.
5. Increased turnover among new employees discouraged by the unwillingness of experienced workers to cooperate in on-the-job training.
6. Elevated levels of mistrust between workers and management.

Source: T. Wilson, "Is It Time to Eliminate the Piece Rate Incentive System?" *Compensation and Benefits Review* 24, no. 2 (1992), pp. 43–49; Pinhas Schwinger, *Wage Incentive Systems* (New York: Halsted, 1975).

EXHIBIT | **11.8** | Lincoln Electric's Compensation System ——————

Description of Culture:	Reservoir of Trust. Long history of employment stability even under severe economic downturns. Employees with 3+ years seniority are guaranteed (on one-year renewable basis) at least 75 percent full-time work for that year. In exchange, employees agree to flexible assignment across jobs.
Base Wages:	Market rate determined. Time study department sets piece rate so average worker can earn market rate.
Bonus (short term):	Board of Directors sets year-end bonus pool as function of company performance. Employee's share in pool is function of semi-annual performance review (see below).
Incentive (long term):	Employees share in long-term company successes/failures in form of employee stock ownership plan (ESOP). Employees now own 28 percent of outstanding stock shares.
Performance Review:	Employees rated on four factors: 1) dependability, 2) quality, 3) output, 4) ideas and cooperation in comparison to others in department. To ensure against rating inflation, the average score in department cannot exceed 100.

Team/Group Incentive Plans: Types

team/group incentive plans

■ incentive pay for meeting or exceeding group performance standards

When we move away from individual incentive systems and start focusing on people working together, we shift to **team/group incentive plans**. The group might be a work team, a department, a division, or the whole company. The basic concept is still the same, though. A standard is established against which worker performance (that is, team performance) is compared to determine the magnitude of the incentive pay. With the focus on groups, we are concerned now with group performance in comparison to some standard, or level of expected performance. The standard might be an expected level of operating income for a division. Or, the measure might be more unusual, as with Litton Industries. One division has a team variable pay measure that is based on whether customers would be willing to act as a reference when Litton solicits other business. The more customers willing to do this, the larger the team variable pay.[13]

As Exhibit 11.9 suggests, the range of performance measures for different types of corporate objectives is indeed impressive.[14] Historically, financial measures have been the most widely used performance indicator for group incentive plans. Increasingly, though, top executives express concern that these measures do a better job of communicating performance to stock analysts than to managers trying to figure out how to improve operating effectiveness.[15] One of the refinements designed in part to address this concern is called *The Balanced Scorecard*. Mobil Oil, for example, uses a constellation of measures that better indicate exactly where a company is succeeding and what needs to be improved. The process begins with a careful analysis of strategic objectives for both the corporation and all of its divisions. Then, leaders of all the strategic business units are challenged to identify measures that best reflect the directions being taken by the business. This leads to a constellation of measures such as customer satisfaction, quality, innovation, employee development, and the ever-familiar financial measures. The balanced scorecard forces discussions about priorities among these different measures. But dissent is viewed positively. A picture begins to emerge about what is most important and what the necessary tradeoffs are to achieve the different objectives. What evolves is a series of objectives with different weights in terms of importance. These objectives send clear signals to managers, and then to their employees, about what is important.

The central point is still that we are now concerned about group performance. This presents both problems and opportunities. As Exhibit 11.10 illustrates, we need to decide whether a group incentive plan is a better choice than an individual plan. Recent evidence, for example, suggests that firms high on business risk—those with uncertain outcomes—are better off not having incentive plans; corporate performance is higher.[16]

Comparing Group and Individual Incentive Plans

In this era of heightened concern about productivity, we frequently are asked whether setting up incentive plans really boosts performance. As we noted in Chapter 10, the answer is yes. We also are asked which is better, group or individual incentive plans. Often this is a misleading question. As we noted in Exhibit 11.6, things such as the type of task, the organizational commitment to teams, and the type of work environment may preclude one or the other. When forced to answer the question anyway, experts agree that individual incentive plans have better potential, and probably better track records, in delivering higher productivity. Group plans suffer from what is called the "free-rider" problem where at least one person doesn't carry his or her share of the load. Yet, when it comes time to divide the rewards, they typically are shared equally. Problems like this have caused some companies to phase out many of its team reward packages. Top-performing employees quickly grow disenchanted with having to carry free riders. End result—turnover of the very group that is most costly to lose.

Recent research on free riders suggests that the problem can be lessened through use of good performance measurement techniques. Specifically, free riders have a harder time loafing when

---

EXHIBIT | **11.9** | A Sampling of Performance Measures ──────────────

Customer-Focused Measures

Time-to-Market Measures
- On-time delivery
- Cycle time
- New product introductions

Customer Satisfaction Measures
- Market share
- Customer satisfaction
- Customer growth and retention
- Account penetration

Financially Focused Measures

Value Creation
- Revenue growth
- Resource yields
- Profit margins
- Economic value added

Shareholder Return
- Return on invested capital
- Return on sales/earnings
- Earnings per share
- Growth in profitability

Capability-Focused Measures

Human Resources Capabilities
- Employee satisfaction
- Turnover rates
- Total recruitment costs
- Rate of progress on developmental plans
- Promotability index
- Staffing mix/head-count ratio

Other Asset Capabilities
- Patents/copyrights/regulations
- Distribution systems
- Technological capabilities

Internal Process-Focused Measures

Resource Utilization
- Budget-to-actual expenses
- Cost-allocation ratios
- Reliability/rework
- Accuracy/error rates
- Safety rates

Change Effectiveness
- Program implementation
- Teamwork effectiveness
- Service/quality index

---

there are clear performance standards. Rather than being given instructions to "do your best," when asked to deliver specific levels of performance at a specific time, the poorer performers actually showed the most performance improvement.[17]

Team Compensation

Despite an explosion of interest in teams and team compensation, many of the reports from the front lines are not encouraging. Companies report they generally are not satisfied with the way their team compensation systems work.[18] Failures can be attributed to at least five causes. First, one of the problems with team compensation is that teams come in many varieties. There are full-time teams (e.g., work group organized as a team). There are part-time teams that cut across functional departments (e.g., experts from different departments pulled together to improve customer relations). There are even full-time teams that are temporary (e.g., cross-functional teams pulled together to help ease the transition into a partnership or joint venture). With so many varieties, it's hard to argue for one consistent type of compensation plan. We are still at the stage of trying to find the *one best way*. Maybe the answer is to look at different compensation approaches for different types of teams.

A second problem with rewarding teams is called "the level problem." If we define teams at a very broad level—the whole organization being an extreme example—much of the motivational

EXHIBIT 11.10   Different Types of Variable Pay Plans: Advantages and Disadvantages ──────

Plan Type	What It Is	Advantages	Disadvantages	Why?
Cash Profit Sharing	▪ Award based on organizational profitability ▪ Shares a percentage of profits (typically above a target level of profitability) ▪ Usually an annual payout ▪ Can be cash or deferred	▪ Simple, easily understood ▪ Low administrative costs	▪ Profit influenced by many factors beyond employee control ▪ May be viewed as an entitlement ▪ Limited motivational impact	▪ To educate employees about business operations ▪ To foster teamwork or "one-for-all" environment
Stock Ownership or Options	▪ Award of stock shares or options	▪ Option awards have minimal impact on the financial statements of the company at the time they are granted ▪ If properly communicated, can have powerful impact on employee behaviour ▪ Tax deferral to employee	▪ Indirect pay/performance link ▪ Many factors outside individual influence affect stock price ▪ Employees may be required to put up money to exercise grants	▪ To recruit top quality employees when organization has highly uncertain future (e.g., startups, high-tech, or biotech industries) ▪ To address employee retention concerns ▪ To focus employees on need to increase shareholder value
Balanced Scorecard	▪ Awards that combine financial and operating measures for organization, business unit, and/or individual performance ▪ Award pool based on achieving performance targets ▪ Multiple performance measures may include: 1. Nonfinancial/ Operating: quality improvements, productivity gains, customer service improvements 2. Financial: EPS, ROE, ROA, Revenues	▪ Communicates organizational priorities	▪ Performance criteria may be met, but if financial targets are not met, there may be a reduced payout or no payout at all ▪ Can be complex	▪ To focus employees on organization, division, and/or individual goals ▪ To link payouts to a specific financial and/ or operational target
Productivity/ Gain-Sharing	▪ Awards that share economic benefits of improved productivity, quality, or other measurable results ▪ Focus on group, plant, department, or division results ▪ Designed to capitalize on untapped knowledge of employees	▪ Clear performance–reward links ▪ Productivity and quality improvements ▪ Employee's knowledge of business increases ▪ Fosters teamwork, co-operation	▪ Can be administratively complicated ▪ Unintended effects, such as a drop-off in quality ▪ Management must "open the books" ▪ Payouts can occur even if company's financial performance is poor	▪ To support a major productivity/quality initiative (such as TQM or reengineering) ▪ To foster teamwork environment ▪ To reward employees for improvements in activities that they control

continued

EXHIBIT 11.10 Different Types of Variable Pay Plans: Advantages and Disadvantages (*continued*)

Plan Type	What It Is	Advantages	Disadvantages	Why?
Team/Group Incentives	▪ Awards determined based on team/group performance goals or objectives ▪ Payout can be more frequent than annual and can also extend beyond the life of the team ▪ Payout may be uniform for team/group members	▪ Reinforces teamwork and team identity/results ▪ Effective in stimulating ideas and problem-solving ▪ Minimizes distinctions between team members ▪ May better reflect how work is performed	▪ May be difficult to isolate impact of team ▪ Not all employees can be placed on a team ▪ Can be administratively complex ▪ May create team competition ▪ Difficult to set equitable targets for all team	▪ To demonstrate an organizational commitment to teams ▪ To reinforce the need for employees to work together to achieve results

impact of incentives can be lost. As a member of a 1,000-person team, I'm unlikely to be convinced that my extra effort will significantly affect our team's overall performance. Why, then, should I try hard? Conversely, if we let teams get too small, other problems arise. Small work teams competing for a fixed piece of incentive awards may tend to gravitate to behaviours that are clearly unhealthy for overall corporate success. Teams may hoard star performers, refusing to allow transfers even for the greater good of the company. Teams may be reluctant to take on new employees for fear that time lost to training will hurt the team—even when the added employees are essential to long-run success. Finally, bickering may arise when awards are given. Because teams have different performance objectives, it is difficult to equalize for difficulty when assigning rewards. Inevitably complaints arise.[19]

The last three major problems with team compensation involve the three Cs: *complexity, control, and communications.* Some plans are simply too *complex.* The second C is *control.* Praxair, a worldwide provider of gases (including oxygen) extracted from the atmosphere, works hard to make sure all its team pay comes from performance measures under the control of the team. If mother nature ravages a construction site, causing delays and skyrocketing costs, workers aren't penalized with reduced team payouts. Such uncontrollable elements are factored into the process of setting performance standards. Indeed, experts assert that this ability to foretell sources of problems and adjust for them is a key element in building a team pay plan.[20] Key to the control issue is the whole question of fairness. Are the rewards fair, given our ability to produce results? Recent research suggests this perception of fairness is crucial. The final C is a familiar factor in compensation successes and failures: *communication.* Team-based pay plans simply are not well communicated. Employees asked to explain their plans often flounder because more effort is devoted by the design team to the mechanics than to deciding how to explain the plan.

Gain-Sharing Plans

gain-sharing plan
group incentive plan where employees share in cost savings

Our discussion of team-based compensation often mentioned **gain-sharing plans** as a common component. As the name suggests, employees share in the gains in these types of group incentive plans. With profit-sharing plans—surprise!—the sharing involves some form of profits. Realistically, though, most employees feel that little they can do will affect profits—that's something top management decisions influence more. So gain-sharing looks at cost components and identifies savings over which employees have more impact (e.g., reduced scrap, lower labour costs, reduced utility costs).

The following issues are key elements in designing a gain-sharing plan:

1. *Strength of reinforcement.* What role should base pay assume relative to incentive pay? Incentive pay tends to encourage only those behaviours that are rewarded.
2. *Productivity standards.* What standard will be used to calculate whether employees will receive an incentive payout? Almost all group incentive plans use a historical standard. A historical standard involves the choice of a prior year's performance to use for comparison with current performance. But which baseline year should be used? If too good (or too bad) a comparison year is used, the standard will be too hard (or easy) to achieve, with obvious motivational and cost effects. One possible compromise is to use a moving average of several years (for example, the average for the past five years, with the five-year block changing by one year on an annual basis).

    One of the major problems with historical standards is the problems that changing environmental conditions can cause. Care must be taken to ensure that the link between performance and rewards is sustained. This means that environmental influences on performance, those not controllable by plan participants, should be factored out when identifying incentive levels.
3. *Sharing the gains: split between management and workers.* Part of the plan must address the relative share paid to management and workers of any profit or savings generated. This also includes discussion of whether an emergency reserve (gains withheld from distribution in case of future emergencies) will be established in advance of any sharing of profits.
4. *Scope of the formula.* Formulas can vary in the scope of inclusions for both the labour inputs in the numerator and productivity outcomes in the denominator.[21] Recent innovations in gain-sharing plans largely address broadening the types of productivity standards considered appropriate. Arguing that organizations are complex and require more complex measures, performance measures have expanded beyond traditional financial measures to include retention of customers, customer satisfaction, delivery performance, safety, absenteeism, turnaround time, and number of suggestions submitted. Great care must be exercised with these alternative measures, though, to ensure that the behaviours reinforced actually affect the desired bottom-line goal.
5. *Perceived fairness of the formula.* One way to ensure that the plan is perceived as fair is to let employees vote on whether implementation should go forward. This and union participation in program design are two elements in plan success.[22]
6. *Ease of administration.* Sophisticated plans with involved calculations of profits or costs can become too complex for existing company information systems. Increased complexities also require more effective communications and higher levels of trust among participants.
7. *Production variability.* One of the major sources of problems in group incentive plans is failure to set targets properly. A good plan ensures that environmental influences on performance, not controllable by plan participants, should be factored out when identifying incentive levels. One alternative would be to set standards that are relative to industry performance. The obvious advantage of this strategy is that economic and other external factors hit all firms in the industry equally. If our company performs better, relatively, it means we are doing something as employees to help achieve success.

    The three primary types of gain-sharing plans, differentiated by their focus on either cost savings (the numerator of the equation) or some measure of revenue (the denominator of the equation), are noted below.

Scanlon Plan.   Scanlon plans are designed to lower labour costs without lowering the level of a firm's activity. Incentives are derived as a function of the ratio between labour costs and sales value of production (SVOP).[23] The SVOP includes sales revenue and the value of goods in inventory. To illustrate how these two figures are used to derive incentives under a Scanlon plan, consider Exhibit 11.11.

EXHIBIT 11.11 Examples of a Scanlon Plan ──────────────────────────────

1997 Data (base year) for Alton, Ltd.

SVOP	=	$10,000,000
Total wage bill	=	4,000,000
$\dfrac{\text{Total wage bill}}{\text{SVOP}}$	=	$4,000,000 \div 10,000,000 = .40 = 40\%$

Operating Month, March 1998

SVOP	=	$950,000
Allowable wage bill	=	.40 ($950,000) = $380,000
Actual wage bill (August)	=	330,000
Savings	=	50,000

$50,000 available for distribution as a bonus.

.NET WORTH Scanlon Plan Effectiveness in Retail Stores

Although the Scanlon plan was first developed more than 60 years ago, Scanlon-type programs only became popular in the 1980s and 1990s. Most work on Scanlon plans has focused on the manufacturing sector, but recently a major retailer implemented the plan in an attempt to improve employee motivation because of sagging sales and loss of market share.

Stores with the Scanlon plan received on average a more favourable response on all customer satisfaction measures of performance than did control stores without a Scanlon plan. Scanlon plan stores had consistently higher sales performance to sales goals than did the control stores. This finding is particularly impressive since sales are affected by many factors beyond the control of store employees. Finally, employee willingness to make suggestions was higher in Scanlon plan stores than in control stores. Employees involved in the implementation of the Scanlon plan were more likely to try to find ways to cut costs, to seek out financial information on company performance, and to share in the consequences of company financial setbacks than were employees not involved in implementation of the Scanlon plans.

These findings support the contribution that Scanlon plans make to the effectiveness of retail stores and, to a somewhat lesser degree, to customer satisfaction. Several lessons were learned in the course of implementing the Scanlon plan. First, it is critical to have senior management support and commitment. Second, this is an initiative that cannot be delegated. Third, there will be inherent skepticism among employees that only time and good leadership can overcome. Fourth, it is difficult to recover from false starts. Finally, the Scanlon plan is not for every store. It is not a panacea; it demands a committed and participative leader, and can create some turmoil when it is initiated. Another lesson learned was the importance of having a systematic and participative implementation process.

Source: K.D. Scott, J. Floyd, P.G. Benson, & J.W. Bishop, "The Impact of the Scanlon Plan on Retail Store Performance." *WorldatWork Journal*, Third Quarter 2002, pp. 25-31.

In practice, the $50,000 bonus in Exhibit 11.11 is not all distributed to the workforce. Rather, 25 percent is distributed to the company, 75 percent of the remainder is distributed as bonus, and 25 percent of the remainder is withheld and placed in an emergency fund to reimburse the company for any future months when a "negative bonus" is earned (i.e., when the actual wage bill is greater than the allowable wage bill). Any excess remaining in the emergency pool is distributed to workers at the end of the year.

Rucker Plan.   The Rucker plan involves a somewhat more complex formula than a Scanlon plan for determining worker incentive bonuses. Essentially, a ratio is calculated that expresses the value of production required for each dollar of total wage bill. Consider the following illustration:[24]

1. Assume accounting records show the company expended $.60 worth of electricity, materials, supplies, and so on, to produce $1.00 worth of product. The value added is $.40 for each $1.00 of sales value. Assume also that 45 percent of the value added was attributable to labour; a productivity ratio (PR) can be allocated from the formula:
2. PR (labour) $\times .40 \times .45 = 1.00$. Solving yields PR = 5.56.
3. If the wage bill equals $100,000, the *expected* production value is the wage bill ($100,000) $\times$ PR (5.56) = $555,556.
4. If *actual* production value equals $650,000, then the savings (actual production value minus expected production value) is $94,444.
5. Since the labour contribution to value added is 45 percent, the bonus to the workforce should be $.45 \times \$94,444 = \$42,500$.
6. The savings are distributed as an incentive bonus according to a formula similar to the Scanlon formula—75 percent of the bonus is distributed to workers immediately and 25 percent is kept as an emergency fund to cover poor months. Any excess in the emergency fund at the end of the year is then distributed to workers.

Implementation of the Scanlon/Rucker Plans.

There are two major components vital to the implementation and success of a Rucker or Scanlon plan: (1) a productivity norm and (2) development of effective worker committees. Development of a productivity norm requires both effective measurement of base year data and acceptance by workers and management of this standard for calculating bonus incentives.

The second ingredient of Scanlon/Rucker plans is a series of worker committees (also known as productivity committees or bonus committees). The primary function of these committees is to evaluate employee and management suggestions for ways to improve productivity and/or cut costs. It is not uncommon for the suggestion rate to be above that found in companies with standard suggestion incentive plans.[25] This climate the Scanlon/Rucker plans foster is probably the element most vital to success.

Improshare.

Improshare (IMproved PROductivity through SHARing) is a gain-sharing plan that has proven easy to administer and to communicate.[26] First, a standard is developed which identifies the expected hours required to produce an acceptable level of output. This standard comes either from time and motion studies conducted by industrial engineers or from a base period measurement of the performance factor. Any savings arising from production of the agreed-upon output in fewer than the expected hours is shared by the firm and by the worker.[27] So, for example, if 100 workers can produce 50,000 units over 50 weeks, this translates into 200,000 hours (40 hours $\times$ 50 weeks) for 50,000 units, or 4 hours per unit. If we implement an Improshare plan, any gains resulting in less than 4 hours per unit are shared 50–50 between employees and management (wages times number of hours saved).[28]

One survey of 104 companies with an Improshare plan found a mean increase in productivity during the first year of 12.5 percent.[29] By the third year the productivity gain rose to 22 percent. A significant portion of this productivity gain was traced to reduced defect rates and downtime (e.g., repair time).

Profit-Sharing Plans

profit-sharing plans

variable pay plans requiring a profit target to be met before any payouts occur

Today, there is less discussion of **profit-sharing plans** and more focus on gain-sharing plans or related variants. An erroneous conclusion to draw from this is that profit sharing is dead. In reality, many variable pay plans still require some profit target to be met before any payouts occur. Profit sharing continues to be popular because the focus is on the measure that matters most to the most people: some index of profitability. When payoffs are linked to these measures, employees spend more time learning about financial measures and the business factors that influence them.

On the downside, most employees don't feel their jobs have a direct impact on profits. Furthermore, even if workers are able to improve operating efficiency, there is no guarantee that profits will automatically increase. Strength of the market, global competition, even the way we enter accounting information into the balance sheet all can affect profits and serve to disenchant workers.

The trend in recent variable pay design is to combine the best of gain-sharing and profit-sharing plans.[30] The company specifies a funding formula for any variable payout that is linked to some profit measure. As experts say, the plan must be self-funding. Dollars going to workers are generated by additional profits gained from operational efficiency. Along with the financial incentive, employees feel they have a measure of control. For example, an airline might give an incentive for reductions in lost baggage, with the size of the payout dependent on hitting profit targets. Such a program combines the need for fiscal responsibility with the chance for workers to affect something they can control.

Earnings-at-Risk Plans

earnings-at-risk plan

incentive plan sharing profits in successful years and reducing base pay in unsuccessful years

Think of incentive plans as falling into one of two categories: success sharing or risk sharing. In success-sharing plans, employee base wages are constant and variable pay adds on during *successful years*. If the company does well, you receive some amount of variable pay. If the company does poorly, you simply forgo any variable pay—there is no reduction in your base pay, though. In a risk-sharing plan, usually called **earnings at risk plan**, base pay is reduced by some amount relative to the level that would be offered in a success-sharing plan. For example, base pay could be reduced 15 percent across the board in year one. That 15 percent could be replaced with a .5 percent increase in base pay for every 1 percent increase in productivity beyond 70 percent of the prior year's productivity. This figure would leave workers whole (no decline in base pay) if they only matched the prior year productivity. Each additional percentage of improvement in productivity could yield a 1.5 percent increase in base wages.

Clearly, at-risk plans shift some of the risk of doing business from the company to the employee. The company hedges against the devastating effects of a bad year by mortgaging some of the profits that would have accrued during a good year. Companies such as DuPont and Saturn report mixed results. DuPont terminated its plan in the second year because of lackluster performance and the expectation of no payout. At-risk plans appear to be met with decreases in satisfaction with both pay in general and with the process used to set pay.[31] It's clear that the long-run success of at-risk plans depends on employee acceptance. At Saturn, for example, storm clouds are on the horizon. Employees suggested that Saturn enter the hot SUV market. This suggestion was ignored by management until it was too late to be an early entrant, angering employees. After all, bad management decisions have a direct impact on worker paycheques. And at-risk programs do direct employee attention to organizational decisions.[32]

One of the reasons for the separation of the United Auto Workers (UAW) in Canada from the international union in 1984 was the UAW decision to enter into an earnings-at-risk plan with General Motors. The Canadian autoworkers rejected this approach to compensation and instead preferred a known, fixed-increment compensation package. The Canadian workers left the UAW and formed the Canadian Auto Workers (CAW) union because of this issue.

Group Incentive Plans: Advantages and Disadvantages

Clearly, group pay-for-performance plans are gaining popularity, while individual plans are stable or declining in interest. Why? A big part of the reason is the changing nature of work processes. Teams as the basic work unit are growing in popularity. The interdependence of jobs and the need for cooperation mean compensation must reinforce working together. Efforts to reinforce these group efforts with compensation generally have been successful (Chapter 10). Exhibit 11.12 outlines some of the general positive and negative features of group pay-for-performance plans.[33]

EXPLOSIVE INTEREST IN LONG-TERM INCENTIVE PLANS

Exhibit 11.13 shows different types of long-term incentives and their definitions. These plans are also grouped by the level of risk faced by employees holding these incentives, as well as the expected rewards that might come from them. Long-term incentives (LTIs) focus on performance beyond the one-year timeline used as the cutoff for short-term incentive plans. Recent explosive growth in long-term plans appears to be spurred in part by a desire to motivate longer-term value creation.[34] In fact, studies indicate that when top management has greater ownership (usually more stock) there is significantly more investment in research and development (an indicator of long-term value creation). Stock ownership also is likely to increase internal growth, rather than more rapid external diversification.[35]

EXHIBIT 11.12 Advantages and Disadvantages of Group Incentive Plans

Advantages

1. Positive impact on organization and individual performance of about 5–10 percent per year.
2. Easier to develop performance measures than for individual plans.
3. Signals that cooperation, both within and across groups, is a desired behaviour.
4. Teamwork meets with enthusiastic support from most employees.
5. May increase participation of employees in decision-making process.

Disadvantages

1. Line of sight may be lessened, i.e., employees may find it more difficult to see how their individual performance affects their incentive payouts.
2. May lead to increased turnover among top individual performers who are discouraged because they must share with lesser contributors.
3. Increases compensation risk to employees because of lower income stability. May influence some applicants to apply for jobs in firms where base pay is larger compensation component.

| EXHIBIT | 11.13 | Long-Term Incentives and Their Risk/Reward Tradeoffs |

Level one: Low risk/reward

1. **Time-based restricted stock.** An award of shares that actually is received only after the completion of a predefined service period. Employees who terminate employment before the restriction lapses must return their shares to the company.
2. **Performance-accelerated restricted stock.** Restricted stock granted only after attainment of specified performance objectives.
3. **Stock purchase plan.** Opportunity to buy shares of a company stock either at prices below market price, or with favourable financing.

Level two: Medium risk/reward

4. **Time-vested stock option.** This is what most stock options are—the right to purchase stock at a specified price for a fixed time period.
5. **Performance-vested restricted stock.** This is a grant of stock to employees upon attainment of defined performance objective(s).
6. **Performance-accelerated stock option.** An option with a vesting schedule that can be shortened if specific performance criteria are met.

Level three: High risk/reward

7. **Premium-priced stock option.** A stock option that has an exercise price above market value at the time of grant. This creates an incentive for employees to create value for the company, see stock prices rise, and thus be eligible to purchase the stock.
8. **Indexed stock option.** An option whose exercise price depends on what peer companies' experiences are with stock prices. If industry stock prices are generally rising, it would be difficult to attribute any similar rise in a specific company to "motivated employees." Therefore, these options require improvements beyond general industry improvement.
9. **Performance-vested stock option.** One that vests only upon the attainment of a predetermined performance objective.

Source: IOMA, "PFP News Brief," Ioma's *Pay for Performance Report,* June 2000, p. 8.

Employee Stock Ownership Plans (ESOPs)

employee stock ownership plan (ESOP)

plan offering employees the opportunity to purchase company stock, often partially or fully matched by employer-paid stock for the employee

Some companies believe that employees can be linked to the success or failure of a company in yet another way—through **employee stock ownership plans**.[36] At places such as PepsiCo, Lincoln Electric, DuPont, Coca-Cola, and others, the goal is to increase employee involvement in the organization, and hopefully this will influence performance.

However, ESOPs are not particularly effective as incentive plans. First, the effects are generally long term. And, my working harder does not mean more for me. Indeed, we can't predict very well what makes stock prices rise—and this is the central ingredient in the reward component of ESOPs. So the performance measure is too complex to figure out how we can control our own destiny. But ESOPs do foster employee willingness to participate in the decision-making process.[37] And a company that takes advantage of that willingness can harness a considerable resource—the creative energy of its workforce.

Stock Options

stock options

the right to purchase
stock at a specified
(exercise) price for a
fixed time period

Stock options provide an employee with the right to purchase stock at a specified (exercise) price for a fixed time period. Beware stock options in declining markets however. After Microsoft stock was battered by its antitrust battle in 2000, employee morale plummeted. Many of the options granted to employees had exercise prices higher than the current market value—in effect making the options all but worthless. In mid-2000 Microsoft issued 70 million shares of stock at $66.25, the then-closing stock price. This price was considerably below that of many options issued in the past and was intended to motivate workers to help drive stock prices back upward.[38]

Broad-Based Option Plans (BBOPs)

**broad-based option
plans**

stock options provided
to employees at all
levels

The latest trend in long-term incentives, and probably the component of compensation generating the most discussion since the late 1990s, is in the area of **broad-based option plans**. BBOPs are stock grants: The company gives employees shares of stock over some time frame. The strength of BBOPs is their versatility. Depending on the way they are distributed to employees, they can either reinforce a strong emphasis on performance (performance culture) or inspire greater commitment and retention (ownership culture) of employees.

Many companies offer stock grants to employees at all levels. For example, Starbucks has a stock grant program called Beanstock, and all employees who work at least 500 hours per year, up to the level of vice president, are eligible (broad-based participation). If company performance goals are reached, all employees receive equal stock grants worth somewhere between 10–14 percent of their earnings. The grants vest 20 percent each year, and the option expires 10 years after the grant date. This program exists to send the CEOs a clear signal that all employees, especially the two-thirds who are part-timers, are business partners. This effort to create a culture of ownership is viewed as the primary reason Starbucks has turnover that is only a fraction of the usually high turnover in the retail industry.

Microsoft's program shares one common feature with Starbucks. The stock grant program, again, is broad based. By rewarding all employees, Microsoft hopes to send a strong signal to all employees that reinforces its culture: Take reasoned risks that have long-run potential for contributing to the company. Microsoft's BBOP is targeted at all permanent employees. Unlike Starbucks' plan, though, the size of the stock grant is linked to individual performance and estimated long-run contribution to the company. Starting 12 months after the stock grant date, 12.5 percent is vested every 6 months.

Kodak provides a third example. Only nonmanagement employees are eligible, and grants are given only to that small percentage of employees who are recognized for extraordinary accomplishments. Kodak prides itself on giving immediate grant options for outstanding contributions based on recommendations by an individual or team's manager.

In conclusion, pay-for-performance plans can work, but the design and effective administration of these plans is key to their success. Having a good idea is not enough. The good idea must be followed up by sound practices that recognize that rewards, if used properly, can shape employee behaviour.

■ PAY-FOR PERFORMANCE FOR SPECIAL GROUPS

All we have to do is open a newspaper to see that some jobs and some people are singled out for special compensation treatment in an organization. Why do professional sports players regularly make millions per year? Why does Frank Stronach (chief executive officer, Magna Corp) regularly make over $10 million per year? Is the value of these jobs determined in the same way that compensation is determined for other jobs in a company? The answer is probably no. But why? To answer this question it is useful to work backwards. What jobs get special compensation treatment in a company? Are they basically the same kinds of jobs across companies? If they are the same kinds of jobs, is there any common characteristic(s) the jobs share that would cause companies to devise special compensation packages?

◼ WHO ARE SPECIAL GROUPS?

When we begin to look at company practices with these questions in mind, a pattern begins to emerge. Special treatment, either in the form of add-on packages not received by other employees, or in the form of compensation components unique in the organization, tends to focus on a few specific groups. We argue that special groups share two characteristics. First, special groups tend to be placed in positions that have built-in conflict, conflict that arises because different factions place incompatible demands on members of the group. And second, simply facing conflict is not sufficient; the way that this conflict is resolved has important consequences for the success of the company.

When both of these characteristics are present, we tend to find distinctive compensation practices adopted to meet the needs of these special groups. Exhibit 11.14 describes the nature of the conflicts faced by such special groups as supervisors, top management, boards of directors, scientists and engineers, sales personnel, and contingent workers.

EXHIBIT 11.14 Conflicts Faced by Special Groups

Special Group	Type of Conflict Faced
Supervisors	Caught between upper management and employees. Must balance need to achieve organization's objectives with importance of helping employees satisfy personal needs. If unsuccessful, either corporate profit or employee morale suffers.
Top Management	Stockholders want healthy return on investment. Government wants compliance with laws. Executive must decide between strategies that maximize short-run gains at expense of long run versus directions that focus on long run.
Board of Directors	Face possibility that disgruntled stockholders may sue over corporate strategies that don't "pan out."
Professional Employees	May be torn between goals, objectives, and ethical standards of their profession (e.g., should an engineer leak information about a product flaw, even though that information may hurt corporate profits) and demands of an employer concerned more with the profit motive.
Sales Staff	Often go for extended periods in the field with little supervision. Challenge is to stay motivated and continue making sales calls even in the face of limited contact or scrutiny from manager.
Contingent Workers	Play an important "safety valve" role for companies. When demand is high, more are hired. When demand drops, these are the first workers downsized. Employment status is highly insecure and challenge is to find low cost ways to motivate.
Dot-Com Employees	Must adjust rapidly to a changing environment where the only rule is: "There are no rules."

■ COMPENSATION STRATEGY FOR SPECIAL GROUPS

Supervisors

Remember, supervisors are caught between the demands of upper management in terms of production and the needs of employees in terms of rewards and reinforcements. The major challenge in compensating supervisors centres on equity. Some incentive must be provided to entice hourly employees to accept the challenges of being a supervisor. For many years, the strategy was to treat supervisors like lower-level managers. But, in so doing, the existing job evaluation system sometimes left these supervisors making less money than the top paid employees they supervised. As you might imagine, this created little incentive to take on the extra work involved. More recently, organizations have devised several strategies to attract workers to supervisory jobs. The most popular method is to key the base salary of supervisors to some amount exceeding the top paid subordinate in the unit (5 percent to 30 percent represents the typical size of the differential). Another method to maintain equitable differentials is simply to pay supervisors for scheduled overtime. The current trend in supervisory compensation centres on increased use of variable pay.

Corporate Directors

A typical board of directors consists of 10 outside and 3 inside directors, each having a term averaging three years. Historically, directors frequently were given the role of "rubber stamping" decisions made by top management. Such boards were stacked with people affiliated in some way with the organization. Modern corporate boards have changed considerably. Approximately two-thirds of boards now include more outside directors than inside directors. Outside members now include unaffiliated business executives and major shareholders. Outside directors usually are paid higher compensation, probably because it takes a greater incentive to get them to participate. Direct compensation includes an annual retainer, attendance fees, and fees for participation on subcommittees.

In addition to cash compensation, there is an increasing emphasis on director rewards that link to corporate performance. Shareholders are holding directors accountable for firm performance. Reflecting this trend of linking pay to performance, more pay is stock based (40 percent of total compensation),[39] with 62 percent of companies giving directors some form of outright stock grant or more restricted stock options.[40]

Executive Compensation

How would you like to make $3.1 million per year? That is the 2002 average (salary plus bonus) for the ten highest-paid Canadian chief executive officers (CEOs). Add long-term incentive plans, and the average dollar value of total compensation for these executives rises to a mind-boggling $16,341,000.[41] The granting of stock options has gradually played a bigger role in executive compensation.

Exhibit 11.15 shows total compensation for the top ten executives in Canada in 2002. Notice that most of the top ten, as is true for many highly paid executives, reap the greatest rewards from long-term incentives, usually by exercising stock options. Many critics argue that this level of compensation for executives is excessive.[42] Are the critics right? One way to answer the question is to look at the different ways people say executive compensation is determined and ask, "Does this seem reasonable?"

Possible Explanations for CEO Compensation.   One approach to explain why executives receive such large sums of money involves *social comparisons*.[43] In this view executive salaries bear a consistent relative relationship to compensation of lower-level employees. When salaries of

EXHIBIT 11.15 Compensation for Executives in Canada 2002

Name	Company	2002 Salary + Bonus	Long-Term Incentive	Total
Frank Stronach	Magna International	$ 314,080	$51,823,200	$52,137,280
Travis Engen	Alcan	$4,444,232	$13,011,410	$17,455,642
Don Wright	TD Bank Financial	$ 800,000	$11,778,675	$12,578,675
Belinda Stronach	Magna International	$6,388,340	$ 6,132,224	$12,520,564
Paul Tellier	CN Railway	$2,357,170	$ 9,904,214	$12,261,385
Gwyn Morgan	EnCana	$3,681,667	$ 8,403,210	$12,084,877
Jean Monty	BCE	$2,028,500	$ 9,769,500	$11,798,000
Paul Hastings	QLT	$1,142,555	$10,509,855	$11,652,410
Vic De Zen	Royal Group Tech.	$6,129,548	$ 4,480,000	$10,609,548
Dominic Dalessandro	Manulife Financial	$3,600,000	$ 6,707,989	$10,307,989

Source: "The Top 1000: Canada's Power Book – 50 Best Paid Executives," *ROB Magazine*, July 2003.

lower-level employees rise in response to market forces, top executive salaries also rise to maintain the same relative relationship. In general, managers who are in the second level of a company earn about two-thirds of a CEO's salary, while the next level down earns slightly more than half of a CEO's salary.[44] Much of the criticism of this theory, and an important source of criticism about executive compensation in general, is the gradual increase in the spread between executives' compensation and the average salaries of the people they employ, particularly in the United States, where in 1980, CEOs received about 42 times the average salary of workers. By 1999 U.S. top executives were paid 475 times the average factory worker.[45] As a point of reference, the corresponding differential in Japan is under 20.[46] Both these pieces of information suggest that a social comparison explanation is not sufficient to explain why executive wages are as high as they are.

A second approach to understanding executive compensation focuses less on the difference in wages between executive and other jobs, and more on explaining the level of executive wages. The premise in this *economic approach* is that the worth of a CEO should correspond closely to some measure of company success, such as profitability or sales. Intuitively, this explanation makes sense. There is also empirical support. Numerous studies over the past 30 years demonstrate that executive pay bears some relationship to company success.[47] A recent article analyzing the results from over 100 executive pay studies found empirical evidence that firm size (sales or number of employees) is by far the best predictor of CEO compensation. The size variables are nine times better at explaining executive compensation than are any of the performance measures. How big the firm is explains what the boss gets paid better than how well he performs![48]

Some evidence contradicts this though. One recent study combined both social comparison and economic explanations to try to better understand CEO salaries. Both of these explanations turned out to be significant. Size and profitability affected level of compensation. But social comparisons did also. In this study the social comparison was between CEOs and the wages of the board of directors. It seems that CEO salaries rose, on average, 51 percent for every $100,000 more that was earned by directors on the board.[49] Recognizing this, CEOs sometimes lobby to get a board loaded with directors who are highly paid in their primary jobs.

A third view of CEO salaries, called *agency theory*, incorporates the political motivations that are an inevitable part of the corporate world. Sometimes, this argument runs, CEOs make decisions that aren't in the economic best interest of the firm and its shareholders. One variant on this view suggests that the normal behaviour of a CEO is self-protective—CEOs make decisions to solidify their position and to maximize the rewards they personally receive.[50]

Agency theory argues that executive compensation should be designed to ensure that executives have the best interests of stockholders in mind when they make decisions. The outcome has been to use some form of long-term incentive plan, most commonly stock options. A survey of 500 firms found the use of long-term incentives rising for CEOs from 33 percent of the package in 1990 to 39 percent in 1995.[51] In the simplest form, an executive is given the option to purchase shares of the company stock at some future date for an amount equal to the fair market price at the time the option is granted. There is a built-in incentive for an executive to increase the value of the firm. Stock prices rise. The executive exercises the option to buy the stock at the agreed-upon price. Because the stock price has risen in the interim, the executive profits from the stock sale.

Although this sounds like an effective tool to motivate executives, there still are many critics.[52] The major complaint is that stock options don't have a downside risk. If stock prices rise, the stock options are exercised. If stocks don't improve, the executive suffers no out-of-pocket losses. Some argue that executive compensation should move more towards requiring executives to own stock, and not just to the option to buy.[53] With the threat of possible financial loss and the hopes of possible substantial gains, motivation might be higher. Some early evidence supports this position. In three industries in which executives had large stock holdings, firms outperformed other industries in which executives had little or no current stock investment.

The second trend in response to complaints about excessive executive compensation is increasing government regulation. For example, the Ontario Securities Commission has rules regarding disclosure of executive compensation for companies listed on the TSX. The chief executive officer's pay always must be disclosed, as well as that of the next four highest paid employees. Furthermore, boards of directors must disclose how they make executive compensation decisions. In the public sector, the Ontario government has required since 1996 that salaries for provincial government employees earning $100,000 or more be publicly disclosed. The law also applies to employees in the broader public sector, including hospitals, universities, school boards, crown agencies, and municipalities.

Components of an Executive Compensation Package.   There are five basic elements of most executive compensation packages: (1) base salary, (2) short-term (annual) incentives or bonuses, (3) long-term incentives and capital appreciation plans, (4) employee benefits, and (5) perquisites. Because of the changing nature of tax legislation, each of these at one time or another has received considerable attention in designing executive compensation packages. Companies are now placing more and more emphasis on incentives at the expense of base salary. Such a change in emphasis signals the growing importance attached to making decisions that ensure profitability and survival of a company.

Base Salary.   As noted earlier, being competitive is a very important factor in the determination of executive base pay. But competitive levels of compensation vary widely across industries. Exhibit 11.16 shows the top base salaries of CEOs in different industries.

Although formalized job evaluation still plays an occasional role in determining executive base pay, other sources are much more important. Particularly important is the opinion of a compensation committee of the company's board of directors.[54] Frequently this compensation committee will take over some of the data analysis tasks previously performed by the chief human resources officer, even going so far as to analyze salary survey data and performance records for executives of comparably sized firms.[55] One empirical study suggests the most common behaviour (60 percent of the cases) of executive compensation committees is to identify major competitors and set the CEO's compensation at a level between the best and worst of these comparison groups.[56]

EXHIBIT 11.16 The Top Base Salaries across Industries

Industry	Name/Company	Base Salary
Publishing	Richard Harrington/Thomson	$1,931,592
Aluminum	Travis Engen/Alcan	$1,923,740
Railway	Paul Tellier/CN Railway	$1,727,440
Manufacturing	Robert Brown/Bombardier	$1,500,000
Business Products	Robert Burton/Moore	$1,480,203
Chemicals	Jeffrey Lipton/Nova Chemicals	$1,413,360
Paper	Pierre-Karl Peladeau/Quebecor	$1,354,305
Banking	Peter Godsoe/Bank of Nova Scotia	$1,350,000
Telecommunications	Frank Dunn/Nortel Networks	$1,295,580
Natural Resources	William Doyle/Potash Corp. of Sask.	$1,275,950

Source: "The Top 1000: Canada's Power Book – 50 Best Paid Executives," *ROB Magazine*, July 2003.

Bonuses. Annual bonuses often play a major role in executive compensation and are primarily designed to motivate better performance. Most striking is the rapid rise in popularity of this type of compensation. Only 15 years ago just 36 percent of companies gave annual bonuses. Today bonuses are given to 90 percent of executives. The types of organizations relying almost exclusively on base salary for total direct compensation typically have one or more of the following characteristics: (1) tight control of stock ownership, (2) not-for-profit institutions, or (3) firms operating in regulated industries.

Long-Term Incentive and Capital Appreciation Plans. Long-term incentives now account for 40 percent of total executive compensation, up from 28 percent a decade ago.[57] By far the most common long-term incentive remains the executive stock option. Because many of the highest reported executive pay packages can be traced to stock options, critics have focused on their use and abuse. One clear complaint is that stock options don't pay for performance of the executive. In a stock market that is rising on all fronts, executives can exercise options at much higher prices than the initial grant price—and the payouts likely will be attributable to general market increases rather than to any specific action by the executive. Efforts to counter this undeserved reward are linked to the rise of other types of long-term incentives, some of which require the executive to "beat the market" or hit certain performance targets specifically linked to firm performance. Exhibit 11.17 identifies other types of long-term incentives and generally describes their main features.[58] Clearly, in today's more turbulent stock market, stock options are not the "mother lode" they were in the 90s. Options granted at one price quickly become poor motivational tools when the stock price drops far below that figure. Many companies now scramble to grant new options at lower prices, reflecting better the realities of a declining market.

Executive Benefits. Since many benefits are tied to income level (e.g., life insurance, disability insurance, pension plans), executives typically receive higher benefits than most other exempt employees. Beyond the typical benefits outlined in Chapter 9, however, many executives also receive additional life insurance, exclusions from deductibles for health-care costs, and supplementary pension income exceeding the maximum limits permissible under legal guidelines for registered (eligible for tax deductions) pension plans.

Executive Perquisites. Perquisites, or "perks," probably have the same genesis as the expression "rank has its privileges." Indeed, life at the top has its rewards, designed to satisfy several

EXHIBIT | **11.17** | Long-Term Incentives for Executives

Type	Description
Incentive Stock Options	Purchase of stock at a stipulated price in a given time period.
Phantom Stock Plans	Cash or stock award determined by increase in stock price at a fixed future date.
Stock Appreciation Rights	Cash or stock award determined by increase in stock price during any time chosen (by the executive) in the option period.
Restricted Stock Plans	Grant of stock at a reduced price with the condition it may not be sold before a specified date.
Performance Share/Unit Plans	Cash or stock award earned through achieving specific goals.

Source: Sibson & Co. 1990 Executive Compensation Report.

types of executive needs. One type of perk could be classified as internal, providing a little something extra while the executive is inside the company: luxury offices, executive dining rooms, special parking. A second category also is designed to be company-related, but for business conducted externally: company-paid membership in clubs/associations, payment of hotel, resort, airplane, and auto expenses.

The final category of perquisites should be totally isolated from the first two because of the differential tax status. This category, called personal perks, includes such things as low-cost loans, personal and legal counselling, free home repairs and improvements, personal use of company property, and expenses for vacation homes.[59]

Compensation of Scientists and Engineers in High-Technology Industries

The compensation of scientists and engineers focuses on rewarding them for their special scientific or intellectual training. Here lies one of the special compensation problems that scientists and engineers face. Consider the freshly minted electrical engineer who graduates with all the latest knowledge in the field. For the first few years after graduation this knowledge is a valuable resource for engineering projects in which new applications of the latest theories are a primary objective. Gradually, though, this engineer's knowledge starts to become obsolete. Team leaders begin to look to newer graduates for fresh ideas. If you track the salaries of these employees, there is a close resemblance between pay increases and knowledge obsolescence. Early years bring larger-than-average (relative to employees in other occupations) increases. After 10 years, increases drop below average, and become downright puny in the 15–20-year time frame. Partly because salary plateaus arise, many scientists and engineers make career changes such as moving into management or temporarily leaving business to update their technical knowledge. In recent years some firms have tried to deal with the plateau effect and also accommodate the different career motivations of mature scientists and engineers.

The result has been the creation of dual career tracks. Exhibit 11.18 shows a typical **dual career ladder**. Notice that dual ladders provide exactly that: two different ways of progressing in an organization, each reflecting different types of contributions to the organization's mission. The first, or managerial ladder, ascends through increasing responsibility for supervision or direction of people. The professional track ascends through increasing contributions of a professional nature which do not mainly entail the supervision of employees. Scientists and engineers have the

dual career ladder

career progression on either a managerial path or a professional path

EXHIBIT **11.18** IBM Dual Ladders

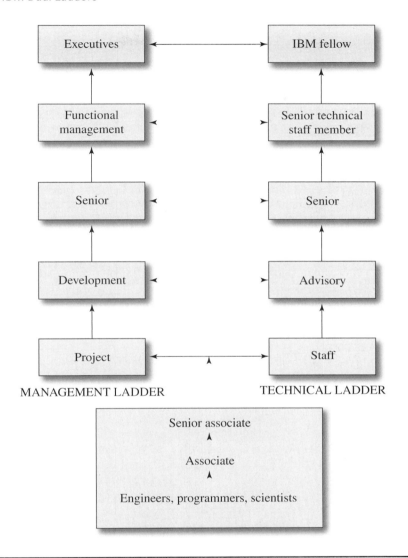

MANAGEMENT LADDER

TECHNICAL LADDER

opportunity at some stage in their careers to consider a management track or to continue along the scientific track. Not only do dual tracks offer greater advancement opportunities for scientists and engineers, but maximum base pay in the technical track can approximate that of upper management positions.

A second problem in designing the compensation package of scientists and engineers centres on the question of equity. The very nature of technical knowledge and its dissemination requires the relatively close association of scientist and engineers across organizations. In fact, scientists and engineers tend to compare themselves for equity purposes with other graduates who entered the labour market at the same time period. Partly because of this, and because of the volatile nature of both jobs and salaries in these occupations, organizations rely heavily on external market data in pricing their base pay.[60] This has resulted in the use of maturity curves.

Maturity curves reflect the relationship between scientist/engineer compensation and years of experience in the labour market. Generally, surveying organizations ask for information about salaries as a function of years since the incumbent(s) last received a degree. This is intended to measure the half-life of technical obsolescence. In fact, a plot of these data, with appropriate smoothing to eliminate aberrations, typically shows curves that are steep for the first five to seven years and then rise more gradually as technical obsolescence erodes the value of jobs. Exhibit 11.19 illustrates such a graph with somewhat greater sophistication built into it, in that different graphs are constructed for different levels of performance.

Scientists and engineers also receive performance-based incentives such as profit sharing and stock ownership incentives.[61] Other incentives link payment of specific cash amounts to

---

EXHIBIT 11.19 Maturity Curve Showing Years since Last Degree Relative to Salary

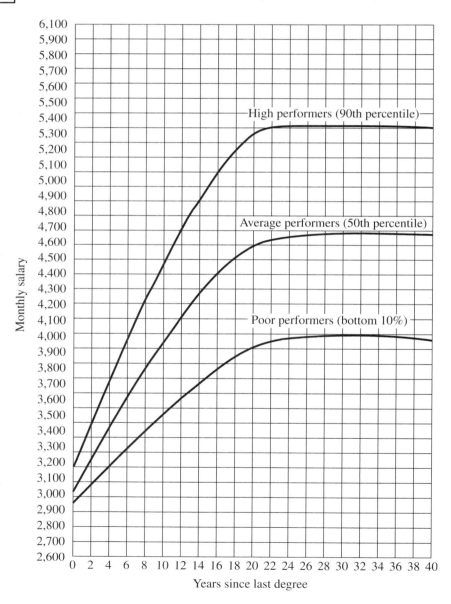

completion of specific projects on or before agreed-upon deadlines. Post-hiring bonuses are also paid for such achievements as patents, publications, election to professional societies, and attainment of professional licenses.

Finally, organizations provide perks that satisfy the unique needs of scientists and engineers, such as flexible work schedules, large offices, campuslike environments, and lavish athletic facilities. The strategic importance of these groups dictates that both mind and body be kept active.

Sales Force Compensation

The sales staff spans the all-important boundary between the organization and consumers of the organization's goods or services. Sales staff must be sensitive to changing consumer tastes, and, therefore, there is a growing trend toward linking sales compensation to customer satisfaction measures, with about one-third of all companies reporting use of such quality-based measures.[62] The role of interacting in the field with customers requires individuals with high initiative who can work under low supervision for extended periods of time, and so, there is much more reliance on incentive payments tied to individual performance. Thus, even when salespeople are in the field—and relatively unsupervised—there is always a motivation to perform. Most sales employees at every organization level have some component of pay, usually a large one, that is an incentive tied to performance.

Designing a Sales Compensation Plan. Four major factors influence the design of sales compensation packages: (1) the nature of people who enter the sales profession, (2) organizational strategy, (3) competitor practices, and (4) product to be sold.

People Who Enter the Sales Profession. Popular stereotypes of salespeople characterize them as heavily motivated by financial compensation. One study supports this perception, with salespeople ranking pay significantly higher than five other forms of reward.[63] These values almost dictate that the primary focus of sales compensation should be on direct financial rewards (base pay + incentives).

Organizational Strategy. A sales compensation plan should link desired behaviours of salespeople to organizational strategy.[64] This is particularly true in the Internet age. As more sales dollars are tied to computer-based transactions, the role of sales personnel also will change.[65] Salespeople must know when to stress customer service and when to stress volume sales. And, when volume sales are the goal, which products should be pushed hardest? Strategic plans signal which behaviours are important. For example, emphasis on customer service to build market share, or movement into geographic areas with low potential, may limit sales volume. Alternatively, an organization may want to motivate aggressive sales behaviour. A straight commission-based incentive plan will focus sales efforts in this direction, to the possible exclusion of supportive tasks such as processing customer returns.

Competitor Practices. The very nature of sales positions means that competitors will cross paths, at least in their quest for potential customers. This provides the opportunity to chat about relative compensation packages, an opportunity which salespeople frequently take. To ensure that the comparison is favourable, the organization should identify a compensation level strategy that explicitly indicates target salaries for different sales groups and performance levels.

Product to Be Sold. Consider a product which, by its very technical nature, takes time to understand and thus to fully develop an effective sales presentation. Such products are said to have high barriers to entry, meaning considerable training is needed to become effective in the field. Compensation in this situation usually includes a large base pay component, minimizing the risk a sales representative will face, and encouraging entry into the necessary training program. At the opposite extreme are products with lower barriers to entry, where the knowledge needed to make an effective sales presentation is relatively easy to acquire. These product lines are sold more often using a higher incentive component, thus paying more for actual sales than for taking the time to learn the necessary skills.

Base compensation tends to be more important with easily sold products but incentives become more important when willingness to work hard may make the difference between success and failure. One recent study argues convincingly that setting sales targets or quotas is the most important, and most difficult, part of sales compensation. Several clues help tell you if your quotas are reasonable: (1) Can the salesforce tell you explicitly how the quotas are set? (2) In periods when the company hits its business plan, does 60–70 percent of the sales force hit quota? (3) Do high performers hit their target consistently? (4) Do low performers show improvement over time?[66]

Most jobs do not fit the ideal specifications for either of the two extremes, represented by straight salary or straight commission plans. A combination plan is intended to capture the best of both these plans. A guaranteed straight salary can be linked to performance of nonsales functions such as customer service, while a commission for sales volume yields the incentive to sell. A plan combining these two features signals the intent of the organization to ensure that both types of activities occur.

Compensation for Contingent Workers

About one of every 10 workers is employed in a nontraditional work relationship.[67] For our purposes let's call contingent workers anyone who works through a temporary help agency, on an on-call basis, through a contract company, or as an independent contractor. The first two of these groups typically earn less than workers in traditional arrangements; the latter two more.

Why the move to contingent workers? Part of the answer may be cost savings. Employee benefit costs are about half for contingent workers.[68] But sometimes wages are higher. The real reason for contingent workers may be the added flexibility such employment offers the employer. In today's fast-paced marketplace, lean and flexible are desirable characteristics. And contingent workers offer this option. In fact, recent evidence suggests that the most rapidly growing segment of contingent workers is "technical experts," added to assist in efforts to build virtual corporations.[69]

A major compensation challenge for contingent workers, as with all our special group employees, is identifying ways to deal with equity problems. Contingent workers may work alongside permanent workers, yet often receive lower wages and benefits for the same work. Employers deal with this potential source of inequity on two fronts, one traditional and one that challenges the very way we think about employment and careers. One company response is to view contingent workers as a pool of candidates for more permanent hiring status. High performers may be moved off contingent status and afforded more employment stability.

A second way to look at contingent workers is to champion the idea of boundaryless careers.[70] At least for high-skilled contingent workers, it is increasingly popular to view careers as a series of opportunities to acquire valuable increments in knowledge and skills. Sometimes these opportunities arise in one organization through transfers across different jobs. But knowledge acquisition may even be faster for employees willing to forgo traditional job security and accept temporary assignments that quickly enhance their skill repertoire. In this framework, contingent status isn't a penalty or cause of dissatisfaction. Rather, employees who accept the idea of boundaryless careers may view contingent status as part of a fast-track developmental sequence. Lower wages are offset by opportunities for rapid development of skills—opportunities that might not be so readily available in more traditional employment arrangements. Companies such as General Electric that promote this reward—enhanced employability status through acquisition of highly demanded skills—may actually have tapped into an underutilized reward dimension.

Compensating Dot-Com Employees

We place dot-com employees, those who work for Internet companies, as a special group because they must adjust to rapidly changing work environments, often with no rules to govern what is essentially a new frontier. The obvious question, then, is, What's different about compensation for these employees? Well, if you look at the components of compensation, nothing appears new.[71] Base pay, short-term variable pay, stock options, and benefits are all part of the package. But the mix of ingredients and the importance of them is certainly different. The most striking difference in dot-com compensation is the early reliance on stock options to lure and retain talented people. Before dot-coms mature, historically (if there is any such thing as history with this rapidly changing industry) they have relied heavily on long-term incentives—stock options and stock grants—to attract and motivate workers. Recent reports, though, indicate movement away from stocks—largely because of the roller coaster market—and greater use of other compensation alternatives.[72] Most of the movement has been towards short-term incentives and, increasingly, competitive base salaries.[73] And here is where the big compensation problem arises for dot-coms: Dot-com jobs tend to be very structured to the individual, moulding the job to personal skills. Moreover, jobs tend to change rapidly, to fit changing demands in a highly volatile industry. These characteristics don't fit at all well with a traditional job evaluation/internal equity approach to base wages. Dot-coms meet this challenge by setting initial base wages at the external market level. Even this is difficult, though. Even good salary surveys tend to be 3–6 months out of date by the time all the information is gathered and analyzed. Dot-com jobs can change literally overnight. And their salaries change with them. Dot-coms have begun to do real-time salary surveys on key price-sensitive jobs. And once market rates are determined, any further salary increase is linked to subjective estimates of value added by specific employees.[74]

CONCLUSION

In conclusion, special groups share two common characteristics: They all have jobs with high potential for conflict, and resolution of this conflict is central to the goals of the organization. Probably because of these characteristics, special groups receive compensation treatment that differs from other employees. Unfortunately, most of this compensation differentiation is prescriptive in nature, and little is known about the specific roles assumed by special groups and the functions compensation should assume in motivating appropriate performance. Future practice and research should focus on answering these questions.

CHAPTER SUMMARY

1. Three short-term individual pay-for-performance plans are: merit pay, lump sum bonuses, and individual spot awards.
2. Four categories of performance measures are: customer-focused measures such as on-time delivery and market share, financially focused measures such as revenue growth and return on invested capital, capability-focused measures such as employee satisfaction and patents, and internal process-focused measures such as budget-to-actual expenses and program implementation.
3. Five causes of problems with team compensation systems are: the need for different compensation programs for different types of teams; the loss of motivational impact if the team is very large; overly complex team compensation plans; lack of control by teams over what they are measured on; and poor communication of team-based plans.

4. Seven key issues in designing a gain-sharing plan are: strength of reinforcement, productivity standards, sharing the gains between management and workers, scope of the formula, perceived fairness of the formula, ease of administration, and production variability.

5. Employee stock ownership plans offer employees the opportunity to purchase company stock, often partially or fully matched by employer-paid stock for the employee. Stock options provide an employee with the right to purchase stock at a specified price for a fixed time period. Broad-based option plans are stock grants to employees over a specified time frame.

6. Three possible explanations for extremely high levels of CEO compensation are: social comparisons to salaries of lower-level employees, the desirability of a relationship between pay and company success, and the agency theory suggestion that CEOs act with a self-protecting, political motivation.

7. The five basic elements of executive compensation packages are: base salary, short-term (annual) incentives or bonuses, long-term incentives and capital accumulation plans, employee benefits, and perquisites.

8. Dual career ladders are two different ways of progressing in an organization, one through a managerial ladder, the other through a scientific ladder. This approach helps to deal with the plateauing effect of gradual technological obsolescence, and accommodates the opportunity for mature scientists and engineers to switch to the management ladder. Maturity curves reflect the relationship between scientist/engineer compensation and years of experience in the labour market, as pay increases sharply for the first five to seven years and then rises more gradually due to the effect of technological obsolescence.

KEY TERMS

REVIEW QUESTIONS

1. How is an earnings-at-risk plan different from an ordinary gain-sharing or profit-sharing plan? How might earnings-at-risk plans affect attraction and retention of employees?

2. Why are firms moving to different types of long-term incentives for executives in a shift away from stock options?

3. For each of the special groups discussed in this chapter, explain how the issue of equity is especially important. Who are the comparison groups to which special group members might compare themselves to determine if compensation is fair?

EXPERIENTIAL EXERCISES

1. Your boss had lunch yesterday with a CEO in the same town who just implemented a gain-sharing plan. You guessed it...he wants to see if it would work in your company. What conditions would you like to see exist before you would be comfortable making a positive recommendation?

2. As VP of HR at Mentholatum (deep heating rub), you are experiencing turnover problems with top-level employees (directors, vice presidents at all levels). President Yamoto has asked you to fix the problem. Although your primary emphasis might be on having competitive base pay, is there anything you can do in the incentive department? Justify your answer.

3. You own Higgins Tool Coating Company, a high-tech firm specializing in coating of cutting tools (e.g., drill bits, cutting blades) that provides longer life before resharpening is needed. You are concerned that the competition is continuing to develop new coating methods and new applications of this coating in different industries. If you wanted to create a work environment where employees offered more new product suggestions and suggested new industries where these suggestions might be applied, what type of compensation plan might you recommend? What are some of the problems you need to be aware of?

WEB EXERCISE

ESOP Feasibility

ESOP Builders Inc. is a Mississauga, Ontario-based company that assists small- and medium-sized businesses in implementing employee stock ownership plans. The first step is to assess whether such a plan would be feasible, and ESOP Builders has prepared a feasibility questionnaire to assist with this process. Go to the ESOP Builders Web site www.esopbuilders.com and click on "feasibility questionnaire." Complete the questionnaire for a small- or medium-sized company that you are familiar with. Submit the questionnaire for analysis and then review the response you get back. Given the material in the chapter, do you agree with the response from ESOP Builders? Explain why or why not.

CASE

Understanding Stock Options

Note: In order to successfully complete this exercise you do not need to have Internet access; the information required to do the exercise can be found on-line as well as on paper (e.g., *Globe and Mail*). Just look up the company's stock symbol. The calculations can also be made by hand.

Information regarding calculations and data can be found on-line at **http://newman.mgt. buffalo.edu/compensation**, including links to sites displaying current share prices.

Exercise 1

You have been working for Sun Microsystems (symbol SUNW) for about four years as a project manager and doing very well. Upon employment (10/1/1998) you were granted 4,000 nonqualified stock options, which vested over 4 years, at 25 percent a year. The stock price at the date of grant was $40.13 (not adjusted for splits and dividends). How much did you gain? Experiment with different values for the stock price to see what would happen if the stock increased or decreased dramatically. How would these numbers change if all of your options had already vested?

Exercise 2

After graduation you and a friend both got great jobs, you with Dell (DELL) and your friend with Microsoft (MSFT). You both started at the same salary and bonus and got 2,000 non-qualified stock options as a signing bonus (good negotiating!). You received 2,000 stock options at July 28, 1996, and the grant price was $43.69. Your options vest over four years, 25 percent a year, and they expire in 10 years. Your friend's information is exactly the same, except the grant price is $69.69. Compare your friend's gain to yours. Whose stock options appreciated more? Did you earn money? If the stocks climbed 40 percent, what would be the gain? Was it reasonable for you to reject an offer of 1,000 more options at the price of $3,000? How much would you (from the ex-post-perspective) pay for those 1,000 stock options?

Exercise 3

You are sales manager of American Express Co (AXP). Today you have been granted 8,000 nonqualified stock options. The exercise price was chosen so that the options would only be in the money if the stock price increased by more than 10 percent in each of the following years. What will be the exercise price for each of the next five years? At what stock price could you take home $1,000,000 after taxes? What would be your gain, if the stock price increased by 15 percent per year?
Hint: Assume for convenience that all shares vest today.

Exercise 4

You have been chosen to set up a stock option program at a new Canadian airline. The CEO and co-founder holds only 63 percent of the shares. He does not want to lose control over the company, so the number of options you can offer is limited. In order to retain control, the CEO needs 50 percent of the shares plus one more share. (The total stock volume can be found on the Nasdaq homepage **www.nasdaq.com**.) Considering that the company will give out new shares to the option holders and not buy back the stock in the market, how

CASE

many stock options can be granted to employees? You would like the stock price to rise within the first three years at an average of 20 percent a year. Which grant price should you select to make sure that the employees will only get rich when the stock price outperforms the 20 percent offset?

You decided to give 5,000 nonqualified stock options to each of the 100 top employees. Imagine the share price rose to $60. How much would a grantee earn from exercising his options? What would be the cost to the company if the money had been paid as a bonus after the third year?

The CEO earned $10,000,000 (before taxes) from exercising stock options this year. How many options did he get if the exercise price was at $10?

As in the last exercise, assume all shares vest at once.

Financial Background: Stock Options

Making money with shares is pretty easy: One buys shares at a certain price and sells the shares at a different price. The win (or loss) can be calculated by multiplying the number of shares with the difference between the buying price and selling price. For example, buying 5,000 shares at $20 and selling them for $15 will generate a loss of ($20 − $15) × 5000 = $25,000. The only problem is that nobody knows what the share price will be in the future.

A stock option entitles the owner to buy (or sell, but that kind of option is of no relevance to the exercise) a share of a certain company at a certain price (the grant price). If you have an option to buy one share of a company for $10 and the stock price is at $20, you will make a gain of $10 exercising this option. You cannot lose any money with an option, as you don't need to exercise the option when the stock price is below the exercise price (this is why it is called option). Yet if the share price rises, the option will be worth more and more, as the gain for exercising the option will increase even faster.

Example: Company X has a stock price of $500. You have an option to buy this stock at $480. Therefore the option is worth $500 − $480 = $20. If the stock price rises by 10 percent, one share will be worth $550 . . . the option is now worth $550 − $480 = $70, equivalent to a price increase of 350 percent. This effect is also called leverage effect.

Attention hobby-brokers: When buying stock options on the real market you have to pay a certain amount for an option. If the stock price stays below the grant price, THIS MONEY WILL BE LOST. Although the risk of total loss is pretty slim when working with shares, it is clear and present when working with options.

The exercise of stock options is usually limited to a certain period of time (e.g., 10 years after issuance). Therefore, it is reasonable to exercise options before that date if they are "in the money."

Financial Background: Stock Options as Incentives

Stock options are a way to compensate employees while saving money. Doling them out doesn't cost any money. In comparison to shares themselves, stock options have a tremendous advantage: Exercising the options grants only the course difference; the basic value of a share will not be part of the compensation.

CASE

A problem that occurs with this kind of compensation is dilution. Since every exercised stock option increases the number of shares (when not bought back from the market), the percentage of stock owned by the previous stockholders diminishes. This might lead to losing control over the company, when the percentage of stock owned decreases to below 50 percent.

In order to keep employees from exercising options and leaving the company as well as to keep them from conducting measures that, in the short run, lead to increasing stock prices but, in the long run, hurt the company (causing stocks to fall), it might prove helpful to permit the exercise of options only after a certain time. The time frame during which the exercise of the options is not allowed is called the vesting period. Stock options typically vest over four years, 25 percent after each year.

The differences between the different types of stock options used in compensation plans are described in Exhibit 11.17.

PART 4

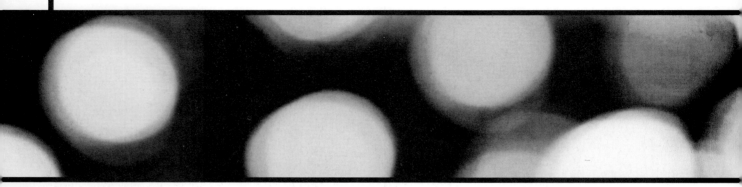

Managing the System

The last part of our total pay model is administration. We have touched on aspects of administration already—the use of budgets in merit increase programs, the "message" that employees receive from their variable pay bonuses, communication and cost control in benefits, and the importance of employee involvement in designing the total compensation system.

Several important issues remain. The first is the significant role that government plays in managing compensation. Laws and regulations are the most obvious government intervention. In Canada, employment standards legislation, pay equity acts, and human rights laws, among others, regulate pay decisions. Government is more than a source of laws and regulations, however. As a major employer, as a consumer of goods and services, and through its fiscal and monetary policies, government affects the supply and demand for labour.

Chapter 13 covers three aspects of managing compensation: costs, communication, and change. One of the key reasons for being systematic about pay decisions is to manage the costs associated with pay decisions. As Chapter 13 will show, a total compensation system is really a device for allocating money in a way that is consistent with the organization's objectives.

Communication and change are linked. What is to be communicated to whom is an important, ongoing issue. In addition to communication, the system must be constantly evaluated to judge its effectiveness. Is it helping the organization achieve the objectives? What information can help us make these judgments? If it is not doing what it should be doing, how do we change it? Any system will founder if it is ineffectively implemented, managed, and communicated.

Chapter 13 also discusses how to organize the compensation department. Which activities should be done in-house and which may be candidates for digitizing and outsourcing are among the issues discussed.

EXHIBIT **IV.1** The Pay Model

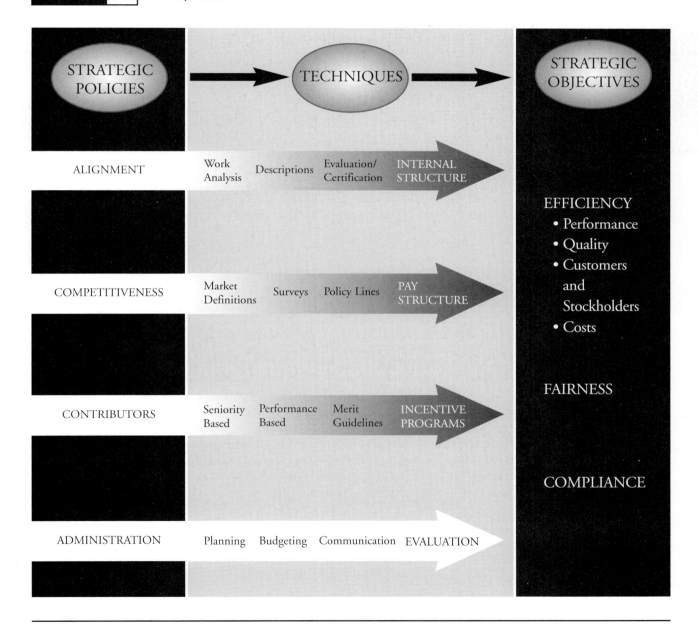

THE ROLE OF GOVERNMENT AND UNIONS IN COMPENSATION

LEARNING OUTCOMES

- *Explain* the role of government in compensation.
- *Describe* the major compensation-related provisions of employment standards legislation.
- *Explain* the impact of human rights legislation on compensation.
- *Discuss* the situation regarding gender discrimination in pay and *explain* what pay equity legislation is intended to accomplish.
- *Describe* four ways in which unions have an impact on wage determination.
- *Explain* why union attitudes regarding pay-for-performance have gradually become more favourable.

A 1939 pay policy handbook for a major corporation outlines this justification for paying different wages to men versus women working on the same jobs:[1]

> The . . . wage curve . . . is not the same for women as for men because of the more transient character of the former, the relative shortness of their activity in industry, the differences in environment required, the extra services that must be provided, overtime limitations, extra help needed for the occasional heavy work, and the general sociological factors not requiring discussion herein. Basically then we have another wage curve . . . for women below and not parallel with the men's curve.

The presumption that people should be paid different wages based on "general sociological factors" was still evident in the 1960s, in newspaper help-wanted ads that specified "perky gal Fridays." The women's movement and subsequent legislation ended such practices. However, legislation does not always achieve what it intends. Nor does it always intend what it achieves. Consequently, *compliance* and *fairness* are continuing compensation issues.

In democratic societies, the legislative process begins when a problem is identified (not all citizens are receiving fair treatment in the workplace) and corrective legislation is proposed (human rights, employment equity, and pay equity). If enough support develops, often as a result of compromises and tradeoffs, the proposed legislation becomes law. Employers, along with other stakeholders, attempt to influence the form any legislation will take.

Once passed, laws are enforced by agencies through rulings, regulations, inspections, and investigations. Companies respond to legislation by auditing and perhaps altering their practices, and perhaps again lobbying for legislative change. The laws and regulations issued by governmental agencies created to enforce the laws have a significant influence on compensation decisions throughout the world.

GOVERNMENT AS PART OF THE EMPLOYMENT RELATIONSHIP

The exact role that government should play in the contemporary workplace depends in part on one's political ideology. Some call for organizations and the government to act in concert to carry out a public policy that protects the interests of employees.[2] Others believe that the best opportunities for employees are created by the constant change and reconfiguring that is inherent in market-based economies; the economy ought to be allowed to adapt and transform, undistorted by government actions.[3] All countries throughout the world must address these issues. However, different countries and cultures have different perspectives. Government is a key stakeholder in compensation decision making. Governments' usual interests are whether procedures for determining pay are fair (e.g., pay equity), safety nets for the unemployed and disadvantaged are sufficient (e.g., minimum wage, unemployment compensation), and employees are protected from exploitation (e.g., overtime pay, child labour). Consequently, company pay practices set the context for national debates on minimum wage, the security and portability of pensions, even the quality of public education and the availability of training. So, in addition to individuals and employers, government is a key party in pay decisions.

Government policy decisions also affect compensation by affecting the supply and demand for labour.

Supply.   Legislation aimed at protecting specific groups also tends to restrict that group's participation in the labour market. For example, compulsory schooling laws restrict the supply of children available to sell hamburgers or to assemble soccer balls. Licensing requirements for certain occupations (plumbers, taxi drivers, psychologists) restrict the number of people who can legally offer a service.

Demand.   Government affects demand for labour most directly as a major employer. A government also indirectly affects labour demand through its purchases (military aircraft, computer systems, paper clips) as well as its public policy decisions. For example, lowering interest rates generally boosts manufacturing of everything from cars to condominiums. Increased business activity translates into increased demand for labour and upward pressure on wages.

This chapter will examine the most important Canadian regulations concerning wages. Because our society continues to wrestle with the issue of discrimination, we will go into some depth about how pay discrimination has been defined and the continuing earnings gap between men and women.

EMPLOYMENT STANDARDS ACTS

Each of the 14 jurisdictions regulating employment across Canada (ten provinces, three territories, and the federal jurisdiction) has enacted legislation, usually named "employment standards acts" specifying minimum terms and conditions of employment.[4] Although there are differences in specific requirements, these laws all specify a minimum hourly wage, paid vacations, paid holidays, standard hours of work and overtime pay, pay for employees who are terminated by the company, minimum age of employment, and equal pay for equal work by men and women. Administrative rules regarding record keeping, statement of wages, and deductions from wages are also prescribed.

Minimum Wage

Minimum wage laws are intended to provide an income floor for workers in society's least productive jobs. The minimum hourly wage varies by jurisdiction, and is increased regularly as the cost of living rises. Workers who are paid slightly above minimum wage often benefit as well when these increases are mandated. As legislation forces pay rates at the lowest end of the scale to move up, pay rates above the minimum often increase to maintain differentials. This shift in pay structure does not affect all industries equally. For example, the lowest rates paid in the software, chemical, oil, and pharmaceutical industries already are well above minimum; any legislative change would have little direct impact in these industries. In contrast, retailing and service firms tend to pay at or near minimum wage for many clerks and sales personnel. When legislation results in substantially higher labour costs for these firms, they may consider substituting non-human forms of capital by using robots, or reducing the number of jobs available.

Minimum wage discussion is also relevant to the social good of the people who are not faring well in the market economy.[5] Some make the case that continuing a low minimum wage permits the continuation of boring, dead-end jobs that ought to be modernized. If employers are forced to pay higher wages, they will find it worthwhile to offer training to employees to increase their economic value. Marriott, for example, boasts of helping its low-wage cleaning staff apply for federal earned income tax credits. Marriott and others can get by paying minimum wages because of all the taxpayer-financed government benefit programs that exist to help low-income wage earners.

So the topic stirs endless debate. What is certain is that people working at or near the minimum wage who continue to work definitely do benefit from mandated minimum wage increases, and other workers in higher-level jobs in those same companies may also benefit. Yet fewer workers will be hired or hours will be cut if the increased costs cannot be passed on to consumers or offset by increased productivity.

Paid Vacation

Each jurisdiction recognizes that vacations are necessary to ensure continued employee health and productivity. The specific amounts of minimum vacation vary across jurisdictions, but the basic structure and philosophy of the laws regarding vacations are similar across the country. In most cases, the minimum amount of vacation is either two weeks or three weeks per year.

Paid Holidays

Each jurisdiction recognizes that there are days of special significance that citizens celebrate together, and provide for paid days off from work to observe these holidays. The number of paid holidays varies from five to nine across the country, but all jurisdictions include New Year's Day, Good Friday, Canada Day, Labour Day, and Christmas.

Standard Hours of Work and Overtime Pay

Employment standards legislation sets out the standard hours of work for employees, and provides for overtime pay when an employee is required to work more than these standard hours. Standard hours of work vary between 40 hours per week and 48 hours per week across jurisdictions, and overtime pay is one-and-one-half times regular pay in almost all cases. Meal breaks and rest periods also are required during working hours, but do not have to be paid. Sometimes counting the hours of work becomes a contest, as shown in Exhibit 12.1.

The original intent of overtime pay laws was to share available work by making hiring additional workers a less costly option than scheduling overtime for current employees. However, the

| **EXHIBIT** | **12.1** | There's no such thing as a free . . . |

Gainers Workers Must Pay to Use Bathroom

EDMONTON—Employees at Gainers Inc. are now docked pay for every bathroom break visit made outside of breaks and lunch hour under regulations brought in last week by company owner Burns Meats Ltd.

A notice posted in the meat-packing plant tells employees that abusing washroom visits has lowered productivity. If employees need to use the bathroom outside of breaks, they must report to a supervisor, who records the time of departure and return. The time is tabulated at the end of the week and pay cheques are deducted based on an employee's hourly wage.

"How can they charge you for going to the washroom?" asked one angry employee.

The man said one worker at the plant had a kidney transplant and has to use the washroom often.

"Because of this system, he had to hold it in [between breaks] for a whole week. He went once for three minutes and was charged 43 cents."

Such washroom rules are rare but there is nothing in the Alberta employment standards code that requires a person to be paid when they don't work, said Kathy Lazowski, a public affairs officer with Alberta Labour.

—Canadian Press

workplace has changed considerably over the years, Today, overtime pay is often the least costly option. Contemporary employers face (1) an increasingly skilled workforce with higher training costs per employee and (2) higher benefit costs, often a fixed cost per employee. These factors have lowered the break-even point at which it pays employers to schedule longer hours and pay the overtime premium, rather than hire, train, and pay benefits for more employees. Additionally, in times of low unemployment, hiring new employees is a difficult and expensive process.

Pay on Termination of Employment

In the event that the company terminates the employment of one of its workers, certain payments are required to be made. The employer must provide a minimum notice of termination during which time the employee continues to be paid or else receives the same payment in lieu of notice. This notice period varies from one week to eight weeks, depending on the employee's length of service. Two jurisdictions (Ontario and federal) require additional severance pay to be provided, in certain circumstances, to an individual employee who is terminated.

In situations where a group of employees are terminated, such as when a business closes or downsizes, employment standards legislation across the country (other than in Prince Edward Island) requires special additional notice (or pay in lieu thereof) to be provided to the workers affected. The minimum number of employees considered a group for this purpose varies between 10 and 50, and the amount of additional notice varies from 4 weeks to 18 weeks, depending on the number of employees being terminated. Some jurisdictions require the employer to take responsibility for organizing a joint planning committee to consider how terminations could be avoided, or to help employees find alternative employment.

Minimum Age of Employment

Restrictions on child labour were one of the primary reasons for the creation of employment laws, in recognition of the importance of ensuring that children have access to education, and of protecting their safe and normal development. All jurisdictions have established a minimum age for employment, ranging from 14 to 17. These rules are qualified by exemptions for specified occupations such as certain types of agricultural work and vocational training programs.

Equal Pay for Equal Work by Men and Women

All jurisdictions require that men and women who are doing similar work be paid equally. The legislation also applies to men and women doing substantially the same work, based on an assessment of skill, effort, responsibility, and working conditions required in each case. For example, if the only difference between the work of a male orderly and a female nursing assistant is that the orderly occasionally does heavy lifting, then the work is considered to be substantially the same.

■ HUMAN RIGHTS LAWS

Canada is a world leader in the protection of basic human rights, and a *Charter of Rights and Freedoms* forms part of its Constitution.[6] As the Canadian workforce has become more diverse, the issue of workplace discrimination has become increasingly important. The Charter specifically permits the development of programs to relieve the situation of historically disadvantaged groups. For example, employment equity programs designed to increase the number of women, visible minorities, Aboriginal people, and people with disabilities in positions where they have been underrepresented in the past, are mandated by law in the federal jurisdiction.

Human rights legislation has been enacted in every jurisdiction in Canada, and guarantees every person equal treatment in regard to employment and opportunity for employment regardless of race, colour, creed/religion, sex, sexual orientation, marital status, age, or mental or physical disability. Employment applications and interviews are in violation of the law if they ask for any information in these areas. Hiring, firing, training, and promotion decisions based on these grounds are prohibited. Compensation decisions based on any of these grounds are also illegal. Employers must ensure that their compensation systems treat all groups neutrally, compensating for merit rather than membership in a particular group.

Enforcement of human rights legislation is complaint-based. Employees who believe they have been discriminated against must make a complaint to the appropriate human rights commission, which will then launch an investigation and assess penalties if discrimination is deemed to have occurred.

■ PAY EQUITY

Across North America, Europe, and Australia, gender remains the best predictor of wages, a factor surpassing in importance education, experience, or unionization. In 2001, Canadian women working full-time earned approximately 70 percent of the amount that full-time male workers earned.[7] This difference is called the "**wage gap**."

The Wage Gap

wage gap

the amount by which the average pay for female workers is less than the average pay for male workers

A variety of factors contribute to the wage gap. Some of the more important factors, shown in Exhibit 12.2, include the following:

1. Differences in the occupational attainment and the jobs held by men and women.
2. Differences in personal work-related characteristics and work behaviours.
3. Differences among industries and firms.
4. Differences in union membership.
5. The presence of discrimination.

First let us examine some data, then some conflicting beliefs.

EXHIBIT | **12.2** | Possible Determinants of Pay Differences

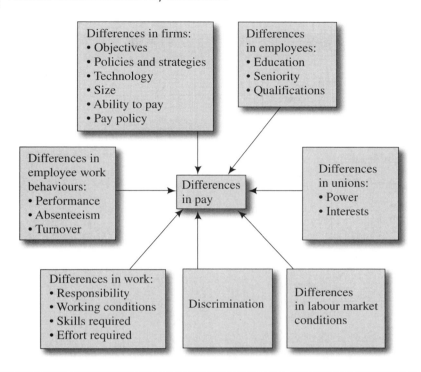

Source: George T Milkovich, "The Emerging Debate," in *Comparable Worth: Issues and Alternatives*, ed. E. Robert Livernash (Washington, DC: Equal Employment Advisory Council, 1980).

Differences in Occupational Attainment

occupational segregation

the historical segregation of women into a small number of occupations such clerical, sales, nursing, and teaching

One of the most important factors in the pay gap is differences in jobs held by men and women. Traditionally, female workers were segregated in occupations such as clerical, sales, nursing, and teaching. Over the last 25 years, not that much has changed, other than an increase in women holding managerial jobs, as shown in Exhibit 12.3. Thus **occupational segregation** is a persistent phenonmenon.

Increased levels of occupational attainment do not automatically mean that the wage gap will close. A study of women in science and engineering professions finds that even though they have already cleared the hurdles of misguided high school guidance counsellors and/or lack of peer support or role models, women scientists and engineers are almost twice as likely as males to leave these occupations.[8]

For a variety of reasons, the relatively small wage gap among younger cohorts (i.e., recent university graduates) tends to increase as the cohort ages.[9] Perhaps women continue to be more likely to drop out of the labour force at some point for family reasons, or perhaps the barriers to continued advancement become more substantial at higher levels in the job hierarchy. A study of MBAs found that 10 to 15 years after graduation, in addition to a pay gap there is also a gender-based chasm in such subjective measures as career satisfaction, boss appreciation, and feelings of discrimination.[10] Fully 46 percent of women said they had experienced discrimination; only 9 percent of men said they had. The most common problem women reported was that less qualified men were chosen for promotions over them. Additionally, they felt that at higher levels discrimination was more subtle and harder to prove. Clearly, many professional women and minorities believe they operate in less supportive work environments than their white male colleagues.[11]

EXHIBIT 12.3 Male/Female Employment by Occupation, 1987, 1994, and 2002

	1987			1994			2002		
	Women	Men	Women as a% of total employed in occupation	Women	Men	Women as a% of total employed in occupation	Women	Men	Women as a% of total employed in occupation
Managerial									
Senior management	0.4	1.6	16.9	0.4	1.5	19.8	0.2	0.6	25.1
Other management	5.8	10.0	30.6	7.4	10.4	36.9	6.2	10.4	34.0
Total management	6.2	11.6	28.9	7.9	12.0	35.1	6.4	11.0	33.6
Professional									
Business and finance	1.9	2.1	40.7	2.4	2.4	44.6	3.1	2.9	48.2
Natural sciences/ engineering/mathematics	1.8	6.6	16.7	1.8	7.4	17.0	3.1	9.8	21.3
Social sciences/religion	2.3	1.9	47.8	3.5	2.2	56.5	4.2	2.2	62.1
Teaching	5.0	2.8	57.3	5.6	3.2	59.4	5.3	2.5	64.4
Doctors/dentists/ other health	0.9	0.9	44.1	1.3	1.1	48.7	1.3	0.9	54.4
Nursing/therapy/other health-related	8.0	0.9	87.3	8.1	1.0	87.1	8.4	1.1	87.3
Artistic/literary/ recreational	2.8	2.0	50.4	3.2	2.3	53.6	3.2	2.4	53.5
Total professional	22.8	17.3	49.8	25.8	19.6	52.2	28.5	21.8	53.1
Clerical and administrative	29.6	7.7	74.4	26.4	7.3	74.9	24.1	6.9	75.0
Sales and service	30.9	18.5	55.7	31.2	19.9	56.4	32.2	19.7	58.6
Primary	2.4	7.3	20.0	2.2	6.7	21.3	1.4	5.2	19.8
Trades, transport, and construction	2.0	27.1	5.3	1.7	25.0	5.4	2.0	24.7	6.5
Processing, manufacturing, and utilities	6.0	10.4	30.2	4.7	9.5	29.2	5.2	10.7	29.6
Total[1]	100.0	100.0	43.0	100.0	100.0	45.3	100.0	100.0	46.4
Total employed (000s)	5,299.3	7,021.4	—	5,934.2	7,177.5	—	7,149.8	8,262.0	—

[1] Includes occupations that are not classified.
Source: *Women in Canada: Work Chapter Updates.* Statistics Canada Catalogue no. 89F0133XIE, p. 21.

Differences in Personal Work-Related Characteristics

Differences in employee attributes and behaviours help explain part of the earnings gap. Work-related differences include experience and seniority within a firm, continuous time in the workforce, education, and the like. Personal characteristics of questionable work-relatedness include obesity and beauty. Yet empirical studies have found both these factors are related to pay differences.[12] Plain people earn less than average-looking people, who earn less than the good-looking. The "plainness penalty" is 5 to 10 percent.

Experience and Seniority.   On average, male full-time workers put in 6 percent more hours per week than women full-time workers. By the time men and women have been out of school for 6 years, women on average have worked 30 percent less than men. After 16 years out of school, women average half as much labour market experience as men.[13] A study of middle-aged law school grads concluded that the women lawyers did work fewer hours—about 91 percent as long as men.[14] However, they were paid substantially (not proportionately) less; they earned only 61 percent of what men earned. Even with differences in work history accounted for, male lawyers continue to enjoy a considerable earnings advantage as well as a higher rate of growth earnings. Women's record of work experience is continuing to grow closer to that of men, for several reasons. First, when a strong demand for employees exists, as it has in recent years, fewer barriers to women's entry exist. Additionally, as women see those above them receive promotions, they become more likely to invest in their own human capital via training, education, and experience to position themselves for such promotions. However, such "feedback effects" can also work in reverse: Small initial discriminatory differences in wages affect women's decisions about their future, including their willingness to stay in the workforce.[15]

Education.   Currently, more women than men graduate from Canadian universities. However, they still tend to choose different majors, although those differences are diminishing. Their major is the single strongest factor affecting income of university graduates.[16]

Combining Factors.   Although many researchers have studied the effects of differences in jobs and occupations and personal characteristics such as experience and education, few studies have looked at their effects on pay differences *over time*. One study controlled for education degree, major, and prior experience. Males had a 12 percent *higher* starting salary than females. When all the variables were included, the current salary differential between male university graduates and female university graduates was less than 3 percent. The implication is that women received greater pay increases after they were hired than men did, but differences in starting salary remain important and persistent contributors to gender-related pay differences.[17]

Another study looked not only at a combination of factors to explain pay differences, but at the combined effects of different areas of discrimination: in hiring, job assignment, and pay. Although initial differences in treatment in each area may be small, when the effects are combined and projected ahead, they can become substantial. The authors call for better measures to combine the effects of different types of discrimination.[18]

Differences in Industries and Firms

Other factors that affect earnings differences between men and women are the industry and the firms in which they are employed. The study of middle-aged lawyers revealed large differences between men and women lawyers in the types of firms that employed them. Men were much more likely than women to be in private practice, and they were twice as likely to practice in large firms (over 50 lawyers). In contrast, men are much *less* likely than women to be in the relatively low-paying areas of government and legal services. Clearly, these differences are related to pay: The most highly paid legal positions are in private practice law firms, and the larger the law firm, the greater the average rate of pay.[19]

Differences in the firm's compensation policies and objectives within a specific industry are another factor that accounts for some of the earnings gap. As noted in Chapters 7 and 8, some firms within an industry adopt pay strategies that place them among the leaders in their industry; other firms adopt policies that may offer more employment security coupled with bonuses and gain-sharing schemes. The issue here is whether *within an industry* some firms are more likely to employ women than other firms and whether that likelihood leads to earnings differences.

Within a firm, differences in policies for different jobs may even exist. For example, many firms tie pay for secretaries to the pay for the manager to which the secretary is assigned. The rationale is that the secretary and the manager function as a team. When the manager gets promoted, the secretary also takes on additional responsibilities and therefore also gets a raise. However, this traditional approach breaks down when layers of management are cut. When IBM went through a major restructuring a few years back, it cut pay by up to 36 percent for secretaries who had been assigned to managerial levels that no longer existed. IBM justified the cuts by saying the rates were way above the market. Prior to the reduction, the highest base salary for a senior executive secretary was $70,000 plus overtime.[20]

We also know that the size of a firm is related systematically to differences in wages. Female employment is more heavily concentrated in small firms. Wages of men in large firms are 54 percent higher than wages of men in small firms. That gap was only 37 percent for women in small versus large firms. Other studies report that employees in some jobs can get about a 20 percent pay increase simply by switching industries in the same geographic area while performing basically similar jobs.[21] On the other hand, recent studies conclude that this pay premium associated with changing jobs is only enjoyed by white males. Women and minorities who were MBA graduates from five universities did not obtain the same pay increases as their white male classmates when they switched jobs.[22] The authors speculate that the failure of women and minorities to receive a comparable premium is that they do not have the well-developed social networks that provide "inside information" on job opportunities. A weaker network may hurt them in the pay bargaining process, too.

To the extent that these differences in job setting are the result of an individual's preference or disposition, they are not evidence of discrimination. To the extent that these differences are the result of industry and firm practices that steer women and minorities into certain occupations and industries, or lower-paying parts of a profession, they may reflect discrimination. At a minimum, they require thoughtful exploration.

Differences in Contingent Pay

Recently, a new and interesting approach was used to examine the gender earnings differential. Total pay was divided into base pay and contingent pay that varies with job performance. After controlling for individual characteristics (e.g., education and experience), occupation, and job level, approximately 34 percent of the unexplained pay gap was due to gender differences in performance-based pay.[23] If these differences occur *within* a firm, several possible explanations exist. Perhaps firms are not offering men and women equal opportunities to earn contingent pay; perhaps men and women are treated differently in the evaluations used to determine contingent pay; perhaps men and women differ substantially on performance.

However, if the differences are *across* firms, then perhaps women prefer less pay risk and choose those occupations and firms with less variable pay.[24] Although their sample size did not permit the authors to say if the differences were within or across firms, if the pay gap is in fact the result of the way people select occupations and employers, then we need to understand how pay practices influence those choices.

Differences in Union Membership

Finally, we also know that belonging to a union will affect differences in earnings. Belonging to a union increases wages.

Presence of Discrimination

So we know that many factors affect pay, and discrimination appears to be one of them.[25] But we are not in agreement as to what constitutes evidence of discrimination. Although 15 to 20 percent of the wage gap that remains after the effects of the above factors are removed is the most frequently cited example, closer inspection reveals the weaknesses in this statistic. A 2002 Statistics Canada analysis of the wage gap concluded that "While earning differences between men and women have narrowed since the 1970s, they continue to be remarkably persistent. Measurement and methodological issues play important roles in studying these differences.[26]

Pay Equity Legislation

pay equity

legislation intended to redress the unexplained portion of the wage gap assumed to be due to gender discrimination

Pay equity legislation has been introduced in almost all Canadian jurisdictions, often for public sector employees only, but increasingly for private sector employees as well. The laws are intended to address the effects of occupational segregation and the historical undervaluing of work done by women by requiring that female-dominated jobs be compensated in the same way as male-dominated jobs of the same value. Thus, pay equity legislation is proactive, rather than complaint-based.[27]

The pay equity process is detailed, technical, and complex, and varies to some extent between jurisdictions. However, the following steps are the basic components of a pay equity process:

- identify the unit for which the pay equity plan will be developed
- identify job classes with similar duties and responsibilities
- identify male and female job classes
- assess the value of jobs using a gender-neutral (free of gender bias) job evaluation system based on the criteria of:
  - *skill*, including intellectual and physical qualifications acquired by experience, training, education, or natural ability, but not considering the methods by which skills are acquired
  - *effort*, including both physical and intellectual effort
  - *responsibility*, for technical, financial, and human resources, and
  - *working conditions*, including both the physical and psychological conditions, such as noise, temperature, isolation, physical danger, health hazards, and stress
- compare male and female job classes using one of:

job-to-job method

method of comparing pay for male- and female-dominated job classes where each female job class is compared to a male job class of equal or comparable value

wage line method

method of comparing pay for male- and female-dominated job classes where the wage line for female job classes is compared indirectly with the wage line for male job classes

  - the **job-to-job method** where each female job class is compared to each male job class of equal or comparable value (Nova Scotia, Ontario, Prince Edward Island, Quebec, Yukon)
  - the **wage line method**, shown in Exhibit 12.4, where the wage line for female job classes is compared indirectly with the wage line for male job classes (Manitoba, New Brunswick, Newfoundland, Quebec, federal)

EXHIBIT 12.4 Job Evaluation Points and Salary

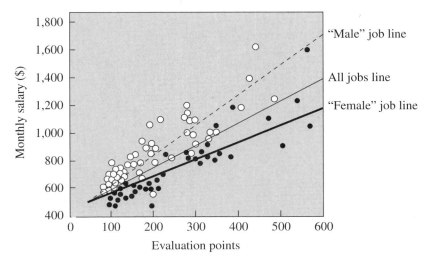

- Female-dominated jobs.   ○ Male-dominated jobs.

proportional value method

method of comparing pay for male- and female-dominated job classes when female job classes have no appropriate male comparators under the job-to-job system, where the relationship between the value of the job and the pay received by male job classes is then applied when setting pay for female job classes

proxy comparison method

method of comparing pay for male- and female-dominated job classes when pay equity cannot be achieved through job-to-job or proportional value methods, where female job classes are compared to similar female job classes that have achieved pay equity with another employer

- the **proportional value method**, for female job classes with no appropriate male comparators under the job-to-job system, where the relationship between the value of the job and the pay received by male job classes is then applied when setting pay for female classes (Ontario). This method has been quite controversial.
- the **proxy comparison method**, when pay equity cannot be achieved through job-to-job or proportional value methods, where female job classes are compared to similar female job classes that have achieved pay equity with another employer (Ontario public sector only). This method has been quite controversial.

- identify where compensation adjustments are required due to disparities in compensation between male and female job classes of equal value
- develop a pay equity plan that sets out how the differences in compensation that were discovered through the pay equity process will be remedied, containing:
  - a description of the unit for which the pay equity plan has been developed
  - an identification of all the job classes that formed the basis of comparisons, including which were female and which were male
  - a description of the gender-neutral job evaluation system used
  - where more than one method of comparison was permissible, the method of comparison used for each job class
  - the results of the comparisons
  - an identification of those job classes where permissible differences in compensation existed
  - for those job classes where differences in compensation exist which are not permissible, a description of how the compensation will be adjusted to achieve pay equity, and
  - a schedule of the payout of compensation adjustments
- make compensation adjustments, up to limits prescribed in the legislation, such as up to one percent of total Ontario payroll in the previous year (Ontario), or over a four-year period (Quebec).

Most pay equity legislation requires that pay equity be maintained over time. Employers must update or revise their pay equity plans when there are significant changes in circumstances, such as the creation or elimination of job classes, changes to the value of job classes, changes to job comparison processes, and mergers or acquisitions.

Conclusion

Governments around the world play varying roles in the workplace. Legislation in any society reflects people's expectations about the role of government. Beyond direct regulation, government affects compensation through policies and purchases that affect the supply and demand for labour.

In Canada, legislation reflects the changing nature of work and the workforce. In the 1930s, legislation was concerned with correcting the harsh conditions and arbitrary treatment facing employees, including children. In the 1980s, legislation turned to the issue of human rights. Such legislation has had a profound impact on Canadian society. Nevertheless, discrimination in the workplace, including pay discrimination, remains an unresolved issue.

Pay equity laws require special attention for several reasons. These laws regulate the design and administration of pay systems. Many of the provisions of these laws simply require sound pay practices that should have been employed in the first place. Achieving compliance with these laws rests in large measure on the shoulders of compensation managers. It is their responsibility to ensure that the pay system is properly designed and managed.

Is all this detail on pay equity really necessary? Yes. Without understanding legislation, compensation managers risk violating the law, exposing their employers to considerable liability and expense, and losing the confidence and respect of all employees when a few are forced to turn to the Pay Equity Commission to gain nondiscriminatory treatment.

THE IMPACT OF UNIONS ON WAGE DETERMINATION

Unions assume an important role in wage determination. Even in a nonunion firm, the protective actions taken by wage and salary administrators are influenced by external union activity. The general factors affecting wages in unionized firms include the impact of the union on: (1) general wage and benefit levels, (2) the structure of wages, (3) nonunion firms (also known as spillover), and (4) wage and salary policies and practices in unionized firms.

Union Impact on General Wage Levels

Do unions raise wages? Are unionized employees better off than they would be if they were nonunion? Unfortunately, comparing what *is* versus *what might have been* is no easy chore. Several measurement problems are difficult to overcome. The ideal situation would be to compare numerous organizations that are identical except for the presence or absence of a union.[28] Any wage differences between these organizations could then be attributed to unionization. Unfortunately, few such situations exist. One alternative strategy adopted has been to identify organizations within the same industry that differ in level of unionization. For example, consider company A which is unionized, and company B which is not. It is difficult to argue with assurance that wage differences between the two firms are attributable to the presence or absence of a union. First, the fact that the union has not organized the entire industry weakens its power base (strike efforts to shut down the entire industry could be thwarted by nonunion firms). Consequently, any union impact in this example might underestimate the role of unions in an industry where percentage of unionization is greater. A second problem in measuring union impact is apparent from this example. What if company B grants concessions to employees as a strategy to avoid unionization? These concessions, indirectly attributable to the presence of a union, would lead to underestimation of union impact on wages.

Another strategy in estimating union impact on wages is to compare two different industries that vary dramatically in the level of unionization.[29] This strategy suffers because nonunionized industries (e.g., agriculture, service) are markedly different from unionized industries in the types of labour employed and their general availability. Such differences have a major impact on wages independent of the level of unionization and make any statements about union impact difficult to substantiate.

Perhaps the best conclusion about union versus nonunion wage differences comes from a summary analysis of 114 different studies.[30] Two important points emerged:

1. Unions do make a difference in wages. Union workers earn approximately 10 percent more than their nonunion counterparts.
2. The size of the gap varies from year to year. During periods of higher unemployment, the impact of unions is greater. During strong economies the union–nonunion gap is smaller. Part of the explanation for this time-based phenomenon is related to union resistance to wage cuts during recessions and the relatively slow response of unions to wage increases during inflationary periods (because of rigidities or lags introduced by the presence of multi-year labour contracts).

Another situation in which unions affect general wage levels occurs when wage cuts are negotiated. This usually happens in extreme situations where the only other alternative is job loss.

.NET WORTH — Why Women Earn Less

Men and women are still treated unequally in the workplace. Women continue to earn less, on average, for the same performance, and they remain underrepresented in top jobs. Research has shown that both conscious and subconscious biases contribute to this problem.

But we have discovered another, subtler source of inequality: Women often don't get what they want and deserve because they don't ask for it. In separate studies, we found that men are more likely than women to negotiate for what they want. This can be costly for companies—and it requires management intervention.

One study found that the starting salaries of male MBAs who had recently graduated from Carnegie Mellon University in Pittsburgh were 7.6%, or almost US$4,000, higher on average than those of females from the same program. That was because most of the women had simply accepted the employer's initial salary offer; only 7% had attempted to negotiate. Yet 57% of their male counterparts—or eight times as many men as women—had asked for more.

Another study tested this gender difference in the lab. Subjects were told they would be observed playing a word game and that they would be paid between $3 and $10 for playing. After each subject completed the task, an experimenter thanked the participant and said, "Here's $3. Is $3 okay?" For the men, it was not OK, and they said so. Their requests for more money exceeded the women's by nine to one.

Women are less likely than men to negotiate for themselves for several reasons. First, they often are socialized from an early age not to promote their own interests and to focus on the needs of others. The messages girls receive—from parents, teachers, other children, the media, and society in general—can be so powerful that when they grow up they may not realize they've internalized this behaviour, or they may realize it but not understand how it affects their willingness to negotiate. Women tend to assume they will be recognized and rewarded for working hard and doing a good job. Unlike men, they have not been taught that they can ask for more.

continued

Canadian workers at Air Canada, Vancouver's Collingwood Neighbourhood House, and Northern British Columbia health care facilities all faced wage cuts in 2003 and 2004.[31] Some experts claim that wage concessions are more prevalent in unionized firms, and this reduces the advantage union workers hold in wages, particularly during downturns in the economy. Recent research suggests that concessions are not a tool used solely in unionized firms.[32]

The Structure of Wage Packages

The second compensation issue involves the structuring of wage packages. One dimension of this issue concerns the division between direct wages and employee benefits. Research indicates that the presence of a union adds about 20–30 percent to employee benefits.[33] Whether because of reduced management control, strong union–worker preference for benefits, or other reasons, unionized employees also have a greater percentage of their total wage bill allocated to employee benefits.[34] Typically the higher costs show up in the form of higher pension expenditures or

.NET WORTH

Second, many companies' cultures penalize women when they do ask—further discouraging them from doing so. Women who assertively pursue their own ambitions and promote their own interests may be labelled as bitchy or pushy. They frequently see their work devalued and find themselves ostracized or excluded from access to important information. These responses are a product of society's ingrained expectations about how women should act.

As a result, women in business often watch their male colleagues pull ahead, receive better assignments, get promoted more quickly, and earn more money.

Managers who believe (rightly) that an important part of their job is to keep their employees happy may give women smaller pieces of the pie simply because they give their employees what they ask for. They do not realize that men are asking for a lot more than the women are.

Managers need to confront this problem. At the individual level, they can mentor the women they supervise, advising them on the benefits (and the necessity) of asking for what they need to do their jobs effectively and fulfill their professional goals.

Managers also can make sure women understand how many aspects of their working lives can be negotiated. This can effectively compensate for women's more limited access to many of the professional and social networks in which men learn these lessons. Our studies found women respond immediately and powerfully to this advice and rapidly begin to see the world as a much more negotiable place.

Managers also can develop detailed and transparent systems to evaluate whether they are doling out opportunities and rewards to all employees based on skills and merit, rather that on who asks and who does not.

Finally, managers should drive larger-scale cultural change. By finding ways to examine different responses, leaders can open eyes to hidden barriers and create an atmosphere in which women and men can ask—and receive—equally.

Source: L. Babcock, S. Laschever, M. Gelfand, and D. Small, "Why Women Earn Less," *Financial Post,* October 8, 2003, p. FP16. Reprinted from Harvard Business School Publishing.

higher insurance benefits.[35] One particularly well-controlled study found unionization associated with a 217 percent higher level of pension expenditures and 127 percent higher insurance expenditures.[36]

A second dimension of the wage structure issue is the evolution of two-tier pay plans. With two-tier pay plans, basically a phenomenon of the union sector, a contract is negotiated which specifies that employees hired after a given target date will receive lower wages than their higher seniority peers working on the same or similar jobs. From management's perspective, wage tiers represent a viable alternative compensation strategy. Tiers can be used as a cost control strategy to allow expansion or investment, or as a cost-cutting device to allow economic survival.[37] Two-tier pay plans spread initially because unions viewed them as less painful than wage freezes and staff cuts among existing employees, even though they represent a radical departure from the most basic precept of unionization—the belief that all members are equal. Two-tier plans are obviously at odds with this principle. Lower-tier employees, those hired after the contract is ratified, may receive wages significantly lower than employees in the higher tier.[38] The contract may specify that the wage differential be permanent, or the lower tier may be scheduled ultimately to catch up with the upper tier. Eventually the inequity resulting from receiving different pay for the same level may cause employee dissatisfaction.[39] Consider the Roman emperor who implemented a two-tier system for his army in ad 217.[40] He was assassinated by his disgruntled troops shortly thereafter. Although such expressions of dissatisfaction are unlikely today, Canadian unions are reluctant to accept a two-tier structure, and may view it as a strategy of last resort.[41]

Union Impact: The Spillover Effect

spillover effect

employers seeking to avoid unionization offer workers the wages, benefits, and working conditions won in rival unionized firms

The impact of unions in general would be understated if we did not account for what is termed the "**spillover effect**." Specifically, employers seek to avoid unionization by offering workers the wages, benefits, and working conditions won in rival unionized firms. A classic example is Dofasco, who pay their non-unionized workforce based on the union pay rates at their heavily unionized competitor, Stelco. The nonunion management continues to enjoy the freedom from union "interference" in decision making, and the workers receive the spillover of rewards already obtained by their unionized counterparts. Several studies document the existence of this phenomenon (although smaller as union power diminishes), providing further evidence of the continuing role played by unions in wage determination.[42]

Role of Unions in Wage and Salary Policies and Practices

Perhaps of greatest interest to current and future compensation administrators is the role unions play in administering wages. The role of unions in administering compensation is outlined primarily in the contract. For example, collective agreements often require union representation on job evaluation committees. The following sections provide further illustrations of this role.

Basis of Pay.   The vast majority of contracts specify that one or more jobs are to be compensated on an hourly basis and that overtime pay will be paid beyond a certain number of hours. Notice the specificity of the language in the following contract clause:

A. Overtime pay is to be paid at the rate of one and one-half (1 1/2) times the basic hourly straight-time rate.
B. Overtime shall be paid to employees for work performed only after eight (8) hours on duty in any one service day or forty (40) hours in any one service week. Nothing in this Section shall be construed by the parties or any reviewing authority to deny the payment of overtime to employees for time worked outside of their regularly scheduled workweek at the request of the Employer.
C. Penalty overtime pay is to be paid at the rate of two (2) times the basic hourly straight-time rate. Penalty overtime pay will not be paid for any hours worked in the month of December.
D. Excluding December, part-time flexible employees will receive penalty overtime pay for all work in excess of ten (10) hours in a service day or fifty-six (56) hours in a service week.

Furthermore, many contracts specify that a premium be paid above the worker's base wage for working nonstandard shifts:

Employees regularly employed on the second or third shift shall receive in addition to their regular pay for the pay period five (5) percent and ten (10) percent additional compensation, respectively.

Alternatively, agreements may specify a fixed daily, weekly, biweekly, or monthly rate. In addition, agreements often indicate a specific day of the week as payday, and sometimes require payment on or before a certain hour.

Much less frequently, contracts specify some form of incentive system as the basis for pay. The vast majority of clauses specifying incentive pay occur in manufacturing (as opposed to non-manufacturing) industries. For example:

> Section 7. Establishment of Labour Standards. The Company and the Union, being firmly committed to the principle that high wages can result only from high productivity, agree that the Company will establish Labour Standards that:
> (a) Are fair and equitable to both the Company and the workers; and
> (b) Are based on the working capacity of a normally qualified worker properly motivated and working at an incentive pace; and
> (c) Give due consideration to the quality of workmanship and product required; and
> (d) Provide proper allowances for fatigue, personal time, and normal delays, and
> (e) Provide for payment of incentive workers based on the earned hours produced on-standard (except when such Employees are working on a Preliminary Estimate, etc.), and for each one per cent (1%) increase in acceptable production over standard, such workers shall receive a one per cent (1%) increase in pay over the applicable incentive rate.
>
> The Company will, at its discretion as to the time and as to jobs to be placed on or removed from incentive, continue the earned-hour incentive system now in effect, and extend it to jobs in such other job classifications which, in the opinion of the Company, can properly be placed on incentive, with the objective of increasing productivity and providing an opportunity for workers to enjoy higher earnings thus made possible. The plan shall be maintained in accordance with the following principles . . .

Occupation–Wage Differentials. Most contracts recognize that different occupations should receive different wage rates. Within occupations, though, a single wage rate prevails.

Occupation	Hourly Wage
Production Line Operator	$ 8.28
Packing Clerk	$ 8.38
QC Inspector	$ 8.48

Although rare, there are some contracts that do not recognize occupational/skill differentials. These contracts specify a single standard rate for all jobs covered by the agreements. Usually such contracts cover a narrow range of skilled groups.

Experience/Merit Differentials. Single rates are usually specified for workers within a particular job classification. Single-rate agreements do not differentiate wages on the basis of either seniority or merit. Workers with varying years of experience and output receive the same single rate. Alternatively, agreements may specify wage ranges. The following example is fairly typical:

Job Title	Start	2 mo	6 mo	1 yr	2 yr	5 yr	7 yr	10 yr
Packing Clerk	$7.02	$7.47	$7.90	$8.38	$9.01	$9.22	$9.56	$9.76
QC Inspector	7.12	7.57	8.00	8.48	9.11	9.32	9.66	9.86

The vast majority of contracts, as in the example above, specify seniority as the basis for movement through the range. Automatic progression is an appropriate name for this type of movement through the wage range, with the contract frequently specifying the time interval between movements. This type of progression is most appropriate when the necessary job skills are within the grasp of most employees. Denial of a raise is rare, and frequently is accompanied by the right of the union to submit any wage denial to the grievance procedure.

A second strategy for moving employees through wage ranges is based exclusively on merit. Employees who are evaluated more highly receive larger or more rapid increments than average or poor performers. Within these contracts, it is common to specify that disputed merit appraisals may be submitted to grievance. If the right to grieve is not explicitly excluded, the union has the implicit right to grieve.

The third method for movement through a range combines automatic and merit progression in some manner. A frequent strategy is to grant automatic increases up to the midpoint of the range and to permit subsequent increases only when merited on the basis of performance appraisal.

Other Differentials.   There are a number of remaining contractual provisions that deal with differentials for reasons not yet covered. A first example deals with different pay to unionized employees who are employed by a firm in different geographic areas. Very few contracts provide for different wages under these circumstances, despite the problems that can arise in paying uniform wages across regions with markedly different costs of living.

A second category where differentials are mentioned in contracts deals with part-time and temporary employees. Few contracts specify special rates for these employees. Those that do, however, are about equally split between giving part-time and temporary employees wages above full-time workers (because they have been excluded from the employee benefits program) or below full-time workers.

Vacations and Holidays.   Vacation and holiday entitlements are among clauses frequently found in labour contracts. They, too, use very specific language, as the following example illustrates:

Observance

The following holidays will be observed

New Year's Day—First Day in January

Canada Day—First day of July

Labour Day—First Monday in September

Thanksgiving Day—Second Monday in October

Christmas Day—Twenty-fifth day of December

When a holiday falls on a Sunday, the holiday is observed on the following Monday. When a holiday falls on a Saturday, the holiday is observed on the preceding Friday. For employees whose work assignment is to a seven (7) day operation, the holiday shall be celebrated on the day it actually falls. A holiday shall start at 12:01 a.m. or with the work shift that includes 12:01 a.m.

Work on Holidays

Employees required to work on a holiday will be compensated at their discretion either at the rate of one and one-half (1 1/2) times their regular rate of pay, or granted compensatory time at the rate of one and one-half (1 1/2) times, plus straight time pay for the holiday. The choice of compensatory time or wages will be made by the employee.

Wage Adjustment Provisions.   Frequently in multi-year contracts some provision is made for wage adjustment during the term of the contract. There are three major ways these adjustments might be specified: (1) deferred wage increases, (2) reopener clauses, and (3) cost-of-living adjustments (COLA) or escalator clauses. A deferred wage increase is negotiated at the time of initial contract negotiations, with the timing and amount specified in the contract. A reopener clause specifies that wages, and sometimes such nonwage items as pension and benefits, will be renegotiated at a specified time or under certain conditions. Finally, a COLA clause, as noted earlier, involves periodic adjustments based typically on changes in the consumer price index:

> Effective May 27, 2001, an Escalation Adjustment will be determined by computing the percentage increase in the Consumer Price Index, hereafter called "CPI" between March 1998 and March 2001.
> (i) If the percentage increase of the CPI exceeds the cumulative percentage increase to the Maximum Rates of each wage schedule for the Initial General Wage Increase (GWI), plus the second, third, and fourth GWI's, an Escalation Adjustment shall be applied by multiplying times the percentage increase in the CPI. The result shall be added to the fourth scheduled GWI and applied to the Maximum Rates and Minimum Rates in effect on May 26, 2001.
> (ii) A partial percentage increase shall be rounded to the nearest one-tenth of one percent.

■ UNIONS AND ALTERNATIVE REWARD SYSTEMS

International competition causes a fundamental problem for unions. If a unionized company settles a contract and the company raises prices to cover the increased wage costs, there is always the threat that an overseas competitor with lower labour costs will capture market share. Eventually, enough lost market share means the unionized company will be out of business. To keep this from happening, unions have become more receptive in recent years to alternative reward systems that link pay to performance. After all, if worker productivity rises, product prices can remain relatively stable, even with wage increases.

Alternative reward systems include lump sum, piece rate, gain-sharing, profit sharing, and skill-based pay.[43] Willingness to try such plans is greater when the firm faces extreme competitive pressure.[44] In unionized firms that do experiment with these alternative reward systems, though, the union usually insists on safeguards that protect both the union and its workers. The union insists on group-based performance measures with equal payouts to members. This equality principle cuts down strife and internal quarrels among the members and reinforces the principles of equity that are at the very foundation of union beliefs. To minimize bias by the company, performance measures tend to be objective in unionized companies. Most frequently the measures rely on past performance as a gauge of realistic targets, rather than some time study or other engineering standard that might appear more susceptible to tampering.[45] Below we offer specific feedback about union attitudes towards alternative reward concepts.

Lump-Sum Awards

As discussed in Chapter 11, lump-sum awards are one-time cash payments to employees that are not added to an employee's base wages. These awards typically are given in lieu of merit increases, which are more costly to the employer. This higher cost results both because merit increases are added on to base wages and because several employee benefits (e.g., life insurance and vacation pay) are calculated as a percentage of base wages. Lump-sum payments are a reality of union contracts. For the past 10 years a stable one-third of all major collective bargaining agreements in the private sector have contained a provision for lump-sum payouts.[46]

Employee Stock Ownership Plans (ESOPs)

An alternative strategy for organizations hurt by intense competition is to obtain wage concessions in exchange for giving employees part ownership in the company. For example, the Teamsters have experimented with contract provisions permitting local trucking companies and Teamster employees to set up ESOP plans.[47] One agreement specified that employees receive 49 percent ownership in a trucking company in exchange for wage concessions of no more than 15 percent over five years. So far, these plans have not been very effective in keeping marginal firms from eventually declaring bankruptcy.[48]

Pay-for-Knowledge Plans

Pay-for-knowledge plans do just that: pay employees more for learning a variety of different jobs or skills. For example, the collective agreement may include provisions giving hourly wage increases for learning new skills on different parts of the assembly process. By coupling this new wage system with drastic cuts in the number of job classifications, organizations have greater flexibility in moving employees quickly into high-demand areas. Unions also may favour pay-for-knowledge plans because they make each individual worker more valuable, and less expendable, to the firm. In turn, this also lessens the probability that work can be subcontracted out to nonunion organizations.

Gain-Sharing Plans

Gain-sharing plans are designed to align workers and management in efforts to streamline operations and cut costs. Any cost savings resulting from employees working more efficiently are split according to some formula between the organization and the workers. Some reports indicate gain-sharing is more common in unionized than nonunionized firms.[49] In our experience, success is dependent on a willingness to include union members in designing the plan. Openness in sharing financial and production data—key elements of putting a gain-sharing plan in place—are important in building trust between the two parties.

Although unions aren't always enthusiastic about gain-sharing, they rarely directly oppose it, at least initially. Rather, the most common union strategy is to delay taking a stand until real costs and benefits are more apparent.[50] Politically, this may be the wisest choice for a union leader.

Profit-Sharing Plans

Unions have debated the advantages of profit-sharing plans for at least 90 years.[51] The goal of unions is to secure sound, stable income levels for their membership. When this is achieved, subsequent introduction of a profit-sharing plan allows union members to share the wealth with more profitable firms, while still maintaining employment levels in marginal organizations. We should note, though, that not all unions favour profit-sharing plans. Inequality in profits among firms in the same industry can lead to wage differentials for workers performing the same work.

CONCLUSION

Other countries continue to make inroads in product areas traditionally the sole domain of North American companies. The impact of this increased competition has been most pronounced in the compensation area. Labour costs must be cut in order to improve our competitive stance. Alternative compensation systems to achieve this end are regularly being devised. Unions face a difficult situation. How should they respond to these attacks on traditional compensation systems? Many unions believe that the crisis demands changing attitudes from both management and unions. Labour and management identify compensation packages that both parties can abide. Sometimes these packages include cuts in traditional forms of wages in exchange for compensation tied more closely to the success of the firm. We expect the future will be dominated by more innovation in compensation design and increased exploration between unions and management for ways to improve the competitive stance of North American business.

CHAPTER SUMMARY

1. The role of government in compensation is to assess whether procedures for determining pay are fair, whether safety nets for the unemployed and disadvantaged are sufficient, and whether employees are protected from exploitation. Governments also affect the supply and demand for people.
2. The major compensation-related provisions of employment standards legislation are minimum pay, paid vacation, paid holidays, standard hours of work and overtime pay, pay on termination of employment, minimum age of employment, and equal pay for equal work by men and women.
3. Human rights legislation affects compensation in that compensation decisions based on any of the prohibited grounds for discrimination are illegal. Employers must ensure that their compensation systems treat all groups neutrally, compensating for merit rather than membership in a particular group.
4. Gender discrimination in pay appears through a persistent wage gap between men and women that cannot be fully explained by other factors. Pay equity legislation is intended to redress the unexplained portion of the wage gap assumed to be due to gender discrimination. The laws are intended to address the effects of occupational segregation and the historical undervaluing of work done by women by requiring that female-dominated jobs be compensated in the same way as male-dominated jobs of the same value.
5. Unions affect wage determination through their impact on (1) general wage and benefit levels, (2) the structure of wages, (3) spillover effect on non-union firms, and (4) wage and salary policies and practices in unionized firms.
6. Union attitudes regarding pay-for-performance have gradually become more favourable because of the threat of overseas competitors with lower labour costs taking so much market share from unionized companies that they go out of business.

KEY TERMS

REVIEW QUESTIONS

1. Consider compensation practices such as skill/competency-based pay, broadbanding, market pricing, and pay-for-performance plans. What are some of the issues related to pay equity that arise when using these practices? How can these issues be resolved?
2. Could the pay objective of regulatory compliance ever conflict with other pay objectives such as consistency, competitiveness, or employee perceptions of fairness? If so, how would you deal with such situations?
3. What factors help account for the male-female wage gap?
4. Most union contracts do not include provisions for merit pay. Given what you have learned here and in Chapter 10, explain why unions oppose merit pay.

EXPERIENTIAL EXERCISES

1. Assume that, as local union president, you have just received valid information that the grocery chain employing your workers is close to bankruptcy. What types of wage concessions might your union be able to make? Which of these are likely to have the least negative impact on your union workers' wages in the short run (one year)? Which is most likely to create internal dissension between different factions of the union?

WEB EXERCISE

Pay Equity Quizzes

The Ontario Pay Equity Commission Web site www.gov.on.ca/lab/pec/index_pec.html contains a wide variety of information about pay equity in general and on the Ontario pay equity legislation in particular. Click on "Go to the PEO" and then click "Interactions." Complete the Pay Equity Quiz and the Women and Work Quiz. How did you score? How much/how little did you know in these areas? Which of the answers did you find most surprising?

CASE

Garfield Technology

The Company

Garfield Technology (GT) is an international producer of burglar alarm systems. To crack the international market, GT must comply with quality standards as set by the International Organization for Standardization (ISO). Compliance requires that all products and processes pass a series of 17 strict criteria, the so-called ISO 9000 audit.

The Union

The Technology Workers of Canada organized GT in 2004. In the last control, both parties agreed to have a three-person panel listen to all disputes between union and management concerning the proper classification of jobs.

Your Role

You are the neutral third party hired to hear the dispute described below. The union representative has voted in the union's favour, and management has sided with management's position. You will break the tie. How do you vote and why? Some experts would argue that enough evidence is presented here for you to make a decision. See if you can figure out what the logic was that led to this conclusion. Also list what other information you would like to have and how that might influence your decision.

The Grievance

A job titled Technical Review Analyst I with responsibility for ISO 9000 audits is slotted as a tier 3 job.[1] Union believes that this job should be evaluated as a tier 4 job. Management contends that both this job and its counterpart in tier 4 (Senior Technical Review Analyst) should be graded in tier 3.

Summary of Important Points in the Union Case

The union asserts, and management agrees, that the only difference historically between auditors classified as Technical Review Analysts I (tier 3) and those classified as Senior Technical Review Analysts (tier 4) was the presence or absence of one task. That task was the performance of systems tests. Only tier 4 personnel performed this work, and this yielded the higher tier classification. With the introduction of ISO 9000 audits, the systems test component of the tier 4 job eventually was phased out, and both tier 3 and tier 4 auditors were asked to perform the ISO 9000 audit. The union and management agree that the systems test work previously performed by tier 4 employees was easier (and less valuable to the company) than the new ISO 9000 work now being performed. However, the union maintains that this added responsibility from the ISO 9000 audit, which involves about 150 hours of training, is sufficiently complex to warrant tier 4 classification. As partial support, the union provided a list of attendees to one ISO 9000 training session and noted that many of the attendees from other companies are managers and engineers, asserting this as evidence of the complexity involved in the audit material and the importance attached to this job by other firms.

The union also presented evidence to support the assertion that tier 3 personnel performing ISO 9000 audits are doing work of substantially the same value as the old grade 310 work.[2] This grade, as agreed by both the union and the company, is equivalent to the new tier 4.

continued

CASE

Summary of Important Points in Management Case

Management's case includes four major points. First, management argues that a Technical Review Analyst performing ISO 9000 audits has a job that is similar in complexity, responsibility, and types of duties to jobs previously classified as grade 308 and 309. Jobs in these old grades are now slotted into tier 3, per the contract.

Second, management presented evidence that many of the duties performed in the ISO 9000 audits were performed in a series of prior audits, variously labelled Eastcore MPA, QSA 1981, and QPS 1982. This long and varied history of similar duties, management contends, is evidence that ISO 9000 does not involve higher level or substantially different (and hence no more valuable) duties than have been performed historically.

Third, management presented both notes and a memorandum from W. P. Salkrist (the company job evaluation expert) in support of its argument that the audit job with ISO 9000 responsibilities should be classified as a tier 4 job. Prior to introduction of the ISO 9000 audit, neither the union nor management had found any reason to complain about the existing prior job evaluations of the tier 3 and tier 4 review analysts.

Fourth, management provided evidence that these jobs at other facilities, with other local contract provisions and conditions, were all classified as tier 3.[3]

[1] Tier 1 is the low end and tier 5 is the high end for all skilled craft jobs. Different evaluation systems are used for management and for clerical employees.

[2] The former job evaluation system broke jobs down into many more grades. As of the last contract, jobs are now classified into one of five tiers or grades.

[3] Union strongly contests the introduction of this information. In the past, management has vehemently argued that conditions at other facilities should not be introduced because local contracts were negotiated, with different tradeoffs being made by the different parties. Union believes that this same logic should now apply if a consistent set of rules is to evolve.

BUDGETS AND ADMINISTRATION

LEARNING OUTCOMES

- *Explain* the three components of labour cost and how they are mathematically combined to create total labour cost.
- *Describe* how salary level can be controlled by a top-down approach and a bottom-up approach.
- *Identify* four inherent controls in compensation design techniques.
- *Explain* the six stages in the compensation communication cycle.
- *Discuss* the various issues regarding how organizations structure the compensation function.

Today, managers of compensation are business partners. The financial status of the organization, the competitive pressures it faces, and budgeting are integral to managing compensation. The cost implications of decisions such as updating the pay structure, merit increases, or gain-sharing proposals are critical for making sound decisions. Consequently, budgets are an important part of managing compensation. They are also part of managing human resources and the total organization.[1]

Creating a compensation budget involves tradeoffs among the basic pay policies—how much of the increase in external market rates should be budgeted according to employee contributions to the organization's success compared to automatic across-the-board increases. Tradeoffs also occur over short- versus long-term incentives, over pay increases contingent on performance versus seniority, and over direct pay (cash) compared to benefits. Budgeting also involves tradeoffs between how much to emphasize compensation compared to other aspects of human resource management.

Managers must decide on the financial resources to deploy toward compensation compared to staffing (e.g., workforce size and job security), compared to training (e.g., workforce skills), and so on. The human resource budget implicitly reflects the organization's human resource strategy; it becomes an important part of the human resource plan. Finally, budgeting in the total organization involves allocating financial resources to human resources and/or technology, capital improvements, and the like. Today's managers of compensation need to demonstrate how compensation decisions help achieve organization success while treating employees fairly.

How the pay systems are used by managers involves the administration of pay.

ADMINISTRATION AND THE TOTAL PAY MODEL

Consider making pay decisions without a formal system. Each manager could pay whatever seemed to work at the moment. Total decentralization of compensation decision making would result in a chaotic array of rates. Employees could be treated inconsistently and unfairly. Managers might use pay to motivate behaviours that achieved their own objectives, not necessarily those of the organization.

This was the situation in Canada in the early 1900s. The "contract system" made highly skilled workers managers as well as workers. The employer agreed to provide the "contractor" with floor space, light, power, and the necessary raw or semifinished materials. The contractor hired *and* paid labour. Pay inconsistencies for the same work were common. Some contractors demanded kickbacks from employees' paycheques; many hired their relatives and friends. Dissatisfaction and grievances became widespread, resulting in legislation and an increased interest in unions.

Lest we pass off the contract system as ancient history dredged up by equally ancient professors, consider the current use of outsourcing. Outsourcing means that organizations secure a range of services from independent, external vendors. Payroll processing and benefits administration are two popular areas to outsource. The danger is that if everything is outsourced, then we are back to the organization as a network of individual contractors.[2] Look back to the early 1900s, replace contracting with outsourcing, and the similarities emerge. Will dissatisfaction, unfair treatment, cost sharing, and risk shifting to employees again be the result? Some see the litigation over the pay of contract workers as history repeating itself.

To avoid this result, any management system must be goal directed. Compensation is managed to achieve the three pay model objectives: efficiency, fairness, and compliance. Properly designed pay techniques help managers achieve these objectives. Rather than goal-directed tools, however, pay systems often degenerate into bureaucratic burdens whose administrators blindly follow the fads and fashions of the day. Techniques become ends in themselves rather than focusing on objectives. Operating managers may complain that pay techniques are more a hindrance than a help. So any discussion of administration must again raise the questions: What does this technique do for us? How does it help us better achieve our objectives? Although it is possible to design a system that includes internal alignment, external competitiveness, and employee contributions, it will not achieve its objectives without competent administration.

Although many pay administration issues have been discussed throughout the book, a few remain to be called out explicitly. Therefore, this chapter covers a variety of compensation administration issues, including (1) managing labour costs, (2) variable pay as a cost control, (3) inherent controls, (4) communication, and (5) structuring the compensation function.

MANAGING LABOUR COSTS

You already know many of the factors that affect labour costs. As shown in Exhibit 13.1,

$$\text{Labour Costs} = \text{Employment} \times \left(\frac{\text{Average cash}}{\text{compensation}} + \frac{\text{Average benefit}}{\text{cost}} \right)$$

Using this model, there are three main factors to control in order to manage labour costs: employment (e.g., number of employees and the hours they work), average cash compensation (e.g., wages, bonuses), and average benefit costs (e.g., health and life insurance, pensions). The cash and benefits factors are this book's focus. However, if our objective is to better manage labour costs, it should be clear that all three factors need attention.

EXHIBIT **13.1** Managing Labour Costs

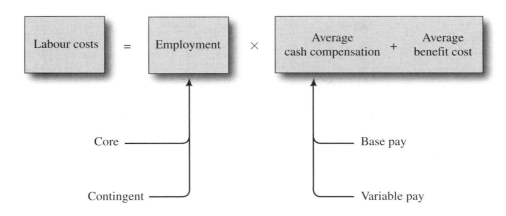

Controlling Employment: Head Count and Hours

Managing the number of employees (head count) and/or the hours worked is the most obvious and perhaps most common approach to managing labour costs. Paying the same wages to fewer employees is less expensive. However, as part of their social contracts, many European countries have legislation that makes it very difficult to reduce head count. Managing labour costs is a greater struggle in such circumstances.

Announcements of layoffs and plant closings often have favourable effects on stock prices, since investors anticipate improved cash flow and lower costs. However, it doesn't always work out that way. Other evidence suggests that the adverse effects of workforce reduction, such as the loss of trained employees and unrealized productivity, often cause the financial gains of the reductions to be less than anticipated.[3]

To manage labour costs better, many employers attempt to buffer themselves and employees by establishing different relationships with different groups of employees. As Exhibit 13.2 depicts, the two groups are commonly referred to as core employees, with whom a strong and long-term relationship is desired, and contingent workers, whose employment agreements may cover only short, specific time periods.[4] Rather than expand or contract the core workforce, many employers achieve flexibility and control labour costs by expanding or contracting the contingent work force.[5] Hence, the fixed portion of labour costs becomes smaller and the variable portion larger. And one can expand or contract the variable portion more easily than the core.

Contingent workers have many and varied compensation packages. It is common to pay more cash (base) but no benefits. Hence, contractors tend to be less expensive. So in the labour cost model, contingent workers' average salary may be greater, but there may be no additional benefits, which can run to one-third or more of total compensation costs.[6] Other issues of contingent worker compensation are covered in the chapter on special groups.

Hours. Rather than defining employment in terms of the number of employees, hours of work often are used. For non-management employees, hours over 40 per week are more expensive (1.5 × regular wage). Hence, another approach to managing labour costs is to examine overtime hours rather than adding to the workforce.

EXHIBIT | **13.2** | Core and Contingent Employees

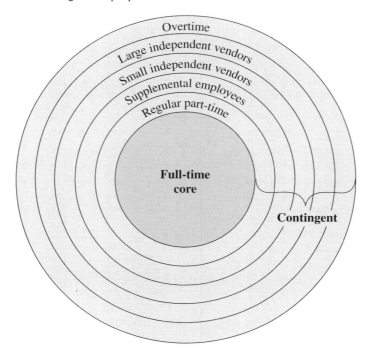

Note that the three factors—employment, cash compensation, and benefits costs—are not independent. Overtime hours require higher wages but avoid the benefits cost of hiring a new employee. Other examples of interdependence are the apparent lower wages (and lack of benefits) for some contingent workers, or a program that sweetens retirement packages to make early retirement attractive. Sweetened retirements drive head count down and usually affect the most expensive head count—older, more experienced employees. Hence, the average wage and health care costs for the remaining (younger) workforce probably will be lowered too.[7]

Controlling Average Cash Compensation

Exhibit 13.1 indicates that controlling the average cash compensation includes managing average salary level and variable compensation payments such as bonuses, gain-sharing, or profit sharing. Two approaches to help manage adjustments to average salary level are: (1) top down, in which upper management determines pay and allocates it "down" to each subunit for the plan year, and (2) bottom up, in which individual employee's pay for the next plan year is forecast and summed to create an organization salary budget.

■ CONTROL SALARY LEVEL: TOP DOWN

top-down budgeting

top management of each organizational unit estimates the pay-increase budget for that unit

Top-down budgeting requires top management of each organizational unit to estimate the pay-increase budget for that unit. Once the total budget is determined, it is then allocated to each manager, who plans how to distribute it among subordinates. There are many approaches to unit-level budgeting in use. A typical one, controlling the planned pay-level rise, will be considered. A planned pay-level rise is simply the percentage increase in average pay for the unit that is planned to occur.

EXHIBIT 13.3 What Drives Level Rise?

Current year's rise
Ability to pay
Competitive market
Turnover effects
Cost of living

⎫
⎬
⎭

Percentage increase
in average pay
in plan year

Exhibit 13.3 lists several factors that influence the decision about how much to increase the average pay level for the next period: how much the average level was increased this period, ability to pay, competitive market pressures, turnover effects, and cost of living.

Current Year's Rise

This is the percentage by which the average wage changed in the past year; mathematically:

$$\text{Percentage level rise} = 100 \times \frac{\text{Average pay at year end} - \text{Average pay at year beginning}}{\text{Average pay at the beginning of the year}}$$

Ability to Pay

The decision regarding how much to increase the average pay level is in part a function of financial circumstances. Financially healthy employers may wish to maintain their competitive position in the labour market or even to share outstanding financial success through bonuses and profit sharing.

Conversely, financially troubled employers may not be able to maintain competitive market positions. The conventional response in these circumstances has been to reduce employment. However, another option is to reduce the rate of increase in average pay by controlling adjustments in base pay and/or variable pay.

Competitive Market

In Chapter 8, we discussed how managers determine an organization's competitive position in relation to their competitors. Recall that a distribution of market rates for benchmark jobs was collected and analyzed into a single average wage for each benchmark. This "average market wage" became the "going market rate." It then was compared to the average wage paid by the organization for its benchmark jobs.[8] The market rates adjust differently each year in response to a variety of pressures.

Turnover Effects

turnover effect

decreased budget required as lower paid workers replace employees who leave, calculated as annual turnover rate times planned average increase

Variously referred to as churn or slippage, the **turnover effect** recognizes the fact that when people leave (through layoffs, quitting, or retiring), they typically are replaced by workers earning a lower wage. Depending on the degree of turnover, the effect can be substantial. Turnover effect can be calculated as annual turnover times planned average increase. For example, assume that an organization whose labour costs equal $1 million a year has a turnover rate of 15 percent and a planned average increase of 6 percent. The turnover effect is 0.9 percent, or $9,000 (0.009 × $1,000,000). So, instead of budgeting $60,000 to fund a 6 percent increase, only $51,000 is needed. The lower average pay also will reduce those benefit costs linked to base pay, such as pensions.

Cost of Living

Although there is little research to support this conclusion, employees undoubtedly compare their pay increases to changes in their costs of living. Unions consistently argue that increasing living costs justify adjustments in pay.[9]

A Distinction.   It is important to distinguish between three related concepts: the cost of living, changes in prices in the product and service markets, and changes in wages in labour markets. As Exhibit 13.4 shows, changes in wages in labour markets are measured by pay surveys. These changes are incorporated into the system through market adjustments in the budget and by updating the policy line and range structure. Price changes for goods and services in the product and service markets are measured by several government indexes, one of which is the Consumer Price Index. The third concept, the cost of living, refers to the expenditure patterns of individuals for goods and services. The cost of living is more difficult to measure because employees' expenditures depend on many things: marital status, number of dependents and ages, personal preferences, and so on. Different employees experience different costs of living, and the only accurate way to measure them is to examine the personal expenditures of each employee.

The three concepts are interrelated. Wages in the labour market are part of the cost of producing goods and services, and changes in wages create pressures on prices. Similarly,

EXHIBIT   13.4 | Three Distinct but Related Concepts and Their Measures

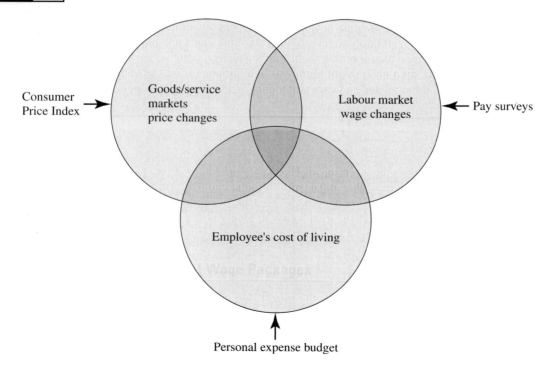

changes in the prices of goods and services create needs for increased wages in order to maintain the same lifestyle.

Consumer Price Index (CPI)

index that measures changes in prices over time

The Consumer Price Index (CPI).   Many people refer to the CPI as a "cost of living" index, and many employers choose, as a matter of pay policy or in response to union pressures, to tie wages to it. However, the CPI does not necessarily reflect an individual employee's cost of living. Instead, it measures *changes in prices over time*. Changes in the CPI indicate only whether prices have increased more or less rapidly in an area since the base period. For example, a CPI of 110 in Halifax and 140 in Vancouver does not necessarily mean that it costs more to live in Vancouver. It does mean that prices have risen faster in Vancouver since the base year than they have in Halifax, since both cities started with bases of 100.

The index is based on a survey of the actual buying habits of Canadians. Categories of major expenditures are derived, and weights assigned based on each category's percentage of total expenditures. For example, a weighting of 5.02 percent for auto purchases means that of the total money spent by all the people in the study, 5.02 percent of it was spent to buy new cars. This weighting plan measures both the price of cars and the frequency of new car purchases. To determine the new car component for today's CPI, today's price of a new car identically equipped to the one purchased in 1993–95 is multiplied by the factor weight of 5.02 percent. The result is called today's market basket price of a new car.

The CPI is of public interest because changes in it trigger changes in labour contracts, Old Age Security payments, federal and military pensions, and social assistance eligibility, as well as employers' pay budgets.[10] Tying budgets or payments to the CPI is called indexing. Note that the cost of living is included in Exhibit 13.3 as an influence on the percentage increase of average salary level. It also may affect cost of benefits, either through health insurance coverage or pension costs.

Rolling It All Together

Let us assume that the managers take into account all these factors—current year's rise, ability to pay, market adjustments, turnover effects, changes in the cost of living, and geographic differentials—and decide that the planned rise in average salary for the next period should be 6.3 percent. This means that the organization has set a target of 6.3 percent as the increase in average salary that will occur in the next budget period. It does not mean that everyone's increase will be 6.3 percent. It means that at the end of the budget year, the average salary calculated to include all employees will be 6.3 percent higher than it is now.

The next question is, How do we distribute that 6.3 percent budget in a way that accomplishes management's objectives for the pay system and meets the organization's goals?

Distributing the Budget to Subunits.   A variety of methods exists to determine what percentage of the salary budget each manager should receive. Some firms use a uniform percentage, in which each manager gets an equal percentage of the budget, based on the salaries of each subunit's employees. Others vary the percentage allocated to each manager based on pay-related problems, such as turnover or performance, which have been identified in that subunit.

Once salary budgets are allocated to each subunit manager, they become a constraint: a limited fund of money that each manager has to allocate to subordinates. Typically, merit increase guidelines are used to help managers make these allocation decisions.

Merit increase grids help ensure that different managers grant consistent increases to employees with similar performance ratings and in the same position in their ranges. Additionally, grids help control costs. Examples of grids are included in Chapter 10.

■ CONTROL SALARY LEVEL: BOTTOM UP

bottom-up budgeting

■ managers forecast the pay increases they will recommend in the coming year

Bottom-up budgeting requires managers to forecast the pay increases they will recommend during the upcoming plan year. Exhibit 13.5 shows the process involved. Each of the steps within this compensation forecasting cycle is described here.

1. *Instruct managers in compensation policies and techniques.* Train managers in the concepts of a sound pay-for-performance policy and in standard company compensation techniques such as the use of pay increase guidelines and budgeting techniques. Also communicate the salary ranges and market data.
2. *Distribute forecasting instructions and worksheets.* Furnish managers with the forms and instructions necessary to preplan increases. More and more, this is done most easily via computer. Each employee's performance rating history, past raises, training background, and past incentives are all included. Guidelines for increases based on merit, promotion, and equity adjustments are provided, and all the worksheets are linked so that the manager can model pay adjustments for each employee and see the budgetary effects of those adjustments immediately.

    Some argue that providing such detailed data and recommendations to operating managers makes the system too mechanical. How would you like your present instructor to look at your overall GPA before giving you a grade in this course? Pay histories ensure that managers are at least aware of this information and that pay increases for any one period are part of a continuing message to individual employees, not some ad hoc response to short-term changes.
3. *Provide consultation to managers.* Offer advice and salary information services to managers upon request. An on-line approach makes it much easier to request and apply such guidance.

EXHIBIT **13.5**   Compensation Forecasting and Budgeting Cycle ——————————

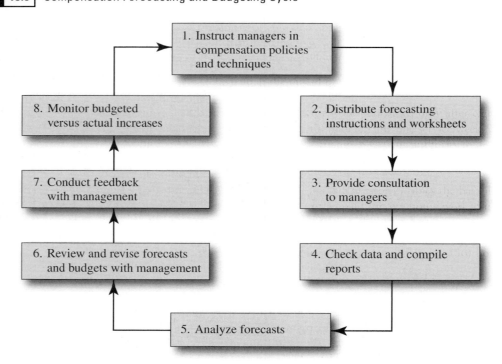

---

4. *Check data and compile reports.* Audit the increases forecasted to ensure that they do not exceed the pay guidelines and are consistent with appropriate ranges. Then use the data to feed back the outcomes of pay forecasts and budgets.
5. *Analyze forecasts.* Examine each manager's forecast and recommend changes based on noted inequities between different managers.
6. *Review and revise forecasts and budgets with management.* Consult with managers regarding the analysis and recommended changes. Obtain top-management approval of forecasts.
7. *Conduct feedback with management.* Present statistical summaries of the forecasting data by department and establish unit goals.
8. *Monitor budgeted versus actual increases.* Control the forecasted increases versus the actual increases by tracking and reporting periodic status to management.

The result of the forecasting cycle is a budget for the upcoming plan year for each organization's unit as well as estimated pay treatment for each employee. The budget does not lock in the manager to the exact pay change recommended for each employee. Rather, it represents a plan, and deviations due to unforeseen changes such as performance improvements, unanticipated promotions, and the like are common.

This approach to pay budgeting requires managers to plan the pay treatment for each of their employees. It places the responsibility for pay management on the managers. The compensation manager takes on the role of advisor to operating management's use of the system.[11]

Managing or Manipulating?

Budgeting average compensation costs is increasingly complicated, for two reasons. First is the increased use of variable forms of pay (i.e., gain-sharing, performance bonuses, and stock options). The second is the use of generally accepted accounting practices that permit earnings to be "managed."

Labour costs associated with performance-based pay typically are included in the budget process by estimating the anticipated profits and then the expected profit-sharing pool. Many organizations seek to ensure that these variable incentive plans are "self-funded," i.e., the bonuses (increase in labour costs) are offset by productivity gains (output/costs).

However, controlling variable pay costs may have a "smoke and mirrors" feel to it. At one organization's compensation strategy session, the chief financial officer observed that it was possible to "manage our reported earnings within several percentage points of the target. We can exceed analysts' and shareholder expectations by 1 to 10 percent." This was relatively easy for this company since about one-third of its earnings came from liquid investments in other companies. The remainder was revenue from its products and services. The implication of managing earnings for employees' profit-sharing payouts was not ignored, but clearly it was a secondary concern. Goodbye "pay for performance strategy," hello managed earnings to "meet or slightly exceed analysts' expectations." The point is that measures of financial performance do not provide an immutable "gold standard." They can be "managed."[12]

Clearly, these accounting practices have implications for managing labour costs, especially costs associated with variable pay programs. Compensation managers need to become active players and knowledgeable about the accounting practices used in their organizations.

■ INHERENT CONTROLS

Pay systems have two basic processes that serve to control pay decision making: (1) those inherent in the design of the techniques and (2) the formal budgeting process.

Think back to the many techniques already discussed: job analysis and evaluation, skill/competency-based plans, policy lines, range minimums and maximums, broad bands, performance evaluation, gain-sharing, and salary increase guidelines. In addition to their primary purposes, these techniques also regulate managers' pay decisions by guiding what managers do. Controls are imbedded in the design of these techniques to ensure that decisions are directed toward the pay system's objectives. A few of these controls are examined below.

Range Maximums and Minimums

These ranges set the maximum and minimum dollars to be paid for specific work. The maximum is an important cost control. Ideally, it represents the highest value the organization places on the output of the work. Under job-based structures, skills and knowledge possessed by employees may be more valuable in another job, but the range maximum represents all that the work produced in a particular job is worth to the organization. For example, the job of airline flight attendant is in a pay range with a maximum that is the highest an airline will pay a flight attendant, no matter how well the attendant performs the job.

Pressures to pay above the range maximum occur for a number of reasons—for example, when employees with high seniority reach the maximum or when promotion opportunities are scarce. If employees are paid above the range maximum, these rates are called **red circle rates**. Most employers "freeze" red circle rates until the ranges are shifted upward by market update adjustments so that the rate is back within the range again.

Range minimums are just that: the minimum value placed on the work. Often rates below the minimum are used for trainees. Rates below minimum may also occur if outstanding employees receive a number of rapid promotions and rate adjustments have not kept up. **Green circle rates** are those that are below the range minimum; they are usually swiftly increased to the range minimum. If red and/or green circle rates become common throughout an organization, the design of the ranges and the evaluation of the jobs should be reexamined.

Broad Bands.   Broad bands are intended to offer managers greater flexibility than a grade-range design. Usually broad bands are accompanied by external market "reference rates" and "shadow ranges" that guide managers' decisions. Bands may be more about career management than pay decisions. From the perspective of managing labour costs, broad bands really don't play a role. Rather, the control is in the salary budgets given to managers. The manager has flexibility in pay decisions, as long as the total pay comes in under the budget.

Compa-Ratios

Range midpoints reflect the pay policy line of the employer in relationship to external competition. To assess how managers actually pay employees in relation to the midpoint, an index called a **compa-ratio** is often calculated.

$$\text{Compa-Ratio} = \frac{\text{Average rates actually paid}}{\text{Range midpoint}}$$

A compa-ratio of less than 1.00 means that, on average, employees in that range are paid below the midpoint. Translated, this means that managers are paying less than the intended policy. There may be several valid reasons for such a situation. The majority of employees may be new or recent hires; they may be poor performers; or promotion may be so rapid that few employees stay in the job long enough to get to the high end of the range.

A compa-ratio greater than 1.00 means that, on average, the rates exceed the intended policy. The reasons for this are the reverse of those mentioned above: a majority of workers with high seniority, high performance, low turnover, few new hires, or low promotion rates. Compa-ratios may be calculated for individual employees, for each range, for organization units, or for functions.

---

red circle rates

pay rates above the range maximum

green circle rates

pay rates below the range minimum

compa-ratio

ratio of average rates actually paid to range midpoint

One control designed into pay techniques is the mutual sign-off on job descriptions required of supervisors and subordinates. Another is slotting new jobs into the pay structure via job evaluation, which helps ensure that jobs are compared on the same factors.

Similarly, an organizationwide performance management system is intended to ensure that all employees are evaluated on similar factors.

Variable Pay

Variable pay depends on performance and is not "rolled into" (added to) employees' base pay. Thus, the compounding effects of merit pay and across-the-board increases do not occur. The essence of variable pay is that it must be re-earned each period, in contrast to conventional merit pay increases or across-the-board increases that are added to base pay each year and that increase the base on which the following year's increase is calculated.

Increases added into base pay have compounding effects on costs, and these costs are significant. For example, $15 a week take-home pay added onto a $40,000 base compounds into a cash flow of $503,116 over 10 years. In addition, costs for some benefits also increase. By comparison, the organization could use that same $503,000 to keep base pay at $40,000 a year and pay a 26.8 percent bonus every single year. As the example shows, the greater the ratio of variable pay to base pay, the more variable (flexible) the organization's labour costs. Go back to the general labour cost model in Exhibit 13.1; note that the greater the ratio of contingent to core workers and variable to base pay, the greater the variable component of labour costs, and the greater the options available to managers to control these costs.

But a caution: Although variability in pay and employment may be an advantage for managing labour costs, it may be less appealing from the standpoint of managing fair treatment of employees. The inherent financial insecurity built into variable plans may adversely affect employees' financial well-being and subsequently their behaviours at work and attitudes toward their employers. Managing labour costs is only one objective of managing compensation; other objectives in the pay model include sustaining competitive advantage (productivity, total quality, customer service, and costs) and equitable treatment of employees.

Analyzing Costs

Costing out wage proposals is commonly done prior to recommending pay increases. It is also used in preparation for collective bargaining. For example, it is useful to bear in mind the dollar impact of a 1-cent per hour wage change or a 1 percent change in payroll when one goes into bargaining. Knowing these figures, negotiators can quickly compute the impact of a request for a 9 percent wage increase. Commercial computer software is available to analyze almost every aspect of compensation information. Computers can provide analysis and data that improve the administration of the pay system. For example, computers can easily compare past estimates to what actually occurred (e.g., the percentage of employees that actually received a merit increase and the amount). Spreadsheet programs can simulate alternate wage proposals and compare their potential effects. Software also can evaluate salary survey data and simulate the cost impact of incentive and gain-sharing options. However, trained compensation decision makers are still required to make decisions based on the results.

Making the Information Useful. Compensation expertise also is required to be sure that all the data generated are useful. An international example illustrates the point. 3M has long been a global company. However, until recently they have always considered compensation and benefit changes on a country-by-country basis, one at a time.[13] When they wanted to start implementing compensation initiatives globally, they found they did not have enough comparable labour cost data to do this. Ensuring comparability across countries and employee categories

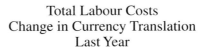

EXHIBIT 13.6   Individual Pay Planning Data for Managers

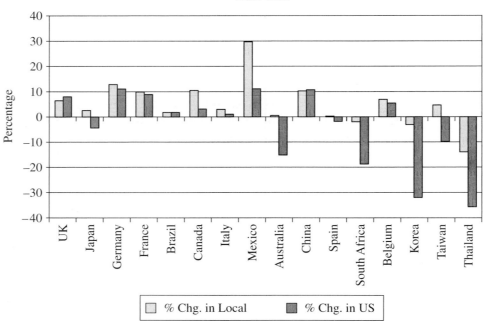

Total Labour Costs
Change in Currency Translation
Last Year

Source: Stan Durda, "Total Labor Cost Overview." 3M presentation, April 2000.

turned out to be a two-year project for their U.S. head office that required a great deal of compensation expertise to decide what data would be necessary and useful. Exhibit 13.6 shows one of their looks at how currency fluctuations between countries affect results. The 3 percent increase in Japan becomes a 5 percent decrease when converted to U.S. currency. The 30 percent increase in Mexico is about a 12 percent increase in U.S. dollars, and the 3 percent decrease in Korea is more than a 30 percent decrease in U.S. dollars. Note that this chart covers a time period of an increasingly strong dollar. A falling dollar might reverse these relationships. What should 3M do to minimize the effect of currency fluctuations on labour costs? Collecting these data and looking at these sorts of comparisons is the first step. The point is to illustrate the need for judgment in converting all kinds of data into useful input for making compensation decisions.

■ COMMUNICATION: MANAGING THE MESSAGE

Compensation communicates. It signals what is important and what is not. If you receive a pay increase for one more year of experience on your job, then one more year is important. If the pay increase is equal to any change in the CPI, then cost of living is important. If the increase is for moving to a bigger job or for outstanding performance, then a bigger job or outstanding performance is important. Pay sends a powerful message about what matters. Therefore, managing that message is important.

Earlier in the book, we stressed that employees must believe that the pay system is fair. Employees' perceptions of fairness of the pay system are shaped through formal communication programs about their pay and performance and through participation in the design of the system.

WorldatWork, an international group of compensation and human resources professionals, recommends a six-stage process of communication, shown in Exhibit 13.7.[14]

Step one is, not surprisingly, defining the objectives of the communication program. Perhaps the objective is to ensure that employees fully understand all the components of the compensation system; perhaps it is to change expectations, or to better capitalize on the motivational aspects built into the compensation systems. Although specifying objectives as a first step seems obvious, it is often overlooked in the rush to design an attractive brochure.

Step two is to collect information from executives, managers, and employees concerning their current perceptions, attitudes, and understanding of the compensation programs in effect. Information may be gathered through opinion survey questionnaires, focus groups, or formal or informal interviews. Some research concludes that employees typically misperceive the pay system by overestimating the pay of those with lower level jobs and underestimating the pay of those in higher level jobs. If differentials are underestimated, their motivational value is diminished.

Furthermore, there is evidence to suggest that the goodwill engendered by the act of being open about pay may affect employees' attitudes toward pay. Interestingly, the research also shows that employees in companies with open pay communication policies are as inaccurate in estimating pay differentials as those in companies in which pay secrecy prevails. However, employees under open pay policies tend to express higher satisfaction with their pay and with the pay system.

EXHIBIT 13.7 The Compensation Communication Cycle

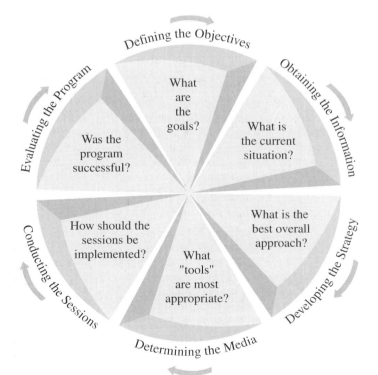

After the information on current attitudes and perceptions is analyzed, *step three* is to develop a communication strategy that will accomplish the original objectives. There is no standard approach about what to communicate to individuals about their own pay or that of their colleagues. Some organizations adopt a *marketing approach* that includes consumer attitude surveys about the product, snappy advertising about the pay policies, and elaborate videotapes expounding policies and strengths. The objective is to manage expectations and attitudes about pay. In contrast, the *communication approach* tends to provide technical details. The marketing approach focuses on the quality and advantages of overall policies and is silent on specifics such as range maximums, increase guides, and the like.

Steps four and five of the communication process are to determine the most effective media, in light of the message and the audience, and to conduct the campaign. Exhibit 13.8 recommends designing the message in terms of detail and emphasis according to the audience. Executives, for example, will be interested in how the compensation programs fit the business strategy (Chapter 2). Managers will need to know how to use the development and motivation aspects of the compensation program for the people they supervise. Employees may want to know the process and policy (procedural justice) as well as specifics about how their pay is determined.

EXHIBIT | **13.8** | Conducting Formal Communication Sessions for Various Audiences

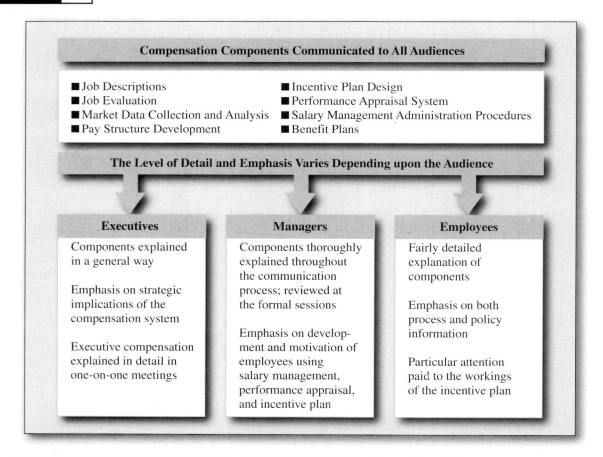

Source: Reprinted from ACA Building Block #4, *Communicating Compensation Programs, An Approach to Providing Information to Employees,* by John A. Rubino, CCP, with permission from the American Compensation Association (ACA), 14040 N. Northsight Blvd., Scottsdale, AZ U.S.A. 85260; telephone (602) 951-9191, fax: (602) 483-8352, © ACA.

Reach versus Richness.   A tradeoff in any communication program is what should they know, and when should they know it. A "richness" approach tailors information to the individual employee on a number of employment-related topics. The danger is overload—information so detailed that employees don't bother sorting through it to find out what they really wanted to know.

Intended and Unintended Consequences.   *Step six* of the communication process suggests that the program be evaluated. Did it accomplish its goals? Pay communication can have unintended consequences. For example, providing accurate pay information may cause some initial short-term concerns among employees. Over the years, employees may have rationalized a set of relationships between their pay and the perceived pay and efforts of others. Receiving accurate data may require that those perceptions be adjusted.

.NET WORTH   Effectiveness of Pay Communication

There are three ways to determine the effectiveness of pay communication. First, examine the timeliness and relevancy of employee communications regarding all new and existing pay programs. Using a variety of communication channels increases the chances that employees will understand messages sent to them. Communication methods and content should differ for different employee groups, such as production hourly, office hourly, and professional. Examining the clarity, frequency, and content of communications can result in a good initial quality assessment of the company's pay communication.

Second, in order to determine if pay messages are reaching employees, ask them. Interviews, group meetings, or employee attitude surveys are ideal ways to garner this information. If trust in management is low, it may be difficult to collect unbiased information unless respondent anonymity is assured. Responses to surveys, interviews, and group meetings can be collected, analyzed, and presented by an outsider in order to help employees feel secure about their anonymity.

Finally, one can confirm that pay programs motivate and reward the desired behaviour and outcomes. To establish this link, performance data for those who receive the rewards must be collected and examined. Comparisons can be made between those who receive the rewards and those who do not. Also, the performance of those who receive the awards can be compared to their own performance before the incentives were offered (using time series analysis). If significant differences are not found, then either the pay plan is flawed or it was not explained properly.

Previous research has found that employees who understand their pay plans perceive these plans to be more effective. Furthermore, employee feelings of pay fairness are often not the result of the amount they are paid, but rather their perception of how management arrives at pay levels. Thus, employees need to have confidence that management uses a systematic, unbiased approach to establishing pay levels. This includes the use of fair internal pay criteria, positioning pay at correct levels in comparison to the relevant labour market, and fairly distributing merit increases and rewards

Source: K.D. Scott, D. Morajda, and J.W. Bishop, "Increase Company Competitiveness: 'Tune Up' Your Pay System," *Worldat Work Journal*, First Quarter 2002, pp. 35-42.

Say What?

If the pay system is not based on work-related or business-related logic, then the wisest course probably is to avoid formal communication until the system is put in order. However, avoiding formal communication is not synonymous with avoiding communication. Employees are constantly receiving intended and unintended messages through the pay treatment they receive.

Many employers communicate the range for an incumbent's present job and for all the jobs in a typical career path or progression to which employees reasonably can aspire. Some also communicate the typical pay increases that can be expected for poor, satisfactory, and top performance. The rationale is that employees exchange data (not always factual) and/or guess at normal treatment, and the rumour mills are probably incorrect. One potential danger in divulging increase schedule data is the inability to maintain that schedule in the future for reasons outside the control of the compensation department (e.g., economic or product market conditions). Nevertheless, providing accurate data may have a positive effect on employee work attitudes and behaviours.

Opening the Books.   There are some who advocate sharing all financial information with employees.[15] All of it. For 10 years, employees at Springfield Remanufacturing, a rebuilder of engines, have been given weekly peeks at everything from revenues to labour costs. The employees, who own 31 percent of the company stock, and others argue that this "open book" approach results in high commitment and an understanding of how to maintain competitiveness. Many employers don't share information with such gusto, but they are increasingly disclosing more to their employees. Some are even providing basic business and financial training to help employees better understand the information. Devotees of opening the books and financial training believe that these methods will improve attitudes and performance, but there is no research to support this conclusion. Web sites increasingly are being used as part of communicating compensation and "opening the books." With salary data available on the Internet (albeit often inaccurate and misleading data), developing in-house compensation sites has appeal.

At a minimum, perhaps the most important information to be communicated is the work-related and business-related rationale on which pay systems are based. Some employees may not agree with this rationale or with the results, but at least it will be made clear that pay is determined by something other than the whims or biases of their supervisors.

Participation: Beliefs, Payoffs, and Practices

An often-unchallenged premise of this book has been that employee (and manager) participation in the design and administration of pay systems pays off through increased understanding and commitment. As you might expect, research on the effects of employee participation in general shows mixed results. Overall, the evidence suggests that participation does have positive effects, but that they are not overwhelming. Generally, employees seem to have input into aspects that are directly related to them (i.e., job descriptions), but not into overall policies, structure, or competitor salary surveys.

■ PAY: CHANGE AGENT IN RESTRUCTURING

Compensation often plays a singular role when organizations restructure. Strategic changes in the business strategy mean that the compensation strategy must be realigned as well.[16] Pay is a powerful signal of change; changing people's pay captures their attention.

Pay changes can play two roles in any restructuring: Pay can be a leading catalyst for change or a follower of the change. Shifts from conventional across-the-board annual increases to profit sharing, or from narrow job descriptions and ranges to broad roles and bands signal major change to employees. To signal yet another of ATT's major restructurings, the company shifted the measures it uses to trigger its bonus plan from 25 percent based on corporate earnings and 75 percent on individual performance, to 75 percent on corporate earnings and 25 percent on individual performance. ATT managers were meant to "understand" the need to focus on improving ATT performance. Unfortunately, two years later ATT restructured again. So it is not clear whether pay alone can be a sufficient catalyst.

Whether pay is a leading catalyst for change or a follower of change, compensation managers need to learn how to implement and manage change. Not only do they need to know the strategic and technical aspects of compensation, they also need to learn how to bargain, resolve disputes, empower employees, and develop teams. Being able to grab bullets in midflight and become airborne à la the "one" in the movie *Matrix* doesn't hurt, either.

■ STRUCTURING THE COMPENSATION FUNCTION

Compensation professionals seem to be constantly reevaluating where the responsibility for the design and administration of pay systems should be located within the organization. The organizational arrangements of the compensation function vary widely.

Centralization–Decentralization

An important issue related to structuring the function revolves around the degree of decentralization (or centralization) in the overall organization structure. *Decentralized* refers to a management strategy of giving separate organization units the responsibility to design and administer their own systems. This contrasts with a *centralized* strategy, which locates the design and administration responsibility in a single corporate unit.

Some firms, such as 3M and Xerox, have relatively large corporate staffs whose responsibility it is to formulate pay policies and design the systems. 3M calls its group the Total Compensation Resource Centre. Administration of these policies and systems falls to those working in various units, often human resources generalists. Such an arrangement runs the risk of formulating policies and practices that are well tuned to overall corporate needs, but less well tuned to each unit's particular needs and circumstances. The use of task forces, with members drawn from the generalists in the affected units, to design new policies and techniques helps to diminish this potential problem.

Other more decentralized organizations, such as TRW and GE, have relatively small corporate compensation staffs (three or four professionals). Their primary responsibility is to manage the systems by which executives and the corporate staff are paid. These professionals operate in a purely advisory capacity to other organization subunits. The subunits, in turn, may employ compensation specialists. Or the subunits may choose to employ only human resources generalists rather than compensation specialists, and may turn to outside compensation consultants to purchase the expertise required on specific compensation issues.

AES, an electrical power company, has no compensation unit at all. Nor any HR department either. Compensation is all handled by teams of managers. Decentralizing certain aspects of pay design and administration has considerable appeal. Pushing these responsibilities (and expenses) close to the units, managers, and employees affected by them may help to ensure that decisions are business related. However, decentralization is not without problems. For example, it may be difficult to transfer employees from one business unit to another. Problems crop up as a result of designing pay systems that support a subunit's objectives but run counter to the overall corporate objectives. So, too, does the potential for pay discrimination.

Flexibility within Corporatewide Principles

The answer to these and related problems of decentralization can be found in developing a set of corporatewide principles or guidelines that all must meet. These principles may differ for each major pay technique. For example, GE's business units worldwide have the flexibility to design incentive plans tailored to each unique business unit's strategies and cultures. The only guidance is to ensure that the plans adhere to GE's basic beliefs, improve financial and business objectives, and maintain or enhance GE's reputation.

Keep in mind that the pay system is one of many management systems used in the organization. Consequently, it must be congruent with these other systems. For example, it may be appealing, on paper at least, to decentralize some of the compensation functions. However, if financial data and other management systems are not decentralized also, the pay system may not fit and may even be at odds with other systems.

Reengineering and Outsourcing

Reengineering the compensation function involves changing the process of paying people. It means reshaping the compensation function to make it more client- or customer-focused. Clients may include employees, managers, owners, and perhaps even real customers of the organization. The basic question asked during reengineering is, "Does each specific activity (technique) directly contribute to our objectives (i.e., to our competitive advantage)?" If some added value isn't apparent, then the technique should be dropped. The next question, directed at those pay activities that do contribute to achieving objectives is, "Should we be doing the specific activity in-house, or can others do it more effectively? That is, should we outsource it?"

Outsourcing is a viable alternative in the compensation (and benefits) field as organizations struggle to cease doing activities that do not directly contribute to strategic objectives.[17] In a recent survey, about 33 percent of over 1,000 firms reported that they already outsourced major responsibilities for their pay (e.g., market surveys and structure design) and benefits administration.

Cost savings is the apparent major short-term advantage of outsourcing. All those compensation experts can be laid off or retrained. Major disadvantages of outsourcing include less responsiveness to unique and specific employee–manager problems, less control over decisions that are often critical to all employees (i.e., their pay), and information leaks to rivals and competitors.[18]

■ CONTROLS AS GUIDELINES: LET (THOUGHTFUL) MANAGERS BE FREE

One of the major attacks on traditional compensation plans is that they often degenerate into bureaucratic nightmares that interfere with the organization's ability to respond to competitive pressures. Some recommend reducing the controls and guidelines inherent in any pay plan. Hence, banding eliminates or at least reduces the impact of range maximums and minimums. Replacing merit grids with awards and bonuses eliminates the link between the pay increase and the employees' salary position in the range and performance rating. Replacing job evaluation with skill-based plans opens up the freedom to assign employees to a wider variety of work, regardless of their pay and the value of the work they perform.

Such approaches are consistent with the common plea that managers should be free to manage pay. Or, as some more bluntly claim, pay decisions are too important to be left to compensation professionals. There is a ring of truth to all this. Our experience with many companies is that their pay systems are bureaucratic nightmares.

Yet permitting managers to be free to pay employees as they judge best rests on a basic premise: Managers will use pay to achieve the organization's objectives—efficiency, fairness, and compliance with regulations—rather than their own objectives. Clearly, some balance between strict controls and chaos is required to ensure that pay decisions are directed at the organization's goals, yet permit sufficient flexibility for managers and employees to respond to unique situations. Achieving the balance becomes part of the art of managing compensation.

A final issue related to pay design and administration involves the skills and competencies required in compensation managers. The grandest strategy and structure may seem well designed, well thought out in the abstract, but could be a disaster if the people qualified to carry it out are not part of the staff.

In view of the importance of a well-trained staff, WorldatWork has professional development programs to entice readers into the compensation field. In addition, the Web sites in the Appendix to this chapter provide a lot more information.

CONCLUSION

We have now completed the discussion of the pay administration process. Administration includes control: control of the way managers decide individual employees' pay as well as control of overall costs of labour. As we noted, some controls are designed into the fabric of the pay system (inherent controls, range maximums and minimums, etc.). The salary budgeting and forecasting processes impose additional controls. The formal budgeting process focuses on controlling labour costs and generating the financial plan for the pay system. The budget sets the limits within which the rest of the system operates.

We also noted that with continuous change in organizations, compensation managers must understand how to manage change and be knowledgeable business partners.

Other aspects of administration we examined in this chapter included the fair treatment of employees in communications and participation. The basic point was that pay systems are tools, and like any tools, they need to be evaluated in terms of usefulness in achieving an organization's objectives.

CHAPTER SUMMARY

1. The three components of labour cost are employment (number of employees and hours they work), average cash compensation, and average benefit cost. Average cash compensation and average benefit cost are added together and then multiplied by employment levels in order to create total labour cost.
2. Salary levels can be controlled by a top-down budgeting approach by requiring top management of each unit to estimate the pay increase budget for the entire unit, and then allocating it to each manager, who plans how to distribute it among subordinates. The bottom-up budgeting approach requires each manager to forecast the pay increases he or she will recommend during the upcoming plan year, which are then reviewed by top management for approval.
3. Four inherent controls on pay decision making in compensation design techniques are range maximums and minimums, compa-ratios, variable pay, and costing of wage proposals.

4. The six stages in the compensation communication cycle are: (1) defining the objectives and goals of the communication program, (2) obtaining information on the current compensation program, (3) developing the strategy for the best overall communication approach--a marketing (sales) approach or a more technical communication approach, (4) determining the media and tools that are most appropriate, (5) conducting communication sessions, and (6) evaluating the success of the program.

5. Various issues regarding how organizations structure their compensation function include: decisions on centralization versus decentralization of compensation management, level of flexibility for compensation management decisions within corporatewide principles for all systems, and consideration of reengineering or outsourcing the compensation function.

KEY TERMS

REVIEW QUESTIONS

1. What are some of the approaches used to control labour costs, based on Exhibit 13.1? Based on budgeting methods? Based on the design of the pay system?

2. Which activities in administering the pay system are likely candidates to be outsourced? Why?

3. How do employee communication and participation influence the effectiveness of the pay system?

EXPERIENTIAL EXERCISES

1. Find a news article or information at hr.com about the impact of layoffs some time after the cuts were made. Was the layoff successful in reducing costs? In achieving corporate objectives?

2. Calculate the compounding effect of an annual 5% merit pay increase on a salary of $60,000 over five years. How much less money would be paid out if the merit pay increase of 5% were not added to base pay and had to be re-earned each year?

3. Consider the top-down and bottom-up approaches to controlling salary levels. Which one do you think would be more effective in a small entrepreneurial company? In a large government department?

WEB EXERCISE

Salary Budgeting at Mohawk College

Some organizations make their salary budgeting process public. Go to the Web site for Mohawk College (www.mohawkc.on.ca) and, in the human resources division area, find the policy document on salary administration guidelines. Does Mohawk College use a top-down or bottom-up salary budgeting process? Explain.

CASE

Two Harbours Teachers

Private school teachers typically are paid according to salary schedules that include:

1. "Steps" that pay for accumulating experience.
2. "Lanes" that pay for extra university credits.

Steps and lanes operate to boost pay even if the school does not grant any across-the-board or cost-of-living increases.

Critics of such schedules say that they guarantee steadily climbing costs, even in times when the school's finances do not permit increases.

Exhibit 1 shows a simplified salary schedule at Two Harbours, a private school that employs 100 teachers and whose enrolment is growing at about 3 percent a year.

A. Calculate the change in salary in year 2 under the following conditions:

1. Six teachers earning an average salary of $43,444 resign.
2. Nine teachers are hired at an average of $25,666.

EXHIBIT | **1** | Two Harbours Salary Schedule Showing Distribution of 100 Teachers ──────────

Year One

	Total salaries for 100 teachers			$3,110,000
	Average salary			$ 31,100

	B.A. degree	B.A. and credits	M.A. degree	M.A. and credits
Step 5	7 teachers $29,000	18 teachers $33,000	14 teachers $36,000	11 teachers $41,000
Step 4	4 teachers $27,000	6 teachers $30,000	5 teachers $34,000	1 teacher $38,000
Step 3	6 teachers $25,000	4 teachers $28,000	3 teachers $31,000	1 teacher $35,000

continued

CASE

	B.A. degree	B.A. and credits	M.A. degree	M.A. and credits
Step 2	6 teachers $23,000	2 teachers $26,000	2 teachers $28,000	0 teachers $32,000
Step 1	8 teachers $22,000	1 teacher $24,000	1 teacher $26,000	0 teachers $28,000

Each step represents four years of service; the vertical columns show levels of university credits. In year 2, the faculty moves from an average of 3.86 steps to 3.93, and the proportion of teachers with master's degrees increases from 38 to 39 percent.

■ APPENDIX 13–A
COMPENSATION WEB SITES

Consulting Firms

Consulting Firms	WWW Address	What does Web site offer?
Hay Group	http://www.haygroup.ca http://www.haypaynet.com	■ News releases, legislative and regulatory updates, and survey data ■ Hay PayNet allows organization to tap into Hay's customized compensation databases
Hewitt Associates	http://was4.hewitt.com/hewitt/worldwide/canada/index.htm	■ Provides press releases, full text articles, and brief items on laws and regulations
Runzheimer International	http://www.runzheimer.com	■ Information on salary differentials, living costs, and travel and moving benefits
Sibson & Company	http://www.segalco.com/sibson/index.html	■ Case studies drawn from client experiences ■ Items on compensation design, organization development, etc.
Towers Perrin	http://www.towers.com/towers/canada/en/default_canada.htm	■ Information on international pay and benefits ■ New legislation, regulations, and new issues in major countries
Watson Wyatt Worldwide	http://www.watsonwyatt.com/canada-english	■ Global news service, including reports and surveys from all over the world
William M. Mercer	http://www.mercerhr.com	■ Surveys on salaries, performance pay, assessment, compensation committees, and executive pay

Broad Listing for Compensation

Employee Compensation	WWW Address	What does Web site offer?
WorldatWork	http://www.worldatwork.org	■ Information on seminars and organization certification programs ■ Listings of publications
Canadian Management Centre	http://www.cmctraining.org	■ Information about training programs, publications, and other resources
Canadian Council of Human Resources Associations	http://www.cchra-ccarh.ca	■ HR news and wide range of links, including compensation and benefits ■ A number of links to human resources service providers

Benefits

Benefits	WWW Address	What does Web site offer?
Employee Benefit Research Institute (EBRI)	http://www.ebri.org	▪ Lists of health care providers and links to other benefits and business Web sites ▪ A list of links to other benefits sources on the Web ▪ EBRI reports on benefit issues
International Foundation of Employee Benefit Plans	http://www.ifebp.org	▪ Industry news ▪ Reports on benefit issues ▪ Full listing of IFEBP services and resources

Pensions and Retirement

Pensions and Retirement	WWW Address	What does Web site offer?
Association of Canadian Pension Management	www.acpm.com	▪ Canada's pension portal ▪ pension consultants ▪ industry organizations ▪ industry publications ▪ regulation
Canadian Pension and Benefits Institute	www.cpbi-icra.ca	▪ seminars ▪ conferences

APPENDIX

INTERNATIONAL PAY SYSTEMS

Around the world, global competitive forces are changing the way people work and the way they get paid. In Japan, Nissan and Fuji Photo have modified their promise of *lifetime employment* to "*long-term security*" within a group of subsidiary companies, not necessarily the parent company.[1] Toyota is dismantling its seniority-based pay system for managers and replacing it with a merit-based system.[2] Toshiba is considering stock awards, something that was not even legal in Japan only a few years ago.[3] European companies such as Deutsche Bank, Nokia, and Seimens are experimenting with variable pay and performance-based (rather than personality-based) appraisal in their search for ways to control labour costs.[4] Some high-tech startups in Germany and Spain are using stock options.[5] Global acquisitions of former competitors also are changing international pay systems. As part of its takeover and restructuring of Tungsram Electric in Poland, General Electric changed the pay system from a rigid seniority-based one to a more flexible one with broad bands, market-based wage rates, and performance bonuses.

Sometimes the changes in pay are directly tied to larger, cataclysmic sociopolitical change. Consider China, Russia, and Eastern Europe.[6] Central and government authorities had dictated pay rates in these communist command-and-control economies. Now companies and governments face the challenge of devising pay systems that are responsive to business and market pressures while trying to maintain a sense of social justice among the people. The Chinese situation is extraordinarily complex. The government is trying to shrink the welfare state at the same time that state-owned enterprises are being asked to become profitable. The only hope of profitability is to cut the massively bloated head count. Yet, an army of unemployed people without social support threatens stability and even government survival. The government's own newspaper, the *People's Daily*, hectors workers to assume responsibility for themselves. "City dwellers are used to eating from one big rice bowl . . . they could learn from rural people how to fend for themselves."[7] As part of the move to make state-owned enterprises more efficient, the government is urging them to emphasize markets, performance, and jobs designed to support the business objectives. Some state-owned enterprises, such as Bao Gang, the country's largest steelmaker, have moved to more "market and performance-based" systems, even though labour markets are just emerging in China. In anticipation of the competition for talent that will accompany China's entry into the World Trade Organization, Shanghai Shenyingwanguo Security Company and Shanghai Bank are examining internal alignment and implementing job-based structures. They want to provide structure that will help them retain key employees and increase pay satisfaction. Privatized enterprises, startups, and joint ventures with foreign firms use a variety of approaches. Most surprising of all is that some town-owned enterprises are using stock awards as part of their employee compensation.[8] China may still be striving to become a worker's paradise, but the experimentation with compensation approaches might already qualify it as a pay specialist's paradise.

However, too much change and experimentation often have a dark side, even threatening further social unrest. There are reports from the Ukraine, Romania, and Russia of people going unpaid for months, without legal recourse.[9] In Russia, a friend maintains that "the most effective pay delivery system is a brown bag under the table." So it is a time of unprecedented global change. Or is it? Let's step back to gain some historical perspective.

> . . . There is hardly a village or town anywhere on the globe whose wages are not influenced by distant foreign markets, whose infrastructure is not financed by foreign capital, whose engineering, manufacturing, and even business skills are not imported from abroad, or whose labor markets are not influenced by the absence of those who had emigrated or by the presence of strangers who had immigrated.[10]

This was not a description of the beginning of the 21st century, but of the beginning of the last century. In the late 1800s, trade barriers were reduced, free trade was promoted, and mass migration of people was underway. Thanks to transoceanic telegraphic cables, the speed of communication increased dramatically, and investment capital flowed between nations. Yet by 1917 these global links had been replaced by a global war. Nations began to raise tariffs to protect domestic companies hurt by foreign competitors. Foreign immigrants were accused of "robbing jobs," factories were moved to lower-wage nations, and citizens became uncomfortable with the greater risks and uncertainty of globalization. Historians conclude that "globalization is neither unique nor irreversible; it has and can again sow seeds of its own destruction."[11]

This warning notwithstanding, wherever you look in the world today, you can find evidence of the effects of globalization on the way people work and get paid. Our challenge is to understand and manage employee compensation in the midst of this changing world.

■ MANAGING VARIATIONS: THE GLOBAL GUIDE

Understanding international compensation begins with recognizing variations (differences and similarities) and figuring out how best to manage them. How people get paid around the world depends on differences (and similarities) in the factors in the global guide depicted in Exhibit A-1. Four general ones are listed: *economic, institutional, organizational,* and *employee.* Each of these has subfactors. For the faithful reader who has managed to get to this appendix, these should be very familiar. They have been discussed throughout the book. Now they can be applied globally. But, once we shift from a domestic to an international perspective, additional factors become important, too. Differences in institutional factors such as cultural traditions and political structures, and economic factors such as differences in ownership of enterprises and the development of capital and labour markets come into play. Furthermore, social contracts, the roles of trade unions, and other institutional factors also must be considered. Detailed discussion of all these factors is well beyond our purpose. (Did we hear you say, "Thank you for large favours"?) But an example using the global guide illustrates their relevance and usefulness.

Reconsider the Daimler-Chrysler situation discussed in Chapter 2. Prior to Daimler's acquisition of Chrysler, the pay for the 10 top Daimler executives equalled the pay of Chrysler's CEO alone. As little as 25 percent of Chrysler managers' total compensation was in the form of base pay, whereas Daimler managers' base pay accounted for up to 60 percent of their total compensation. The merged Daimler-Chrysler seems to have adopted a Chrysler-like approach for its management. Some have even claimed that Chrysler's more attractive pay was the reason Daimler executives were eager to acquire it!

The Daimler and Chrysler managerial pay systems are contrasted in Exhibit A-2, using the specific factors in the global guide in Exhibit A-1. At Daimler, the roots of today's pay system reach back to postwar Germany and efforts to rebuild an economy devastated by two world

EXHIBIT **A-1** Guide to International Compensation

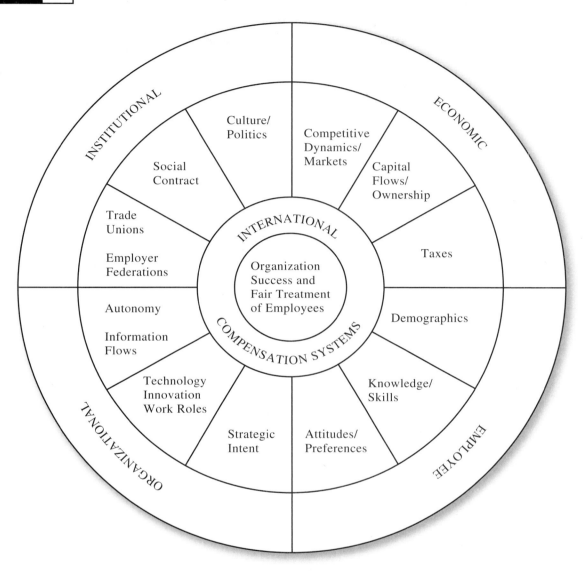

© George T. Milkovich

wars. Rather than aggressive wage competition that risked inflation, trade union federations, employer associations, government agencies, and financial institutions participated in centralized negotiations. The result was industrywide negotiated pay systems called tariff agreements. They included predictable annual increases, government-provided social welfare programs, and well-defined internal structures. All companies competing in the same product markets (e.g., Daimler, Volkswagen, and Opel) used the same pay structures. Daimler could pay above these negotiated rates but had little reason to do so. Instead, it competed for employees based on its reputation as a place to work, its quality of training, and the like. As a result, managers were less likely to consider pay as an instrument of strategy. Instead, pay looked more like a constraint to them, determined by people and processes outside the organization.

EXHIBIT A-2 Applying the Global Guide

Pressures	Daimler	Chrysler
ECONOMIC		
Competitive markets	Moderately competitive	Highly competitive
Capital/Ownership	Few shareholders	Many shareholders
Taxes	High taxes	Moderate taxes
INSTITUTIONAL		
Culture/Politics	Centralized process	Decentralized process
Regulations	Strong government/trade union involvement	Limited government involvement
Trade union/Employer federations	Tripartite-based social contract	Individual/employer-based social contract
ORGANIZATIONAL		
Strategic intent	High margins/High-end vehicles	Lower-margin passenger vehicles, higher-margin SUVs, minivans
Autonomy	Lower autonomy	Moderate autonomy
Work roles	Defined roles	More flexible roles
EMPLOYEE		
Skill/knowledge	Continuous learning	On-the-job
Attitudes/behaviours	High commitment	Committed but contentious
Demographics	Older, experienced	Older, experienced
TOTAL PAY SYSTEM	Sensitive to social contract; hierarchical; well-defined jobs	Aligned with strategy, sensitive to competitive markets
	Base and benefits; annual increase	Base/performance bonuses, stock ownership
	Focus on commitment and continuous learning	Focus on performance and cost control

German tax policies and labour regulations supported this approach.[12] A typical Daimler employee's marginal tax rate (percentage tax on each additional euro earned) is 30 percent higher than a Chrysler employee's tax rate on an additional dollar in the United States. As a result, the financial returns for working smarter (and longer and harder) in order to receive performance bonuses are significantly smaller at Daimler. Plus, until very recently, broad-based stock options for employees were illegal; even now, they are highly taxed. Consequently, base salary and across-the-board pay increases (rather than performance bonuses and stock options) are most common. On the other hand, Daimler employees receive generous welfare and unemployment payments, plus subsidized college and apprenticeship programs, in exchange for higher taxes. As Exhibit A-2 shows, this description of centralized wage setting, with predictable annual pay increases, concentrated financial ownership, and high taxes that support a wide social safety net still characterizes the pay system at Daimler-Chrysler's German locations.

Now let us apply the global guide to Chrysler. Chrysler reflects the competitive dynamics in North American labour and product markets as well as the social contract in North America, which values individual choice. Pay setting for managers is highly decentralized. It is influenced by labour markets in which thousands of employers and individuals and/or unions agree to pay rates with limited government involvement (e.g., ensuring conformance with minimum wage, tax, and discrimination laws). Chrysler's managerial pay system arguably is aligned with its business strategy, sensitive to market conditions, and includes significant performance bonus and stock ownership. The pay system is considered a strategic tool intended to competitively attract, retain, and motivate managers, but also to support customer satisfaction and improve shareholder value (a litany now familiar to faithful readers). Canadian and U.S. tax codes support the use of stock options by granting lower tax rates (capital gains) and favourable treatment under accounting practices. A recent study contrasted US and German pay systems thus: "In the US you work hard to advance to keep a good job, to keep from falling into a shallow social safety net . . . . whereas the German pay system and social benefits system is close to a guaranteed annual income."[13]

So the factors in the global guide serve as tools in a tool kit. By using each, we can gain increased understanding of the differences (and similarities) we see in international pay. Let's turn to five of these factors that are particularly salient. These are variations in (1) social contracts, (2) cultures, (3) trade unions, (4) ownership and capital markets, and (5) managers' autonomy. Although we separate the factors to clarify our discussion, they do not separate so easily in reality. Instead, they overlap and interact.

■ THE SOCIAL CONTRACT

The top of Exhibit A-3 depicts the employment relationship between an individual and an organization. Employees believe that certain actions are expected of them; in exchange they expect to receive certain returns (total value of employment). Now let us expand to the level of all stakeholders and institutions in a society. The relationship now includes the government, all enterprise owners, sometimes acting individually and sometimes collectively through owner associations, and all employees, sometimes acting individually and sometimes in trade unions. The relationships of these parties form the social contract. Variations in these social contracts

EXHIBIT A-3 Social Contract: Government, Organizations, and Employees

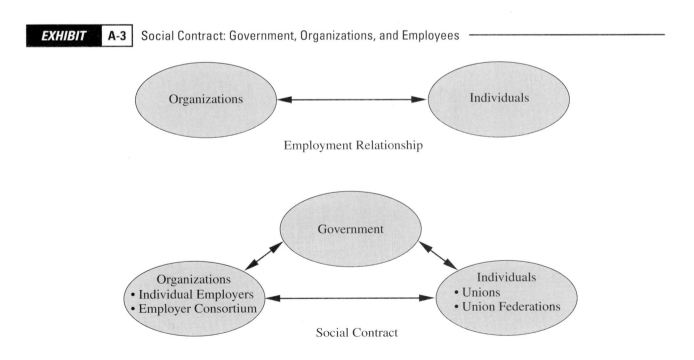

around the world are keystones of modern societies' economic and social well-being. As you think about how people get paid around the world, especially about the differences in the forms of pay, it will be clear that different people in different countries hold differing beliefs about the roles and responsibilities of government, employees, unions, and employers. These beliefs underlie differences in social contracts.

Understanding how to manage employee compensation in any country requires an understanding of the social contract; that is, understanding the roles played by government, employees, and employers in that country. Efforts to change employee compensation systems—for example, to make them more responsive to customers, encourage innovative and quality service, or control costs—require changing the mutual expectations of parties to the social contract.

Centralized–Localized Decision Making.   Perhaps the most striking example of the social contract's effects on pay systems is to contrast the degree of centralization of pay setting between countries.[14] Exhibit A-4 differentiates between countries such as the United States, the United Kingdom, Canada, Hong Kong, and Brazil with their highly decentralized approach and very little government involvement, and the moderately centralized-by-industry-sector approach found in Japan, Germany, Belgium, and some Central European nations, and a highly centralized approach, which creates the national pay systems in Sweden, Denmark, Austria, and Slovakia. The degree of centralization of pay setting closely parallels the growth in government. Public spending as a percentage of gross domestic product is higher in Sweden (56 percent), France (55 percent), and Germany (55 percent) than in the United Kingdom (39 percent) and the United States (30 percent).[15]

EXHIBIT A-4 Social Contracts and Pay Setting

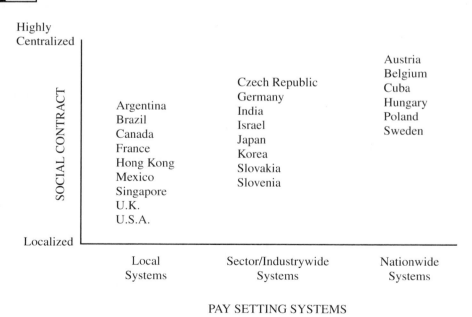

■ CULTURE

Culture is often defined as shared mental programming.[16] It is rooted in the values, beliefs, and assumptions shared in common by a group of people, and it influences how information is processed. How critical is culture in managing international pay? Very important, according to some. The assumption that pay systems must be designed to fit different national cultures is based on the belief that most of a country's inhabitants share a national character. Therefore, the job of the global manager is to search for national characteristics whose influence is assumed to be critical in managing international pay systems.

Typical of this thinking is the widely used list of national cultural attributes proposed by Hofstede (power distance, individualism–collectivism, uncertainty avoidance, and masculinity–femininity).[17] According to this view, "it is crucial that companies adjust their compensation practices to the cultural specifics of a particular host country."[18] Accordingly, in nations where the culture emphasizes respect for status and hierarchy (high power distance, attributed to Malaysia and Mexico), more hierarchical pay structures are appropriate. In "low power distance" nations (Australia and the Netherlands), more egalitarianism is called for.[19]

Advice can be even more specific. Companies operating in nations with "collectivistic" cultures, such as Singapore, Japan, Israel, and Korea, should use egalitarian pay structures (small differences between levels of work), equal pay increases, and group-based rather than individual-based performance incentives. Employers in the more "individualistic" national cultures such as the United States, United Kingdom, and Hong Kong prefer individual-based pay and increases that are proportional to contributions.

One might well react to such thinking by pointing out that it engenders blatant stereotyping.[20] It parallels such broad notions as "all women desire time off because of their caring and nurturing values, while all men desire more time at work to pursue their more aggressive values." The idea that culture is uniquely national overlooks the variations (diversity) between subgroups and regions within nations (e.g., within companies, city versus rural, older versus younger people, and so on).[21] So the issue to resolve is not what are the cultural differences between nations. Rather, the question is, Whose culture matters?[22]

Any group of people may exhibit a culture, a shared set of beliefs. Look around your university or workplace; engineers, lawyers, accountants, technicians may each hold unique shared mindsets. Organizations may, too. Your school's "culture" probably differs from Microsoft's, Toshiba's, or the London Symphony Orchestra's. In fact, you are likely part of many cultures. You are part of your university, but also part of your family; your social, political, interest groups; your region of the state or country, and so on. Cultures may be similar or different between all these groupings.

Interesting, but *so what* for understanding and managing total compensation around the world?

Culture Matters, but So Does Cultural Diversity

You will not be surprised to hear that culture classifiers consider the United States a country of risk takers who rank high on the individualistic (rather than collectivist) scale. In contrast, the country of Slovenia has been classified as more collectivist and security-conscious (as opposed to risk taking).[23] Slovenia was the first country to break off from the former Yugoslavia. (How is that for taking a risk?) It has a population of under three million, and by most standards would be considered very homogeneous. So you would expect Slovenian MBA students to be very different from US MBA students. However, a study found that Slovenian MBAs tended on average to be more risk taking and individualistic than US MBAs. The most striking finding, as shown in Exhibit A-5, was that the degree of variation between students on cultural

EXHIBIT A-5 Understanding the "Full House" of Variation within a Culture

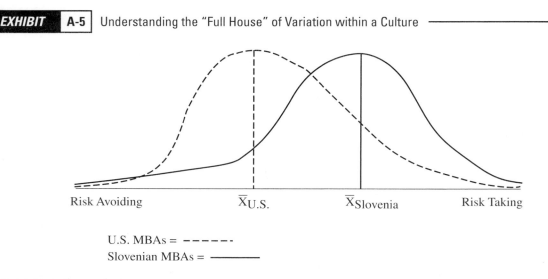

Risk Avoiding $\overline{X}_{U.S.}$ $\overline{X}_{Slovenia}$ Risk Taking

U.S. MBAs = − − − − − −
Slovenian MBAs = ————

dimensions was virtually the same in both the Slovene and US data. Thus, one can find risk-averse collectivists and risk-taking individualists in both nations.

So how useful is the notion of a national culture? In the absence of better data on variations such as in Exhibit A-5, it may offer a starting point. However, it is only a starting point. National culture can be thought of as the "average" in Exhibit A-5. It provides some information about what kinds of pay attitudes and beliefs you are likely to find in an area. But over-reliance on the "average" can even be harmful. This point is critical for managing international pay. As the paleobiologist Stephen Jay Gould noted, "Failure to consider the 'full house' of cases plunges us into serious error again and again."[24] Although Gould may not have been talking about compensation, we can still extend his point to global pay. To claim that all organizations and people in Germany or Japan or Canada use the same shared mind-set ignores variations and differences within each nation. Considerable diversity between companies and people within any country exists. So keep in mind our basic premise in this chapter: The interplay between economic, institutional, organizational, and individual conditions within each nation or region, taken as a whole, forms distinct approaches to total comparisons. Understanding these factors in the global guide is useful for managing employee compensation. However, do not assume uniformity (the average) within a country. Understanding the full range of individuals within nations is important in managing international pay.

TRADE UNIONS AND EMPLOYEE INVOLVEMENT

As Exhibit A.6 shows, Europe is highly unionized: In Sweden, 91 percent of the workforce belongs to unions; in the United Kingdom, 33 percent; and in Italy, 44 percent. Asia is less heavily unionized. Japan's unionization rate is 24 percent and South Korea's almost 13 percent. Although the exhibit might cause you to conclude that union power is declining in Europe, caution is in order. In many countries, workers' pay is set by collective agreements, even though they may not be union members. In France, for example, 90 percent of workers are covered by collective agreements, even though only 9 percent are members of unions.[25]

EXHIBIT | **A-6** | Trade Union Density

	1995	% change since 1985
Sweden	91.1	+8.7
Italy	44.1	–7.4
South Africa	40.9	+130.8
Australia	35.2	–29.6
U.K.	32.9	–27.7
Germany	28.9	–17.6
New Zealand	24.3	–55.1
Japan	24.0	–16.7
U.S.	14.2	–21.1
South Korea	12.7	+2.4
France	9.1	–37.2

In addition to higher rates of unionization, Belgium, Germany, and the European Union (EU) require the establishment of worker councils. Although the exact rules may vary between nations, worker councils and unions significantly affect any proposed changes in pay. The European Union is committed to maintaining the role of the *social partners*, as it calls employers and trade unions. The European Union is trying to provide common labour standards in all its member countries. The purpose of standards is to avoid "social dumping," or the relocation of a business in a country with lower standards and labour costs. At present, hourly labour costs and productivity vary substantially between the EU countries. Often the higher labour costs are off-set by greater productivity.[26]

Exhibits A-7 and A-8 sample some of the different approaches to social legislation, and what they cost. Britain specifies the fewest requirements, with no minimum wage, no maximum hours, and no formal methods for employee participation. France and Germany have the most generous social insurance. Trade unions based in each European nation have launched initiatives to coordinate social legislation across national borders. For example, the European Metalworkers Federation EU seeks regular pay increases that match inflation and a share in all productivity gains.

Some even foresee the eventual "Europeanization" of pay determination.[27]

◼ OWNERSHIP AND FINANCIAL MARKETS

Ownership and financing of companies differ widely around the world. These differences are also important to understanding and managing international pay. Fifty percent of American households own stock in companies either directly or indirectly through mutual funds and pension funds.[28] Direct stock ownership is only a few mouse clicks away. In Korea, six conglomerates control a significant portion of the Korean economy, and the six are closely linked to specific families (e.g., Hyundai and Samsung).[29] In Germany, the national Bundesbank and a small number of other influential banks have ownership interests in most major companies. These patterns of ownership make certain types of pay systems almost nonsensical. For example, linking performance bonuses to increased shareholder value or offering stock options to employees makes

Time and the clock

France, already among the most generous of nations in providing vacation time and short workdays, has instituted a 35-hour week in hopes of reducing unemployment. Opponents say the program will do little to dent the French jobless rate.

	AVERAGE HOURS WORKED Per employee, annually. 40 hours a week, with 2 weeks vacation, equals 2,000 hours.	JOBLESS RATE* Adjusted to be comparable across nations.
UNITED STATES ('97)	1,966 hours	4.3%
JAPAN ('95)	1,899	4.9%
BRITAIN ('97)	1,731	5.9%
FRANCE ('97)	1,656	11.1%
GERMANY ('97)	1,574	9.1%

*As of July, seasonally adjusted

Sources: International Labor Office; Bureau of Labor Statistics

little sense in the large conglomerates in Germany, Korea, or Japan. On the other hand, ownership in small startups in these nations is outside these traditional channels, so they are offering stock options to attract new employees.[30] Recent tax law changes in these countries have made options more attractive, but the ownership of the major employers is slow to change.

The most vivid illustrations of the importance of ownership occur in China and in Eastern Europe (Poland, Hungary, Slovenia, Czech Republic, and Slovakia), where a variety of forms are emerging. Although state-owned enterprises still employ two-thirds of all workers in China, township enterprises, wholly privately owned enterprises, joint ventures with foreign companies, and wholly owned foreign enterprises (WOFEs) account for 50 percent of the profits. Chinese employees switching from government-owned enterprises to these newer organizations find that both the pay and the employer expectations (i.e., the social contract) are substantially different.[31] The point is that understanding international compensation requires recognition that ownership differs, and that these differences may influence what forms of pay make sense. It is misleading to assume that every place is like home.

■ MANAGERIAL AUTONOMY

Managerial autonomy, an organizational factor in the global guide in Exhibit A-1, refers to the degree of discretion managers have to make the choices that make total compensation a strategic

EXHIBIT | **A-8** | Employment Practices Differ between Nations—II

The Cost of an Employee

For an employer, the cost of social insurance as a percentage of salary is higher in France than in some other places.

The hourly cost of a production worker in manufacturing . . .	. . . is made up from the salary paid directly to the worker before deductions . . .	. . . and what an employer pays in social insurance and labour taxes.	What those extra costs are as a percentage of salary.
France	$17.97	$12.36	$5.61	45.4%
Germany*	$28.28	$20.94	$7.34	35.1%
United States	$18.24	$14.34	$3.90	27.2%
Japan	$19.37	$16.52	$2.85	17.3%
Britain	$15.47	$13.47	$2.00	14.8%

*Former West Germany

Sources: Bureau of Labor Statistics; International Labor Office

---

tool. It is inversely related to the degree of centralization discussed earlier. Thus, most US- and UK-based organizations have relatively greater freedom to change employee pay practices than do most European companies. 3M, a global company based in St. Paul, Minnesota, recently created a worldwide performance-based pay plan for its managers in order to sustain innovation and growth. 3M units in the United States are trying out a variety of gain-sharing and bonus plans. At many 3M global locations, the notion of performance-based bonuses is old hat. On the other hand, 3M Europe, headquartered in Brussels, was told by the Belgian government that its proposed performance-based pay plan was illegal. In an effort to control inflation and promote egalitarian values, Belgium passed a law that made all forms of new pay beyond that set by the nationally negotiated labour agreements illegal. As already noted, centralized pay setting found in European Union countries limits organizations' autonomy to align pay to business strategies and changing market conditions.[32]

But not only institutions such as governments and trade unions limit managerial autonomy. Corporate policies often do as well.[33] Compensation decisions made in the home country corporate offices and exported to subunits around the world may align with the corporate strategy but discount local economic and social conditions. Although IBM corporate in Armonk, New York, expects all its worldwide operations to "differentiate people on performance" with total compensation, some IBM units in Tokyo remain convinced that local Japanese IBMers prefer more egalitarian practices. Nevertheless, managers in IBM Japan are expected to comply with Armonk. Is IBM trying to attract those people in Japan who are seeking more performance-based pay and signal to others that IBM has a performance-based culture around the world? Sounds like a research project to us.

In sum, as the global guide depicts, international compensation is influenced by economic, institutional, organizational, and individual conditions. And globalization really means that these conditions are changing—hence international pay systems are changing as well. Cultural, economic, and organizational forces interact. Culture and laws shape the social contracts, which in turn shape how organizations and employees compete economically. Economic competitiveness recalibrates and forces changes in the culture and laws. Thus, the forces are inevitably intertwined.

■ COMPARING COSTS

In Chapter 8 we discussed the importance of obtaining accurate information about what competitors pay in domestic markets. Similar comparisons of total compensation between nations can be misleading. Even if wage rates appear the same, expenses for health care, living costs, and other employer-provided allowances for such expenses as housing and commuting all complicate the picture. Health care and benefits are examples. Most industrialized nations other than the United States offer some form of national health care. An organization may pay indirectly for it through payroll taxes, but its value as part of total compensation is diminished, since all people in a nation may share similar coverage. Consequently, comparing data in global and local markets around the world is a major challenge. Comparisons between a specific Canadian firm and a specific foreign competitor may be even more misleading. Accurate data usually are difficult to obtain. Although consulting firms are improving their global databases, much of their data are still from North American companies' operations in global locations. Other foreign and local–national companies' data often are not available. So caution is required in using international data; it may be incomplete and biased toward North American practices.

Mexico provides a close-to-home example of the difficulties in comparing data between countries. A US government comparison of hourly compensation costs shows wages in Mexico at only 11 percent of those in the United States. However, another source, Hewitt Associates, computes an "effective labour cost" in Mexico at about 33 percent of the US rate.[34] The difference between the two estimates stems largely from supplemental pay required by Mexican law and custom. Hewitt reports that it is standard practice in Mexico to pay one month's pay as a Christmas bonus plus 80 percent of base for vacation bonuses plus punctuality bonuses. In addition, Mexican law dictates that workers be paid 365 days per year.[35] Andersen Consulting reports that due to shortages of trained Mexican managers, they often earn 20 to 30 percent more than their US counterparts. The point of including all this detail is to show that some data are useful only for gross comparisons and understanding trends over time. But anyone designing a pay system in one of these countries must obtain current local data and understand local regulations and practices.

Standard of Living: Basket of Goods versus Big Mac

If comparing total compensation is difficult, comparing living costs and standards is even more complex. The Bank of Switzerland uses a uniform basket of goods based on European consumer habits, which includes the prices for 137 items from clothing to transportation to personal care.[36] You may think the whole world shops at the Gap. Not so. A woman shopping for a summer dress, jacket, skirt, shoes, and stockings will find Tokyo the most expensive place to shop ($1,760), whereas Manila ($130) and Bombay ($120) are best buys. Tokyo is equally expensive for a man. If he wants a blazer, shirt, jeans, socks, and shoes, he will need to come up with $1,050 to pay for a medium-priced outfit.

If your tastes don't run to blazers and jackets, the *Economist* takes a Big Mac approach. Rather than pricing a complex basket of goods and services, the magazine uses the price of a Big Mac in different locations.[37] (Yes, the whole world does eat at McDonald's.) According to Exhibit A-9, the average price of a Big Mac in the United States is $2.51 (average of 4 cities), in China 9.90 yuan ($1.20 U.S.), in Canada $2.85 ($1.94 U.S.), and in Indonesia 14,500 rupiah ($1.83).

So what does a Big Mac have to do with compensation? Companies use cost comparisons in adjusting pay for employees who transfer between countries. The objective is to maintain *purchasing power parity*.[38]

There are several ways to calculate purchasing power. A common approach is to divide hourly wages by the cost of a standard basket of goods and services. Another approach is to

EXHIBIT **A-9** The Hamburger Standard

	Big Mac Prices	
	in local currency	in dollars
United States*	$2.51	2.51
Argentina	Peso2.50	2.50
Australia	A$2.59	1.54
Brazil	Real2.95	1.65
Britain	£1.90	3.00
Canada	C$2.85	1.94
Chile	Peso1,260	2.45
China	Yuan9.90	1.20
Czech Rep	koruna54.37	1.39
Denmark	DKr24.75	3.08
Euro area	EURO2.56	2.37
France	FFr18.50	2.62
Germany	DM4.99	2.37
Italy	Lire4,500	2.16
Spain	Pta375	2.09
Hong Kong	HK$10.20	1.31
Hungary	Forint339	1.21
Indonesia	Rupiah14,500	1.83
Israel	Shekel14.5	3.58
Japan	¥294	2.78
Malaysia	M$4.52	1.19
Mexico	Peso20.90	2.22
New Zealand	NZ$3.40	1.69
Poland	Zloty5.50	1.28
Russia	Rouble39.50	1.39
Singapore	S$3.20	1.88
South Africa	Rand9.00	1.34
South Korea	Won3,000	2.71
Sweden	SKr24.00	2.71
Switzerland	SFr5.90	3.48
Taiwan	NT$70.00	2.29
Thailand	Baht55.00	1.45

*Average of New York, Chicago, San Francisco, and Atlanta.
Source: McDonald's

calculate the working time required to buy an item such as a one-kilogram loaf of bread: 7 minutes in London, 15 minutes in Tokyo, 27 minutes in Montreal, and 12 minutes in Chicago. Or to buy a Big Mac: 14 minutes in Chicago, 36 minutes in London, and 90 minutes in Mexico City. The Big Mac (plus fries) attains luxury status in Nairobi, Caracas, and Lagos; an employed person must toil three hours (Nairobi), four hours (Caracas), or almost two days (Lagos) to afford it. (Hold the fries.)

■ COMPARING SYSTEMS

We have made the point that pay systems differ around the globe, and that those differences relate to variations in economic pressures, sociopolitical institutions, and the diversity of organizations and employees. In this section we compare several compensation systems. The caution about stereotyping raised earlier applies here as well. Even in nations described by some as homogeneous, pay systems differ from business to business. For example, two well-known Japanese companies, Toyota and Toshiba, have designed different pay systems. Toyota places greater emphasis on external market rates, uses far fewer levels in its structure, and places greater emphasis on individual-based merit and performance pay than does Toshiba. So, as we discuss "typical" systems, remember that differences exist, and change in these systems is occurring everywhere.

The Total Pay Model: Strategic Choices

The total pay model used throughout the book guides our discussion of pay systems in different countries. We have already examined how all organizations face similar strategic issues, but that the relative importance among them differs. You will recognize the basic choices, which seem universal:

- Objectives of pay systems
- External competitiveness
- Internal alignment
- Employee contributions
- Administration

But, if the choices are universal, the results are not. We have noted that each nation has its own laws regulating pay determination. We further noted in Exhibit A.4 that some of these support centralized, national-level pay setting, others industrywide decision making, and still others operate at the organization level. In Sweden, centralized negotiation involves national union leaders, government officials, and representatives from leading Swedish employers. The nationwide compensation agreement that results guarantees equal pay for equal work across all employers, regardless of differences in each company's performance strategy. Sweden is so constrained by laws and national agreements that all Swedish organizations have very similar pay systems. In effect, decisions about pay are taken out of the hands of the organization and placed in the hands of regulators and nationwide associations. In other countries such as Germany, each industry group negotiates its own central agreement.

In the central European country of Slovenia, where nationwide agreements also exist, companies may use the nationwide agreement as a starting point. The building fabrication company Trimo adds three steps to each base rate set by the agreements. Trimo hopes to establish a lead position in its market and to attract and hold on to more highly educated and skilled workers. However, Trimo's structure is the exception. More often, when national-level negotiations establish the "going rate," pay is no longer used to help achieve competitive advantage. In contrast to North American companies, organizations in the European Union place relatively less importance on market surveys and competitive positions.

So, although regulation in many countries is so strict that it is difficult to manage any part of employee compensation to help achieve competitive advantage, a central theme in this chapter is that global competitive forces are pressuring organizations in all countries to control labour costs and to consider performance-based pay plans. This in turn is putting pressure on regulators and negotiators to modify their social contracts. Although the choices in the pay model are universal, their strategic importance differs around the globe.

■ NATIONAL SYSTEMS

A national system mindset assumes that most employers in a company adopt similar pay practices; analysis then consists of comparing Japanese, German, US, and other systems. This approach is most useful in nations with centralized approaches (see Exhibit A-5) or where homogeneous economic and cultural conditions exist (e.g., Sweden). Some writers abstract even more and describe broader regional systems, as in the European Way, the Asian Way, or the North American Way. Obviously, this approach paints with an even broader brush. We shall describe the Japanese and German national systems below. But please approach this information with care. The national or regional mindset overlooks variations among organizations within each nation. It overlooks the possibility that organizations may design total pay practices that are strategically aligned with the business strategy, unique, and difficult for competitors to copy.

Japanese National System

Traditionally, Japan's employment relationships were supported by "three pillars":

1. Lifetime security within the company.
2. Seniority-based pay and promotion systems.
3. Enterprise unions (decentralized unions that represent workers within a single company).

Japanese pay systems tend to emphasize the person rather than the job; seniority and skills possessed rather than job or work performed; promotions based upon supervisory evaluation of trainability, skill/ability levels, and performance rather than performance alone; internal alignment over competitors' market rates; and employment security based on the performance of the organization and the individual (formerly lifetime security).

Total Compensation in Japan

It is convenient to describe Japanese pay systems in terms of three basic components: base pay, bonuses, and allowances/benefits.[39]

Base Pay.   Base pay accounts for 60 to 80 percent of an employees' monthly pay, depending on the individual's rank in the organization. Base pay is not based on job evaluation or market pricing (as predominates in North America), nor is it attached to specific job titles. Rather, it is based on a combination of employee characteristics: career category, years of service, and skill/performance level.

Career.   Five career categories prevail in Japan: (1) general administration, (2) engineer/ scientific, (3) secretary/office, (4) technician/blue collar job, and (5) contingent. Workers in the first two categories are called white-collar workers.

Years of Service.   Seniority remains a major factor in determining base pay. Management creates a matrix of pay and years of service for each career category. Exhibit A-10 shows a matrix for general administration work. Companies meet periodically to compare their matrices, which accounts for the similarity among companies. In general, salary increases with age until 50 years of age and then is reduced. Employees can expect annual increases no matter what their performance level until age 50, though the amount of increase varies according to individual skills and performance.

EXHIBIT **A-10** Salary and Age Matrix for General Administration Work in a Japanese Company ————

*Age	†Salary	Age	Salary	Age	Salary	Age	Salary
		31	$1,900	41	$2,900	51	$3,800
22	$1,000	32	2,000	42	3,000	52	3,700
23	1,100	33	2,100	43	3,100	53	3,600
24	1,200	34	2,200	44	3,200	54	3,500
25	1,300	35	2,300	45	3,300	55	3,400
26	1,400	36	2,400	46	3,400	56	3,300
27	1,500	37	2,500	47	3,500	57	3,200
28	1,600	38	2,600	48	3,600	58	3,100
29	1,700	39	2,700	49	3,700	59	3,000
30	1,800	40	2,800	50	3,800	60	2,900

Notes: *Age 22 is typical entry with college degree.
†Monthly salary, converted to dollars.

Skills and Performance. Each skill is defined by its class (usually 7–13) and rank (1–9) within the class. Exhibit A-11 illustrates a skill salary chart for the General Administration career category. Classes 1 and 2 typically include associate (entry) and senior associate work; 2, 3, and 4, supervisor and managerial; 5, 6, and 7, managerial, general director, and so on. Employees advance in rank as a result of their supervisor's evaluation of their:

- Effort (e.g., enthusiasm, participation, responsiveness).
- Skills required for the work (e.g., analytical, decision making, leadership, planning, process improvement, teamwork).
- Performance (typical MBO-style ratings).

Mitsui's appraisal form in Exhibit A-12 is typical of most appraisals.

To illustrate how the system works, let us consider a graduate fresh from university who enters at class 1, rank 1. After one year, this new *salaryman* and all those hired at the same time

EXHIBIT **A-11** Skill Chart for General Administration Work ————

	Associate	Senior Associate	Supervisor		Manager	General Director	
	Class 1	*Class 2*	*Class 3*	*Class 4*	*Class 5*	*Class 6*	*Class 7*
Rank 1	$ 600	$1,600	$2,600	$3,100	$3,600	$4,500	$5,500
Rank 2	700	1,700	2,650	3,150	3,750	4,700	6,000
Rank 3	800	1,800	2,700	3,200	3,800	4,900	
Rank 4	900	1,900	2,750	3,250	3,900	5,100	
Rank 5	1,000	2,000	2,800	3,300	4,000		
Rank 6	1,100	2,100	2,850	3,350	4,100		
Rank 7	1,200	2,200	2,900	3,400			
Rank 8	1,300	2,300	2,950	3,450			
Rank 9	1,400	2,400	3,000	3,500			

EXHIBIT | **A-12** | Mitsui Annual Appraisal of Performance (Summary)

Name: Job grade:

Age: Years in the grade:

School:

Appraisal	Rating				
	A	B	C	D	E
Last year's appraisal: First-half appraisal Second-half appraisal					
Attendance					
Performance: Quantity Quality					
Ability: Planning/judgment Improvement Negotiation Leadership					
Work attitude: Positiveness Cooperation Responsibility					
General Appraisal First appraisal Second appraisal Adjustment General appraisal All-company adjustment Final decision					

Key: Outstanding (A); Superior (B); Standard (C); Inferior (D); Very inferior (E).

are evaluated by their supervisors on their effort, abilities, and performance. Early in the career (the first three years), effort is more important; in later years abilities and performance receive more emphasis. The number of ranks an employee moves each year (and therefore the increase in base pay) depends on this supervisory rating (e.g., receiving an A on the appraisal form lets you move up three ranks within the class, a B moves you two ranks, and so on).

Theoretically, a person with an A rating could move up three ranks in class each year and shift to the next class in three years. However, most companies require both minimum and maximum years of service within each class. So, even if you receive four straight A ratings, you would still remain in class 1 for the minimum of six years. Class 2 may also have a six-year minimum time, and so on. Conversely, if you received four straight D grades, you would still get promoted to the next skill class after spending the maximum of 10 years in class 1. These minimum and maximum times in class effectively change this skill system into one based on both seniority and skill.

The logic underlying this approach is revealing. On the one hand, setting a minimum time in each class helps ensure that the employee knows the work and returns value to the company. On the other hand, the system also slows the progress of high-potential performers. And even the weakest performers eventually advance. Indeed, some report that weak performers eventually can get to the top of the pay structure though they do not get the accompanying job titles or responsibility.

The system reflects the traditional Japanese saying, "A nail that is standing too high will be pounded down." An individual employee will not want to stand out. Employees work to advance the performance of the group or team rather than themselves.

Information from the two matrices is combined to determine an individual's salary. Going into his 11th year, an individual hired right out of university is now age 33, which corresponds to $2,100/month in base pay. This individual is class 2, rank 9. His performance would make him eligible to move to class 3; however, he has not yet spent the minimum time required in class 2. He needs to wait another year. So this adds $2,400 to his base pay, for a total of $4,500 per month, or $54,000 per year.

Under the traditional Japanese system, increases in annual base pay are relatively small (7 percent in our example of superior performance, compared to 10 to 12 percent for star performers in many Canadian merit systems), though they compound over time just as conventional merit and across-the-board increases in Canada. However, since the Japanese system is so seniority based, labour costs increase as the average age of the workforce increases. In fact, a continuing problem facing Japanese employers is the increasing labour costs caused by the cumulative effects of annual increases combined with lifetime employment security. Early retirement incentives and "new jobs" with lower salaries are programs being used to contain these costs.

Bonuses.   Bonuses account for between 20 and 40 percent of annual salary, depending on the level in the organization. Generally, the higher up you are, the larger the percentage of annual salary received as bonus. Typical Japanese companies pay bonuses twice a year (July and December). Some still assume that the Japanese bonus is similar to the Canadian profit-sharing bonus in that it is based on some measure of performance. But caution is required in interpretation. For blue-collar and unionized employees, management calls the bonus a *gratuity*. Unions avoid this term, however; they describe bonuses as an *expectable* additional payment to be made twice a year, even in bad financial times.

The amount of bonuses is calculated by multiplying employees' monthly base pay by a multiplier (typically 2.0–3.0 in each payout). The size of the multiplier is determined by collective bargaining between employers and unions in each company. Sometimes the multiplier may also vary according to an employee's performance evaluation. In a recent year, the average multiplier was 4.8 (2.3 in summer and 2.5 in winter) for white-collar workers. Applied to our example, the individual whose monthly base pay was $4,500 would receive a bonus of $10,350 ($4,500/month × 2.3) in July and $11,250 ($4,500/month × 2.5) in December.

According to the Japan Institute of Labour, for most employees (managers excepted), bonuses are in reality variable pay that helps control the employers' cash flow and labour costs but that are not intended to act as a motivator or to support improved corporate performance. Japanese labour laws encourage the use of bonuses to achieve cost savings by omitting bonuses from calculations of many other benefits costs. For example:

- Calculations for pension plan contributions (2.25 percent of each employees' salary) exclude bonuses.
- Health insurance premiums are 4.1 percent of salary, but only .5 percent of bonus.
- Overtime pay calculations (at least 25 percent of base pay) exclude bonuses.
- Calculations for severance pay and earlier retirement allowances exclude bonuses.

So the cost savings offered by emphasizing bonuses rather than base pay can add up.

The timing of the bonuses is very important. In Japan both the summer festival and new year are traditional gift-giving times; in addition, consumers tend to make major purchases during these periods. Employees use their bonuses to cover these expenses. Thus, the tradition of the bonus system is deeply rooted in Japanese life and is still considered an indispensable form of pay.

Benefits and Allowances.   The third characteristic of Japanese pay systems, the allowance, comes in a variety of forms: family allowances, commuting allowances, housing and geographic differential allowances, and so on. Company housing in the form of dormitories for single employees or rent or mortgage subsidies is a substantial amount. Life-passage payments are made when an employee marries or experiences a death in the immediate family. Commuting allowance is also important. One survey reported that employees who took public transportation received about 9,000 yen (approximately $90 per month) for commuting. Family allowances vary with the number of dependents. Toyota provides about 17,500 to 18,000 yen ($175 to $180) a month for the first dependent and about 4,500 to 5,500 yen ($45 to $55) for additional dependents. Some employers even provide matchmaking allowances for those who tire of life in company dorms.

The history of some of these allowances reveals very pragmatic roots. But, like many practices in Canada, the allowances remain long after the need. An example is the contemporary family allowance that originated as a "rice allowance" during food shortages following World War II.

One important allowance in the Japanese system is the retirement allowance. Typically, the amount of payout is calculated by multiplying employees' monthly base pay as of retirement by a multiplier, which is determined based on years of service. Exhibit A-13 illustrates the relationship between the years of employees' service and a multiplier in a Japanese organization. The quadratic relationship shows that the retirement allowance encourages employees to stay in the organization throughout their careers. This retirement allowance is now a heavy financial burden for Japanese companies because of their aging labour force. In response to this problem, some companies have introduced a new system in which an employee can choose either to (1) receive the traditional retirement allowance at retirement, or (2) receive an additional monthly cash payment in exchange for giving up retirement allowance. Experience at companies such as Mitsubishi Electric and Panasonic suggests that younger workers opt for (2)—signalling their preference for cash and perhaps their expectation of changing employers at some time in their career.

Legally Mandated Benefits.   Legally mandated benefits in Japan include health insurance, social security, unemployment, and workers' compensation. Although these four are similar to Canada, Japanese employers also pay premiums for preschool child support, and employment of the handicapped.

The lack of economic growth that Japan has been experiencing over the last decade, coupled with its heavy emphasis on seniority-based pay, means that Japanese labour costs have climbed faster than those of their global competitors. Faced with these pressures, many companies are trying to maintain *long-time* (rather than lifetime) employment while they look for other ways to reward younger and more flexible employees. These younger employees, who have been paid relatively poorly under the seniority-based pay system, are finding the pay in non-Japanese firms

EXHIBIT **A-13** Years of Service as Multiplier for Retirement Allowance in Japanese National System

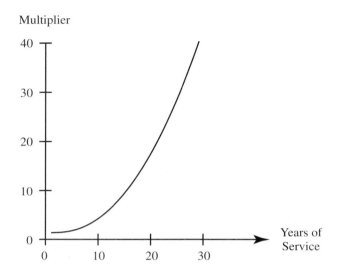

operating in Japan more attractive. Their willingness to move is creating a more active labour market. North American firms are succeeding in hiring such young Japanese by offering them more competitive base pay plus performance-based pay. In order to retain younger employees, many Japanese firms such as Toyota, Toshiba, and Mitsubishi are introducing new pay systems similar to North American pay systems. Stock options, which were just made legal only a few years ago, are increasingly used. As a result, considerable variation in pay systems is beginning to emerge between traditional Japanese companies.[40]

German National System[41]

The social contract in which traditional German pay systems are embedded is marked by a generous *vater staat*, or "nanny state," created through the social partnership between business, labour, and government. Pay decisions are highly regulated; over 90 different laws apply. Different *tariff agreements* (pay rates and structures) are negotiated for each industrial sector (e.g., banking, chemicals, metals manufacturing) by the major employers and unions. Thus, the pay rates at Adam Opel AG, a major car company, are quite similar to those at Daimler, Volkswagen, and any other German car company. Methods for job evaluation and career progression are included in the tariff agreements. However, these tariff agreements do not apply to managerial jobs.

In some companies, the pay rates set in these tariff agreements become minimums to which improvements are added. Local plant agreements use the sector-wide tariffs as guidelines. Even small organizations that are not legally bound by tariffs tend to use them as guidelines. Article 87 of the Works Constitution Act specifies co-determination on all aspects of the pay system and any changes to it. For example, the metal trades agreement that covers manufacturing plants states that "a Christmas bonus" of between 25 and 55 percent of the monthly base wage must be granted. Opel AG started with this as the minimum and negotiated a plan that tied a larger bonus to absentee goals.

Total Compensation in Germany

Vergutung is the most common German word for compensation. Although most employees only think of their monthly salary as being part of *vergutung*, managers worldwide know that compensation includes base, bonuses, allowances, and benefits.

Base Pay Base pay accounts for 70 to 80 percent of employees' total compensation, depending on their job level. Base pay is based on job descriptions, job evaluations, and employee age. The tariff agreement applicable to Adam Opel AG, for example, sets the following *tariff groups* (akin to job families and grades):

wage earners	8 groups (L2–L9)
salary earners	6 office/administrative (K1–K6)
	6 technical (T1–T6)
	4 supervisory (M1–M4)

Exhibit A-14 shows the rates established in the tariff agreement for the office and administration group (K1–K6).

Note that each tariff group K1–K6 is a percentage of the rate negotiated for K2 (the "corner rate"). Base pay and the percentages depend on the work content (job evaluation) and employee age (up to age 28). So an HR specialist (K4) receives between 1796 and 2370 euros, depending on age, which is presumed to reflect professional experience. These negotiated pay rates for K1 through K6 are equivalent across all German car companies. A different tariff exists in companies in the banking or chemicals sector.

EXHIBIT A-14 Base Pay Rates for Office/Administrative Jobs in Adam Opel AG's Tariff Agreement

Tariff Group (Salaried Employees)	Example Jobs	% of Corner Rate	EURO (as of March, 2000)
K1 (simple tasks)	Mail clerk	80–100	€ 1,149–1,437
K2 (corner rate = salary for employees aged 23 – 25) (simple administration)	Receptionist Typist	85–120 100	€ 1,221–1,724 € 1,437
K3 (general administration)	Secretary Clerk	100–140	€ 1,437–2,011
K4 (capable of independent work)	HR specialist	125–165	€ 1,796–2,370
K5 (capable of independent work PLUS specialized knowledge)	Senior specialist	165–190	€ 2,370–2,730
K6 (broader range of responsibility)	Supervisor	200–220	€ 2,874–3,160

Bonuses   Although there is a trend to increase variable-performance-based bonuses, they have not been part of a traditional German pay system for unionized workers. Performance is believed to depend on experience (seniority) and qualifications. In contrast, managerial pay does include performance bonuses.

Adam Opel AG's tariff agreement stipulates that an average 13 percent of the total base wages must be paid as "efficiency allowances." Systems to measure this efficiency are negotiated with the works councils for each location. In reality, these efficiency allowances become expected annual bonuses. Performance bonuses for managerial positions not included in tariffs are based on company earnings and other company objectives. Until recently stock options were not legal in Germany. Currently only about one-third of top executives receive them.

Allowances and Benefits   Germany's social contract includes generous social benefits. These nationally mandated benefits, paid for through taxes on employers and employees, include liberal social security, unemployment protection, health care, nursing care, and other programs. Employer and employee contributions to the social security system can add up to more than one-third of wages. Additionally, companies commonly provide additional benefits and services such as pension plans, savings plans, building loans, and life insurance. Company cars are always popular. The make and model of the car and whether or not the company provides a cell phone are viewed as signs of status in an organization. German workers also receive 30 working days of vacation plus about 12 national holidays annually (compared to an average of nine or ten days in Canada).

Trends   Germany today is not all traditional manufacturing, machine tools, and Mercedes's. It has over half of the top Internet companies in Europe. Even the German post office has been privatized. And nearly one in five German adults own stock, double the rate in the late 1990s. As in most developed economies, global competitive pressures and technological changes are forcing many of these changes. High social security expenses and other costly benefits, unacceptable levels of unemployment, insufficient job creation, and ambivalence over foreign immigrants underlie a rethinking of the traditional German social contract as well as the resulting total compensation systems. Companies are asking for greater flexibility in tariff agreements to better reflect economic conditions, use of performance in total compensation in addition to seniority and qualifications, and ways to link job security to company performance. On the other hand, many are reluctant to change the present system for fear it will destabilize German society.

Strategic Comparisons: Japan, Germany, Canada

Japanese and German traditional systems appear to have different strategic approaches than Canadian pay systems. Exhibit A-15 uses the basic strategic choices outlined in the total pay model—objectives, internal alignment, competitiveness, contribution, and administration—as a basis for comparisons. Both the Japanese and German systems constrain organizations' use of pay as a strategic tool. German companies face pay rates, job evaluation methods, and bonuses identical to those of their competitors, set by negotiated tariff agreements. The basic strategic premise, that competitive advantage is sustained by aligning with business strategy, is limited by laws and unions. Japanese companies do not face pay rates fixed industrywide; rather, they voluntarily meet to exchange detailed pay information. So the end result appears to be the same: similar pay structures across companies competing within an industry. In contrast, managers in Canadian companies possess considerable flexibility to align pay systems with business strategies. As a result, greater variability between companies exists.

The pay objectives in traditional German systems include long-term commitment, greater egalitarianism, and cost control through the negotiation of tariff agreements, which apply to competitors' labour costs, too. Japanese organization set pay objectives that focus on the long term (age and security), support high commitment (seniority/ability-based), are more egalitarian

| **EXHIBIT A-15** | Strategic Similarities and Differences: An Illustrated Comparison |

	Japan	**Canada**	**German**
Objectives	Long-term focus High commitment Egalitarian—internal fairness Flexible work force Control cash flow with bonuses	Short/intermediate focus High commitment Peformance—market—meritocratic Flexible work force Cost control; varies with performance	Long term High commitment Egalitarian—fairness Highly trained Cost control through tariff negotiations
Internal alignment	Person based: age, ability, performance determines base pay Many levels Small pay differences	Work based: jobs, skills, accountabilities Fewer levels Larger pay differences	Work based: jobs and experience Many levels Small pay differences
External competitiveness	Monitor age–pay charts Consistent with competitors	Market determined Compete on variable and performance-based pay	Tariff based Same as competitors
Employee contribution	Bonuses vary with performance only at higher levels in organization Performance appraisal influences promotions and small portion of pay increases	Bonuses an increasing percentage of total pay Increases based on individual, unit, and corporate performance	Tariff negotiated bonuses Smaller performance bonuses for managers
Advantages	Supports commitment and security Greater predictability for companies and employees Flexibility—person based	Supports performance—competitor focus Costs vary with performance Focus on short-term payoffs (speed to market)	Supports commitment and security Greater predictability for companies and employees Companies do not compete with pay
Disadvantage	High cost of aging work-force Discourages unique contributors Discourages women and younger employees	Skeptical workers, less security Fosters "What's in it for me?" No reward for investing in long-term projects	Inflexible; bureaucratic High social and benefit costs Not a strategic tool

(smaller pay differences), signal the importance of company and individual performance (company bonuses, individual promotions), and encourage flexible workers (person-based pay). Canadian companies, in contrast, focus on the shorter term (less job security); are market sensitive (competitive total pay); emphasize cost control (variable pay based on performance); reward performance improvement (bonuses, options, etc.), meritocracy, and innovation (individual rewards); and encourage flexibility (broadbanding and skill based).

Canadian firms generally set base pay according to relevant market (competitive position), the work (job and person), and employee contributions (performance-based pay). In Japan, person-based factors (seniority, ability, and performance) are used to set base pay. Market comparisons are monitored in Japan, but internal alignment based on seniority remains far more important. Job-based factors (job evaluation) and age (experience) are also used in Germany. Labour markets in Germany are highly regulated, and tariff agreements set pay for union workers. So, like the Japanese system, the German system places much greater emphasis on internal alignment than on markets.

Each approach has advantages and disadvantages. Clearly, the Japanese approach is consistent with low turnover/high commitment, greater acceptance of change, and the need to be flexible. Canadian firms face higher turnover (which is not always a disadvantage) and greater skepticism about change (i.e., What's in it for me?). Canadian firms encourage innovation; they also recognize the enormous talent and contributions to be tapped from workforce diversity. German traditional systems tend to be more bureaucratic and rule-bound. Hence, they are more inflexible. However, they also offer more predictability and stability for people. The Japanese national system faces challenges from the high costs associated with an aging white-collar workforce, its limited use of women's capabilities, and emerging efforts to reward innovative individuals. The Canadian challenges include the impact of increased uncertainty and risk among employees, a short-term focus, and employees' stress and skepticism about continuous change.

▉ STRATEGIC MARKET MINDSET

Some believe that the pressures of globalization require rethinking the national system mindset described earlier. A strategic market mindset is an alternative. It depicts companies following either a multiple-nation strategy (where business units in each country or region operate relatively independently in national markets), or a global strategy (where there is a high degree of integration and coordination among the different units and corporate headquarters).[42] In a global study of pay systems used by companies with worldwide operations, three general compensation strategies capture the different approaches: (1) localizer, (2) exporter, and (3) globalizer.[43]

Localizer: "Think Globally, Act Locally"

This approach designs pay systems to be consistent with local conditions. The company's business strategy is to seek competitive advantage by providing products and services tailored to local customers. Localizers operate independently of the corporate headquarters. One manager in the study compared his company's pay system to McDonald's. "It's as if McDonalds used a different recipe for hamburgers in every country. So, too, for our pay system." Another says, "We seek to be a good citizen in each nation in which we operate. So should our pay system." One side effect of aligning with local conditions is multiple systems: One-hundred-fifty countries, 150 systems.

Exporter: "One Size Fits All"

This approach designs a basic total pay system at headquarters and "exports" it worldwide for implementation at all locations. Exporters are the virtual opposites of localizers. Exporting a basic system (with some adjustments for national laws and regulations) makes it easier to move managers and professionals between locations (e.g., between European countries) without having to change how they are paid. The practice also communicates consistent corporatewide objectives. Managers say that "one plan from headquarters gives all managers around the world a common vocabulary and a clear message about what the leadership values." On the other hand, not everyone likes the idea of simply implementing what others have designed. One manager complained that headquarters rarely consulted managers in the field: "There is no idea or interest in a bridge, the notion that ideas can go both ways."

Globalizer: "Think and Act Globally and Locally"

Similar to exporters, globalizers seek a common system that can be used as part of the "glue" to support consistency across all global locations. But headquarters and the operating units are heavily networked to shared ideas and knowledge. Managers with this view stated that "No one has a corner on good ideas about how to pay people. We need to get them for all our locations." "Home country begins to lose its meaning; you measure performance where it makes sense for the business and you design pay structures to support the business." "Compensation policy depends more on tax policies and the dynamics of our business than it does on 'national' culture. I suppose you could argue that tax policies reflect a country's dominant culture, but from where I sit it depends on the political aims of the ruling coalitions and our ability to effectively work with them. The culture argument is something politicians hide behind."

Note that the focus in all three of these strategic global approaches is no longer on matching national systems. Instead, it shifts to aligning the total pay system with the global business strategy. Even the localizer adapts to local (national) systems because they are aligned with the company's business strategy. If, for example, IBM is competing by integrating its solutions offered to customers around the world, then it is likely to use a globalizer approach. If Toshiba operates locally or nationally and emphasizes the differences between national markets, then it is likely to adopt a localizer approach. The challenge is for managers to rethink international compensation in the face of global competition, to align global pay with the way the business is aligned.

■ EXPATRIATE PAY

When multinationals decide to open facilities in an international location, one of the many decisions they face is the type of personnel to hire. International subsidiaries choose from a mix of expatriates ("expat": someone whose citizenship is that of the employer's base country; for example, a Japanese citizen working for Sony in Toronto), third-country nationals (TCN: someone whose citizenship is neither the employer's base country nor the location of the subsidiary; for example, a German citizen working for Sony in Toronto), and local country nationals (LCN: citizens of the country in which the subsidiary is located; for example, Canadian citizens working for Sony in Toronto). Hiring LCNs has advantages. The company saves relocation expenses and avoids concerns about employees adapting to the local culture. Employment of LCNs satisfies nationalistic demands for hiring locals. Only rarely do organizations decide that hiring LCNs is inappropriate.

Expats or TCNs may be brought in for a number of reasons.[44] The foreign assignment may represent an opportunity for selected employees to develop an international perspective; the position may be sufficiently confidential that information is entrusted only to a proven domestic veteran; the particular skills required for a position may not be readily available in the local labour pool. Exhibit A-16 catalogues a number of reasons for asking employees to take work assignments in another country.

Japanese multinational companies use expatriates more frequently than multinationals headquartered in other countries.[45] About 4.2 percent of the international workforce for Japanese manufacturing companies are expatriates. Among US and European multinationals, only about 1 percent of the international workforce composed of US and European multinational companies are expatriates. The number of expatriates per large US multinational company has declined over the past decade. One reason for the decline is that the objectives for overseas assignments are shifting. Earlier, transferring technologies and the need for specific skills that were in scarce supply in local economies were the primary reasons for hiring expatriates. More recently, developing a global perspective (globalists) among key employees has become more important. This shift is consistent with the global competition discussed throughout this chapter and the growing impor-

EXHIBIT **A-16**   Why Expatriates Are Selected

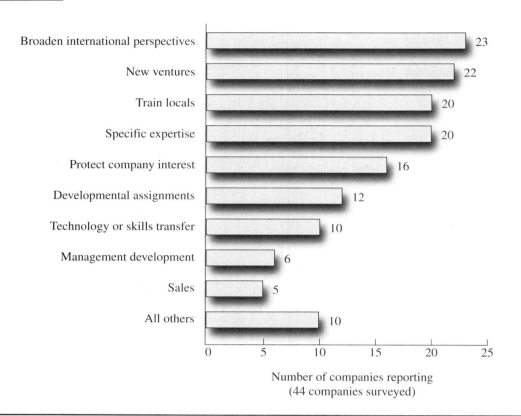

Number of companies reporting
(44 companies surveyed)

tance of international markets and revenues to all major firms. Today, two very different groups of employees are receiving global assignments. One group is higher level managers and executives (globalists) who must make strategic decisions about global opportunities and competition. The other group is recent university graduates who receive relatively short overseas assignments as part of their career development. Designing expatriate pay systems that help achieve such varied objectives is a challenge. A company that sends a Canadian employee (base salary of $80,000) with a spouse and two children to London for three years can expect to spend $800,000 to $1,000,000. Obviously, the high cost of expatriate assignments needs to be offset by the value of the contributions the employee makes.[46]

Elements of Expatriate Compensation

A shopping list of items (such as those in Exhibit A-17) that can make up expatriate compensation includes everything from household furnishing allowances to language and culture training, spousal employment assistance, and rest and relaxation leaves for longer-term assignments. Usually such lists are organized into four major components: salary, taxes, housing, and allowances and premiums.

Salary.   The base salary plus incentives (merit, eligibility for profit sharing, bonus plans, etc.) for expatriate jobs is usually determined via job evaluation or competency-based plans. 3M applies a global job evaluation plan for its international assignments. Common factors describe different 3M jobs around the world. With this system, the work of a regional human resource

EXHIBIT A-17 Common Allowances in Expatriate Pay Packages

Financial Allowances
- Reimbursement for tax return preparation
- Tax equalization
- Housing differential
- Children's education allowance
- Temporary living allowance
- Goods and services differential
- Transportation differential
- Foreign service premium
- Household furnishing allowance
- Currency protection
- Hardship premium
- Completion bonus

Family Support
- Language training
- Assistance locating schools for children
- Training for local culture's customs (family)
- Child care providers
- Assistance locating spousal employment

Social Adjustment Assistance
- Emergency leave
- Home leave
- Company car/driver
- Assistance with locating new home
- Access to Western-style health care
- Club membership
- General personal services (e.g., translation)
- Personal security (manager and family)
- General culture-transition training (manager)
- Social events
- Career development and repatriation planning
- Training for local culture customs (manager)
- Orientation to community (manager and family)
- Counselling services
- Rest and relaxation leave
- Domestic staff (excluding child care)
- Use of company-owned vacation facilities

manager in Brussels can be compared to the work of a human resource manager in Vancouver or Singapore. Most companies try to use the same procedures to value domestic operations and expatriate jobs.

Beyond salaries and incentives, the intent of the other components is *to help keep expatriate employees financially whole and minimize the disruptions of the move.* This basically means maintaining a standard of living about equal to their peers in their home or base country. This is a broad standard, one that often has resulted in very costly packages from the company's perspective, but one that provides good deals for the expatriate.

Taxes.   Income earned in foreign countries has two potential sources of income tax liability.[47] With few exceptions (Saudi Arabia is one), foreign tax liabilities are incurred on income earned in foreign countries. For example, money earned in Japan is subject to Japanese income tax, whether earned by a Japanese or a Korean citizen. The other potential liability is the tax owed in the employees' home country. The United States has the dubious distinction of being the only developed country that taxes its citizens for income earned in another country, even though that income is taxed by the country in which it was earned. Employers handle this through *tax equalization*.[48] The employer takes the responsibility of paying whatever income taxes are due to either the host country and/or the home country. Taxes are deducted from employees' earnings up to the same amount of taxes they would pay had they remained in their home country.

This allowance can be a substantial amount. For example, the marginal tax rates in Belgium, the Netherlands, and Sweden can run between 70 and 90 percent. So, if a Swedish expatriate is sent to a lower-tax country, say, Great Britain, the company keeps the difference. If a British expatriate goes to Sweden, the company makes up the difference in taxes. The logic here is that if the employee kept the windfall from being assigned to a low-tax country, getting this person to accept assignments elsewhere would become difficult.

Housing.   Providing expatriates with appropriate housing seems to have a major impact on their success. Most international companies pay allowances for housing or provide company-owned housing for expatriates. "Expatriate colonies" often grow up in sections of major cities where many different international companies group their expatriates. The difficulty comes in determining what is appropriate housing, and in some cases, finding affordable versions of it. Depending on the type of package used, an employee may be given some or complete choice in the matter.

Allowances and Premiums.   A friend in Moscow cautions that when we take the famed Moscow subway, we should pay the fare at the beginning of the ride. Inflation is so high there that if we wait to pay until the end of the ride, we won't be able to afford to get off! Cost of living allowances, club memberships, transportation assistance, child care and education, spousal employment, local culture training, and personal security are some of the many service allowances and premiums expatriates receive.

The logic supporting these allowances is that foreign assignments require the expatriate to (1) work with less direct supervision than a domestic counterpart, (2) often live and work in strange and sometimes uncongenial surroundings, and (3) represent the employer in the host country. The size of the premium is a function of both the expected hardship and hazards in the host country and the type of job. So an assignment in London will probably yield fewer allowances than one in Tehran, where Death to Americans Day is still a national holiday.[49]

The Balance Sheet Approach

Most North American, European, and Japanese global firms combine these elements of pay in a balance sheet approach.[50] The name stems from accounting, where credits and debits must balance. It is based on the premise that employees on overseas assignments should have the same spending power as they would in their home country. Therefore, the *home country is the standard* for all payments. The objective is to:

1. Ensure mobility of people to global assignments as cost effectively as is feasible.
2. Ensure that expatriates neither gain nor lose financially.
3. Minimize adjustments required of expatriates and their dependents.

Notice that none of these objectives link to performance.

Exhibit A-18 depicts the balance sheet approach. Home country salary is the first column. A person's salary (based on job evaluation, market surveys, merit, and incentives) must cover taxes, housing, goods and services, plus other financial obligations (a "reserve"). The proportions set for each of the components in the exhibit are *norms* (i.e., assumed to be "normal" for the typical expatriate) set to reflect consumption patterns in the home country for a person at that salary level with that particular family pattern. They are not actual expenditures. These norms are based on surveys conducted by consulting firms. Using these norms is supposed to avoid negotiating with each individual, though substantial negotiation still occurs.

So let us assume that the norms suggest that a typical manager with a spouse and one child, earning $84,000 in Canada, will spend $2,000 per month on housing, $2,000 on taxes, $2,000 on goods and services, and put away a reserve of $1,000 per month. The next building block is the equivalent costs in the host country where the assignment is located. For example, if similar housing costs $3,000 in the host country, the expatriate is expected to pay the same $2,000 paid in Canada, and the company pays the employee the difference (in our example, the extra $1,000 per month). In the illustration, taxes, housing, and goods and services components are all greater in the host country than in the home country. The expatriate bears the same level of costs (white area of column two) as at home. The employer is responsible for the additional costs (shaded area). (Changing exchange rates among currencies complicate these allowance calculations.)

EXHIBIT A-18 Balance Sheet Approach

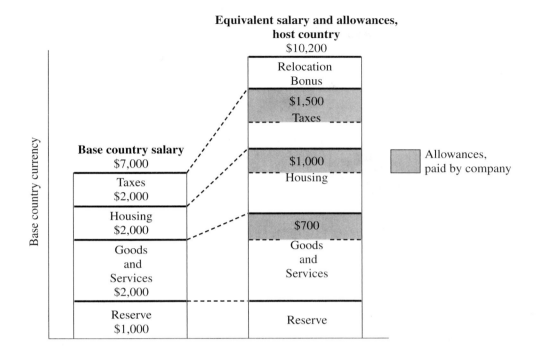

However, equalizing pay may not motivate an employee to move to another country, particularly if the new location has less personal appeal. Therefore, many employers also offer some form of financial incentive or bonus to encourage the move. Column 2 of Exhibit A-18 includes a relocation bonus. Four out of five North American multinational corporations pay relocation bonuses to induce people to take expatriate assignments.

If gaining international experience is really one of the future competencies required by organizations, then the need for such bonuses ought to be reduced, since the expatriate experience should increase the likelihood of future promotions. Either the experience expatriates obtain is unique to each situation and therefore not transferable, or companies simply do not know how to value it. Whatever the reason, research reveals that North American expatriates feel that their organizations still do not value their international expertise.[51] So the rhetoric of the value of global competencies has yet to match the reality; hence the need for relocation incentives.

Alternatives to Balance Sheet Approach.   The balance sheet approach was refined in the 1960s and 1970s when most expatriates were technical employees of North American oil companies. But the business environment and the reasons for expatriate assignments have changed since then. Consequently, many employers are exploring changes.

Negotiation simply means that the employer and employee find a mutually agreeable package. This approach is most common in smaller firms with very few expatriates. The arrangements tend to be relatively costly (or generous, depending on your point of view), create comparability problems when other people are asked to locate overseas ("but Mike and Sarah got . . ."), and need to be renegotiated with each transfer ("You are going to take away my chauffeur and three domestic servants here in the Philippines just to send me to London? Guess again!").

Another alternative, *localization*, ties salary to the *host* (local) *country* salary scales and provides some cost of living allowances for taxes, housing, and dependents. The allowances tend to be similar to those under the balance sheet, but the salary can vary. The downside is that individual salaries vary with the location (average rate for an engineer in Geneva is $55,000, compared to $41,300 in Rome and $32,000 in Bristol) rather than with the job or performance.

The balance sheet approach ties salary to the home country; the *modified balance sheet* ties salary to a *region* (Asia-Pacific, Europe, North America, Central America, and South America). The logic is that if an employee of a global business who relocates from Winnipeg to Halifax receives only a moving allowance, why should all the extras be paid for international moves of far less distance (e.g., from Germany to Spain)? In Europe, many companies no longer view those European managers who work outside their home country as expats. Instead, they are Europeans running their European businesses. And the use of a common currency, the euro, makes this easier.

Another common modification is to decrease allowances over time. The logic is that the longer the employee is in the host country, the closer the standard of living should come to that of a local employee. For example, if Canadians eat a $10 pizza twice a week at home, should they eat a $30 pizza twice a week in Tokyo, at the employer's expense? More typically, after a couple of months, the expatriate will probably learn where the nationals find cheaper pizza or switch to sushi. So, although these modified plans minimize the impact of changes in standards of living at the first stage (one to three years) of the assignment, after three to five years some of the allowance becomes equal to allowances paid to local national employees, with the exception of taxes and housing. The main purpose of the modified balance sheet seems to be to reduce costs; it pays little attention to performance, ensuring fairness, or satisfying preferences of expats.

The *lump-sum/cafeteria approach* offers expats more choices. This approach sets salaries according to the home-country system and simply offers employees lump sums of money to offset differences in standards of living. So, for example, a company will still calculate differences in cost of living. But instead of breaking them into housing, transportation, goods and services, and so on, the employee simply receives a total allowance. Perhaps one employee will trade less spacious housing for private schooling and tutors for the children; another employee will make different choices. We know of one expatriate who purchased a villa and a winery in Italy with his allowance. He has been reassigned to Mexico City, but still owns and operates his winery. This arrangement probably was not an objective of the expatriate pay system; however, the expatriate made tradeoffs in his living arrangements to retain most of his lump sum. A recent survey of these different approaches shows that the balance sheet is by far the most commonly used (68 percent). There is little evidence that companies have developed a truly international pay strategy for their global employees.[52]

Expatriate Systems → Objectives? *Quel Dommage*!

Talk to experts in international compensation, and you soon get into complexities of taxes, exchange rates, housing differences, and the like. What you do not hear is how the expatriate pay system affects competitive advantage, customer satisfaction, quality, or other performance concerns. It does emphasize maintaining employee purchasing power and minimizing disruptions and inequities. But the lack of attention to improving performance or ensuring that the expatriate assignment is consistent with organization objectives is glaring.

Expatriate compensation systems are forever trying to be not too high, not too low, but just right. The expatriate pay must be sufficient to encourage the employee to take the assignment, yet not so attractive that local nationals will feel unfairly treated or that the expatriate will refuse any future reassignments. However, the relevant standard for judging fairness may not be home-country treatment. It may be the pay of other expats, that is, the expat community, or it may be local nationals. And how do local nationals feel about the allowances and pay levels of their expat co-workers? Very little research tells us how expats and those around them judge the fairness of expat pay.

Employee Preferences. Beyond work objectives, costs, and fairness, an additional consideration is employees' preferences for international assignments. For many Europeans, working in another country is just part of a career. Yet for many Canadian employees, leaving Canada means leaving the action. They may worry that expatriate experience will sidetrack rather than enhance their career. Employees undoubtedly differ in their preferences for overseas jobs, and preferences can vary over time. Having children in high school or elderly parents to care for, divorce, working spouses, and other life factors exert a strong influence on whether an offer to work overseas is a positive or negative opportunity. Research does inform us of the following:

- 68 percent of expatriates do not know what their jobs will be when they return home.
- 54 percent return to lower level jobs. Only 11 percent are promoted.
- Only 5 percent believe their company values overseas experience.
- 77 percent have less disposable income when they return home.
- More than half of returning expatriates leave their company within one year.
- Only 13 percent of US expatriates are women (49 percent of all US managers and professionals are women).

Unfortunately, although research does highlight the problem, it does not offer much guidance for designers of expat pay systems.[53] Consequently, we are at the mercy of conjecture and beliefs.

BORDERLESS WORLD → BORDERLESS PAY? GLOBALISTS

Many multinational corporations are attempting to create a cadre of globalists: managers who operate anywhere in the world in a borderless manner. They expect that during their career, they will be located in and travel from country to country. According to Jack Welch, former CEO of General Electric, "The aim in a global business is to get the best ideas from everyone, everywhere."[54] To support this global flow of ideas and people, some are also designing borderless or at least regionalized pay systems. One testing ground for this approach is the European Union. As our global guide, discussed earlier, points out, one difficulty with borderless pay is that base pay levels and the other components depend too much on differences in each nation's laws and customs about managerial pay.

Nevertheless, perhaps the strongest pressure to harmonize managerial pay systems is that some managers in globalizing companies are no longer expatriates from their home countries, but are becoming global managers running global businesses.

Focusing on expatriate compensation may blind companies to the issue of adequate rewards for employees who are seeking global career opportunities. Ignoring such employees causes them to focus only on local operations and pay less attention to the broader goals of the global firm. It is naive to expect commitment to a long-term global strategy in which local managers have little input and receive limited benefits. Paradoxically, attempts to localize top management in subsidiaries may reinforce the gap in focus between local and global management.

Are We Global Yet?

Globalizing an organization goes beyond developing and paying a cadre of people who move around the world to different assignments. It involves a *mindset*—adapting alternative courses to create a common mental programming that views the company's operations on a worldwide scale. This view requires balancing priorities of corporate, business unit, and different regions. Total pay systems can support such a mindset.

A successful global organization must learn from its experiences in each locality in order to become truly global rather than "multilocal." Designing pay systems that simultaneously support national customs and reflect local conditions helps create global minds—thinking and acting globally and locally.

The belief is that those companies that do manage to mobilize global intellectual capital will gain a substantial competitive edge. However, global utilization of intellectual capital probably will not be achieved without a rethinking of reward systems.

CONCLUSION

Studying employee compensation only in your neighbourhood, city, or country is like being a horse with blinders. Removing the blinders by adopting a global perspective will deepen your understanding of local or national issues. Anyone interested in compensation needs to adopt a global perspective. The globalization of businesses, financial markets, trade agreements, and even labour markets is affecting every workplace and every employment relationship. And employee compensation, so central to the workplace, is embedded in the different political–socioeconomic arrangements found around the world. Examining employee compensation with the factors in the global pay model offers insights into managing total compensation internationally.

The basic premise of this book has been that compensation systems have a profound impact on individual behaviour, organization success, and social well-being. We believe this holds true within and across all national boundaries.

ENDNOTES

Chapter 1

[1]L. Gomez-Mejia and D. Balkin; *Compensation, Organizational Strategy, and Firm Performance* (Cincinnati, OH: Southwestern Publishing, 1992); P. Zingheim and J. R. Schuster, *Pay People Right!* (San Francisco: Jossey Bass, 2000); B. Gerhart, "Pay Strategy and Firm Performance," in S. L. Rynes and B.E. Gerhart, eds. *Compensation in Organizations: Current Research and Practice* (San Francisco; Jossey-Bass, 2000); B. E. Becker and M. Huselid, "High Performance Work Systems and Firm Performance: A Synthesis of Research and Management Implications," in G. Ferris ed. *Research in Personnel and Human Resources* (Greenwich, CT: JAI Press, 1998).

[2]M. Drolet, "The Male-Female Wage Gap," *Perspectives*, Spring 2002, pp. 29-35. Statistics Canada Catalogue No. 75-001-XPE.

[3]C. Sparks and M. Greiner, "U.S. and Foreign Productivity and Unit Labor Costs," *Monthly Labor Review*, February 1997, pp. 26–35.

[4]S. Greenhouse, "Anti-Sweatshop Movement is Achieving Gains Overseas," *New York Times*, January 26, 2000, p. A10; S. Greenhouse, "Activism Surges at Campuses Nationwide, and Labor Is at Issue," *New York Times*, March 29, 1999, p. A14.

[5]D. Olive, "Many CEOs Richly Rewarded for Failure," *Toronto Star*, August 25, 2002, pp. A1, A10, A11.

[6]*Industry Total Labor Cost Studies* (Philadelphia: The Hay Group, 1997); J. E. Triplett, *An Essay on Labor Costs* (Washington, D.C.: Office of Research and Evaluation, U.S. Bureau of Labor Statistics, 1997).

[7]E. Lawler III, *Rewarding Excellence* (San Francisco: Jossey Bass, 2000); B. E. Becker and M. Huselid, "High Performance Work Systems and Firm Performance: A Synthesis of Research and Management Implications," in *Research in Personnel and Human Resources*, ed. G. Ferris (Greenwich, CT: JAI Press, 1998).

[8]G. T. Milkovich and M. Bloom, "Rethinking International Compensation: From National Cultures to Markets and Strategic Flexibility," *Compensation and Benefits Review*, January 1998, pp. 1–10; M. Bloom and G. Milkovich, "A SHRM Perspective on International Compensation and Reward Systems," *Research in Personnel and Human Resources Management,* Supplement 4 (Greenwich, CT: JAI Press, 1999), pp. 283–303; R. B. Freeman and L. F. Katz, *Differences and Changes in Wage Structures* (Chicago: University of Chicago Press, 1995); C. Brown and M. Corcoran, "Sex-based differences in school content and the male-female wage gap," *Journal of Labor Economics* 15 (3) (1997), pp. 431–65; J. Waldfogel, "Understanding the 'Family Gap' in Pay for Women with Children," *Journal of Economic Perspectives* 12(1), (1998), pp. 157–70; P. Cappelli, J. Constantine, and C. Chadwick, "It Pays to Value Family: Work and Family Tradeoffs Reconsidered," *Industrial Relations* 39 (2), April 2000, pp. 175–98; F. Blau and L. Kahn, "Gender Differences in Pay," Cambridge, MA: NBER working paper 7732, June 2000.

[9]E. E. Lawler, *Rewarding Excellence* (San Francisco: Jossey Bass, 2000).

[10]Participants in an international compensation seminar at Cornell University provided the information on various meanings of compensation.

[11]D. Rousseau, *Psychological Contracts in Organizations* (Thousand Oaks, CA: Sage, 1995).

[12]*Compensation Planning Outlook 2003* (Ottawa, ON: Conference Board of Canada).

[13]R. S. Kaplan and D. P. Norton, *The Balanced Scorecard: Translating Strategy into Action* (Boston: Harvard Business School Press, 1996).

[14]See the Web site for F. W. Cook, www.fredericwcook.com.

[15]Some believe greater stock ownership motivates performance; others argue that the link between individual job behaviours and the vagaries of the stock market are tenuous at best. J. L. Pierce, S. A. Rubenfeld, and S. Morgan, "Employee Ownership: A Conceptual Model of Process and Effects," *Academy of Management Review* 16 (1991), pp. 121–44; S. Rodrick, *The Stock Options Book of 1998* (Oakland, CA: The National Center for Employee Ownership, 1998) (see also their Web site at www.nceo.org); D. Kruse and J. Blasi, "Employee Ownership, Employee Attributes and Firm Performance," *Journal of Employee Ownership, Law and Finance*, April 2000, pp. 37–48; "Web Sites for Employees with Stock Options," *Employee Ownership Report*, November/December 2000, p. 11.

[16]Employee Benefits Research Institute's Web site at http://www.ebri.org. See also the EBRI's *Fundamentals of Employee Benefits* (Washington, D.C.: EBRI, 1997) and EBRI *Health Benefits Databook* (1999); D. J. B. Mitchell, "Employee Benefits in Europe and the United States" in *Research Frontiers*

in IR and HR, ed. D.Lewin (Madison, WI: IRRA, 1996), pp. 587–625.

[17] T. Humber, "Creating a Culture of Wellness," *Canadian HR Reporter*, April 7, 2003, pp. 21, 26.

[18] Further information on each company's philosophy and way of doing business can be deduced from their Web sites: www.medtronic.com and www.aesc.com. Readers of earlier editions of this book will note that fairness is substituted for equity. Equity has taken on several meanings in compensation, e.g., stock ownership, and pay discrimination. We decided that fairness better conveyed our meaning in this book.

[19] J. Brockner, Y. Chen, K. Leung, and D. Skarlicki "Culture and Procedural Fairness: When the Effects of What You Do Depend on How You Do It," *Administrative Science Quarterly* 45 (2000), pp. 138–59; M. P. Miceli, "Justice and Pay System Satisfaction" in *Justice in the Workplace: Approaching Fairness in Human Resource Management* (Lawrence Erlbaum Associates, 1993).

Chapter 2

[1] John L. Nesheim, *High Tech Start Up* (Saratoga, CA: John L. Nesheim, 1997); Michael Wanderer, "Dot-Comp: A 'Traditional' Pay Plan with a Cutting Edge," *WorldatWork Journal*, Fourth Quarter 2000, pp. 15–24.

[2] M. Lewis, *The New New Thing* (New York: Norton & Company, 2000); Rodney K. Platt, "Dot-Com Companies: Changing the Rules of Rewards," *Workspan*, June 2000, pp. 41–46; Mike Wanderer, "Dot-Comp: A 'Traditional' Pay Plan with a Cutting Edge," *WorldatWork Journal*, Fourth Quarter 2000, pp. 15–24.

[3] D. Vaughan Whitehead, "Wage Reform in Central and Eastern Europe," in *Paying the Price*, ed. Vaughn-Whitehead (St. Martin's Press, New York, 2000); R. Boisot and J. Child, "From Fiefs to Clans to Network Capitalism: Explaining China's Emerging Economic Order," *Administrative Science Quarterly* 41 (1996), pp. 600–28.

[4] Henry Mintzberg, "Five Tips for Strategy," in *The Strategy Process: Concepts and Contexts*, eds. Henry Mintzberg and James Brian Quinn (Englewood Cliffs, NJ: Prentice-Hall, 1992); J. E. Delery and D. H. Doty, "Models of Theorizing in Strategic Human Resource Management," *Academy of Management Journal* 39 (4), pp. 802–35; Helen L. DeCieri and Peter Dowling, "Theoretical and Empirical Developments in Strategic International HRM," in *Research and Theory in Strategic HRM: An Agenda for the Twenty-First Century*, eds. Pat Wright et al. (Greenwich, CT: JAI Press, 1999); L. R. Gomez-Mejia and D. B. Balkin, *Compensation, Organization Strategy, and Firm Performance* (Cincinnati: Southwestern, 1992); P. K. Zingheim and R. Schuster, *Pay People Right!* (San Francisco: Jossey Bass, 2000); Ediberto F.

Montemayer, "Aligning Pay Systems with Market Strategy," *ACA Journal*, Winter 1994, pp. 44–53.

[5] B. Gerhart, "Pay Strategy and Firm Performance," in *Compensation in Organizations: Current Research and Practice*, S. L. Rynes and B. Gerhart, ed. (San Francisco; Jossey-Bass, 2000).

[6] A. Richter, "Paying the People in Black at Big Blue," *Compensation and Benefits Review*, May/June 1998, pp. 51–59. Also see H. A. Thompson, "Supporting Sears' Turnaround with Compensation," *ACA Journal* (1997) pp. 8–12.

[7] M. Porter, "What is Strategy?" *Harvard Business Review*, November–December 1996, pp. 61–78; J. Jackson, "Why Being Different Pays," *Financial Times*, June 23, 1997, p. B1; M. Treacy and F. Wiersma, *The Discipline of Market Leaders* (Reading, MA: Addison-Wesley, 1997).

[8] V. Pucik, N. Tichy, and C. Barnett, eds., *Globalizing Management: Creating and Leading the Competitive Organization* (Wiley, 1992); L. R. Gomez-Mejia, "Structure and Process of Diversification, Compensation Strategy, and Firm Performance," *Strategic Management Journal*, October 1992, pp. 44–56.

[9] Howard Schultz and Dori Jones Yang, *How Starbucks Built a Company One Cup at a Time* (New York: Hyperion 1997); J. Lee-Young, "Starbucks Expansion in China," *Wall Street Journal*, March 12, 2000, p. B6.

[10] H. Mintzberg, "Crafting Strategy," *Harvard Business Review*, July–August 1970, pp. 66–75.

[11] S. Brown and K. Eisenhart, *Competing on the Edge* (Boston: Harvard Business School Press, 1998).

[12] P. Gooderham, O. Nordhaug, and K. Ringdal, "Institutional and Rational Determinants of Organization Practices: Human Resource Management in European Firms," *Administrative Science Quarterly* 44, September 1999, pp. 507–31; M. Bloom, G. Milkovich, and A. Mitra, "Rethinking International Compensation and Reward Systems: A Grounded Theory Perspective," Ithaca, NY: ILR School/CAHRS working paper, 2000; M. Bloom and G. Milkovich, "Strategic Perspectives on International Compensation and Reward Systems," in *Research and Theory in Strategic HRM: An Agenda for the Twenty-First Century*, eds. Pat Wright et al (Greenwich, CT: JAI Press, 1999); D. D. McKenna and J. J. McHenry, *Microsoft's Maniacal Work Ethic* (Redmond, WA: Microsoft, 1996); A. Sorge, "Strategic Fit and Societal Effect: Cross National Comparisons of Technology, Organization, and HR," *Organization Studies*, July 1991, pp. 1–2; G. Hoefstede, *Culture's Consequences: International Differences in Work Relationships and Values* (Thousand Oaks, CA: Sage Publications, 1980).

[13] See the Bureau of Labor Statistics Web site for most current figures on international wage comparisons.

[14]A. Harney, "Toyota Plans Pay Based on Merit," *Financial Times*, July 8, 1999, p. 20.

[15]S. Greenhouse, "Mission Statements: Words That Can't Be Set to Music," *New York Times*, June 21, 2000, p. C1.

[16]*Competing in a Global Economy* (Bethesda, MD: Watson Wyatt Worldwide, 1998); Jiing-Lih Farh, Rodger W. Griffeth, and David B. Balkin, "Effects of Choice of Pay Plans on Satisfaction, Goal Setting, and Performance," *Journal of Organizational Behavior* 12 (1991), pp. 55–62; Dan Cable and Tim Judge, "Pay Preferences and Job Search Decisions: A Person-Organization Fit Perspective," *Personnel Psychology*, Summer 1994, pp. 317–48.

[17]R. Winslow and C. Gentry, "Give Workers Money and Let Them Buy a Plan," *Wall Street Journal*, February 8, 2000, p. A1.

[18]Melissa Barringer and George Milkovich, "Employee Health Insurance Decisions in a Flexible Benefit Environment," *Human Resource Management* 35 (1996), pp. 293–315; M. P. Patterson, "Health Benefit Evolutions for the 21st Century: Vouchers and Other Innovations?" *Compensation and Benefits Review* 32(4), July/August 2000, pp. 6–14.

[19]D. C. Johnson, "On Pay Day, Union Jobs Stack Up Very Well," *New York Times*, August 31, 1997, p. B1; Henry Farber and Alan B. Krueger, "Union Membership in the United States: The Decline Continues," in *Employee Representation: Alternatives and Future Directions*, eds. Bruce E. Kaufman and Morris M. Kleiner (Madison, WI: Industrial Relations Research Association, 1993), pp. 135–68; E. Applebaum and Rosemary Batt, *The New American Workplace* (Ithaca, NY: ILR Press, 1994); T. A. Kochan and P. Osterman, *The Mutual Gains Enterprise: Forging a Winning Partnership among Labor, Management, and Government* (Boston: Harvard Business School Press, 1994).

[20]"Noranda Smelter Workers Agree to Freeze on Wages," *Toronto Star*, April 1, 2003, p.C4.

[21]S. Pigg, "Air Canada CEO Tells Union More Layoffs, Pay Cuts Needed," *Toronto Star*, May 22, 2003, p.C1.

[22]Richard B. Freeman and Lawrence F. Katz, eds., *Differences and Changes in Wage Structures* (Chicago: University of Chicago Press, 1995); M. Mendenhall and G. Oddou, *Readings and Cases in International HRM*, 3rd ed. (Cincinnati: Southwest, 2000); C. Brewster and H. Harris, *International HRM: Contemporary Issues in Europe* (London: Routledge, 1999); and R. Bronstein, "Labour Law Reform in Latin America: Between State Protection and Flexibility," *International Labour Law Review*, Spring 1997, pp. 327–33.

[23]J. Barney, "Firm Resources and Sustained Competitive Advantage," *Journal of Management* 17 (1997), pp. 99–120; P. M. Wright, G. C. McMahan, and A. McWilliams, "Human Resources and Sustained Competitive Advantage: A Resource-Based

Perspective," *International Journal of Human Resource Management* 5 (1994), pp. 301–26.

[24]J. Pfeffer, "When It Comes to 'Best Practices', Why Do Smart Organizations Occasionally Do Dumb Things?" *Organizational Dynamics* 25 (1997), pp. 33–44; and J. Pfeffer, *The Human Equation: Building Profits by Putting People First* (Boston: Harvard Business School Press, 1998); R. Kanigel, *The One Best Way: Frederick Winslow Taylor and the Enigma of Efficiency* (New York: Viking Press, 1997); P. Wright, L. Dyer, and M. Takla, "Executive: The Critical 'What's Next' in Strategic HRM," Ithaca, NY: CAHRS working paper 99–11, 1999; D. Koys, "Describing the Elements of Business and HR Strategy Statements," *Journal of Business and Psychology* 15, Winter 2000.

[25]K. Kerwin, "Workers of the World, Log On," *Business Week*, February 21, 2000, p. 52; K. Bradsher, "Ford Offers Workers PC's and Internet Service for $5 a Month," *New York Times*, February 4, 2000, p. C1.

[26]G. Milkovich and J. Stevens, "Back to the Future: A Century of Compensation," *ACA Journal*, January 2000, pp. 1–15; Connie Willis, *Bellwether* (London: Bantam Books, 1996); M. Gladwell, *The Tipping Point; The Next Big Thing* (Boston: Little, Brown, and Co., 2000).

[27]Wright, McMahan, and McWilliam, "Human Resources and Sustained Competitive Advantage," *International Journal of Human Resource Management* 5 (1994), pp. 301–26; J. Purcell, "Best Practices and Best Fit: Chimera or Cul-De-Sac?" *Human Resources Management Journal* 9(3), pp. 26–41; Andrew S. Grove, *Only the Paranoid Survive* (New York: Doubleday, 1996).

[28]T. Kochan and P. Osterman, *The Mutual Gains Enterprise* (Boston: Harvard Business School Press, 1994); P. K. Zingheim and J. R. Schuster, *Pay People Right!* (San Francisco: Jossey Bass, 2000); J. Pfeffer, "Pitfalls on the Road to Measurement: The Dangerous Liaison of HR with Ideas of Accounting and Finance," *Human Resource Management* 36, (3), Fall 1997, pp. 357–65; J. Pfeffer, "Seven Practices of Successful Organizations," *California Management Review* 49 (2) (1998), pp. 96–124.

[29]B. Gerhart, "Pay Strategy and Firm Performance," in S. Rynes and B. Gerhart, *Compensation in Organizations: Current Research and Practice* (San Francisco: Jossey-Bass, 2000); B. Gerhart and G. Milkovich, "Employee Compensation" in *Handbook of Industrial and Organization Psychology* 3, M. Dunnette and L. Hough, eds. (Palo Alto, California: Consulting Psychologists Press, 1992); B. Gerhart, C. Trevor, and M. E. Graham, "New Directions in Compensation Research," in *Research in Personnel and Human Resource Management*, ed. G. R. Ferris (Greenwich, CT: JAI Press 1996); M. Bloom, "The Performance Effects of Pay Dispersion on Individuals and Organizations," *Academy of Management Journal* 42 (1) (1999), pp. 7–24; H. Tosi, S. Werner, J. Katz, L. Gomez-Mejia, "How Much Does

Performance Matter? A Meta-Analysis of CEO Pay Studies," *Journal of Management* 26 (2), (2000), pp. 301–39; E. Montemayer, "Aligning Pay Systems with Market Strategy," *ACA Journal, Winter* 1994, pp. 44–53.

[30]B. Gerhart and G. Milkovich, "Organization Differences in Managerial Compensation and Financial Performance," *Academy of Management Journal* 33 (1990), pp. 663–91; K. Murphy and M. Jensen, "It's Not How Much, but How You Pay," *Harvard Business Review*, 1993, pp. 32–45.

[31]Brian Becker and Mark Huselid, "High Performance Work Systems and Firm Performance: A Synthesis of Research and Managerial Implications," in *Research in Personnel and Human Resource Management*, ed. G. R. Ferris (Greenwich, CT: JAI Press, 1997).

[32]S. A. Snell and J. W. Dean, Jr. "Strategic Compensation for Integrated Manufacturing: The Moderating Effects of Job and Organizational Inertia," *Academy of Management Journal* 37 (1994), pp. 1109–14.

[33]J. P. MacDuffie, "Human Resource Bundles and Manufacturing Performance: Organizational Logic and Flexible Production Systems in the World Auto Industry," *Industrial and Labor Relations Review* 48 (1995), pp. 197–221; J. B. Arthur, "Effects of Human Resource Systems on Manufacturing Performance and Turnover," *Academy of Management Journal* 37 (1994), pp. 670–87; C. Ichniowski, K. Shaw, and G. Prennush, "The Effects of HRM Practices on Productivity: A Study of Steel Finishing Lines," *American Economic Review* 87 (3) (1998), pp. 291–313.

[34]B. Gerhart and C. O. Trevor, "Employment Variability under Different Managerial Compensation Systems," *Academy of Management Journal* 39 (6) (1996), pp. 1692–1712. Also see R. Gibbons and M. Waldman, "Careers in Organizations: Theory and Evidence," in *Handbook of Labor Economics* 3, eds. O. Ashenfelder and D. Card (New Elsevier Science Press, 1999).

[35]B. Gerhart, "Pay Strategy and Firm Performance," in *Compensation and Organizations: Progress and Prospects*, S. Rynes and B. Gerhart (eds.) (San Francisco, New Lexington Press, 2000); J. Abowd, "Does Performance Based Managerial Compensation Affect Corporate Performance?" *Industrial and Labor Relations Review* 435 (1990), pp. 52S–73S; B. Gerhart and G. Milkovich, "Organization Differences in Managerial Compensation and Financial Performance," *Academy of Management Journal* 90 (33), pp. 663–91; B. Becker and M. Huselid, "High Performance Work Systems and Firm Performance: A Synthesis of Research and Managerial Implications," *Research in Personnel and Human Resources*, ed. G. Ferris (Greenwich, CT: JAI Press, 1997); S. Werner and H. Tosi, "Other People's Money: The Effects of Ownership on Compensation Strategy," *Academy of Management Journal* 38 (6), pp. 1672–91; B. Hall and J. Liebman, "Are CEOs Really Paid Like Bureaucrats?" *Quarterly Journal of Economics*, August 1998, pp. 653–91.

[36]M. Bloom and G. Milkovich, "Relationships Among Risk, Incentive Pay, and Organization Performance," *Academy of Management Journal* 41 (3) (1998) pp. 283–97.

[37]M. Bloom and G. Milkovich, "Relationships Among Risk, Incentive Pay, and Organization Performance," *Academy of Management Journal* 41 (3) (1998), pp. 283–97; J. Abowd, "Does Performance Based Managerial Compensation Affect Corporate Performance?" *Industrial and Labor Relations Review* 435 (1990), pp. 52S–73S.

[38]M. Bloom, "The New Deal: Understanding Compensation in the Employment Relationship," *ACA Journal* 8 (4), (1999), pp. 58–67.

[39]I. R. Macneil, "Relational Contracts: What We Do and Do Not Know," *Wisconsin Law Review*, 1985, pp. 483–525; A. S. Tsui, J. L. Pearce, L. W. Porter, and J. P. Hite, "Choice of Employee-Organization Relationships," in *Research in Personnel and Human Resource Management*, ed. G. R. Ferris (Greenwich, CT: JAI Press, 1995); and Marvin H. Kosters, "New Employment Relationships and the Labor Market," *Journal of Labor Research* XVIII (4), Fall 1997, pp. 551–59.

[40]Steve Balmer speech quoted in *Wall Street Journal* Interactive Edition, May 11, 1999, www.wsj.com; D. McKenna and J. McHenry, *Microsoft's Maniacal Work Ethic* (Redmond, Wa: Microsoft, 1996).

[41]R. Thomkins, "Touchy-Feely Coffee Company," *Financial Times*, October 9, 1997, p. 14.

Chapter 3

[1]Matthew 20: 1–16.

[2]For a history of the different standards for pay, see Thomas Mahoney, *Compensation and Reward Perspectives* (Burr Ridge, IL: Richard D. Irwin, 1979); G. Milkovich and J. Stevens, "From Pay To Rewards: 100 Years of Change" *ACA Journal* 9 9(1), (2000) pp. 6–18; D. F. Schloss, *Methods in Industrial Remuneration* (New York: G. P. Putnam's Sons, 1892).

[3]Several Japanese firms still base a small portion of a worker's pay on the number of dependants. In the early 1900s, workers who were "family men" received a pay supplement in some US firms as well. The "iron rice bowl," which prevailed until recently in China's state enterprises, provided entire families with cradle-to-grave welfare.

[4]S. G. Cohen and D. E. Bailey, "What Makes Teams Work: Group Effectiveness Research from the Shop Floor to Executive Suite," *Journal of Management* 23 (1997), pp. 239–91; M. Apgar,

"The Alternative Workplace: Changing Where and How People Work," *Harvard Business Review*, May–June 1998, pp. 125–37; R. A. Guzzo and M. W. Dickson, "Teams in Organizations: Recent Research in Performance and Effectiveness," *Annual Review of Psychology* 47 (1996), pp. 307–38; N. Nohria and S. Ghoshal, *The Differential Network: Organizing Corporations for Value Creation* (San Francisco: Jossey-Bass, 1998).

[5]Marcia P. Miceli and Paul Mulvey, "Satisfaction with Pay Systems: Antecedents and Consequences," paper presented at National Academy of Management meetings, San Diego, 1998; G. Hundley and J. Kim, "National Culture and the Factors Affecting Perception of Pay Fairness in Korea and the U.S.," *The International Journal of Organization Analysis* 5, pp. 325–41; M. A. Konovsky, "Understanding Procedural Justice and Its Impact on Business Organizations," *Journal of Management* 26(3) (2000), pp. 489–511.

[6]S. Rynes and G. Gerhart, *Compensation in Organizations: Current Research and Practice* (San Francisco: Jossey-Bass, 2000); R. H. Thaler, "From Homo Economicus to Homo Sapiens," *Journal of Economic Perspectives* 14(1), Winter 2000, pp. 133–41; and P. Milgrom and J. Roberts, "An Economic Approach to Influence Activities in Organizations," *American Journal of Sociology* 94 (1988), pp. S154–S179.

[7]C. Tucker, ed., *The Marx-Engels Reader* (New York: W. W. Norton, 1978).

[8]Allan M. Cartter, *Theory of Wages and Employment* (Burr Ridge, IL: Richard D. Irwin, 1959); P. Milgrom and J. Roberts, *Economics, Organization, and Management* (Englewood Cliffs, NJ: Prentice Hall, 1992).

[9]M. Bloom, G. Milkovich, and A. Mitra, "Toward a Model of International Compensation" (Ithaca, NY: CAHRS Working Paper, 2000); S. Finkelstein and D. Hambrick, *Strategic Leadership: Top Executives and their Effects on Organizations* (St. Paul: West Publishing, 1996); S. Brown and K. Eisenhardt, *Competing on the Edge: Strategy and Structured Chaos* (Boston: Harvard Business Press, 1998).

[10]M. Bloom, G. Milkovich, and A. Mitra, "Toward a Model of International Compensation" (Ithaca, NY: CAHRS Working Paper, 2000); M. Mendenhall and G. Oddou, *Readings and Cases in International HRM* (Cincinnati: Southwestern Publishing, 2000).

[11]G. Hofstede, *Culture's Consequences: International Differences in Work Relationships and Values* (Thousand Oaks, CA: Sage Publications, 1980); M. Bloom, G. Milkovich, and A. Mitra, "Toward a Model of International Compensation" (Ithaca, NY: CAHRS Working Paper, 2000); F. Trompenaars, *Riding the Waves of Culture: Understanding Diversity in Global Business* (Burr Ridge, IL: Irwin,1995); J. Brockner, Y. Chen, K. Leung, and D. Skarlick, "Culture and Procedural Fairness: When the Effects of What You Do Depend on How You Do It," *Administrative Science Quarterly* 45 (2000), pp. 138–59.

[12]D. Levine, D. Belman, G. Charness, E. Groshen, and K. C. O'Shaugnessy, *The New Employment Contract: How Little Wage Structures at U.S. Employers Have Changed* (Kalamazoo: Upjohn, 2001).

[13]R. Batt, "Explaining Wage Inequities, Customer Segmentation, HR Practices, and Unions," *Industrial and Labor Relations Review*, in print; P. Milgrom and J. Roberts, *Economics, Organization, and Management* (Englewood Cliffs, NJ: Prentice Hall, 1992).

[14]Paul Schumann, Dennis Ahlburg, and Christine B. Mahoney, "The Effects of Human Capital and Job Characteristics on Pay," *The Journal of Human Resources* XXIX (2), pp. 481–503.

[15]A. Kohn, *Punished by Rewards: The Trouble with Gold Stars, Incentive Plans, A's, Praise and Other Bribes* (Boston, MA: Houghton Mifflin Co. 1993); Jerald Greenberg and Suzy N. Ornstein, "High Status Job Titles as Compensation for Underpayment: A Test of Equity Theory," *Journal of Applied Psychology* 68 (2) (1983), pp. 285–97.

[16]Thomas A. Mahoney, "Organizational Hierarchy and Position Worth," *Academy of Management Journal*, December 1979, pp. 726–37.

[17]Philip Moss, "Earnings Inequality and the Quality of Jobs," in *Corporate Governance and Sustainable Prosperity*, W. Lazonick and M. O'Sullivan, eds. (New York: MacMillan, 2001); Peter Cappelli, Laurie Bassi, Harry Katz, David Knoke, Paul Osterman, and Michael Useem, *Change at Work* (New York: Oxford University Press, 1997); Erica L. Groshen and David I. Levine, "The Rise and Decline (?) of U.S. Internal Labor Markets," Research Paper No. 9819 (New York: Federal Reserve Bank, 1998); Philip Moss, Harold Salzman, and Chris Tilly, "Limits to Market-Mediated Employment: From Deconstruction to Reconstruction of Internal Labor Markets," working paper, University of Massachusetts at Lowell, 2000.

[18]E. Robert Livernash, "The Internal Wage Structure," in *New Concepts in Wage Determination*, eds. G. W. Taylor and F. C. Pierson (New York: McGraw-Hill, 1957), pp. 143–72.

[19]T. Judge and H. G. Heneman, III, "Pay Satisfaction," in S. Rynes and G. Gerhart, *Compensation in Organizations: Current Research and Practice* (San Francisco: Jossey-Bass, 2000); Robert Folger and Mary Konovsky, "Effects of Procedural and Distributive Justice on Reactions to Pay Raise Decisions," *Academy of Management Journal*, March 1989, pp. 115–30; Jerald Greenberg, "Looking Fair vs. Being Fair: Managing Impressions of Organizational Justice," in *Research in Organizational Behavior*, Vol. 12, eds. B. M. Staw and L. L. Cummings (Greenwich, CT: JAI Press, 1990).

[20]C. W. Hill, M. A. Hitt, and R. E. Hoskisson, "Cooperative Versus Competitive Structures in Related and Unrelated Diversified Firms," *Organization Science* (1992), pp. 501–21.

[21]D. M. Cowherd and D. I. Levine, "Product Quality and Pay Equity between Lower-Level Employees and Top Management: An Investigation of Distributive Justice Theory," *Administrative Science Quarterly* 37 (1992), pp. 302–20; M. Bloom and G. Milkovich, "Money, Managers, and Metamorphosis," in *Trends in Organizational Behavior*, 3rd ed., eds. D. Rousseau and C. Cooper (New York: John Wiley & Sons, 1996).

[22]E. E. Lawler III, "From Job-Based to Competency-Based Organizations," *Journal of Organization Behavior* 15 (1994), pp. 3–15.

[23]Elliot Jaques, "In Praise of Hierarchies," *Harvard Business Review*, January–February 1990, pp. 32–46; M. Bloom and J. Michel, "Understanding the Causes and Consequences of Pay Structures: The Importance of Organization Context" (Notre Dame working paper, 2000).

[24]R. D. Bretz and S. L. Thomas, "Perceived Equity, Motivation, and Final-Offer Arbitration in Major League Baseball," *Journal of Applied Psychology* 77 (1992), pp. 280–87; M. Bloom and J. Michel, "Understanding the Causes and Consequences of Pay Structures: The Importance of Organization Context" (Notre Dame working paper, 2000).

[25]Daniel Z. Ding, Keith Goodall, and Malcolm Warner, "The End of the 'Iron Rice-Bowl': Whither Chinese Human Resource Management?" *International Journal of Human Resource Management* 11(2), April 2000, pp. 217–36.

[26]M. Ingram, "How Much Does Frank Deserve?" *Globe & Mail.com*, May 1, 2003.

[27]Previous editions of this textbook have used an example of a unique job taken from Cornell University's School of Veterinary Medicine. Former students have expressed great affection for the "Cornell cows." However, in light of a changing environment, we are trying to move from the agrarian to the aquarian.

[28]Edward Lazear, "Labor Economics and Psychology of Organization," *Journal of Economic Perspectives* 5 (1991), pp. 89–110; David Wazeter, "Determinants and Consequences of Pay Structures" (PhD. Dissertation, Cornell University, 1991).

[29]E. Robert Livernash, "The Internal Wage Structure," in *New Concepts in Wage Determination*, eds. G. W. Taylor and F. C. Pierson (New York: McGraw-Hill, 1957), pp. 143–72.

[30]Elliot Jaques, "In Praise of Hierarchies," *Harvard Business Review*, January–February 1990, pp. 32–46.

[31]E. E. Lawler, *Pay and Organizational Effectiveness: A Psychological View* (NY: McGraw-Hill, 1971); T. A. Mahoney,

Compensation and Reward Perspectives (Homewood, IL: Richard D. Irwin, 1979).

[32]T. Judge and H. G. Heneman, III, "Pay Satisfaction," in *Compensation in Organizations: Current Research and Practice*, S. Rynes and G. Gerhart (San Francisco: Jossey-Bass, 2000).

[33]B. E. Becker and M. A. Huselid, "The Incentive Effects of Tournament Compensation Systems," *Administrative Science Quarterly* 37 (1992), pp. 336–50; E. Lazear and S. Rosen, "Rank-Order Tournaments as Optimum Labor Contracts," *Journal of Political Economy* 89 (1981), pp. 841–64; Matthew C. Bloom, "The Performance Effects of Pay Structures on Individuals and Organizations," *Academy of Management Journal* 42(1) (1999), pp. 25–40.

[34]R. G. Ehrenberg and M. L. Bognanno, "The Incentive Effects of Tournaments Revisited: Evidence from the European PGA Tour," *Industrial and Labor Relations Review* 43 (1990), pp. 74S–88S.

[35]Matthew C. Bloom, "The Performance Effects of Pay Structures on Individuals and Organizations," *Academy of Management Journal* 42(1) 1999, pp. 25–40.

[36]M. Bloom and J. Michel, "Understanding the Causes and Consequences of Pay Structures: The Importance of Organization Context" (Notre Dame working paper, 2000); W. Jurgens, "Look Out Below," *Wall Street Journal*, April 1, 2000, p. R-3.

[37]L. G. Zucker, "Institutional Theories of Organization," *American Review of Sociology* 13 (1987), pp. 443–64; M. Barringer and G. Milkovich, "A Theoretical Exploration of the Adoption and Design of Flexible Benefit Plans: A Case of HR Innovation," *Academy of Management Review* 23(2) (1998), pp. 305–24.

[38]Harry Levinson, "Why the Behemoths Fell: Psychological Roots of Corporate Failure," *American Psychologist* 49(5) (1994), pp. 428–36.

[39]R. H. Frank and P. J. Cook, *The Winner-Take-All Society* (New York: Penguin Books, 1995); T. A. Kochan and P. Osterman, *The Mutual Gains Enterprise: Forging a Winning Partnership Among Labor, Management, and Government* (Boston, MA: Harvard Business School Press, 1994).

[40]R. L. Heneman, *Merit Pay: Linking Pay Increases to Performance Ratings* (Reading, MA: Addison-Wesley Pub. Co, 1992); H. H. Meyer, "The Pay-For-Performance Dilemma," *Organization Science* 33 (1975), pp. 39–50.

Chapter 4

[1]William Bridges, "The End of the Job," *Fortune*, September 19, 1994, pp. 62–68.

[2]Janet Marler and George Milkovich, "Thriving or Surviving? Preferences for Contingent Employment" (Ithaca, NY: CAHRS Working Paper Series, #00-03, 2000); Sanford M. Jacoby, "Are Career Jobs Headed for Extinction?" Kenneth M. Piper Memorial Lecture at Chicago-Kent Law School, April 1999.

[3]Lee Dyer and Richard A. Shafer, "From HR Strategy to Organizational Effectiveness," in *Strategic Human Resources Management in the Twenty-First Century Supplement* 4, eds. Patrick M. Wright, Lee D. Dyer, John W. Boudreau, and George T. Milkovich (Stamford, CT: JAI Press, 1999); Towers Perrin Internetworked Organization Survey Findings: Report Snapshots (New York: Towers Perrin, February 2000).

[4]*Raising the Bar: Using Competencies to Enhance Employee Performance* (Scottsdale, AZ: American Compensation Association, 1996).

[5]Cynthia Lee, Kenneth S. Law, and Philip Bobko, "The Importance of Justice Perceptions on Pay Effectiveness: A Two-Year Study of a Skill-Based Pay Plan," *Journal of Management* 25 (6) (1999), pp. 851–873.

[6]Peter Cappelli, *The New Deal at Work: Managing the Market-Driven Workforce* (Boston, MA: Harvard Business School Press, 1999).

[7]Most human resource management texts discuss these multiple uses of job analysis information. See, for example, Chapter 3 in G. Milkovich and J. Boudreau, *Human Resource Management* (Burr Ridge, IL: Irwin, 1997).

[8]E. J. McCormick, "Job and Task Analysis," in *Handbook of Industrial and Organizational Psychology*, ed. M. D. Dunnette (Chicago: Rand McNally, 1976), pp. 651–96; E. J. McCormick, *Job Analysis: Methods and Applications* (New York: AMACOM, 1979).

[9]Robert J. Harvey, "Job Analysis," in *Handbook of Industrial and Organizational Psychology*, Vol. 2, ed. M. D. Dunnette and L. Hough (Palo Alto, CA: Consulting Psychologists Press, 1991), pp. 72–157.

[10]Steven G. Allen, Robert L. Clark, and Sylvester J. Schieber, "Has Job Security Vanished in Large Corporations?" NBER Working Paper 6966 (1999).

[11]www.tbs-sct.gc.ca/Classification/Standards/

[12]Much of the developmental and early applications of the PAQ was done in the 1960s and 1970s. See, for example, McCormick, "Job Analysis"; McCormick, "Job and Task Analysis"; McCormick et al., "A Study of Job Characteristics and Job Dimensions as Based on the Position Analysis Questionnaire" (West Lafayette, IN: Occupational Research Center, Purdue University, 1969). The PAQ is distributed by the University Book Store, 360 West State St., West Lafayette, IN 47906. For more recent discussions, see PAQ Newsletters.

[13]V. L. Huber, S. Crandall, and G. B. Northcraft, "A Rose by Any Other Name Is Not as Sweet: Effects of Job Titles and Upgrade Requests on Job Evaluation and Wage Decisions" (unpublished manuscript, University of Washington, 1992).

[14]Robert Harvey, "Incumbent vs. Superior Perception of Jobs," Presentation at SIOP Conference, Miami, FL, 1990.

[15]Link Group Consultants, Limited, Chester, U.K.

[16]V. L. Huber and S. R. Crandall, "Job Measurement: A Social-Cognitive Decision Perspective," in *Research in Personnel and Human Resources Management* 12, ed. Gerald R. Ferris (Greenwich, CT: JAI Press, 1994, pp. 223–69.)

[17]K. C. O'Shaughnessy, David Levine, and Peter Cappelli, "Changes in Management Pay Structures, 1986–1992 and Rising Returns to Skill," University California at Berkeley Institute of Industrial Relations Working Paper, Berkeley, CA, 1998.

[18]S. G. Cohen and D. E. Bailey, "What Makes Teams Work: Group Effectiveness Research from the Shop Floor to Executive Suite," *Journal of Management* 23 (1997), pp. 239–91.

[19]E. M. Ramras, "Discussion," in *Proceedings of Division of Military Psychology Symposium: Collecting, Analyzing, and Reporting Information Describing Jobs and Occupations*, 77th Annual Convention of the American Psychological Association, Lackland Air Force Base, TX, September 1969, pp. 75–76.

[20]Ronald A. Ash and Edward L. Levine, "A Framework for Evaluating Job Analysis Methods," *Personnel* 57, (6) (November–December 1980, pp. 53–59; R. A. Ash, E. L. Levine, and F. Sistrunk, "The Role of Jobs and Job Based Methods in Personnel and Human Resources Management," *Research in Personnel and Human Resources Management* 1 (1983), pp.45–84; Edward L. Levine, Ronald A. Ash, Hardy Hall, and Frank Sistrunk, "Evaluation of Job Analysis Methods by Experienced Job Analysts," *Academy of Management Journal* 26 (2) (1983), pp. 339–48.

[21]M. D. Dunnette, L. M. Hough, and R. L. Rosse, "Task and Job Taxonomies as a Basis for Identifying Labor Supply Sources and Evaluating Employment Qualifications," in *Affirmative Action Planning*, ed. George T. Milkovich and Lee Dyer (New York: Human Resource Planning Society, 1979), pp. 37–51.

Chapter 5

[1]Liz Hodgson, "Spielberg Raises Slave Wages," *South China Morning Post*, April 30, 1997, p. 16.

[2]Donald P. Schwab, "Job Evaluation and Pay Setting: Concepts and Practices," in *Comparable Worth: Issues and Alternatives*, ed. E. Robert Livernash (Washington, DC: Equal Employment Advisory Council, 1980), pp. 49–77.

[3]Alvin O. Bellak, "Comparable Worth: A Practitioner's View," in *Comparable Worth: Issue for the 80's*, Vol. 1 (Washington, DC: U.S. Civil Rights Commission, 1985).

[4]M. A. Konovsky, "Understanding Procedural Justice and Its Impact on Business Organizations," *Journal of Management* 26 (3) (2000), pp. 489–511; R. Crepanzano, *Justice in the Workplace, Volume 2: From Theory to Practice.* (Mahwah, NJ: Lawrence Erlbaum Associates, 2000); R. Folger, R. and R. Crepanzano, *Organizational Justice and Human Resource Management* (Thousand Oaks, CA: Sage, 1998); R. B. Foreman and J. Rogers, *What Workers Want* (Ithaca, NY: ILR/Cornell University Press, 1999); B. H. Sheppard, R. J. Lewicki, and J. W. Minton, *Organizational Justice: The Search for Fairness in the Workplace* (New York: Macmillan, 1992).

[5]M. S. Viteles, "A Psychologist Looks at Job Evaluation," *Personnel* 17 (1941), pp. 165–76.

[6]Vandra Huber and S. Crandall, "Job Measurement: A Social-Cognitive Decision Perspective," in *Research in Personnel and Human Resources Management*, Vol. 12, ed. Gerald R. Ferris (Greenwich, CT: JAI Press, 1994).

[7]Factor comparison, another method of job evaluation, bears some similarities to the point method in that compensable factors are clearly defined and the external market is linked to the job evaluation results. However, factor comparison is used by less than 10 percent of employers who use job evaluation. The method's complexity makes it difficult to explain to employees and managers, which limits its usefulness.

[8]M. K. Mount and R.A. Ellis, "Investigation of Bias in Job Evaluation Ratings of Comparable Worth Study Participants," *Personnel Psychology* 40 (1987), pp.85–96; H. Remick, "Strategies for Creating Sound, Bias-Free Job Evaluation Plans," Paper presented at the I.R.C. Colloquium, Atlanta, GA, September 1978.

[9]D. F. Harding, J.M. Madden, and K. Colson, "Analysis of a Job Evaluation System," *Journal of Applied Psychology* 44 (1960), pp. 354–57.

[10]R. Nisbett, D. Krantz, C. Jepson, and A. Kunda, "The Use of Statistical Heuristics in Everyday Intuition," *Psychological Review* 90 (1983), pp. 339–63.

[11]See a series of studies conducted by C. H. Lawshe and his colleagues published in the *Journal of Applied Psychology* from 1944–47. For example, C. H. Lawshe, "Studies in job evaluation: II. The adequacy of abbreviated point ratings for hourly paid jobs in three industrial plans," *Journal of Applied Psychology* 29 (1945), pp. 177–84.

[12]www.tbs-sct.gc.ca/Classification/Standards/TC-TI/TCTI_e.doc (August 5, 2003)

[13]Charles Fay and Paul Hempel, "Whose Values? A Comparison of Incumbent, Supervisor, Incumbent-Supervisor Consensus and Committee Job Evaluation Ratings" (Working paper, Rutgers University, 1991); John Doyle, Rodney Green, and Paul Bo Homley, "Judging Relative Importance: Direct Rating and Point Allocation Are Not Equivalent," *Organization Behavior and Human Decision Processes*, April 1997, pp. 65–72.

[14]Paul M. Edwards, "Statistical Methods in Job Evaluation," *Advanced Management* (December 1948), pp. 158–63.

[15]Donald J. Treiman, "Effect of Choice of Factors and Factor Weights in Job Evaluation," in *Comparable Worth and Wage Discrimination*, ed. H. Remick (Philadelphia: Temple University Press, 1984), pp. 79–89.

[16]One of the key findings of a National Academy of Science report that examined virtually all research on pay was that the process used to design pay plans is vital to achieving high commitment. George Milkovich and Alexandra Wigdor, eds., *Pay and Performance* (Washington, DC: National Academy Press, 1991). Also see Carl F. Frost, John W. Wakely, and Robert A. Ruh, *The Scanlon Plan for Organization Development: Identity, Participation, and Equity* (East Lansing: Michigan State Press, 1974); E. A. Locke and D. M. Schweiger, "Participation in Decision Making: One More Look," *Research in Organization Behavior* (Greenwich, CT: JAI Press, 1979); G. J. Jenkins, Jr. and E. E. Lawler III, "Impact of Employee Participation in Pay Plan Development," *Organizational Behavior and Human Performance* 28 (1981), pp. 111–28.

[17]R. Crepanzano, *Justice in the Workplace, Volume 2: From Theory to Practice.* (Mahwah, NJ: Lawrence Erlbaum Associates, 2000); R. Folger, R. and R. Crepanzano, *Organizational Justice and Human Resource Management* (Thousand Oaks, CA: Sage, 1998).

[18]B. Carver and A. A. Vondra, "Alternative Dispute Resolution: Why It Doesn't Work and Why It Does," *Harvard Business Review*, May–June 1994, pp. 120–29.

[19]Theresa M. Welbourne and Charlie O. Trevor, "The Roles of Departmental and Position Power in Job Evaluation," *Academy of Management Journal* 43 (2000), pp. 761–71.

[20]A. G. P. Elliott, *Staff Grading* (London: British Institute of Management, 1960); N. Gupta and G. D. Jenkins, Jr., "The

Politics of Pay," Paper presented at the annual meeting of the Society for Industrial and Organizational Psychology, Montreal, 1992.

[21]Vandra Huber and S. Crandall, "Job Measurement: A Social-Cognitive Decision Perspective" in *Research in Personnel and Human Resources Management*, Vol. 12, ed. Gerald R. Ferris (Greenwich, CT: JAI Press, 1994).

Chapter 6

[1]Robert Kanigel, *The One Best Way* (New York: Viking, 1997).

[2]Gupta, N. and Shaw, J.D., "Successful Skill-Based Pay Plans," in *The Compensation Handbook* (2nd Ed.), ed. C. Fay (Free Press, in press).

[3]Diana Southall and Jerry Newman, *Skill-Based Pay Development* (Buffalo NY: HR Foundations, Inc., 2000).

[4]G. Douglas Jenkins, Jr., Gerald E. Ledford, Jr., Nina Gupta, and D. Harold Doty, *Skill-Based Pay* (Scottsdale, AZ: American Compensation Association, 1992).

[5]Gerald E. Ledford, Jr., "Three Case Studies of Skill-Based Pay: An Overview," *Compensation and Benefits Review* (March/April 1991), pp. 11–23.

[6]B. Murray and B. Gerhart, "An Empirical Analysis of a Skill-Based Pay Program and Plant Performance Outcomes," *Academy of Management Journal* 41 (1998), pp. 68–78.

[7]Gerald E. Ledford, Jr., "Three Case Studies of Skill-Based Pay: An Overview," *Compensation and Benefits Review*, March/April 1991, pp. 11–23. Pages 23–77 of this issue contain case studies of applications at General Mills, Northern Telecom, and Honeywell.

[8]N. Fredric Crandall and Marc J. Wallace, Jr., "Paying Employees to Develop New Skills," in *Aligning Pay and Results*, ed. Howard Risher (New York: American Management Association 1999).

[9]Cynthia Lee, Kenneth S. Law, and Philip Bobko, "The Importance of Justice Perceptions on Pay Effectiveness: A Two-Year Study of a Skill-Based Pay Plan," *Journal of Management* 25 (6) (1999), pp. 851–73.

[10]K. Parrent and C. Weber, "Case Study: Does Paying for Knowledge Pay Off?" *Compensation and Benefits Review*, September–October 1994, pp. 44–50; B. Murray and B. Gerhart, "An Empirical Analysis of a Skill-Based Pay Program and Plant Performance Outcomes," *Academy of Management Journal* 41 (1998), pp. 68–78.

[11]Kenneth Mericle and Dong-One Kim, "Determinants of Skill Acquisition and Pay Satisfaction under Pay-for-Knowledge

Systems" (Working Paper, Institute of Industrial Relations, University of California Berkeley, 1996).

[12]Jason D. Shaw, Nina Gupta, Gerald E. Ledford, Jr., and Atul Mitra, "Survival of Skill-Based Pay Plans," Paper presented at the Annual Meetings of the Academy of Management, Toronto, 2000.

[13]E. E. Lawler, III, S. A. Mohrman, and G. E. Ledford, Jr., *Strategies for High Performance Organizations* (San Francisco: Jossey-Bass, 1998); B. Gerhart, C. O. Trevor, and M. E. Graham, "New Directions in Compensation Research: Synergies, Risk, and Survival," *Research in Personnel and Human Resources Management* 14, 1996, pp. 143–203.

[14]N. Fredric Crandall and Marc J. Wallace, Jr., "Paying Employees to Develop New Skills," in *Aligning Pay and Results*, ed. Howard Risher (New York: American Management Association 1999).

[15]Patricia Zingheim, Gerald E. Ledford, Jr., and Jay R. Schuster, "Competencies and Competency Models: Does One Size Fit All?" *ACA Journal*, Spring 1996, pp. 56–65.

[16]Vandra Huber and S. Crandall, "Job Measurement: A Social-Cognitive Decision Perspective," in *Research in Personnel and Human Resources Management*, Vol. 12, ed. Gerald R. Ferris (Greenwich, CT: JAI Press, 1994).

[17]Lyle M. Spencer, Jr. and Signe M. Spencer, *Competence at Work* (New York: John Wiley and Sons, 1993).

[18]Patricia Zingheim, Gerald E. Ledford, Jr., and Jay R. Schuster, "Competencies and Competency Models: Does One Size Fit All?" *ACA Journal*, Spring 1996, pp. 56–65.

[19]*Competencies, Performance and Pay* (New York: William M. Mercer Companies, Inc. 1995).

[20]James T. Kochanski and Howard Risher, "Paying for Competencies: Rewarding Knowledge, Skills, and Behaviors," in *Aligning Pay and Results*, ed. Howard Risher (New York: American Management Association 1999).

[21]C. A. Bartlett and Sumantra Ghoshal, "The Myth of the Generic Manager: New Personal Competencies for New Management Roles," *California Management Review* 40 (1) (1997), pp. 92–105.

[22]P. Tierney, "Work Relations as a Precursor to a Psychological Climate for Change: The Role of Work Group Supervisors and Peers," *Journal of Organizational Change Management* 12 (2) (1999), pp. 120–33.

[23]Y. Stedham and A. D. Engle, *Multinational and Transnational Strategies: Implications for Human Resource Management*, Paper presented at the 8th Biannual Research Symposium of the Human Resource Planning Society, Ithaca, New York,

1999; J. R. Fulkerson and M. F. Tucker, "Diversity: Lessons from Global Human Resource Practices," in *Evolving Practices in Human Resource Management*, eds. A. I. Kraut and A. K. Korman (San Francisco, CA.: Jossey-Bass Publishers, 1999), pp. 249–71.

[24]Edward E. Lawler III, "From Job-Based to Competency-Based Organizations," *Journal of Organizational Behavior* 15 (1994), pp. 3–15.

[25]R. H. Dorr and Thomas Gresch, *Human Resources Concept: Europe* (General Motors Acceptance Corporation, Wiesbaden, Germany, 1996); Graham L. O'Neill and David Doig, "Definition and Use of Competencies by Australian Organizations: A Survey of HR Practitioners," *ACA Journal*, Winter 1997, pp. 45–56.

[26]Margaret E. Allredge and Kevin J. Nilan, "3M's Leadership Competency Model: An Internally Developed Solution," *Human Resource Management* 39, Summer/Fall 2000, pp. 133–45.

[27]Zingheim, Ledford, and Schuster, "Competencies and Competency Models," *Raising the Bar: Using Competencies to Enhance Employee Performance* (Scottsdale, AZ: American Compensation Association, 1996).

[28]S. Ghoshal and C. A. Bartlett, *The Individualized Corporation* (New York: Harper Business Publishers, 1997).

[29]Odd Nordhaug, "Competence Specificities in Organizations," *International Studies of Management and Organization* 28 (1), Spring 1998, pp. 8–29.

[30]Lee Dyer and Richard A. Shafer, "From HR Strategy to Organizational Effectiveness," in *Strategic Human Resources Management in the Twenty-First Century*, supplement 4, eds. Patrick M. Wright, Lee D. Dyer, John W. Boudreau, and George T. Milkovich (Stamford, CT: JAI Press, 1999).

[31]Dyer and Shafer, "From HR Strategy to Organizational Effectiveness."

[32]Scott A. Snell, David P. Lepak, and Mark A. Youndt, "Managing the Architecture of Intellectual Capital," in *Strategic Human Resources Management in the Twenty-First Century*, supplement 4, eds. Patrick M. Wright, Lee D. Dyer, John W. Boudreau, and George T. Milkovich (Stamford, CT: JAI Press, 1999).

[33]This is a variation of the resource dependence ideas discussed in the strategy chapter (Chapter 2).

[34]C. A. Bartlett and S. Ghoshal, "Changing the Role of Top Management (part 3): Beyond Systems to People," *Harvard Business Review* 73, May–June 1995, pp. 132–43.

[35]Allen D. Engle, Sr., and Mark E. Mendenhall, "Spinning the Global Competency Cube: Toward a Timely Transnational Human Resource Decision Support System" (working paper, Eastern Kentucky University, Richmond, 2000).

[36]Lyle M. Spencer, Jr., and Signe M. Spencer, *Competence at Work* (New York: John Wiley and Sons, 1993).

[37]Sharon A. Tucker and Kathryn Cofsky, "Competency Based Pay on a Banding Platform," *ACA News* 3 (1) , Spring 1994, pp. 30–40.

[38]G. S. Becker, *Human Capital* (New York: Columbia University Press, 1964).

[39]Edward E. Lawler III, "From Job-Based to Competency-Based Organizations," *Journal of Organizational Behavior* 15 (1994), pp. 3–15.

[40]Cynthia Lee, Kenneth S. Law, and Philip Bobko, "The Importance of Justice Perceptions on Pay Effectiveness: A Two-Year Study of a Skill-Based Pay Plan," *Journal of Management* 25 (6) (1999), pp. 851–73.

[41]Vandra Huber and S. Crandall, "Job Measurement: A Social-Cognitive Decision Perspective," in *Research in Personnel and Human Resources Management* 12, ed. Gerald R. Ferris (Greenwich, CT: JAI Press, 1994), pp. 223–69.

[42]R. M. Madigan and D. J. Hoover, "Effects of Alternative Job Evaluation Methods on Decisions Involving Pay Equity," *Academy of Management Journal*, March 1986, pp. 84–100.

[43]D. Doverspike and G. Barrett, "An Internal Bias Analysis of a Job Evaluation Instrument," *Journal of Applied Psychology* 69 (1984), pp. 648–62; Kermit Davis, Jr., and William Sauser, Jr., "Effects of Alternative Weighting Methods in a Policy-Capturing Approach to Job Evaluation: A Review and Empirical Investigation," *Personnel Psychology* 44 (1991), pp. 85–127.

[44]Judith Collins, "Job Evaluation" (Working paper, University of Arkansas-Little Rock, 1992).

[45]D. Lipsky and R. Seeber, "In Search of Control: The Corporate Embrace of Alternative Dispute Resolution," *Journal of Labor and Employment Law* 1 (1) Spring 1998, pp. 133–57.

[46]D. J. Treiman and H. I. Hartmann, eds., *Women, Work and Wages: Equal Pay for Jobs of Equal Value* (Washington, DC: National Academy of Sciences, 1981); H. Remick, *Comparable Worth and Wage Discrimination* (Philadelphia: Temple University Press, 1984).

[47]D. Schwab and R. Grams, "Sex-Related Errors in Job Evaluation: A 'Real-World' Test," *Journal of Applied Psychology* 70 (3) (1985), pp. 533–59; Richard D. Arvey, Emily M. Passino, and John W. Lounsbury, "Job Analysis Results as Influenced by Sex of Incumbent and Sex of Analyst," *Journal of Applied Psychology* 62 (4) (1977), pp. 411–16.

48Michael K. Mount and Rebecca A. Ellis, "Investigation of Bias in Job Evaluation Ratings of Comparable Worth Study Participants," *Personnel Psychology*, Spring 1987, pp. 85–96.

49S. Rynes, C. Weber, and G. Milkovich, "The Effects of Market Survey Rates, Job Evaluation, and Job Gender on Job Pay," *Journal of Applied Psychology* 74 (1989), pp. 114–23.

50D. Schwab and R. Grams, "Sex-Related Errors in Job Evaluation: A 'Real-World' Test," *Journal of Applied Psychology* 70 (3) (1985), pp. 533–59.

51N. Fredric Crandall and Marc J. Wallace, Jr., "Paying Employees to Develop New Skills," in *Aligning Pay and Results*, ed. Howard Risher (New York: American Management Association 1999); B. Murray and B. Gerhart, "An Empirical Analysis of a Skill-Based Pay Program and Plant Performance Outcomes," *Academy of Management Journal* 41 (1998), pp. 68–78.

52Howard Risher, ed. *Aligning Pay and Results* (New York: American Management Association 1999).

Chapter 7

1"2003 Comp Increases," *Canadian HR Reporter*, March 24, 2003, p.3.

2S. L. Rynes and B. Gerhart, eds., *Compensation in Organizations: Current Research & Practice* (San Francisco: Jossey-Bass, 2000); Margaret L. Williams and George Dreher, "Compensation System Attributes and Applicant Pool Characteristics," *Academy of Management Journal*, August 1992.

3The National Association of Colleges and Employers, Bethlehem, PA, publishes a quarterly survey of starting salary offers to college graduates. Data are reported by curriculum, by functional area, and by degree. It is one of several sources employers may use to establish the offers they extend to new graduates. www.naceweb.org

4Adapted from our analysis of CHIPS 2000 data set, by arrangement with Executive Alliance, Boston, Massachusetts.

5Barry Gerhart and George Milkovich, "Employee Compensation: Research and Practice," in *Handbook of Industrial and Organizational Psychology*, 2nd ed., eds. M. D. Dunnette and L. M. Hough (Palo Alto, CA: Consulting Psychologists Press, 1992).

6Barry Gerhart and Sara Rynes, "Determinants and Consequences of Salary Negotiations by Male and Female MBA Graduates," *Journal of Applied Psychology* 76, (2) (1991), pp. 256–62. Also see S. L. Rynes and B. Gerhart, eds., *Compensation in Organizations: Current Research & Practice* (San Francisco: Jossey-Bass, 2000).

7Robert Pindyck and Daniel Rubinfeld, *Microeconomics*, 5th ed. (Upper Saddle River, NJ: Prentice Hall, 2001).

8Thomas A. Mahoney, *Compensation and Reward Perspective* (Burr Ridge, IL: Richard D. Irwin 1979), p. 123.

9David Levine, D. Belman, G. Charness, E. Groshen, and K. C. O'Shaughnessy, *The New Employment Contract: Evidence About How Little Wage Structures Have Changed* (Kalamazoo: Upjohn Institute, 2001); C. Murphy, "Inequality," *Fortune*, September 4, 2000, pp. 253–57; Edward P. Lazear, *Personnel Economics* (New York: John Wiley & Sons, 1998); Carl M. Campbell III, "Do Firms Pay Efficiency Wages? Evidence with Data at the Firm Level," *Journal of Labor Economics* 11, (3) (1993), pp. 442–69.

10Peter Cappelli and Keith Chauvin, "An Interplant Test of the Efficiency Wage Hypothesis," *Quarterly Journal of Economics*, August 1991, pp. 769–87.

11L. Rynes and J. W. Boudreau, "College Recruiting in Large Organizations: Practice, Evaluation, and Research Implications," *Personnel Psychology* 39 (1986), pp. 729–57.

12E. Groshen and A. B. Krueger, "The Structure of Supervision and Pay in Hospitals," *Industrial and Labor Relations Review*, February 1990, pp. 134S–46S.

13Allison Barber, "Pay as a Signal in Job Choice" (Working paper, Graduate School of Business Administration, Michigan State University); A. VanVinnen, "Person-Organization Fit: The Match Between Newcomers' and Recruiters' Preferences for Organization Cultures," *Personnel Psychology* 53 (2000), pp. 115–25.

14Daniel M. Cable and Timothy A. Judge, "Pay Preferences and Job Search Decisions: A Person-Organization Fit Perspective," *Personnel Psychology*, Summer 1994, pp. 317–48.

15C. Brown, "Firms' Choice of Method of Pay," *Industrial and Labor Relations Review*, February 1990, pp. S165–S182.

16Gary S. Becker, *Human Capital* (Chicago: University of Chicago Press, 1975); Barry Gerhart, "Gender Differences in Current and Starting Salaries: The Role of Performance, College Major, and Job Title," *Industrial and Labor Relations Review* 43 (1990), pp. 418–33.

17David I. Levine, "Fairness, Markets, and Ability to Pay: Evidence from Compensation Executives," *American Economic Review*, December 1993, pp. 1241–59; B. Klaas, "Containing Compensation Costs: Why Firms Differ in Their Willingness to Reduce Pay," *Journal of Management* 25 (6) (1999), pp. 829–50.

18David I. Levine, "Fairness, Markets, and Ability to Pay: Evidence from Compensation Executives," *American Economic Review*, December 1993, p. 1250.

19Family and Work Institute, 1992 Survey; K. Grimsley, "U.S. Corporations Look at Incentives to Entice Low-Wage Workers to Stay," *International Herald Tribune*, March 24, 1997, p. 1.

[20]Erica L. Groshen and David Levine, *The Rise and Decline (?) of Employer Wage Structures* (New York: Federal Reserve Bank, 2000); John Haltowanger, *The Creation and Analysis of Employer-Employee Matched Data* (Amsterdam: North Holland, 1999).

[21]D. M. Raff, "The Puzzling Profusion of Compensation Systems in the Interwar Automobile Industry," *NBER*, 1998. Raff attributes the fantastic diversity of compensation programs for blue-collar employees (firm-based, piece rate, company-wide, team-based) to differences in technology employed among competitors.

[22]J. Abowd and I. Kramarz, "Interindustry and Firm Size Wage Differentials: New Evidence," working paper: ILR-Cornell Institute of Labor Market Policies, July 2000; Walter Oi and Todd L. Idson, "Firm Size and Wages," in *Handbook of Labor Economics*, eds., O. Ashenfelter and D. Card (Amsterdam: North Holland, 1999), pp. 2165–214.

[23]H. Heneman and T. Judge, "Pay and Employee Satisfaction," in *Compensation in Organizations: Current Research & Practice*, eds. S. L. Rynes and B. Gerhart (San Francisco: Jossey-Bass, 2000); T. R. Mitchell and A. E. Mickel, "The Meaning of Money: An Individual Differences Perspective," *Academy of Management Review* (24) (1999), pp. 568–78; *Playing to Win: Strategic Rewards in the War for Talent* (New York: Watson Wyatt, 2001); Gerry Ledford, Paul Mulvey, and Peter LeBlanc, *The Rewards of Work: What Employees Value* (Scottsdale, AZ: World at Work, 2000).

[24]R. Ehrenberg and R. Smith, *Modern Labor Economics*, 5th ed. (New York: Harper Collins, 1998); Alex Colvin, R. Batt, and H. Katz, "How HR Practices and IR Institutions Affect Managerial Pay," working paper, ILR School/Cornell University, 2000.

[25]www.erieri.com (August 12, 2003).

[26]Charlie Trevor and M. E. Graham, "Discretionary Decisions in Market Wage Derivatives: What Do Cheeseheads Rely Upon and Does It Really Matter?" Working paper, University of Wisconsin, Madison, 2000; Chockalingham Viswesvaran and Murray Barrick, "Decision Making Effects on Compensation Surveys: Implications for Market Wages," *Journal of Applied Psychology* 77, (5) (1992), pp. 588–97.

[27]Audrey Freedman, *The New Look in Wage Policy and Employee Relations* (New York: The Conference Board, 1985).

[28]David I. Levine, "Fairness, Markets, and Ability to Pay: Evidence from Compensation Executives," *American Economic Review*, December 1993, pp. 1241–59.

[29]See, for example, any of the surveys conducted by leading consulting firms. Hewitt, www.hewitt.com; Wyatt Watson, www.watsonwyatt.com; Hay, www.haygroup.com; Mercer, www.mercer.com; Towers Perrin, www.towersperrin.com; Executive Alliance, www.executivealliance.com.

[30]Brian S. Klaas and John A. McClendon, "To Lead, Lag, or Match: Estimating the Financial Impact of Pay Level Policies," *Personnel Psychology* 49 (1996), pp. 121–40.

[31]R. B. Freeman and J. Rogers, *What Workers Want* (Ithaca, NY: Cornell University Press, 1999); P. D. Lineneman, M. L. Wachter, and W. H. Carter, "Evaluating the Evidence on Union Employment and Wages," *Industrial and Labor Relations Review* 44 (1990), pp. 34–53.

[32]M. B. Tannen, "Is the Army College Fund Meeting Its Objectives?" *Industrial and Labor Relations Review* 41 (1987), pp. 50–62; Hyder Lakhani, "Effects of Pay and Retention Bonuses on Quit Rates in the U.S. Army," *Industrial and Labor Relations Review* 41 (1988), pp. 430–38.

[33]B. Gerhart and G. Milkovich, "Organizational Differences in Managerial Compensation and Financial Performance," *Academy of Management Journal* 33 (1990), pp. 663–91; M. Bloom and J. Michel, "The Relationships among Organization Context, Pay, and Managerial Theories," working paper, University of Notre Dame Department of Management, 2000; M. Bloom and G. Milkovich, "Relationships among Risk, Incentive Pay, and Organization Performance," *Academy of Management Journal* 41 (3) (1998), pp. 283–97; B. Hall and J. Liebman, "Are CEOs Really Paid Like Bureaucrats?" *Quarterly Journal of Economics*, August 1998, pp. 653–91. Variable pay is discussed in Chapters 9 through 11. "Variable" indicates that the pay increase (bonus) is not added to base pay; hence, it is not part of fixed costs but is variable, since the amount may vary next year.

[34]David I. Levine, "Fairness, Markets, and Ability to Pay: Evidence from Compensation Executives," *American Economic Review*, December 1993, pp. 1241–59.

[35]Stephenie Overman, "In Search of Best Practices," *HR Magazine*, December 1993, pp. 48–50.

[36]L. Gaughan and J. Kasparek, "Employees as Customers: Using Market Research to Manage Compensation and Benefits," *Workspan* (9) (2000), pp. 31–38; M. Sturman, G. Milkovich, and J. Hannon, "Expert Systems' Effect on Employee Decisions and Satisfaction," *Personnel Psychology* (1997), pp. 21–34; J. Shaw and Schaubrock, "The Role of Spending Behavior Patterns in Monetary Rewards," working paper, University of Kentucky, 2001.

[37]B. Mackay, "Coke Moves to Stop a Stream of Worker Defections," *Wall Street Journal*, April 11, 2000, p. B1.

[38]Barry Gerhart and George Milkovich, "Employee Compensation: Research and Practice," in *Handbook of Industrial and Organizational Psychology*, 2nd ed., eds. M. D. Dunnette and L. M. Hough (Palo Alto CA: Consulting Psychologists Press, 1992).

[39]Brian Klaas and John A. McClendon, "To Lead, Lag, or Match: Estimating the Financial Impact of Pay Level Policies," *Personnel Psychology* 49 (1996), pp. 121–40.

[40]H. Heneman and T. Judge, "Pay and Employee Satisfaction," in *Compensation in Organizations: Current Research & Practice*, eds. S. L. Rynes & B. Gerhart, (San Francisco: Jossey-Bass, 2000).

Chapter 8

[1]Adapted from each company's compensation strategy statements.

[2]Consulting firms' Web sites list their specialized surveys. See, for example Towers Perrin (www.towers.com); Hay (http://www.haypaynet.com); Hewitt www.hewitt.com; Wyatt Watson (www.watsonwyatt.com); Mercer (www.mercer.com)

[3]Gerry Ledford, Paul Mulvey, and Peter LeBlanc, *The Rewards of Work: What Employees Value* (Scottsdale, AZ.: World at Work, 2000).

[4]Charlie Trevor and Mary E. Graham, "Discretionary Decisions in Market Wage Derivatives: What Do Managers Rely Upon and Does It Really Matter?" Working paper, University of Wisconsin, Madison, 2000; Brian Klaas and John A. McClendon, "To Lead, Lag, or Match: Estimating the Financial Impact of Pay Level Policies," *Personnel Psychology* 49(1996), pp. 121–40.

[5]Charlie Trevor and Mary E. Graham, "Discretionary Decisions in Market Wage Derivatives: What Do Managers Rely Upon and Does It Really Matter?" Working paper, University of Wisconsin, Madison, 2000.

[6]Barry Gerhart and George Milkovich, "Employee Compensation," in *Handbook of Industrial and Organizational Psychology*, 2nd ed., eds. M. D. Dunnette and L. M. Hough (Palo Alto, CA: Consulting Psychologists Press, 1992).

[7]In addition to these consultants, international organizations also do surveys. See Income Data Services Web site (www.incomesdata.co.uk) and their publication *Employment Europe Pay Objectives 2000*, or Link Group Consultants, Limited, Chester, UK. Also see William M. Mercer's International Compensation Guidelines 2000 (information on 61 nations); Towers Perrin's Global Surveys, and Organization Resource Counselors on-line survey for positions in countries ranging from Azerbaijan to Yugoslavia (http://www.orcinc.com). Mercer and Towers Perrin Web site addresses are provided in footnote 2.

[8]Daniel Vaughn-Whitehead, *Paying the Price: The Wage Crisis in Central and Eastern Europe* (McMillin Press Ltd, Handmill Hampshire, UK, 1998); Sheila M. Puffer and Stanislav V. Shekshnia, "Compensating Local Employees in Post-Communist Russia: In Search of Talent or Just Looking for a Bargain?" *Compensation and Benefits Review*, September–October 1994, pp. 35–43.

[9]M. Bloom, G. Milkovich, and A. Mitra, "Toward a Model of International Compensation and Rewards: Learning from How Managers Respond to Variations in Local-Host Conditions," Ithaca, NY: ILR-CAHRS Working Paper, 2000.

[10]Mike Wanderer, "Dot-Comp: A 'Traditional' Pay Plan with a Cutting Edge," *World at Work Journal*, Fourth Quarter 2000, pp. 15–24.

[11]For consultancies' Web sites, see the appendix at the end of this book as well as footnotes 4 and 5 in this chapter.

[12]Hay (http://www.haypaynet.com)

[13]Chockalingam Viswesvaran and Murray Barrick, "Decision-Making Effects on Compensation Surveys: Implications for Market Wages," *Journal of Applied Psychology* 77 (5)(1992), pp. 588–97.

[14]"The Value of Pay Data on The Web," *Workspan*, September 2000, pp. 25–28.

[15]L. S. Hartenian and N. B. Johnson, "Establishing the Reliability and Validity of Wage Surveys," *Public Personnel Management* 20 (3)(1991), pp. 367–83; Sara L. Rynes and G. T. Milkovich, "Wage Surveys: Dispelling Some Myths about the 'Market Wage,'" *Personnel Psychology*, Spring 1986, pp. 71–90; Frederic Cook, "Compensation Surveys Are Biased," *Compensation and Benefits Review*, September–October 1994, pp. 19–22.

[16]Joseph R. Rich and Carol Caretta Phalen, "A Framework for the Design of Total Compensation Surveys," *ACA Journal*, Winter 1992–93, pp. 18–29.

[17]Letter from D. W. Belcher to G. T. Milkovich, in reference to D. W. Belcher, N. Bruce Ferris, and John O'Neill, "How Wage Surveys Are Being Used," *Compensation and Benefits Review*, September– October 1985, pp. 34–51.

[18]Users of Milkovich and Milkovich's *Cases in Compensation* will recognize the small software company FastCat. Visit them at www.HR-Education-Gateway.com.

[19]"Alternative Base Salary Approaches," in *Compensation Guide* (New York: Warren Gorham Lamont, 1995), Ch. 22.

[20]*Users of Cases in Compensation* will note that the SSAP software in FastCat uses the "20 percent above and 20 percent below" approach.

[21]Kenan S. Abosch and Beverly L. Hmurovic, "A Traveler's Guide to Global Broadbanding," *ACA Journal*, Summer 1998, pp. 38–47.

[22]"Life with Broadbands," ACA Research Project, 1998; "Broad Banding Case Study: General Electric," *World at Work Journal*, Third Quarter 2000, p. 43.

[23]Kenan S. Abosch and Janice S. Hand, *Broadbanding Models* (Scottsdale, AZ: American Compensation Association, 1994).

[24]Hill, "Get Off the Broadband Wagon," *Journal of Compensation and Benefits*, January–February 1993, pp. 25–29; Michael Enods and Greg Limoges, "Broadbanding: Is That Your Company's Final Answer?" *World at Work Journal*, Fourth Quarter 2000, pp. 61–68.

[25]Robert Kanigel, *The One Best Way* (New York: Viking, 1997).

[26]S. Rynes, C. Weber, and G. Milkovich, "Effects of Market Survey Rates on Job Evaluation, and Job Gender on Job Pay," *Journal of Applied Psychology* 74 (1989), pp. 114–23.

[27]Frederic W. Cook, "Compensation Surveys Are Biased," *Compensation and Benefits Review*, September–October 1994, pp. 19–22.

[28]S. Rynes and G. Milkovich, "Wage Surveys: Dispelling Some Myths about the 'Market Wage,'" *Personnel Psychology*, Spring 1986, pp. 71–90; Frederic W. Cook, "Compensation Surveys Are Biased," *Compensation and Benefits Review*, September–October 1994, pp. 19–22.

[29]Vandra Huber and S. Crandall, "Job Measurement: A Social-Cognitive Decision Perspective," in *Research in Personnel and Human Resources Management*, Vol. 12, ed. Gerald R. Ferris (Greenwich, CT: JAI Press, 1994), pp. 223–69.

Chapter 9

[1]Katherine Macklem, "The Top 100 Employers," *Macleans*, October 28, 2002.

[2]"Benefits Make the Fortune '100 Best Companies' Great," *IOMA's Report on Managing Benefits Plans*, Issue 99-03 (March 1999).

[3]US Chamber of Commerce, "Employee Benefits 1999" (U.S. Chamber of Commerce: Washington D.C. 1999).

[4]Rebecca Blumenstein, "Seeking a Cure: Auto Makers Attack High Health-care Bills with a New Approach," *The Wall Street Journal*, December 9, 1996, p. A1.

[5]John Hanna, "Can the Challenge of Escalating Benefits Costs Be Met?" *Personnel Administration* 27, no. 9 (1977), pp. 50–57

[6]McCaffery, *Managing the Employee Benefits Program* (New York: American Management Association, 1983).

[7]This table was compiled from three different sources. Some of the reward components rated in some of the studies were not traditional employee benefits and have been deleted from the rankings here. The three studies were: "The Future Look of Employee Benefits," *The Wall Street Journal*, September 8, 1988, p. 23 (Source: Hewitt Associates); Kermit Davis, William Giles, and Hubert Feild, *How Young Professionals Rank Employee Benefits: Two Studies* (International Foundation of Employee Benefit Plans: Brookfield, WI, 1988); Kenneth Shapiro and Jesse Sherman, "Employee Attitude Benefit Plan Designs," *Personnel Journal*, July 1987, pp. 49–58.

[8]Mary Fruen and Henry DiPrete, *Health Care in the Future* (Boston, MA: John Hancock, 1986); HRM Update, "Health Plan Increases" (New York: The Conference Board, May 1988); Kintner and Smith, "General Motors Provides Health Care Benefits to Millions"; Health Research Institute, "1985 Health Care Cost Containment Survey" (Walnut Creek, CA: Health Research Institute); North West National Life Insurance Co., "Ten Ways to Cut Employee Benefit Costs," 1988; *American Demographics*, May 1987, 44–45.

[9]Foegen, "Are Escalating Employee Benefits Self-Defeating?" *Pension World* 14 (9), September 1978, pp. 83–84, 86.

[10]Employee Benefit Research Institute, *America in Transition: Benefits for the Future* (Washington, D.C.: EBRI 1987).

[11]Carol Danehower and John Lust, "How Aware are Employees of Their Benefits?" *Benefits Quarterly* 12(4), pp. 57–61.

[12]Burton Beam, Jr., and John J. McFadden, *Employee Benefits* (Chicago: Dearborn Financial Publishing 1996).

[13]Burton Beam, Jr., and John J. McFadden, *Employee Benefits* (Chicago: Dearborn Financial Publishing 1996).

[14]Burton Beam, Jr., and John J. McFadden, *Employee Benefits* (Chicago: Dearborn Financial Publishing 1996).

[15]Burton Beam, Jr., and John J. McFadden, *Employee Benefits* (Chicago: Dearborn Financial Publishing 1996).

[16]Burton Beam, Jr., and John J. McFadden, *Employee Benefits* (Chicago: Dearborn Financial Publishing 1996).

[17]Melissa W. Barringer and George T. Milkovich, "A Theoretical Exploration of the Adoption and Design of Flexible Benefit Plans: A Case of Human Resource Innovation," *Academy of Management Review* 23 (1998) pp. 306–8; Commerce Clearing House, *Flexible Benefits* (Chicago: Commerce Clearing House, 1983); American Can Company, *Do It Your Way* (Greenwich, Conn.: American Can Co., 1978); L. M. Baytos, "The Employee Benefit Smorgasbord: Its Potential and Limitations," *Compensation Review*, First Quarter 1970, pp. 86–90; "Flexible Benefit Plans Become More Popular," *The Wall Street Journal*, December 16, 1986, p. 1; Richard Johnson, *Flexible Benefits: A How To Guide* (Brookfield, WI: International Foundation of Employee Benefit Plans, 1986).

[18]EBRI, *Employee Benefits Research Institute Databook on Employee Benefits* (Employee Benefits Research Institute, 1995).

[19]Donald P. Crane, *The Management of Human Resources*, 2nd ed. (Belmont, CA: Wadsworth, 1979); Foegen, "Are Escalating Employee Benefits Self-Defeating?" *Pension World* 14(9) (September 1978), pp. 83–84, 86.

[20]Olivia Mitchell, "Fringe Benefits and Labor Mobility," *Journal of Human Resources* 17(2) (1982), pp. 286–98; Bradley Schiller and Randal Weiss, "The Impact of Private Pensions on Firm Attachment," *Review of Economics and Statistics* 61(3) (1979), pp. 369–80.

[21]Olivia Mitchell, "Fringe Benefits and the Cost of Changing Jobs," *Industrial and Labor Relations Review* 37(1) (1983), pp. 70–78; William E. Even and David A. MacPherson, "Employer Size and Labor Turnover: The Role of Pensions," *Industrial and Labor Relations Review* 49(4) July 1996, p. 707.

[22]Christopher Conte, "Flexible Benefit Plans Grow More Popular as Companies Seek to Cut Costs," *The Wall Street Journal*, March 19, 1991, p A1.

[23]Christopher Conte, "Flexible Benefit Plans Grow More Popular as Companies Seek to Cut Costs," *The Wall Street Journal*, March 19, 1991, p A1.

[24]George Dreher, Ronald Ash, and Robert Bretz, "Benefit Coverage and Employee Cost: Critical Factors in Explaining Compensation Satisfaction," *Personnel Psychology* 41 (1988), 237–54.

[25]George Dreher, Ronald Ash, and Robert Bretz, "Benefit Coverage and Employee Cost: Critical Factors in Explaining Compensation Satisfaction," *Personnel Psychology* 41 (1988), 237–54.

[26]"ESOPs Key to Performance," *Employee Benefit News* 5 (1987), p. 16.

[27]Lynn Densford, "Bringing Employees Back to Health," *Employee Benefit News* 2 (February 1988), p. 19.

[28]William F. Glueck, *Personnel: A Diagnostic Approach* (Plano, Tex.: Business Publications, 1978).

[29]Ludwig Wagner and Theodore Bakerman, "Wage Earners' Opinions of Insurance Fringe Benefits," *Journal of Insurance*, June 1960, pp. 17–28; Brad Chapman and Robert Otterman, "Employee Preference for Various Compensation and Benefits Options," *Personnel Administrator* 25 (November 1975), pp. 31–36.

[30]Stanley Nealy, "Pay and Benefit Preferences," *Industrial Relations* (October 1963), pp. 17–28.

[31]George T. Milkovich and Michael J. Delaney, "A Note on Cafeteria Pay Plans," *Industrial Relations*, February 1975, pp. 112–16.

[32]McCaffery, *Managing the Employee Benefits Program* (New York: American Management Association, 1983).

[33]D. McElroy, "Six Golden Rules of Intranet Benefit Communication," *Canadian HR Reporter*, October 18, 1999, pp. 6,9; F.G. Kuzmits, "Communicating Benefits: A Double Click Away," *Compensation and Benefits Review*, September/October 1998, pp. 60-64.

[34]"Towers Perrin Survey Finds Dramatic Increase in Companies Utilizing the Web for HR Transactions: Two- to Threefold Increase Compared to 1999 Survey." Retrieved October 20, 2000 from the World Wide Web: http://www.towers.com/towers/news; Towers, Perrin, Forster, and Crosby, "Corporate Benefit Communication . . . Today and Tomorrow," 1988.

[35]"Towers Perrin Survey Finds Dramatic Increase in Companies Utilizing the Web For HR Transactions: Two- to Threefold Increase Compared to 1999 Survey." Retrieved October 20, 2000 from the World Wide Web: http://www.towers.com/towers/news; Towers, Perrin, Forster, and Crosby, "Corporate Benefit Communication . . . Today and Tomorrow," 1988.

[36]"Towers Perrin Survey Finds Dramatic Increase in Companies Utilizing the Web for HR Transactions: Two- to Threefold Increase Compared to 1999 Survey." Retrieved October 20, 2000 from the World Wide Web: http://www.towers.com/towers/news; Towers, Perrin, Forster, and Crosby, "Corporate Benefit Communication . . . Today and Tomorrow," 1988.

[37]B. Jackson, "Communicating Total Rewards Real-Time," *Workspan*, May 2003, pp. 68-70.

[38]"Yoder-Heneman Creativity Award Supplement," *Personnel Administration* 26(11) (1981), pp. 49–67.

[39]Frank E. Kuzmits, "Communicating Benefits: A Double-Click Away," *Compensation & Benefits Review* 61, September/October 1998.

[40]Frank E. Kuzmits, "Communicating Benefits: A Double-Click Away," *Compensation & Benefits Review* 61, September/October 1998.

[41]Jonathan A. Segal, "Don't Let the Transmission of Bits of Data Bite You in Court," *HR Magazine* 45, June 2000.

[42]Stephanie Armour, "Workers Just Click to Enroll for Benefits," *USA Today*, November 8, 2000, B1.

[43]Stephanie Armour, "Workers Just Click to Enroll for Benefits," *USA Today*, November 8, 2000, B1.

[44]"Towers Perrin Survey Finds Dramatic Increase in Companies Utilizing the Web for HR Transactions: Two- to Threefold Increase Compared to 1999 Survey" Retrieved October 20, 2000 from the World Wide Web: http://www.towers.com/towers/news.

[45]Judith N. Mottl, "Cereal Killer," *Human Resources Executive*, May 2000, pp. 74–75.

[46]"How Do You Communicate? It May Not Be Nearly as Well as You Think," *Benefits*, December 1988, pp. 13–15; Kevin Greene, "Effective Employee Benefits Communication," in David Balkin and Luis Gomez-Mejia, *New Perspectives on Compensation* (Englewood Cliffs, NJ: Prentice-Hall 1987).

[47]Bennet Shaver, "The Claims Process," in Employee Benefit Management, ed. H. Wayne Snider, pp. 141–52.

[48]Thomas Fannin and Theresa Fannin, "Coordination of Benefits: Uncovering Buried Treasure," *Personnel Journal*, May 1983, pp. 386–91.

[49]E. Scott Peterson, "From Those Who've Been There . . . Outsourcing Leaders Talk about Their Experiences," *Benefits Quarterly* 6(1), First Quarter 1997, pp. 6–13.

[50]E. Scott Peterson, "From Those Who've Been There . . . Outsourcing Leaders Talk about Their Experiences," *Benefits Quarterly* 6(1), First Quarter 1997, pp. 6–13.

[51]G. Dee, N. McCombie and G Newhouse, *Workers' Compensation in Ontario Handbook* (Toronto, ON: Butterworths, 1999).

[52]J. Greenan, *The Handbook of Canadian Pension and Benefits Plans* (12th edition) (Toronto, ON: CCH Canadian Ltd., 2002).

[53]J. Greenan, *The Handbook of Canadian Pension and Benefits Plans* (12th edition) (Toronto, ON: CCH Canadian Ltd., 2002).

[54]Institute of Management & Administration (IOMA), "Managing 401(k) Plans," Institute of Management & Administration, August 2000.

[55]Employee Benefit Research Institute, *Fundamentals of Employee Benefit Programs* (Washington, DC: EBRI, 1997), pp. 69–73.

[56]Kevin Dent and David Sloss, "The Global Outlook for Defined Contribution Versus Defined Benefit Pension Plans," *Benefits Quarterly*, First Quarter 1996, pp. 23–28.

[57]B. Cohen and B. Fitzgerald, *The Pension Puzzle: Your Complete Guide to Government Benefits, RRSPs, and Employer Plans.* Toronto, ON: John Wiley & Sons, 2002.

[58]*Canadians and Their Group Health Benefits.* Aventis Canadian Consumer Survey on Healthcare, 2000.

[59]KPMG, Employee Benefit Costs in Canada, 1998.

[60]S. Lebrun, "Keeping the Lid on Drug Benefit Costs," *Canadian HR Reporter*, December 16, 1996, p.12.

[61]Shelly Reese, "Can Employers Halt the Price Hikers?" *Business & Health* 17, December 1999, p. 29; Regina Herzlinger and Jeffrey Schwartz, "How Companies Tackle Health Care Costs: Part I," *Harvard Business Review* 63, July–August 1985, pp. 69–81.

[62]David Rosenbloom, "Oh Brother, Our Medical Costs Went Up Again." Paper presented for the Health Data Institute, March 16, 1988.

[63]Nicholas A. DiNubile, MD. and Carl Sherman, "Exercise and the Bottom Line," *Physician and Sportsmedicine* 27, February, 1999, p. 37.

[64]R. Bunning, "A Prescription for Sick Leave," *Personnel Journal* 67 (August 1988), pp. 44-49.

[65]M. Acharya, " Depressed Workers Cost Firms Billions, Business Panel Says," *Toronto Star*, July 21, 2000, p. C3.

[66]F. Engel, " Lost Profits, Increased Costs: The Aftermath of Workplace Trauma," *Canadian HR Reporter*, September 7, 1998, pp. 21-22.

Chapter 10

[1]R. Mayer and J. Davis, "The Effect of the Performance Appraisal System on Trust for Management," *Journal of Applied Psychology* 84(1), (1999), pp. 123–36.

[2]Rodney A. McCloy, John P. Campbell, and Robert Cuedeck, "A Confirmatory Test of a Model of Performance Determinants," *Journal of Applied Psychology* 79(4) (1994), pp. 493–505.

[3]Brian Becker and Barry Gerhart, "The Impact of Human Resource Management on Organizational Performance: Progress and Propsects," *Academy of Management Journal* 39(4) (1996), pp. 779–801.

[4]This table extrapolates the findings from two studies: Matthew C. Bloom and George T. Milkovich, "The Relationship between Risk, Incentive Pay, and Organizational Performance," *Academy of Management Journal*, forthcoming; Anne Tsui, Jone L. Pearce, Lyman W. Porter, and Angela M. Tripoli, "Alternative Approaches to the Employee–Organization Relationship: Does Investment in Employees Pay Off?" *Academy of Management Journal* 40(5) (1997), pp. 1089–121.

[5]Anne Tsui, Jone L. Pearce, Lyman W. Porter, and Angela M. Tripoli, "Alternative Approaches to the Employee-Organization Relationship: Does Investment in Employees Pay Off?" *Academy of Management Journal* 40(5) (1997), pp. 1089–1121.

[6]A. Mamman, M. Sulaiman, and A. Fadel, "Attitude to Pay Systems: An Exploratory Study within and across Cultures," *The International Journal of Human Resource Management* 7(1), February 1996, pp. 101–121.

[7]IOMA, "Are You Ready to Serve Cafeteria Style Comp?" *Pay for Performance Report*, June 2000, pp. 1, 13.

[8]J. S. Adams, "Toward an Understanding of Inequity," *Journal of Abnormal and Social Psychology* 67 (1963), pp. 422–36; J. S. Adams, "Injustice in Social Exchange," *Advances in Experimental Social Psychology*, Vol. 2, ed. L. Berkowitz (New York: Academic Press, 1965); R. Cosier and D. Dalton, "Equity Theory and Time: A Reformulation," *Academy of Management Review* 8 (1983), pp. 311–19.

[9]B. Oviatt, "Agency and Transaction Cost Perspectives on the Manager-Shareholder Relationship: Incentives for Congruent Interests," *Academy of Management Review* 13 (1988), pp. 214–25.

[10]E. A. Locke, K. N. Shaw, L. M. Saari, and G. P. Latham, "Goal Setting and Task Performance: 1969–1980," *Psychological Bulletin* 90 (1981), pp. 125–52.

[11]M. R. Louis, B. Z. Posner, and G. N. Powell, "The Availability and Helpfulness of Socialization Practices," *Personnel Psychology* 36 (1983), pp. 857–66; E. H. Schein, "Organizational Socialization and the Profession of Management," *Industrial Management Review* 9 (1968), pp. 1–16.

[12]IOMA, "Pay for Performance Report," *IOMA Pay for Performance Report*, January 1998, p. 8; P. Stang and B. Laird, "Working Women's Motivators," reported in *USA Today*, February 9, 1999, p. B1 for Nationwide Insurance/Working Women Magazine Survey.

[13]E. L. Deci and R. M. Ryan, *Intrinsic Motivation and Self-Determination in Human Behavior* (New York: Plenum Press, 1985). Note, however, the evidence is not very strong.

[14]J. R. Schuster and P. K. Zingheim, *The New Pay: Linking Employee and Organizational Performance* (New York: Lexington Books, 1992).

[15]E. J. Conlon and J. M. Parks, "Effects of Monitoring and Tradition on Compensation Arrangements: An Experiment with Principal-Agent Dyads," *Academy of Management Journal* 33 (1990), pp. 603–22.

[16]E. J. Conlon and J. M. Parks, "Effects of Monitoring and Tradition on Compensation Arrangements: An Experiment with Principal-Agent Dyads," *Academy of Management Journal* 33 (1990), pp. 603–22.

[17]W. N. Cooke, "Employee Participation Programs, Group Based Incentives, and Company Performance," *Industrial and Labor Relations Review* 47 (1994), pp. 594–610; G. W. Florkowski, "The Organizational Impact of Profit Sharing," *Academy of Management Review* 12 (1987), pp. 622–36; R. Heneman, *Merit Pay: Linking Pay Increases to Performance Ratings* (Reading, MA: Addison-Wesley, 1992); J. L. McAdams and

E. J. Hawk, *Organizational Performance and Rewards* (Phoenix, Ariz.: American Compensation Association, 1994); D. McDonaly and A. Smith, "A Proven Connection: Performance Management and Business Results," *Compensation and Benefits Review*, January–February 1995, pp. 59–64; G. T. Milkovich, "Does Performance-Based Pay Really Work? Conclusions Based on the Scientific Research," Unpublished document for 3M, 1994; G. Milkovich and C. Milkovich, "Strengthening the Pay Performance Relationship: The Research," *Compensation and Benefits Review* (1992), pp. 53–62.

[18]Mark A. Huselid, "The Impact of Human Resource Management Practices on Turnover, Productivity, and Corporate Financial Performance," *Academy of Management Journal* 38 (3) (1995), pp. 635–72.

[19]R. Heneman, *Merit Pay: Linking Pay Increases to Performance Ratings* (Reading, MA: Addison-Wesley, 1992).

[20]B. Gerhart and G. Milkovich, "Organizational Differences in Managerial Compensation and Financial Performance," *Academy of Management Journal* 33 (1990), pp. 663–90.

[21]E. E. Lawler, *Pay and Organizational Effectiveness: A Psychological View* (New York: McGraw-Hill, 1971); E. E. Lawler and G. D. Jenkins, "Strategic Reward Systems" in *Handbook of Industrial and Organizational Psychology*, eds. M. D. Dunnette and L. M. Hough (Palo Alto, CA: Consulting Psychologist Press, 1992), pp. 1009–55; W. Mobley, *Employee Turnover: Causes, Consequences and Control* (Reading, MA: Addison-Wesley, 1982).

[22]D. M. Cable and T. A. Judge, "Pay Preferences and Job Search Decisions: A Person-Organization Fit Perspective," *Personnel Psychology* 47 (1994), pp. 317–48.

[23]B. Turban and T. A. Judge, "Pay Preferences and Job Search Decisions: A Person-Organization Fit Perspective," *Personnel Psychology* 47 (1994), pp. 317–48.

[24]D. M. Cable and T. L. Keon, "Organizational Attractiveness: An Interactionist Perspective," *Journal of Applied Psychology* 78 (1993), pp. 184-93.

[25]D. M. Cable and T. A. Judge, "Pay Preferences and Job Search Decisions: A Person-Organization Fit Perspective," *Personnel Psychology* 47 (1994), pp. 317–48; A. Kohn, *Punished by Rewards: The Trouble with Gold Stars, Incentive Plans, A's, Praise and Other Bribes* (Boston: Houghton-Mifflin, 1993).

[26]D. M. Cable and T. A. Judge, "Pay Preferences and Job Search Decisions: A Person-Organization Fit Perspective," *Personnel Psychology* 47 (1994), pp. 317–48.

[27]T. R. Zenger, "Why Do Employers Only Reward Extreme Performance? Examining the Relationships Among Performance Pay and Turnover," *Administrative Science Quarterly* 37(1992), pp. 198–219.

[28]David A. Harrison, Meghna Virick, and Sonja William, "Working Without a Net: Time, Performance, and Turnover Under Maximally Contingent Rewards," *Journal of Applied Psychology* 81(4) (1996), pp. 331–45.

[29]M. R. Carrell and J. E. Dettrich, "Employee Perceptions of Fair Treatment," *Personnel Journal* 55 (1976), pp. 523–24.

[30]A. Weiss, "Incentives and Worker Behavior: Some Evidence" in *Incentives, Cooperation and Risk Sharing*, ed. H. R. Nalbantian (Totowa, NJ: Rowan & Littlefield, 1987), pp. 137–50.

[31]R. Heneman and T. Judge, "Compensation Attitudes: A Review and Recommendations for Future Research," in *Compensation in Organizations: Progress and Prospects*, S. L. Rynes and B. Gerhart, eds. (San Francisco: New Lexington Press, 1999).

[32]P. W. Hom and R. W. Griffeth, *Employee Turnover* (Cincinnati: Southwestern. M. Kim, 1995); "Where the Grass is Greener: Voluntary Turnover and Wage Premiums," *Industrial Relations* 38, October 1999, p. 584.

[33]A. Kohn, *Punished by Rewards: The Trouble with Gold Stars, Incentive Plans, A's, Praise and Other Bribes* (Boston: Houghton-Mifflin, 1993).

[34]P. Zingheim and J. R. Shuster, *Pay People Right* (San Francisco: Jossey-Bass, 2000); J. Boudreau, M. Sturman, C. Trevor, and B. Gerhart, "Is It Worth It to Win the Talent War? Using Turnover Research to Evaluate the Utility of Performance-Based Pay," Working Paper 99-06 (Center for Advanced Human Resource Studies, Cornell University, 2000).

[35]IOMA, "Report on Salary Surveys," May 1997, p. 14; Kevin J. Parent and Caroline L. Weber, "Does Paying for Knowledge Pay Off?" *Compensation and Benefits Review*, September 1994, pp. 44–50.

[36]A. Kohn, *Punished by Rewards: The Trouble with Gold Stars, Incentive Plans, A's, Praise and Other Bribes* (Boston: Houghton-Mifflin, 1993).

[37]E. Deci, R. Ryan, and R. Koestner, "A Meta-Analytic Review of Experiments Examining the Effects of Extrinsic Rewards on Intrinsic Motivation," *Psychological Bulletin* 125(6) (1999), pp. 627–68.

[38]R. McKensie and D. Lee, *Managing Through Incentives*. (Oxford University Press: NY, 1998); R. Eisenberger and J. Cameron, "Detrimental Effects of Rewards," *American Psychologist*, November 1996, pp. 1153–56.

[39]L. Dyer, D. P. Schwab, and R. D. Theriault, "Managerial Perceptions Regarding Salary Increase Criteria," *Personnel Psychology* 29 (1976), pp. 233–42.

[40]J. Fossum and M. Fitch, "The Effects of Individual and Contextual Attributes on the Sizes of Recommended Salary Increases," *Personnel Psychology* 38 (1985), pp. 587–603.

[41]L. V. Jones and T. E. Jeffrey, "A Quantitative Analysis of Expressed Preferences for Compensation Plans," *Journal of Applied Psychology* 48 (1963), pp. 201–10; Opinion Research Corporation, *Wage Incentives* (Princeton, NJ: Opinion Research Corporation, 1946); Opinion Research Corp., *Productivity from the Worker's Standpoint* (Princeton, NJ: Opinion Research Corporation, 1949).

[42]D. Koys, T. Keaveny, and R. Allen, "Employment Demographics and Attitudes That Predict Preferences for Alternative Pay Increase Policies," *Journal of Business and Psychology* 4 (1989), pp. 27–47.

[43]B. Major, "Gender, Justice and the Psychology of Entitlement," *Review of Personality and Social Psychology* 7 (1988), pp. 124–48.

[44]IOMA, "Incentive Pay Programs and Results: An Overview," *IOMA*, May 1996, p. 11; G. Green, "Instrumentality Theory of Work Motivation," *Journal of Applied Psychology* 53 (1965), pp. 1–25; R. D. Pritchard, D. W. Leonard, C. W. Von Bergen, Jr., and R. J. Kirk, "The Effects of Varying Schedules of Reinforcement on Human Task Performance," *Organizational Behavior and Human Performance* 16 (1976), pp. 205–30; D. P. Schwab and L. Dyer, "The Motivational Impact of a Compensation System on Employee Performance," *Organizational Behavior and Human Performance* 9 (1973), pp. 215–25; D. Schwab, "Impact of Alternative Compensation Systems on Pay Valence and Instrumentality Perceptions," *Journal of Applied Psychology* 58 (1973), pp. 308–12.

[45]Mark A. Huselid, "The Impact of Human Resource Management Practices on Turnover, Productivity, and Corporate Financial Performance," *Academy of Management Journal* 38(3), pp. 635–72.

[46]Barry Gerhart, "Pay Strategy and Firm Performance" in S. Rynes and B. Gerhart (eds), *Compensation in Organizations: Progress and Prospects*. (San Francisco: New Lexington Press) (1999).

[47]W. N. Cooke, "Employee Participation Programs, Group Based Incentives, and Company Performance," *Industrial and Labor Relations Review* 47 (1994), pp. 594–610; D. L. Kruse, *Profit Sharing: Does It Make a Difference?* (Kalamazoo, Mich.: Upjohn Institute, 1993); G. T. Milkovich, "Does Performance-Based Pay Really Work? Conclusions Based on the Scientific Research," Unpublished document for 3M, 1994; M. M. Petty, B. Singleton, and D. W. Connell, "An Experimental Evaluation of an Organizational Incentive Plan in the Electric Utility Industry," *Journal of Applied Psychology* 77 (1992), pp. 427–36; J. R. Schuster, "The Scanlon Plan: A Longitudinal Analysis," *Journal of Applied Behavioral Science* 20 (1984), pp. 23–28.

[48]M. M. Petty, B. Singleton, and D. W. Connell, "An Experimental Evaluation of an Organizational Incentive Plan in the

Electric Utility Industry," *Journal of Applied Psychology* 77 (1992), pp. 427–36.

[49]McAdams and Hawk, *Organizational Performance and Rewards*, 1994.

[50]B. Gerhart and G. Milkovich, "Organizational Differences in Managerial Compensation and Financial Performance," *Academy of Management Journal* 33 (1990), pp. 663–90.

[51]K. Murphy and J. Cleveland, *Understanding Performance Appraisal* (Thousand Oaks, Ca.: Sage, 1995).

[52]Susan E. Jackson, Randall S. Schuler, and J. Carlos Rivero, "Organizational Characteristics as Predictors of Personnel Practices," *Personnel Psychology* 42 (1989), pp. 727–86.

[53]Robert L. Cardy and Gregory H. Dobbins, *Performance Appraisal: Alternative Perspectives* (Cincinnati: Southwestern Publishing, 1994).

[54]W. E. Deming, *Out of the Crisis* (Cambridge, Mass.: MIT Press, 1986).

[55]David Waldman, "The Contributions of Total Quality Management of a Theory of Work Performance," *Academy of Management Review* 19 (1994), pp. 510–36.

[56]David Antonioni, "Improve the Performance Management Process before Discontinuing Performance Appraisals," *Compensation and Benefits Review*, May–June 1994, pp. 29–37.

[57]Timothy D. Schellhardt, "Annual Agony," *The Wall Street Journal*, November 19, 1996, p. A1.

[58]R. Arvey and K. Murphy, "Performance Evaluation in Work Settings," *Annual Review of Psychology* 49 (1998), pp. 141–68.

[59]J.P. Campbell, R. McCloy, S. Oppler, and C. Sager, "A Theory of Performance," in *Personnel Selection in Organizations*, N. Schmitt and W. Borman, eds. (San Francisco: Jossey-Bass, 1993), pp. 25–70.

[60]W. Borman and D. Brush, "More Progress towards a Taxonomy of Managerial Performance Requirements," *Human Performance* (1993), 6 (1), pp. 1–21.

[61]D. Coleman, *Working with Emotional Intelligence* (New York: Bantam Books, 1998).

[62]Daniel Ilgen and Jack Feldman, "Performance Appraisal: A Process Focus," *Research in Organizational Behavior* 5 (1983), pp. 141–97.

[63]Lloyd S. Baird, Richard W. Beatty, Craig Eric Schneider, and Douglas G. Shaw, *The Performance, Measurement, Management, and Appraisal Sourcebook* (Amherst, MA: Human Resources Development Press, 1995).

[64]Mark L. McConkie, "A Clarification of the Goal Setting and Appraisal Processes in MBO," *Academy of Management Review* 4 (1) (1979), pp. 29–40.

[65]Bruce McAfee and Blake Green, "Selecting a Performance Appraisal Method," *Personnel Administrator* 22 (5) (1977), pp. 61–65.

[66]H. John Bernardin, "Behavioral Expectation Scales v. Summated Ratings: A Fairer Comparison," *Journal of Applied Psychology* 62 (1977), pp. 422–27; H. John Bernardin, Kim Alvares, and C. J. Cranny, "A Re-comparison of Behavioral Expectation Scales to Summated Scales," *Journal of Applied Psychology* 61 (1976), pp. 284–91; C. A. Schriesheim and U. E. Gattiker, "A Study of the Abstract Desirability of Behavior-Based v. Trait-Oriented Performance Rating," *Proceedings of the Academy of Management* 43 (1982), pp. 307–11; and F. S. Landy and J. L. Farr, "Performing Rating," *Psychological Bulletin* 87 (1980), pp. 72–107.

[67]Michael Keeley, "A Contingency Framework for Performance Evaluation," *Academy of Management Review* 3, July 1978, pp. 428–38.

[68]Mark R. Edwards and Ann J. Ewen, *360 Degree Feedback: The Powerful New Model for Employee Assessment and Performance Improvement* (Toronto: American Management Association, 1996).

[69]Susan E. Jackson, Randall S. Schuller, and J. Carlos Rivero, "Organizational Characteristics as Predictors of Personnel Practices," *Personnel Psychology* 42 (1989), pp. 727–86.

[70]E. Pulakos and W. Borman, *Developing the Basic Criterion Scores for Army-wide and MOS-specific Ratings* (Alexandria, VA: U.S. Army Research Institute, 1992).

[71]Deniz S. Ones, Frank L. Schmidt, and Chockalingam Viswesvaran, "Comparative Analysis of the Reliability of Job Performance Ratings," *Journal of Applied Psychology* 81 (5) (1996), pp. 557–74.

[72]F. S. Landy and J. L. Farr, "Performance Rating," *Psychological Bulletin* 87 (1980), pp. 72–107.

[73]M. M. Harris and J. Schaubroeck, "A Meta Analysis of Self-supervisor, Self-peer and Peer-supervisor ratings," *Personnel Psychology* 4 (1988), pp. 43–62.

[74]Harris and Schaubroeck, "A Meta Analysis of Self-supervisor, Self-peer and Peer-supervisor Ratings."

[75]D. Antonioni, "The Effects of Feedback Accountability on Upward Appraisal Ratings," *Personnel Psychology* 47 (1994), pp. 349–56.

[76]K. Murphy and J. Cleveland, *Understanding Performance Appraisal* (Thousand Oaks, CA.: Sage, 1995).

[77]G. Alliger and K. J. Williams, "Affective Congruence and the Employment Interview," in *Advances in Information Processing in Organizatons*, Vol. 4, eds. J. R. Meindl, R. L. Cardy, and S. M. Puffer (Greenwich, CT: JAI Press).

[78]Landy and Farr, "Performance Rating"; A. S. Denisi, T. P. Cafferty, and B. M. Meglino, "A Cognitive View of the Performance Appraisal Process: A Model and Research Propositions," *Organizational Behavior and Human Performance* 33 (1984), pp. 360–96; Jack M. Feldman, "Beyond Attribution Theory: Cognitive Processes in Performance Appraisal," *Journal of Applied Psychology* 66 (2) (1981), pp. 127–48; and W. H. Cooper, "Ubiquitous Halo," *Psychological Bulletin* 90 (1981), pp. 218–44.

[79]Angelo Denisi and George Stevens, "Profiles of Performance, Performance Evaluations, and Personnel Decisions," *Academy of Management* 24 (3) (1981), pp. 592–602; Wayne Cascio and Enzo Valtenzi, "Relations among Criteria of Police Performance," *Journal of Applied Psychology* 63 (1) (1978), pp. 22–28; William Bigoness, "Effects of Applicant's Sex, Race, and Performance on Employer Performance Ratings: Some Additional Findings," *Journal of Applied Psychology* 61 (1) (1976), pp. 80–84; Dorothy P. Moore, "Evaluating In-Role and Out-of-Role Performers," *Academy of Management Journal* 27 (3) (1984), pp. 603–18; W. Borman, L. White, E. Pulakos, and S. Oppler, "Models of Supervisory Job Performance Ratings," *Journal of Applied Psychology* 76 (6) (1991), pp. 863–72.

[80]H. J. Bernardin and Richard Beatty, *Performance Appraisal: Assessing Human Behavior at Work* (Boston: Kent Publishing, 1984).

[81]G. Dobbins, R. Cardy, and D. Truxillo, "The Effects of Purpose of Appraisal and Individual Differences in Stereotypes of Women on Sex Differences in Performance Ratings: A Laboratory and Field Study," *Journal of Applied Psychology* 73 (3) (1988), pp. 551–58. Edward Shaw, "Differential Impact of Negative Stereotyping in Employee Selection," *Personnel Psychology* 25 (1972), pp. 333–38; Benson Rosen and Thomas Jurdee, "Effects of Applicant's Sex and Difficulty of Job on Evaluation of Candidates for Managerial Positions," *Journal of Applied Psychology* 59 (1975), pp. 511–12; Gail Pheterson, Sara Kiesler, and Philip Goldberg, "Evaluation of the Performance of Women as a Function of Their Sex, Achievement, and Personal History," *Journal of Personality and Social Psychology* 19 (1971), pp. 114–18; W. Clay Hamner, Jay Kim, Lloyd Baird, and William Bignoness, "Race and Sex as Determinants of Ratings by Potential Employers in a Simulated Work Sampling Task," *Journal of Applied Psychology* 59 (6) (1974), pp. 705–11; and Neal Schmitt and Martha Lappin, "Race and Sex as Determinants of the Mean and Variance of Performance Ratings," *Journal of Applied Psychology* 65 (4) (1980), pp. 428–35.

[82]D. Turban and A. Jones, "Supervisor-subordinate Similarity: Types, Effects and Mechanisms," *Journal of Applied Psychology* 73 (2) (1988), pp. 228–34.

[83]Angelo Denisi and George Stevens, "Profiles of Performance, Performance Evaluations, and Personnel Decisions," *Academy of Management Journal* 24(3) (1981), 592–602; William Scott and Clay Hamner, "The Influence of Variations in Performance Profiles on the Performance Evaluation Process: An Examination of the Validity of the Criterion," *Organizational Behavior and Human Performance* 14 (1975), pp. 360–70; Edward Jones, Leslie Rock, Kelly Shaver, George Goethals, and Laurence Ward, "Pattern of Performance and Ability Attributions: An Unexpected Primacy Effect," *Journal of Personality and Social Psychology* 10 (4) (1968), pp. 317–40.

[84]F.S. Landy and J.L. Farr, *Psychological Bulletin* 87(1980), 72–107; H.J. Bernardin and Richard Beatty, *Performance Appraisal: Assessing Human Behavior at Work* (Boston: Kent Publishing, 1984).

[85]B. P. Maroney and R. M. Buckely, "Does Research in Performance Appraisal Influence the Practice of Performance Appraisal? Regretfully Not," *Public Personnel Management* 21 (1992), pp. 185–96.

[86]Robert Liden and Terence Mitchell, "The Effects of Group Interdependence on Supervisor Performance Evaluations," *Personnel Psychology* 36 (2) (1983), pp. 289–99.

[87]G. R. Ferris and T. A. Judge, "Personnel/Human Resource Management: A Political Influence Perspective," *Journal of Management* 17 (1991), pp. 1–42.

[88]Yoav Ganzach, "Negativity (and Positivity) in Performance Evaluation: Three Field Studies," *Journal of Applied Psychology* 80, no. 4 (1995), pp. 491–99.

[89]R. Heneman and K. Wexley, "The Effects of Time Delay in Rating and Amount of Information Observed on Performance Rating Accuracy," *Academy of Management Journal* 26 (4), 1983, pp. 677–686.

[90]L. L. Cummings and D. P. Schwab, *Performance in Organizations* (Glenview Ill: Scott Foresman, 1973).

[91]Neal P. Mero and Stephan J. Motowidlo, "Effects of Rater Accountability on the Accuracy and the Favorability of Performance Ratings," *Journal of Applied Psychology* 80 (4) (1995), pp. 517–24.

[92]H. J. Bernardin and M. R. Buckley, "Strategies in Rater Training," *Academy of Management Review* 6 (2) (1981), pp. 205–12; D. Smith, "Training Programs for Performance Appraisal: A Review," *Academy of Management Review* 11 (1) (1986), pp. 22–40; B. Davis and M. Mount, "Effectiveness of Performance Appraisal Training Using Computer Assisted

Instruction and Behavioral Modeling," *Personnel Psychology* 3 (1984), pp. 439–52; H. J. Bernardin, "Effects of Rater Training on Leniency and Halo Errors in Student Ratings of Instructors," *Journal of Applied Psychology* 63 (3) (1978), pp. 301–8; and J. M. Ivancevich, "Longitudinal Study of the Effects of Rater Training on Psychometric Error in Ratings," *Journal of Applied Psychology* 64 (5) (1979), pp. 502–8.

[93] Bernardin and Buckley, "Strategies in Rater Training."

[94] Robert Heneman, *Merit Pay: Linking Pay Increases to Performance Ratings* (Reading, MA: Addison-Wesley 1992).

[95] Ann Podolske, "Creating a Review System That Works," IOMA's Pay for Performance Report, March 1996, pp. 2–4.

[96] A. DeNisi, T. Robbins, and T. Cafferty. "Organization of Information Used for Performance Appraisals: Role of Diary-keeping," *Journal of Applied Psychology* 74 (1) (1989), pp. 124–29.

[97] Angelo S. Denisi, Lawrence H. Peters, and Arup Varma, "Interpersonal Affect and Performance Appraisal: A Field Study," *Personnel Psychology* 49 (1996), pp. 341–60; F. J. Landy, J. L. Barnes, and K. R. Murphy, "Correlates of Perceived Fairness and Accuracy of Performance Evaluations," *Journal of Applied Psychology* 63 (1978), pp. 751–54.

[98] S. Snell and K. Wexley, "Performance Diagnosis: Identifying the Causes of Poor Performance," *Personnel Administrator*, April 1985, pp. 117–27.

[99] Ann Podolske, "Creating a Review System That Works," IOMA's Pay for Performance Report, March 1996, pp. 2–4.

[100] IOMA, "When Are Bonuses High Enough to Improve Performance?" *IOMA*, November 1996, p. 12.

[101] A. Richter, "Paying the People in Black at Big Blue," *Compensation and Benefits Review*, May/June 1998, pp. 51–59.

[102] John Thibaut and Laurens Walker, *Procedural Justice: A Psychological View* (Hillsdale, NJ: John Wiley & Sons, 1975).

[103] Robert Folger and Mary Konovsky, "Effects of Procedural and Distributive Justice on Reactions to Pay Raise Decisions," *Academy of Management Journal* 32, 1, (1989) 115–30.

[104] S. Alexander and M. Ruderman, "The Role of Procedural and Distributive Justice in Organizational Behavior," *Social Justice Research* 1 (1987), pp. 177–98.

[105] G. S. Leventhal, J. Karuza, and W. R. Fry, "Beyond Fairness: A Theory of Allocation Preferences," in *Justice and Social Interaction*, G. Mikula, ed. (New York: Springer Verlag 1980), pp. 167–218.

[106] Milkovich and Milkovich, "Strengthening the Pay-for-Performance Relationship. . . ," *Compensation and Benefits Review*, May–June 1996, pp. 27–33.

[107] Compensating Salaried Employees During Inflation: General vs. Merit Increases (New York: Conference Board, Report no. 796, 1981).

[108] Jackson, Schuller, and Rivero, "Organizational Characteristics as Predictors of Personnel Practices."

Chapter 11

[1] American Management Association, "Merit Raises Remain Popular Among Fortune 1000," *Compflash*, December 1994, p. 1.

[2] Jerry M. Newman and Daniel J. Fisher, "Strategic Impact Merit Pay," *Compensation and Benefits Review*, July/August 1992, pp. 38–45.

[3] Glenn Bassett, "Merit Pay Increases Are a Mistake," *Compensation and Benefits Review*, March/April, 1994, pp. 20–25.

[4] Robert Heneman, *Merit Pay: Linking Pay Increases to Performance Ratings* (Reading, MA: Addison-Wesley, 1992).

[5] Cincinnati Federation of Teachers, "Teacher Quality Update" (August 2000), Cincinnati Federation of Teachers.

[6] IOMA, "Four Studies Reveal How Alternative Pay Is Being Put to Work," *IOMA's Pay For Performance Report*, March 2000, p. 7.

[7] American Management Association, "A Growing Trend: Variable Pay for Lower Level Employees," *Compflash* (1992), p. 1.

[8] Bob Nelson, *1001 Ways to Reward Employees* (New York: Workman Publishing, 1994).

[9] Thomas Patten, *Pay: Employee Compensation and Incentive Plans* (New York: Macmillan, 1977).

[10] Thomas Wilson, "Is It Time to Eliminate the Piece Rate Incentive System?" *Compensation and Benefits Review*, March–April 1992, pp. 43–49.

[11] Kenneth Chilton, "Lincoln Electric's Incentive System: A Reservoir of Trust," *Compensation and Benefits Review*, Nov.–Dec. 1994, pp. 29–34.

[12] Jon Katzenbach and Douglas Smith, *The Wisdom of Teams* (New York: Harper Collins, 1993).

[13] P. Zingheim and J. R. Shuster, *Pay People Right* (San Francisco, Jossey-Bass, 2000).

[14] F. McKenzie and M. Shilling, "Ensuring Effective Incentive Design and Implementation," *Compensation and Benefits Review*, May–June 1998, pp. 57–65.

[15]F. McKenzie and M. Shilling, "Ensuring Effective Incentive Design and Implementation," *Compensation and Benefits Review*, May–June 1998, pp. 57–65.

[16]M. Bloom and G. Milkovich, "Relationships Among Risk, Incentive Pay, and Organizational Performance," *Academy of Management Journal* 11(3) (1998), pp. 283–97.

[17]American Management Association, "Team-Based Pay: Approaches Vary, but Produce No Magic Formulas," *Compflash* (April 1994), p. 4.

[18]Conversation with Thomas Ruddy, Manager of Research, Xerox Corporation, 1997.

[19]John G. Belcher, *Results Oriented Variable Pay System* (New York: AMACOM, 1996); Steven E. Gross, *Compensation for Teams* (New York: AMACOM, 1995).

[20]Theresa M. Welbourne, David B. Balkin, and Luis R. Gomez-Mejia, "Gainsharing and Mutual Monitoring: A Combined Agency-Organizational Justice Interpretation," *Academy of Management Journal* 38(3) (1995), pp. 881–99.

[21]John G. Belcher, "Gainsharing and Variable Pay: The State of the Art," *Compensation and Benefits Review*, May/June 1994, pp. 50–60.

[22]D. Kim, "Determinants of the Survival of Gainsharing Programs," *Industrial and Labor Relations Review* 53(1) (1999), pp. 21–42.

[23]A. J. Geare, "Productivity from Scanlon Type Plans," *Academy of Management Review* 1 (3) (1976), pp. 99–108.

[24]A. J. Geare, "Productivity from Scanlon Type Plans," *Academy of Management Review* 1(3) (1976), pp. 99–108.

[25]T. Patten, *Pay: Employee Compensation and Incentive Plans* (New York: Macmillan, 1977); Pinhas Schwinger, *Wage Incentive Plans* (New York: Halsted, 1975).

[26]Newman, "Selecting Incentive Plans to Complement Organizational Strategy," in *Current Trends in Compensation Research and Practice*, eds. L. Gomez-Mejia and D. Balkin (Englewood Cliffs, NJ: Prentice Hall, 1987).

[27]Marhsall Fein, "Improshare: A Technique for Sharing Productivity Gains with Employees," *The Compensation Handbook*, eds. M. L. Rock, and L. A. Berger (New York: McGraw-Hill, 1993), pp. 158–75.

[28]R. Kaufman, "The Effects of Improshare on Productivity," *Industrial and Labor Relations Review* 45 (2) (1992), pp. 311–22.

[29]Darlene O'Neill, "Blending the Best of Profit Sharing and Gainsharing," *HR Magazine*, March 1994, pp. 66–69.

[30]K. Brown and V. Huber, "Lowering Floors and Raising Ceilings: A Longitudinal Assessment of the Effects of an Earnings-at-Risk Plan on Pay Satisfaction," *Personnel Psychology* 45 (1992), pp. 279–311.

[31]These observations are drawn from a variety of sources, including: K. Brown and V. Huber, "Lowering Floors and Raising Ceilings: A Longitudinal Assessment of the Effects of an Earnings-at-Risk Plan on Pay Satisfaction," *Personnel Psychology* 45 (1992), pp. 279–311; D. Collins, L. Hatcher, and T. Ross (1993), "The Decision to Implement Gainsharing: The Role of Work Climate, Expected Outcomes and Union Status," *Personnel Psychology* 46 (1993), pp. 77–103; "Team-Based Pay: Approaches Vary but Produce No Magic Formulas," *Compflash*, April 1994, p. 4; W. N. Cooke, "Employee Participation Programs, Group Based Incentives and Company Performance," *Industrial and Labor Relations Review* 47 (1994), pp. 594–610; G. W. Florowski, "The Organizational Impact of Profit Sharing," *Academy of Management Review* 12(4) (1987), pp. 622–36.

[32]IOMA, "Why Saturn's Famous At-Risk Program Is Now at Risk Itself," *IOMA's Pay for Performance Report*, May 1998, pp. 4–5.

[33]T. H. Hammer and R. N. Stern, "Employee Ownership: Implications for the Organizational Distribution of Power," Academy of Management Journal 23 (1980), pp. 78–100.

[34]B. J. Hall, "What You Need to Know About Stock Options," *Harvard Business Review*, March–April 2000, pp. 121–29.

[35]Barry Gerhart, "Pay Strategy and Firm Performance," in S. Rynes and B. Gerhart (eds.), *Compensation in Organizations: Progress and Prospects* (San Francisco: New Lexington Press, 1999).

[36]Chilton, "Lincoln Electrics' Incentive System: A Reservoir of Trust," *Compensation and Benefits Review*, Nov.–Dec. 1994, pp. 29–34; Howard Rudnitsky, "You Have to Trust the Workforce," *Forbes*, July 19, 1993, pp. 78–81.

[37]IOMA "Another Pan of Stock Option Plans," *IOMA's Pay for Performance Report*, January 1999, p. 11.

[38]R. Buckman, "Microsoft Uses Stock Options to Lift Morale," *Wall Street Journal*, April 26, 2000, p. A3.

[39]IOMA, "Company Stock Is Increasingly Used in Board of Director Pay," *Report on Salary Surveys*, March 1998, p. 6.

[40]American Management Association, "More Companies Pay Board Members with Stock," *Compflash*, September 1995, p. 4.

[41]The Top 1000: Canada's Power Book – 50 Best Paid Executives. *ROB Magazine*, July 2003. www.globeinvestor.com/series/top1000/tables/executives/2003/

[42] Graef S. Crystal, *In Search of Excess* (New York: W.W. Norton, 1991).

[43] Herbert A. Simon, *Administrative Behavior*, 2nd ed. (New York: MacMillan, 1957).

[44] The Conference Board, *Top Executive Compensation: 1995.*

[45] "Executive Pay," *Business Week*, April 17, 2000, p. 110.

[46] This comparison needs to be interpreted with some caution. One counterargument (the Hay Group, *Compflash*, April 1992, p. 3) notes that American companies are generally much larger than their foreign counterparts. When compared to like-sized companies in other countries, the US multiple is comparable to the international average.

[47] Marc J. Wallace, "Type of Control, Industrial Concentration, and Executive Pay," *Academy of Management Proceedings* (1977), pp. 284–88; W. Lewellan and B. Huntsman, "Managerial Pay and Corporate Performance," *American Economic Review* 60 (1977), pp. 710–20.

[48] H. L. Tosi, S. Werner, J. Katz, and L. Gomez-Mejia, "A Meta Analysis of CEO Pay Studies," *Journal of Management* 26 (2) (2000), pp. 301–39.

[49] Charles O'Reilly, Brian Main, and Graef Crystal, "CEO Compensation as Tournament and Social Comparison: A Tale of Two Theories," *Administrative Science Quarterly* 33 (1988), pp. 257–74.

[50] Kathryn M. Eisenhardt, "Agency Theory: An Assessment and Review," *Academy of Management Review* 14 (1989), pp. 57–74.

[51] "Executives' Pay: On the Rise but Increasingly at Risk," *Compflash*, November 1995, p. 5.

[52] Nancy C. Pratt, "CEOs Reap Unprecedented Riches While Employees' Pay Stagnates," *Compensation and Benefits Review*, September/October 1996, p. 20

[53] Ira T. Kay, "Beyond Stock Options: Emerging Practices in Executive Incentive Programs," *Compensation and Benefits Review* 23(6) (1991), pp. 18–29.

[54] C. Daly, J. Johnson, A. Ellstrand, and D. Dalton, "Compensation Committee Composition as a Determinant of CEO Compensation," *Academy of Management Journal* 41(2) (1998), pp. 209–220; H. Barkema and L. Gomez-Mejia, "Managerial Compensation and Firm Performance: A General Research Framework," *Academy of Management Journal* 41(2) (1998), pp. 135–48.

[55] Ernest C. Miller, "How Companies Set the Base Salary and Incentive Bonus Opportunity for Chief Executive and Chief Operating Officers. . . A Compensation Review Symposium," *Compensation Review* 9 (Fourth Quarter, 1976), pp. 30–44;

Monci Jo Williams, "Why Chief Executives' Pay Keeps Rising," *Fortune*, April 1, 1985, pp. 66–72, 76.

[56] Daniel J. Miller, "CEO Salary Increases May Be Rational After All: Referents and Contracts in CEO Pay," *Academy of Management Journal* 38(5) (1995), pp. 1361–85.

[57] *IOMA's* Pay for Performance Report, May 1998, p. 11. p. 2.

[58] Other tax reform issues are discussed in Gregory Wiber, "After Tax Reform, Part I: Planning Employee Benefit Programs," *Compensation and Benefits Review* 19(2) (1987), pp. 16–25; and Irwin Rubin, "After Tax Reform, Part 2," *Compensation and Benefits Review* 20(1) (1988), pp. 26–32.

[59] Michael F. Klein, "Executive Perquisites," *Compensation Review* 12 (Fourth Quarter 1979), pp. 46–50.

[60] Jo C. Kail, "Compensating Scientists and Engineers," in *New Perspectives on Compensation*, eds. David B. Balkin and Luis R. Gomez-Mejia (Englewood Cliffs, NJ: Prentice-Hall, 1987), pp. 247–81.

[61] George T. Milkovich, "Compensation Systems in High Technology Companies," in *New Perspectives on Compensation*, eds. Balkin & Gomez-Mejia, pp. 269–77, 1987.

[62] "Sales Compensation Is Increasingly Tied to Quality," *Compflash*, July 1995, p.1.

[63] N. Ford, O. Walker, and G. Churchill, "Differences in the Attractiveness of Alternative Rewards among Industrial Salespeople: Additional Evidence," *Journal of Business Research* 13(2) (1985), pp. 123–38.

[64] Bill O'Connell, "Dead Solid Perfect: Achieving Sales Compensation Alignment," *Compensation and Benefits Review*, March/April 1996, pp. 41–48.

[65] B. Weeks, "Setting Sales Force Compensation in the Internet Age," *Compensation and Benefits Review*, March/April 2000, pp. 25–34.

[66] S. Sands, "Ineffective Quotas: The Hidden Threat to Sales Compensation Plans," *Compensation and Benefits Review*, March/April 2000, p. 35–42.

[67] S. Matusik and C. Hill, "The Utilization of Contingent Work, Knowledge Creation and Competitive Advantage," *Academy of Management Review* 23 (4) (1998), pp. 680–97.

[68] Kim Clark, " Manufacturing's Hidden Asset: Temp Workers," *Fortune*, November 10, 1997, pp. 28–29.

[69] Matusik and Hill, "The Utilization of Contingent Workers . . ."

[70] Janet H. Marler, George T. Milkovich, and Melissa Barringer, "Boundaryless Organizations and Boundaryless Careers: A New Market for High Skilled Temporary Work" (Unpublished paper

submitted to 1998 Academy of Management Annual Conference, Human Resource Division).

[71]M. Wander, "Is Dot.Comp Something New?" *World at Work* (forthcoming).

[72]L. Enos, "Dot—Compensation Going Mainstream," *E Commerce Times*, August 22, 2000, p. 1.

[73]P. Platten and C. Weinberg, "Shattering the Myths About Dot.Com Employee Pay," *Compensation and Benefits Review*, January–February 2000, pp. 21–27.

[74]L. Enos, "Dot—Compensation Going Mainstream," *E Commerce Times*, August 22, 2000, p. 1.

Chapter 12

[1]The job evaluation manual was introduced as evidence in *Electrical Workers (IUE) v. Westinghouse Electric Corp.*, 632 F.2d 1094, 23 FEP Cases 588 (3rd Cir. 1980), cert. denied, 452 U.S. 967, 25 FEP Cases 1835 (1981).

[2]Bruce Kaufman, ed. *Government Regulation of the Employment Relationship* (Ithaca, NY: Cornell University Press, 1998); Arthur Gutman, EEO Law and Personnel Practices, 2nd ed. (Thousand Oaks, CA: Sage Publications, 2000).

[3]*Keeping America Competitive* (Washington, DC: Employment Policy Foundation, 1994).

[4]This section based on T. A. Opie, *You Asked? Your Employment Standards Questions Answered,* 2nd edition. Toronto, ON: CCH Canadian Ltd., 2002, and S. D. Saxe, *Ontario Employment Law Handbook: An Employer's Guide*, sixth edition.Toronto, ON: Butterworths Canada, 2002.

[5]Oren M. Levin-Waldman, "Do Institutions Affect the Wage Structure? Right-to-Work Laws, Unionization, and the Minimum Wage," No. 57, Public Policy Brief (Washington, DC: National Academy of Sciences, 1999).

[6]This section based on T. A. Opie, *You Asked? Your Employment Standards Questions Answered,* 2nd edition. Toronto, ON: CCH Canadian Ltd., 2002.

[7]This section based on T. A. Opie, *You Asked? Your Employment Standards Questions Answered,* 2nd edition. Toronto, ON: CCH Canadian Ltd., 2002.

[8]Anne E. Preston, "Why Have All the Women Gone? A Study of Exit of Women from the Science and Engineering Professions," *American Economic Review*, December 1994, pp. 1446–62.

[9]Joy A. Schneer and Frieda Reitman, "The Importance of Gender in Mid-Career: A Longitudinal Study of MBAs," *Journal of Organizational Behavior* 15 (1994), pp. 199–207; F. Blau and L.

Kahn, "Gender Differences in Pay" (Cambridge, MA: NBER working paper 7732, June 2000).

[10]Joy A. Schneer and Frieda Reitman, "The Importance of Gender in Mid-Career: A Longitudinal Study of MBAs," *Journal of Organizational Behavior* 15 (1994), pp. 199–207.

[11]Alison M. Konrad and Kathy Cannings, "Of Mommy Tracks and Glass Ceilings: A Case Study of Men's and Women's Careers in Management," *Relations Industrielles* 49 (2) (1994), pp. 303–33.

[12]Daniel S. Hamermesh and Jeff E. Biddle, "Beauty and the Labor Market," *The American Economic Review*, December 1994, pp. 1174–94; Mark Roehling, "Weight-Based Discrimination in Employment: Psychological and Legal Aspects," *Personnel Psychology* 52 (1999), pp. 969-1016; John Cawley, "Body Weight and Women's Labor Market Outcomes" (Cambridge, MA: NBER working paper 7841, August 2000).

[13]Francine Blau and Marianne Ferber, "Career Plans and Expectations of Young Women and Men," *Journal of Human Resources* 26 (4) (1991), pp. 581–607.

[14]Robert G. Wood, Mary E. Corcoran, and Paul N. Courant, "Pay Differences among the Highly Paid: The Male–Female Earnings Gap in Lawyers' Salaries," *Journal of Labor Economics* 11 (3) (1993), pp. 417–41.

[15]Barry A. Gerhart and George T. Milkovich, "Salaries, Salary Growth, and Promotions of Men and Women in a Large, Private Firm," *Pay Equity: Empirical Inquiries* (Arlington, VA: National Science Foundation, 1989); Jane Waldfogel, "Understanding the 'Family Gap' in Pay for Women with Children," *Journal of Economic Perspectives* 12 (1) (1998), pp. 157–70; C. Brown, C. and M. Corcoran, "Sex-Based Differences in School Content and the Male–Female Wage Gap," *Journal of Labor Economics* 15 (3) (1997), pp. 431–65.

[16]Andrew M. Gill and Duane E. Leigh, "Community College Enrollment, College Major, and the Gender Wage Gap," *Industrial and Labor Relations Review* 54 (1), October 2000, pp. 163–81; Catherine J. Weinberger, "Race and Gender Wage Gaps in the Market for Recent College Graduates," *Industrial Relations* 37 (1) (1998), pp. 67–84; John M. McDowell, Larry D. Singell Jr., and James P. Ziliak, "Cracks in the Glass Ceiling: Gender and Promotion in the Economics Profession," *American Economic Review* 89 (2) (1999), p. 392–96.

[17]Catherine J. Weinberger, "Race and Gender Wage Gaps in the Market for Recent College Graduates," *Industrial Relations* 37 (1) (1998), pp. 67–84.

[18]Mary E. Graham, Julie L. Hotchkiss, and Barry Gerhart, "Discrimination by Parts: A Fixed-Effects Analysis of Starting Pay Differences Across Gender," *Eastern Economic Journal* 26 (1), Winter 2000, pp. 9–27.

[19]Robert G. Wood, Mary E. Corcoran, and Paul N. Courant, "Pay Differences among the Highly Paid: The Male-Female Earnings Gap in Lawyers' Salaries," *Journal of Labor Economics* 11 (3) (1993), pp. 417–41.

[20]Laurie Hays, "IBM Plans to Slash Secretaries' Salaries in Sweeping Review," *Wall Street Journal*, May 18, 1995, pp. A3, A7.

[21]Jerry Jacobs, "The Sex Segregation of Occupations: Prospects for the 21st Century," in *Handbook of Gender in Organizations*, Gary N. Powell, ed. (Newbury Park, CA: Sage Publications, 1999), pp. 125–41.

[22]George F. Dreher and Taylor H. Cox, Jr., "Labor Market Mobility and Cash Compensation: The Moderating Effects of Race and Gender," *Academy of Management Journal* 43 (5) (2000), pp. 890–900; J. M. Brett and L. K. Stroh, "Jumping Ship: Who Benefits from an External Labor Market Career Strategy?" *Journal of Applied Psychology* 82 (1997), pp. 331–41; G. F. Dreher and T. H. Cox, Jr., "Race, Gender, and Opportunity: A Study of Compensation Attainment and the Establishment of Mentoring Relationships," *Journal of Applied Psychology* 81 (1996), pp. 297–308; J. H. Greenhaus, S. Parasuraman, and W. J. Wormley, "Effects of Race on Organizational Experiences, Job Performance Evaluations, and Career Outcomes," *Academy of Management Journal* 33 (1990), pp. 64–86.

[23]Keith W. Chauvin and Ronald A. Ash, "Gender Earning Differentials in Total Pay, Base Pay, and Contingent Pay," *Industrial and Labor Relations Review*, July 1994, pp. 634–49.

[24]Patti Walmeir, "Employers Facing More Stock Option Lawsuits," *Financial Times*, October 21, 1999, p. 1.

[25]Donald J. Treiman and H. J. Hartmann, eds., *Women, Work and Wages* (Washington, DC: National Academy Press, 1981); Gregory Attiyeh and Richard Attiyeh, "Testing for Bias in Graduate School Admissions," *Journal of Human Resources* 32 (3), pp. 524–48.

[26]M. Drolet, "The Male-Female Wage Gap," *Perspectives*, Spring 2002, pp. 29-37. Statistics Canada Catalogue no. 75-001-XPE.

[27]This section based on T. A. Opie, *You Asked? Your Employment Standards Questions Answered,* 2nd edition. Toronto, ON: CCH Canadian Ltd., 2002.

[28]Ilan M. Carter and F. Ray Marshall, *Labor Economics* (Homewood, Ill.: Richard D. Irwin, 1982).

[29]Allan M. Carter and F. Ray Marshall, *Labor Economics* (Homewood, Ill.: Richard D. Irwin, 1982).

[30]Stephen B. Jarrell and T.D. Stanley, "A Meta Analysis of the Union–Non-Union Wage Gap," *Industrial and Labor Relations Review* 44, (1) (1990), pp. 54–67.

[31]Robert Gay, "Union Contract Concessions and Their Implications for Union Wage Determination" (Working paper no. 38, Division of Research & Statistics, Board of Governors of the Federal Reserve System, 1984).

[32]Linda A. Bell, "Union Wage Concessions in the 1980s: The Importance of Firm-Specific Factors," *Industrial and Labor Relations Review* 48 (2), January 1995, pp. 258–75.

[33]Richard Freeman and James Medoff, *What Do Unions Do?* (New York: Basic Books, 1981).

[34]Bureau of Labor Statistics, "Employer Costs for Employee Compensation Summary" (Washington DC: Bureau of Labor Statistics 1999). Retrieved November 3, 2000, from the World Wide Web: http://stats.bls.gov/news.release/ecec.nws.htm.

[35]Bureau of Labor Statistics, "Table 7: Private Industry, by Region and Bargaining Status" (Washington DC: Bureau of Labor Statistics 1999). Retrieved November 3, 2000, from the World Wide Web: http://stats.bls.gov/news.release/ecec.t07.htm; Robert Rice, "Skill, Earnings and the Growth of Wage Supplements," *American Economic Review*, Fall 1972, pp. 139–47; William Bailey and Albert Schwenk, "Employer Expenditures for Private Retirement and Insurance Plans," *Monthly Labor Review* 95 (1972), pp. 15–19.

[36]Loren Solnick, "Unionism and Fringe Benefits Expenditures," *Industrial Relations* 17 (1) (1978), pp. 102–7.

[37]James E. Martin and Thomas D. Heetderks, *Two-Tier Compensation Structures: Their Impact on Unions, Employers and Employees* (Kalamazoo, MI: W.E. Upjohn Institute for Employment Research, 1990).

[38]Mollie Bowers and Roger Roderick, "Two-Tier Pay Systems: The Good, The Bad, and The Debatable," *Personnel Administrator* 32(6) (1987), pp. 101–12.

[39]James Martin and Melanie Peterson, "Two-Tier Wage Structures: Implications for Equity Theory," *Academy of Management Journal* 30(2) (1987), pp. 297–315.

[40]"Two-Tier Systems Falter as Companies Sense Workers' Resentment," *The Wall Street Journal*, June 16, 1987, p. 1.

[41]Fehmida Sleemi, "Collective Bargaining Outlook for 1995," *Compensation and Working Conditions* 47 (1), January 1995, pp. 19–39.

[42]Richard B. Freeman and Joel Rogers, *What Workers Want* (Ithaca, NY: ILR Press, 1999); David Neumark and Michael L. Wachter, "Union Effects on Nonunion Wages: Evidence from Panel Data on Industries and Cities," *Industrial and Labor Relations Review* 31(1) (1978), pp. 205–16.

[43]J. L. McAdams and E. J. Hawk, *Organizational Performance and Reward: 663 Experiences in Making the Link* (Scottsdale, AZ: American Compensation Association, 1994).

[44]L. B. Cardinal and I. B. Helbrun, "Union versus Nonunion Attitudes toward Share Agreements," Proceedings of the 39th Annual Meeting of the Industrial Relations Research Association (Madison, WI 1987), pp. 167–173.

[45]R. L. Heneman, C. von Hippel, D. E. Eskew, and D. B. Greenberger, "Alternative Rewards in Union Environments," *ACA Journal*, Summer 1997, pp. 42–55.

[46]Fehmida Sleemi, "Collective Bargaining Outlook for 1995," *Compensation and Working Conditions* 47 (1), January 1995, pp. 19–39.

[47]*Changing Pay Practices: New Developments in Employee Compensation* (Washington, DC: Bureau of National Affairs, 1988).

[48]*Changing Pay Practices: New Developments in Employee Compensation* (Washington, DC: Bureau of National Affairs, 1988).

[49]R. L. Heneman, C. von Hippel, D. E. Eskew, and D. B. Greenberger, "Alternative Rewards in Unionized Environments." *ACA Journal*, Summer 1997, pp. 42–55.

[50]T. Ross and R. Ross, "Gainsharing and Unions: Current Trends," in *Gainsharing: Plans for Improving Performance*, ed. B. Graham-Moore and T. Ross (Washington, DC: Bureau of National Affairs), pp. 200–13.

Chapter 13

[1]Stan Durda, "Total Labor Costs: Overview," 3M presentation, April 2000; Robert H. Meehan, "Analyzing Compensation Program Costs," in *Compensation Guide*, ed. William Caldwell (Boston, MA: Warren Gorham and Lamont, 1994).

[2]"The New World of Work," and "Sixty-Five Years of Work in America," *Business Week*, October 17, 1994, pp. 76–148.

[3]K. P. DeMeuse, P. A. Vanderheiden, and T. J. Bergmann, "Announced Layoffs: Their Effect on Corporate Financial Performance," *Human Resource Management* 33 (4) (1994

[4]E. A. Lenz, "Flexible Employment: Positive Work Strategies for the 21st Century," *Journal of Labor Research XVII*, no. 4 (1996), pp. 555–65.

[5]Janet H. Marler, George T. Milkovich, and Melissa Barringer, "Boundaryless Organizations and Boundaryless Careers: A New Market for High-Skilled Temporary Work" (Ithaca, New York: Center for Advanced Human Resource Studies working paper #98-01, 1998); P. S. Tolbert, "Occupations, Organizations, and Boundaryless Careers," in *Boundaryless Careers*, eds. M. Arthur and D. M. Rousseau (New York: Oxford University Press, 1996), pp. 331–49

[6]L. M. Segal and D. G. Sullivan, "The Growth of Temporary Services Work," *Journal of Economic Perspectives* 11 (2) (1997), pp. 117–36; M. W. Barringer and M. Sturman, "Exploring The Effects of Variable Work Arrangements on the Organizational Commitment of Contingent Workers" (Working Paper, University of Massachusetts, Amherst, 1998); Scott Lever, "An Analysis of Managerial Motivations behind Outsourcing Practices in Human Resources," *Human Resource Planning* 20 (2) (1997), pp. 37–47; Leslie King, "Microsoft Rulings and Contingent Workers: What Does It All Mean for Employers?" *Workspan*, October 2000, pp. 79–81.

[7]M. Carnoy, M. Castells, and C. Benner, "Labour Markets and Employment Practices in the Age of Flexibility: A Case Study of Silicon Valley," *International Labour Review* 136 (1) (1997), pp. 27–48.

[8]S. Snell and M. A. Youndt, "Human Resource Management and Firm Performance: Testing a Contingency Model of Executive Controls," *Journal of Management*, issue 4, 1995.

[9]J. Barney, "Organizational Economics: Understanding the Relationship Between Organizations and Economic Analysis," in *Handbook of Organization Studies*, eds. S. Clegg, C. Hardy, and W. Nord (London: Sage Publishers, 1997), pp. 115–47.

[10]For information on the CPI, see the Government of Canada Web site for Statistics Canada; Mary Kokoski, "Alternate CPI Aggregations: Two Approaches," *Monthly Labor Review*, November 2000, pp. 31–39.

[11]Ronald T. Albright and Bridge R. Compton, *Internal Consulting Basics* (Scottsdale, AZ: American Compensation Association, 1996

[12]Nancy Emmons, "Managed and Manipulated Earnings: Implications for Compensation Managers" (working paper, ILR/Cornell University, 2000); Flora Guidry, Andrew J. Leon, and Steve Rock, "Earnings-Based Bonus Plans and Earnings Management by Business-Unit Managers," *Journal of Accounting and Economics* 26 (1999), pp. 113–42

[13]Stan Durda, "Total Labor Costs: Overview," 3M presentation, April 2000

[14]John A. Rubino, *Communicating Compensation Programs* (Scottsdale, AZ: American Compensation Association, 1997).

[15]"Rethinking Ways to Present Financial Information to Employees," *Employee Ownership Report*, March/April 2000, pp. 7, 10.

[16]Michael Beer and Mitin Nohria, "Cracking the Code of Change," Harvard Business Review, May–June 2000, pp. 133–41; Dave Ulrich, "A New Mandate for Human Resources," *Harvard Business Review*, January–February 1998, pp. 125–34.

[17]Brian Hackett, *Transforming the Benefit Function* (New York: The Conference Board, 1995); *Outsourcing HR Services* (New York: The Conference Board, 1994).

[18]Robert M. Dodd and Barbara M. Renterghem, "Increasing Benefit Plan Value through Outsourcing," *Benefits Quarterly*, First Quarter 1997, pp. 14–19.

Appendix

[1]S. Strom, "In Japan, from Lifetime Job to No Job at All," *New York Times* Online, February 3, 1999.

[2]A. Harney, "Toyota Plans Pay Based on Merit," *Financial Times*, July 8, 1999, p. 20.

[3]Interviews with Toshiba Managers, included in G. Milkovich, M. Bloom, and A. Mitra, "Research Report: Rethinking Global Reward Systems," working paper, Cornell University, 2000.

[4]Income Data Services, *IDS Employment Europe* January 2000, 457, p. 20.

[5]Also see *Pay in Europe 2000, Remuneration Policy and Practices* (Surrey, England: Federation of European Employers, 2000) and the FEE's Web site at www.euen.co.uk.

[6]A. Puffer and S. Shekshnia, "Compensating Local Employees in Post-Communist Russia," *Compensation and Benefits Journal*, September–October 1994, pp. 35–42; D. Soskice, "Wage Determination: The Changing Role of Institutions in Advanced Industrialized Countries," *Oxford Review of Economic Policy* 6 (4), pp. 36–61; *Paying the Price: Crisis in Central and Eastern Europe*, ed. D. Vaughan Whitehead (Geneva: ILO, 1999); L. Bajzikova, "Transition Process of HRM in the Slovak Republic," *Journal of HRM* 2 (2001), in press; N. Zupan, "HRM in Slovenian Transitional Companies," working paper, Faculty of Economics, Ljubljana University, Slovenia, 2000.

[7]"China Tries to Shrink Welfare State," *Wall Street Journal*, January 20, 1997, p. C12; D. Dong, K. Goodall, and M. Warner, "The End of the Iron Rice Bowl," *International Journal of Human Resource Management*, April 2, 2000, pp. 217–36.

[8]Zhong-Ming Wang, presentation to Cornell University Global HRM Distance Learning seminar, Shanghai China, March 2000; comments by Ningyu Tang, instructor in Shanghai for Global HRM Distance Learning seminar.

[9]D. Woodruff, "Germany's Ties Among Government, Corporations, and Labor are Unraveling," *Wall Street Journal*, March 11, 1999, p. A18; G. T. Khulikov, "Ukraine Wage Decentralization in a Nonpayment Crisis," Chapter 11 in *Pay the Price* (Geneva: ILO, 2000); R. Yokovlev, "Wage Distortions in Russia," Chapter 9 in *Pay the Price* (Geneva: ILO, 2000).

[10]Kevin O'Rourke and J. G. Williamson, *Globalization and History: The Evolution of a 19th Century Atlantic Economy* (Cambridge, MA: MIT Press, 1999), p. 2.

[11]Kevin O'Rourke and J. G. Williamson, *Globalization and History: The Evolution of a 19th Century Atlantic Economy* (Cambridge, MA: MIT Press, 1999), Chapter 14. Also see D. Rodrik, "Has Globalization Gone Too Far?" *California Management Review* 39 (3), Spring 1997; W. Keller, L. Pauly, and S. Reich, *The Myth of the Global Corporation* (Princeton University Press, 1998); B. Kogut, "What Makes A Company Global? Harvard Business Review, January–February 1999, pp. 165–70; "Blaming Immigrants" editorial in *New York Times*, October 14, 2000, p. 18; Deborah Hargreaves, "Europe: Immigration: Rocky Road from Control to Management," *Financial Times*, October 12, 2000, p. 8.

[12]Lowell Turner, ed. *Negotiating the New Germany: Can Social Partnership Survive?* (Ithaca, New York: Cornell University Press, 1998).

[13]Linda Bell and Richard Freeman, "Why Do Americans and Germans Work Different Hours?" (Working Paper 4808, National Bureau of Economic Research, 1994).

[14]R. Freeman and L. F. Katz, *Differences and Changes in Wage Structures* (University of Chicago Press, 1994); Income Data Services Employment Europe 2000 monthly newsletter.

[15]Vito Tanzi, *Public Spending in the 20th Century* (Cambridge University Press, 2000); M. Wolf, "The Golden Age of Government," *Financial Times*, July 12, 2000, p. 17.

[16]F. Trompenaars, *Riding the Waves of Culture: Understanding Diversity in Global Business* (Burr Ridge, IL: Irwin, 1995); H. C. Triandis, "Cross-Cultural Industrial and Organizational Psychology," in M. D. Dunnette and L. M. Hough, eds. *Handbook of Industrial and Organizational Psychology* (Palo Alto, CA: Consulting Psychologists Press, 1994), pp. 103–72, H. C. Triandis, *Individualism and Collectivism* (Boulder, CO: Westview Press, 1995).

[17]G. Hofstede, "Cultural Constraints in Management Theories," *International Review of Strategic Management* 5 (1994), pp. 27–51.

[18]R. Schuler and N. Rogovsky, "Understanding Compensation Practice Variations Across Firms: The Impact of National Culture," Journal of International Business Studies 29 (1998), pp. 159–78.

[19]L. R. Gomez-Mejia and T. Welbourne, "Compensation Strategies in a Global Context," *Human Resource Planning* 14 (1994), pp. 29–41.

[20]G. Milkovich and M. Bloom, "Rethinking International Compensation: From Expatriates and National Cultures to Strategic Flexibility," *Compensation and Benefits Review*, April 1998; L. Markoczy, "Us and Them," *Across the Board*, February 1998, pp. 44–48.

[21]F. Trompenaars, *Riding the Waves of Culture: Understanding Diversity in Global Business* (Burr Ridge, IL: Irwin, 1995); M. Bloom, G. Milkovich, and A. Mitra, "Toward a Model of International Compensation and Rewards: Learning from How Managers Respond to Local Conditions," CAHRS working paper, Cornell University, #2015; G. Hundley and J. Kim, "National Culture and the Factors Affecting Perceptions of Pay Fairness in Korea and the U.S.," *International Journal of Organization Analysis* 5 (4), October 1997, pp. 325–41; L. Kim and G. Yi, "Transformation of Employment Practices in Korean Business," *International Studies of Management and Organizations* 28 (4) (1998–99), pp. 73–83.

[22]F. Trompenaars, *Riding the Waves of Culture: Understanding Diversity in Global Business* (Burr Ridge, IL: Irwin, 1995); G. Hofstede, "Cultural Constraints in Management Theories," *International Review of Strategic Management* 5 (1994), pp. 27–51; P. C. Earley and C. B. Gibson, "Taking Stock in our Progress on Individualism–Collectivism: 100 Years of Solidarity and Community," *Journal of Management* 24 (1998), pp. 265–304; David Landes, *Culture Matters: How Values Shape Human Progress* (New York: Basic Books, 2001).

[23]M. Bloom, G. Milkovich, and N. Zupan, "Contrasting Slovenian and U.S. Employment Relations: The Links Between Social Contracts and Psychological Contracts" *CEMS Business Review* 2 (1997), pp. S95–S109.

[24]Stephen Jay Gould, *Full House: The Spread of Excellence from Plato to Darwin* (New York: Three Rivers Press, 1996).

[25]H. Katz and Owen Darbishire, *Converging Divergences: Worldwide Changes in Employment Systems* (Ithaca, NY: Cornell University Press, 2000).

[26]Christopher L. Erickson and Sarosh Kuruvilla, "Labor Costs and the Social Dumping Debate in the European Union," *Industrial and Labor Relations Review*, October 1994, pp. 28–47; K. Schwab, M. Porter, J. Sachs, A. Warner, and M. Levison, *The Global Competitiveness Report 2000*, World Economic Forum (Harvard University Press, 2000).

[27]Chris Brewster and Hilary Harris, *International HRM: Contemporary Issues in Europe* (London: Routledge Press, 1999); P. Dowling and R. Schuler, *International Dimensions of Human Resource Management* (Boston, MA: PWS Kent, 2000); Matthew F. Davis, "Global Compensation in the New Economy," *International HR Journal* Fall 2000 (9) (3), pp. 45–50.

[28]The Web site for the National Center for Employee Ownership (NCEO) has information and referrals concerning employee stock ownership plans (ESOPs) and other forms of employee ownership: .www.esop.org. Worker Ownership around the world is discussed at www.activistnet.org.

[29]Michael Byungnam Lee, "Bonuses, Unions, and Labor Productivity in South Korea," *Journal of Labor Research* (1997); G. R. Ungson, R. J. Steers, and S. H. Park, *Korean Enterprises: The Quest for Globalization* (Boston: Harvard Business School Press, 1997).

[30]Lowell Turner, ed. *Negotiating the New Germany: Can Social Partnership Survive?* (Ithaca, New York: Cornell University Press, 1998); D. Soskice, "Wage Determination: The Changing Role of Institutions in Advanced Industrialized Counties," *Oxford Review of Economic Policy* 6 (4), pp. 36–61.

[31]Zhong-Ming Wang, interview of Shang Gua Gao, President of the Economic Reforms Foundation, *American Management Executive* 14 (1), February 2000, pp. 8–12; G. Breton, H. Lan, and Yuan Lu, "China's Township and Village Enterprises," *American Management Executive* 14 (1), February 2000, pp. 19–30; W. Van Honacher, "Entering China: An Unconventional Approach," *Harvard Business Review*, March–April 1992, pp. 130–40.

[32]Giuseppe Fajertag, ed. *Collective Bargaining in Europe 1998–1999* (European Trade Union Institute, Brussels, 2000). The European Trade Union Institute's Web site is at http://www.etuc.org/etui/default.cfm

[33]K. Roth and S. O'Donnell, "Foreign Subsidiary Compensation Strategy: An Agency Theory Perspective," *Academy of Management Journal* 39 (3) (1996), pp. 678–703; Ingmar Bjorkman and Patrick Furu, "Determinants of Variable Pay for Top Managers of Foreign Subsidiaries in Finland," *International Journal of Human Resource Management* 11 (4), August 2000, pp. 698–713.

[34]"Mexican Labor's Hidden Costs," *Fortune*, October 17, 1994, p. 32.

[35]*International Benefit Guidelines* (New York: William M. Mercer, 2000).

[36]Daniel Kalt and Manfred Gutmann, eds., *Prices and Earnings Around the Globe* (Zurich: Union Bank of Switzerland, 2000).

[37]"Big Mac Currencies," *Economist*, April 29, 2000, p. 75.

[38]J. Abowd and M. Bognanno, "International Differences in Executive & Managerial Compensation," in *Differences and Changes in Wage Structures*, R. B. Freeman and L. Katz, eds. (Chicago: NBER, 1995), pp. 67–103.

[39]C. Hitoshi, S. Osamu, and I. Ryuko, "Salaryman Today and into Tomorrow," *Compensation and Benefits Review*, September–October 1997, pp. 67–75; M. Yashiro, *Human Resource Management in Japanese Companies in the Future* (New York: Organization Resource Counselors, 1996); *International Benefit Guidelines* (New York: William M. Mercer, 2000).

[40]S. Strom, "In Japan, from Lifetime Job to No Job at All," *New York Times* Online, February 3, 1999; M. Bloom, G. Milkovich, and A. Mitra, "Toward a Model of International Compensation

and Rewards: Learning from How Managers Respond to Local Conditions," CAHRS working paper, Cornell University, #2015; Michiyo Wakamoto, "Leaving the Fold," *Financial Times*, April 2000, p. 18.

[41]We thank Thomas Gresch and Elke Stadelmann whose manuscript, *Traditional Pay System in Germany* (Ruesselsheim, Germany: Adam Opel AG, 2001), is the basis for this section of the chapter.

[42]J. W. Walker, "Are We Global Yet?" *Human Resource Planning*, First Quarter 2000, pp. 7–8; R. Locke and K. Thelen, "Apples and Oranges Revisited: Contextualized Comparisons and Comparative Labor Policies," *Politics and Society* 23 (2) (1996), pp. 337–67; Tom Redburn, "Asian Values Trumped by the New Economy," *New York Times*, April 2, 2000, p. B4; H. Mehlinger and M. Krain, *Globalization and the Challenges of the New Century* (Indiana University Press, 2000); M. Mendenhall and Gary Oddou, *Readings and Cases in International Human Resource Management* (Cincinnati: Southwestern College Publishing, 2000); J. S. Black, H. Gregerson, M. E. Mendenhall, and L. Stroh, *Globalizing People through International Assignments* (Reading, MA: Addison Wesley, 1999).

[43]M. Bloom, G. Milkovich and A. Mitra, "Toward a Model of International Compensation and Rewards: Learning from How Managers Respond to Local Conditions," CAHRS working paper, Cornell University, #2015. See also N. Napier and Van Tuan Vu, "International HRM in Developing and Transitional Economy Context," *Human Resource Management Review* 8 (1) (1998), pp. 39–71.

[44]C. Reynolds, "Expatriate Compensation in Historical Perspective," *International Human Resource Journal*, Summer 1997, pp. 118–31.

[45]Vlado Pucik, "The Challenges of Globalization: The Strategic Role of Local Managers in Japanese-Owned U.S. Subsidiaries" (Paper presented at Cornell Conference on Strategic HRM, Ithaca, NY, October 1997).

[46] *What It Costs to House Expatriates Worldwide* (New York: Runzheimer International, 2000); Orley Ashenfelter and Stepan Jurajda, "Cross-Country Comparisons of Wage Rates: The Big Mac Index," paper presented at Ninth Annual Policy Conference, Labor Markets in Comparative Perspective, Ithaca, New York, October 7, 2000.

[47] Monica M. Sabo, "Tax-Effective Compensation Planning for International Assignments," *International Compensation and Benefits*, January–February 1995, pp. 24–28; Paul Bailey, "The Role of Cost of Living Data in Creating Cost-Effective Expatriate Assignments," *International HR Journal*, Winter 2001 (9) (4), pp. 27–30.

[48]C. Reynolds, "Expatriate Compensation in Historical Perspective," *International Human Resource Journal*, Summer 1997, pp. 118–31.

[49] *Guide to Major Holidays Around the Globe* (Zurich: Union Bank of Switzerland, 1998).

[50] *International Total Remuneration*, certification course T9 (Scottsdale, AZ: WorldatWork, 2000); Cal Reynolds, "International Compensation," in *Compensation Guide*, ed. William A. Caldwell (Boston: Warren, Gorham and Lamont, 1998).

[51]Fred K. Piker, "Attracting, Retaining, Motivating Senior-Level Expatriates: What's Fair to Both Company and Employee," *Innovations in International HR*, Summer 1997, pp. 1–5; Hal B. Gregersen and Linda K. Stroh, "Coming Home to the Arctic Cold: Antecedents to Finnish Expatriate and Spouse Repatriation Adjustment," *Personnel Psychology* 50 (1997), pp. 635–54; Richard A. Guzzo, Katherine A. Noonan, and Efrat Elron, "Expatriate Managers and the Psychological Contract," *Journal of Applied Psychology* 7 (4) (1994), pp. 617–26; "Focusing on International Assignments," ACA News, July/August 1999.

[52]Hal B. Gregersen and Linda K. Stroh, "Coming Home to the Arctic Cold: Antecedents to Finnish Expatriate and Spouse Repatriation Adjustment," *Personnel Psychology* 50 (1997), pp. 635–54; Richard A. Guzzo, Katherine A. Noonan, and Efrat Elron, "Expatriate Managers and the Psychological Contract," *Journal of Applied Psychology* 7 (4) (1994), pp. 617–26.

[53] *Expatriate Dual Career Survey Report* (New York: Windham International and National Foreign Trade Council, 1997); Garry M. Wederspahn, "Costing Failures in Expatriate Human Resources Management," *Human Resource Planning* 15, no. 3, pp. 27–35; Michael S. Schell and Ilene L. Dolins, "Dual-Career Couples and International Assignments," *International Compensation and Benefits*, November–December 1992, pp. 25–29; Carolyn Gould, "Can Companies Cut Costs by Using the Balance-Sheet Approach?" *International Compensation and Benefits*, July–August 1993, pp. 36–41; David E. Molnar, "Repatriating Executives and Keeping Their Careers on Track," *International Compensation and Benefits*, November–December 1994, pp. 31–35; Ken I. Kim, Hun-Joon Park, and Nori Suzuki, "Reward Allocations in the United States, Japan, and Korea: A Comparison of Individualistic and Collectivistic Cultures," *Academy of Management Journal* 33, no. 1 (1990), pp. 188–98; Anne S. Tsui, Jone L. Pearce, Lyman W. Porter, and Angela M. Tripoli, "Alternative Approaches to the Employee-Organization Relationship: Does Investment in Employees Pay Off?" *Academy of Management Journal* 40, no. 5 (1997), pp. 1089–121.

[54] "The Global Company: Series on Global Corporations," *Financial Times*, November 7, 1995.

GLOSSARY

agency theory—motivation theory stating that employees and management/owners both will act opportunistically to obtain the most favourable exchange possible

allowances—compensation to provide for items that are in short supply

alternation ranking—ranking the best employee, then the worst employee, then the next best and worst, and so on

alternation ranking method—ranking the highest- and lowest-valued jobs first, then the next highest- and lowest-valued jobs, repeating until all jobs have been ranked

behaviourally anchored rating scales (BARS)—performance rating scale using behavioural descriptions as anchors for different levels of performance on the scale

benchmark job—a job whose contents are well known, relatively stable, and common across different employers

benefit maximums—limitations on benefits payable

best fit—aligning compensation decisions with the environment and the business strategy

best practices—a set of pay practices that yields better performance with almost any business strategy

bottom-up budgeting—managers forecast the pay increases they will recommend in the coming year bourse market—prices are subject to barter or negotiation

broadbanding—a large band of jobs containing several pay grades

broad-based option plans—stock options provided to employees at all levels

Canada/Quebec Pension Plan (C/QPP)—a mandatory government-sponsored pension plan for all employed Canadians, funded equally by employers and employees

central tendency error—avoiding extremes in ratings across employees

classification—job evaluation method based on job class descriptions into which jobs are categorized

coinsurance—percentage of insurance premiums paid for by the employer

compa-ratio—ratio of average rates actually paid to range midpoint

compensable factors—characteristics in the work that the organization values, that help it pursue its strategy and achieve its objectives

compensating differentials theory—higher wages must be offered to compensate for negative features of jobs

compensation—all forms of financial returns and tangible services and benefits employees receive as part of an employment relationship

competencies—underlying, broadly applicable knowledge, skills, and behaviours that form the foundation for successful work performance

competency analysis—a systematic process to identify and collect information about the competencies required for successful work performance

competency-based pay structure—links pay to work-related competencies

competency indicators—observable behaviours that indicate the level of competency within each competency set

competency sets—specific components of a competency

competitive advantage—a business practice or process that results in better performance than other competitors

Consumer Price Index (CPI)—index that measures changes in prices over time

coordination of benefits—reduction of benefits by any amount paid under a spouse's plan

core competencies—competencies required for successful work performance in any job in the organization

cost-of-living adjustment—percentage increment to base pay provided to all employees regardless of performance

deductible—specified dollar amount of claims paid by the employee each year before insurance benefits begin

defined-benefit plan—pension plan in which an employer agrees to provide a specific level of retirement pension, the exact cost of which is unknown

defined-contribution plan—pension plan in which an employer agrees to provide specific contributions but the final benefit is unknown

differentials—pay differences between levels

distributive justice—fairness of the result or outcome of a decision

dual career ladder—career progression on either a managerial path or a professional path

earnings-at-risk plan—incentive plan sharing profits in successful years and reducing base pay in unsuccessful years

efficiency wage theory—high wages may increase efficiency and lower labour costs by attracting higher-quality applicants who will work harder

employee assistance plan (EAP)—employer-sponsored program that provides employees with confidential counselling and/or treatment programs for personal problems including addiction, stress, and mental health issues

employee benefits—part of the total compensation package, other than pay for time worked, provided to employees in whole or in part by employer payments, such as life insurance, pension plan, workers' compensation, vacation, etc.

employee stock ownership plan (ESOP)—plan offering employees the opportunity to purchase company stock, often partially or fully matched by employer-paid stock for the employee

Employment Insurance—a mandatory government-sponsored plan for all employed Canadians that provides workers with temporary income replacement as a result of employment interruptions due to circumstances beyond their control, funded by employer and employee contributions

equity theory—motivation theory stating that people are concerned about fairness of the reward outcomes exchanged for employee inputs

evaluation format—the method used to evaluate an employee's performance, either ranking against other employees or rating on one or more performance criteria

expectancy theory—motivation theory stating that people cognitively evaluate potential behaviours in relation to rewards offered in exchange

external competitiveness—comparison of compensation with that of competitors

factor degree/level—description of several different degrees or levels of the factor in jobs. A different number of points is associated with each degree/level.

factor weights—weighting assigned to each factor to reflect differences in importance attached to each factor by the employer

first impression error—developing a negative or positive opinion of an employee early in the review period and allowing that to influence negatively or positively all later perceptions of performance

flexible benefit plans—benefit plans in which the employee is provided with a specified amount of money and then chooses which benefits to spend the money on, according to their attractiveness and cost

gain-sharing plan—group incentive plan where employees share in cost savings

gini coefficient—statistic that varies between zero and one, increasing with pay differentials between levels

green circle rates—pay rates below the range minimum

halo error—an appraiser giving favourable ratings to all job duties based on impressive performance in just one job function. For example, a rater who hates tardiness rates a prompt subordinate high across all performance dimensions exclusively because of this one characteristic.

human capital—the education, experience, knowledge, abilities, and skills that people possess

human capital theory—higher earnings are made by people who improve their potential productivity by acquiring education, training, and experience

implicit contract—an unwritten understanding between employers and employees about their reciprocal obligations and returns

incentives/variable pay—one-time payments for meeting previously established performance objectives

internal alignment (internal equity)—the pay relationships between the jobs/skills/competencies within a single organization. The relationships form a structure that can support the work flow, is fair to the employees, and directs their behaviour toward organization objectives

internal labour markets—rules and procedures that determine the pay for different jobs within a single organization, and allocate employees to those different jobs

job analysis—the systematic process of collecting information about the nature of specific jobs

job competition theory—workers compete through qualifications for jobs with established wages

job description—written summary of a job, including responsibilities, qualifications, and relationships

job evaluation—the process of systematically determining the relative worth of jobs to create a job structure for the organization. The evaluation is based on a combination of job content, skills required, value to the organization, organizational culture, and the external market.

job specification—qualifications required to be hired for a job; may be included in the job description

job structure—hierarchy of all jobs based on value to the organization; provides the basis for the pay structure

job-to-job method—method of comparing pay for male- and female-dominated job classes where each female job class is compared to a male job class of equal or comparable value

leniency error—consistently rating someone higher than is deserved

line-of-sight—link between an individual employee's work and the achievement of organizational objectives

long-term disability plans—employer-sponsored plans that provide income protection due to long-term illness or injury that is not work-related

loosely coupled structure—pay structure for jobs that are flexible, adaptable, and changing

management by objectives (MBO)—performance rating method based on meeting objectives set at the beginning of the performance review period

marginal product of labour—the additional output associated with the employment of one additional human resources unit, with other production factors held constant

marginal productivity theory—Unless an employee can produce something of value from his/her job equal to the value received in wages, it will not be worthwhile for an employer to hire that employee.

marginal revenue of labour—the additional revenue generated when the firm employs one additional unit of human resources, with other production factors held constant

market pay line—links a company's benchmark jobs on the horizontal axis (internal structure) with market rates paid by competitors (market survey) on the vertical axis

market pricing—establishing pay structure by relying almost exclusively on external market pay rates

maturity curves—curves on a graph depicting the relationship between salaries and years of work experience since attaining a degree

merit increase—increment to base pay in recognition of past work behaviour

merit pay—increase in base pay related to performance

motivation—a process involving the determination of what is important to a person, and offering it in exchange for desired behaviour

negative halo error—the opposite of a halo error; downgrading an employee across all performance dimensions exclusively because of poor performance on one dimension

occupational segregation—the historical segregation of women into a small number of occupations such as clerical, sales, nursing, and teaching

organizational agility—the capacity to be infinitely adaptable without having to change

outlier—a data point that falls outside the majority of the data points

paired comparison method—listing all jobs across columns and down rows of a matrix, comparing the jobs in each cell and indicating which one is of greater value, then ranking jobs based on the total number of times each one is ranked as being of greater value

paired comparison performance ranking—ranking each employee against all other employees, one pair at a time

pay equity—legislation intended to redress the unexplained portion of the wage gap assumed to be due to gender discrimination

pay forms—the mix of the various types of payments that make up total compensation

pay grade—grouping of jobs considered substantially equal for pay purposes

pay level—the average of the array of rates paid by an employer: $\sum$ base + bonuses + benefits + options/$\sum$ employees

pay policy line—pay line representing an adjustment to the market pay line to reflect the company's external competitive position in the market (i.e., lead, match, lag)

pay range—an upper and lower limit on pay for all jobs in a pay grade

pay structure—the array of pay rates for different work or skills within a single organization. The number of levels, differentials in pay between the levels, and the criteria used to determine those differences create the structure.

pension plan—plan that provides income to an employee at retirement as compensation for work performed now

performance appraisal—process of evaluation or appraising an employee's performance on the job

point method—job evaluation method that assigns a number of points to each job, based on compensable factors that are numerically scaled and weighted

position analysis questionnaire (PAQ)—a structured job analysis questionnaire used for analyzing jobs on the basis of 194 job elements that describe generic work behaviours

procedural fairness—fairness of the process used to make a decision

procedural justice—perceived fairness of the procedures used to determine pay or other work outcomes

profit-sharing plans—variable pay plans requiring a profit target to be met before any payouts occur

proportional value method—method of comparing pay for male- and female-dominated job classes when female job classes have no appropriate male comparators under the job-to-job system, where the relationship between the value of the job and the pay received by male job classes is then applied when setting pay for female job classes

proxy comparison method—method of comparing pay for male- and female-dominated job classes when pay equity cannot be achieved through job-to-job or proportional value methods, where female job classes are compared to similar female job classes that have achieved pay equity with another employer

quoted price market—prices are specifically indicated

ranking—job evaluation method that ranks jobs from highest to lowest based on a global definition of value

recency error—the opposite of first impression error. Allowing performance, either good or bad, at the end of the review period, to play too large a role in determining an employee's rating for the entire period.

red circle rates—pay rates above the range maximum

reference rates—pay rates from market data used in pricing broad bands

relational returns—psychological returns employees believe they receive in the workplace

reliability—consistency of results from repeated applications of a measure

reservation wage theory—job seekers have a reservation wage level below which they will not accept a job

salary—pay calculated at an annual or monthly rate

short-term disability plans/salary continuation plans—employer-sponsored plans that provide a continuation of all or part of an employee's earnings when the employee is absent from work due to an illness or injury that is not work-related

sick leave—employer-sponsored plans that grant a specified number of paid sick days per month or per year

signalling theory—pay levels and pay mix are designed to signal desired employee behaviours

similar-to-me error—giving better ratings to individuals who are like the rater in behaviour and/or personality

skill analysis—a systematic process to identify and collect information about skills required to perform work in an organization

skill-based pay structures—link pay to the depth or breadth of the skills, abilities, and knowledge a person acquires that are relevant to the work

spillover effect—employers seeking to avoid unionization offer workers the wages, benefits, and working conditions won in rival unionized firms

spillover error—continuing to downgrade an employee for performance errors in prior rating periods

stock options—the right to purchase stock at a specified (exercise) price for a fixed time period

strategic objectives—goals identified by an organization as necessary for the achievement of its strategy for success

strategic perspective—a focus on compensation decisions that help the organization gain and sustain competitive advantage

strategy—the fundamental business decisions that an organization has made in order to achieve its strategic objectives, such as what business to be in and how to obtain competitive advantage

strictness error—the opposite of leniency error; rating someone consistently lower than is deserved

survey—the systematic process of collecting and making judgments about the compensation paid by other employers

survey levelling—multiplying survey data by a factor to adjust for differences between the company job and the survey job

tailored structure—pay structure for well-defined jobs with relatively small differences in pay

team/group incentive plans—incentive pay for meeting or exceeding group performance standards

360-degree feedback—performance appraisal method including feedback from up to five sources: supervisor, peers, self, customers, and subordinates

top-down budgeting—top management of each organizational unit estimates the pay-increase budget for that unit

total reward system—all rewards (in at least 13 general categories) provided by organizations

turnover effect—decreased budget required as lower paid workers replace employees who leave, calculated as annual turnover rate times planned average increase

validity—accuracy of a measure

vesting—waiting period for entitlement to employer-paid pension benefits

wage—pay calculated at an hourly rate

wage gap—the amount by which the average pay for female workers is less then the average pay for male workers

wage line method—method of comparing pay for male- and female-dominated job classes where the wage line for female job classes is compared indirectly with the wage line for male job classes

Workers' Compensation—a mandatory, government-sponsored, employer-paid, no-fault insurance plan that provides compensation for injuries and diseases that arise out of, and while in the course of, employment

SUBJECT INDEX

NAME INDEX

A

Adam Opel AG, 367, 384, 385, 385*f*, 386
AES, 10, 12, 27, 28*f*, 357
Air Canada, 29, 330
Alcan, 301*f*, 303*f*
Algoma Steel, 157, 166
Amazon.com, 147*f*, 153
American Airlines, 88
American Express Co., 31, 312
Amistad, 88
Angus Reid, 234
AON Consulting, 205
Aristotle, 47
Association of Canadian Pension Management, 364
ATT, 357
AT&T, 253
Austin, Deborah, 147*f*

B

Balzer's Tool Coating, 119–120, 120*f*, 124
Banff Centre for Leadership, 143
Bank of Nova Scotia, 303*f*
Bank of Switzerland, 376
Bao Gang, 365
B.C. Hydro, 173
BCE Inc., 3, 301*f*
Belcher, David, 190
Ben and Jerry's Homemade, 54–55
Best Buy, 200
Bezos, Jeff, 147*f*
Blue Cross, 221
Bombardier, 163, 166, 303*f*
Borong, Zhou, 147*f*
Bristol-Myers Squibb (BMS), 19–21, 20*f*, 30, 34
Brown, Duncan, 147*f*
Brown, Robert, 303*f*
Bullock, Sandra, 147*f*
Bundesbank, 373
Burger King, 264
Burlington Northern, 100
Burns Meats Ltd., 321

Burton, Robert, 303*f*
Bush, George W., 147*f*

C

Canada Customs and Revenue Agency, 234
Canadian Auto Workers, 296
Canadian Auto Workers (CAW), 235
Canadian Council of Human Resource Associations (CCHRA), 17, 363
Canadian Management Centre, 363
Canadian Pension and Benefits Institute, 364
Career Edge, 18
Carnegie Mellon University, 330
Cats, 1
CBS, 146, 163–164
CHEX, 163–164
Chrysler Corporation, 27, 366–369
Clarkson, Adrienne, 147*f*
CN Railway, 301*f*, 303*f*
Coca-Cola Co., 169, 297
Cohen, Ben, 55
Colgate, 176, 199
Collingwood Neighbourhood House, 330
Compensation and Benefits Review, 17
Conference Board, 166

D

Daimler-Benz, 27, 366, 367
DaimlerChrysler, 27, 31, 366–368, 384
Dalessandro, Dominic, 301*f*
Dalzell, Richard, 147*f*
De Zen, Vic, 301f
Dell Computer, 312
Deming, Edward, 256
Deutsche Bank, 365
Digital Equipment Corporation, 228
Dofasco, 332
Don, Michael, 147*f*
Doyle, William, 303*f*
DreamWorks SKG, 88
Dunn, Frank, 303*f*

DuPont, 295, 297
Dutton, Bryan, 147*f*

E

Economist, 376
Employee Benefits Research Institute (EBRI), 17, 364
EnCana, 301f
Engen, Travis, 301*f*, 303*f*
ETHICON, 30
European Metalworkers Federation EU, 373

F

FastCat, 190–191, 195, 196–197, 200
Firepond, 19–21, 20*f*, 30, 34
FMC, 122, 123f, 124
Ford Canada, 31
Ford Motor Company, 21, 31, 40, 43, 45, 65, 246
Fortune magazine, 64
France Telecom, 147*f*
Fuji Photo, 365

G

Gainers Inc., 321
the Gap, 376
Gates, William (Bill), 147*f*
General Electric, 12, 181, 203, 204, 308, 357, 358, 365, 395
General Mills, 121, 122*f*, 166
General Motors, 31, 163, 215, 296
George Weston Ltd., 10
Getty, William, 147v
Global Business and Economic Roundtable on Addiction and Mental Health, 236
Globe and Mail, 312
Godsoe, Peter, 303*f*
Gould, Stephen Jay, 372
Greenfield, Jerry, 55
Gretzky, Wayne, 246